OneStream Workspaces and Assemblies

Eric Telhiard and Jessica Toner

OneStream Press

Published in 2026 by OneStream Press.

ISBN: 9781068333842

 OneStream Press is an imprint of Play Technologies (England) Limited. 6 Woodside, Churnet View Road, Oakamoor, ST10 3AE, United Kingdom.

www.OneStreamPress.com

Disclaimer

While the advice and information in this book is believed to be true and accurate at the date of publication, OneStream Press, the authors, and OneStream Software LLC do not guarantee the accuracy, adequacy, or completeness of any information, and are not responsible for any errors or omissions or the results obtained from the use of such information.

OneStream Press, the authors, and OneStream Software LLC make no warranty, express or implied, with respect to the material contained herein, and hereby disclaim any liability to any party for any loss, damage, or disruption caused by errors or omissions, whether such errors or omissions result from negligence, accident, or any other cause.

About the Authors

Eric Telhiard is the Senior Director of Demo Engineering at OneStream Software. Since joining the company in 2020, he has played a pivotal role in shaping the demo development experience, leading vertical industry-build initiatives, and driving innovation across the demo engineering organization. With more than 25 years in Corporate Performance Management (CPM), Eric has helped global organizations navigate complex planning, forecasting, and profitability challenges by crafting tailored, scalable solutions. Eric approaches every challenge with a blend of precision and curiosity, and hopes this book encourages fellow implementers and administrators to explore the full creative potential of the OneStream platform.

To my OneStream teammates – thank you for your brilliance, grit, and the occasional well-timed sarcasm. And to my incredible wife, Michelle, who puts up with more than anyone should have to: you make it all worthwhile.

Jessica Toner is the Director of Vertical Demo Engineering at OneStream Software. She joined the OneStream Software services team in 2017, where she played a vital role in the successful implementation of OneStream's inaugural Federal customer solution. In 2020, she shifted her focus to Partner Enablement as a Partner Engagement Manager, providing partner implementation support and project management for the OneStream Public Sector practice. In 2021, she advanced to the Presales organization as a Lead Solution Consultant, where she was responsible for managing and enhancing the Public Sector practice's demo asset portfolio.

Jessica currently oversees the architecture, development, and governance of all Vertical Demo Assets across the enterprise. She also provides technical advisory support to cross-functional teams, ensuring consistency, quality, and innovation in demo build practices throughout the organization.

Prior to joining OneStream in 2017, she amassed over a decade of experience in accounting and finance across diverse industries, enabling her to acquire a deep understanding of the complex financial challenges that many organizations face. Jessica currently resides in Royal Oak, Michigan.

To my amazing Vertical Demo Engineering team – thank you. Your creativity, dedication, and constant support have shaped this work in more ways than I can count. I'm deeply grateful for every idea shared, every challenge tackled together, and the heart you bring to everything you do. I'm honored to work alongside you.

Technical Reviewers

Jack Lacava is a Platform Product Manager at OneStream, with just enough technical skills to be dangerous. He knew Python before it was cool, rides motorbikes, and actually comes from Italy. His wife can't understand how anybody would ever pay him to do what he does.

Jérôme Marcq is a Lead Solutions Consultant at OneStream, known for his ability to make complex financial and operational data feel simple and manageable. With more than a decade of experience, he has spent his career helping organizations bring structure, clarity, and confidence to their reporting and decision-making processes.

Errata

Despite best efforts, mistakes can sometimes creep into books. If you spot a mistake, please feel free to email us at errata@onestreampress.com (with the book title in the subject line).

The errata page for this book is hosted at *www.onestreampress.com/Workspaces*

Contents

1

Introduction

We are very excited to introduce the next evolution of the OneStream Extended Finance Platform, the Workspace. At first glance, this might just seem like a more intuitive way to organize dashboards and all their components, but Workspaces do much more than that. Workspaces bring together historically distinct application objects, such as Cube Views and data management objects, while also introducing new development concepts to OneStream with Assemblies and Assembly Services.

My OneStream education journey has involved many trial-and-error sessions while attempting to tackle various use cases over the course of my job. My approach to retaining different concepts is to create little “How To...” documents with snippets describing the issue to be solved, the steps to solve it, and a detailed screenshot walkthrough of the various screens and settings to accomplish the mission. I hope you find this approach helpful in your journey to understand the new Workspaces and everything that comes with them.

Although the *OneStream Advanced Reporting and Dashboards* book from OneStream Press is not a prerequisite for understanding Workspaces, it provides a detailed understanding of all the components within dashboards. It was written to teach the intricacies of designing and configuring dashboards to make robust user experiences that meet the needs of your user community. Since all of these concepts are still valid, we won’t be diving deep into these topics again, but will instead focus on how the introduction of Workspaces enhances a developer’s ability to customize the user experience.

Who is this book for?

The goal of this book is to help you get a solid understanding of Workspaces and where they fit into your OneStream journey. From experienced OneStream developers to new users and new developers, this book will guide you to make the most out of your OneStream investment.

For experienced developers, you need to understand the transition from pre-Workspace development concepts to post-Workspace development concepts, where and why you should embrace using Workspaces for future development, and how to convert your current environment. For developers just beginning their OneStream journey, this book explains how and why all the Workspace components fit together to provide a best-practice approach to building your OneStream application.

For new OneStream users, this book will introduce you to the fundamentals of Workspaces, guiding you through the basics of dashboard organization and how contained solutions can streamline your workflow. You’ll learn the importance of collaboration and how enhanced security measures ensure your application development remains protected. Through step-by-step instructions and practical examples, you will gain a solid foundation to start building and managing Workspaces effectively.

Experienced users and developers will find this book invaluable in delving deeper into advanced topics such as Assembly Services. We will showcase how these new features can revolutionize your existing development processes and significantly enhance your overall productivity. Understanding these concepts will enable you to leverage the full potential of Workspaces in your projects.

Additionally, we will explore the critical aspect of moving from development to production (Dev to Prod) and provide best practices and strategies to ensure smooth transitions. By understanding how Workspaces integrate with the OneStream platform, you will be equipped with the knowledge to implement this powerful tool effectively, driving greater efficiency and success in your organization's financial operations.

In the subsequent sections, we will cover a range of topics, from setting up your Workspace to managing complex components like Assemblies and dynamic dashboards. Each chapter is crafted to guide you step by step, offering practical examples and best practices to help you navigate the OneStream landscape. You'll learn how to create new Workspaces, configure settings, and navigate the interface with ease.

Join us as we delve into the world of OneStream Workspaces, exploring their potential to transform your development processes and drive greater efficiency in your organization's financial operations. This journey will equip you with the skills and knowledge to harness the full power of OneStream Workspaces, making you an adept and confident user.

Let's get started!

2

Understanding Workspaces

In this chapter, we will dive into the core concept of Workspaces in OneStream, a powerful feature that significantly enhances how you manage, build, and interact with data. Workspaces are designed to streamline your development process, provide better organization, and ensure that users can collaborate more efficiently while maintaining security and control over the definition of the objects contained in the Workspace.

You'll learn how Workspaces function as an organized, flexible development area that allows users to manage and build multiple solutions without impacting other users or processes. The concept of separating environments into Workspaces introduces a new layer of dashboard development security, segregation of duties, and efficiency, allowing developers, analysts, and administrators to work in parallel while minimizing disruption to business operations.

This chapter will introduce you to the key components of a Workspace, the benefits of using them, and how to use them. We will also explore best practices and real-world examples that will help you unlock the full potential of Workspaces in OneStream. Whether you are new to the platform or looking to refine your approach, this chapter will provide the foundational knowledge you need to leverage Workspaces in your OneStream environment.

By the end of this chapter, you will have a clear understanding of what Workspaces are, how they fit into the OneStream ecosystem, and how they can make your development process more efficient, secure, and manageable. In the following chapter, we will walk through an exercise on how to set up a Workspace.

Definition and Concept of Workspaces

What is a Workspace?

Workspaces serve as a foundational framework for building software within software environments. They function as structured, sandbox-like development spaces where teams can create, modify, and test solutions without interfering with other work streams.

At their core, Workspaces store **Maintenance Units**, which serve as organizational containers that streamline solution development by *grouping* related components, configurations, and enhancements together. This ensures that changes remain structured and manageable, reducing complexity as solutions evolve.

By enabling isolated yet collaborative development, Workspaces empower developers to work independently on different features, updates, or fixes without the risk of disrupting others. This fosters innovation, accelerates development cycles, and improves overall efficiency. As organizations strive to enhance agility and maintain structured development practices, Workspaces will play a critical role in keeping teams organized while providing the flexibility needed for independent and scalable solution development.

Purpose of Workspaces

Workspaces were designed to facilitate seamless collaboration and efficient solution development across teams, applications, and even environments. They serve as dedicated spaces where developers can independently build, test, and refine solutions while maintaining a structured and organized workstream.

One of the key advantages of Workspaces is their ability to promote modularity and reuse, allowing developers to create solutions that can be easily *shared* across different teams or migrated between environments. This reduces redundancy and ensures consistency across applications, ultimately accelerating the development process.

Additionally, Workspaces act as controlled development containers that help preserve application integrity. Developers can experiment with new features, implement enhancements, and troubleshoot issues without impacting production systems or other ongoing projects. This level of isolation minimizes risks while enabling teams to innovate with confidence.

By providing a flexible yet structured framework, Workspaces empower organizations to speed up solution delivery, enhance collaboration, and maintain stability across their software ecosystems.

How Workspaces Work

Workspaces are like compartmentalized development areas within a single application. Maintenance units are stored in Workspaces, and dashboards are stored in maintenance units.

Think about file storage platforms like SharePoint; you most likely have files within folders within folders, right? Imagine you have a folder named "Vendors", and within that folder you have a folder named "Microsoft" and a folder named "Amazon" where you store vendor-specific invoices. It's possible to receive invoices from vendors with the same invoice number since you can't control your vendor's invoice numbering or naming convention, but since you have separate folders for each vendor, you're able to save "Invoice1412512.pdf" from Microsoft under the Microsoft folder, and also save "Invoice1412512.pdf" from Amazon under the Amazon folder.

Once you grasp the concept of the folder hierarchy structure and its ability to accept different files with the same file name – in separate folders, of course – the concept of Workspaces becomes a little clearer.

Benefits of Using Workspaces

Isolated Development Workspaces

Provide Developers with Dedicated Sandboxes

Workspaces are like dedicated development spaces; they allow developers to build dashboards within the same application without impacting existing dashboards. Prior to Workspaces, developers were hamstrung by the application's existing dashboard objects' naming conventions, meaning they had to use different names when creating objects to avoid naming conflicts.

Solving the Naming Conflict Problem

Before Workspaces, developers were constrained by the application's global naming conventions for dashboard objects, which meant they had to manually adjust object names to prevent conflicts. This not only added complexity but also increased the risk of errors when integrating new dashboards into existing applications. With Workspaces, these limitations are removed, enabling developers to work on dashboards independently while the system manages object relationships in the background.

Eliminating Environment Guesswork

Consider a scenario where you've built dashboards in a true sandbox environment and then needed to export and load them into a live environment for testing or deployment. One of the biggest challenges in this process is uncertainty about changes in the destination environment – were any dashboards modified or new objects added since your last export? Manually tracking these changes is impractical, and conflicts often lead to overwritten work, inconsistencies, or broken dashboards.

Imagine you built a dashboard that has been tested in the sandbox environment, and you give the administrator the green light to port the solution over to the live environment. The next day, your administrator comes back to you and says they are getting the following error message upon loading the export:

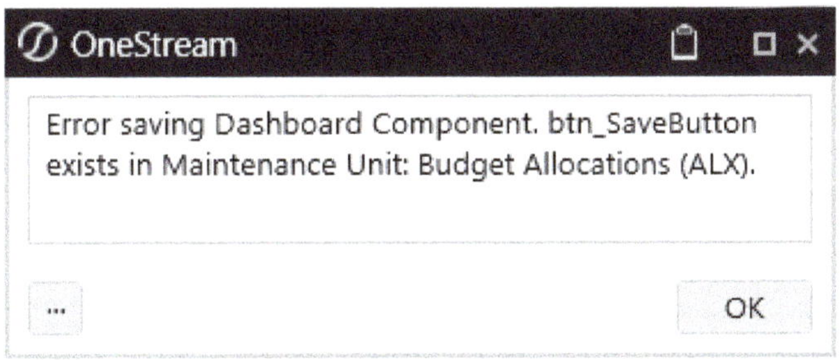

Figure 2.1

As it turns out, there was a button recently created in the live environment with the same name you used for a button in development. The error the administrator sees is just the first naming conflict, but this is potentially the tip of the iceberg. Once you change the button name in your sandbox environment and re-export the dashboard, your administrator attempts to load the dashboard and alerts you that another naming conflict occurred.

You can see how this can quickly snowball and turn what should be a half-day exercise into a week's worth of trial and error. Workspaces solve this problem by isolating development efforts to reduce errors and promote efficiency.

With Workspaces, guesswork is eliminated. Developers can confidently build, refine, and deploy dashboards without worrying about conflicts or unintended disruptions. The structured environment allows teams to focus on creating dashboard content, not troubleshooting deployment issues.

Flexibility and Sharing

Limit Access to Workspaces

Workspaces seamlessly integrate with the platform's built-in security model, ensuring that access control remains both flexible and secure. By leveraging security groups, administrators can define who can access and modify a Workspace, maintaining a clear distinction between those who can access content and those who can actively develop and maintain it.

Granular Access Control

Each Workspace has two levels of security assignments:

1. **Maintenance Groups** – These groups contain users responsible for building, editing, and maintaining the Workspace content. Only members of these groups can make changes, ensuring controlled development.
2. **Access Groups** – These groups allow broader visibility into the Workspace. Users in access groups can view or review the content without being able to modify or disrupt it.

Example: Controlled Collaboration

Imagine a scenario where multiple teams need access to a Workspace. The development team (maintenance group) is responsible for creating dashboards, reports, or application components, while the QA team and business stakeholders (access group) need visibility to review progress without modifying the work. By assigning different security groups to these roles, Workspaces enable controlled collaboration – ensuring that development remains organized while still allowing transparency across teams.

Benefits of Workspace Security Controls

- **Prevents Unauthorized Changes** – Only designated maintenance group members can edit, reducing accidental modifications.
- **Encourages Cross-Team Visibility** – Stakeholders and reviewers can access Workspaces without disrupting development.
- **Maintains Data Integrity** – Ensures that only the right people can push changes to production.
- **Supports Compliance and Governance** – Security groups align with organizational policies, making auditing and user management easier.

By incorporating security groups at both the maintenance and access levels, Workspaces provide a structured yet collaborative development environment, enabling teams to work efficiently while maintaining strong access controls. The ability to leverage your existing security model allows you to facilitate who can modify and who can access dashboards by creating security groups for different development teams and QA or business stakeholder teams that may be responsible for multiple Workspace projects.

In the Practical Use Cases section, later in this chapter, we'll walk you through an example of how to configure Workspace security using **Security Group** role assignments, and explain how different users can have access to multiple Workspaces while limiting maintenance rights – this is incredibly powerful when you're managing multiple development projects and need to ensure that dashboards are not accidentally modified by users that you have not assigned maintenance rights to.

Selectively Share Workspace Objects

Workspaces provide a more controlled method of sharing objects with other development teams by allowing you to select whether a Workspace is **Shareable** or not. Before the inception of Workspaces, sharing objects between maintenance units was enabled for all objects in an application's dashboard library. The inability to restrict what could be shared meant that you had limited control over dashboard object independence and could risk unintentionally breaking solution A by updating solution B. OneStream has effectively added a layer of protection to ensure that only content flagged as shareable would be made available for dashboard display.

For example, say you have an existing Workspace for KPI dashboards with various standardized layouts parameterized to display KPIs defined by the security groups. Your organization uses these KPI dashboards in various areas within the application to ensure that users view the appropriate and correct information. You've been tasked with building a landing page for users that includes specific menu options defined by the users' security group rights, and also displays relevant KPI information based on the users' security group rights. Rather than copy the dashboard objects from the KPI Workspace into your Landing Page Workspace, you can reuse the KPI dashboards. This eliminates redundant work, minimizes clutter in your Workspace, and follows your company policy of using the prescribed KPI dashboards. It also enables the creation of libraries containing reusable, shared objects – promoting more standardized and consistent interfaces across solutions.

So how does it work? Let's look at an example of where and how to make the KPI dashboards available for reuse on your Landing Page dashboard. The figure below shows a new set of properties on the Workspace page under the Sharing section, which will be addressed in two steps. In the first step, you see that the Key Performance Indicators (OP_KPI) Workspace's Is Shareable Workspace setting has been set to True, allowing other Workspaces to reuse objects from this Workspace.

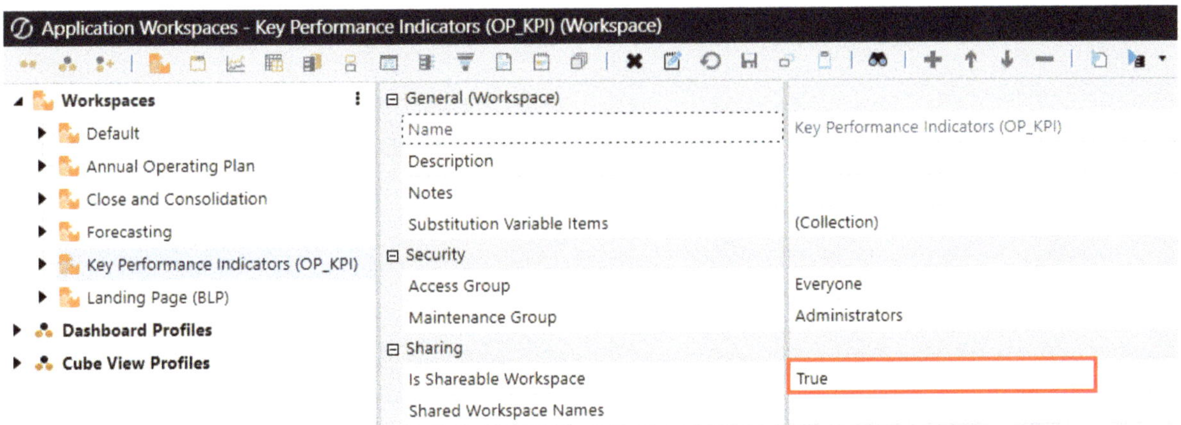

Figure 2.2

Step two of establishing object sharing is defining the Shared Workspace Names setting. On the Landing Page Workspace, this is where you define the Workspaces from which you need to reuse objects.

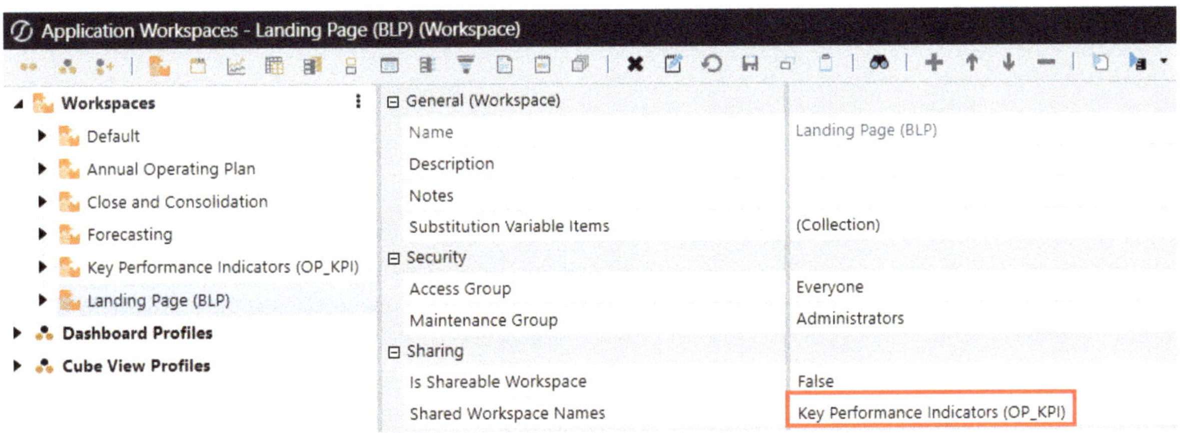

Figure 2.3

Note: Hover over the Shared Workspace Names field to display the tool tip.

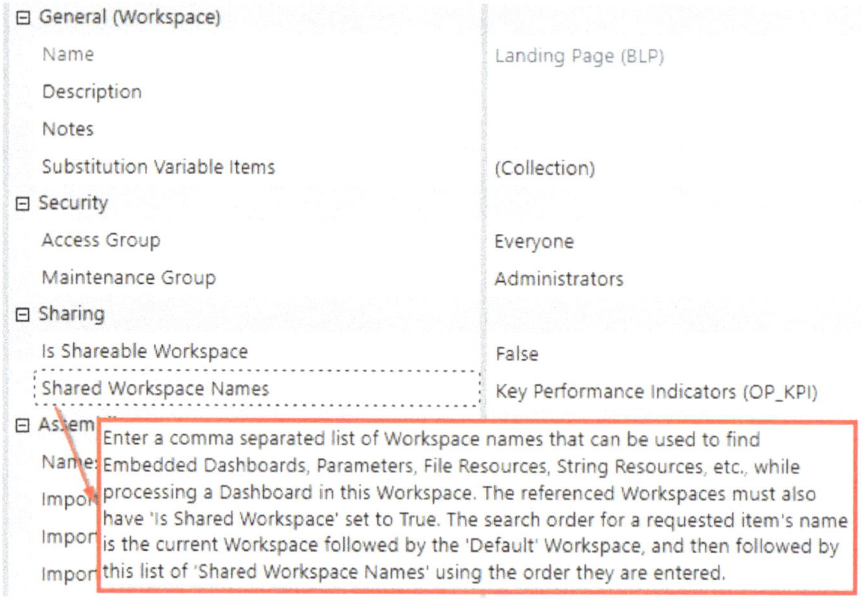

Figure 2.4

Naming Conventions

You can now use the same name of an object multiple times, as long as the object with the same name is in a separate Workspace. Prior to the release of Workspaces, it was something of a challenge naming new dashboards and components if the object name already existed, meaning that you could not use the same name for a dashboard or component if it already existed, even if it was stored in a separate maintenance unit.

To explain this more explicitly, say you need to add a new button to a dashboard to open a file, and you name the button `btn_OpenFile`. If another button in the application already exists with the name `btn_OpenFile`, you previously could not save the new button until you gave it a different name, maybe `btn_OpenFile2`. Assuming you are not aware of the existing `btn_OpenFile` button, wouldn't you wonder if there was supposed to be a button named `btn_OpenFile1`? The ability to reuse object names in separate Workspaces means you can now name the new button `btn_OpenFile` to stay organized and clean.

The same concept applies to all objects in the Workspace, including maintenance units, dashboards, Cube Views, data management jobs, components, data adapters, files, strings, and Assemblies.

Foundation For Future Development

Central Workspace Design Templates

Solutions downloaded from the Solution Exchange have started transitioning how the solutions are built using Workspaces, with solutions fully packaged within the Workspace. This means that when you load solutions from the Solution Exchange, the Workspace will include Assemblies with the code files housed in the Workspace rather than importing them directly into the application's business rules library.

Developers can build standard dashboard layout templates in dedicated Workspaces for the sole purpose of sharing them with other team members in the organization, ensuring a consistent end-user experience. The more familiar you are with Workspaces, the more value you will see as you develop content.

Product Packaging for Creating, Deploying, and Migrating Solutions

Developers now have a whole new way to create and share solutions in a way that is centrally managed for streamlined navigation, troubleshooting, and deployment. As with any software, organizations typically have a separate environment for building and testing new solutions and updates before migrating them to the live environment; this is commonly known as a "sandbox" environment. The introduction of Workspaces now allows developers to work in a sandbox environment and quickly and easily port solutions between the sandbox and live environments.

Cube View Groups

Cube Views can be built and managed within a Workspace's maintenance unit without navigating out of the Workspace and into the Cube Views page.

Data Management Groups

Data management groups can be built and managed within a Workspace's maintenance unit without navigating out of the Workspace and into the Data Management page.

Assemblies

Assemblies, also known as business rules, can be stored and maintained within a Workspace's maintenance unit as well, making this part of a solution especially powerful when developing logic that will control the functionality of a given solution.

Packaging The Solution

OneStream solutions are built on the framework and mindset of a dashboard being the "main" product; however, there are other objects to consider when thinking about a solution. In terms of sharing solutions or migrating a solution between environments, developers have previously had to extract multiple objects from an application in order to load the full solution into another application.

The figure below shows the Load/Extract window with the items that would need to be individually extracted highlighted. This process of extracting all solution items can be confusing and cause solutions not to work as designed if any one item is missed when exporting from the development environment, adding risk to a seemingly simple porting objective.

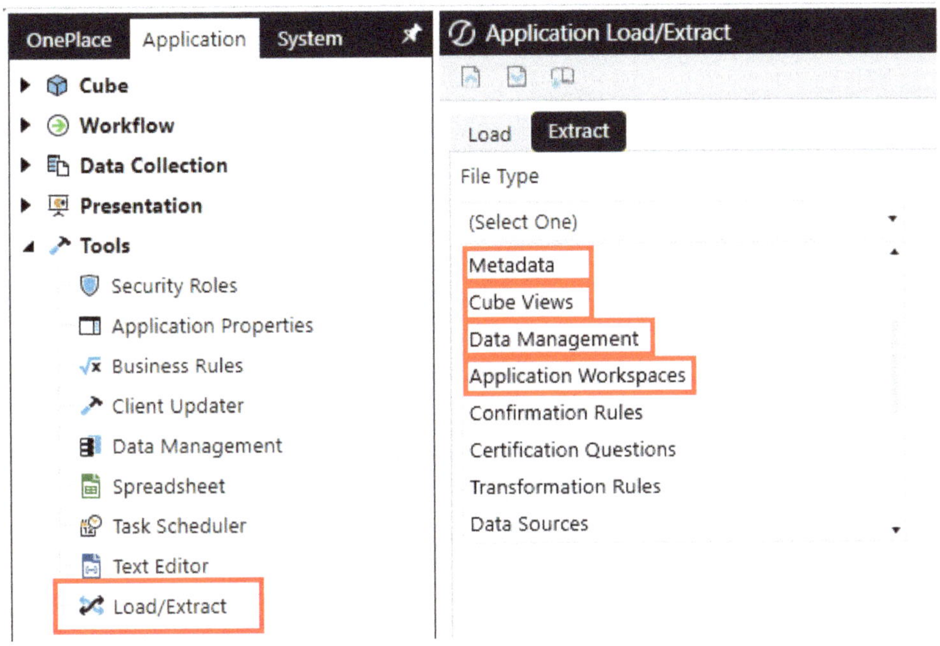

Figure 2.5

Once development becomes fully built within a Workspace, the extract process is much simpler and reduces the risk of forgetting to extract items such as Cube Views, data management jobs, and Assemblies. The figure below shows the process of extracting a single item (Application Workspaces) from the File Type drop-down menu and selecting the Workspace with all related items neatly packaged in a single XML file.

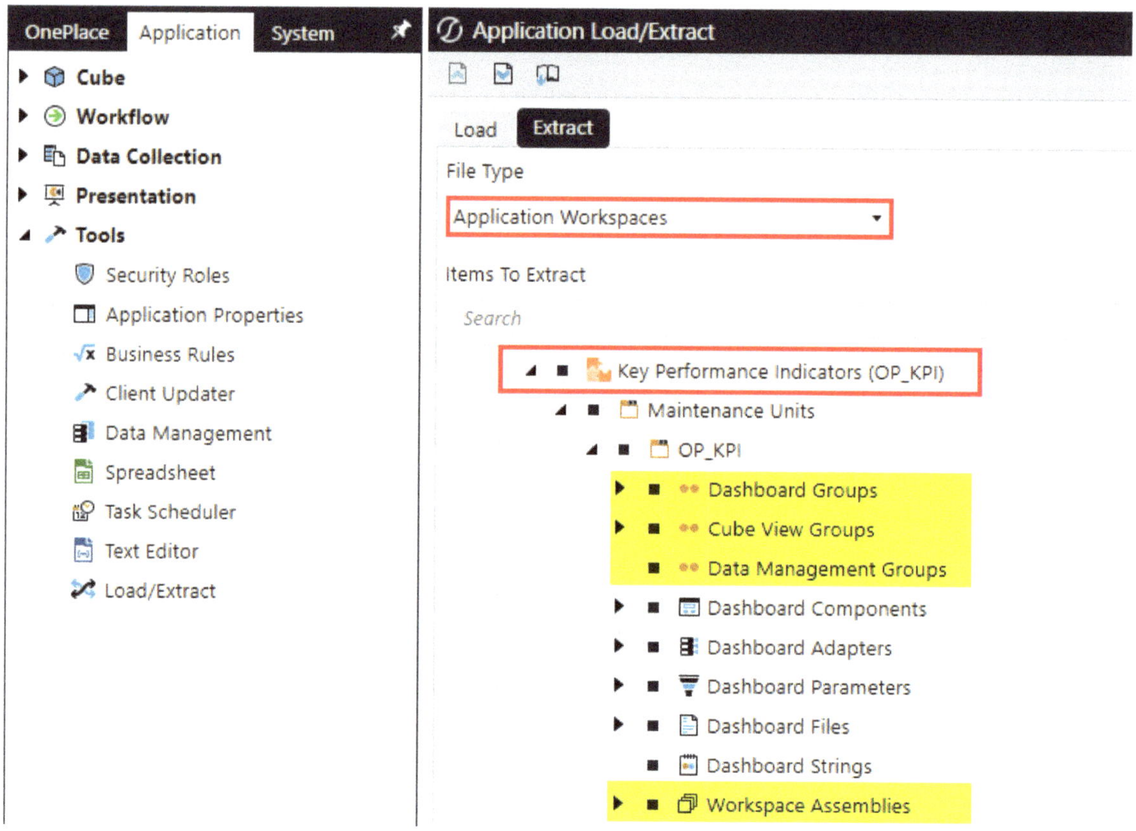

Figure 2.6

Practical Use Cases

Organizing Dashboards

OneStream allows you to organize your dashboards and related objects by grouping them into Workspaces, providing a cleaner view of what solutions are in your application. When you need to make changes to a Cube View or data management job, you can simply navigate to the object's Workspace to find the object you need to update.

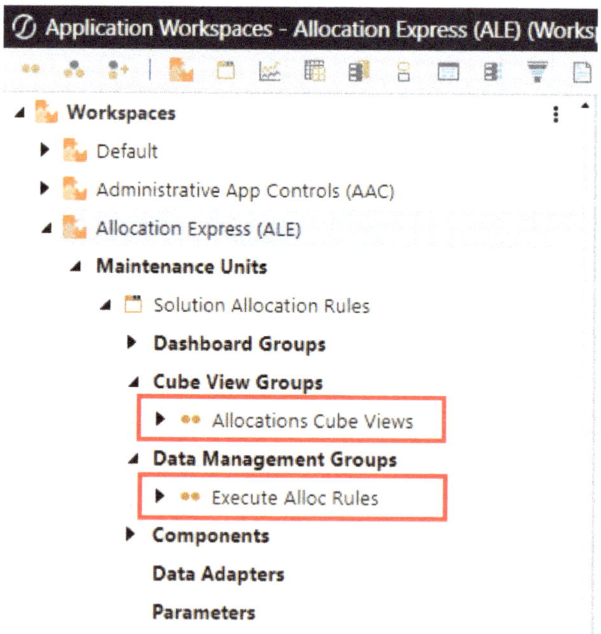

Figure 2.7

Workspaces can be organized in many ways, whether it be by function area, development projects, or however your organization wants to group specific workstreams. The figure below is an example of Workspace categorization by functional area, making it much easier to find what you're looking for and troubleshoot when needed.

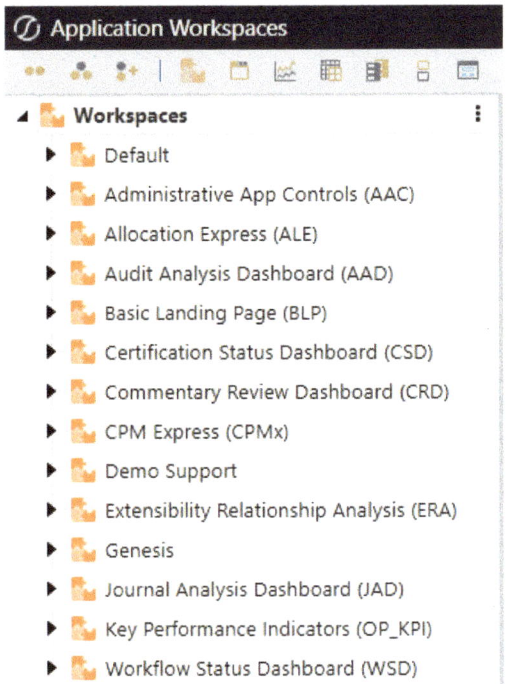

Figure 2.8

Sharing Packaged Solutions

You now have the ability to package solutions into Workspaces for export and sharing. This is especially powerful when you consider the standard way of exporting solutions requires you to export piecemeal items from the Load/Extract page. In this use case, we've developed a solution, below, to display KPIs and are ready to share the solution with other developers, applications, or even publish the solution on OneStream's Community Solutions forum.

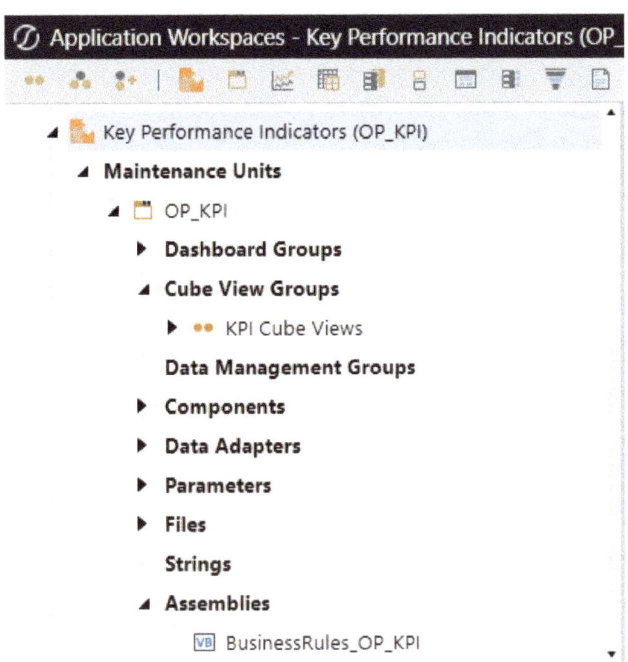

Figure 2.9

With Workspaces, you can easily export the Workspace and all related objects with one extract file.

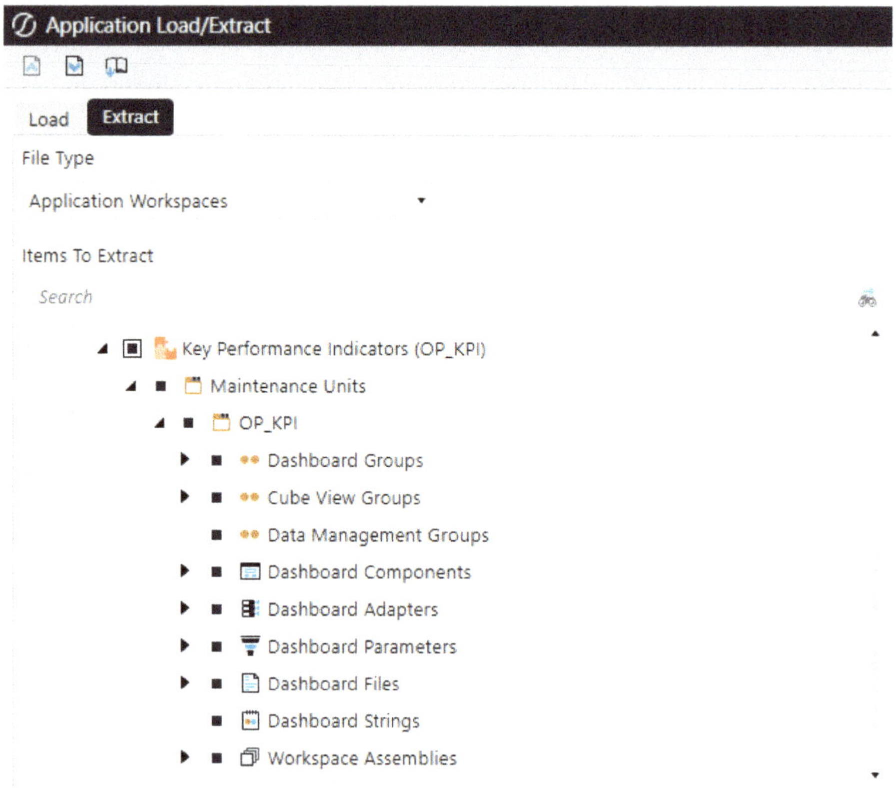

Figure 2.10

Enable Multiple Developers to Build Simultaneously

For this use case, we'll show how to configure Workspaces to grant access and maintenance rights to developers working on separate workstreams, how to add an overarching security group with rights to multiple Workspaces, and how the specified security groups are configured.

Use Case

We have two developers currently building dashboard solutions and one QA user responsible for reviewing and ultimately signing off on the solutions before they can be made available for end-users. Below is our development team and their security group assignments, as well as their role in development, and which solutions they are responsible for.

Security Group	Name	Role	Workspace
DeveloperGroup1	EricTelhiard	Maintenance	Annual Operating Plan
DeveloperGroup2	JessicaToner	Maintenance	Close and Consolidation
DevelopmentQA	TomShea	Access	Annual Operating Plan Close and Consolidation

Figure 2.11

Application Security Roles

There are three primary security role assignments that control access to the Workspaces page, Workspace management, and Workspace Assemblies. To configure these roles, navigate to the Security Roles page located under the Tools section of the Application tab. OneStream's flexible security model allows you to tailor access and permissions across various Workspace components, enabling you to assign appropriate rights based on user responsibilities.

The image below illustrates the Workspace-specific security roles (left) and the corresponding permissions they grant (right).

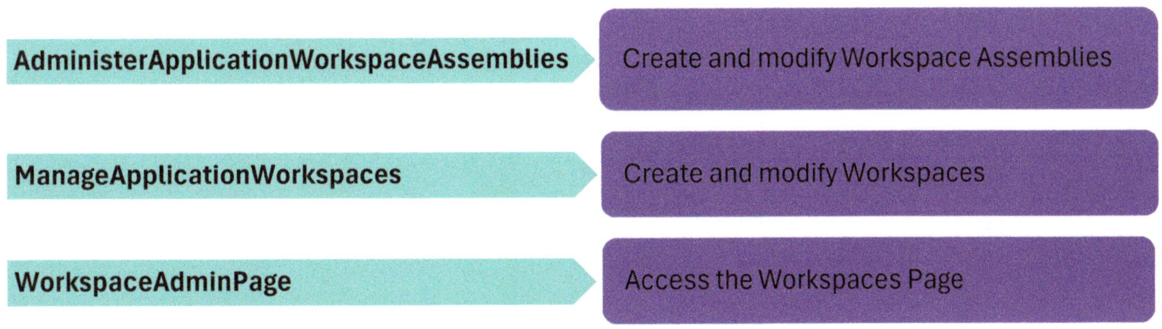

Figure 2.12

To grant users access to the Workspaces page and the ability to manage Workspaces and Workspace Assemblies, they must be added to the appropriate Application Security Role-assigned groups. Once the security groups shown in Figure 2.11 are created, they can be added as Child Groups to the relevant Application Security Role groups in your application settings. This ensures proper inheritance of access and management rights.

Refer to Chapter 3 for a step-by-step walkthrough on how to navigate and configure these settings.

Security Configuration

Before security is assigned to the Workspace, start by creating the security groups (if they don't already exist) and adding the appropriate users to the groups. In this example, we only have one developer under `DeveloperGroup1`; however, you could have as many users in these groups as necessary.

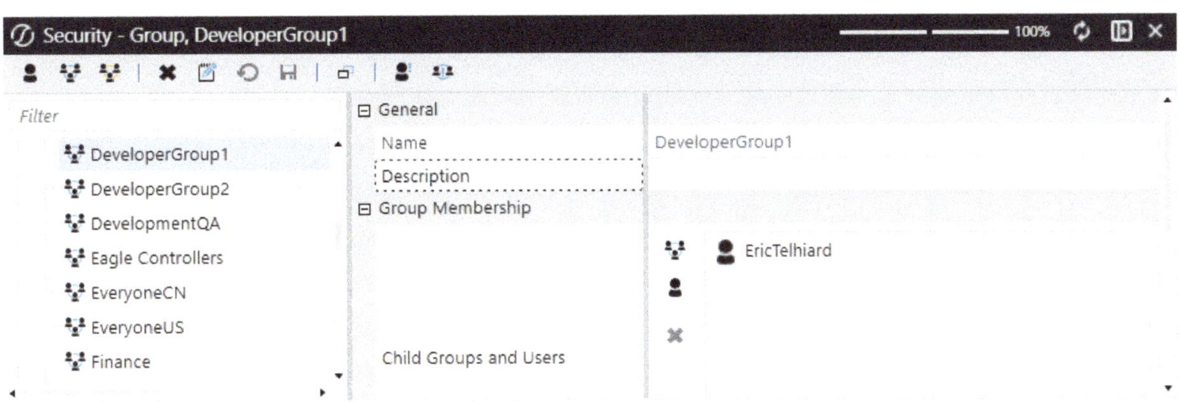

Figure 2.13

The next security group we need to create is `DeveloperGroup2`, and we need to assign a developer to it.

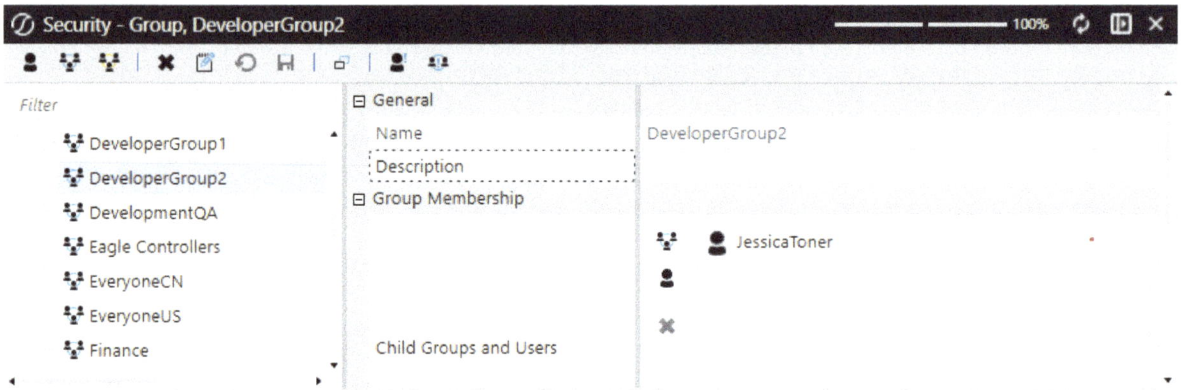

Figure 2.14

Now that we've established our two dedicated developer security groups, we need to create a group for QA users or business stakeholders.

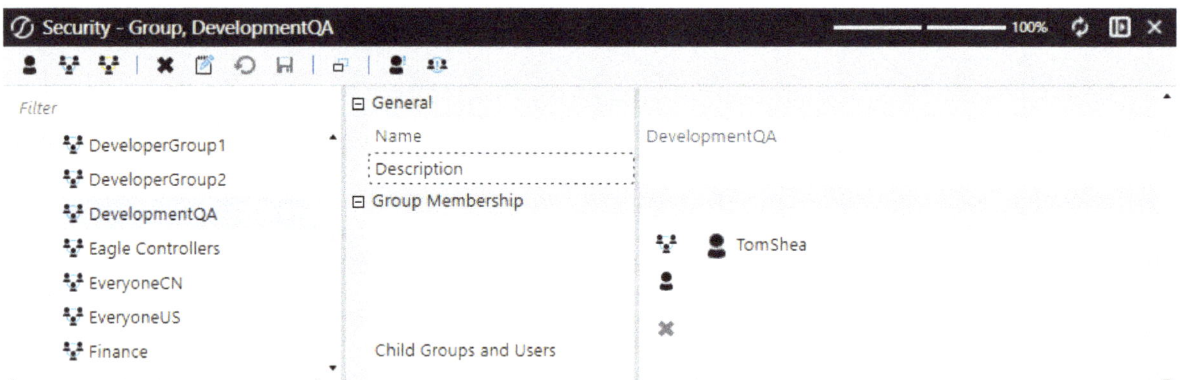

Figure 2.15

Workspace Security Assignment

Once our developers and QA users are in the appropriate security groups, we can assign the rights to the Workspaces. We've assigned `DeveloperGroup1` and `DeveloperGroup2` to the maintenance groups of the `Annual Operating Plan` and `Close and Consolidation` Workspaces. The Access Group for both Workspaces is assigned to DevelopmentQA, which is how we give access rights to our QA team without giving them rights to modify anything within the Workspaces.

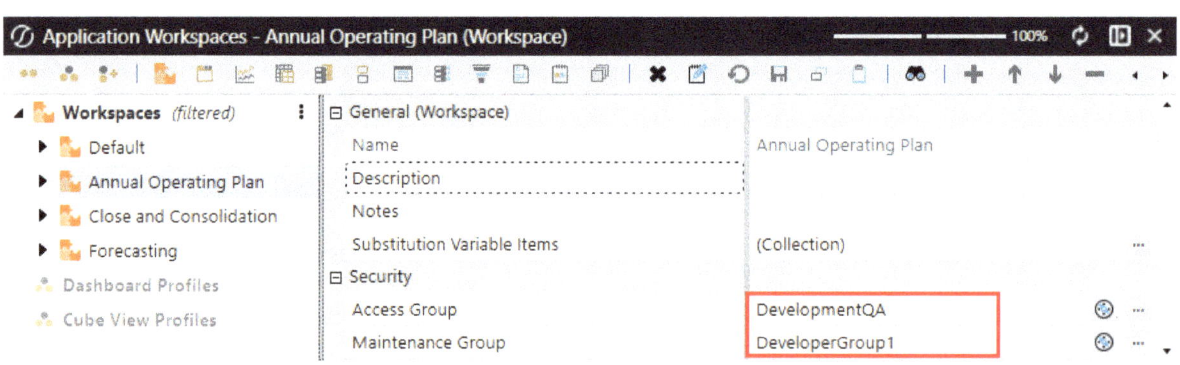

Figure 2.16

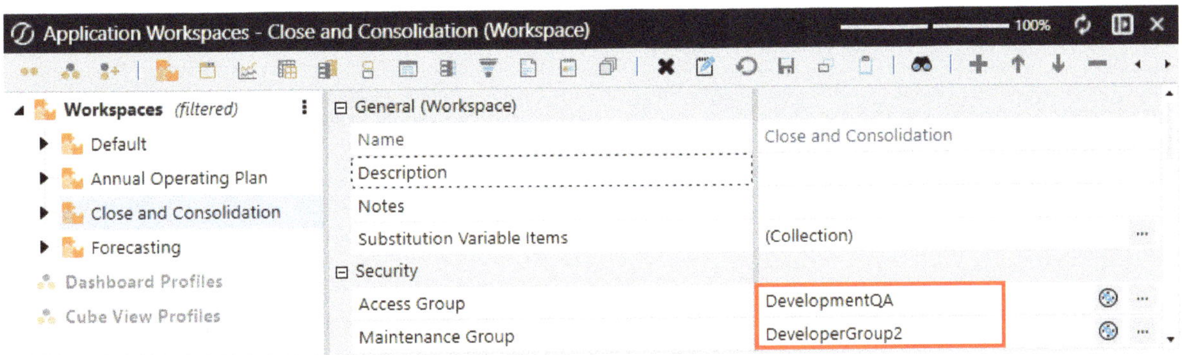

Figure 2.17

Testing Security Assignments

EricTelhiard logs into OneStream and only sees the Workspace that he is responsible for.

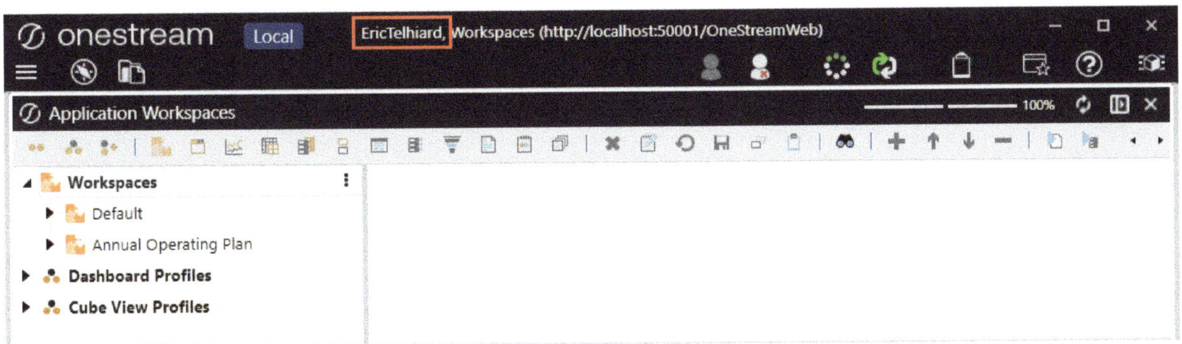

Figure 2.18

JessicaToner logs into OneStream and only sees the Workspace that she is responsible for.

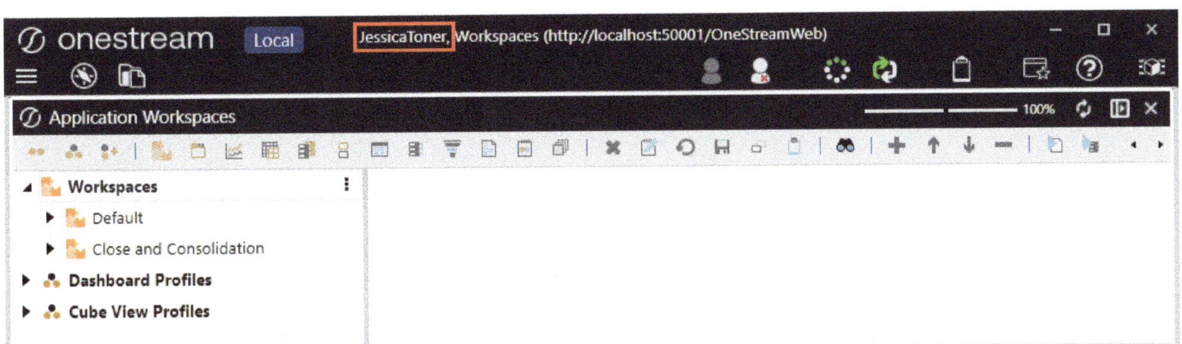

Figure 2.19

TomShea logs into OneStream and sees both Workspaces that he is responsible for (`Annual Operating Plan` & `Close and Consolidation`), but he cannot modify anything in the Workspaces (which is what we would expect, having given him access-only rights). The grey text on the right upon `Maintenance Unit` selection denotes that this is read-only.

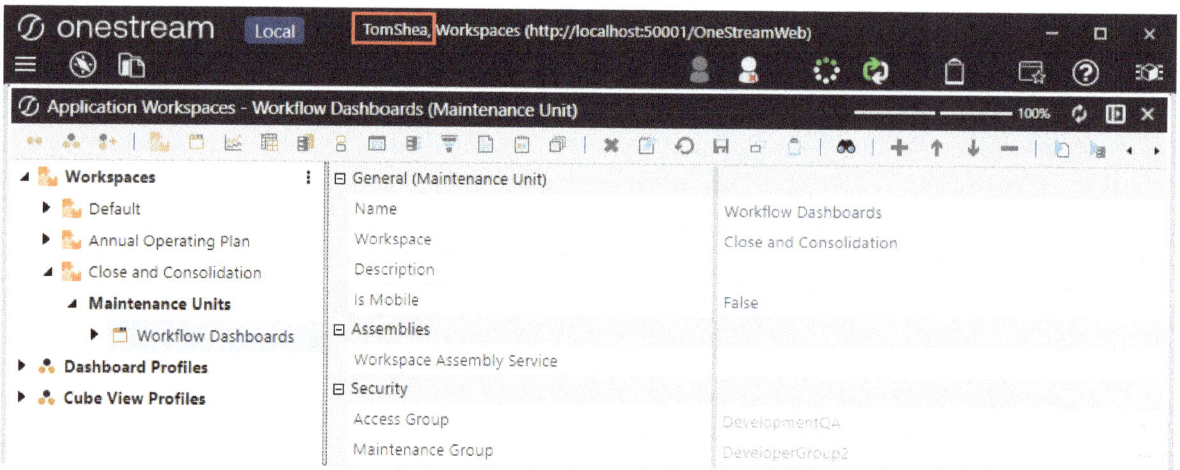

Figure 2.20

That's it! That's how easy it is to set up Workspace security to enable multiple developers to build simultaneously within OneStream without disrupting other developers or build activity. It's worth noting that users can be added and removed from security groups as needed, so once you establish a security structure for Workspace development, you can reuse it over and over again.

Workspace vs Traditional Development Environments

Many organizations follow a development lifecycle that involves building and testing solutions in a sandbox environment before deploying them to a live production environment. Traditionally, this process can be time-consuming and disruptive, as administrators must take the application offline to copy the sandbox environment over to production.

This downtime creates several challenges:

- **End-user disruptions:** Taking the application offline can temporarily block users from accessing critical reports, dashboards, or other functionalities needed for daily operations.
- **Developer delays:** While the update process is underway, developers are unable to make further changes, which slows down progress and iteration cycles.
- **Risk of errors:** Moving an entire environment can be complex, requiring careful coordination to avoid data loss or configuration issues.

How Workspaces Improve This Process

Workspaces provide a modernized approach that allows development, testing, and deployment to happen more seamlessly within the same instance – eliminating the need for disruptive environment swaps.

- **Parallel development:** Developers can continue working on new solutions without interfering with live business operations.
- **Seamless QA testing:** Users can test updates in real-time within the same instance, making quality assurance (QA) more efficient and accelerating feedback loops.
- **Concurrent collaboration:** Developers and business users can work in the same Workspace at the same time, refining solutions independently without waiting for a full environment migration. Updates become visible upon refresh, enabling efficient coordination.

By leveraging Workspaces, organizations can streamline their development cycles, reduce downtime, and create a more agile, collaborative approach to solution development and deployment.

Potential Misconceptions About Workspaces

Too Complicated to Set Up

False. Setting up Workspaces is just as simple as configuring maintenance units. In the next chapter, you'll find a hands-on exercise guiding you through the process of setting up a Workspace step by step.

Need to Rebuild Solutions

That statement is false because there is no need to rebuild existing solutions when adopting Workspaces in OneStream. Workspaces are an optional but powerful organizational tool designed to enhance structure and navigation, not a fundamental change that requires the redevelopment of existing solutions.

When you download and implement solutions from the OneStream Solution Exchange, any solutions that have been upgraded to use the Workspace methodology are designed to seamlessly integrate with your existing environment. These upgraded solutions automatically recognize and categorize existing objects – such as business rules, dashboards, and reports – placing them into the appropriate Workspace upon loading into the application. This ensures a smooth transition without requiring users to manually reorganize or rewrite their solutions.

Rather than replacing or restructuring your current framework, Workspaces function as an additional tool in your development toolbox, helping to improve organization and accessibility while maintaining backward compatibility. You can continue using OneStream as you always have, but with the added benefit of a more structured approach to managing your assets going forward.

In summary, Workspaces enhance the way you interact with your solutions, but they do not require redevelopment. They simply provide a more intuitive, organized way to manage content, making it easier for developers and end users to navigate and maintain their OneStream applications efficiently.

No Benefit to My Organization

That statement is false because OneStream's Workspaces provide value to all users, regardless of their role or the complexity of their development needs. Whether you're managing multiple development projects or simply looking for a way to make dashboard navigation more intuitive, Workspaces enhance organization, accessibility, and efficiency across the board.

For developers and administrators handling multiple projects, Workspaces serve as a structured environment where assets such as dashboards, reports, and business rules can be logically grouped. This makes it easier to manage different development efforts without confusion or overlap, improving overall workflow efficiency.

For power users, Workspaces contribute to a better user experience by organizing content in a way that makes navigation more intuitive. Rather than sifting through a cluttered interface, users can quickly locate and interact with the dashboards and reports that are most relevant to their role.

Additionally, Workspaces help enforce security and access control by allowing organizations to assign permissions at a more granular level. This means that different teams or individuals can be granted access to only the content they need, reducing the risk of unauthorized modifications while keeping the user experience streamlined.

Ultimately, whether you are deeply involved in development or just need an easy way to navigate OneStream's reporting and analysis tools, Workspaces provide undeniable benefits that enhance usability, organization, and security.

Tips for Optimizing Workspaces

Assign Role-Based Security

When implementing security controls in your development environment, it's crucial to leverage your existing security model rather than building something entirely new from scratch. This approach ensures efficiency and consistency across your organization while reducing administrative overhead.

By using your current security model, you can streamline the segregation of duties, ensuring that developers, QA teams, and other stakeholders have access only to the data and functionalities they need. This also allows you to apply and restrict modification rights appropriately, preventing unauthorized changes that could compromise system integrity. Additionally, it enhances the organization of dashboards and Workspaces, making it easier for developers to navigate and access relevant tools and data.

A key strategy for managing access control effectively is to create predefined security groups for development and QA teams. Establishing these groups from the outset enables quick and systematic assignment of security permissions at multiple levels – such as Workspaces and maintenance units. This granular control ensures that security policies align with your organization's needs, maintaining compliance while fostering a structured and secure development environment.

By adopting this approach, you not only enhance security but also improve operational efficiency by reducing the time and effort required to manage access controls manually.

Leverage Solution Exchange Solutions

Solutions available on the OneStream Solution Exchange are designed to be highly robust, feature-rich, and well-structured, making them excellent references for best practices in solution development. These solutions are built with real-world use cases in mind, offering organizations pre-configured functionality that can be leveraged, modified, or studied to improve their own implementations.

The Shift to Workspace-Driven Solutions

As OneStream continues evolving, more solutions are being developed using the Workspace methodology. This shift enhances organization and usability by grouping relevant objects – such as business rules, data management jobs, and Assemblies – within a dedicated Workspace, providing a clearer and more structured way to manage solution components.

Example: Navigation Center Solution

A great example of this transition is the **Navigation Center solution** from the Solution Exchange. When you download and load this solution into your application, you'll see that:

- Data management jobs and business rules are neatly organized within the Workspace.
- The solution is structured to be easily navigable, allowing users to quickly understand how different components interact.
- Developers can use it as a reference, analyzing the built-in data management jobs, business rules, and Assemblies to learn how similar functionality can be applied to their own solutions.

By downloading and exploring these Workspace-driven solutions, users can gain valuable insights into OneStream's best practices, understand how complex processes are structured, and accelerate their own development efforts without starting from scratch. As more solutions adopt the Workspace approach, this will further streamline the implementation and customization process, making it easier for organizations to deploy and manage powerful financial and operational solutions.

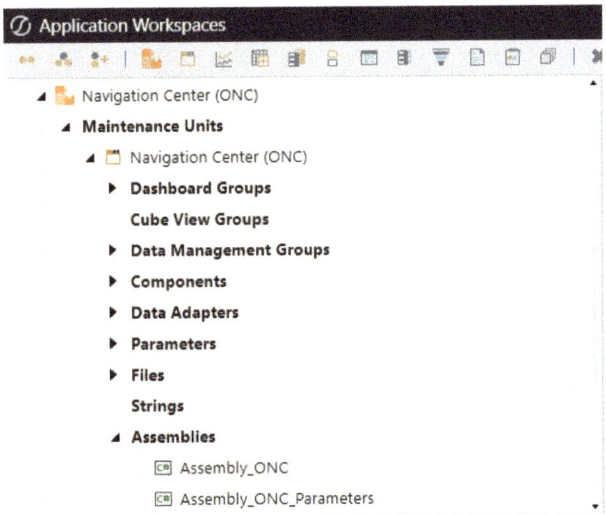

Figure 2.21

You can also extract an existing Workspace, open the XML and change the Workspace name shown below, then load the XML back into the application. Once you've loaded the file, navigate to the Workspaces page, and you'll see a new Workspace where you can change, add objects, and test.

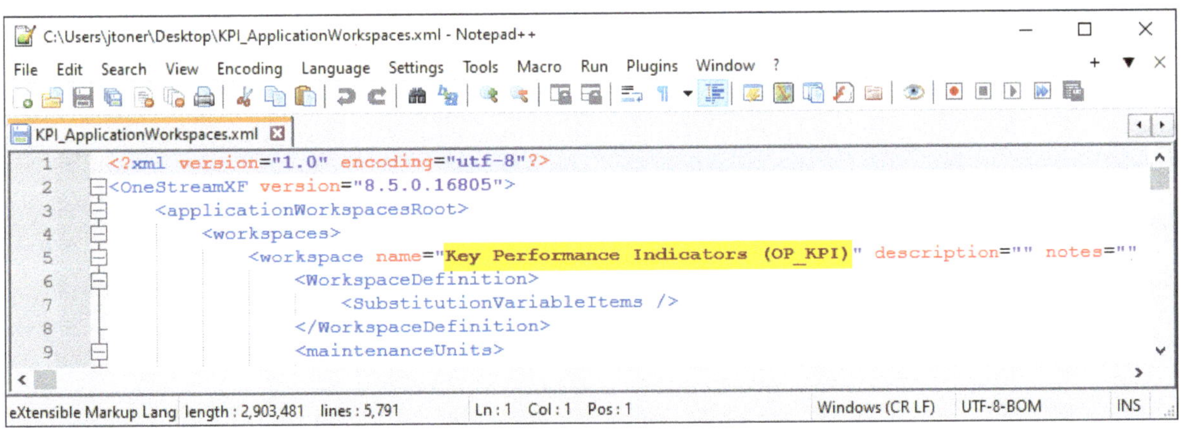

Figure 2.22

Encourage Adoption of Development

The earlier you start incorporating Workspaces into your development workflow, the more benefits you'll unlock in terms of efficiency, organization, and flexibility. Workspaces are designed to streamline development, making it easier to manage multiple projects simultaneously without disrupting ongoing operations.

Why Workspaces Are a Game-Changer for Developers

For developers, Workspaces provide a structured, isolated environment where they can build, test, and refine dashboards, reports, and business rules independently. This eliminates common bottlenecks that occur when multiple developers need to work within the same application environment.

Key Benefits:

- **Parallel Development**: Developers can work on new dashboards and features at the same time as others, without the risk of interfering with each other's progress.

- **No Disruptions to Existing Processes**: Unlike traditional methods that might require taking an application offline to implement changes, Workspaces let you continue building without affecting production or other development efforts.
- **Greater Autonomy**: Developers don't have to wait for others to finish their work before they can start their own. Workspaces provide independent environments that allow for faster iteration and experimentation.
- **More Agile Development**: With Workspaces, changes can be tested and refined in real time, making it easier to gather feedback and optimize solutions before they're deployed across the organization.

A No-Brainer for Future-Proofing Your Development

By adopting Workspaces early, you're setting up your organization for greater scalability and smoother collaboration. As OneStream continues evolving toward Workspace-driven solutions, being proactive in integrating this methodology will maximize your development flexibility and efficiency going forward.

Dashboard Types

When creating a new dashboard in OneStream, the **Dashboard Type** setting defaults to (Use Default). This means that the system applies the standard dashboard type configuration unless manually changed. Users, however, have the flexibility to adjust this setting to better fit the specific use case and functionality required.

Top Level

The dashboard type can be configured to determine how a dashboard is displayed within the OnePlace interface. By setting the Dashboard Type to Top Level, you control which dashboard is exposed at the highest level in the OnePlace navigation menu.

Scenario Explanation

Imagine you have a dashboard group that contains multiple dashboards. For instance, you might have several dashboards, like `0_ImageSelection_BLP_OnePlace`, and `0_LandingPage_BLP_OnePlace`, all grouped together under a single Dashboard Group. This group is assigned to a dashboard profile that is exposed from OnePlace, but you only want one of these dashboards to be shown in the OnePlace dashboard menu at the top level – specifically, `0_LandingPage_BLP_OnePlace`.

How It Works

- The dashboard group is part of a larger dashboard profile that defines the dashboards available to specific users or roles.
- By default, when multiple dashboards are part of the group, they may all be accessible or visible to users, which could lead to navigation clutter or an inefficient user experience.
- To manage this, you can go into the Behavior settings of the specific dashboard and set the Dashboard Type to Top Level. This ensures that only the chosen dashboard (`0_LandingPage_BLP_OnePlace`) is exposed at the top level in the OnePlace menu, making it easily accessible from the main dashboard menu.

Why Is This Important?

- **Streamlined User Experience:** Users don't have to sift through unnecessary options in the OnePlace menu. They can go straight to the most important or frequently used dashboard.
- **Focused Navigation:** By restricting which dashboards appear in the top-level menu, you guide users to the most relevant content, improving workflow efficiency and reducing confusion.

- **Improved Dashboard Management:** This setting ensures that only one or more key dashboards are highlighted for users, while others can remain accessible at a lower navigation level or hidden as needed.

In the figure below, we see two dashboards within the Dashboard Group assigned to the dashboard profile, but by setting the Dashboard Type of 0_LandingPage_BLP_OnePlace to Top Level, we ensure it is the only one visible from the OnePlace dashboard menu. This makes it the primary entry point for users, improving accessibility and overall experience.

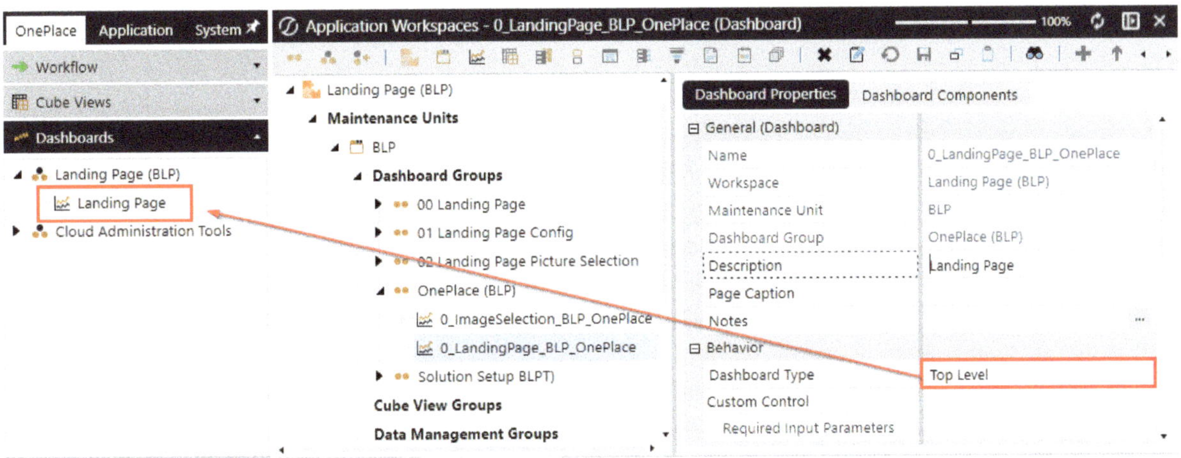

Figure 2.23

Top Level Without Parameter Prompts

The **Top Level Without Parameter Prompts** dashboard type is a powerful tool when you want to simplify the user experience and control which parameters are available for user interaction in your dashboards. This type is particularly useful when you want to show users a specific view of data – such as a financial report or an operational dashboard – without giving them the option to modify certain parameters, like time periods or dimensions.

Embedded

The **Embedded** dashboard type is one of the most commonly used when creating hierarchical or layered dashboards, especially in scenarios where you're building dashboards on top of dashboards. This approach allows you to create a more dynamic and interactive dashboard structure by combining multiple dashboard elements, such as buttons, Cube Views, charts, and other dashboard components, in a nested or integrated format.

Scenario Explanation

Imagine you have several dashboards that work together to form a larger, more complex interface. For instance, you might have:

1. A **button dashboard** that lets users navigate to different sections or trigger specific actions.
2. A **Cube View dashboard** that displays detailed financial or operational data.
3. A **combined dashboard** that brings the button dashboard and the Cube View dashboard together, creating a seamless, unified experience.

In this case, the button dashboard and the Cube View dashboard are embedded into the combined dashboard. This allows users to interact with the button (to navigate or trigger actions) and view the cube data in the same space, *without having to open separate dashboards.*

In your application, you may have a Landing Page dashboard exposed at the top level (via the Top-Level setting) in the OnePlace menu. However, within this landing page, you could have an embedded dashboard that contains detailed financial data (Cube View), which should not be exposed directly in OnePlace. By setting the Embedded Dashboard Type, users can access it through the Landing Page interface without cluttering the OnePlace menu.

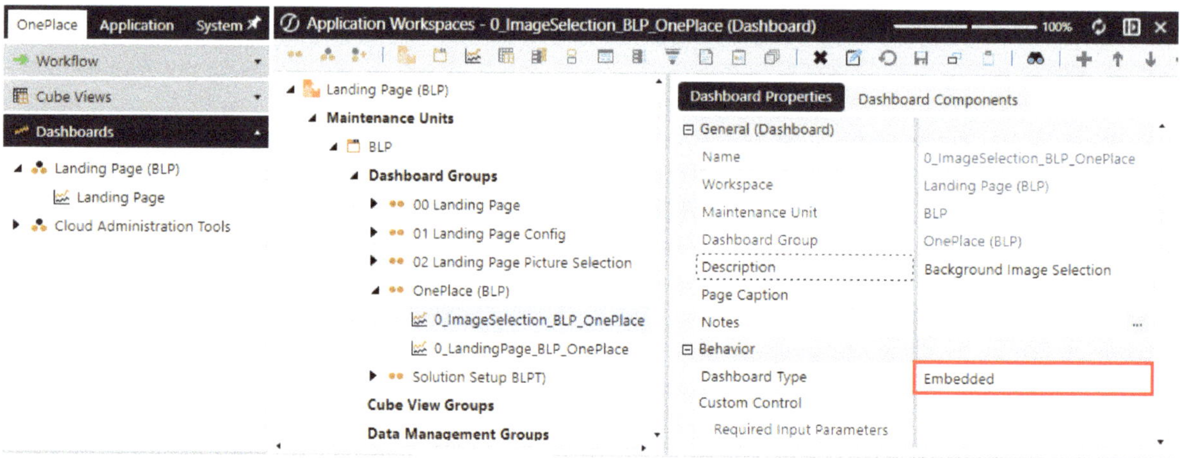

Figure 2.24

Embedded Dynamic

Embedded Dynamic dashboards are used when creating objects defined in the Workspace's Assemblies. The concept of Embedded Dynamic dashboard usage and configuration will be explained in more detail in Chapter 8.

Embedded Dynamic Repeater

The **Embedded Dynamic Repeater** dashboard type is designed for scenarios where you want to display multiple instances of a single object within a dashboard. This is achieved by utilizing the Component Template Repeat Items property, which allows you to define a set of items that will each use the same object to display repeated content, based on the template properties. This approach is particularly useful when you need to dynamically display a list of buttons, such as workflow navigation buttons.

The concept of configuring and using the Embedded Dynamic Repeater dashboard type will be explored in more detail in Chapter 8, where we will delve into how to leverage this functionality effectively.

Custom Control

Custom Control dashboards allow you to use dashboard templates in order to change the behavior of the underlying components using **Event Listeners**.

Conclusion

In this chapter, we explored the core concept of Workspaces in OneStream and how they enhance data management, organization, and collaboration. You've learned how Workspaces function as flexible environments that allow multiple users to build and manage solutions independently while maintaining security and efficiency. By understanding their key components and best practices, you are now equipped to leverage Workspaces to streamline development and improve overall system performance.

With this foundational knowledge, you are ready to take the next step. In the following chapter, we will walk through a hands-on exercise to set up a Workspace, allowing you to apply what you've learned and experience the benefits firsthand!

3

Setting Up Your Workspace

A well-organized Workspace is the foundation of a productive and efficient OneStream experience. Whether you're a new user exploring the platform for the first time, an experienced administrator looking to fine-tune your environment, or a developer eager to better manage your development projects in an organized way, setting up your Workspace correctly ensures seamless navigation, improved workflow efficiency, and quick access to essential tools and data.

OneStream is a powerful and flexible platform designed to unify financial processes such as budgeting, forecasting, reporting, and consolidation. However, to fully leverage its capabilities, it's crucial to *tailor* your Workspace to *your specific needs*. From customizing dashboards and setting up workflow structures to adjusting user preferences and configuring security settings, a properly configured Workspace enables you to work smarter and faster.

In this chapter, we'll guide you through the key steps to optimize your OneStream environment. You'll learn about:

- **Navigating the OneStream interface** to understand its layout and key components.
- **Workspace Properties explained** to provide detailed explanations of Workspace properties and how to use and configure them.
- **Managing security and access controls** to ensure the right users have appropriate permissions.
- **How to set up a Workspace** to serve as a starting point for future development.
- **Workspace Filter Functionality** to help you focus on what you're working on and/or reviewing.

By the end of this chapter, you'll have a fully customized OneStream Workspace that enhances your efficiency and gives you the tools to leverage OneStream Workspaces and extend your use of the OneStream platform.

Let's dive in and start setting up your Workspace for success!

Navigating the Workspace Interface

OneStream's Workspace interface is designed for efficiency, providing users with seamless access to key tools, reports, and workflows. Understanding how to navigate the interface ensures a smoother experience, allowing users to maximize productivity while leveraging OneStream's powerful financial planning, reporting, and analytics capabilities. This section provides an in-depth guide to the key components of the OneStream Workspace and how to navigate them effectively.

Toolbar Buttons

Below is a complete inventory of the Workspace toolbar buttons and a description of their function.

1. **Create Group**: Create a new Cube View group (if the cursor is on the Cube View groups icon), dashboard group (if on the dashboard groups text of a maintenance unit), or data management group (if the cursor is on the data management icon).
2. **Create Profile:** Create a new Cube View Profile (if you have selected a Cube View Profile) or dashboard profile (if you have selected a dashboard profile).

3. **Manage Profile Members:** Displays the profile builder dialog box if you have selected either a Cube View Profile or a dashboard profile. If the Cube View or dashboard is not in the default Workspace, a tool tip will display the Workspace prefix when you hover the cursor over the group name.
4. **Create Workspace:** Create a new Workspace (security role-based).
5. **Create Maintenance Unit:** Create a new maintenance unit to store dashboards.
6. **Create Dashboard:** Create a new dashboard to attach components to.
7. **Create Cube View:** Create a new Cube View when viewing Cube View groups.
8. **Create Sequence:** Create a new sequence within data management groups.
9. **Create Step:** Create a new step within data management groups.
10. **Create Dashboard Component:** Opens a dialog listing components to pick to create.
11. **Create Data Adapter:** Create a new data adapter to add to a dashboard component.
12. **Create Parameter:** Create a new parameter to create lists or use in formatting.
13. **Create File:** Create a new file to be used in the Workspace.
14. **Create String:** Create a new string to use on Cube View headers.
15. **Create Assembly:** Create a new Workspace Assembly.
16. **Delete Selected Item:** Delete selected component item. You can select multiple Cube Views, Cube View groups, and data management group steps and sequences. You can only delete empty Cube View groups, and multi-select more than one data management sequence and step to delete within the same data management group. Multiple Cube Views can only be selected and deleted if they are in the same Cube View group. You cannot delete data management sequences or steps within different data management groups at the same time. For an Assembly, you must be on the Properties tab to be able to delete it.
17. **Rename Selected Item:** Opens the Rename dialog box.
18. **Cancel All Changes Since Last Save:** Will undo all changes made to an object.
19. **Save:** The button is visible when adding or modifying an object.
20. **Copy:** Makes a copy of the selected items. Select more than one item of the same type by pressing and holding the Ctrl button and clicking each item with the mouse. You can also select the items to copy, then right-click to open a context menu. You can only copy items of the same type.
21. **Paste:** Pastes copied items into the selected destination. `_Copy` is appended to the name of the newly pasted item.
22. **Search:** Search for a component using the Select Workspace Object dialog box. Cube Views and data management sequences and steps are added to the list of searchable objects.
23. **Plus Sign:** Adds a data management group sequence or step, Cube View row or column, or dashboard component.

24. **Move Up:** Moves up a data management group sequence or step, Cube View row or column, or dashboard component.

25. **Move Down:** Moves down a data management group sequence or step, Cube View row or column, or dashboard component.

26. **Minus Sign:** Removes a data management group sequence or step, Cube View row or column, or dashboard component.

27. **View Dashboard:** Displays dashboard.

28. **View Dashboard in Design Mode:** Displays dashboard with the structure outlined to visually select objects to navigate to directly.

29. **Show Objects That Reference the Selected Item:** Opens the Object Usage Viewer and lists all objects that reference the selected item.

30. **Object Lookup:** Opens the Object Lookup dialog box, letting you search for any object in the application, such as all Workspaces that contain data management sequences and any other object.

Workspace Structure

Workspaces are incredibly powerful when it comes to organizing dashboards. They also provide developers with dedicated development environments where they can build dashboards and application functionality within an isolated Workspace. With the recently added capability to build Cube Views, data management sequences, and Workspace Assemblies within Workspaces, solutions can truly be developed for packaging and distribution, whether you want to share a solution or create a solution for the Partner Exchange or Community Exchange.

The introduction of Workspaces has led to some changes to the Workspaces (formerly dashboards) user interface, as the Workspaces, profiles, and default objects are stored slightly differently than before Workspaces were available in the OneStream Platform.

Below are some main differences, as well as items that have remained the same.

Cube View groups and data management groups that are not built within a new Workspace are located under the default maintenance unit, which is a child of the default Workspace. Maintenance units that existed before Workspaces were available are under the default Workspace.

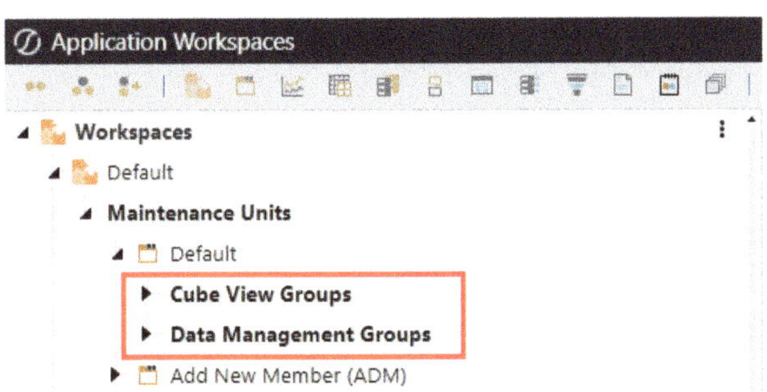

Figure 3.1

Dashboard profiles and Cube View Profiles are globally located under the Workspaces tree; these profiles are not Workspace-specific and have remained in the same location.

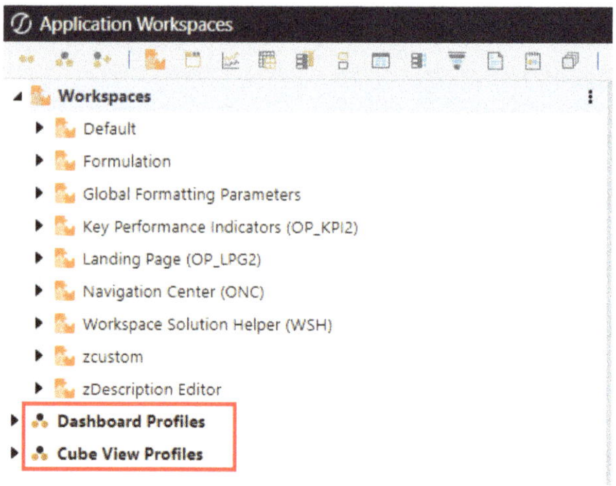

Figure 3.2

New Workspaces that have been created manually, as well as some solutions from the Solution Exchange that began using Workspaces upon deployment of the solution, contain their own maintenance units, Cube View groups, data management groups, and Workspace Assemblies.

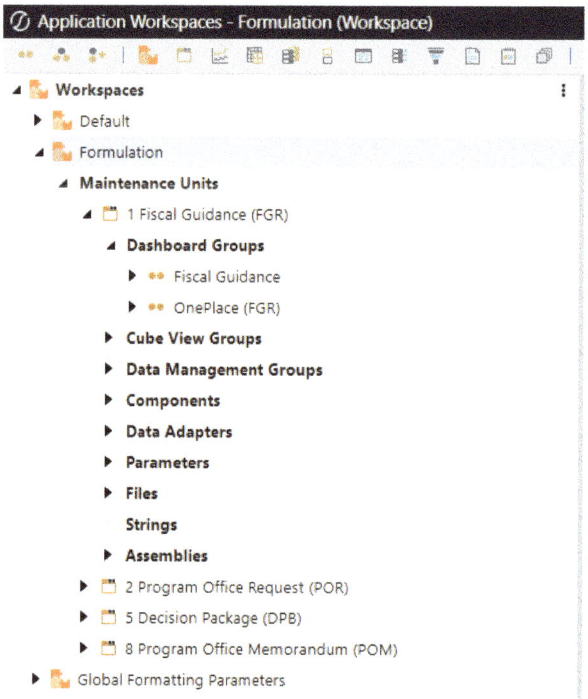

Figure 3.3

Workspace Properties Explained

General (Workspace)

Name

The name of your Workspace should reflect its purpose and how you plan to organize your work. There are several approaches you can take when naming Workspaces:

- **By Development Groups** – Useful if your organization has distinct teams working on different aspects of OneStream.
- **By Functionality** – Ideal for grouping dashboards and tools, based on their specific purpose, such as reporting, analysis, or automation.

- **By Workstreams** – A great option for aligning Workspaces with business processes, such as Financial Close, Planning, or Forecasting.
- **By Personas** – Where Workspaces are named, based on user roles and the dashboards they interact with, ensuring easy navigation and usability.
- **By Development Teams** – If OneStream is used as a development platform, Workspaces can be named after development teams, allowing for clear ownership and organization.

Choosing the right naming convention helps maintain clarity, improves collaboration, and ensures that users can easily locate and work within their designated environments.

Description

This field provides a brief description of the Workspace to help users understand its purpose and intended use. Sometimes, the name of the Workspace alone doesn't clearly convey its function, so the description offers an opportunity to provide additional context that the name may not capture.

For example, I often include details about how and where the Workspace's dashboards will be used. If I have a Workspace named `Financial Close`, I might enter the description as "Financial Close Workflow Dashboards" to clarify its specific role.

While descriptions are not mandatory, they are a helpful way to provide more clarity and ensure users know exactly what they are looking at and how it fits into the broader workflow. This added context can make navigation and understanding much easier for everyone involved.

Notes

This free-form text field allows you to enter notes that provide valuable context about the Workspace. Developers can use this field to document important information, such as completion dates, the status of dashboards in progress, or reminders about ongoing projects. While entering notes is not required, doing so can significantly enhance collaboration and clarity within the Workspace.

By using this field, developers can easily track progress and communicate key updates or tasks associated with the Workspace. For example, you might note when a particular task was completed, outline any pending issues, or list goals for upcoming work. These notes not only serve as a helpful reference for the person working on the Workspace but can also provide useful context to other team members or users who interact with the Workspace in the future.

Ultimately, this field adds contextual value, based on the *specific* purpose of the Workspace and any additional information that may be useful to users, making it easier to manage projects and collaborate efficiently.

Substitution Variable Items

Substitution variables are a convenient way to create and manage variable references within a Workspace, allowing developers to use the same value or text throughout the Workspace without needing to retype it. These variables are not displayed directly on the Workspace interface; instead, the field shows as **(Collection)** with an ellipsis button. Clicking this button opens a dialog where you can view or manage the substitution variables.

To view or add substitution variables, simply click the ellipsis button, which will open a dialog box containing any existing variables. Add substitution variables as needed from this window by clicking the Add Item button and then entering the substitution variables suffix name and substitution variables value. When using substitution variables in your Workspace, remember to prefix them with `WSSV` when referencing them on a dashboard or object. For example, if you have a substitution variable named `Developer`, you would reference it as `|WSSVDeveloper|`. The exercise below demonstrates how to create and use this example.

Security

Access Group

The **Access Group** determines who can access the Workspace. Users in this access security group are granted permission to view the Workspace and its dashboards, but they do not have the ability to modify the Workspace or any of its objects. This ensures that while they can interact with the content, they cannot make changes to the Workspace's structure or underlying components.

Maintenance Group

The **Maintenance Group** controls who can manage and administer the Workspace. Users in the maintenance security group can access the Workspace, view its dashboards, and have the necessary permissions to modify the Workspace and its objects.

Depending on your OneStream security structure, users may belong to multiple or nested security groups. This flexibility allows you to apply layered security, offering more granular control rather than limiting access to a simple *either/or* selection. This approach enables you to tailor permissions based on specific roles and responsibilities within the Workspace.

Sharing

Is Shareable Workspace

This setting allows you to control whether objects, such as parameters or dashboards within the Workspace, can be shared with other Workspaces for re-use or reference.

For example, if your Workspace contains objects like parameters that are used in other Workspaces, you would want to set this property to True to make the Workspace shareable. This ensures that the parameters, as well as other dashboard objects, are accessible to other Workspaces. An important step to keep in mind is that the Workspace name will need to be added to the Shared Workspace Names property on the Workspaces it will be shared with.

If the property is set to False, and another Workspace tries to use a parameter from your Workspace, the parameter will not be recognized. As a result, the user will be prompted to input the parameter manually.

In essence, this property facilitates outward sharing, allowing other Workspaces to access your objects. The next property, on the other hand, is designed to allow inward sharing, enabling your Workspace to use objects from other Workspaces.

Shared Workspace Names

This setting allows you to define the Workspaces from which your Workspace can re-use or reference objects. The **Default Workspace** is always shared and accessible by any other Workspace, regardless of whether it's explicitly listed in this field.

To re-use objects from other Workspaces, enter the names of the Workspaces you want to include in a comma-separated list. Be sure to order the list based on how you want shared items to appear in any search results when referencing them within your Workspace.

The list of shared Workspaces can be modified at any time. However, it's important that the Workspaces you list here have the Is Shareable Workspace setting set to True in order for the sharing to work properly.

Assemblies

Namespace Prefix

This field is important when working with **Workspace Assemblies** in OneStream, as it allows you to write syntax that can execute code from other Workspaces or from within the same (current) Workspace. This property lets you define a shorter or code-based name, making it easier to reference and use in your Workspace Assemblies.

Imports Namespace 1–8

When a Workspace Assembly depends on another Workspace, these properties allow you to dynamically reference that dependency by specifying the source code Assembly in this field. The reference is then passed into the current Workspace Assembly.

This is especially helpful when managing changes to Assemblies, as the reference is stored in the Workspace properties. This eliminates the need to search for and update the reference within the Assembly itself, streamlining maintenance and reducing the chance of errors.

Workspace Assembly Service

Here, you define the name of the Workspace Assembly Service Factory. The correct syntax is `AssemblyName.FactoryName`, where `AssemblyName` refers to the name of the Workspace Assembly, and `FactoryName` is the specific Service Factory type within that Assembly. `FactoryName` is the actual name of the Service Factory, which is typically the same as the name of the file containing its code (minus its extension; e.g., ".cs" or ".vb").

For a more detailed explanation of Workspace Assemblies, including their concepts and various examples, refer to Chapter 5, where these topics are explored in depth.

Text 1-8

The **Text1-8 fields** enable you to store string values that can be easily referenced within Workspace Assemblies.

For instance, if you have a string that needs to be referenced in an Assembly – but may change over time – the typical approach would require developers to update the Assembly every time the string changes, adding unnecessary administrative burden.

However, by utilizing the Workspace text fields, developers can directly access these fields within the Assembly, eliminating the need to modify the Assembly itself. This approach not only reduces maintenance efforts but also makes the Assembly rules more dynamic and flexible, allowing them to automatically adapt to changes without requiring manual intervention.

For example, to reference a `Text1` field within an Assembly, you can use the following syntax:

```
Dim WSText1 As String = BRApi.Dashboards.Workspaces.GetWorkspace(si,
False, args.PrimaryDashboard.WorkspaceID).Text1
```

This allows the Assembly to dynamically use the value stored in the Text1 field, making it easier to manage updates without modifying the Assembly code.

Configuring Application Security for Workspaces

To ensure your developers have the required access to the Workspaces page, and can create or modify Workspaces, it's crucial to first review the **Application Security Role** assignments. These roles define what users can and cannot do within the OneStream platform, including their ability to access certain pages and perform specific actions such as Workspace creation or modification.

Here's how to approach it:

1. **Review Existing Role Assignments**: Check the current security roles assigned to developers. You'll want to confirm whether they have the appropriate permissions to access the Workspaces page, which includes both viewing and modifying Workspace configurations.
2. **Identify Required Permissions**: Ensure that the necessary security rights are granted, such as the ability to create new Workspaces, modify existing ones, and manage security settings within the Workspaces. You may need to assign specific roles like "Workspace Administrator" or "Workspace Creator", depending on the level of access required.
3. **Administrator Involvement**: In most cases, your administrator will need to take the lead in reviewing and adjusting these security role assignments. This may involve adding or

removing specific roles for developers, ensuring they have the appropriate level of access based on their responsibilities.

4. **Make Modifications if Necessary**: If roles and permissions are not configured correctly, your administrator will need to modify them. This can include granting access to certain features or restricting actions to ensure that only authorized users can make significant changes, such as creating new Workspaces or modifying security settings.
5. **Testing and Verification**: After adjustments are made, it's important to test whether developers can successfully access the Workspaces page and perform the necessary tasks. This ensures that the role assignments are working as intended and that developers have the permissions they need to be productive.

By reviewing and fine-tuning the application security role assignments, you can ensure that developers have the right level of access to efficiently work within the OneStream platform while maintaining the necessary security controls.

From the Application tab, navigate to Security Roles under the Tools section. This page displays the security assignments for both Application Security Roles and Application User Interface Roles.

In the Application Security Roles section, review the security groups assigned to the following roles:

- **AdministerApplicationWorkspaceAssemblies**: Users in this group have the ability to modify existing Assemblies as well as create new ones.
- **ManageApplicationWorkspaces**: Users in this group can create new Workspaces. Depending on your organizational needs, you may want to limit Workspace creation to certain users or administrators. This ensures that only approved users can create Workspaces, helping to prevent unnecessary clutter. With this approach, developers can still build and modify Workspaces with the appropriate security assignments, but they will need an administrator to initially create the Workspace for them.

By carefully reviewing these security roles, you can maintain control over Workspace creation and Assembly modifications while still empowering developers to work within the platform.

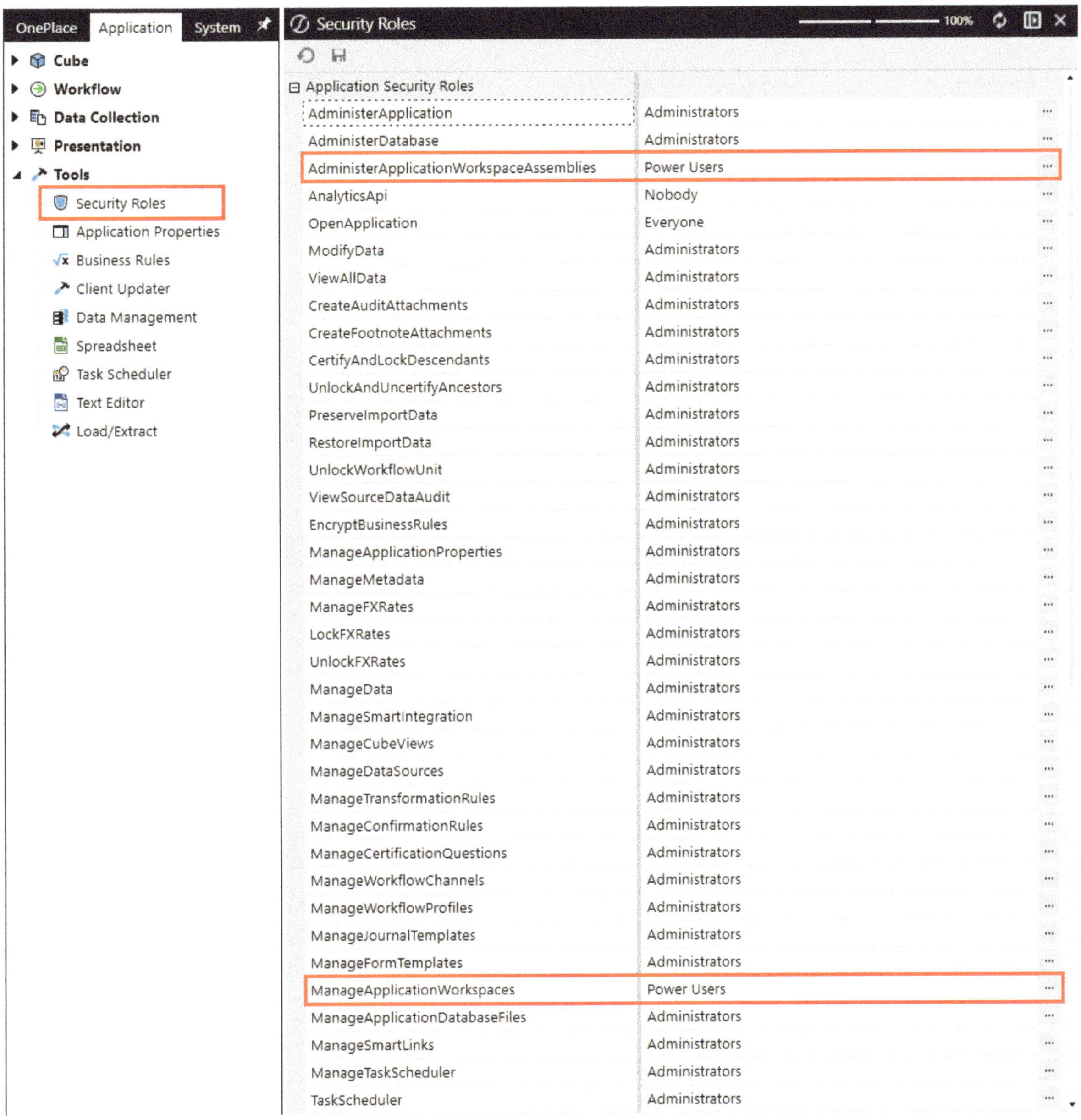

Figure 3.4

In the Application User Interface Roles section, review the WorkspaceAdminPage security role assignment. To grant developers access to the Workspaces page from the Application tab, assign a security group that includes your developers to this role. Without this assignment, they will not have access to the Application tab and, consequently, will be unable to navigate to the Workspaces Admin Page.

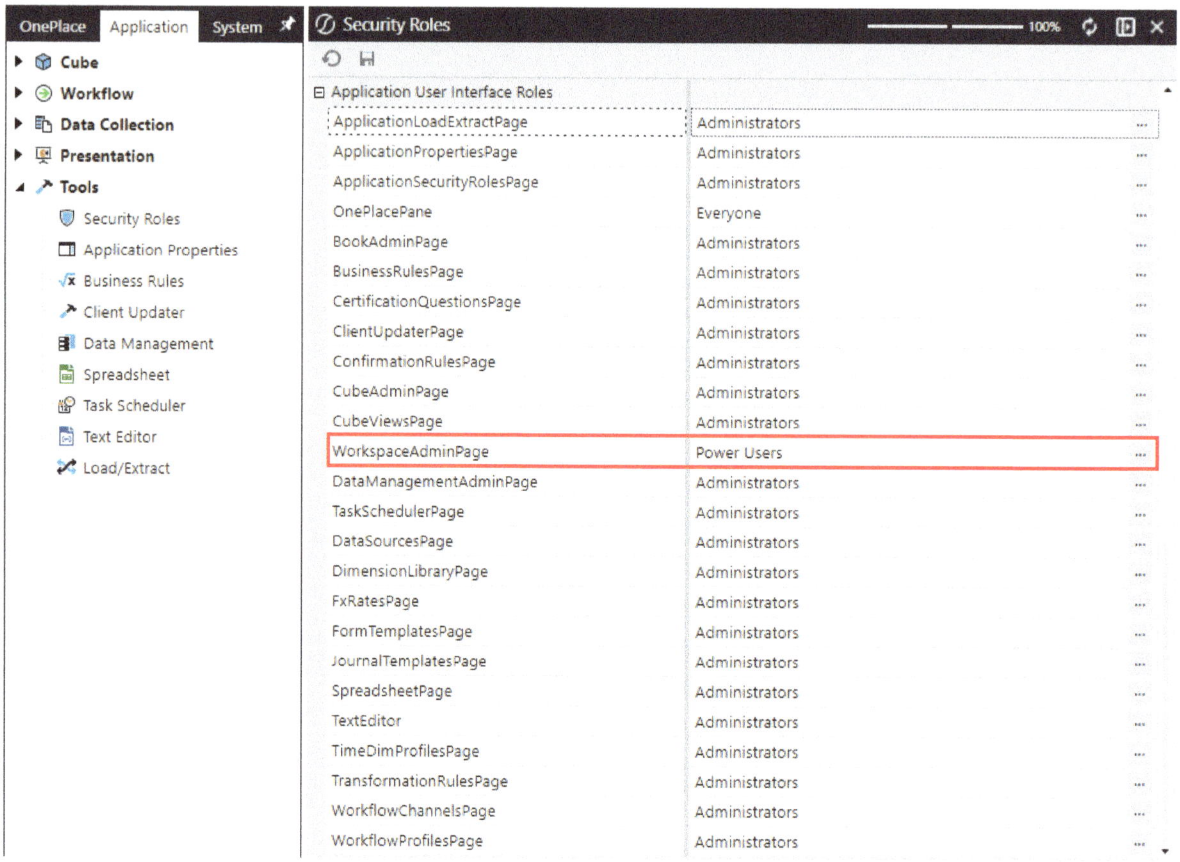

Figure 3.5

Creating a New Workspace

Creating Workspaces in OneStream is simpler than you might expect. With just a few clicks, you can set up multiple Workspaces, each with tailored security settings to ensure the seamless separation of workstreams. This allows your developers to dive straight into their dedicated environments without delay.

Now that you understand Workspace properties and how to use security groups to assign the right roles, let's walk through a straightforward yet powerful example of setting up a Workspace effectively. This exercise will give you hands-on experience configuring Workspaces, reinforcing key concepts such as security assignment, access control, and environment customization. By the end, you'll be equipped with the practical knowledge needed to structure Workspaces efficiently, empowering your teams to collaborate effectively while maintaining security and organization.

This exercise will be continued in Chapter 10, where we walk through an end-to-end Workspace exercise, incorporating Workspace Assemblies, showing examples of sharing between Workspaces, and how to export a packaged solution with a single application export.

Navigate to the Application tab and select `Workspaces` under the `Presentation` section.

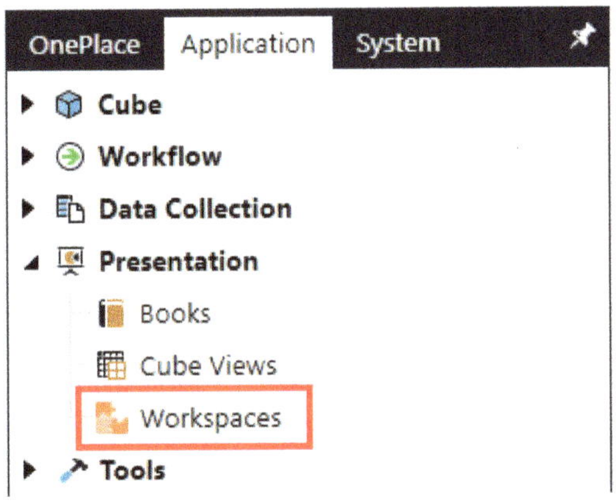

Figure 3.6

Click on `Workspaces` and then click the Create Workspace button from the toolbar menu.

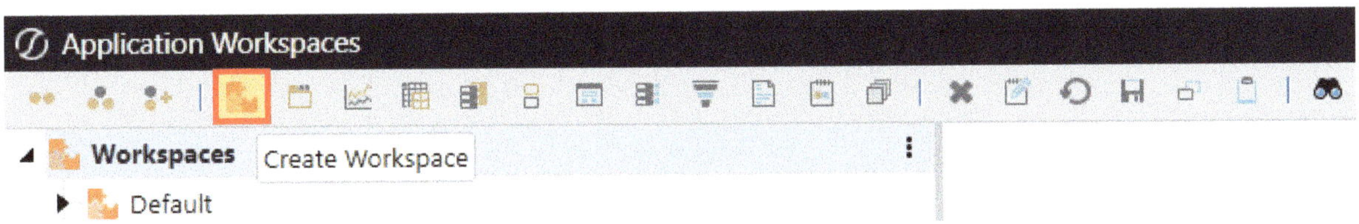

Figure 3.7

Type in the name of your Workspace and then click Save. For this exercise, we'll name our Workspace `Formulation`, as this Workspace will encompass all Workflow dashboards related to the budget formulation process.

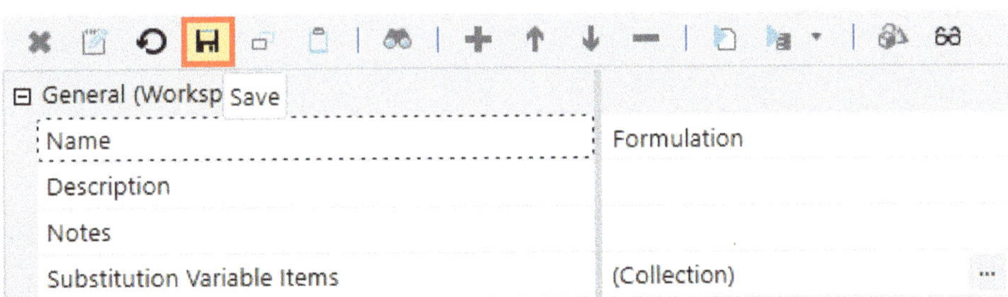

Figure 3.8

Note: When renaming Workspaces, check the Workspace inventory for any Workspaces that list your Workspace as a **Shared Workspace**; these will need to be updated to reflect the new name and allow sharing to remain undisturbed.

Figure 3.9

Type into the following properties (optional):

- **Description**: Formulation Workflow Dashboards
- **Notes**: Fiscal Guidance completed 2/20. Decision Package completed 3/15.

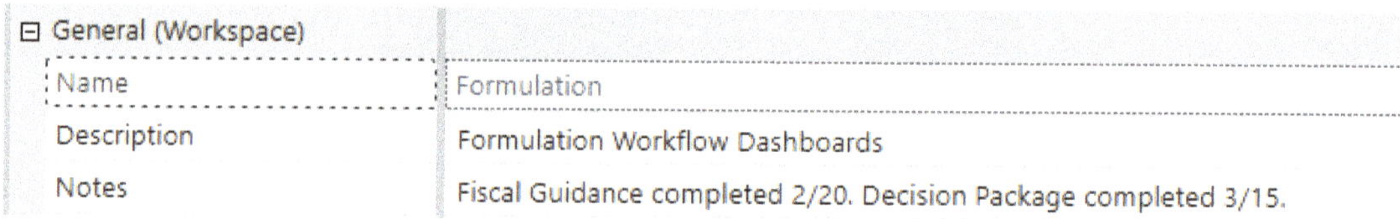

Figure 3.10

Click the Edit button on the Substitution Variable Items property; this will open a dialog box where you can add substitution variables. For this exercise, we will create two substitution variables that we will display on dashboards in a later step.

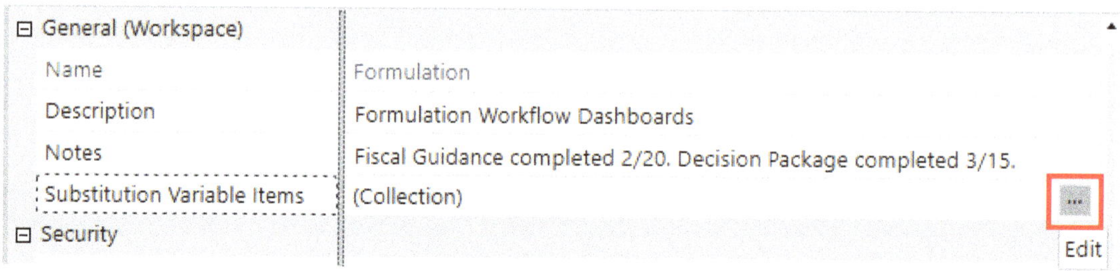

Figure 3.11

Once the Substitution Variable Items dialog box opens, click the Add Item (+) button.

Type Developer into the Substitution Variable Name Suffix, and Jessica into the Substitution Variable Value.

Click the Add Item (+) button again. Type StartDate into the Substitution Variable Name Suffix, and 3/1/2025 into the Substitution Variable Value.

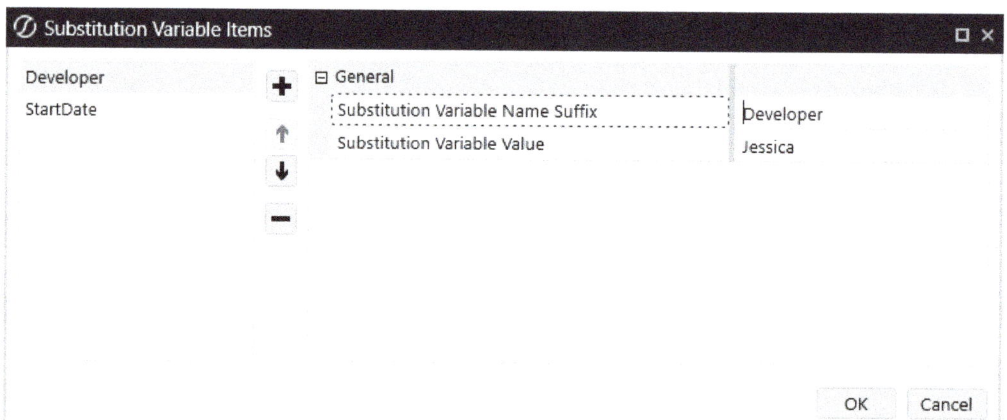

Figure 3.12

To display Workspace substitution variables, the syntax is `WSSV` followed by the substitution variable name suffix. For the variables we created, you would use `|WSSVDeveloper|` and `|WSSVStartDate|` to display their respective values.

From the Substitution Variable Items dialog box, hover over the Suffix field to view the tool tip, which will provide additional guidance on the syntax.

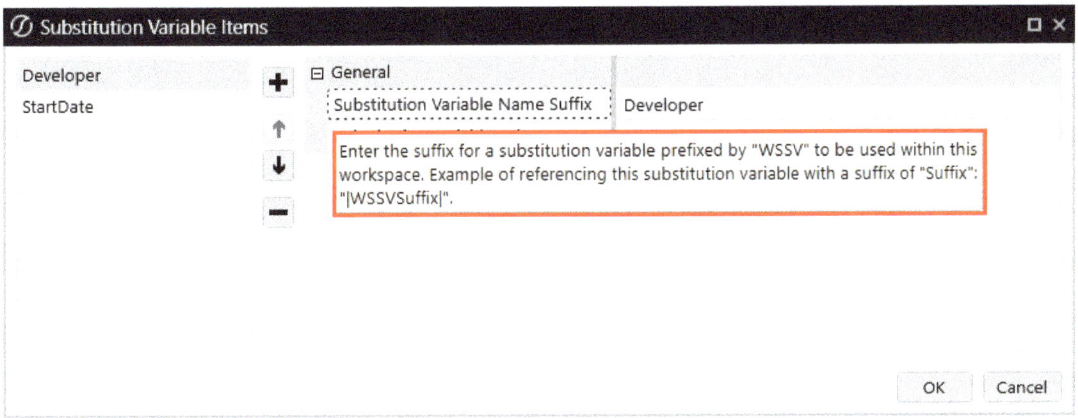

Figure 3.13

Click the Edit button on the Access Group property and select a security group. Repeat this step to select a security group for the Workspace's Maintenance Group property.

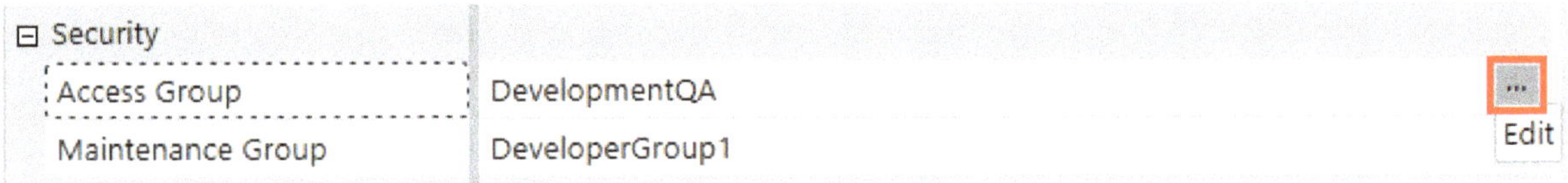

Figure 3.14

Set the Is Shareable Workspace property to True. Enabling this property allows us to open a dashboard within the Workspace directly from a button on the landing page, which is stored in the `Landing Page (OP_LPG)` Workspace.

In this exercise, our Workspace will contain Cube Views that use parameters to dynamically apply Cube View formatting, eliminating the need to recreate the parameters. To enable this functionality, we'll add the Shared Workspace Name for Global Formatting Parameters, allowing these global parameters to be shared with our new Workspace and ensuring the appropriate formatting is applied.

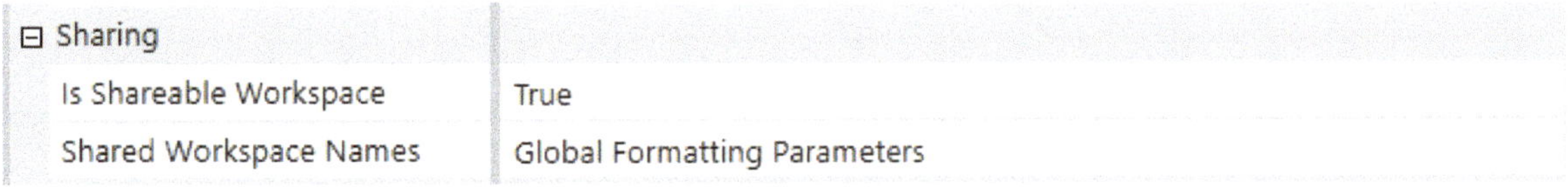

Figure 3.15

> **Note**: We must also add the `Formulation` Workspace name to the `Landing Page (OP_LPG)` Workspace's Shared Workspace Names to enable shared navigation.

The Workspace should look like the following figure, once all the preceding steps have been completed.

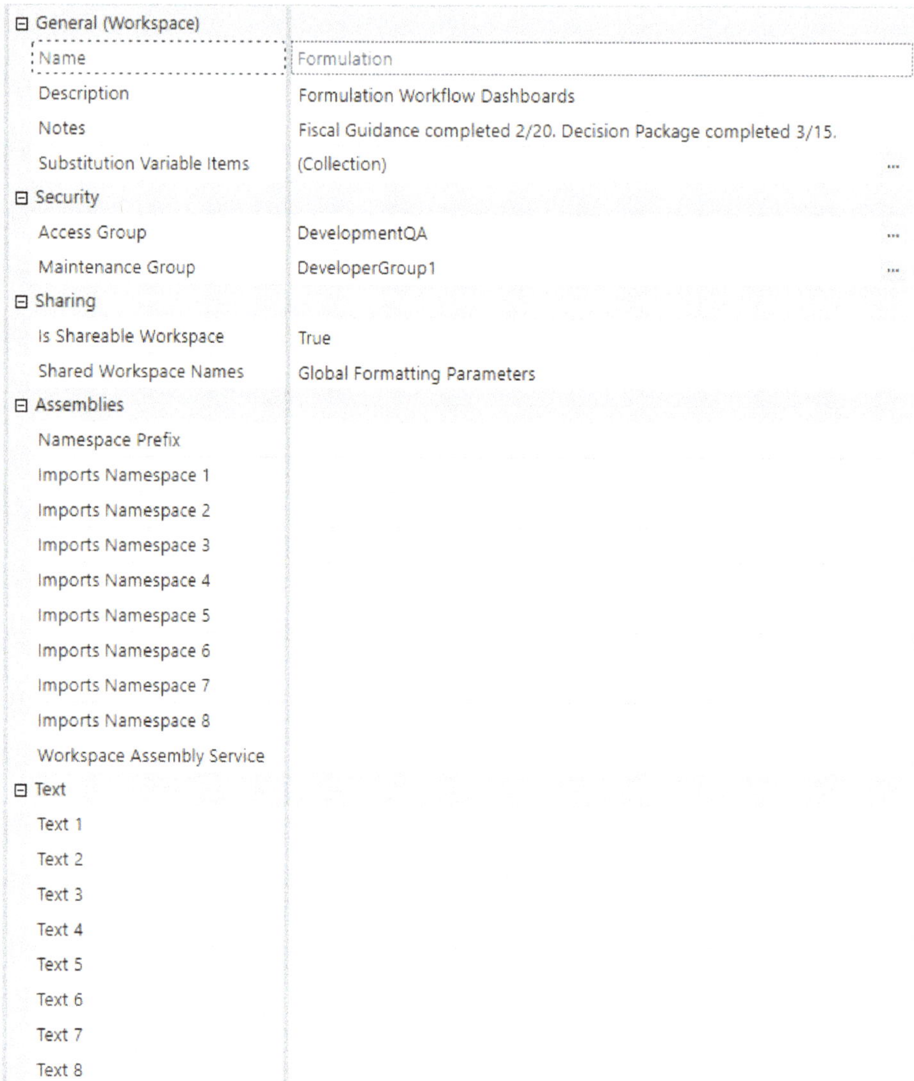

Figure 3.16

In Chapter 10, we will walk through an end-to-end Workspace exercise where we'll demonstrate how to build maintenance units within the Workspaces and configure Workspace Assemblies within the Workspace.

For the final step of this exercise, let's explore how to use the substitution variables we created earlier. Remember the substitution variables we set for Developer and StartDate? We'll use these variables to display key information on the dashboard's Page Caption, such as the developer's name and the date when development started.

On the dashboard shown below, notice that the Page Caption property has been filled in with the following syntax: `Developer: |WSSVDeveloper| - StartDate: |WSSVStartDate|`.

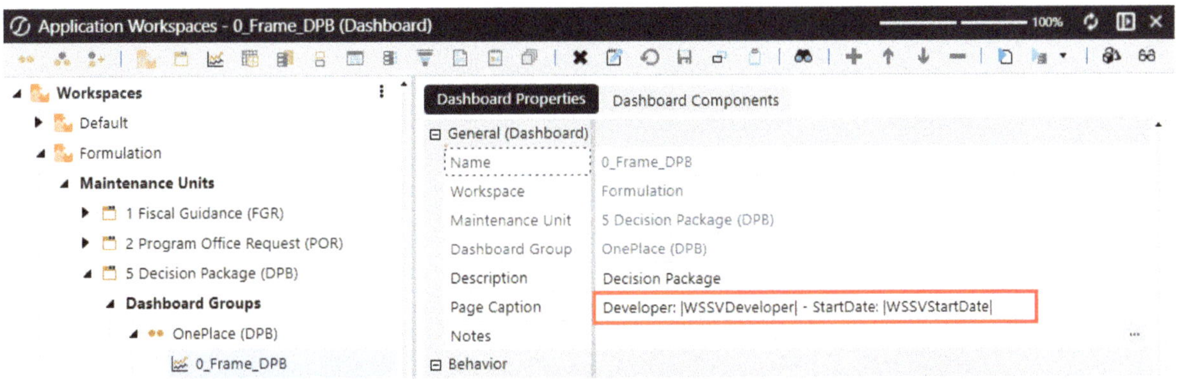

Figure 3.17

When the dashboard is rendered, notice the dashboard's title now displays the substitution variable values that we defined in the Workspace properties and entered into the dashboard's Page Caption property.

Figure 3.18

Workspaces Filter Functionality

In OneStream, **Workspace Filters** allow users to refine the Workspaces displayed within their filter selections. This allows developers to focus on their dedicated development Workspaces, and power users can limit what they want to see without cluttering the screen with Workspaces they are not concerned with.

This filtering functionality enhances navigation and organization, allowing users to quickly access relevant Workspaces without having to manually search through potentially long lists of Workspaces used throughout the organization.

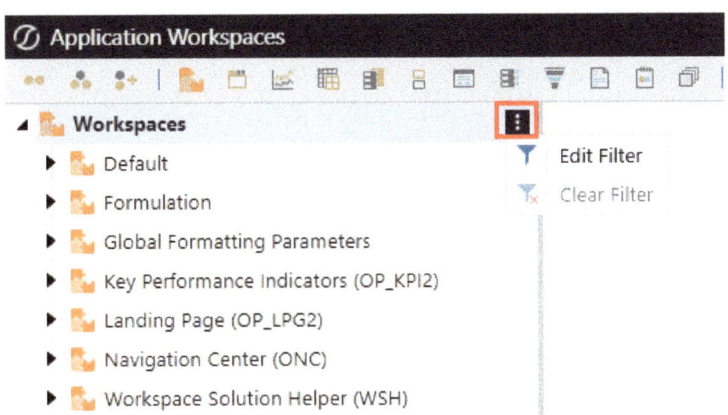

Figure 3.19

By effectively using Workspace filters, users can focus their own view on prioritized Workspaces, optimizing their overall experience within OneStream.

Conclusion

Setting up your OneStream Workspace is a crucial step toward maximizing efficiency and productivity. By customizing dashboards, configuring workflows, adjusting user preferences, and managing security settings, you can create an environment tailored to your specific needs. A well-organized Workspace structure allows you to navigate the platform seamlessly, access critical data quickly, and streamline your financial processes.

In this chapter, we covered:

- **Navigating the OneStream interface** to understand its layout and key components.
- **Workspace Properties Explained** to provide detailed explanations of Workspace properties and how to use and configure them.
- **Managing security and access controls** to ensure the right users have appropriate permissions.
- **How to set up a Workspace** to serve as a starting point for future development.
- **Workspace Filter Functionality** to help you focus on what you're working on, and/or reviewing.

By applying these principles, you can build a Workspace that not only meets your operational requirements but also enhances your ability to analyze data and make informed decisions efficiently. As you continue using OneStream, don't hesitate to refine your setup further to adapt to changing business needs.

Now that your Workspace is properly configured, you're ready to explore the next steps in leveraging OneStream's full capabilities. We will move forward and complete another exercise in Chapter 10.

4

Components of Workspaces

In this chapter, we'll delve into the various elements that constitute Workspaces within OneStream. This chapter provides a comprehensive overview of maintenance units, dashboard groups, Cube View groups, data management groups, and other essential components that enhance the functionality and efficiency of OneStream applications. Users can achieve refined workflows and streamlined processes by organizing and developing solutions through these components. By the end of this chapter, you'll be equipped with the knowledge to leverage these components effectively, thereby optimizing Workspace solutions for better performance and usability.

Maintenance Units

Maintenance Units are groups of dashboards and related components that make up solutions in OneStream. When you load solutions from the Solution Exchange, the file contains the building blocks of a maintenance unit, which makes organizing and developing solutions more cohesive.

While Workspaces increase development efficiency, maintenance units allow for further refinement and the separation of unique workstreams to provide another tool in taking your OneStream application to the next level.

The example below shows a Workspace with four maintenance units that contains dashboard solutions used in workflow steps.

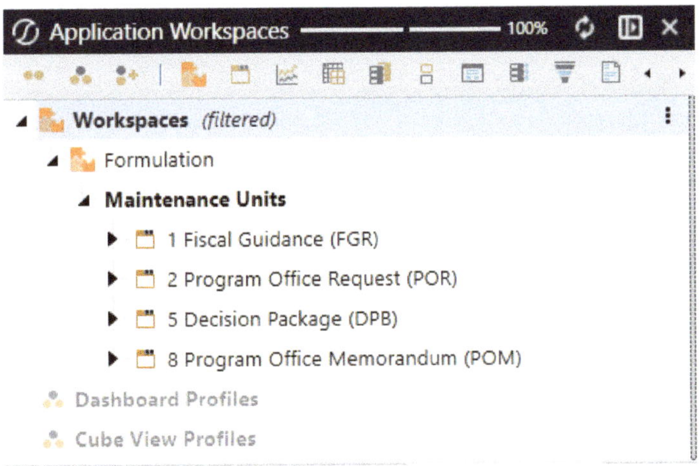

Figure 4.1

Dashboard Groups

Dashboards can be built and grouped by functionality or any method you prefer. In the example below, we've built a solution named `Decision Package`, which comprises multiple dashboard tabs and dialogs that are organized by tab and a `OnePlace (DPB)` group. The top-level dashboard is made available from OnePlace by attaching the dashboard group to a dashboard profile.

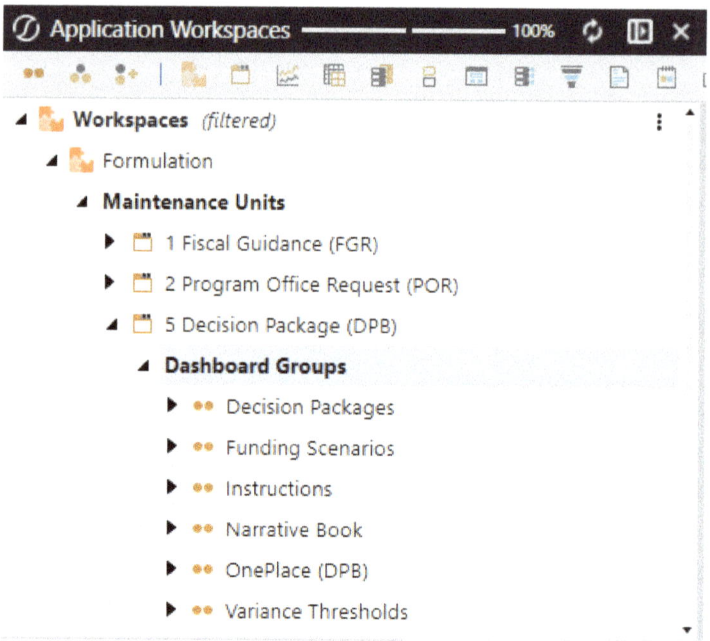

Figure 4.2

Cube View Groups

Cube Views are used for reporting, analysis, and data entry. You can create Cube Views on the Cube Views page under the Application tab, or you can create them within Workspaces to truly organize and group fully packaged Workspace solutions that can be packaged for deployment.

Additional Cube Views created outside of the Default Workspaces – within other Workspaces – cannot be accessed from the Cube View page.

Cube Views can be found in three areas within the Workspace menu:

1. From the `Default` Workspace, under the `Default` maintenance unit. Here is where you will find all legacy Cube Views.

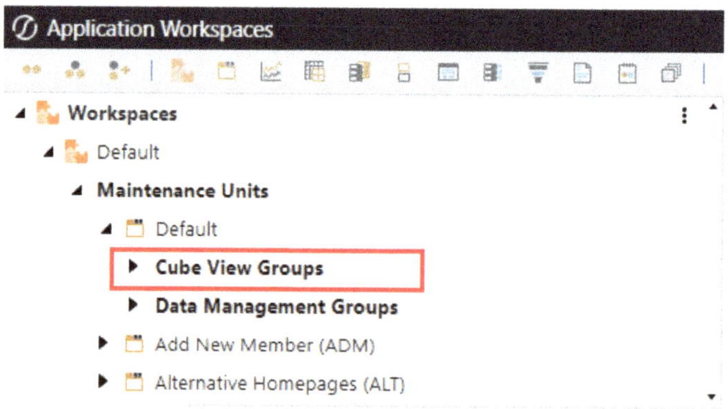

Figure 4.3

2. From the `Default` Workspace, under the specified maintenance unit. When modifying or building out maintenance units within the `Default` Workspace, you now have the ability to create Cube Views packaged within the respective maintenance unit.

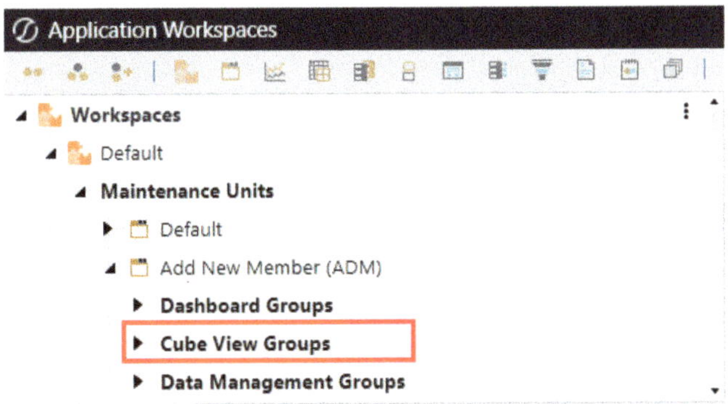

Figure 4.4

3. From non-default Workspaces, under the specified maintenance unit. When creating new Workspaces for development, building Cube Views within the Workspace allows you to export the application Workspace without the need to export a separate file for the Cube Views.

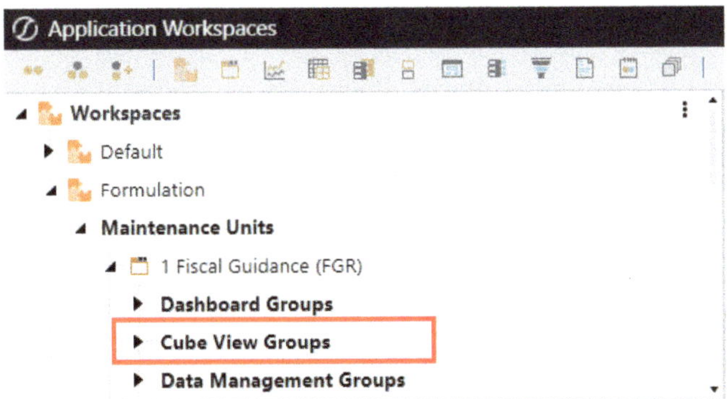

Figure 4.5

Data Management Groups

Data management objects are used to automate and organize tasks in OneStream – like loading data, running calculations, or triggering business rules. These objects work together to form structured process flows that execute in a specific order. You can create data management objects on the Data Management page under the Application tab, or you can create them within Workspaces to truly organize and group fully packaged Workspace solutions that can be packaged for deployment.

Data management objects can be found in three areas within the Workspace menu:

1. From the `Default` Workspace, under the default maintenance unit. Here is where you will find all legacy data management objects.

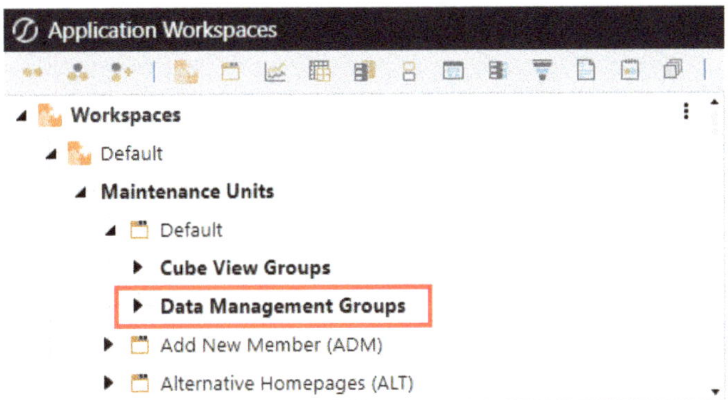

Figure 4.6

2. From the `Default` Workspace, under the specified maintenance unit. When modifying or building out maintenance units within the `Default` Workspace, you now have the ability to create data management objects packaged within the respective maintenance unit.

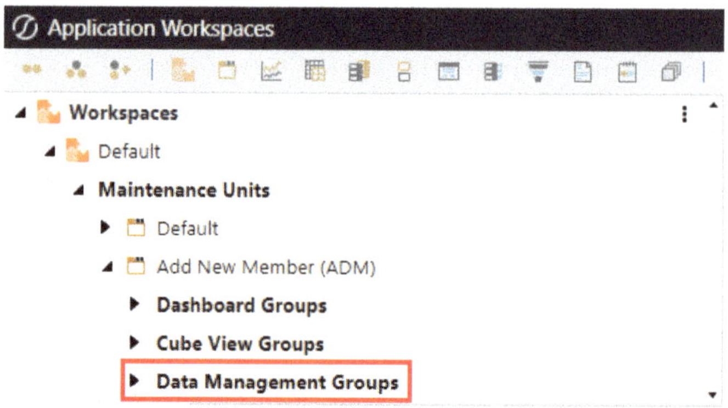

Figure 4.7

3. From non-default Workspaces, under the specified maintenance unit. When creating new Workspaces for development, building data management jobs within the Workspace allows you to export the application Workspace without the need to export a separate file for the data management objects.

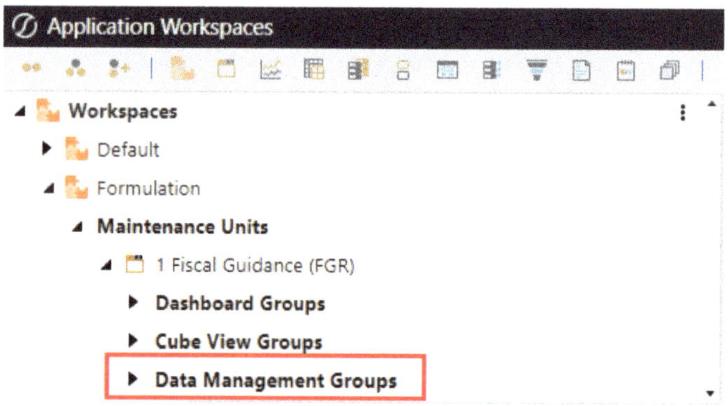

Figure 4.8

Steps

Steps are the building blocks for creating and adding new processes that can be combined within sequences to run a single action that triggers all steps assigned to the sequence.

Click from the Workspace toolbar to create a new data management sequence.

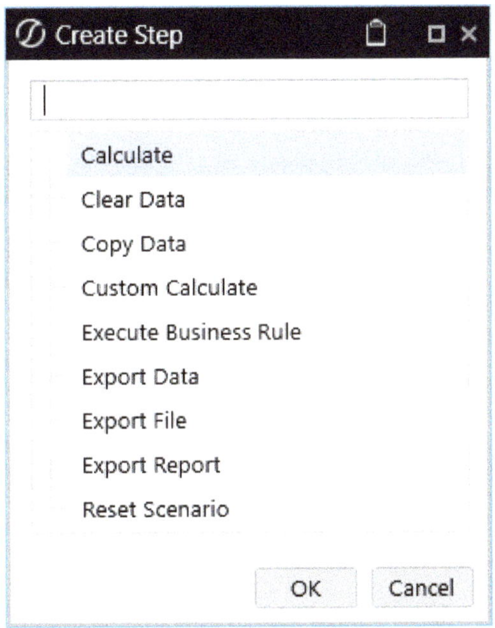

Figure 4.9

Below is an example of a custom calculate data management step using a business rule function to trigger an action following the processing of a sequence (and its steps).

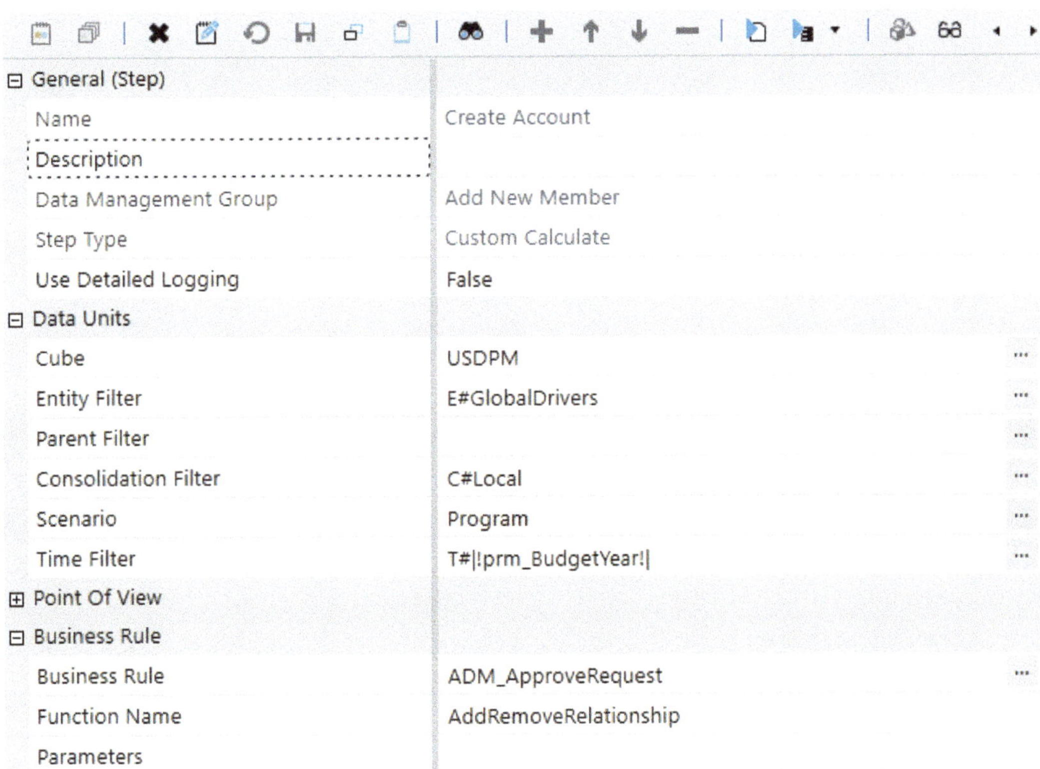

Figure 4.10

Sequences

A sequence is an ordered series of one or more data management steps that will execute in the order in which the steps are organized. The sequence name is used to trigger actions when calling business rules from dashboard components such as buttons.

Click from the Workspace toolbar to create a new data management sequence. Next, click on the Sequence Steps tab and the + button to add steps to your sequence.

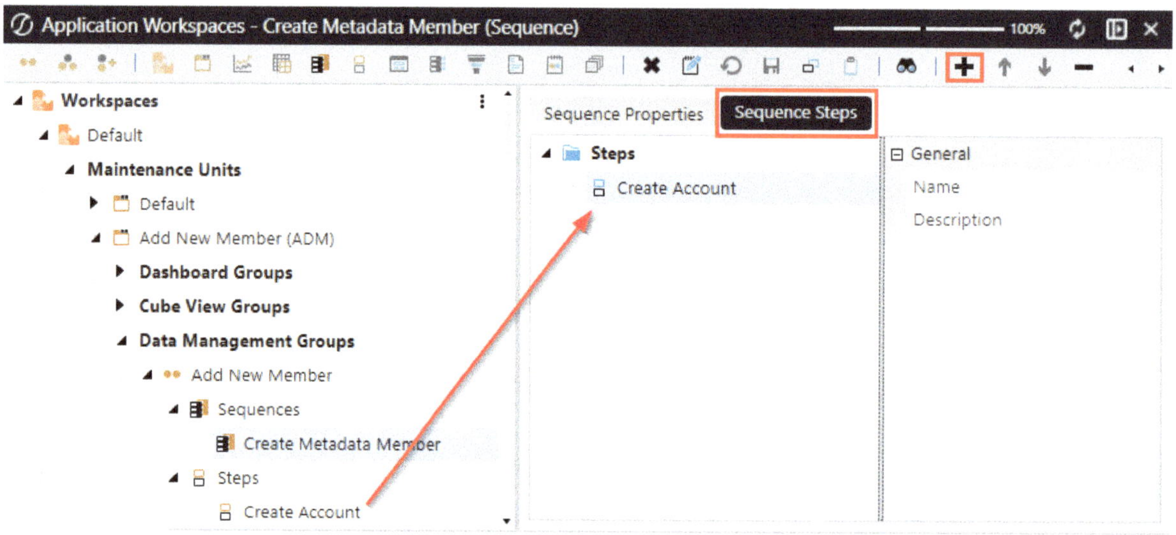

Figure 4.11

Data Adapters

These objects are attached to various dashboard components to provide a live connection from the database tables to the dashboard, allowing users to interact with the data.

Data adapters are objects used to supply various dashboard components with data. They use the following available methods:

- **Cube View** – This command type allows for a preconfigured Cube View to be the data source for a dashboard, and is the primary data source for most components.

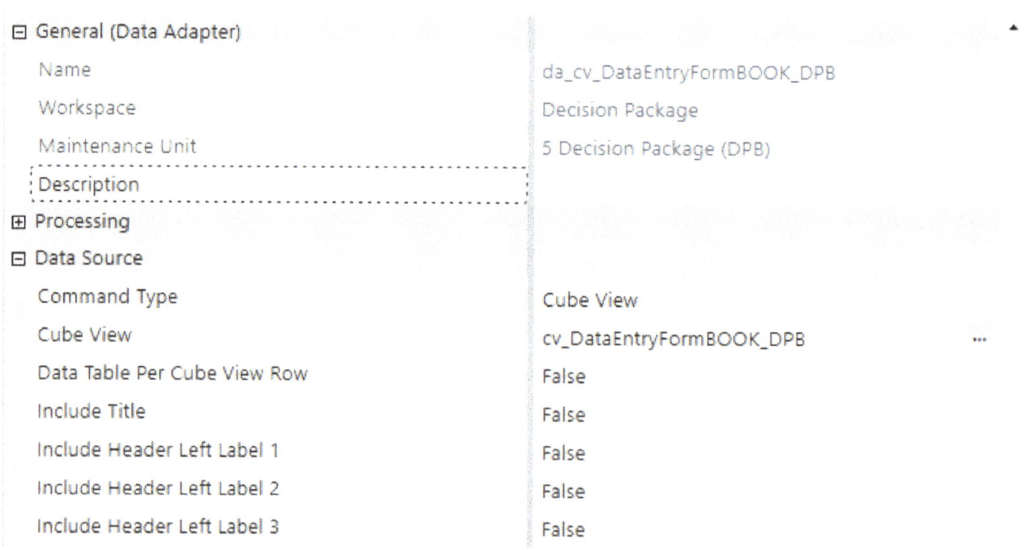

Figure 4.12

- **Cube View MD** – This command type will return the selected Cube View as a multidimensional fact table that simplifies report building using BI Viewer components.

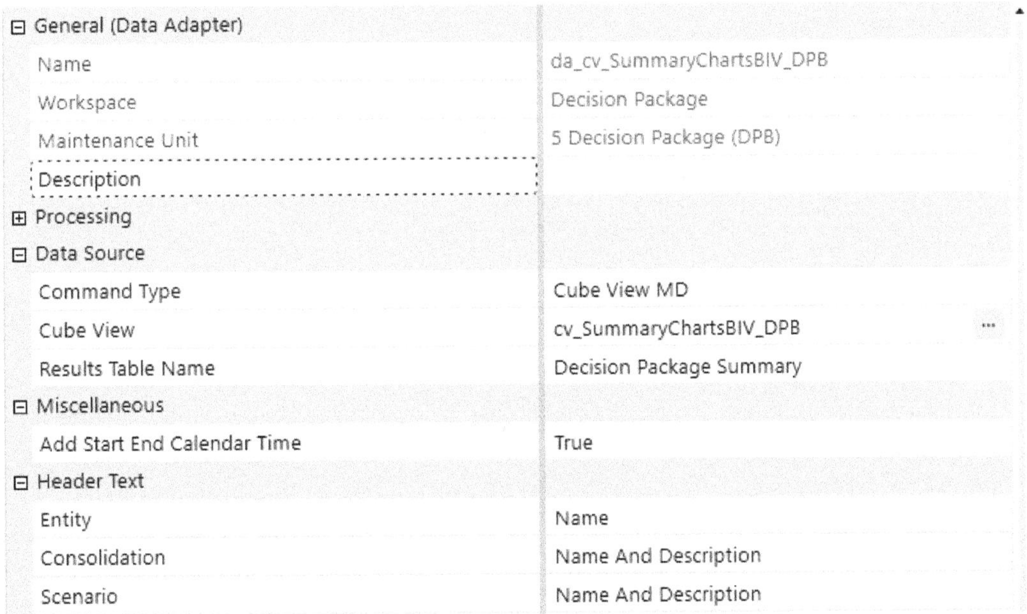

Figure 4.13

- **Method** – Use the Business Rule option when creating a custom rule to incorporate within a Method query. Upon selecting this method type, the data adapter will display various out-of-the-box queries that can be used in addition to any custom business rule logic.

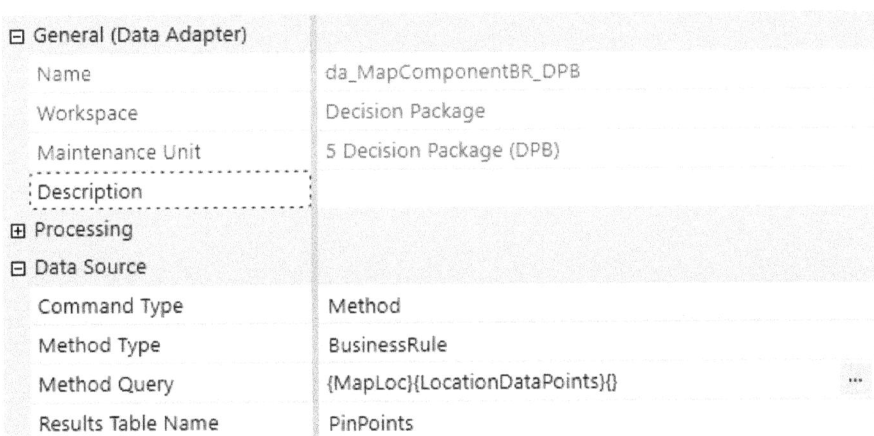

Figure 4.14

- **SQL** – Queries against the application or framework database can be written as a data source.

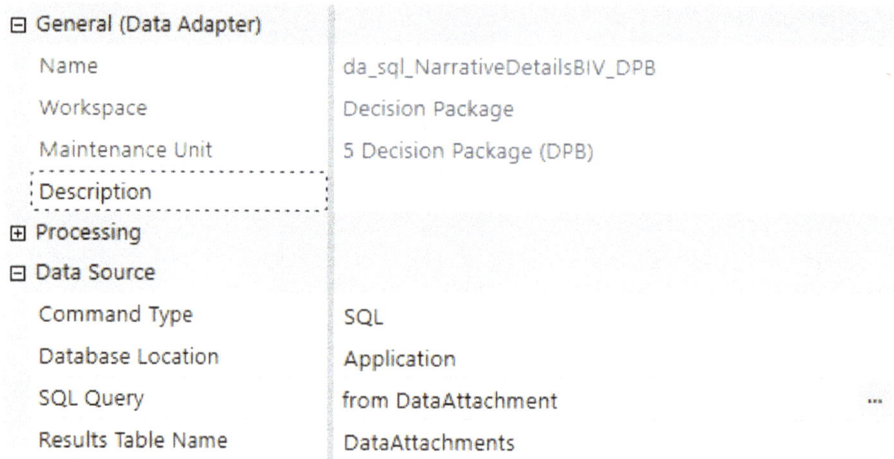

Figure 4.15

- **BI-Blend** – The purpose of the BI Blend adapter is to provide dashboard designers with a predefined interface for querying BI Blend tables.

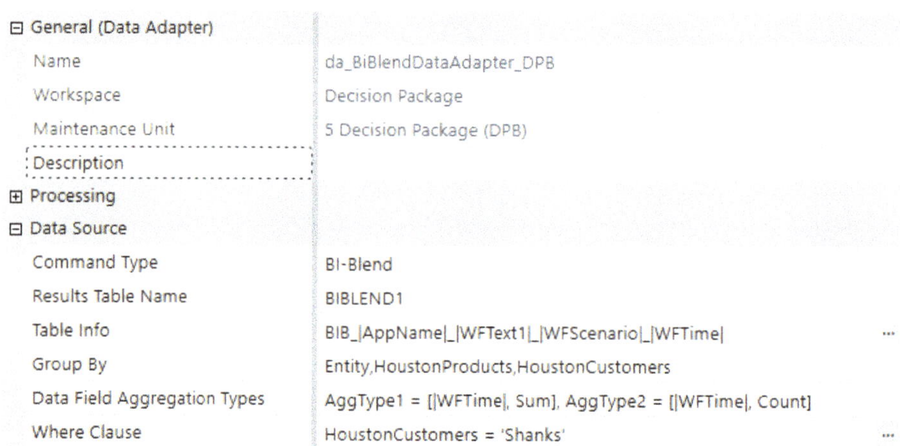

Figure 4.16

Parameters

Parameters allow you to make dashboards and reports dynamic and reusable by creating lists of metadata members, values, selections, and literal values you want to remain static. The use of parameters is highly recommended to reduce report duplication and streamline data quality.

Listed below are the parameter types available in OneStream:

- **Literal Value** – Explicit value that can be updated with dashboard actions via business rules or Assemblies.

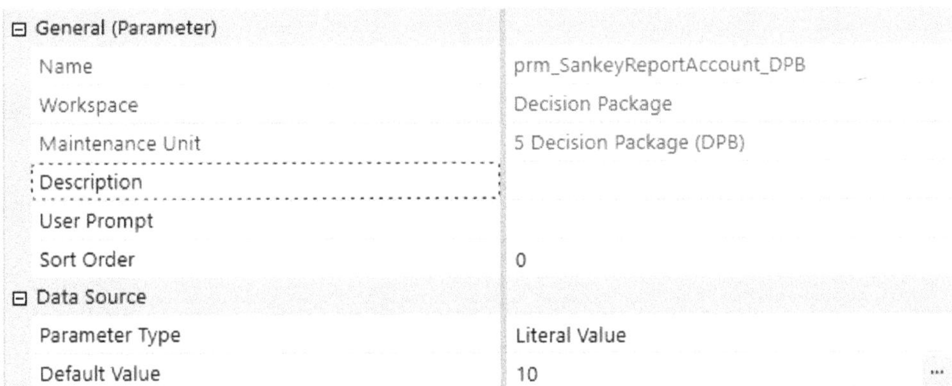

Figure 4.17

- **Input Value** – Holding parameter that dashboard actions pass values into for use in business rules or Assemblies.

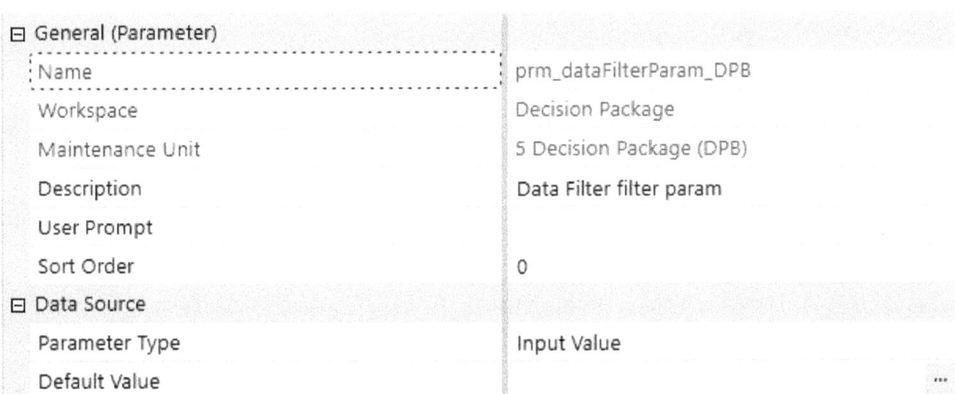

Figure 4.18

- **Delimited List** – Manually list out items to be available from a selection component.

⊟ General (Parameter)	
Name	prm_AttachDoc_DPB
Workspace	Decision Package
Maintenance Unit	5 Decision Package (DPB)
Description	
User Prompt	Right Click to Attach Files
Sort Order	0
⊟ Data Source	
Parameter Type	Delimited List
Default Value	True ...
Display Items (comma delimited)	True,False
Value Items (comma delimited)	True,False

Figure 4.19

- **Bound List** – Create lists of various application members and properties by using different Method Types.

⊟ General (Parameter)	
Name	prm_SelectMultiPrograms_DPB
Workspace	Decision Package
Maintenance Unit	5 Decision Package (DPB)
Description	
User Prompt	
Sort Order	0
⊟ Data Source	
Parameter Type	Bound List
Default Value	...
Result Format String Type	Custom
Result Custom Format String	U1#{0}
Command Type	Method
Method Type	Members
Method Query	{UD1}{BUD_Programs}{UD1#11200.Descendants}{} ...
Results Table Name	Programs
Display Member	Description
Value Member	Name

Figure 4.20

- **Member List –** Uses Member Filter Builder to create a list of metadata members.

⊟ General (Parameter)	
Name	Organization_DPB
Workspace	Decision Package
Maintenance Unit	5 Decision Package (DPB)
Description	
User Prompt	Select Field Office:
Sort Order	0
⊟ Data Source	
Parameter Type	Member List
Default Value	10010
Display Member	Description
Cube	USDPM
Dimension Type	Entity
Dimension	Organization
Member Filter	E#USDPM.Base

Figure 4.21

- **Member Dialog –** Metadata member list that is used in the member tree component or in a button that exposes the member tree structure.

⊟ General (Parameter)	
Name	prm_AccountMemberTree_DPB
Workspace	Decision Package
Maintenance Unit	5 Decision Package (DPB)
Description	
User Prompt	
Sort Order	0
⊟ Data Source	
Parameter Type	Member Dialog
Default Value	
Cube	USDPM
Dimension Type	Account
Dimension	BOC
Member Filter	A#[Total BOC].tree

Figure 4.22

Components

OneStream currently has 38 **Component Types**. In the following section, we'll explain the various components and provide examples of what they look like.

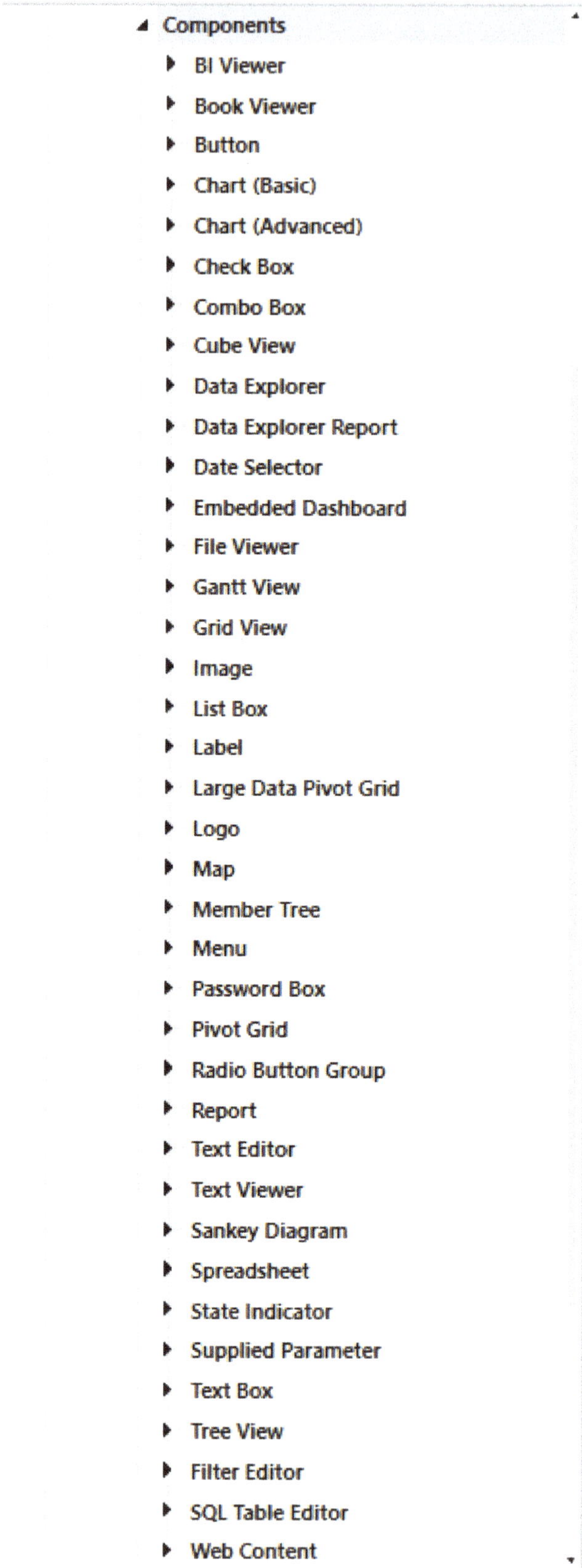

Figure 4.23

Data & Visualization Components

BI Viewer

The interactive presentation engine enables users to rapidly build Business Intelligence (BI) visualizations using data from existing or newly created data adapters. It provides a streamlined way to create BI dashboards that support rich data analysis and visualization.

These dashboards are highly dynamic and empower users to build components such as charts, gauges, maps, grids, and cards. The BI component integrates seamlessly with the Cube View MD data adapter and offers robust design-time capabilities, including:

- Adding calculated fields and custom measures
- Defining drill-down paths
- Enabling multi-select filters
- Applying conditional formatting for runtime interactivity
- Customizing color palettes for a tailored visual experience

The BI Viewer component in the figure below retrieves data from a Cube View MD data adapter.

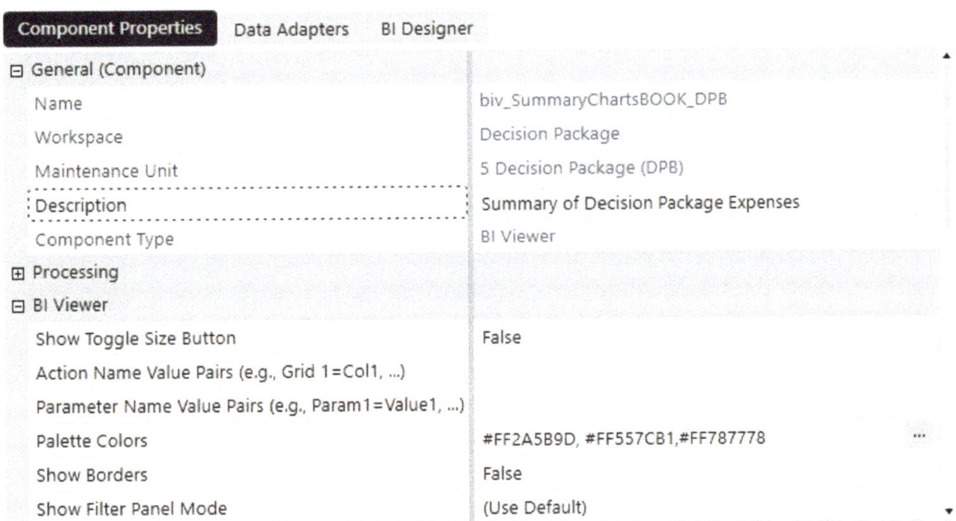

Figure 4.24

Component Display

The Cube View supplying the data adapter is made up of years in the columns and accounts in the rows, making this a quick and simple visualization to create, based on dashboard parameters.

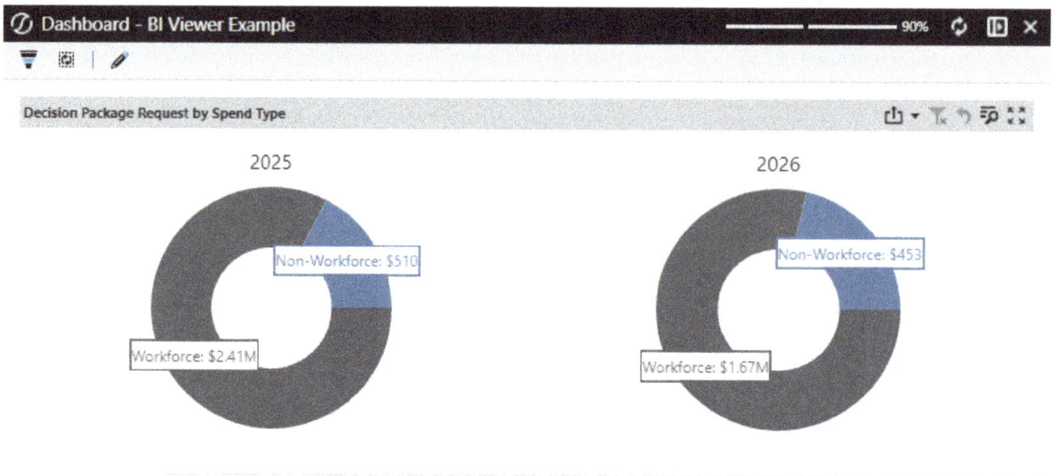

Figure 4.25

Book Viewer

Displays a bound report book (.pdf, Word, Excel) inside the dashboard. Books are created in OneStream from the Application → Books menu.

Books can be saved as the following file location types:

- Workspace file
- Application Database file
- System Database file
- File Share file

In the Component property, you are able to enter a description that displays in the header, specify the book location, select the book, and modify display settings when the component is displayed on a dashboard.

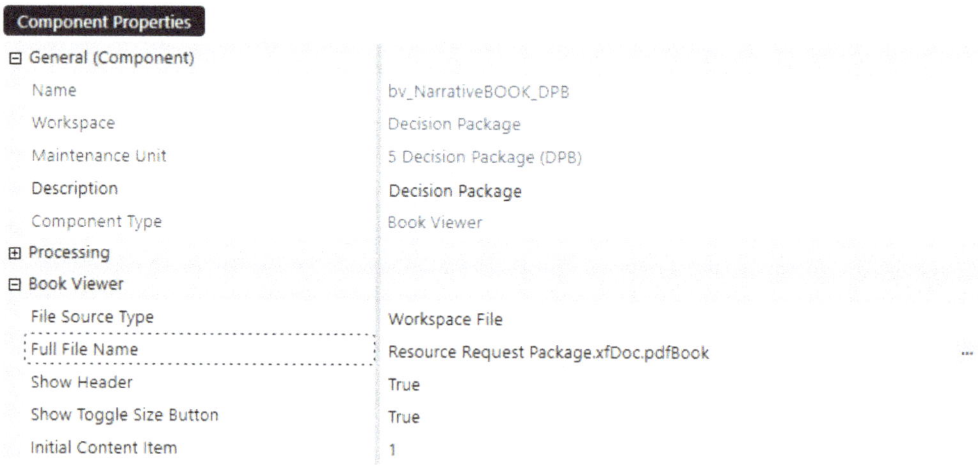

Figure 4.26

Component Display

This component allows you to view book sections individually, or check the box to Combine All Items, effectively merging the book content that can be exported as a PDF.

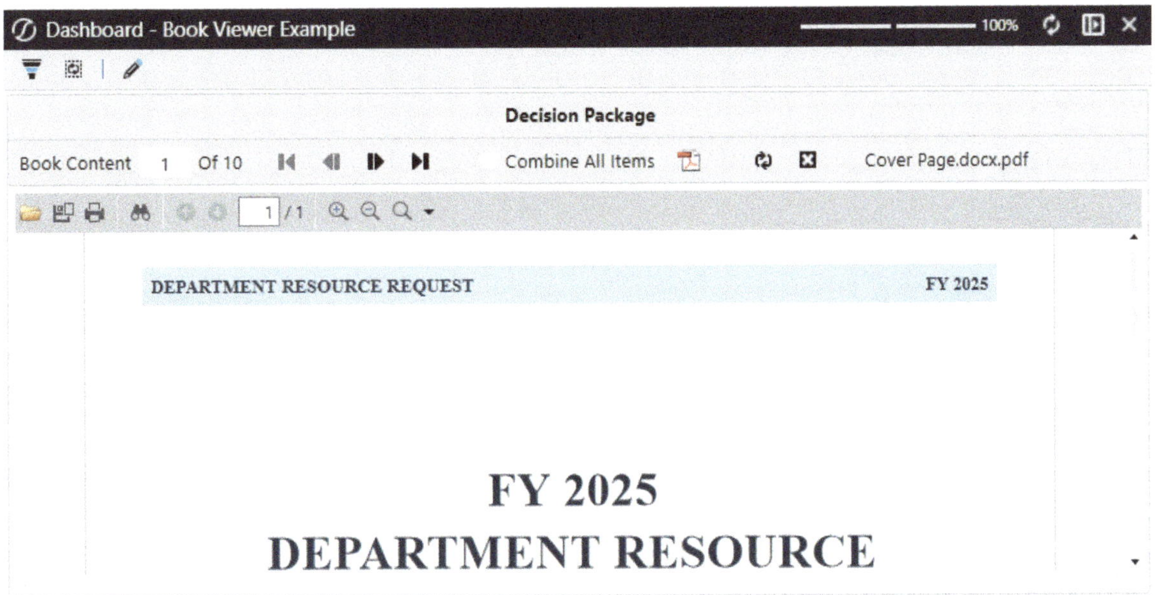

Figure 4.27

Chart (Basic)

Simple chart types (bar, line, pie, etc.) for quick data visualization.

In the Component property, you can enter a description to display in the header, pick the Chart Type, modify basic X-axis and Y-axis settings, and select the Data Series Source Type.

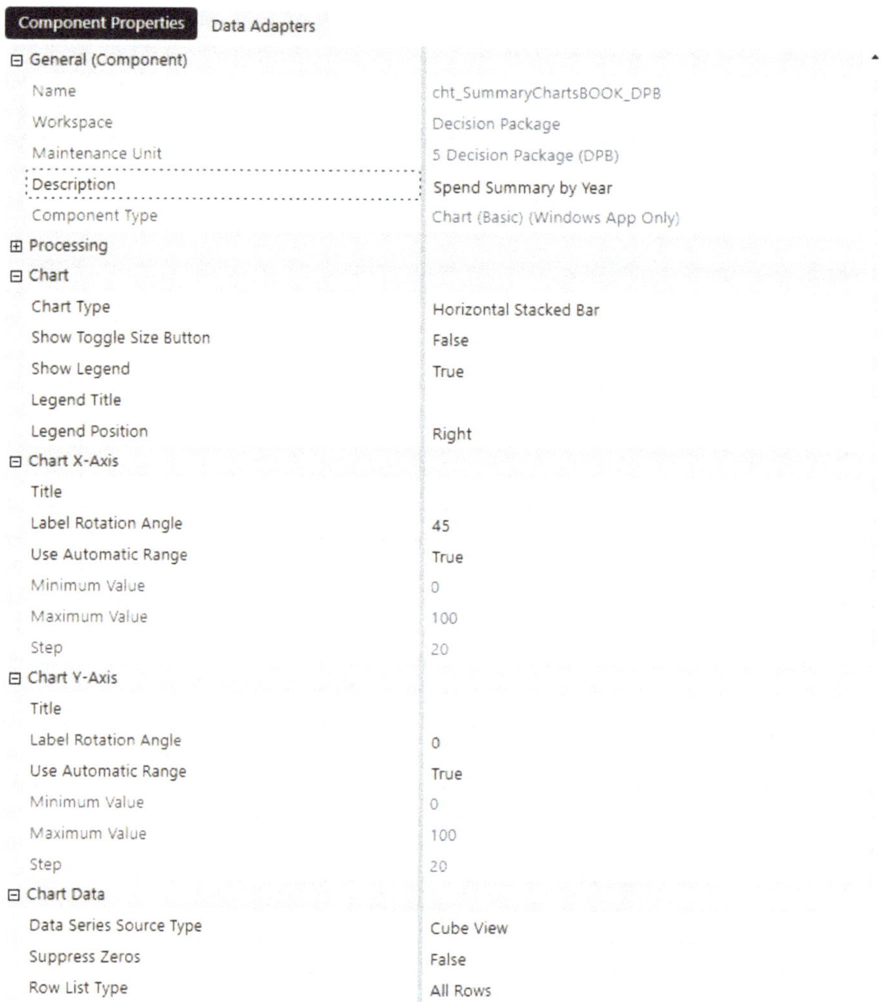

Figure 4.28

Component Display

The basic chart component provides limited control over display formatting – compared to advanced charts – but is a quick and easy visualization to create in a pinch.

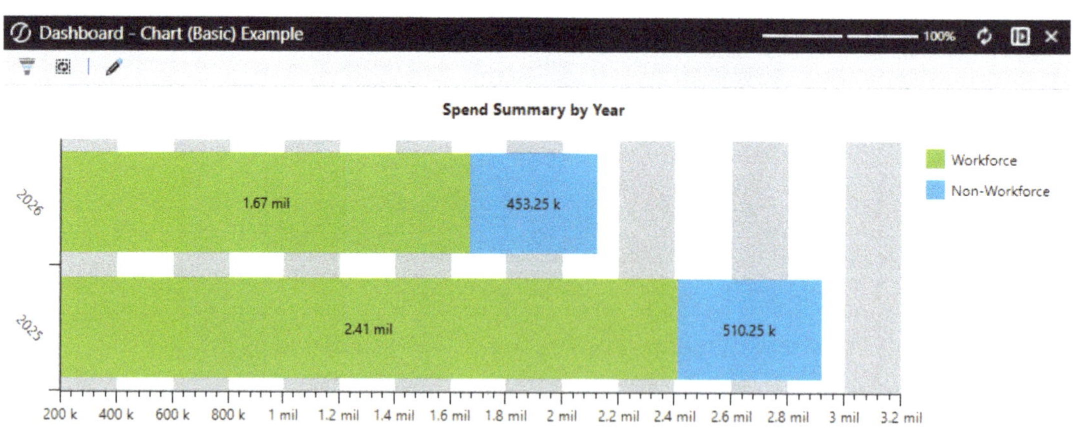

Figure 4.29

Chart (Advanced)

Advanced charts provide significantly more flexibility with formatting and interactive behavior that can be configured. In the figures below, we've configured the chart to display a side-by-side stacked bar chart to provide a visual representation of Workforce vs Non-workforce spend contribution by year. The chart explains how a multi-year funding request is allocated by spend category in an easy-to-understand visual.

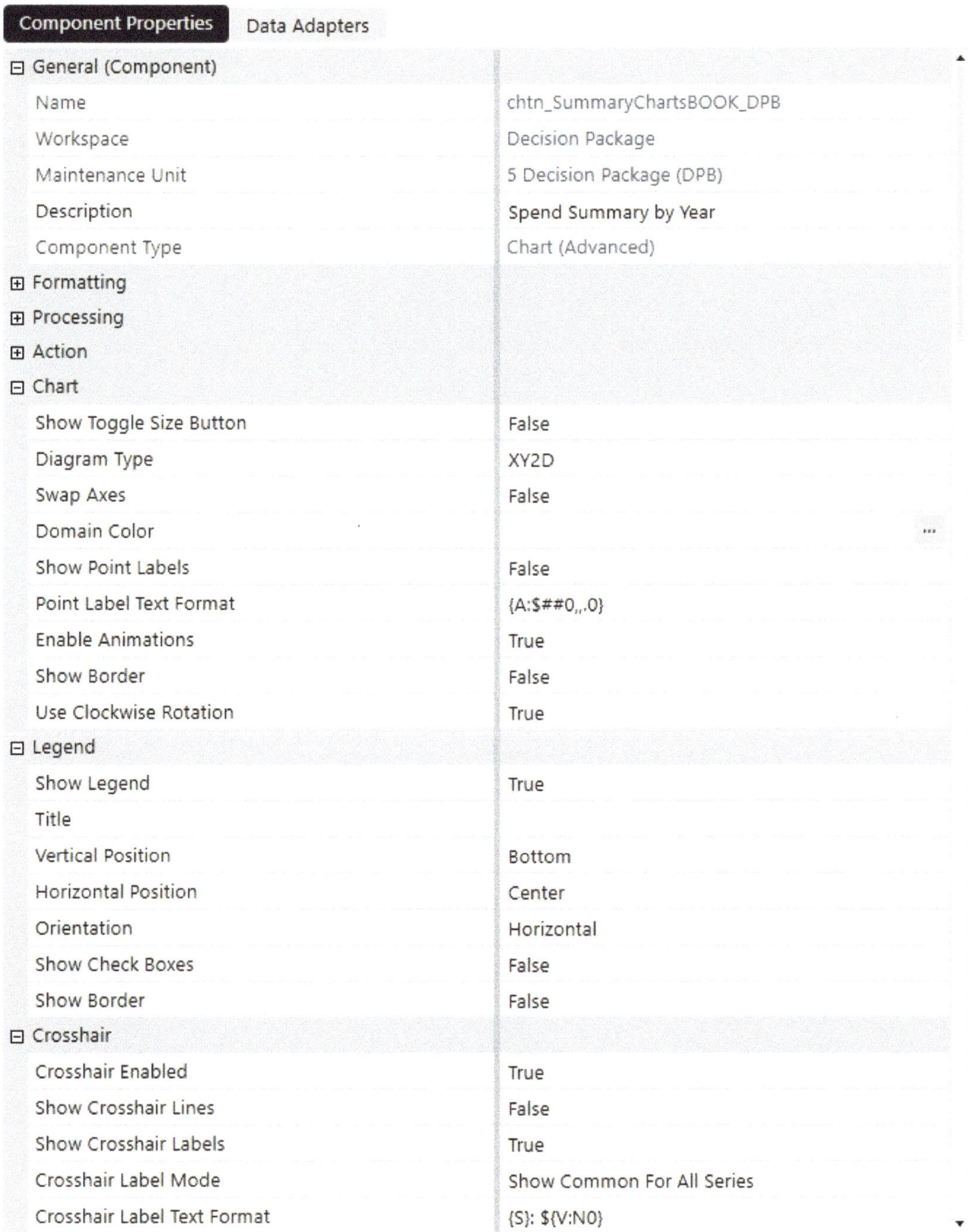

Figure 4.30

In the Chart Data section of the advanced chart properties, the Data Series Source Type should be selected based on the data adapter that supplies the component with its relevant data. The default setting is Cube View, but you can change this to Business Rule from the drop-down menu when configuring the component. For heavy customization, developers may prefer to use business rules to fine-tune chart formatting.

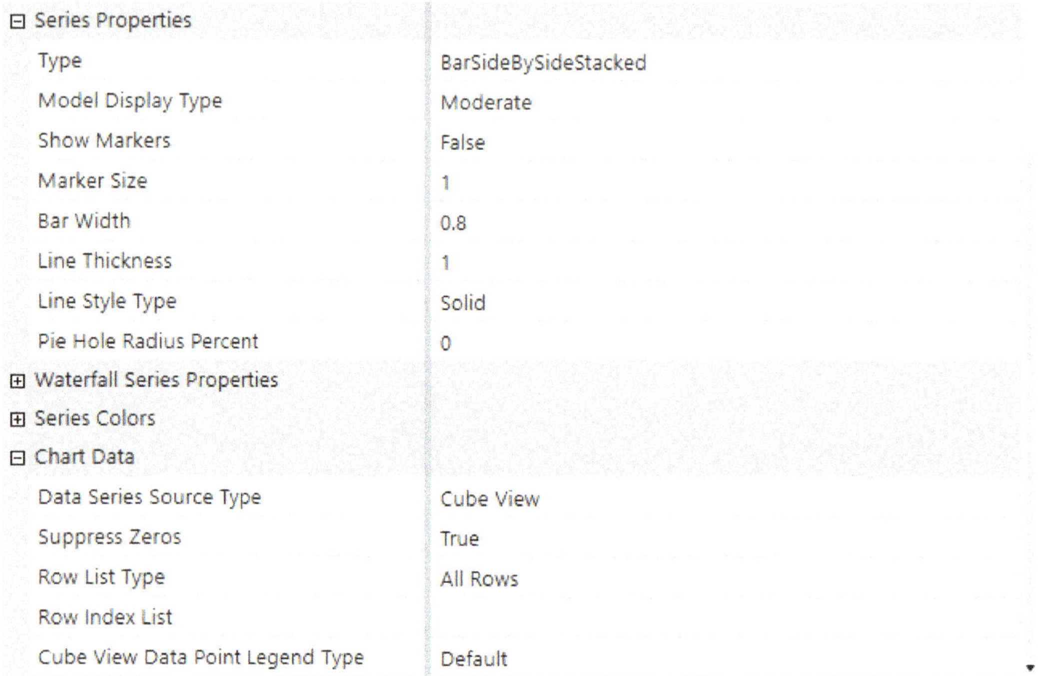

Figure 4.31

To use a business rule, simply change the Data Series Source Type to Business Rule and attach a data adapter with a Method command type and BusinessRule method type. Here is an example of a Dashboard Data Set business rule:

```
If args.DataSetName.XFEqualsIgnoreCase("WaterFallFormat") Then

    Dim dataAdapter As String = args.NameValuePairs.XFGetValue("DataAdapter")

    Dim dataRows As New XFSeriesCollection()
    dataRows.FillUsingCubeViewDataAdapter(si,False,String.Empty,dataAdapter,xfdatarowlisttype.Allrow
    s, String.Empty,xfChartCubeViewDataPointLegendType.Default,False,
    XFChart2seriesType.BarRangeSideBySideWaterfall,args.CustomSubstVars)

    For Each dataRow As XFSeries In dataRows.Series
        dataRow.ModelType   = XFChart2ModelType.BarRange2DTransparent
        dataRow.BarWidth    = .90
        dataRow.Transparency = .7

        For Each dataPoint As XFSeriesPoint In dataRow.Points
            If dataPoint.Value > 0 Then
                dataPoint.Color = "Green"     'If this datapoint is an increase, paint it green
            Else
                dataPoint.Color = "Red"           'If this datapoint is a decrease, paint it red
            End If
        Next

        dataRow.Points(0).Color                          = "OSLightGray"'Paint the first bar OSLightGray
        dataRow.Points(dataRow.Points.Count-1).Color = "OSDarkGray" 'Paint the last bar OSDarkGray

    Next

    Return dataRows.CreateDataSet(si)

End If
```

Component Display

The appearance of advanced charts is vastly improved compared to basic charts. Their dynamic components give you the tools to really take advantage of additional formatting, as well as trigger actions to open or refresh other dashboards – with a simple click – on any area within the chart.

Within the component's property, you can configure these charts to run business rules, open dialogs, or navigate within the application, based on the bound parameter and server tasks or user interface actions, located under the **Actions** section.

Formatting the chart's colors, legend, crosshairs, as well as X and Y axis display settings, are available with this component, making this chart much more visually and interactively appealing than the basic chart component.

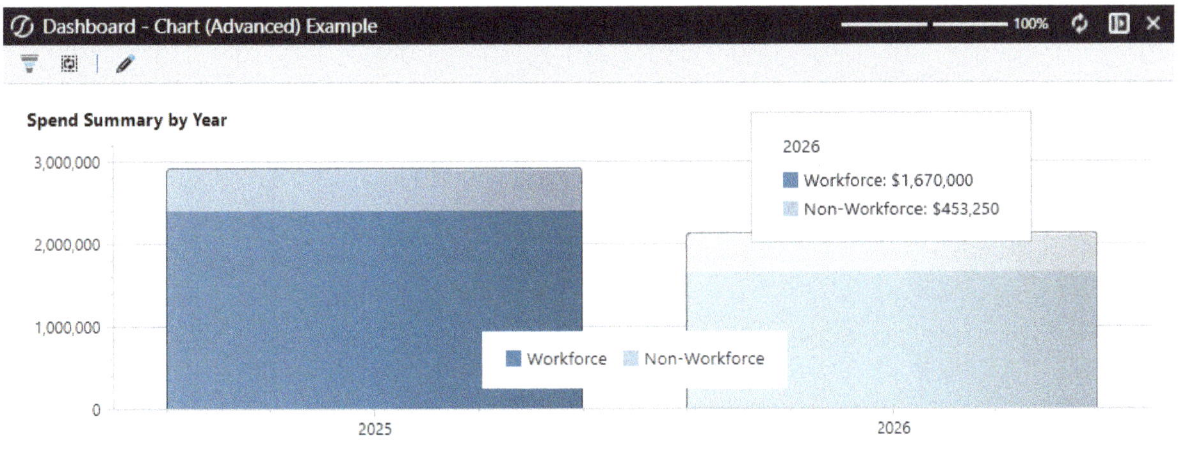

Figure 4.32

Cube View

Displays multidimensional data from the cube in grid format, which can be used for input or reporting. It's important to note that Cube View components differ from Cube Views themselves; Cube View components are objects placed on dashboards that display a Cube View – *with* the ability to control what should happen when a user interacts with the Cube View (refresh a different part of the dashboard, for example).

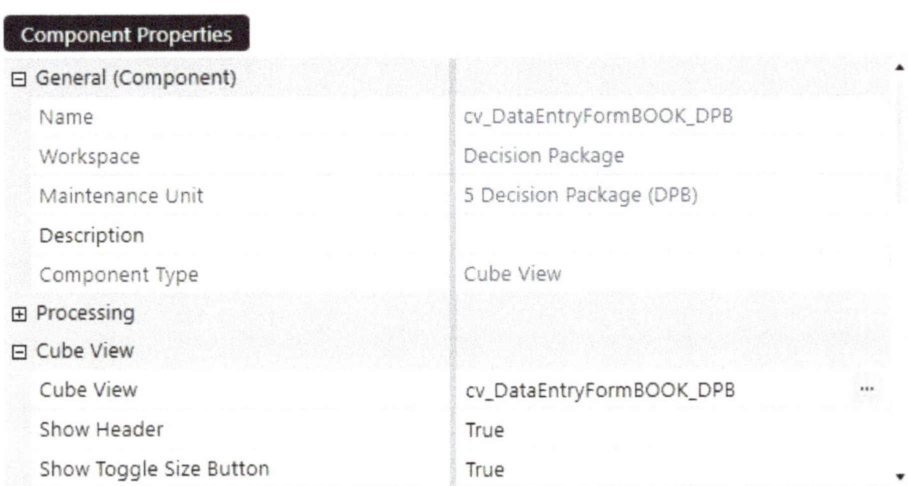

Figure 4.33

Component Display

Cube View components display identically to the same processed Cube View in the user interface. This component serves as a method by which Cube Views are displayed on dashboards, whether for reporting or data entry.

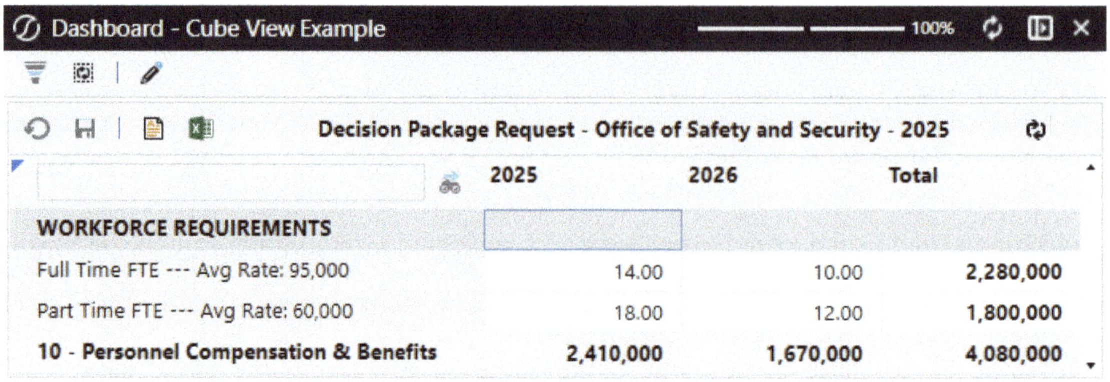

Figure 4.34

Data Explorer

This component is another method of displaying a Cube View in the standard Data Explorer view, when you click Open Data Explorer from the Cube View item itself. To use this component, enter a name and attach a Cube View Method Data Adapter to the component's Data Adapters tab.

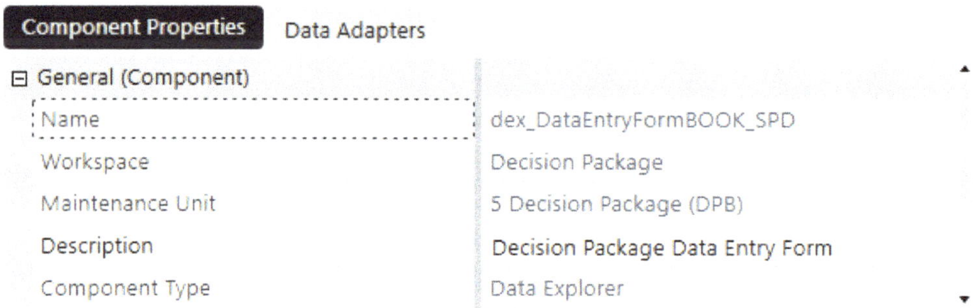

Figure 4.35

Component Display

The Data Explorer component's display is the same as the Cube View component. However, you do not have the ability to hide the header or remove certain buttons from the header toolbar.

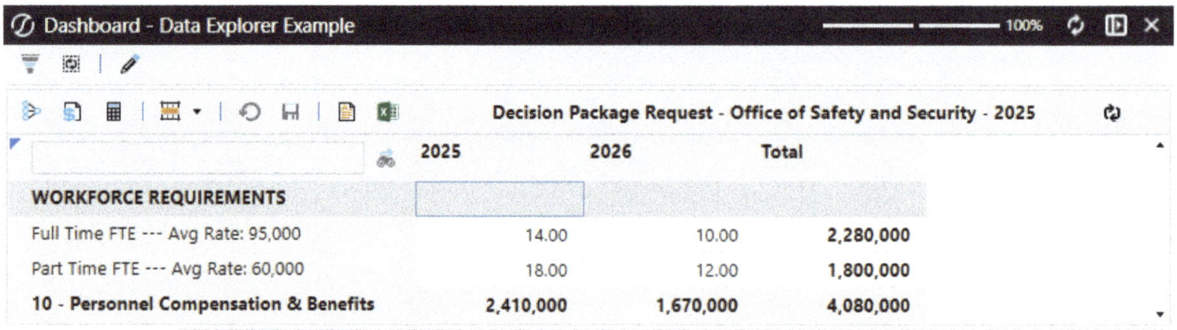

Figure 4.36

Data Explorer Report

A static version of a Data Explorer result for viewing or exporting (PDF, Excel, etc.).

This component's display mirrors the Report View of a processed Cube View. To use this component, enter a name and attach a Cube View Method Data Adapter to the component's Data Adapters tab.

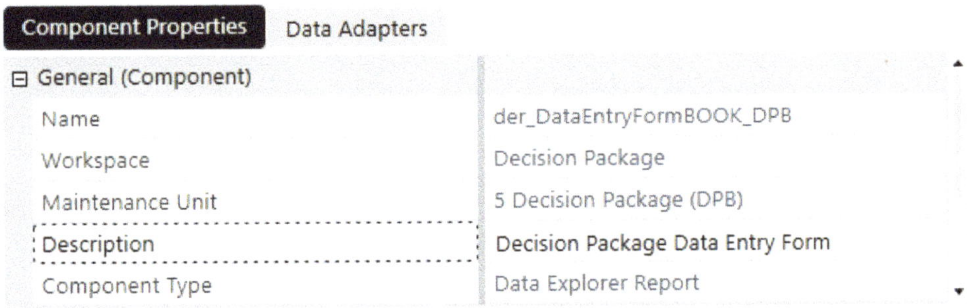

Figure 4.37

Component Display

The Data Explorer Report component's display is identical to what you see when viewing a processed Cube View report. This component is especially useful when enabling navigation links from Cube View rows that have been configured to open other dashboards in dialog boxes.

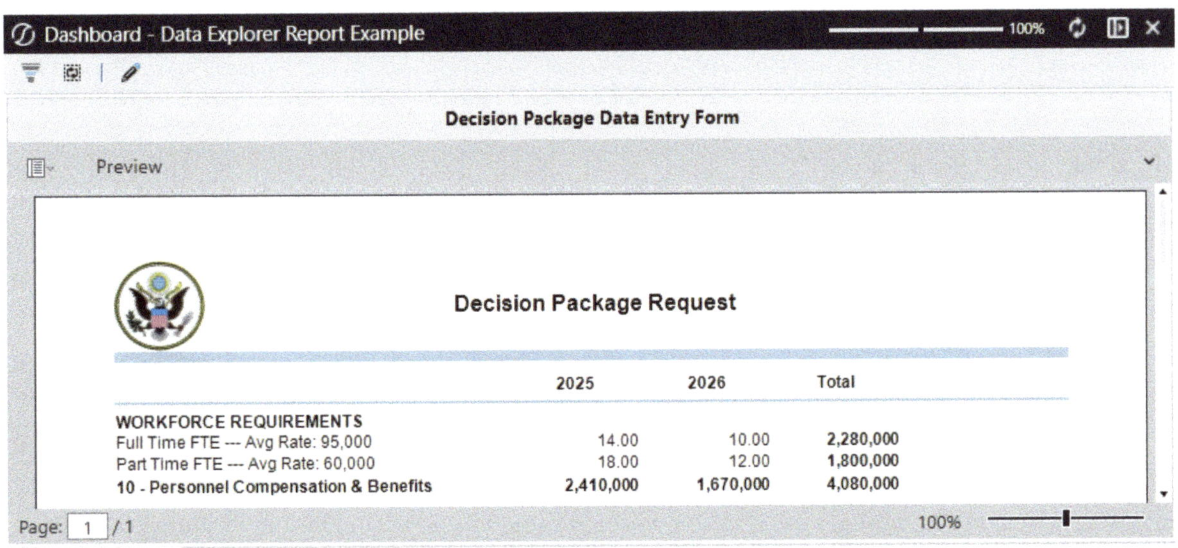

Figure 4.38

Gantt View

For visualizing tasks, events, or project timelines, a Gantt view is great for planning and project dashboards!

A Gantt View is best known for its use in Task Manager. This component displays a timeline visualization for a given process, project, or set of tasks, which helps your users quickly understand the status of groups of items.

Another added benefit of this component is the ability to trigger actions based on item selection, making it incredibly interactive and actionable, based on the visual indicators.

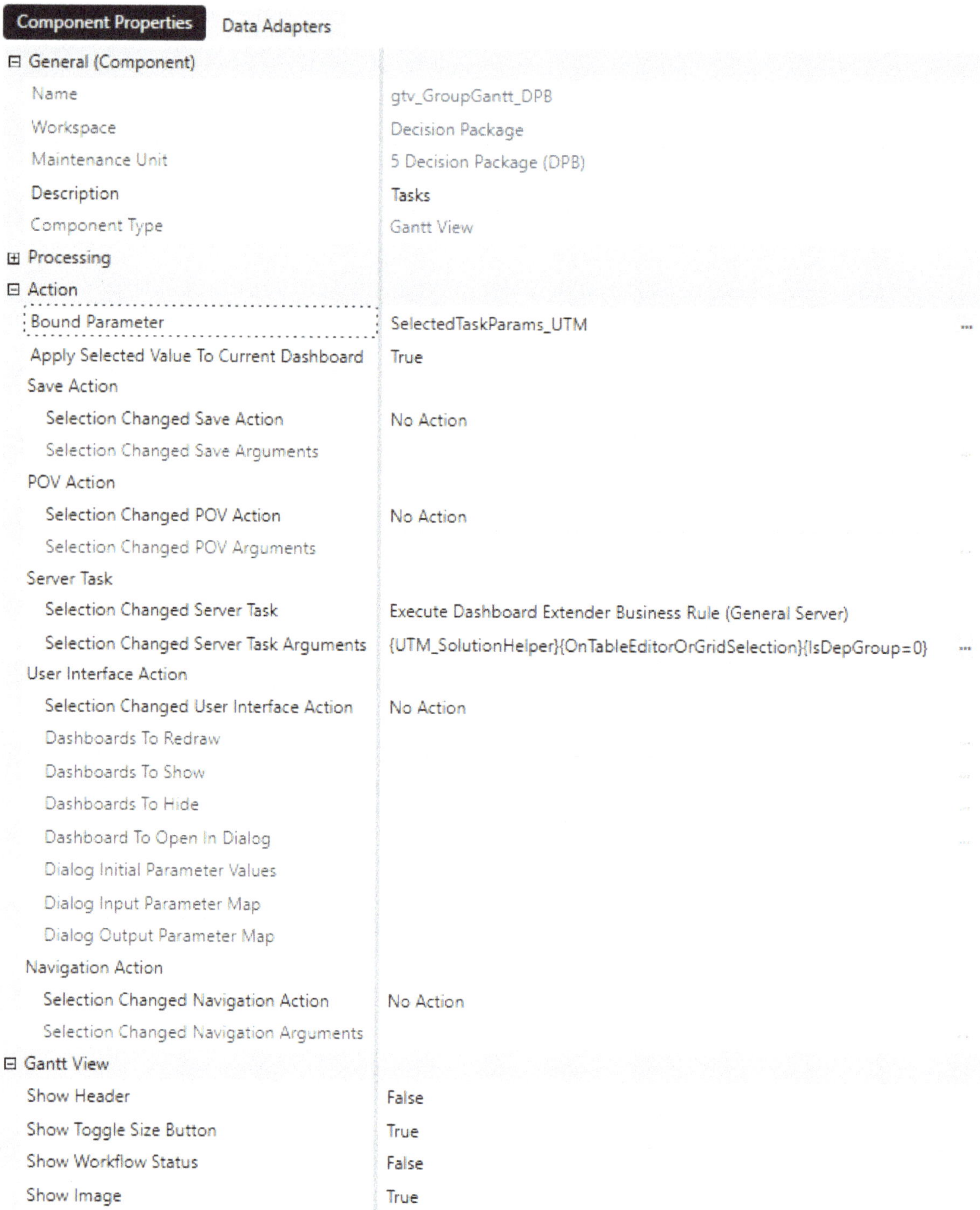

Figure 4.39

Component Display

Below is a sample set of tasks from Task Manager, with a Gantt View that shows the steps to be completed to close the books for a given period. The orange image indicator means that the task has a **dependency**, meaning that the preceding tasks must be completed before Load Trial Balance can be completed.

You can easily see the start and end dates for any task, whether by viewing the columns or viewing the timeline on the right of the tasks. The Details column surfaces buttons that can launch navigation or expose additional information about the task.

This is just an example of how Gantt Views can be used to enhance the user experience. Now, imagine how project or resource planning (or any other planning process) could be visually displayed to enable users to act faster and more efficiently, with the ability to realize bottlenecks or delays.

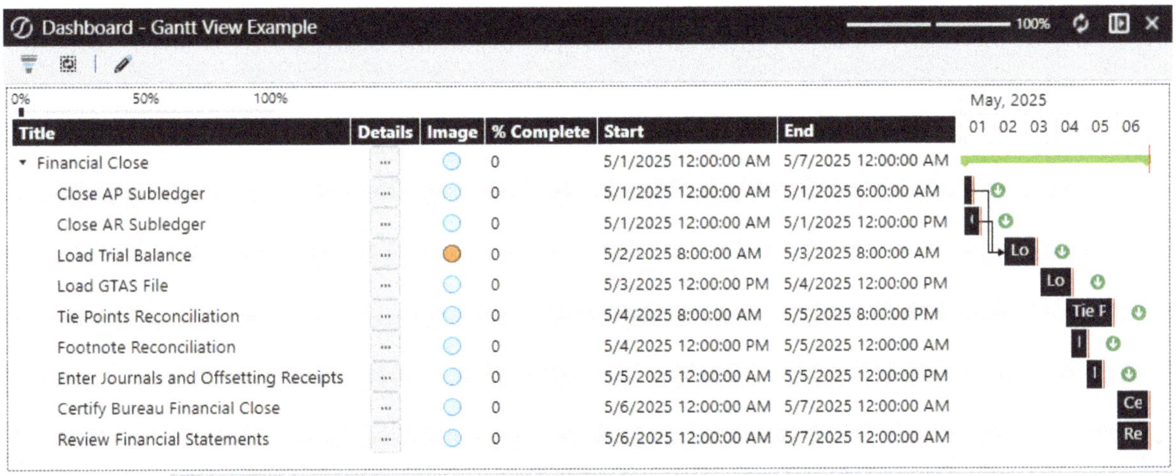

Figure 4.40

Grid View

A tabular display of data from SQL or cube queries. Good for listing or editing records.

Grid views are blank canvases for displaying data from various sources – all based on the data adapter attached to the component. In the figure below, a SQL Command Type data adapter has been created that queries the `DataAttachment` application database table to source the component with text entered into various annotation view members. In the grid view's properties, formatting options allow you to make columns multi-line text in order to apply word-wrap and fit within the column's width setting.

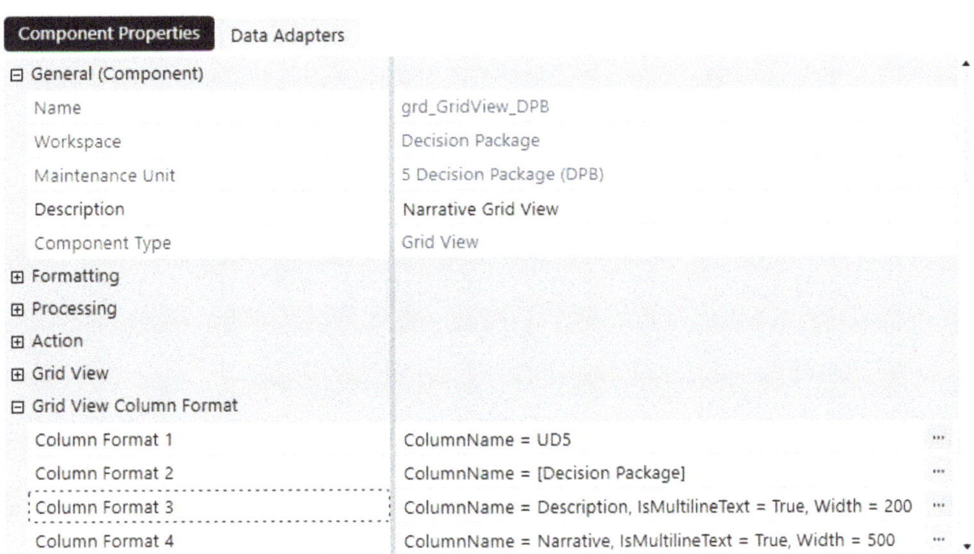

Figure 4.41

Component Display

Grid views are a great way to display cube data, relational data, or a combination of both, depending on how you configure the data adapter that sources the data and other information. They perform best with datasets up to a few thousand records, ensuring a smooth and responsive user experience.

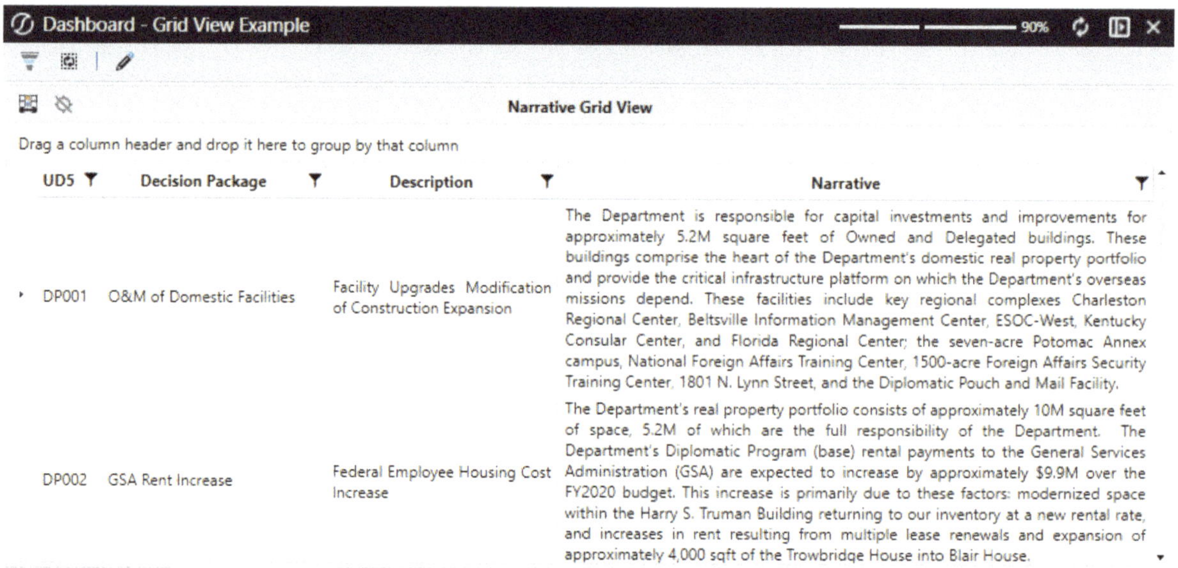

Figure 4.42

Large Data Pivot Grid

Optimized for high-volume cube data with pivoting, sorting, and filtering. Think "power-user" view.

When working with large data sets, you may need to analyze data that may not be within the OneStream application due to performance or data modification requirements. To address this, the Large Data Pivot Grid component allows you to query tables directly that you can sort, organize, and analyze – even on data that is not actually in the application. Thanks to Pagination, this component can be responsive and performant even on datasets with millions of records.

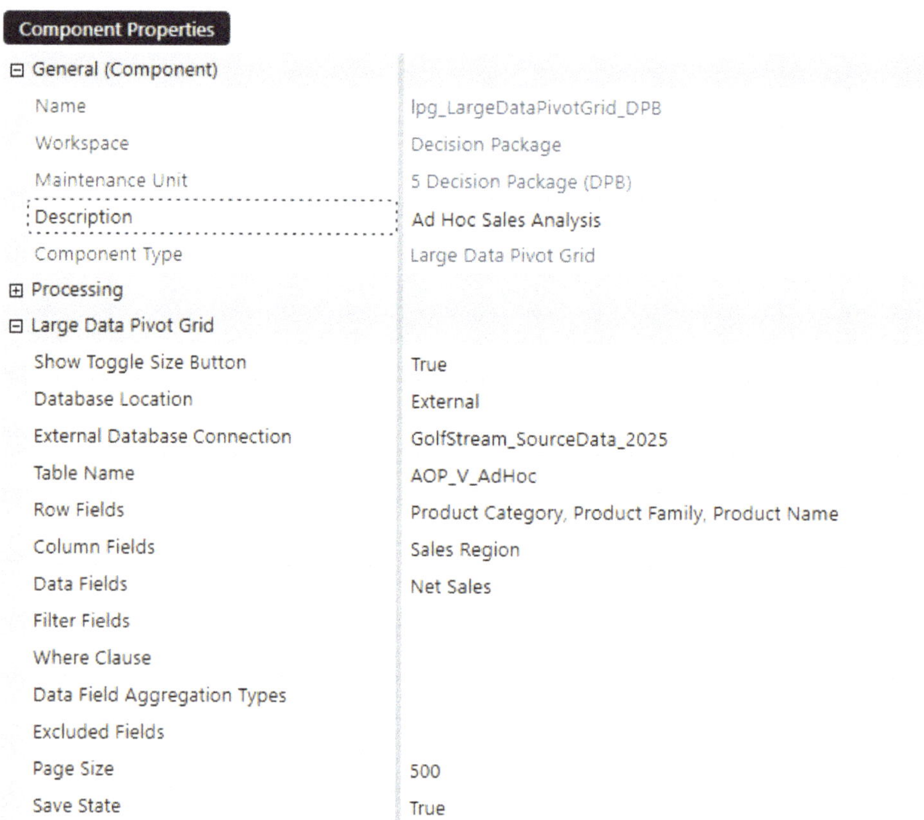

Figure 4.43

Component Display

This component displays external data from the server connection string, empowering users to analyze and act on data at a more granular level than what has been loaded to the cube.

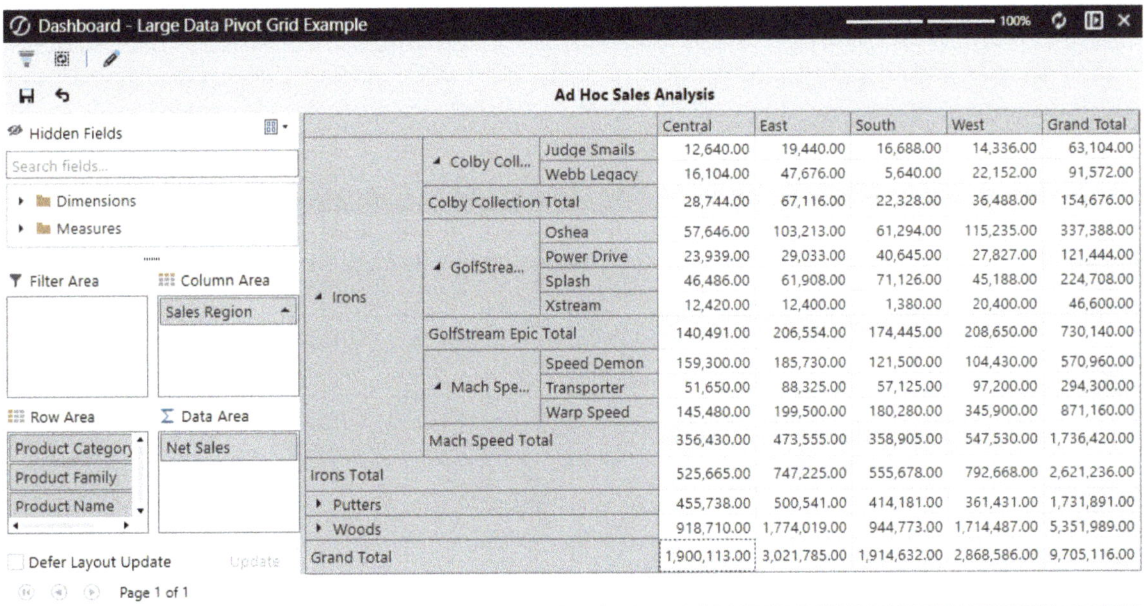

Figure 4.44

Map

A geo-visualization tool for data displayed on maps (region-based KPIs, etc.).

Using the map component requires no data adapters or coding out-of-the-box. You can, however, customize the map and interactivity with the use of **data set business rules**.

- **Display Type** – Humanitarian, Standard, and Transport map display types are available.
- **Zoom Level** – The distance at which you want to view the map. A lower zoom level will display a broader view of the area, while a higher zoom level will show a closer view.
- **Center Latitude & Longitude** – These coordinates determine the central location of the map.

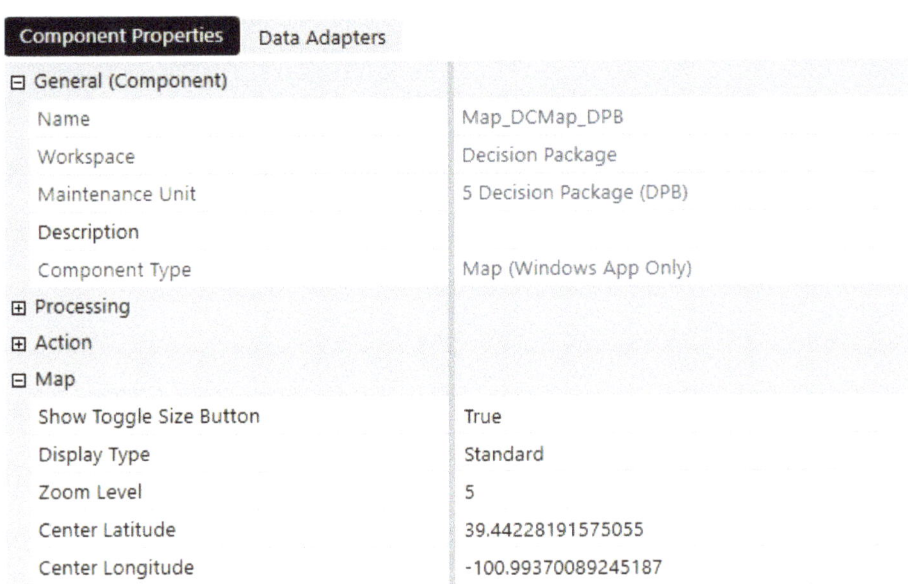

Figure 4.45

Component Display

This component can be configured to pass in parameters based on map points, allowing you to navigate to region/location-specific data based on coordinates that are assigned to a metadata member's text properties, simply by clicking on the map point.

To enable this functionality, you would use a data set business rule and attach it to a data adapter that displays points on the map. Once the data adapter is configured and attached to the component, you can assign a **bound parameter** to the map component and configure the server task settings to refresh the page with member-filtered data when a user clicks on a point on the map.

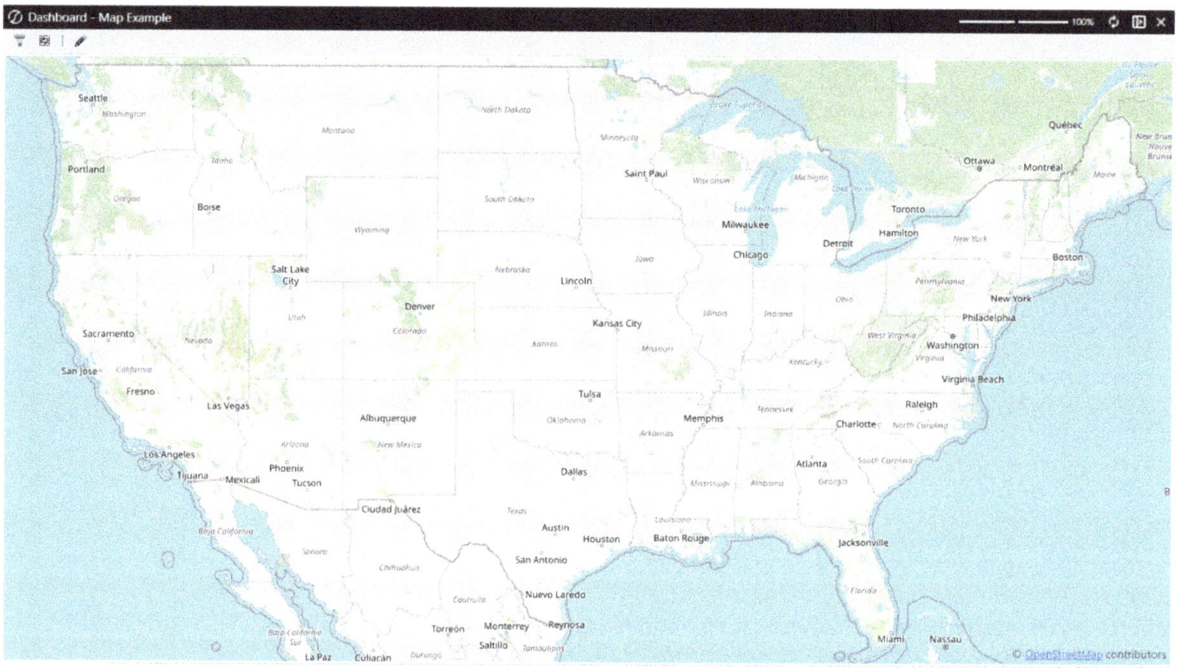

Figure 4.46

Pivot Grid

An interactive grid for analyzing cube data – pivot fields, sort, filter, drill. Unlike the Large Data Pivot Grid, this component is powered by a standard data adapter – you can source data from Cube Views or business rules. However, it is not intended for displaying datasets containing hundreds of millions of records.

Below is an example of the data adapter querying the People Planning Register table. You can refine the SQL query to limit the fields users can view, and add a `WHERE` clause to filter the table's records.

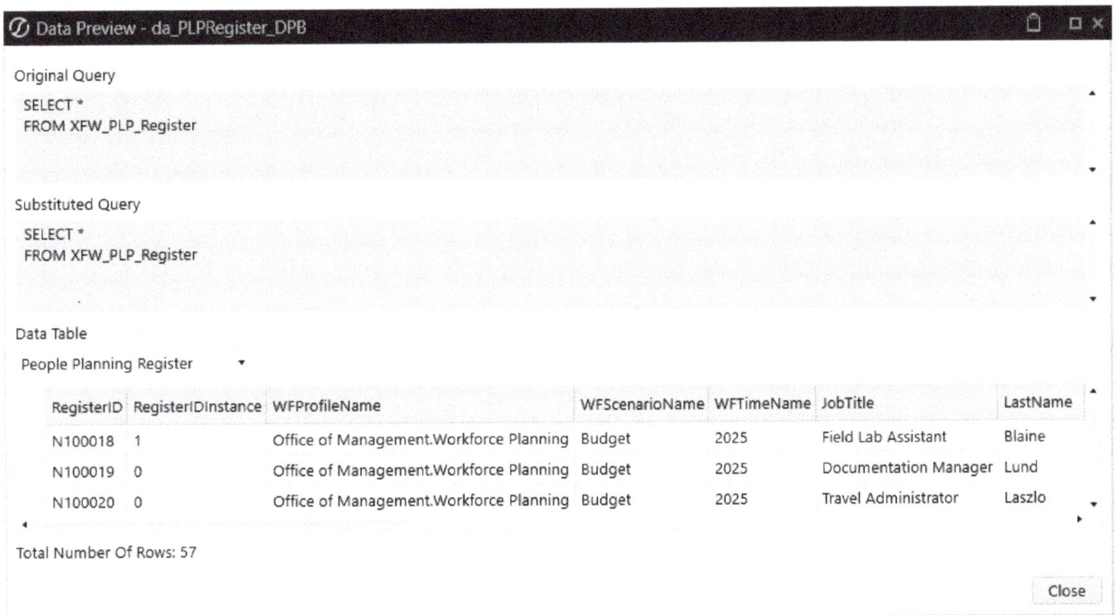

Figure 4.47

In the Component Properties, you can set the default Column, Row, and Data Fields.

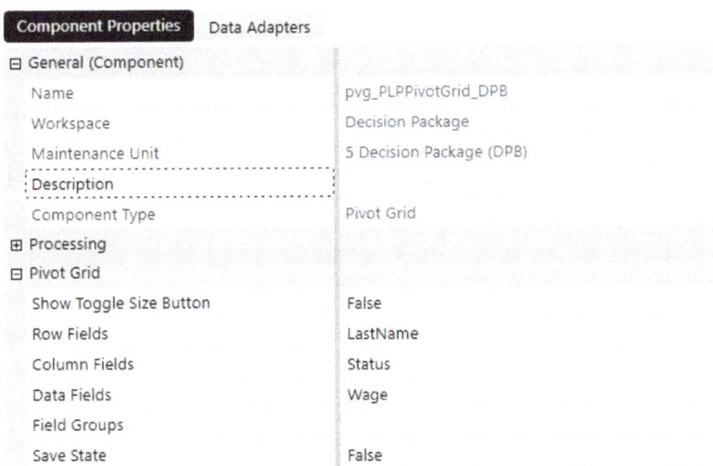

Figure 4.48

Component Display

When the component is initially displayed, default settings are applied. However, by nature of the component, the user can easily change the view, add additional nesting in rows or columns, and essentially slice the data – in whatever way they need to – when analyzing the data.

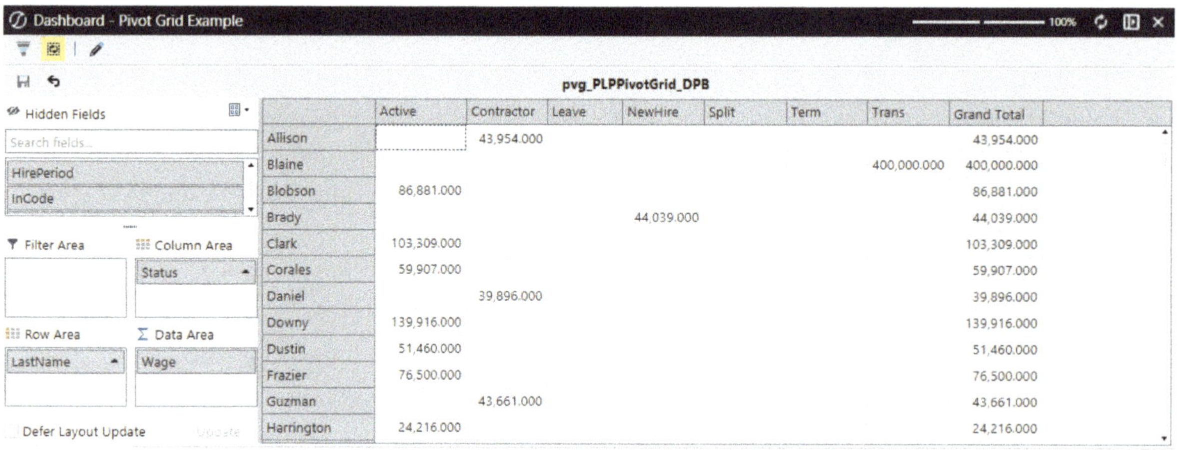

Figure 4.49

Report

Displays formatted, printable reports that can be displayed on dashboards or even incorporated into Books. Within the Report Designer, you can place and format fields, create reports that loop through data members, and insert a Table of Contents.

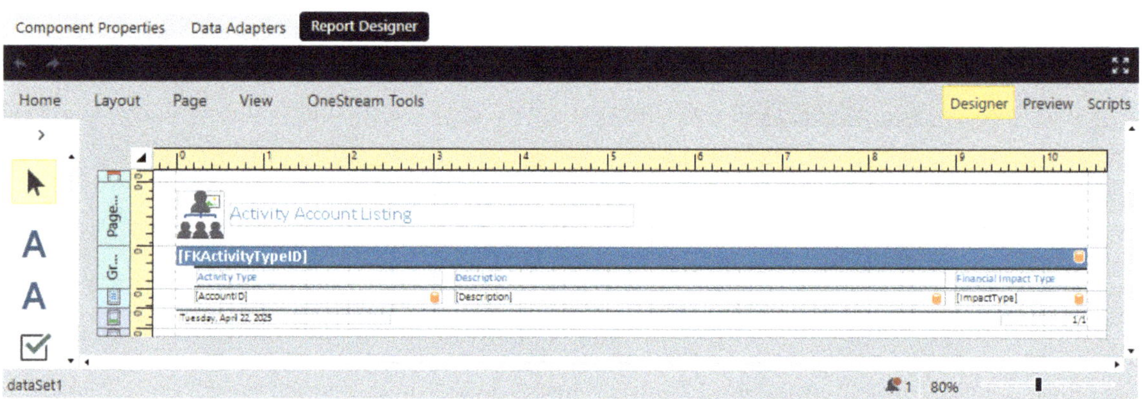

Figure 4.50

Component Display

The figure below is one of the many reports included in the out-of-the-box People Planning solution from the Solution Exchange.

Designing these reports from scratch can be an intimidating task. The way I learned how to make and modify them is by copying an existing report and making minor changes, then previewing the report from the Report Designer. Once you grasp how these report outputs are constructed, you'll better understand how you can use these reports to loop through large data sets and create lengthy books rather than duplicate the same report.

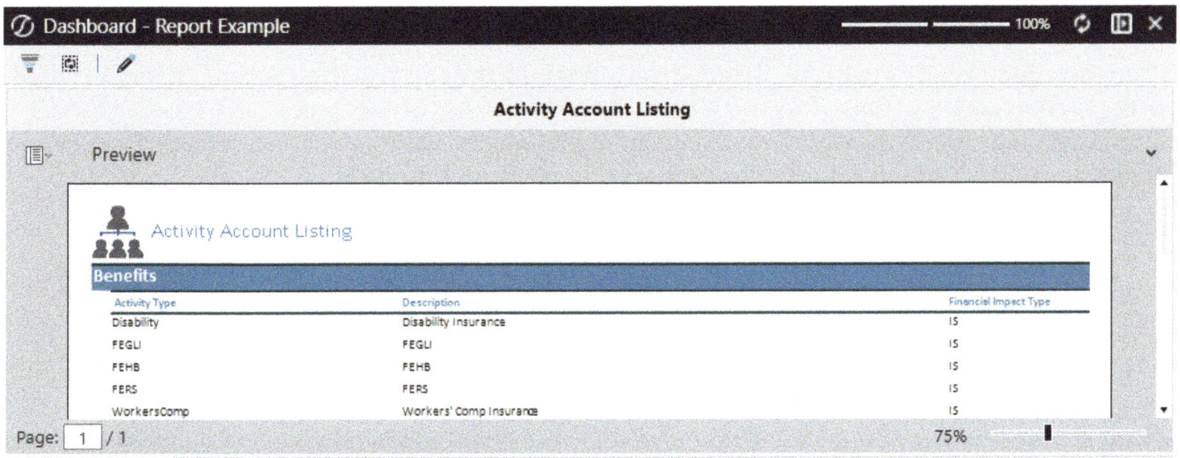

Figure 4.51

Sankey Diagram

A flow diagram showing how values split and merge, a Sankey diagram is great for cost allocations and data movement.

This component requires a BusinessRule data adapter to create datasets on the fly. The Sankey diagram shows the flow of data from one dimension to another, as well as tiered flows, based on how the code is written.

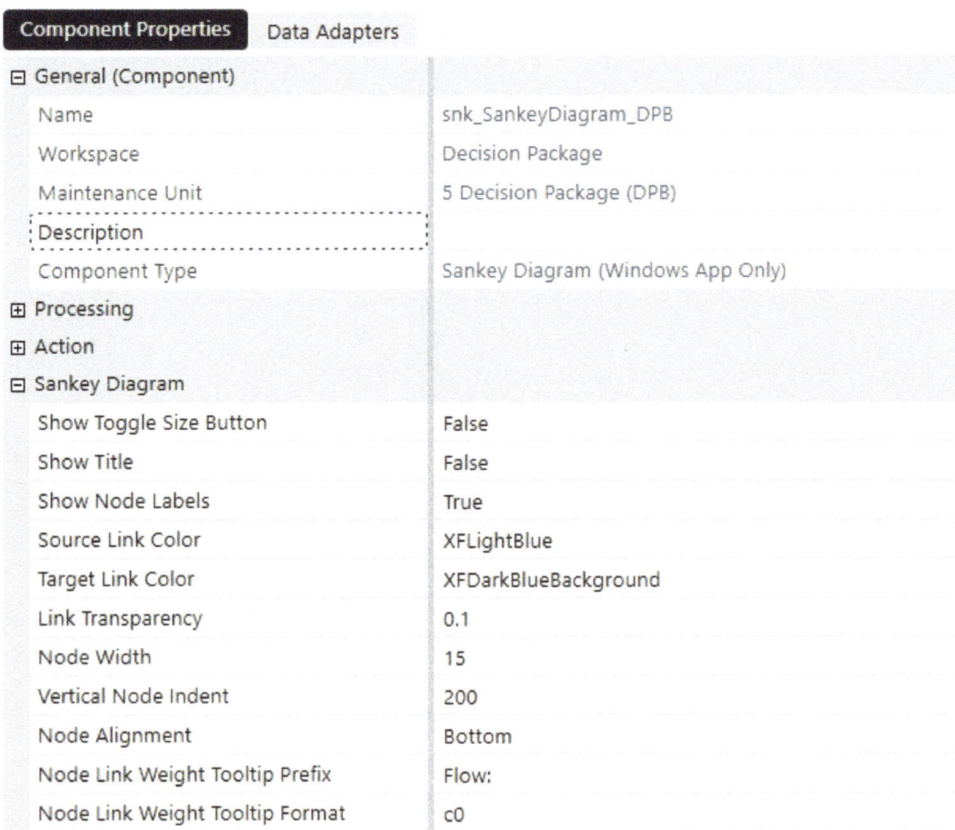

Figure 4.52

Component Display

The component displays the flow, based on how the business rule has been coded. This is a simple example showing how values from entities on the left contribute to programs on the right. You're able to pass parameters through the component to provide the ability to click on a specific flow stream and display additional detail or expose other navigation features.

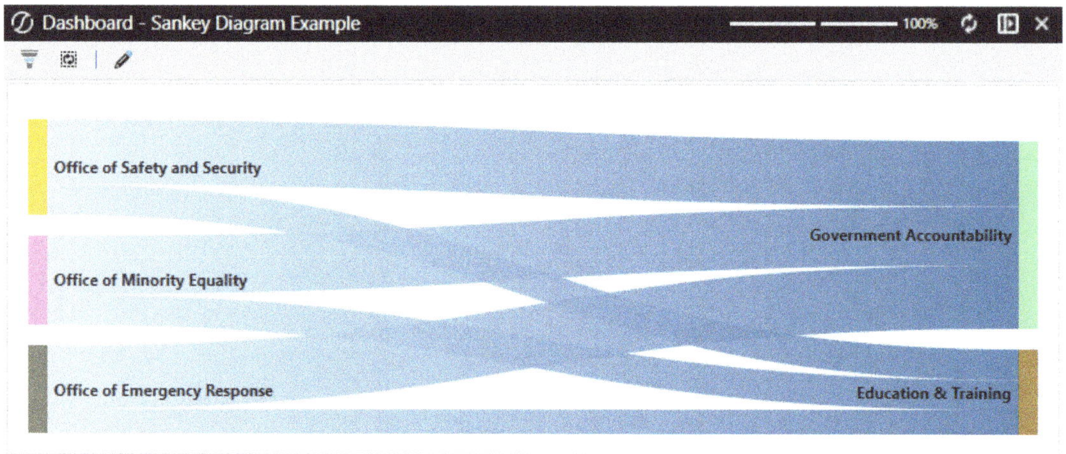

Figure 4.53

Spreadsheet

An embedded Excel-like spreadsheet interface where users can work with familiar Excel tools inside OneStream. To use this component, you'll need to either upload an Excel file into OneStream or open the Spreadsheet tool under Applications and save the file into one of the folder structures.

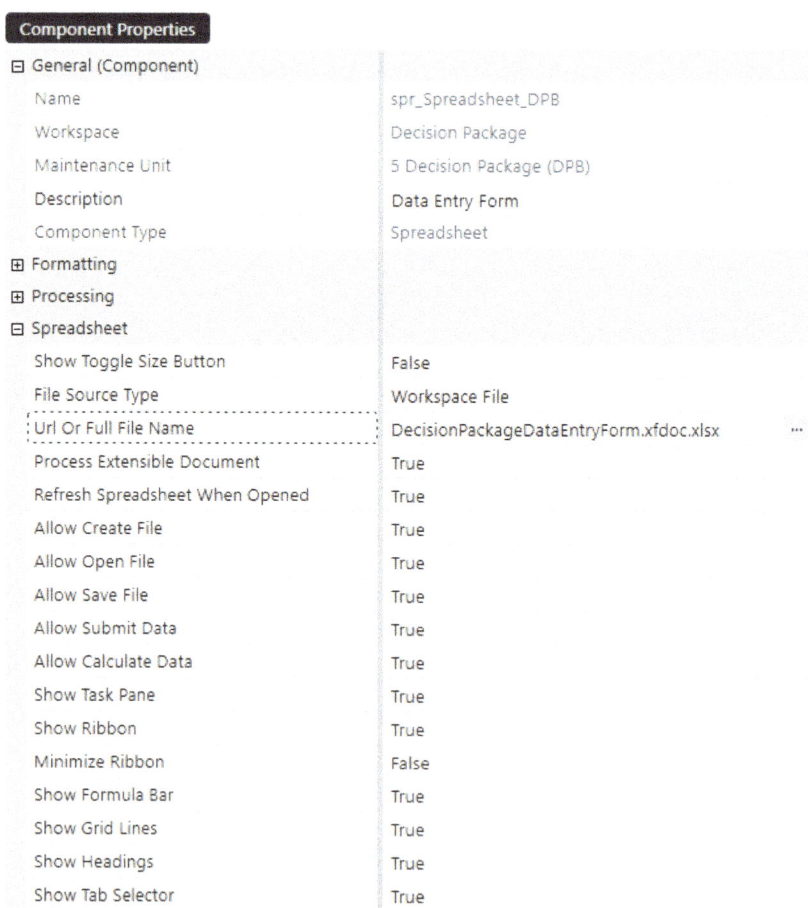

Component Properties

⊟ General (Component)	
Name	spr_Spreadsheet_DPB
Workspace	Decision Package
Maintenance Unit	5 Decision Package (DPB)
Description	Data Entry Form
Component Type	Spreadsheet
⊞ Formatting	
⊞ Processing	
⊟ Spreadsheet	
Show Toggle Size Button	False
File Source Type	Workspace File
Url Or Full File Name	DecisionPackageDataEntryForm.xfdoc.xlsx ...
Process Extensible Document	True
Refresh Spreadsheet When Opened	True
Allow Create File	True
Allow Open File	True
Allow Save File	True
Allow Submit Data	True
Allow Calculate Data	True
Show Task Pane	True
Show Ribbon	True
Minimize Ribbon	False
Show Formula Bar	True
Show Grid Lines	True
Show Headings	True
Show Tab Selector	True

Figure 4.54

Component Display

In this example, the source Excel file we inserted into the component has a Cube View connection, which displays the contents and layout of the Cube View in Excel. Spreadsheets can also use table views to display raw tables that provide more reporting capabilities. To do this, you'll need to create a Spreadsheet business rule that can be called and inserted into the Spreadsheet from the OneStream ribbon.

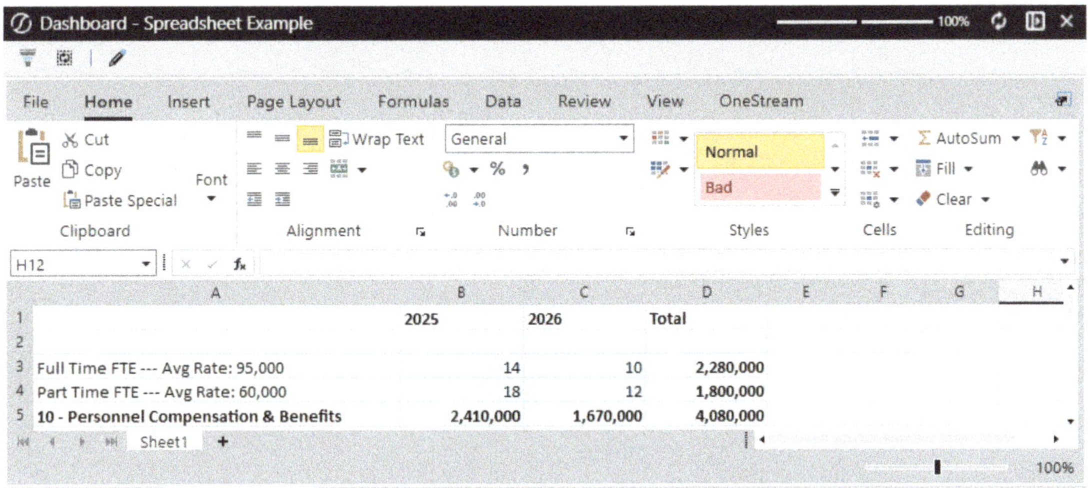

Figure 4.55

Navigation & Input Components

Button

Executes actions, opens dashboards, runs business rules, refreshes data, etc.

Buttons are commonly used on dashboards to allow users to interact with the software. All Solution Exchange solutions contain buttons in some fashion, and I encourage you to dissect the different buttons within these solutions to understand what they are doing and how they are configured.

Listed below are the highlights of button functionality:

- **Save** – Saves data that has been changed on a dashboard
- **Refresh** – Refreshes dashboards after data has been changed
- **Execute Actions** – Runs calculations, business rules, and data management jobs
- **Navigation** – Navigates to workflows, dashboards, files, webpages, or application pages (based on user security)
- **Change POV** – Changes the Cube POV, workflow, or both
- **Open Dialogs** – Opens dialog boxes with instructions, other information, etc.

In the figure below, the button has been formatted with a label and tool tip, and the button itself is configured to execute a dashboard extender business rule, which sends a dashboard report to email recipients defined by security groups.

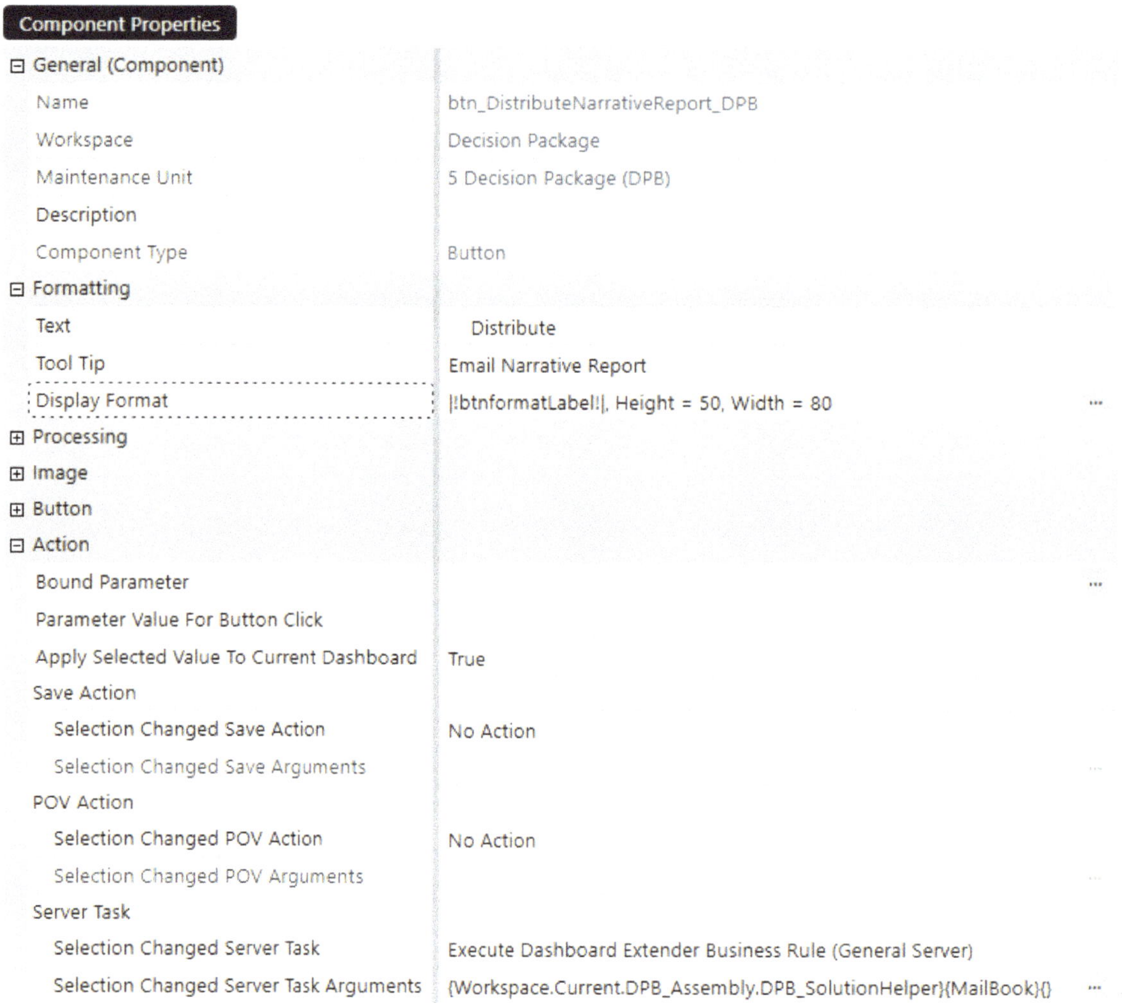

Figure 4.56

Component Display

When you hover over the button, you can easily see the tool tip as configured in the button properties. This is especially helpful when you want to display buttons without text, and you can enter instructions, descriptions (or whatever you want) in the tool tips field to help users navigate dashboards.

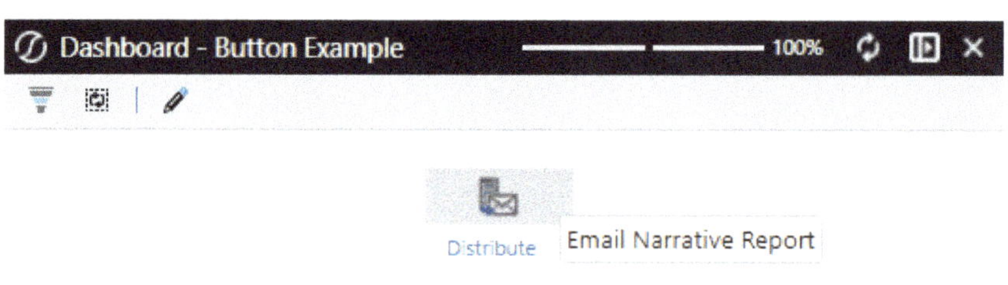

Figure 4.57

Check Box

Allows binary user input (on/off, true/false).

We primarily see the use of this component in Solution Exchange solutions, typically on the administrative setup or management dashboards that control solution settings.

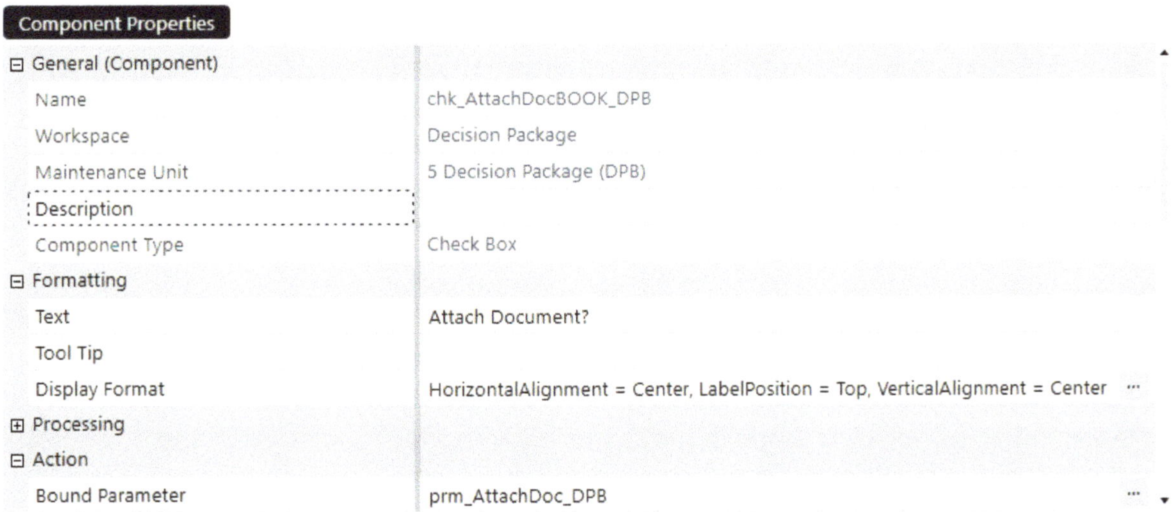

Figure 4.58

Component Display

This component's bound parameter is a delimited list parameter type with true/false options. When the box is checked, you could trigger an action to open a dialog where the user would attach a document to the file path dictated in the component's properties.

This component would typically be used in conjunction with a button to save the selections and run any necessary steps (such as saving the selection or executing an action based on the selection).

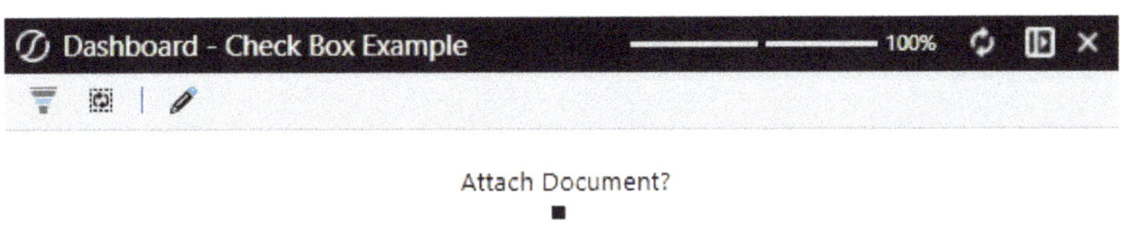

Figure 4.59

Combo Box

A drop-down list to select a single item for binding to dimensions, parameters, or hardcoded lists.

These components, in the simplest use case, should be set up to refresh a dashboard or dashboards. That way, the selection refreshes the dashboard automatically to display data that is relevant to the combo box selection. You have the same functionality available in button components; you can change POV, navigate to other dashboards, or execute actions.

Some of the newer features of combo box components are the Display Format settings:

- **IsMultiSelect** – useful when displaying components with multiple selected items
- **ShowSearch** – useful when you have lengthy lists of options from a parameter

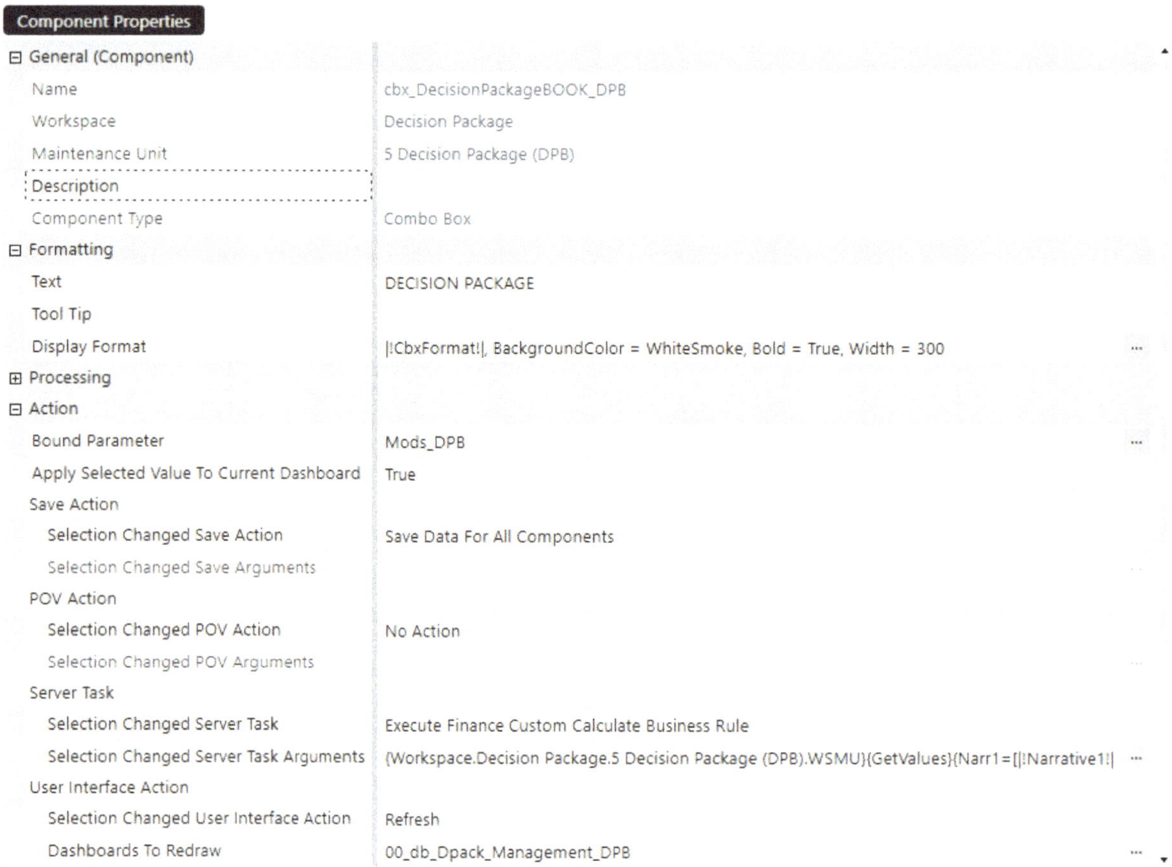

Figure 4.60

Component Display

The combo box in the figure below shows how this component is displayed on a dashboard. This is just an example of a combo box we've built, and you can certainly change the appearance of the combo box by modifying the component's Display Format properties.

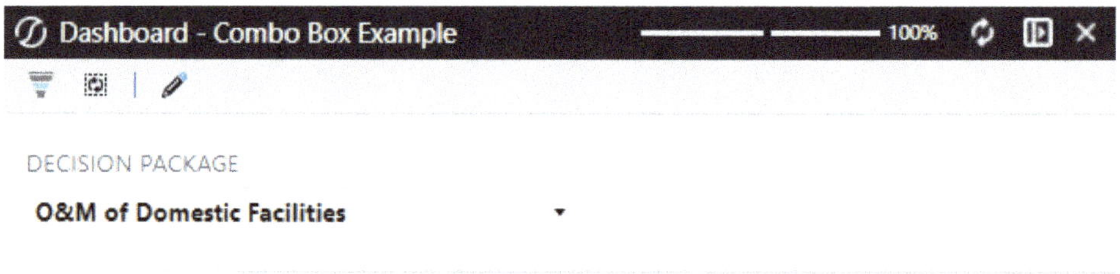

Figure 4.61

Date Selector

A calendar-style picker for date inputs; data selectors can drive time parameters.

Date selectors can be used in various ways, whether that's collecting attributes about a project plan or querying the OneStream database tables to view audit reports within a specified date range. This component requires no business rules or coding, and you can set Min and Max Dates to guide your users to applicable date ranges when populating this component on a dashboard.

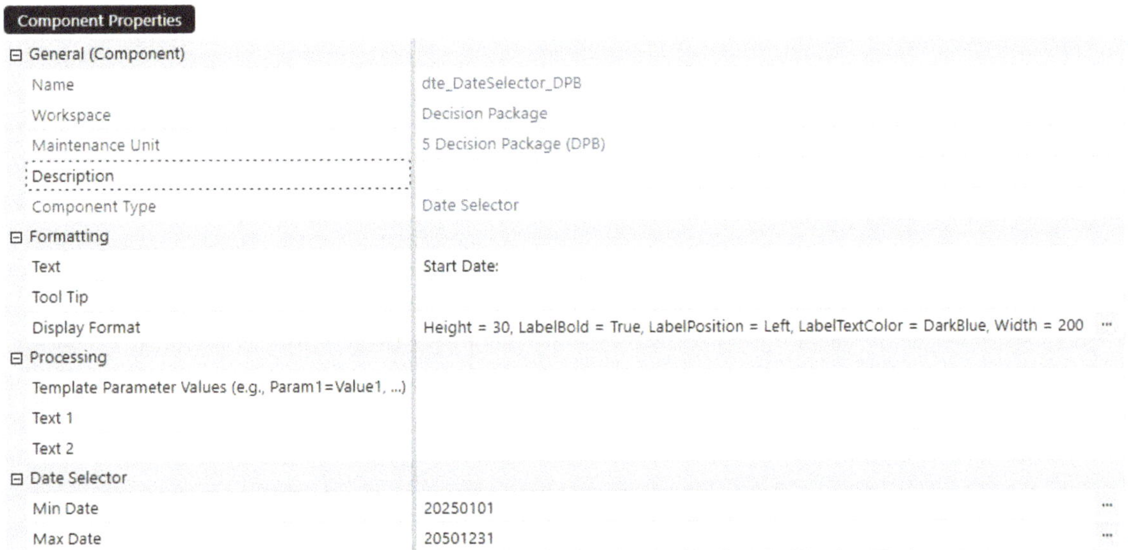

Figure 4.62

Component Display

When placed on a dashboard, users have the ability to key in the date, or select a specific date by clicking on the calendar icon within the box. This component is used widely throughout the **Application Reports solution** from the Solution Exchange, specifically in the audit reports, where the reports query the database tables for date ranges.

Suppose you want to plan long-term project profitability. You could use this component to capture the start and completion dates to get a timespan, and the timespan could then be used in calculations to forecast allocated costs by period, factoring in partial months up to the proportion of days in the start and completion date.

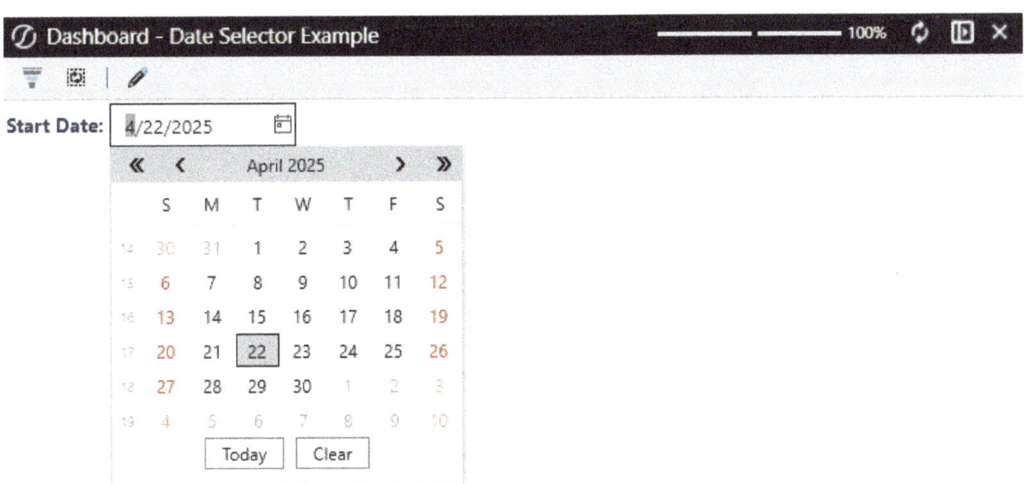

Figure 4.63

Embedded Dashboard

Embedded dashboard components are automatically created when you create dashboards for the purpose of **nesting** dashboard objects. These components are also the mechanism for reusing dashboards from other Workspaces or maintenance units.

In the example below, we've created a new embedded dashboard component that we will use to pull a dashboard from another Workspace. The native dashboards shown below are components that were automatically created when we added actual dashboards to our dashboard groups, while the added component is the item we created.

When adding embedded dashboards to a tab layout-style dashboard, the tab label defaults to the name of the embedded dashboard. For example, if you attach the first two embedded dashboard components shown below, the first tab would display `emb WorkflowButtons_DPB` and the second would display `Embedded 0_Frame_DPB`. To present more user-friendly tab names, you can set the Description property of each embedded dashboard – helping users quickly understand what each tab contains.

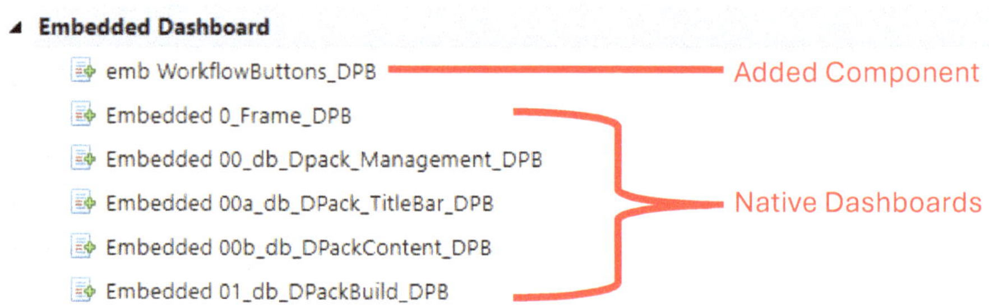

Figure 4.64

Component Display

Dashboards are a collection of objects laid out in a user-defined layout. In the figure below, you can see that two embedded dashboard components have been added to the `00_db_Dpack_Management_DPB dashboard`.

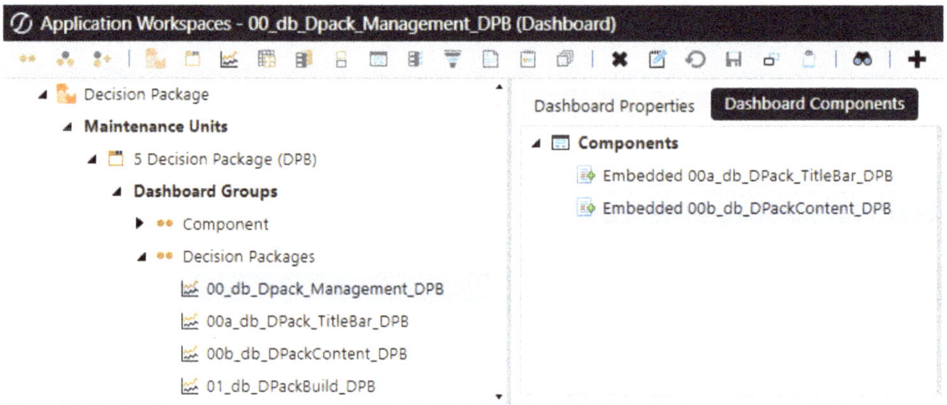

Figure 4.65

Filter Editor

Enables users to build and modify filters dynamically; often tied to Cube Views or reports.

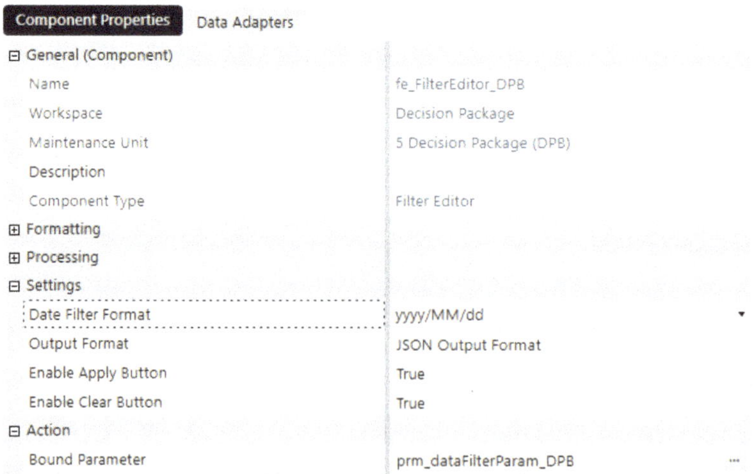

Figure 4.66

Component Display

This component is used to allow users to filter data from another component, such as a grid view component (shown below, for example), which can be filtered using multiple conditions. To the right of the filter component, the filter query is displayed to show the user any applied filters.

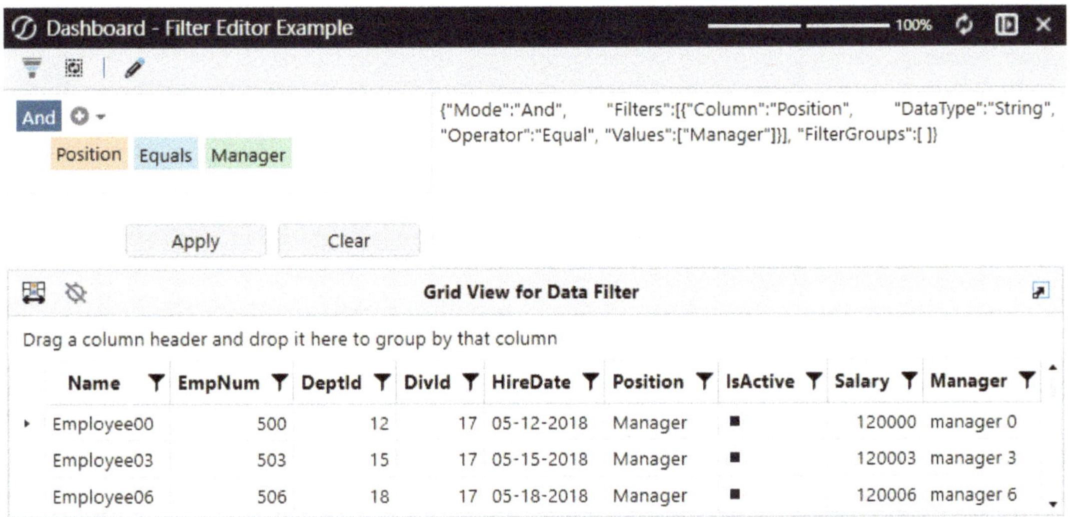

Figure 4.67

List Box

Displays a scrollable list, single or multi-selection.

The list box component shown below uses a bound parameter based on a Method Command Type parameter, and you can enable the multi-select feature from the component's Display Format properties.

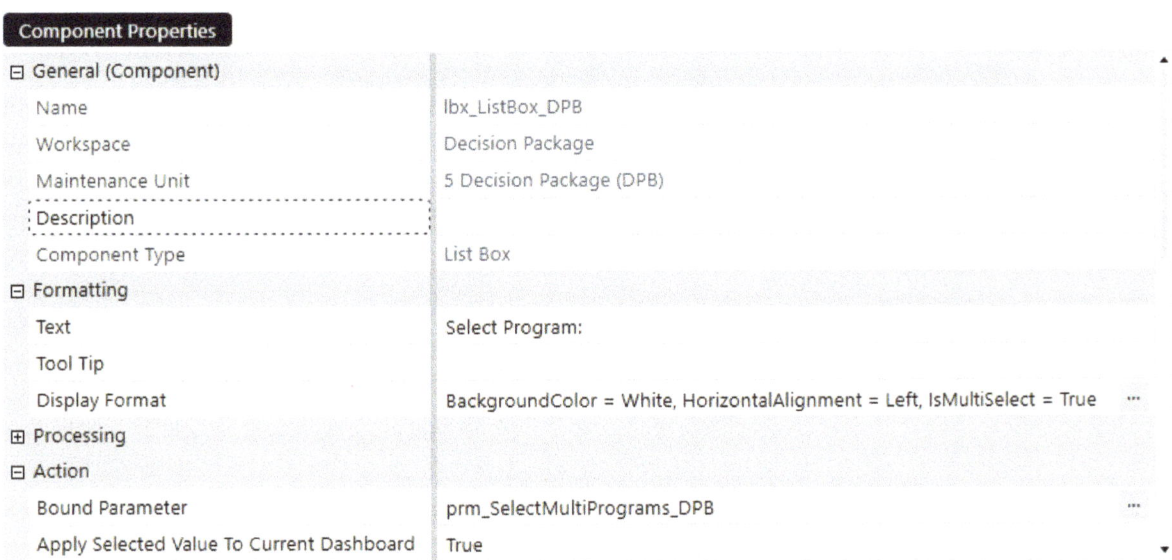

Figure 4.68

The parameter used to supply the list box component is shown below. In the method query, our dimension type, name, and filter are defined.

⊟ General (Parameter)	
Name	prm_SelectMultiPrograms_DPB
Workspace	Decision Package
Maintenance Unit	5 Decision Package (DPB)
Description	
User Prompt	
Sort Order	0
⊟ Data Source	
Parameter Type	Bound List
Default Value	...
Result Format String Type	Custom
Result Custom Format String	U1#{0}
Command Type	Method
Method Type	Members
Method Query	{UD1}{BUD_Programs}{UD1#11200.Descendants}{} ...
Results Table Name	Programs
Display Member	Description
Value Member	Name

Figure 4.69

Component Display

When the component is placed on a dashboard, we see the query results from the parameter, as well as check boxes on each list row to allow selection. This component could be used on a dashboard to allow users to pick multiple members that would populate a Cube View or any other component to display data, based on the selections made from the list box component. The dashboard that is refreshed – based on the list box selection – could either be automatically refreshed each time the list box selections are changed, or you could use a button to refresh the dashboard once item selections are made and ready to refine the dashboard.

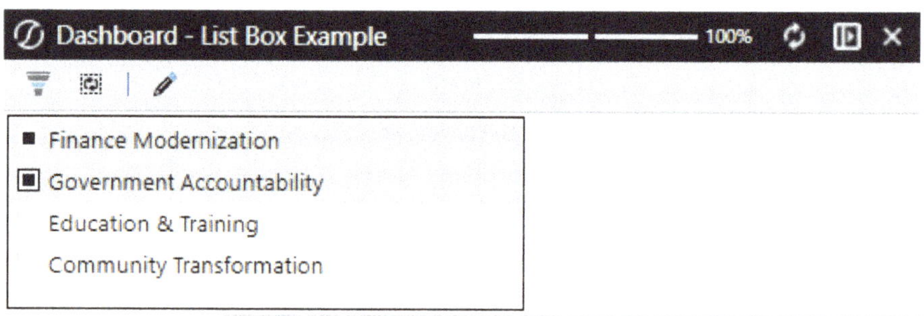

Figure 4.70

Menu

A drop-down or pop-up navigation menu; able to launch dashboards, functions, etc.

This component is one of the most recent additions to OneStream's component library, and it is widely used in the Genesis Framework. It allows you to create parameterized lists of options that streamline navigation.

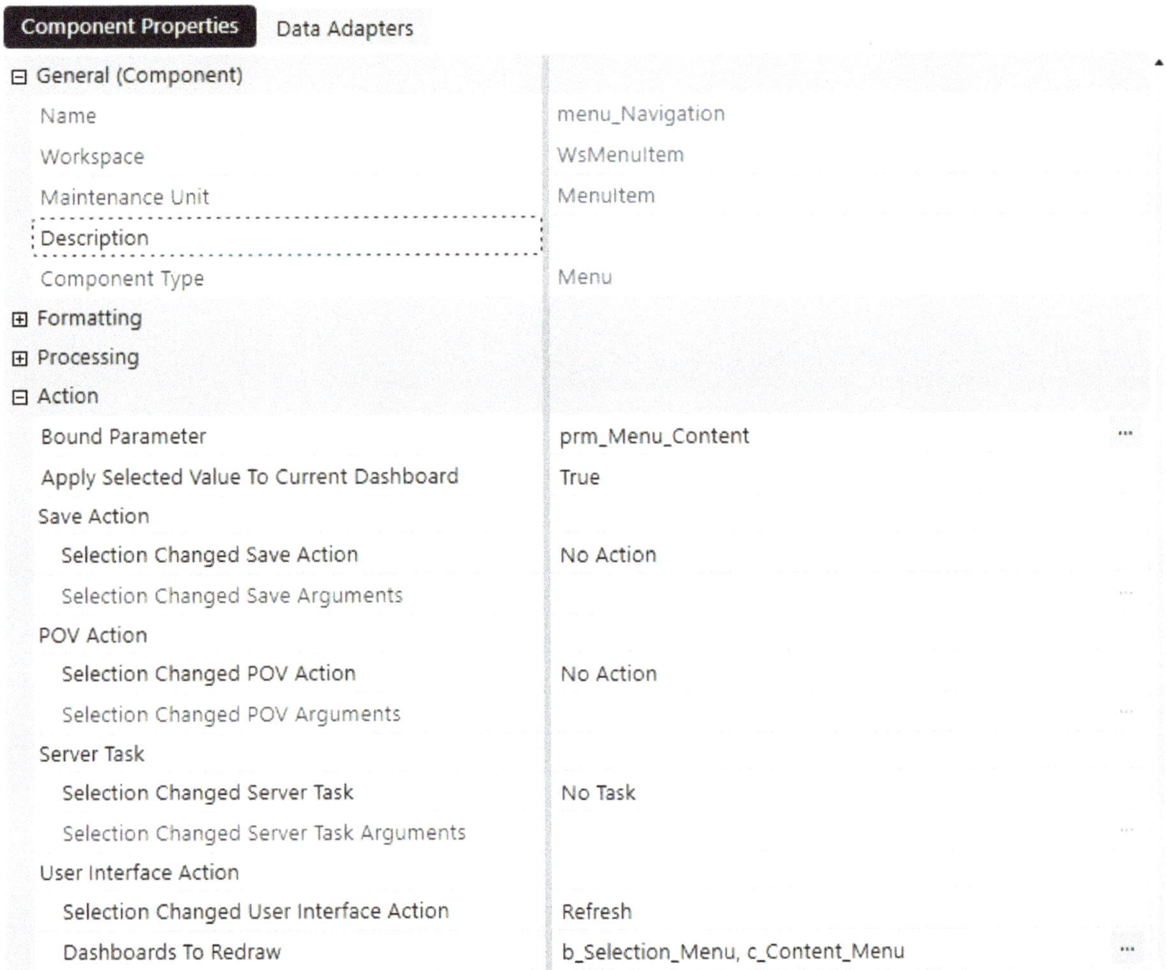

Figure 4.71

Component Display

The menu component is configured using a data adapter driven off a business rule or Workspace Assembly, making this a developer's go-to when developing dashboards with wizard-like interactivity. Upon menu item selection, this component can swap dashboards, refresh content on a user-role-based filter, and expose even more content as defined during the development process.

Figure 4.72

The content and the format of the menu are controlled by a data set business rule or a data set service Assembly. Here is an example:

```
'Display settings
Dim width As Integer = 140
Dim height As Integer = 28
Dim menuBackgroundColor  As String = "Black"
Dim menuTextColor As String = "White"
Dim subMenuBackgroundColor  As String = "OSLightGray"
Dim subMenuTextColor As String = "Black"

If args.DataSetName.XFEqualsIgnoreCase("GetMainMenu") Then

    Dim L1 As New XFMenuItem("L1","Admin",subMenuTextColor,subMenuBackgroundColor,
    True,False,True,False,width,height,5,5,5,5,Nothing,Nothing,"0","Admin","Admin View",Nothing)
    Dim L2 As New XFMenuItem("L2","Config",subMenuTextColor,subMenuBackgroundColor,
    True,False,True,False,width,height,5,5,5,5,Nothing,Nothing,"0","Config","Config View",Nothing)
    Dim L3 As New XFMenuItem("L3","Help",subMenuTextColor,subMenuBackgroundColor,
    True,False,True,False,width,height,5,5,5,5,Nothing,Nothing,"0","Help","Help View",Nothing)
    Dim L4 As New XFMenuItem("L4","Home",subMenuTextColor,subMenuBackgroundColor,
    True,False,True,False,width,height,5,5,5,5,Nothing,Nothing,"0","Home","Home View",Nothing)

    Dim LMain As List (Of XFMenuItem) = New List (Of XFMenuItem)
      LMain.Add(L1)
      LMain.Add(L2)
      LMain.Add(L3)
      LMain.Add(L4)

    Dim TopMenuItem As XFMenuItem = New XFMenuItem("Main","MainMenu",
    menuTextColor,menuBackgroundColor,True,False,True,False,width,height,5,5,5,5,Nothing,Nothing,0,
    "MENU","Navigate to Menu Selection",LMain)

    Dim Menu As XFMenuItemCollection = New XFMenuItemCollection()
    menu.MenuItems.Add(TopMenuItem)

    Return menu.CreateDataSet(si)

End If
```

Password Box

A password box is a UI control (often used in dashboards or business rules within OneStream) that lets users enter sensitive information like passwords or tokens. The key feature is that the characters typed into the box are hidden (displayed as dots or asterisks), ensuring confidentiality during input.

It's especially useful when you are building a solution that requires secure inputs, such as:

- Connecting to an external system (via REST API, FTP, etc.)
- Running a custom process that needs authentication
- Allowing admin users to securely store or pass credentials at runtime

When creating a password box, you can enter tool tip text that gives users instructions or explains how to interact with the component.

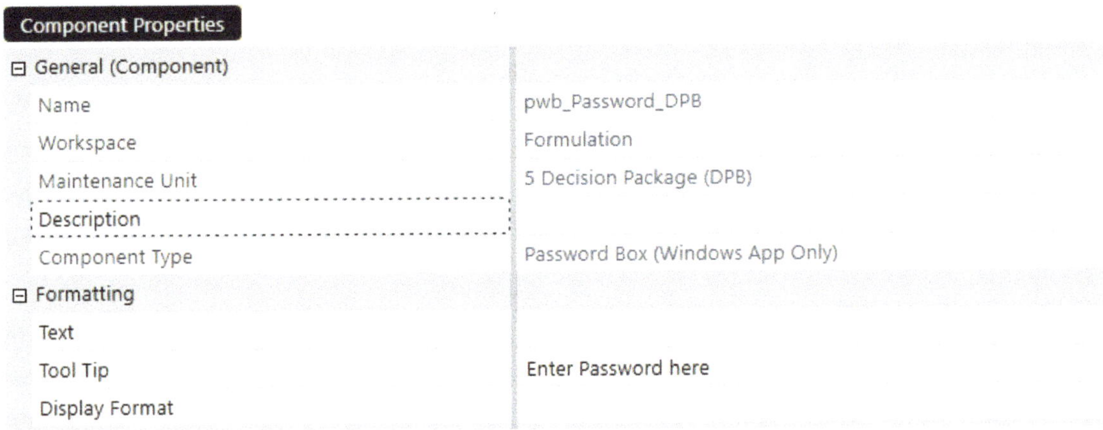

Figure 4.73

Component Display

When users hover over the password field, the tool tip appears with guidance. This component provides an added layer of security to your most secure data. Whether you want to password-protect data that the user sees, or require a password when the user changes data on a dashboard, this component really adds value to data securitization.

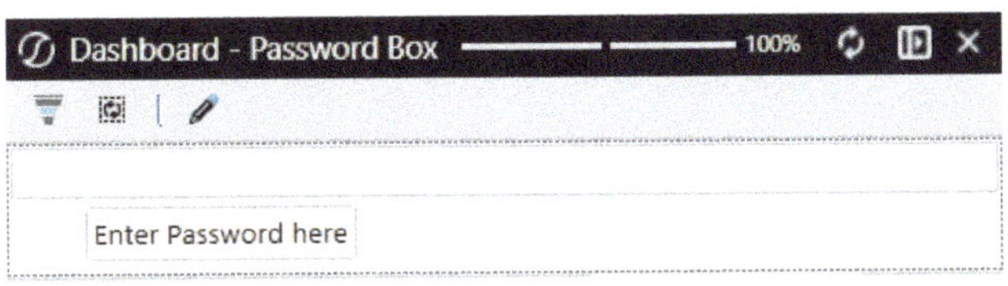

Figure 4.74

Radio Button Group

An alternative option to a combo box, this component lets you display the parameter options in a vertical or horizontal stack display so that users can toggle selections and see dashboards refreshed.

In the example below, not only are we refreshing a dashboard, but we are also leveraging the component's inherent ability to trigger action-based business rules to display alternative content in additional dashboard components.

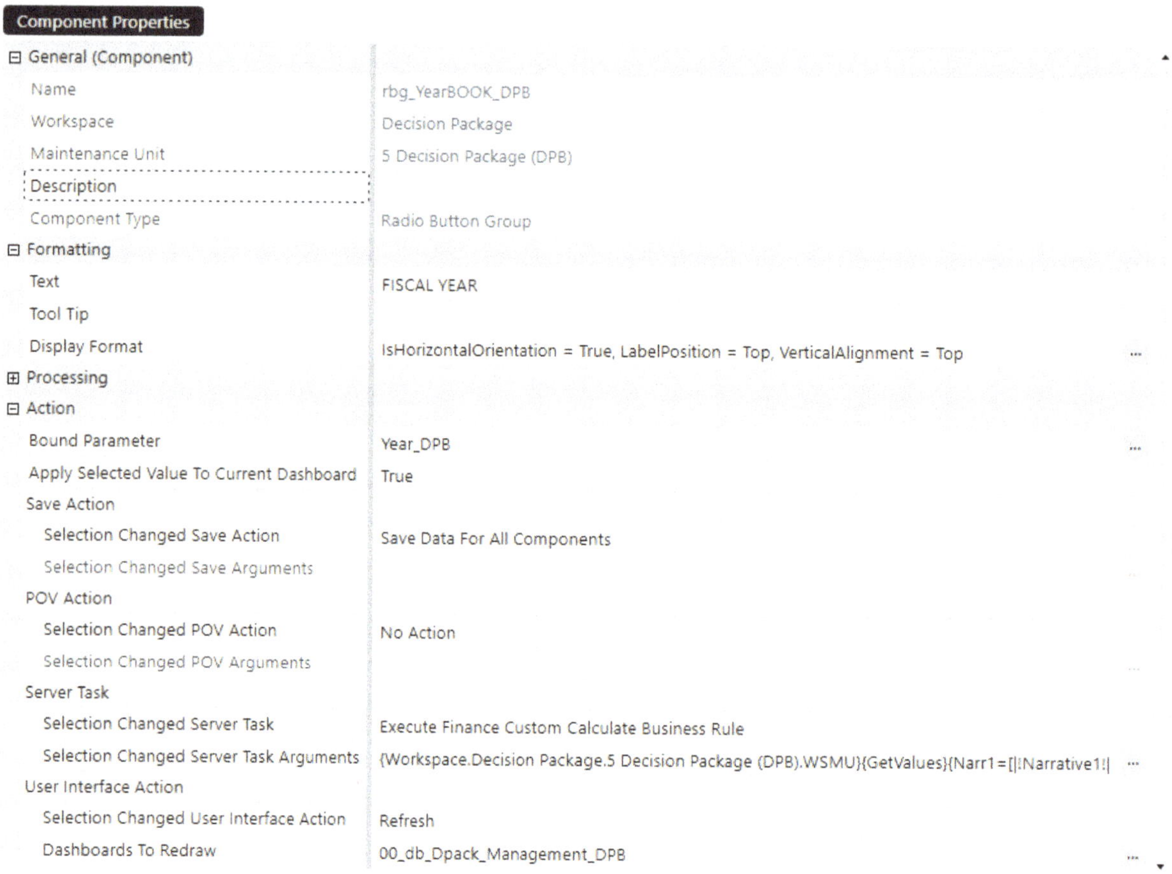

Figure 4.75

Component Display

The radio button group display is shown below, with available options based on the bound parameter assigned to the component. The default display settings of this component display the parameter options vertically, but we have set the IsHorizontalOrientation property on the component to True, allowing us to preserve dashboard real estate by horizontally stacking the options.

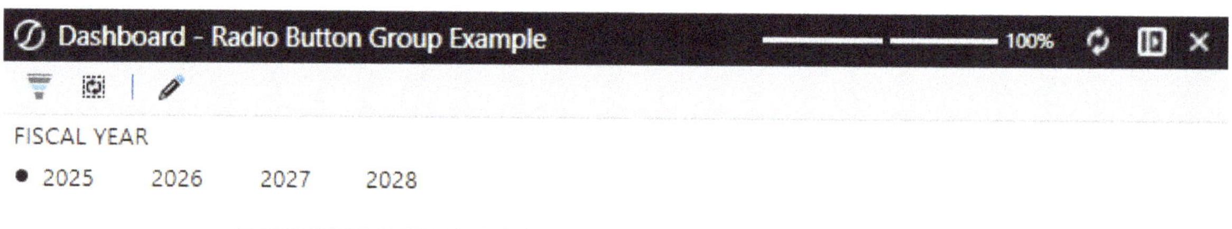

Figure 4.76

Supplied Parameter

A hidden or background parameter supplied automatically; typically used for context like user, entity, or time.

This component preserves the parameter selections from one dashboard and passes them to a dashboard that is opened in a dialog box.

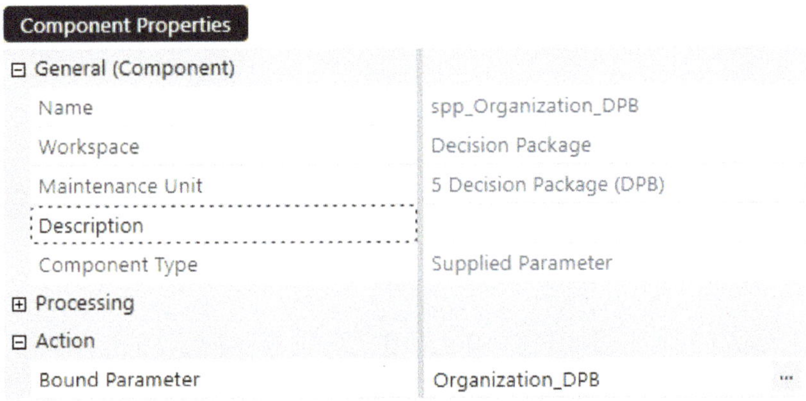

Figure 4.77

Component Display

Supplied parameters are hidden from view and prevent OneStream from prompting the user to enter a value in the standard dialog box that appears when processing a dashboard or Cube View with undefined parameters. This is particularly useful when launching a dashboard as a dialog and passing parameters to it, or when certain parameters are defined through "on load" business rules.

In the example below, you'll see a dashboard that a button on our main dashboard displays when clicked.

The dashboard being opened in a dialog box (named `1_NarrativeBook_DPB`) is a Book Viewer component that has been parameterized to display report data based on user selections. Without attaching these supplied parameters to the `1_NarrativeBook_DPB` dashboard, the user would be prompted to make selections when the button is clicked. But with the supplied parameters attached, the dashboard is rendered with the selections made on the source dashboard where the button is surfaced.

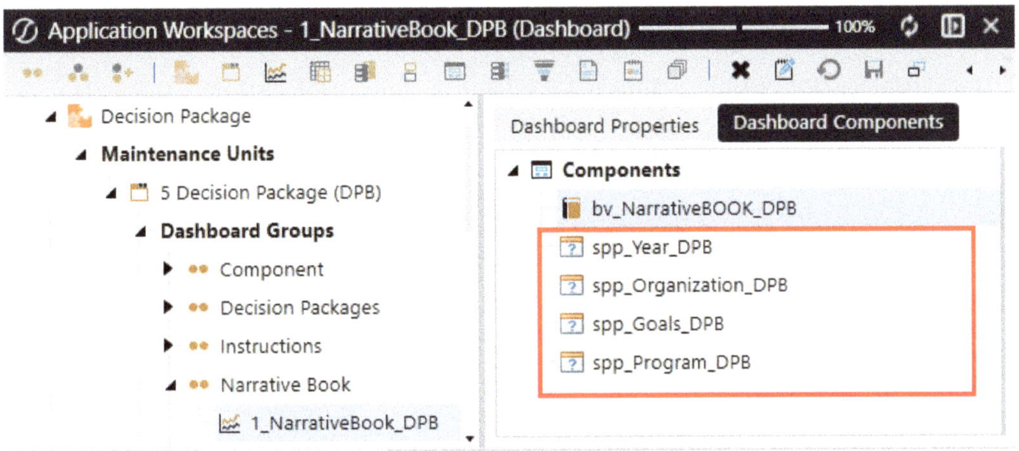

Figure 4.78

Text Box

User input for short text; can be bound to parameters or saved values.

Text boxes are useful for collecting commentary or other annotation data to add context to your data. In the example component configuration below, we set the Allow Rich Text property to True, allowing users to format the text within the text box as they add and enter text. This is a recently available and popular component.

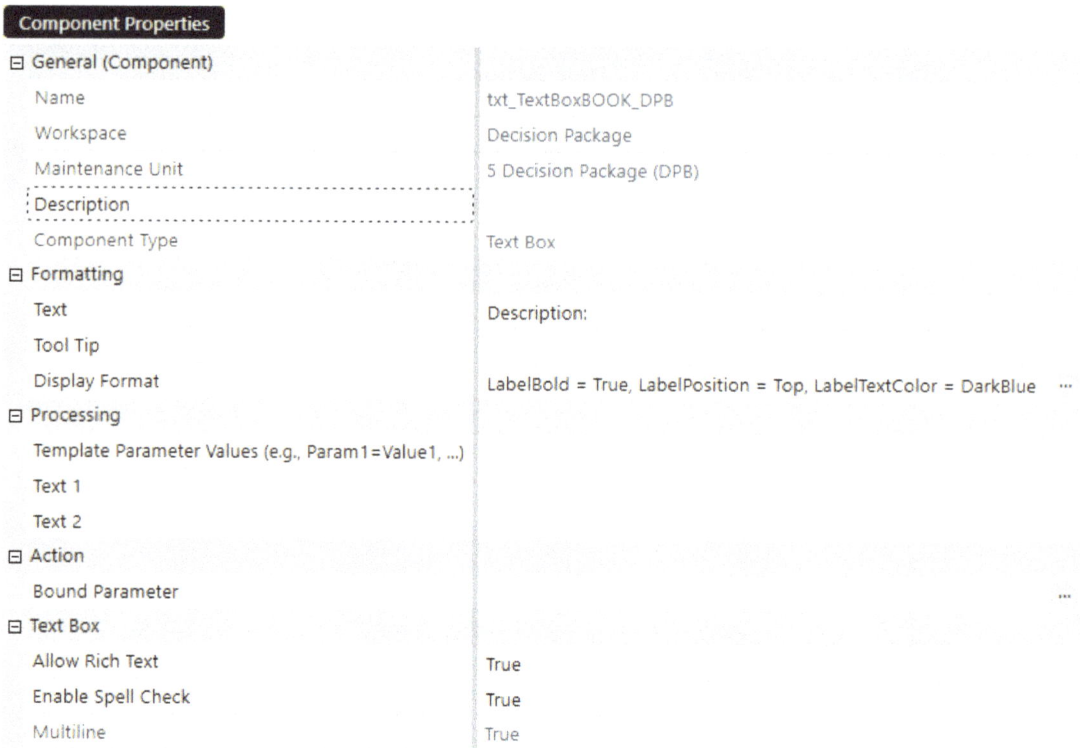

Figure 4.79

Component Display

When the component is displayed, users have the ability to format the text and background, as well as leverage spell checking. This not only displays the formatting as defined by the user on a given dashboard, but this format can also be leveraged to display as defined in XFDocs.

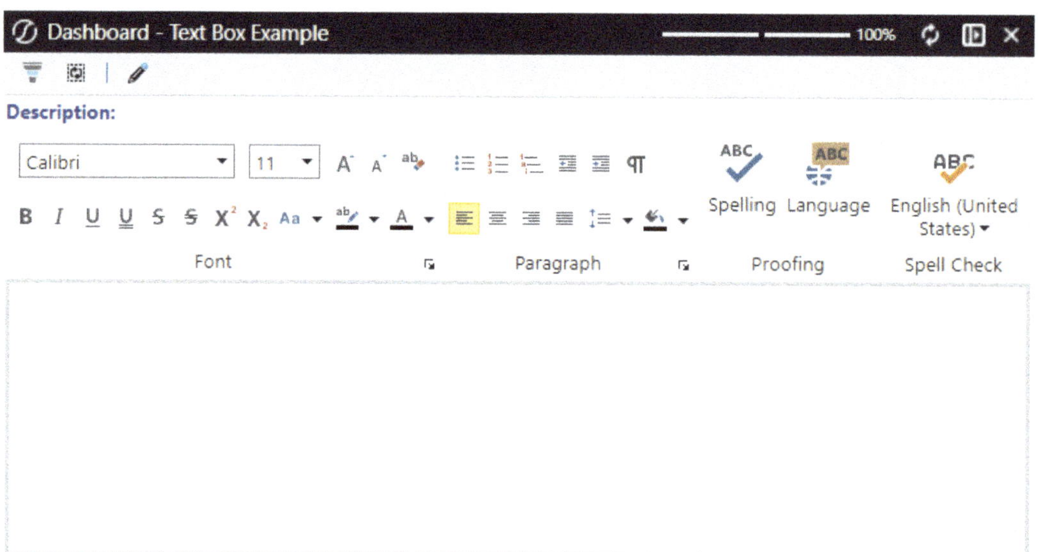

Figure 4.80

Text Editor

A rich text input file that supports Microsoft Word editing and processing.

This component is heavily used in OneStream's **Narrative Reporting** solution, which can be downloaded from the Solution Exchange. The Text Editor can be used as a plain Word document, or it can be used to surface an XFDoc, where users can embed parameters and contents like charts, data grids, etc.

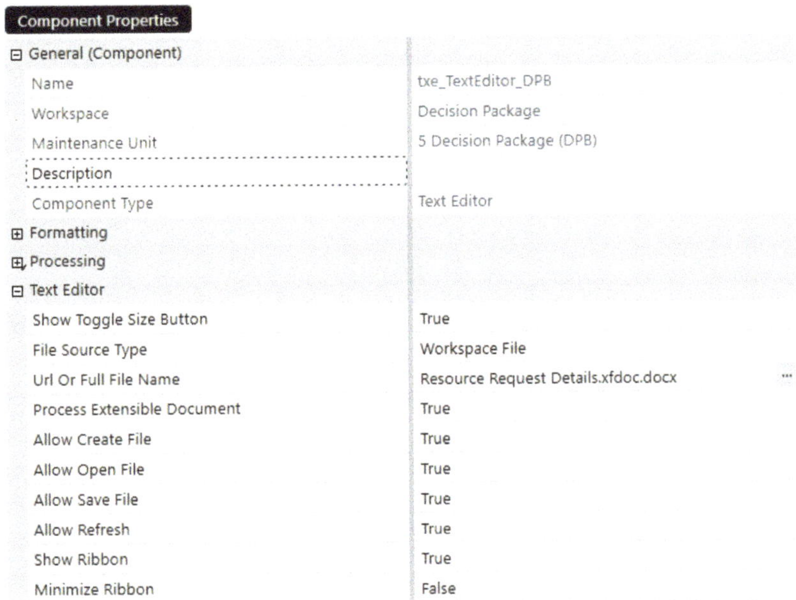

Figure 4.81

Component Display

The Text Editor can be used to create XFDocs or add text to existing XFDocs linked to data sources to support Book creation and the dynamic, rapid deployment of reporting.

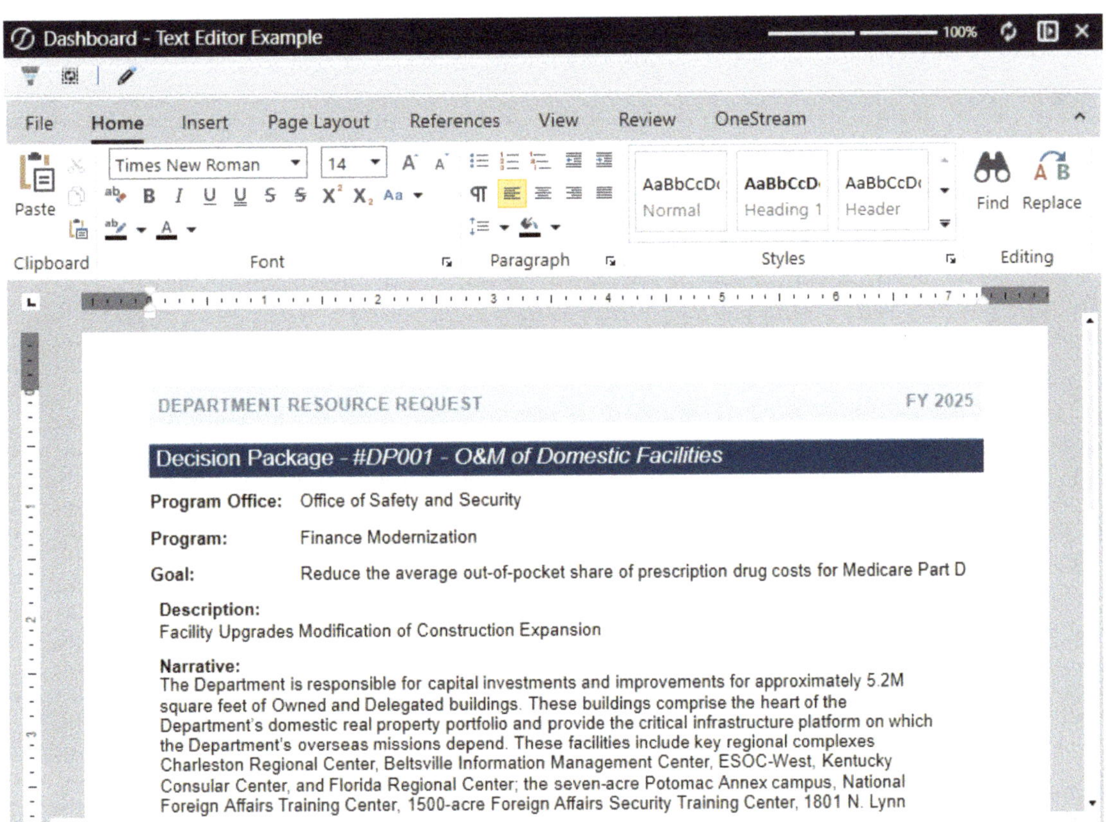

Figure 4.82

Tree View

Tree views support a hierarchical display of items (like a dimension or folder structure) so you can see relationships between data points or records. The data adapter below uses a Workspace Assembly rule where records from the `XFW_TCM_Register` table are surfaced in a tree view structure.

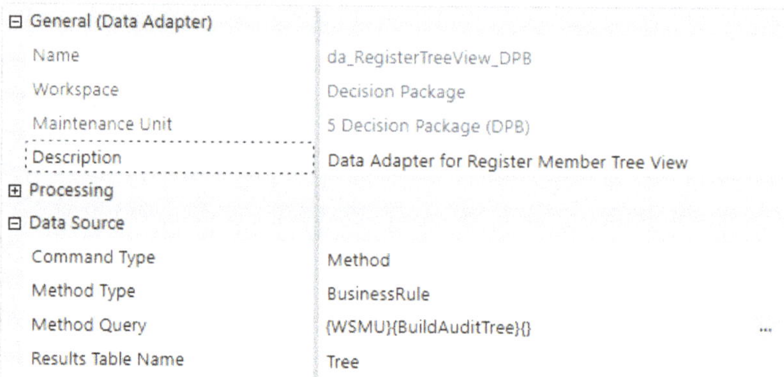

Figure 4.83

In this example, the register contains audit engagement records which need to be resolved and ultimately progressed to Complete status as Corrective Actions are closed out by users.

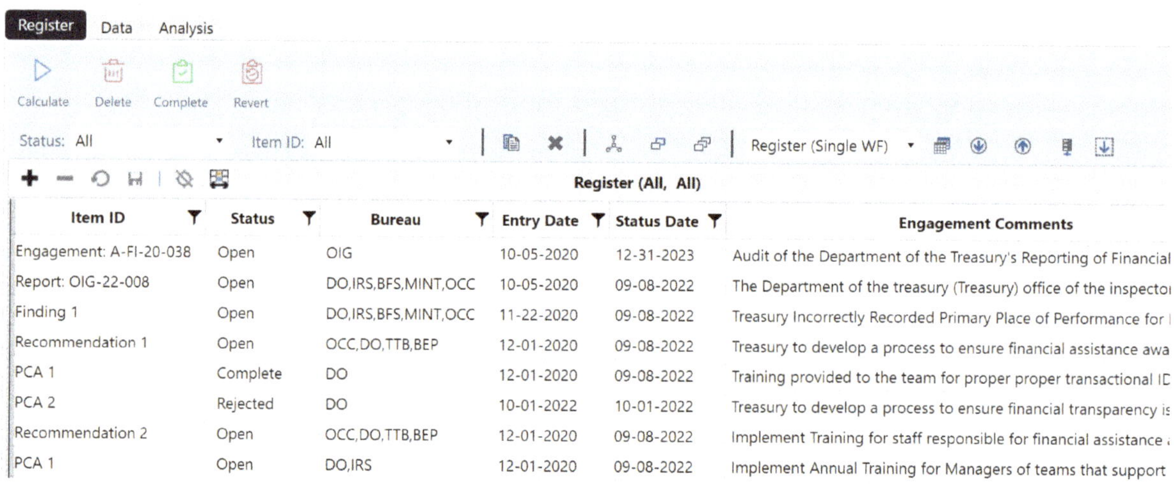

Figure 4.84

The solution has been configured to create and maintain metadata members that facilitate the hierarchical structure. The figure below shows the correlation from register to dimension members, as noted in the member description property.

Note that member creation is not necessary when using register-based solutions; this is purely to demonstrate the visual structure using a data set business rule to control the tree structure.

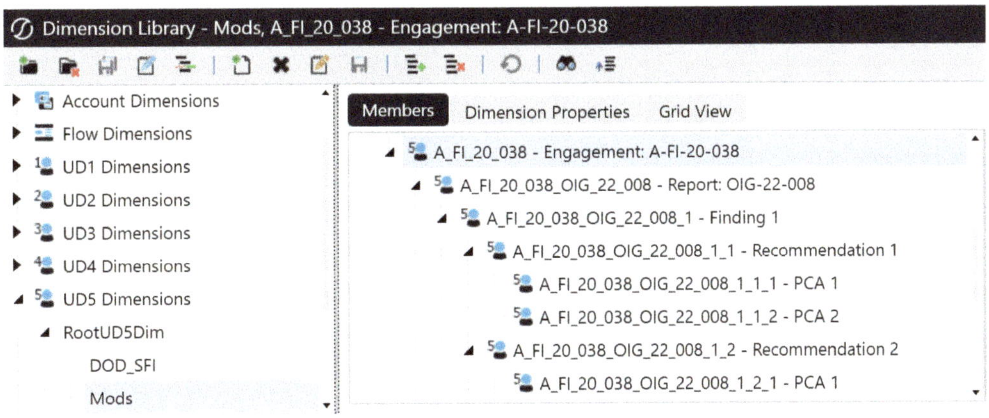

Figure 4.85

The data adapter is attached to the tree view component, which is then displayed on a dashboard.

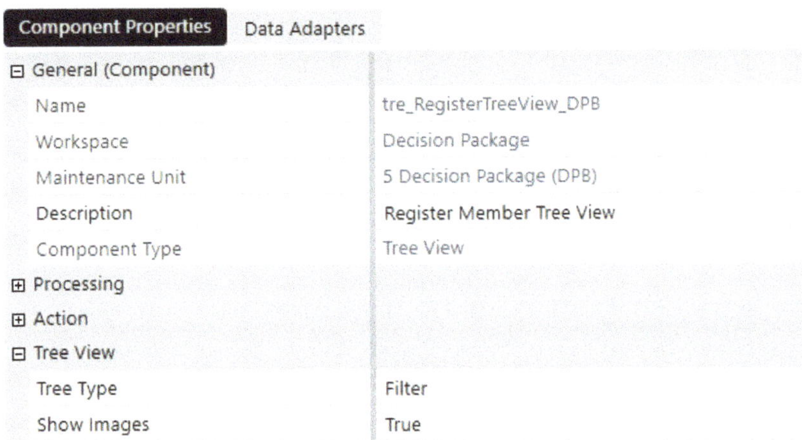

Figure 4.86

Component Display

In the figure below, we have a tree view of items – collected from a table that has relationships defined – to create the tree structure displayed at runtime. PCAs or **Corrective Actions** are detailed items that must be addressed following an audit engagement. These corrective actions are specific to overarching **Recommendations**, which roll up to **Findings** reported during audit engagement.

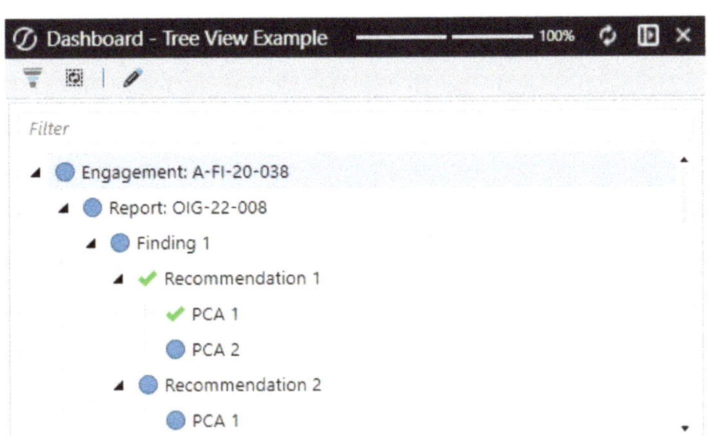

Figure 4.87

Member Tree

Specifically for dimension member selection in a hierarchy (e.g., accounts, entities).

To use this component, the parameter type must be a **Member Dialog** that includes the `.tree` extension to display a tree visual in the output.

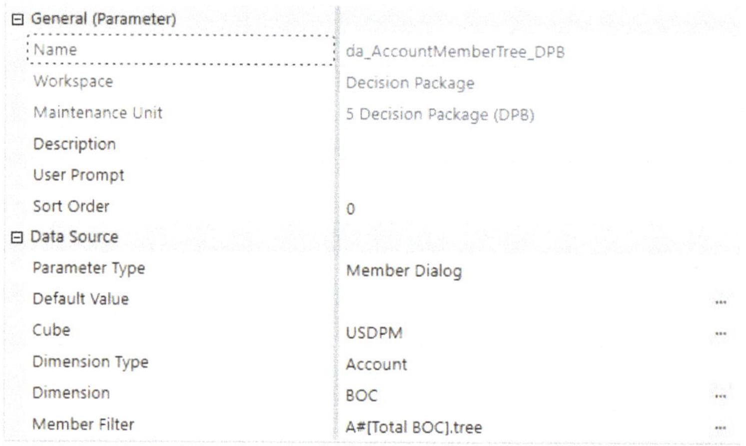

Figure 4.88

The component itself is pretty straightforward. Once you've created the parameter and inserted the parameter name into the Bound Parameter property, the component can be attached to a dashboard.

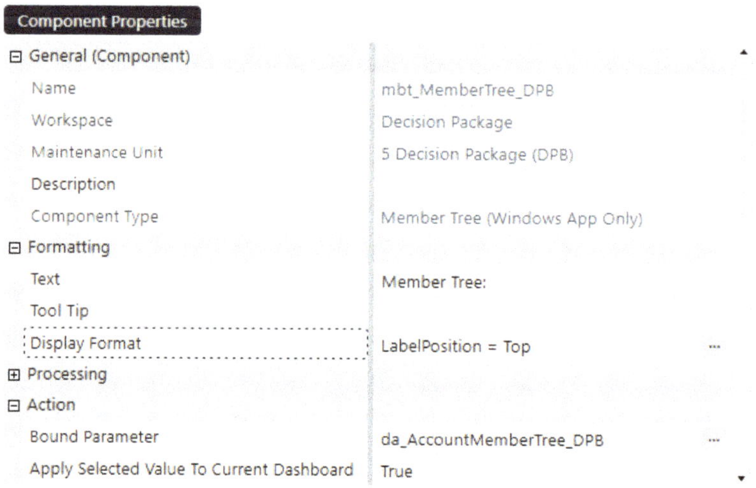

Figure 4.89

Component Display

When the component is displayed, you are able to see a visual tree of the defined parameter. This component type would be best suited for a dashboard where you want users to easily click on a member within the tree and expose or refresh member properties on a right-pane dashboard.

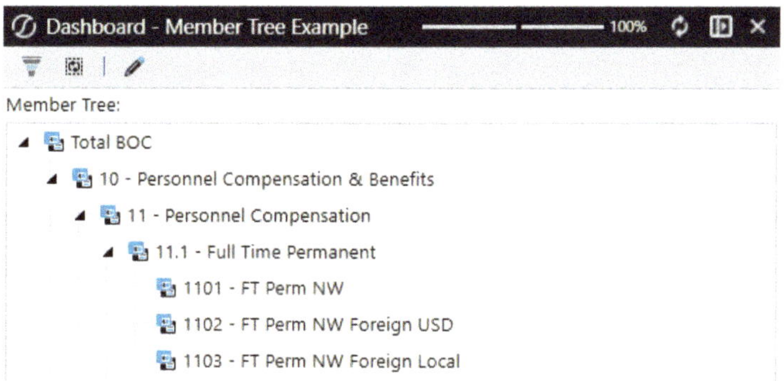

Figure 4.90

SQL Table Editor

An editable table connected to SQL data; can add/update/delete rows based on user interaction.

This is one of my favorite components due to its powerful querying built right into the component. There's no need for data adapters or fancy business rules, but you do need some knowledge of what application or system tables you want to query and expose to users. With this component, you can define the fields displayed and select the applicable `DataFormatString` to format the data in the appropriate format.

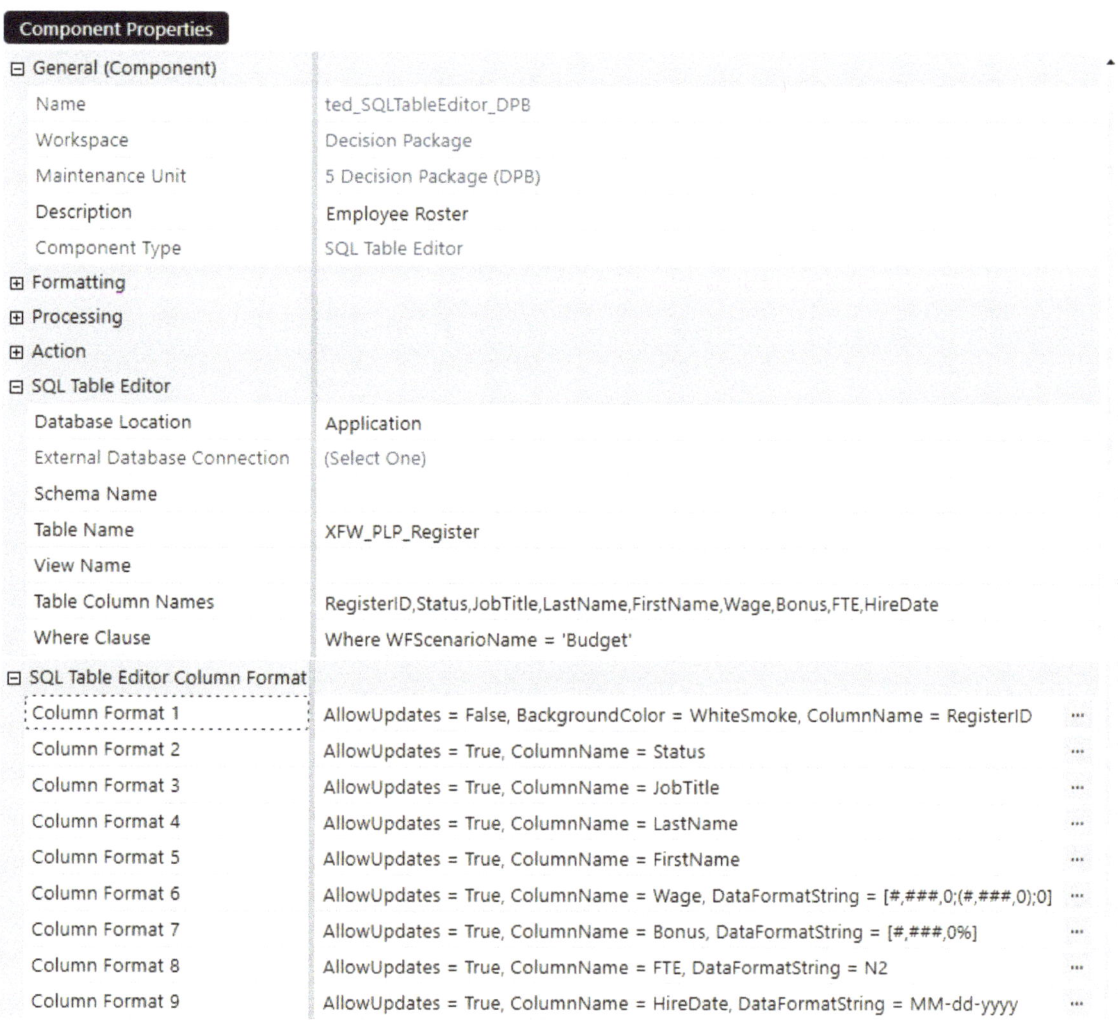

Figure 4.91

Component Display

The resulting component is a clean, grid-looking view of table data, all configured, filtered, and formatted from the SQL Table Editor table component.

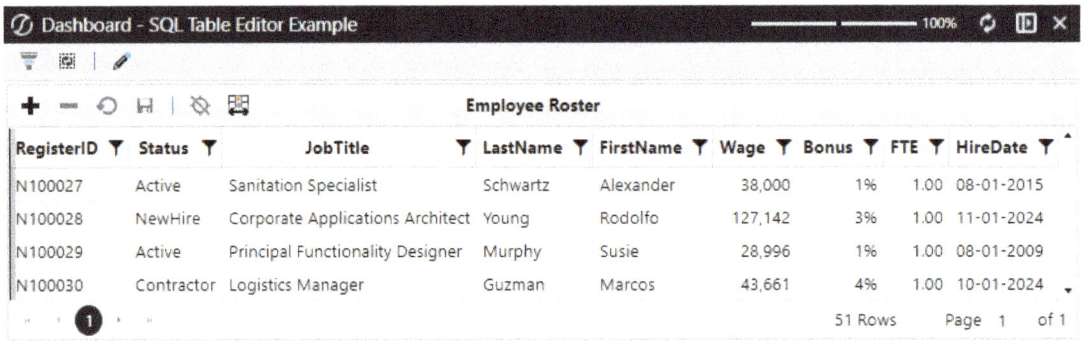

Figure 4.92

Static Content / Display Components

File Viewer

Displays uploaded files (PDFs, images, docs) inside the dashboard.

Files can be loaded into any one of OneStream's file collection locations and displayed on dashboards.

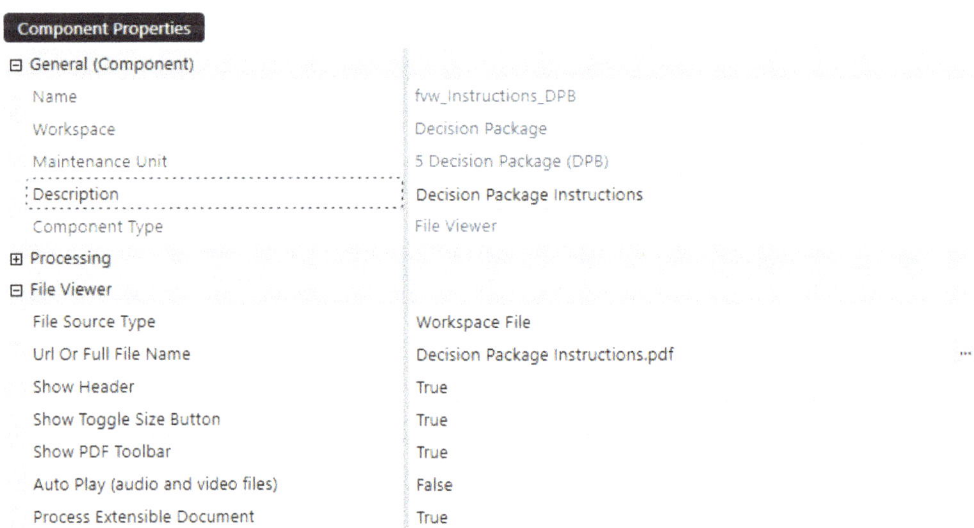

Figure 4.93

Component Display

In the example below, we have a PDF file with instructions that we want to make available to end-users as they progress through their workflows. The component displays an instruction guide – that can be exposed from a button – so users can click to get help on any given task.

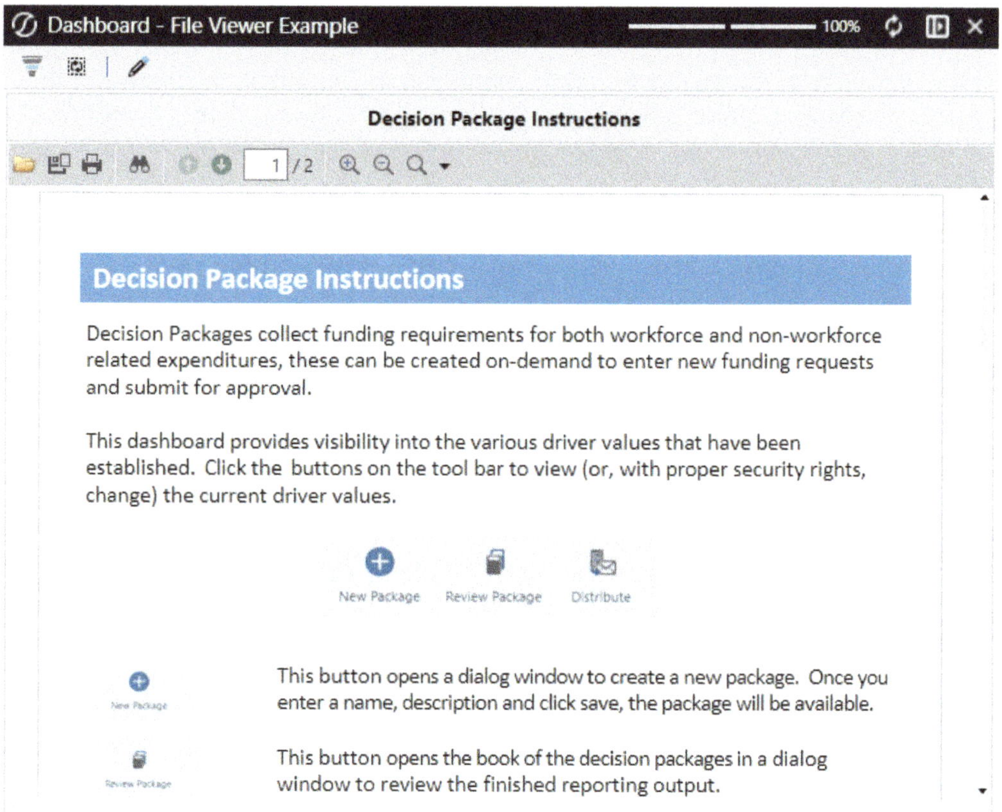

Figure 4.94

Image

Embeds an image: logos, charts, diagrams, etc.

Images can be displayed on any dashboard to personalize the user experience. These are commonly used on the landing page when users login to the application. Developers can dynamically select images for the background, based on user roles, names, or (as a bonus) they can allow users to personalize their own user experience by selecting an image that they want to see when navigating to the landing page or initially logging into OneStream.

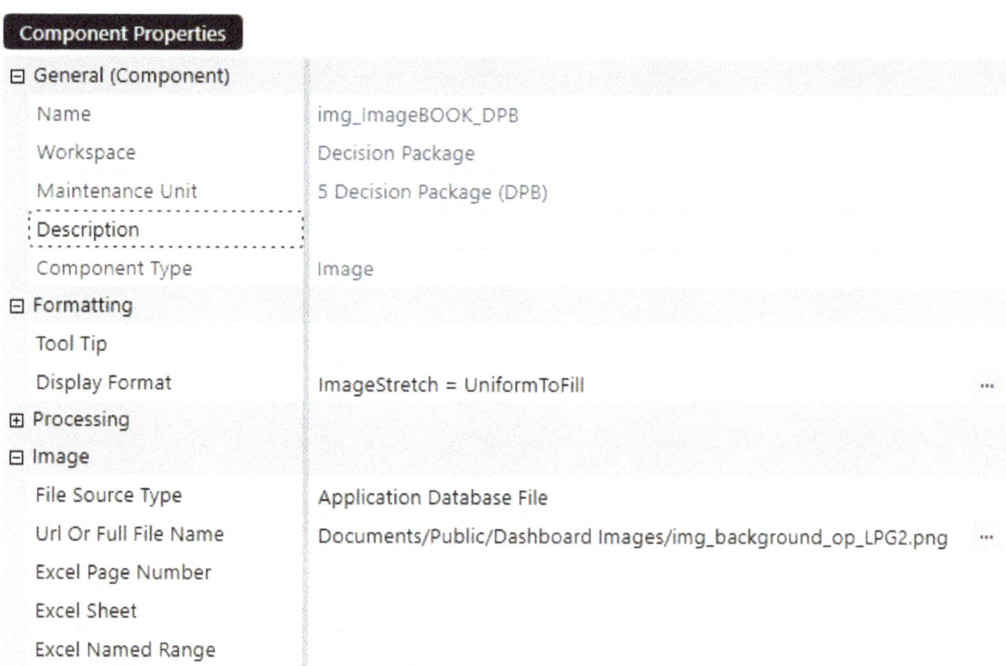

Figure 4.95

Component Display

For those of you who have seen a OneStream demonstration, you might recognize this image. It is displayed when the demonstration begins, and it is the standard image defined in the GolfStream demo application, nested just between the menu buttons at the top and the KPIs displayed at the bottom of the landing page dashboard.

Figure 4.96

Label

Static or dynamic text used to label or describe other dashboard elements.

OneStream's demonstration applications use labels on nearly all dashboard headers to describe the dashboard or its functionality to help users understand what they are looking at.

Figure 4.97

Component Display

The example below shows the explicit label text as entered into the component's properties. Check out the Strings section, later in this chapter, to see how you can make this display flexible and dynamic to show culture-specific settings.

Figure 4.98

Logo

Typically, a predefined image placeholder for company logos or branding.

The logo component does not require any inputs or data adapters. Instead, it pulls the logo loaded into the Application Properties field from the Application tab.

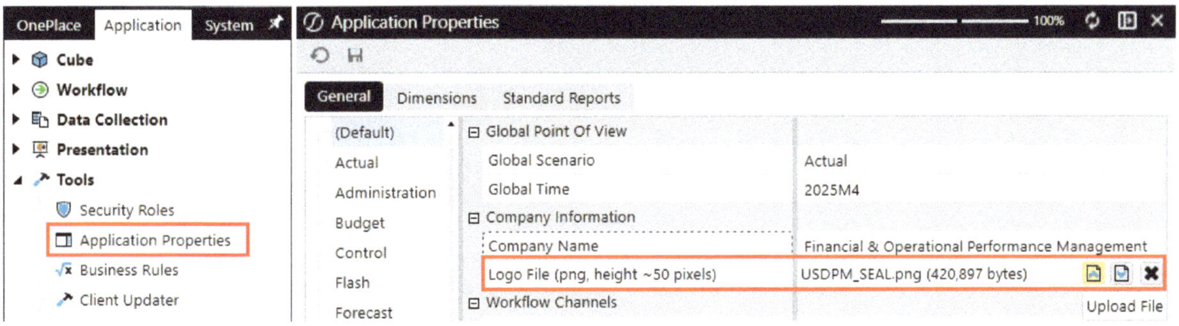

Figure 4.99

To surface the logo on a dashboard, simply create a logo component and modify the Display Format properties as needed.

Figure 4.100

Component Display

Any logo components that are created throughout Workspaces will display the logo image as defined in the Application Properties.

Figure 4.101

State Indicator

Displays status with visual cues (colors, icons); commonly used for health checks or KPIs.

The component below uses a Cube View data adapter to query the calculation status by entity.

Component Properties | Data Adapters

⊟ General (Component)	
Name	sti_StateIndicator_DPB
Workspace	Decision Package
Maintenance Unit	5 Decision Package (DPB)
Description	
Component Type	State Indicator (Windows App Only)
⊟ Formatting	
Text (use {1}, {2} for Data Table Cells)	|!!Organization_DPB!!| [{1}]
Tool Tip	OK = No Data has Changed, CA = Calculation Needed, CN = Consolidation Needed
Display Format	Height = 100, HorizontalAlignment = Left, LabelPosition = Top ...
⊞ Processing	
⊟ Data Table Cells From Adapter	
Number Of Data Table Cells	1
Cell 1	
Data Row Selection Type	Key Column Name And Value
Key Column Name	RowHdr0Name
Key Column Value Or Row Index	|!Organization_DPB!|
Result Column Name	Col0ValueAsText
Number Format	
⊟ States	
State Indicator Type	Traffic Lights
Default State Index	0
State 0	
State Selection Type (Image = Off)	(Not Used)
Minimum Amount	
Maximum Amount	
Text Items	
State 1	
State Selection Type (Image = Green)	Contains Text Item
Minimum Amount	
Maximum Amount	
Text Items	OK
State 2	
State Selection Type (Image = Yellow)	Contains Text Item
Minimum Amount	
Maximum Amount	
Text Items	CA
State 3	
State Selection Type (Image = Red)	Contains Text Item
Minimum Amount	
Maximum Amount	
Text Items	CN

Figure 4.102

Component Display

When displaying the component, a visual indicator explains the calculation status of an intersection.

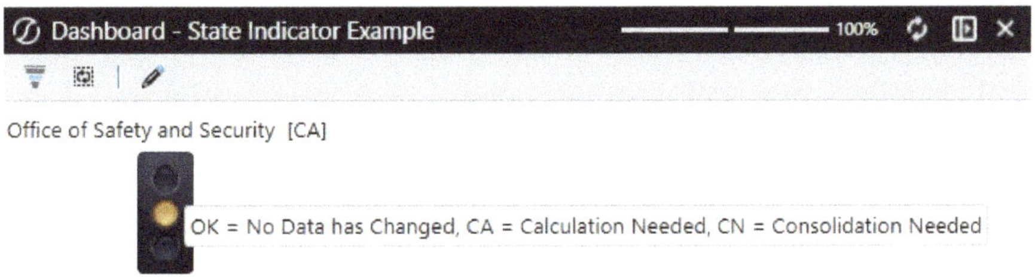

Figure 4.103

Text Viewer

Displays static or dynamic text; often bound to variables or results from business rules.

Files to display using this component need to be saved in any of the file source types: 1. Workspace file; 2. Application Database file; 3. System Database file; 4. File Share file.

Figure 4.104

Component Display

The component displayed on a dashboard shows the file indicated in the component properties, which may be parameter-driven and require user selection to display data dynamically. The example below has been run from a dashboard type **Top Level Without Parameter Prompts**. This omits the user selection prompts and applies the parameter defaults to populate the variables at runtime.

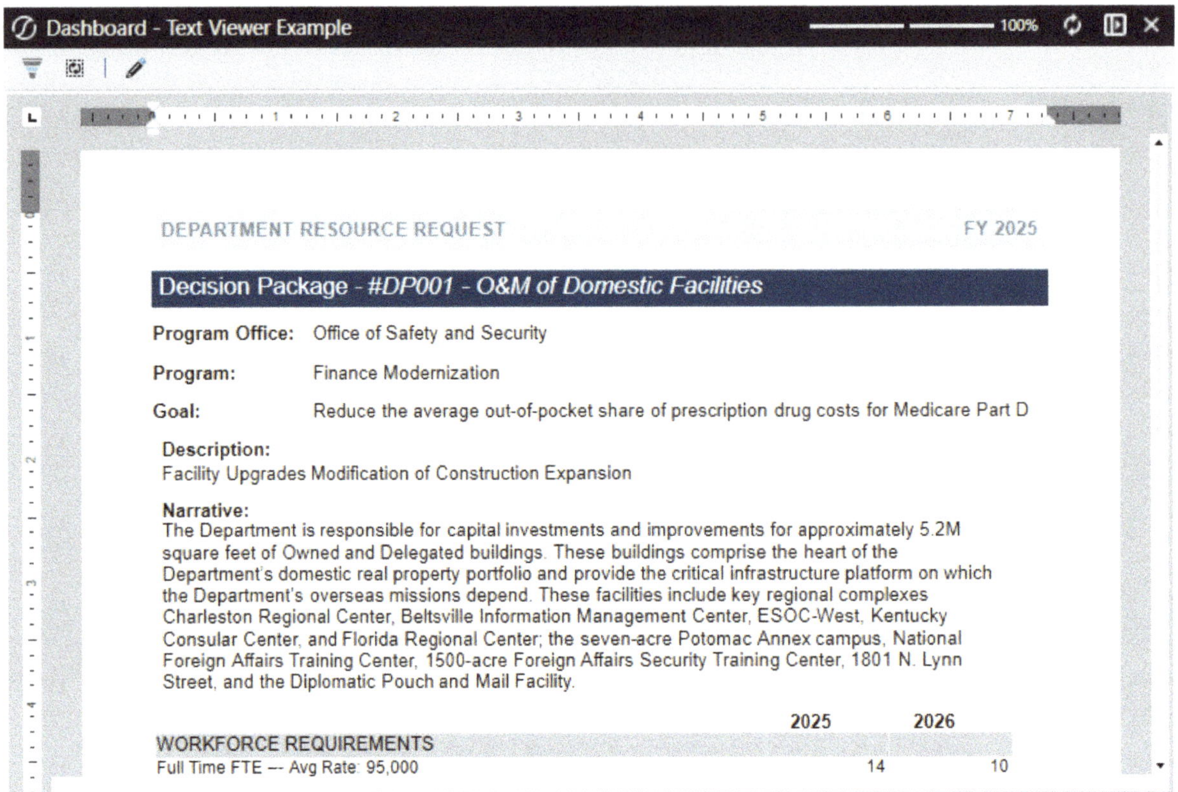

Figure 4.105

Web Content

Embeds external websites on dashboards; used for custom visualizations or integrations.

This component is especially useful when users need to access website pages. It allows you to surface URLs within the OneStream application interface by placing the component on a dialog that can be exposed from a button click.

This component is intended to launch a URL within the OneStream application interface, without needing to open multiple windows. When viewing the component from the browser, the Open Content in New Tab (Web Only) property should be set to True – this allows the user to open the URL in a new tab. Some example use cases include the following:

- Open the Federal Reserve FX Rates website
- View Futures prices on indices websites
- Navigate to your company's website

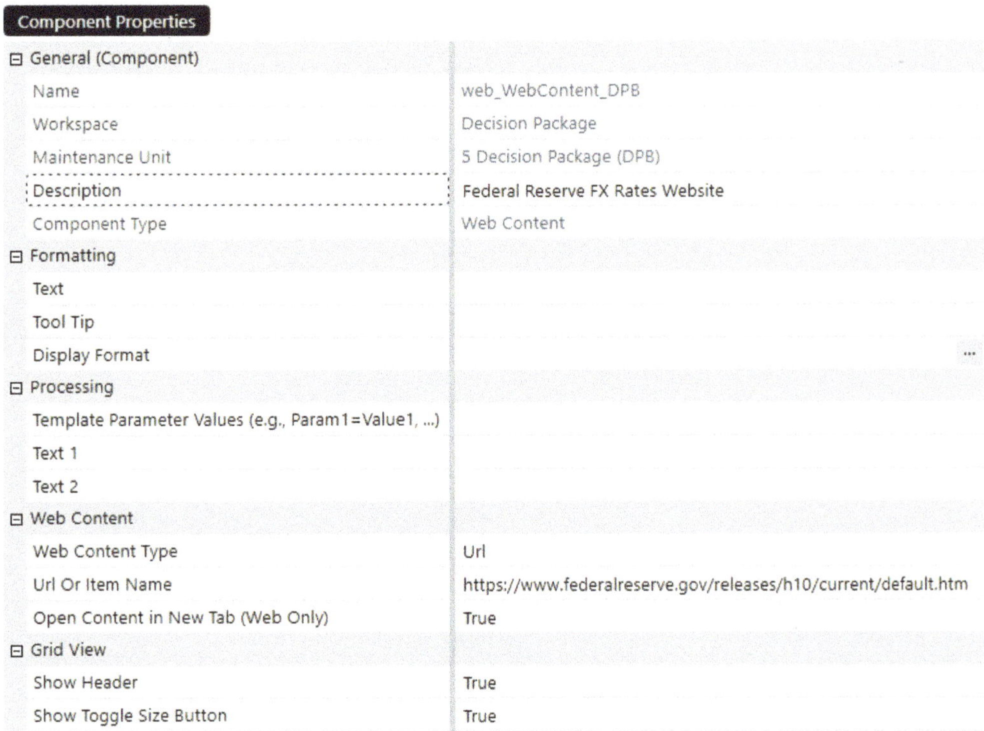

Figure 4.106

Component Display

This component can be attached to a dashboard and directly displayed within the OneStream user interface, or you can use a button to open the webpage in a separate dialog box window.

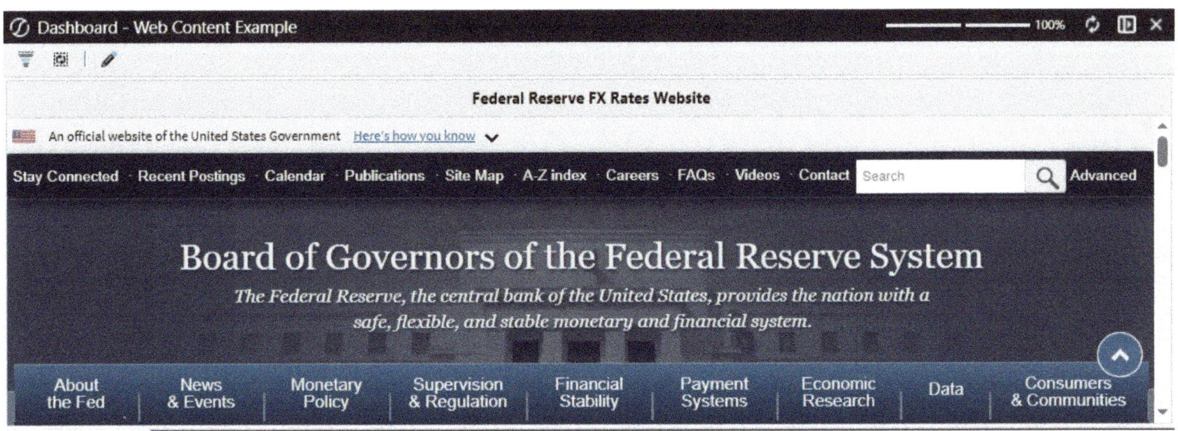

Figure 4.107

Files

Files that are used for specific processes can be stored in default maintenance units as well as new Workspace maintenance units to keep dashboard objects together. To create a new file, click on Files, then click Create File, then name the file and click Upload File to import your file.

These files can be referenced or displayed on dashboards using components such as File Viewer, Text Editor, Spreadsheet, etc., promoting another level of organization of Workspace objects.

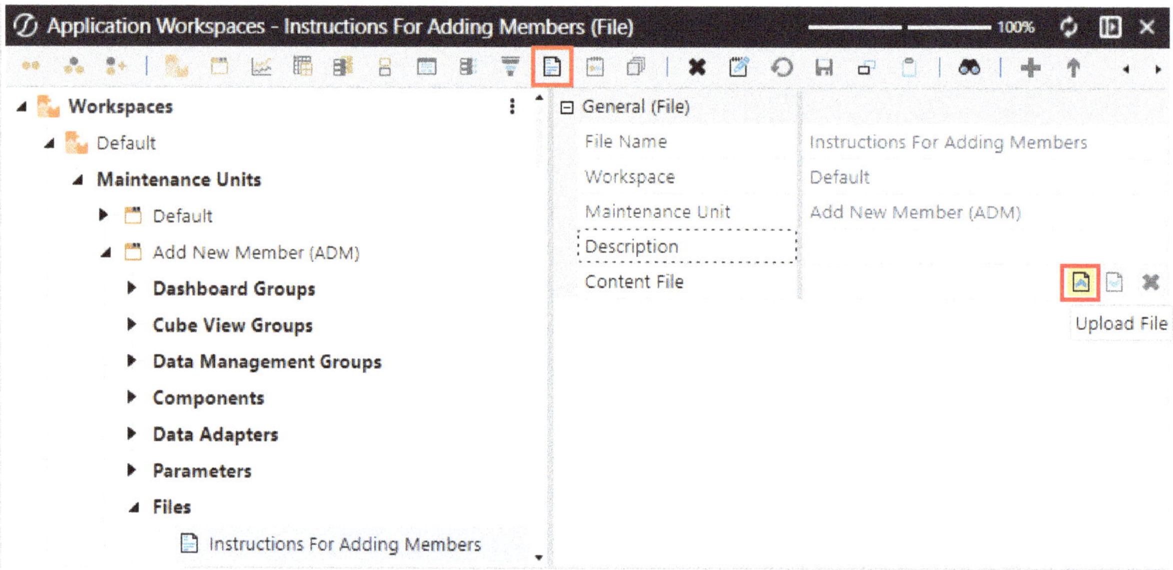

Figure 4.108

Strings

Strings are objects that allow you to display different text, based on a user's culture settings.

In the example below, we've translated the title Decision Packages for our French and Spanish-speaking users, which will be displayed on a dashboard title. Languages on the string's property correspond to the culture codes enabled on our server settings, and the culture code is then assigned to user profiles to ensure users have a localized experience.

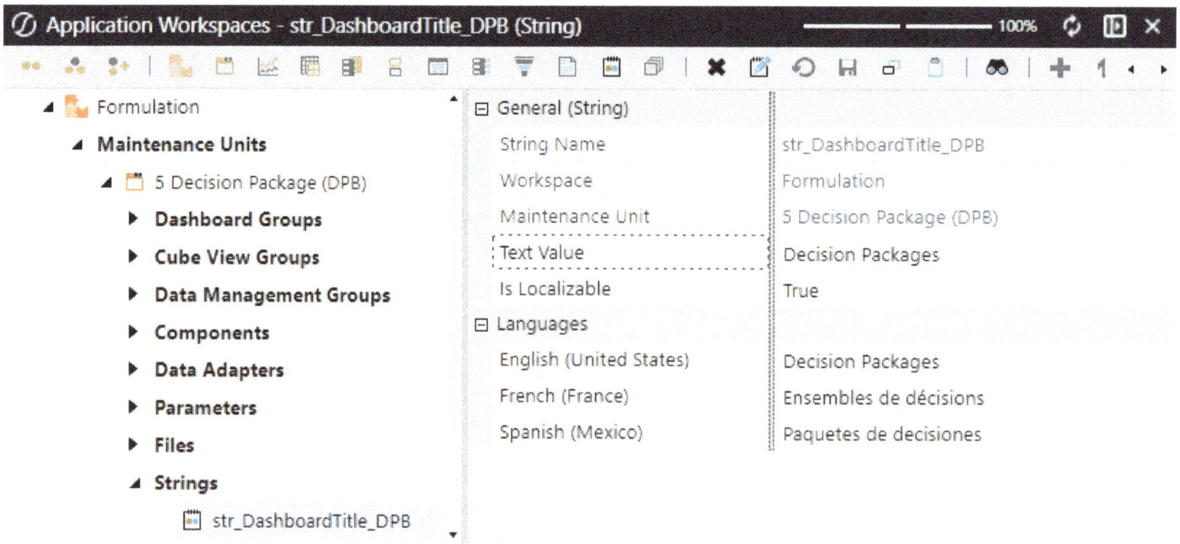

Figure 4.109

The syntax for using strings is `xfstring(YourStringName)`, and below is an example of how to use the string to display the name in the appropriate language by the user.

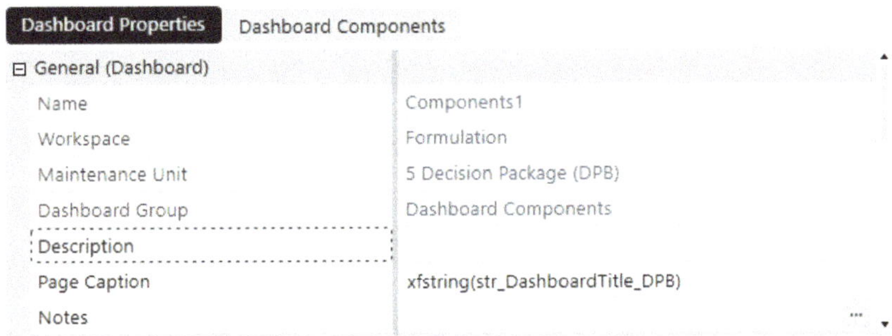

Figure 4.110

When we login with an English culture user, they will see the English alias on the dashboard's page caption.

Figure 4.111

When we login with a user who has a Spanish culture code, they will see the Spanish alias on the dashboard's page caption.

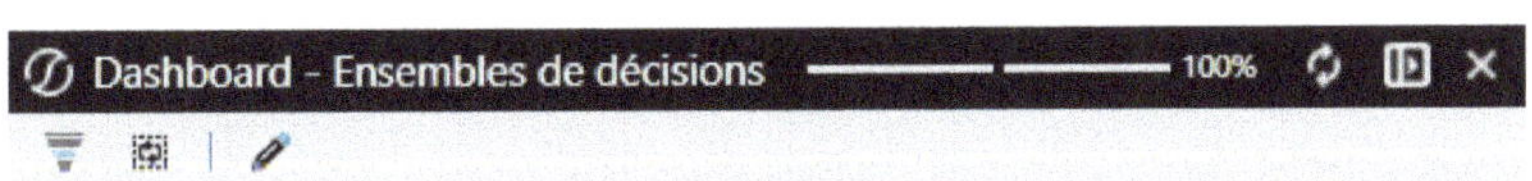

Figure 4.112

Assemblies

Assemblies provide the ability to build and organize syntax within a Workspace. This means that developers are able to code solutions without leaving the Workspace page. Below is an example of a Workspace maintenance unit calling a Service Factory from the maintenance unit's Assemblies.

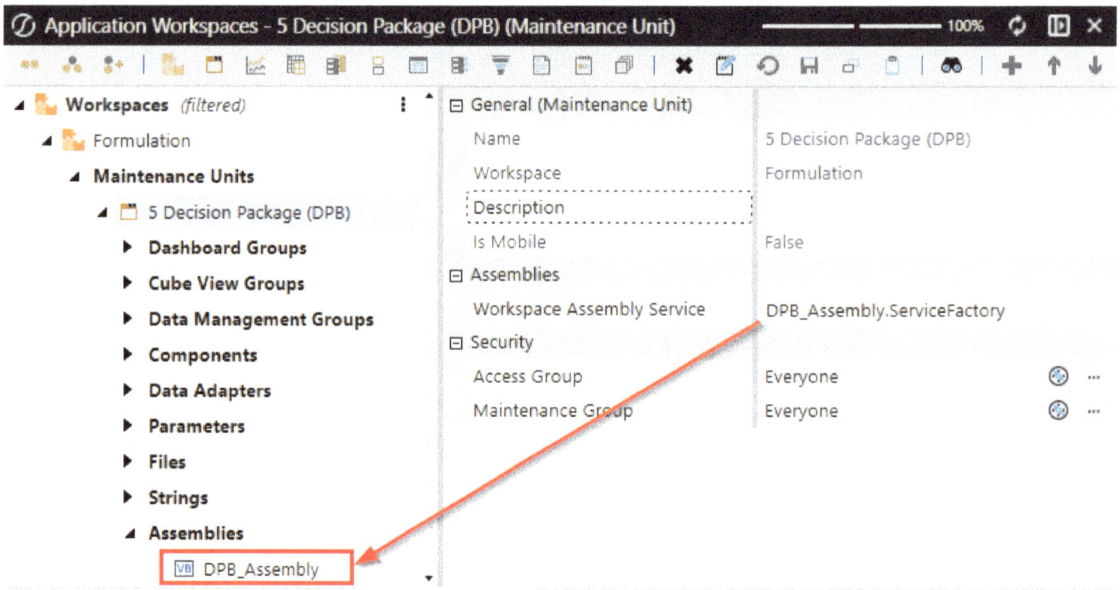

Figure 4.113

The Assemblies are where you can build out logic and call the appropriate service from the Service Factory. Chapters 5-7 explain in detail how to use these Assemblies.

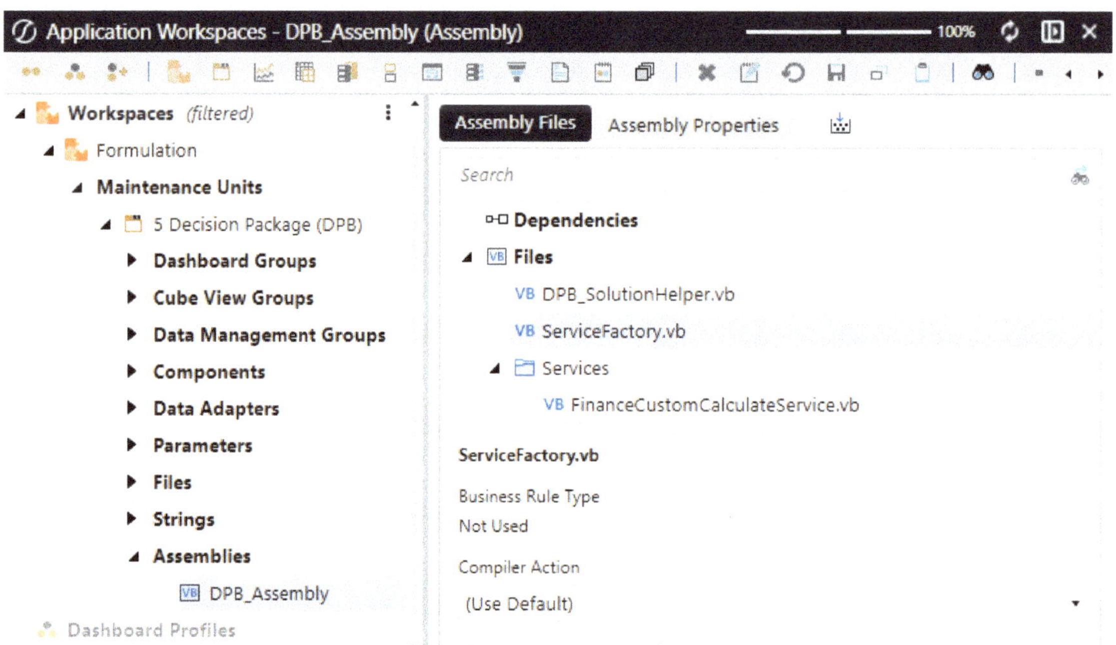

Figure 4.114

Conclusion

Phew! A long chapter where we have outlined the diverse components that form the backbone of Workspaces in OneStream. From maintenance units to data management groups, each component plays a crucial role in structuring and automating tasks, facilitating data analysis, and enhancing user interaction through dynamic dashboards and visualizations.

Users can significantly improve their application development and deployment processes by understanding and utilizing these components. The insights provided in this chapter serve as a valuable resource for maximizing the potential of OneStream Workspaces, ensuring that users can create robust, efficient, and user-friendly solutions.

5

Understanding Assemblies

The New Business Rules

My wife used to tell me that 40 was the new 30 (until she turned 50 😊). Similarly, Assemblies are the new business rules. Now, almost all types of business rules are available as Assemblies. If you are unfamiliar with Assemblies, no worries; I will walk you through the concepts and the transition from business rules to Assemblies.

OneStream has a unique and powerful approach to business rules: we have different rule types for various aspects of the application. We have finance BRs, Cube View Extender BRs, dashboard data set BRs, dashboard extender BRs, dashboard XFBR string BRs, extensibility rules BRs, and Spreadsheet BRs.

Business Rules 101

For users new to OneStream, a quick explanation of business rules is in order. The OneStream platform is very powerful and has the flexibility to configure almost every part of your application through code called business rules. Many parts of the application can be configured and customized, things like dashboards, Cube Views, reports, cube data, relational data, connectors, etc. Because of the breadth of everything that can be customized, there are several types of business rules.

Here is a list of the types of business rules that users can configure through the application:

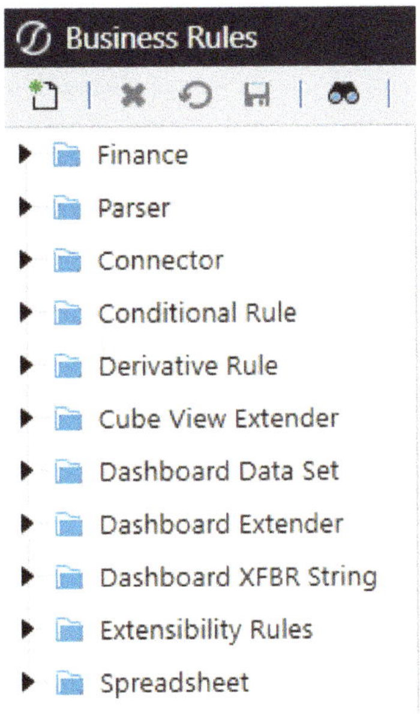

Figure 5.1

Each of these business rules serves a slightly different purpose and, together, they make OneStream incredibly powerful for designing the perfect application for your business. These rules are written in either **VB.Net** or **C#** and adhere to all the conventions of these two languages, in addition to incorporating OneStream platform API calls. If you are familiar with Visual Basic and/or C#, you will just need to understand the OneStream API calls to write the necessary business rules.

The intent of this book is not to deep dive into all these business rule types, but to point out how Assemblies within Workspaces treat these distinct types of rules. For a more detailed exploration of these rule types, please refer to the OneStream Design and Reference Guide.

Assemblies 101

The introduction of Assemblies in Workspaces has brought some new basic terminology that you will need to understand. Here are some new terms.

- **Assembly**: the entire group of files and dependencies.
- **Codebase**: VB.Net or C# will be declared at the Assembly level, and every file within that Assembly will have that selected codebase.
- **Source Code Type**: when creating a new Assembly file, you select the source code type to create the file with the correct libraries (we will cover this later).
- **Dependencies**: external libraries, other Workspace Assemblies, or business rules required by an Assembly to function properly, ensuring it has access to the resources or functionality it depends on.
- **Assembly Business Rule**: a file within an Assembly that has specific source code that defines its purpose.
- **Assembly Service Factory**: a file within an Assembly that is a central place to route references to the correct Assembly service files.
- **Assembly Service**: a file within an Assembly that contains specific source code. This file is executed by the Service Factory.
- **Assembly Standard Class**: a file within an Assembly that does not contain predetermined OneStream code and is open to building generic classes of code.

Here is a screenshot of where these different components (with the exception of the source code type) are situated within the Workspace.

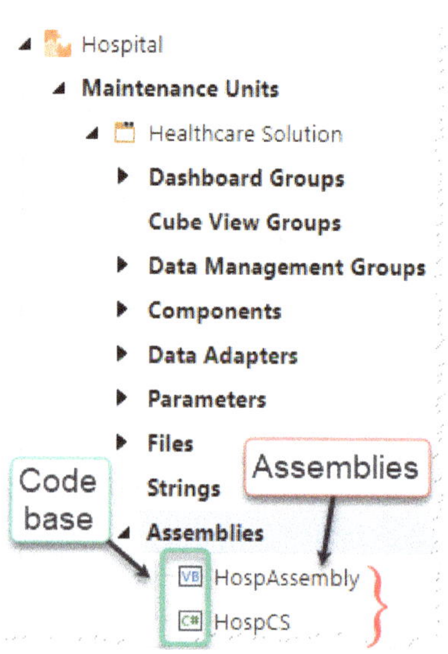

Figure 5.2

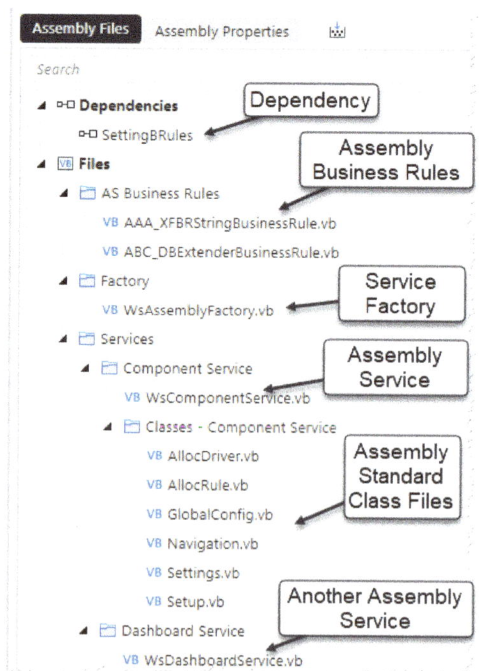

Figure 5.3

Location of Assemblies and Traditional Business Rules

All Assemblies, including Assembly business rules and Assembly Services, are now contained within Workspaces and located within a **Workspace Maintenance Unit** (WSMU), as shown in Figure 5.2.

This organization makes it much easier to keep business rules and logic in the same functional space as dashboards, Cube Views, data management jobs, parameters, etc., facilitating easier troubleshooting and enhancement of these rules as needed.

Before the introduction of Assemblies in Workspaces, all code was stored in a central repository (as shown in Figure 5.4). This often made it difficult to locate and analyze various pieces of code if there was a lack of disciplined naming conventions. As we discussed in the prior section, traditional business rules are grouped by type and – as they are contained in this central repository – it can be challenging to find all the components used for a specific functional area when multiple business rule types are involved.

With Assembly files now organized within Workspaces, a developer working on a specific functional area of the application can access all the necessary code in one place because all business rule types are contained within the same Assembly (as shown in Figure 5.5). This organization also ensures that work in one functional area does not impact developers working on other areas.

The bottom line is that the code required to configure areas of the application – such as forecasts or annual operating plans – can be stored right alongside all related components. This makes it easier to find and locate code that is specific to these functional areas of the application and allows for easy portability of the functional solutions, especially when moving from development to production servers.

Here is an example to illustrate the distinction between the traditional business rule repository and Assemblies, emphasizing how business rules are organized and how the Assembly concept ensures that different rule types are contained within the same functional area.

Central Repository
Organized by Rule Type

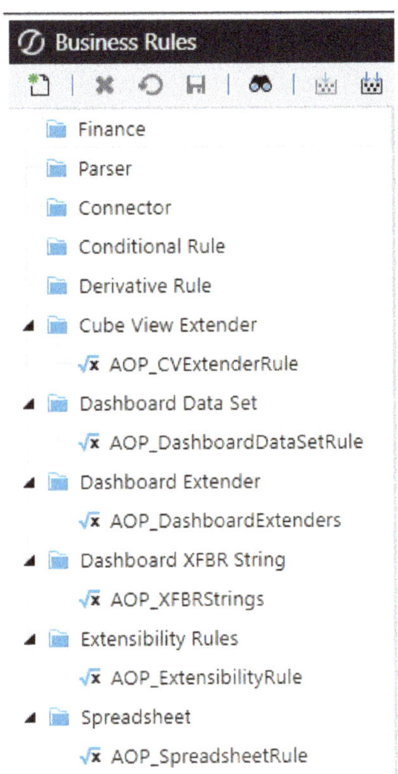

Figure 5.4

Assemblies Within Workspace
Organized by Functional Area
(All Rule Types together)

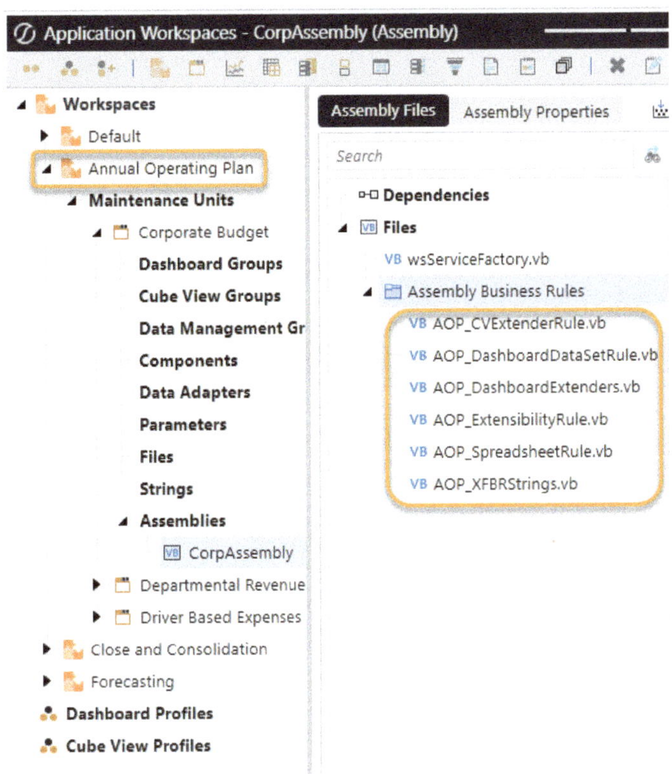

Figure 5.5

Location of Traditional Business Rules in Central Repository

This is probably obvious to anyone who has used OneStream before, but for comparison's sake, and to be complete, traditional business rules are located in a central place under the Application tab under Tools:

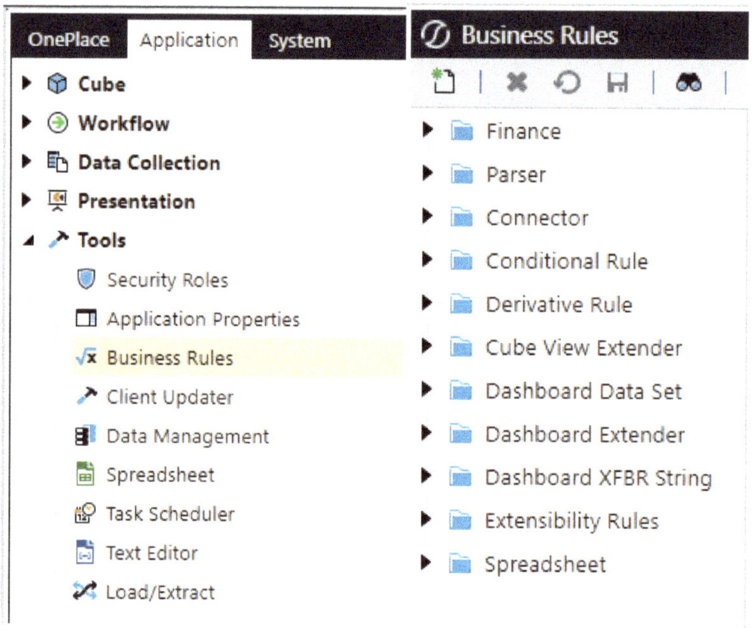

Figure 5.6

Here is an example (Figure 5.7) of the central repository concept and a typical number of business rules within a single business rule type. Notice all of the different rules that represent different functional areas of the application. Contrast this with a more focused approach to grouping business rules within a Workspace that only pertain to items within the Workspace (as shown above in Figure 5.5). This illustrates the advantage of Workspace Assemblies, where all relevant code for that Workspace is organized together.

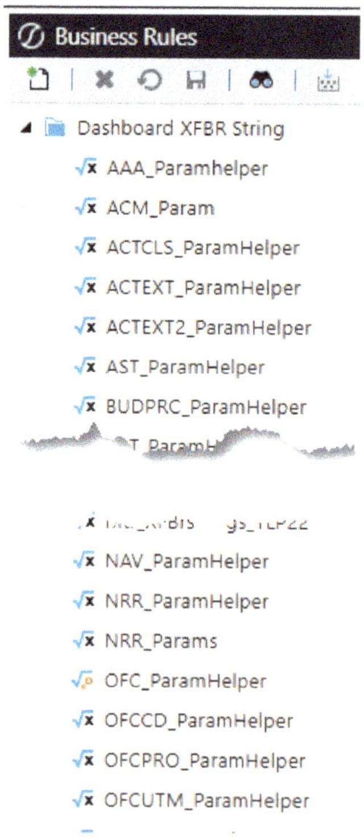

Figure 5.7

Location of Assemblies

Assembly business rules and Assembly Services are located in the maintenance units within Workspaces on the Application tab and in the Presentation section. Each Workspace can have multiple maintenance units, and each maintenance unit can have multiple Assemblies. We will discuss the proper way to organize and reference the appropriate Assemblies in the upcoming chapters.

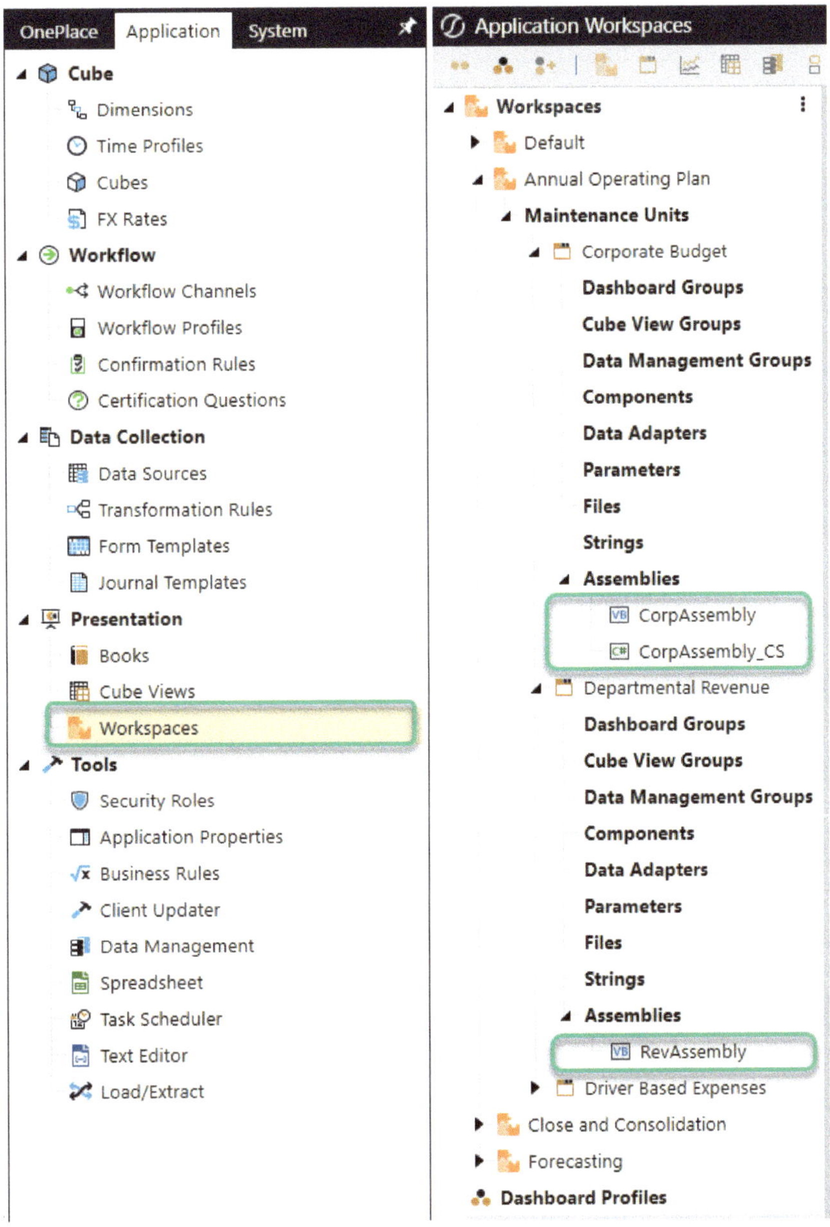

Figure 5.8

Benefits of Assemblies within Workspaces

OneStream's use of Assemblies offers several improvements over traditional business rules:

1. **Organization and Segmentation:** Assemblies allow developers to organize code more efficiently by grouping related logic together. This segmentation of related code makes it easier to manage and maintain, reducing the risk of errors and improving overall performance.
2. **Reduced Complexity:** Traditional business rules often involve a single large file with hundreds of lines of code, which can be difficult to manage and optimize. Assemblies

break down this complexity into smaller, more manageable files, making it easier to optimize and troubleshoot code.

3. **Improved Portability:** Assemblies can be easily moved between different environments with the related dashboard components, such as development and production servers, without the need for extensive reconfiguration. This improves the portability of functional solutions and reduces downtime during deployment.
4. **Dynamic Services:** Assemblies enable the creation of dynamic services like dynamic dashboards and dynamic cubes, which can adapt to changing data and user-specific needs in real-time, providing more flexible and responsive solutions.
5. **Improved Performance:** Assemblies support multithreading, which allows for the concurrent processing of tasks. This can significantly boost performance, especially when dealing with large datasets or complex calculations.
6. **Development Tools:** Assemblies can be developed using external tools like Visual Studio, which provide advanced debugging, code analysis, and other features that can enhance performance and productivity.
7. **Enhanced Security:** Assemblies bring improved security measures for managing the code. By writing code within Assemblies, access is more tightly controlled, reducing the risk of unauthorized modifications and protecting sensitive logic.
8. **Support for Advanced Solutions:** Assemblies are particularly useful for advanced application solutions, allowing technical teams to build sophisticated, customized solutions for clients.

Overall, the use of Assemblies in OneStream leads to more efficient coding practices, better performance, and easier maintenance compared to traditional business rules.

More than One Type of Assembly Logic

There are two main types of Assembly approaches within Workspaces, which can sometimes cause confusion: **Assembly Business Rules** and **Assembly Services**. I'll describe the differences between these two shortly, but first, let me share a graphic that shows how traditional business rule types can be converted to the two Assembly types, and how they map:

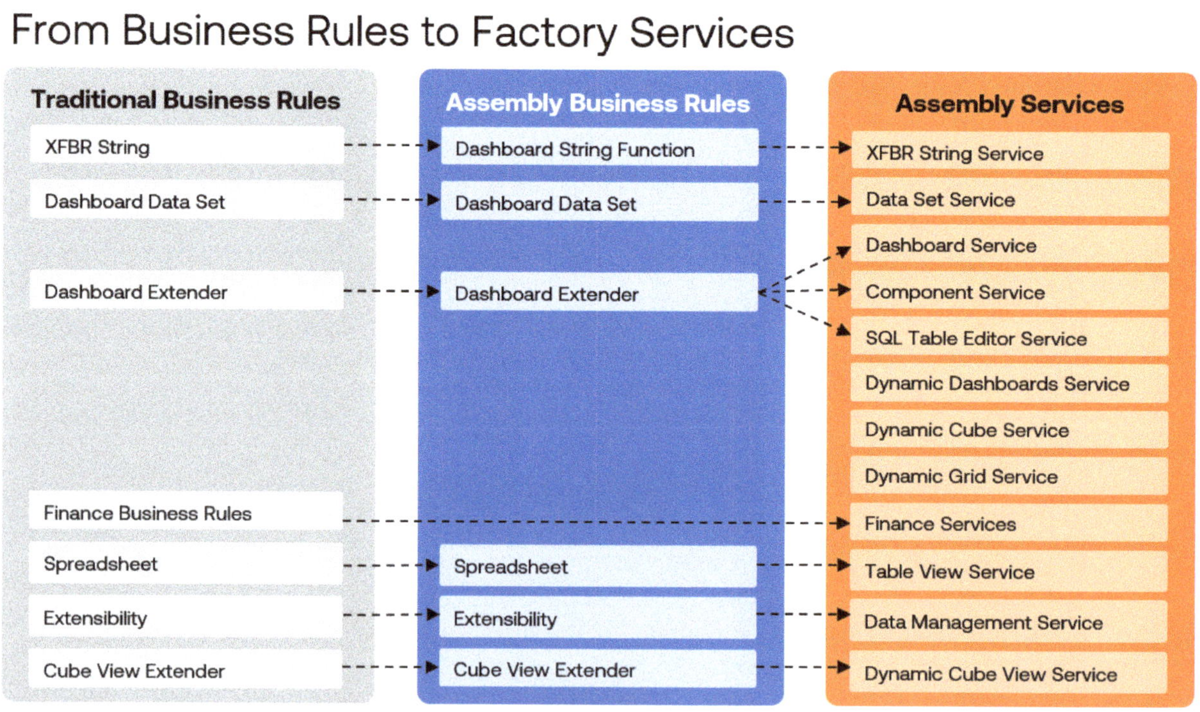

Figure 5.9

Workspaces were first introduced in OneStream version 7.3 and initially included only Assembly business rules. The first Assembly Services were introduced in version 8.0, finance Assembly Services followed in version 8.4, and additional Assembly Services will continue to be added in the future.

What is an Assembly Business Rule?

Assembly business rules are files within a Workspace that contain code to alter various parts of the application, similar to traditional business rules. They help organize the code within the functional area represented by the Workspace and serve as an initial transition from traditional business rules to Workspaces. The ultimate goal is to encourage developers to adopt Assembly Services within Workspaces, and Assembly business rules provide a stepping stone toward that goal.

While Assembly business rules share the same purpose and code structure as traditional business rules, their key distinction is their location. They reside within a Workspace maintenance unit (WSMU) rather than the central repository. Converting traditional business rules to Assembly business rules is a straightforward, one-to-one process. The new Assembly business rule can retain the same name as its traditional counterpart, with nearly identical code. When updating references, the only thing that will change is the prefix with the Workspace and Assembly location, reflecting its new structure.

Limitations of the Assembly Business Rules

As I just mentioned, the Assembly business rules are meant to be a transition from traditional business rules to Assembly Services. Because of this, there are limitations on the types of business rules that can be created as Assembly business rules. Namely, there are no finance business rule types for Assembly business rules. There are also no dynamic dashboards or dynamic cubes in Assembly business rules.

Benefits of Using Assembly Business Rules

The transition from pre-Workspace to Workspace-aware applications is straightforward with Assembly business rules. Since they are quite similar to traditional business rules in terms of how they are called and the syntax used, it is easy to transition existing business rules to these new Assembly business rules. The code remains the same and is surfaced in the same way; the only difference is how they are called. Essentially, it involves placing the rules in a different folder and updating the reference to that folder, which now resides inside Workspace > Maintenance Unit > Assembly instead of the root directory of traditional business rules. I will show examples of this in a later section, describing the differences between Assembly business rules and Assembly Services.

Conclusion

The bottom line is that Assembly business rules contain all of the advantages of the object-oriented programming approach (as listed at the beginning of this chapter) and are a very handy tool to convert an existing OneStream application from a pre-Workspace application to a Workspace-aware application. However, OneStream recommends using Assembly Services for more sophisticated logic in your application.

Here are some graphics that point out the transition of the traditional business rule types to Assembly business rules.

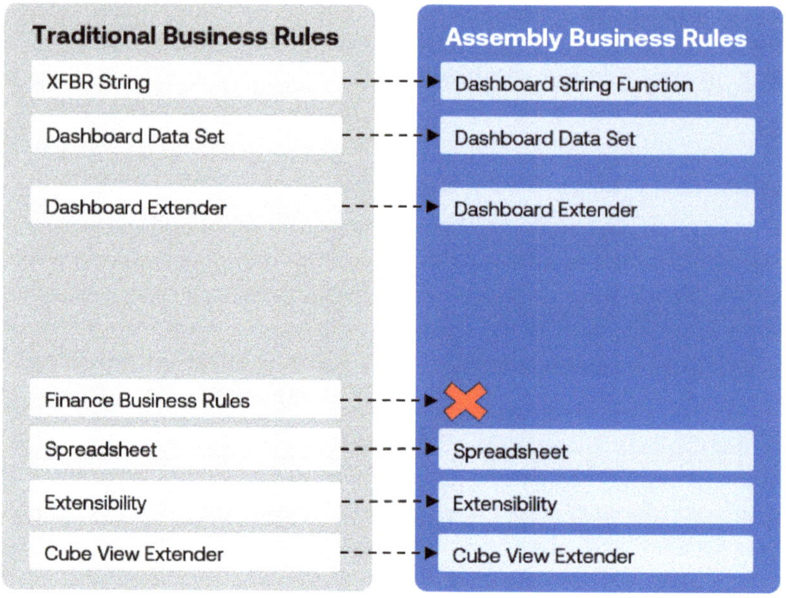

Figure 5.10

Traditional Business Rule Groups

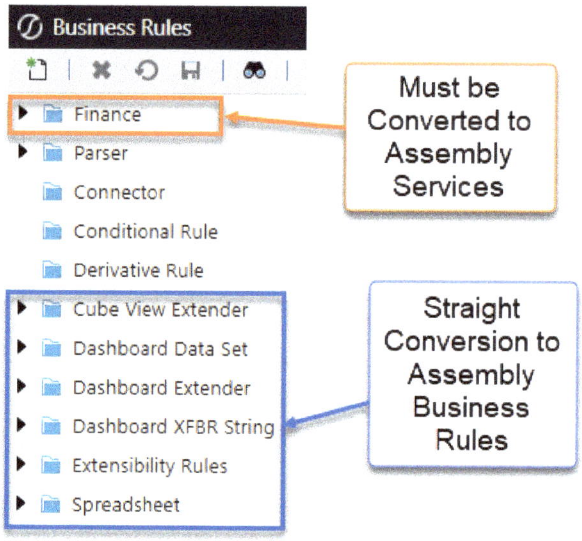

Figure 5.11

When creating a new Assembly file, we select whether this file will be an Assembly business rule or an Assembly service. This dropdown (Figure 5.12) has all the different choices for source code types. This is important because each of these selections seeds different code libraries as a starting point for you to build your business logic. You can see the selection of the Assembly business rules highlighted in blue.

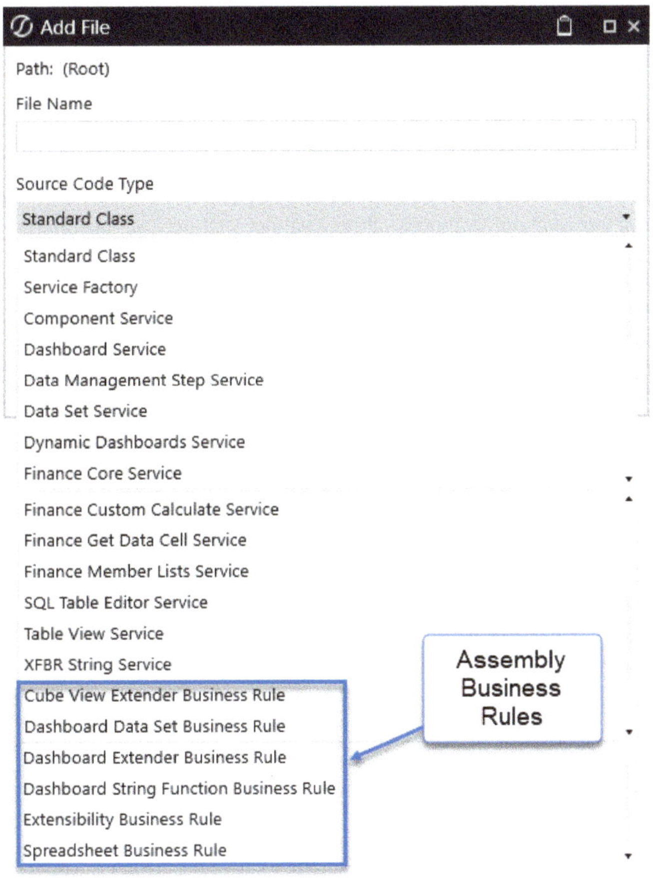

Figure 5.12

What are Assembly Services?

Assembly Services are files containing code that can be called from various places within the application. These services are defined in a file called an **Assembly Service Factory**, which routes specific request types to the appropriate service file. This approach significantly improves coding efficiency and organization while enabling the use of external development tools like Visual Studio.

Limitations of Assembly Services

While not a technical limitation, the learning curve for mastering the differences in the Assembly Services approach can seem intimidating. However, my hope is that the next few chapters will help to ease that process and make your learning journey just a little better.

Benefits of Using Assembly Services

Transitioning to Assembly Services from traditional business rules may be less straightforward than working with Assembly business rules. Nonetheless, once you are comfortable with them, Assembly Services allow you to segment business logic into smaller, more manageable units, enhancing organization and maintainability. By leveraging Workspace Assembly Services, we can boost performance and security while preserving the familiar structure of traditional business rules. Transitioning involves encapsulating rules within Assemblies and updating references to point to the new Assemblies within the OneStream platform.

One of the key advantages of Assembly Services is their ability to support advanced, in-memory solutions like dynamic dashboards, dynamic cubes, and dynamic Cube Views. These features unlock significant functionality for creating flexible and responsive applications.

Conclusion

The bottom line is that by embracing Assembly Services, you can create a well-organized, efficient, and maintainable codebase that enhances the functionality and performance of your OneStream application. These advantages make Assembly Services a powerful tool for developing robust and scalable financial applications.

Here is a graphic of how traditional business rules map to the new Assembly Services:

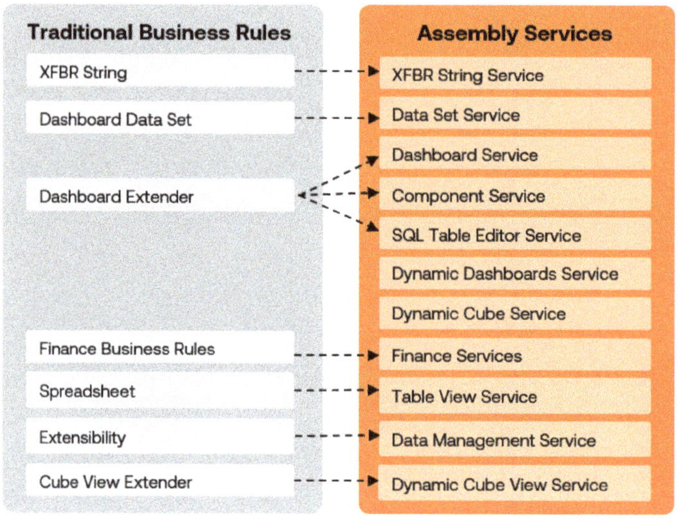

Figure 5.13

As we discussed in the previous section, when creating a new Assembly file, you must choose the source code type to make these files Assembly Services or Assembly business rules (Figure 5.14). Pay attention to the suffixes of business rules against the suffixes of the services. Once selected, the new file will have certain libraries and sample source code that will be a starting point to build your logic.

Also, note that there is a selection for a Service Factory. This is very important when working with Assembly Services because this file will route the request to the appropriate service file.

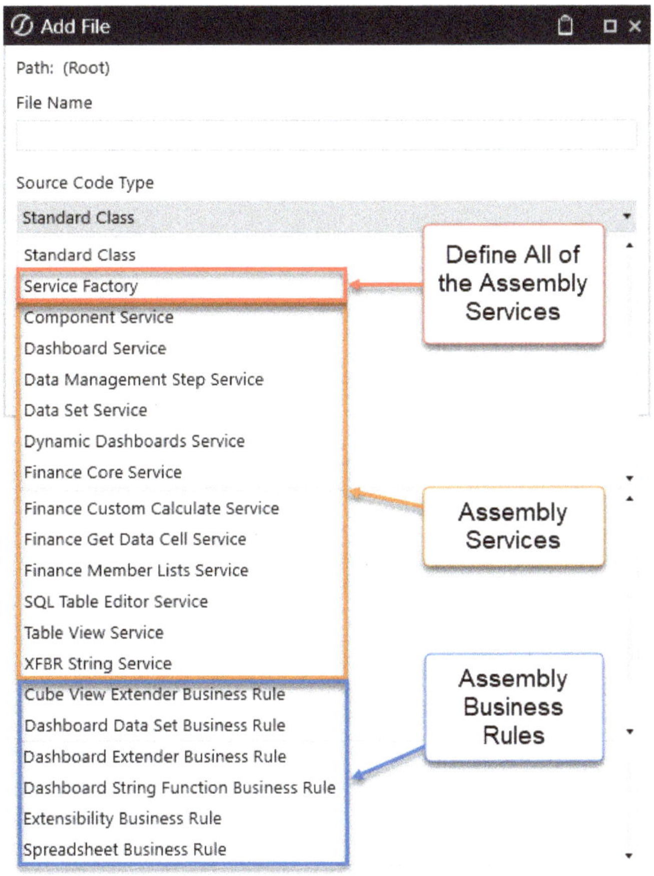

Figure 5.14

Main Differences Between Assembly Business Rules and Assembly Services

Given my experience in developing OS applications and working with traditional business rules, transitioning to Assembly business rules was a very straightforward process for me. However, understanding the intricacies of Assembly Services and Assembly service factories was very challenging for me. In the upcoming chapters, my goal is to clarify these differences so you will be comfortable with Assembly Services. This understanding is crucial, as Assembly Services are where we implement finance logic and all of the nice dynamic services.

One nuanced difference between Assembly business rules and Assembly Services is how they are invoked. Assembly business rules are Assembly files that can be named whatever you like, and when they are invoked, you will call the name of the Assembly file, very much like we have always done with all traditional business rules. As such, most application developers who have been building traditional business rules will see almost no difference when working with Assembly business rules, other than where this file is located within the Workspace and Assembly.

Examples of Invoking Code

To illustrate the differences in how the code is invoked from these different approaches, let me give examples of how a dashboard extender rule is invoked from these three methods:

1. Traditional business rules from a central repository
2. Assembly business rules from within a Workspace
3. Assembly service from a Service Factory inside a Workspace

I've created the same dashboard extender rule in all three places. We will call this logic from a Cube View component within a dashboard.

1. Traditional Business Rules from Central Repository

We are calling a dashboard extender rule from the Server Task setting of a Cube View DB component.

Traditional Reference:

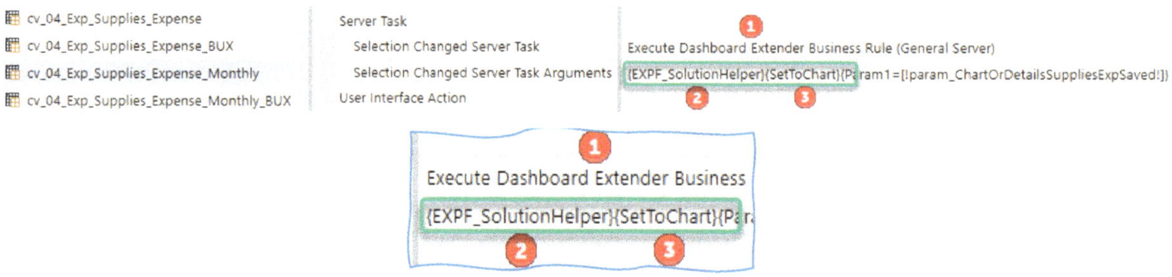

Figure 5.15

This statement is telling OS to look in the business rules repository for a dashboard extender business rule ❶ named `EXPF_SolutionHelper` ❷ and run the function `SetToChart` ❸. Here is where OS will go and find the code (Figure 5.16):

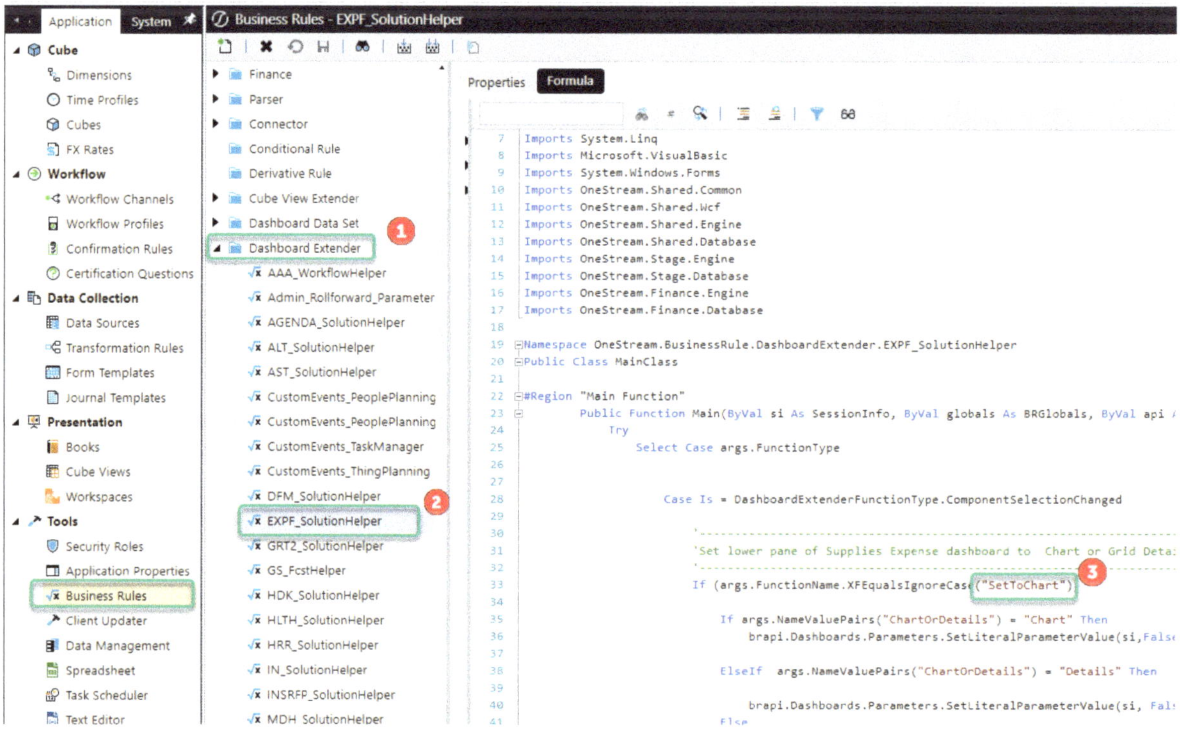

Figure 5.16

2. Assembly Business Rules from within a Workspace

We are calling a dashboard extender rule from the Server Task setting of a Cube View DB component.

Assembly Business Rule Reference:

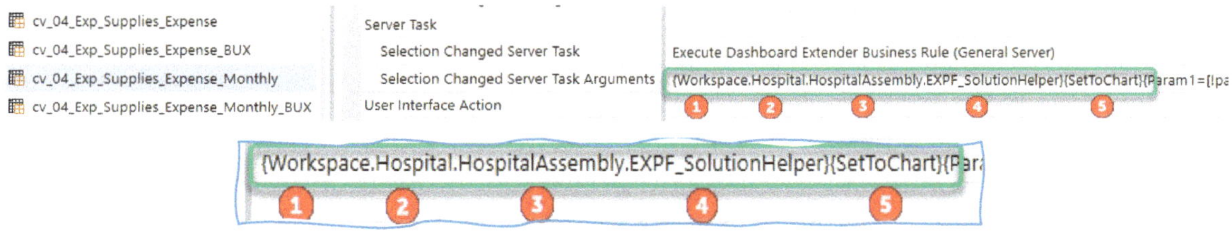

Figure 5.17

This statement is telling OS to look in the Workspace ① named `Hospital` ② and look in the Assembly named `HospAssembly` ③ for an Assembly file named `EXPF_SolutionHelper` ④ and run the function `SetToChart` ⑤. Here is where OS will go and find the code (Figure 5.18):

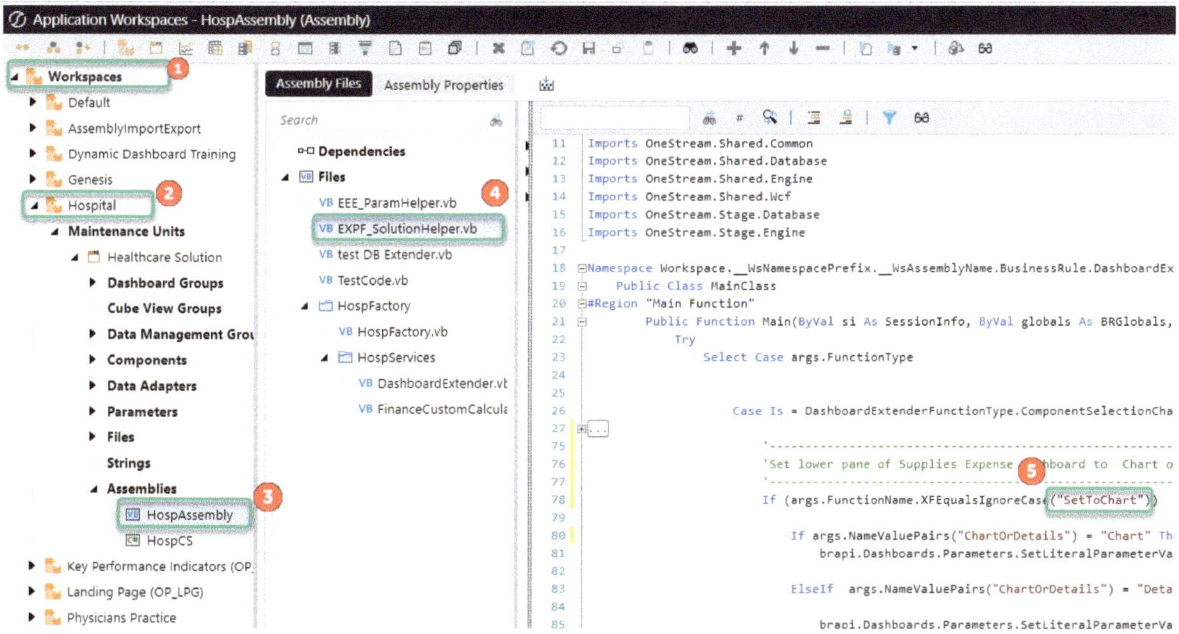

Figure 5.18

> **Note:** This is very similar to the traditional business rule, where OS is looking for the name `EXPF_SolutionHelper`, but it is just located in a new place within the Workspace and Assembly.

3. Assembly Service from within a Workspace

We are calling a dashboard extender rule from the Server Task setting of a Cube View DB component.

Assembly Service Reference:

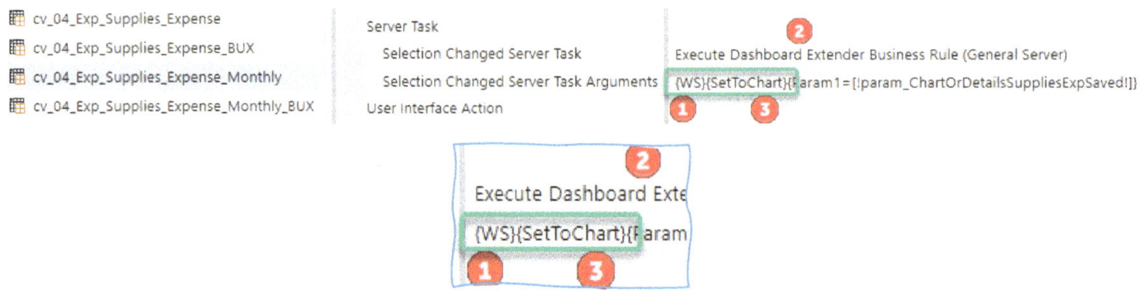

Figure 5.19

This is telling OS to look in the current Workspace where the Assembly is defined ❶ and the Service Factory will find the service for dashboard extender ❷ and run the function `SetToChart` ❸ Here is where OS will go and find the code (Figure 5.20):

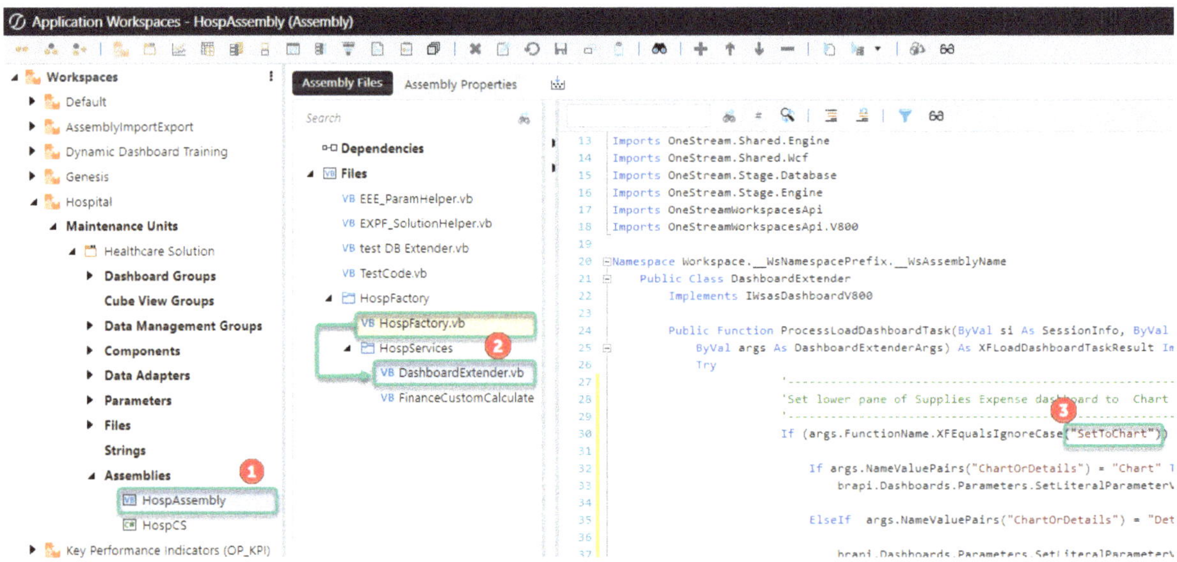

Figure 5.20

With Assembly Services, the names of the files are not invoked during the call; rather, the Workspace has an Assembly and Service Factory defined and will get routed to the correct code. The Service Factory is a file that points to other Assembly service files that contain the code.

We will get into the details around Assembly Services in Chapter 7, but I wanted to mention it here because this nuance can get very confusing when you are converting from pre-Workspaces to Workspaces.

The bottom line is that the Assembly business rules know exactly which file to route to because you give the exact name of the Assembly file when you call the action. Assembly Services are different because we don't tell the server task the exact name of the Assembly file to look for. We just tell the action (e.g., execute dashboard extender business rule (general server)) to look in the Workspace and Assembly Service Factory to look for the corresponding service file (e.g.,

DashboardExtender.vb). The Service Factory then routes the action to the correct Assembly file to run the appropriate function (e.g., SetToChart).

Object-Oriented Programming (OOP) in OneStream: A Beginner's Guide

I don't have a programming background, more of a finance and math background, so I needed to learn these programming concepts while working with CPM software. Understanding how namespaces, classes, functions, subroutines, objects, and modules come together to make your code well-organized and portable will truly help you appreciate OneStream's Workspaces, which allow for Assembly business rules and Assembly Services.

Here is a basic introduction to OOP for those new to these concepts or, like me, years of writing business rules without fully grasping these concepts. If you're already familiar with these concepts, feel free to skip ahead to Chapter 6.

This book is not a comprehensive guide to VB.Net or C#. However, to grasp why Assemblies and Assembly Services are a more efficient way to develop OneStream applications, you need a fundamental understanding of OOP. Both VB.Net and C# are OOP languages, and they are the foundation upon which OneStream is built.

Imagine you have a complex financial puzzle to solve. Instead of tackling it all at once, you break it down into smaller, manageable pieces. This is where Object-Oriented Programming (OOP) comes in.

OOP allows you to break down your code into smaller, reusable parts that can be referenced in different areas, eliminating the need to repeatedly write the same type of code over and over to accomplish similar tasks in different parts of your application.

For the purpose of getting a basic understanding of OOP, I will stick to VB.Net for these examples and not go into C#. For VB.Net, we are mainly using the following parts in our OneStream Assembly files:

- Namespaces
- Classes
- Methods
  - Subroutines
  - Functions
- Objects (as in "Object" Oriented Programming)
- Public vs Private

> **Note:** We will only cover the elements pertinent to Assemblies for organizing code, so we won't delve into other aspects of VB.Net like data types (e.g., string vs. integer vs. decimal) and collection classes (e.g., List(Of ValueClass) vs. Dictionary(Of KeyClass, ValueClass)).

Components of OOP

Namespace

Namespace is a container that allows you to organize your code into groups. Typically, you will have one namespace per business rule or per Assembly.

Classes

A **class** is a blueprint for creating objects. It defines the attributes (properties) and behaviors (methods) that the objects created from the class will have.

```
Public Class Car

   Public Property Make As String
   Public Property Model As String
   Public Property Price As Decimal

      Public Sub SetPrice(amount As Decimal)
         Price = amount
      End Sub

      Public Function StartEngine()
         Return "Engine started."
      End Function

End Class
```

Methods

Methods are functions or subroutines (Subs) defined within a class. They represent the actions that objects created from the class can perform. There are two different types of methods that are common in OOP:

1. Subroutines (Subs): Methods that perform an action, but which *do not return a value*.

```
      Public Sub SetPrice(amount As Decimal)
         Price = amount
      End Sub
```

2. Functions: Methods that perform an action and *return a value*.

```
      Public Function StartEngine()
         Return "Engine started."
      End Function
```

Properties

Properties are attributes meant to encapsulate data within a class.

```
   Public Property Make As String
   Public Property Model As String
   Public Property Price As Decimal
```

Objects – {Important}

Objects are instances of classes, and this is a key concept because a new object inherits all the properties and methods of its class. They are created from classes and have the properties and methods defined by the class.

```
Dim myCar As New Car()
   myCar.Make = "Toyota"
   myCar.Model = "Corolla"
   myCar.SetPrice(25000)
   myCar.StartEngine()
```

It is crucial to understand that once `myCar` is defined as a new object of the `Car` class, it becomes a completely new variable with all the properties, attributes, and methods of the class. In OneStream, we can create these classes once and reference them in various places, eliminating the need to rewrite all the code within the class.

Public vs Private

As the names suggest, public members are accessible from any other code within the namespace (the business rules or Assemblies). Private members, in comparison, are only accessible within the same class or module in which they are declared. They are not accessible from outside the class or module.

Note that you can also import public members from another namespace through dependencies and imports.

This introductory section provides a simplified view of OOP concepts, which is essential for understanding Assemblies and Assembly Services in OneStream. By leveraging these principles, you can create well-organized, efficient, and maintainable code.

Example Problem to solve:

To illustrate these OOP principles, here is a simple example of how these concepts work.

For this example, we need to write VB.Net code that can be reused to calculate a simple calculation for a customer's banking accounts. Here is a summary of the steps that we will execute, as each step is meant to illustrate different concepts of OOP.

1. Create a `Customer` class with properties `Name` and `Balance`, and a method to calculate a balance. (Organized Structure)
2. Create multiple customer objects using the `Customer` class. (Reusability)
3. Update the `Customer` class to include an additional item in the balance calculation. This update will apply to all customers who use this class. (Maintainability)
4. Create a new `Customer2` class that utilizes a private variable and methods to calculate the deposit balance and then a method to return that value. (Encapsulation)
5. Create a new customer object that uses the new `Customer2` class, showing how you need to reference the methods to set and return balance values. (Abstraction)
6. Create a new `SavingsAccount` class that inherits from the `Customer2` class to demonstrate inheritance and reusability. (Inheritance)

1. Organized Structure (Formal Structure Helps Usability)

Create a `Customer` class with properties `Name` and `Balance`, and a method to calculate a balance.

- **Classes and Objects**: In OOP, we create "classes" as blueprints for objects, allowing us to call them in different parts of our code. For example, we might have a Customer class with properties like Name and Balance and methods like UpdateBalance(). This helps us organize our code logically.

- **Example:** This class defines two properties and also has a method to update the Balance property with a deposit amount when called.

```
Public Class Customer
    Public Property Name As String
    Public Property Balance As Decimal
        Public Sub UpdateBalance(deposit As Decimal)
            Balance = Balance + deposit   'Adds the deposit amount to the existing balance
        End Sub
End Class
```

2. Reusability (Build Once, Reference Everywhere)

Create multiple customer objects using the Customer class.

- **Code Reuse**: Once we create a class, we can use it multiple times across different parts of our project. This saves time and effort because we don't have to write the same code repeatedly.
- **Example:** Using the Customer class from above, the variables customer1 and customer2 both have all the properties and methods of the Customer class. We can define the public properties Name and Balance for these customers. Public components can be referenced outside of the class where they are defined.

```
Dim customer1 As New Customer()
Dim customer2 As New Customer()

customer1.Name = "Alice"
customer1.Balance = 500
customer2.Name = "Bob"
customer2.Balance = 900

customer1.UpdateBalance(1000)
```

3. Maintainability (Update in One Place, Permeated Throughout Code)

Update the Customer Class to include an additional item in the balance calculation. This update will apply to all customers who use this class.

- **Easy Updates**: If we need to change how a Customer works, we only need to update the Customer class. All objects created from that class will automatically reflect the changes.
- **Example:** By updating the Sub UpdateBalance method to include a withdrawal amount in the formula, customer1 and customer2 will automatically use the new formula when this method is called. Thus, we update customer1 and customer2 without modifying their individual code.

```
' Updating the UpdateBalance method will affect all Customer objects
Public Sub UpdateBalance(deposit As Decimal, withdrawal As Decimal)
    Balance = Balance + deposit - withdrawal   'Updated formula to deduct the withdrawal amount
End Sub
```

4. Encapsulation (Bundle Code into a Single Unit)

Create a new Customer2 class that utilizes a private variable and methods to calculate the deposit balance, and then a method to return that value.

- **Code Protection**: OOP allows us to hide the internal details of our classes (like the private properties), exposing only what is necessary. This ensures that the code is safe and only accessible through defined methods.
- **Example:** This example creates a new Customer2 class utilizing a private variable _balance that cannot be referenced outside the class. When we create an object from this class, we must set the new balance using the public SetBalance subroutine instead of referencing the internal _balance variable directly. In the previous example, we could set the Balance property because it was defined as a public property. Here, we must call the public SetBalance method and let the internal logic handle the details.

```
Public Class Customer2
    Private _balance As Decimal

    Public Sub SetBalance(amount As Decimal)
        _balance = amount
    End Sub

    Public Function GetBalance() As Decimal
        Return _balance
    End Function
End Class
```

5. Abstraction (Reference Other Classes)

Create a new customer object that uses the new Customer2 class, showing how you need to reference the methods to set and return balance values.

- **Simplified Interaction**: By focusing on what an object does rather than how it does it, OOP allows us to work with complex systems more easily.
- **Example**: We can use the SetBalance method of the Customer class to write a new balance amount and the GetBalance method to retrieve the balance without worrying about the formulas that are performing the calculations.

```
Dim customer As New Customer2()

customer.SetBalance(1000)    'This method (Sub) calculates a value
customer.GetBalance()        'This method (Function) returns a value
```

6. Inheritance (Allows Methods from One Class to Be Used for New Classes)

Create a new SavingsAccount class that inherits from the Customer2 class to demonstrate inheritance and reusability.

- **Building on Existing Code**: OOP allows us to create new classes that inherit properties and methods from existing ones. This promotes code reuse and helps us build more complex applications efficiently.
- **Example:** We create a new class that inherits from the Customer2 class above. This gives us all the methods (subs and functions) from the parent class to use in

our new class. Notice that we can call `SetBalance` and `GetBalance` to create a new subroutine.

```
Public Class SavingsAccount
    Inherits Customer2
    Public Sub AddInterest(rate As Decimal)
        SetBalance(GetBalance() * rate)
    End Sub
End Class
```

By utilizing these OOP concepts, you can configure your OneStream application with VB.Net and C# to create a well-organized, efficient, and maintainable codebase that helps tackle complex financial tasks with ease.

Conclusion

The introduction of Assemblies really marks a transformative leap forward for the OneStream platform. By adopting Assembly business rules and Assembly Services, you can organize code more effectively, unlock advanced functionality like dynamic dashboards and cube services, and create portable, scalable solutions. These innovations not only enhance the development experience but also future-proof your applications by offering robust, modular, and maintainable architectures.

While the transition from traditional business rules may require some adjustment, the benefits far outweigh the challenges. Assemblies empower developers to leverage Object-Oriented Programming principles, streamline workflows, and deliver high-performing solutions that align with modern best practices. As you embrace these tools, you'll find that Assemblies open the door to new possibilities, laying the groundwork for a more dynamic and efficient approach to financial application development.

6

Managing Assembly Business Rules

When I embarked on my journey to learn Workspaces and Assemblies, I set out to convert existing applications that I had previously built into the **Workspace Aware** framework. I quickly realized that converting my traditional (non-financial) business rules into an Assembly business rule was actually trivial. The concepts between the two are identical except for the fact that you will have a new, more detailed reference to where the new Assembly business rule is located.

The bigger differences come with Assembly Services, which we will go over in detail in Chapter 7.

Remember, the overarching goal here is to segment the different code within a Workspace to keep everything related together for portability, ease of use, and improved performance. When converting from pre-Workspace to now separating and converting all items to individual Workspaces, the easiest way to convert traditional business rules is by creating Assembly business rules.

In this chapter, I will walk you through the process of creating, maintaining, and invoking Assembly business rules. The steps are straightforward and easy, but will take a little time to get used to.

Assembly business rules are an excellent bridge between the traditional way of writing code and the Assembly approach within Workspaces. While I have mentioned that Assembly business rules are a transition from traditional to Assembly Services, it is perfectly acceptable to continue using Assembly business rules for as long as you like. This structure is not going away, so if you are more comfortable with Assembly business rules, by all means, continue to build them. Just keep in mind that Assembly Services are needed for finance business rules and all dynamic content, so plan accordingly.

Components of Assembly Business Rules

Before we start creating an Assembly business rule, let's revisit the terminology around Assemblies to ensure we understand the moving parts.

- **Assembly:** The entire group of files and dependencies.
- **Compiler Language**: VB.Net or C# will be declared at the Assembly level, and every file within that Assembly will have that selected codebase.
- **Assembly Business Rule**: A file within an Assembly that has specific source code defining its purpose.
- **Source Code Type**: When creating a new Assembly file, you select the source code type to create the file with the correct libraries.
- **Dependencies**: External libraries, other Workspace Assemblies, or business rules required by an Assembly to function correctly, ensuring it has access to the resources or functionality it depends on.

Now, we will explain and demonstrate the process of creating and executing different Assembly rules. We will first walk through the process of creating an Assembly, then move through the steps of creating Assembly business rules, and lastly, show the various methods and syntax of executing these rules.

Create Assembly First

The first thing we do is create an Assembly. Note that you can create more than one Assembly within a maintenance unit; although this is not very common, there may be reasons that make your particular situation more efficient. As an example of where this may be useful, when I was starting to convert applications to C#, I would create two Assemblies, where one would have Visual Basic as the compiler language and the other would have C# as the language. This allowed me to start switching over to C# incrementally. Another example is to have multiple versions of the business rules saved in your development Workspace. As you will see later, two Assemblies with different names (`MyAssembly_Old` and `MyAssembly`) can contain business rules with the same name. This can be very useful if you want to quickly rollback changes in your business rules.

As a reminder, an Assembly is a collection of files that contain code, and an Assembly business rule is a file within the Assembly. So, whichever compiler language you set for the Assembly, *all files* within that Assembly will have the same language.

Within a maintenance unit, select the `Assemblies` group and then the toolbar icon to open Create Assembly. Click that icon, and a new Assembly Properties screen will open for you to name the Assembly and select the compiler language. Click the Save button, and you now have an Assembly defined.

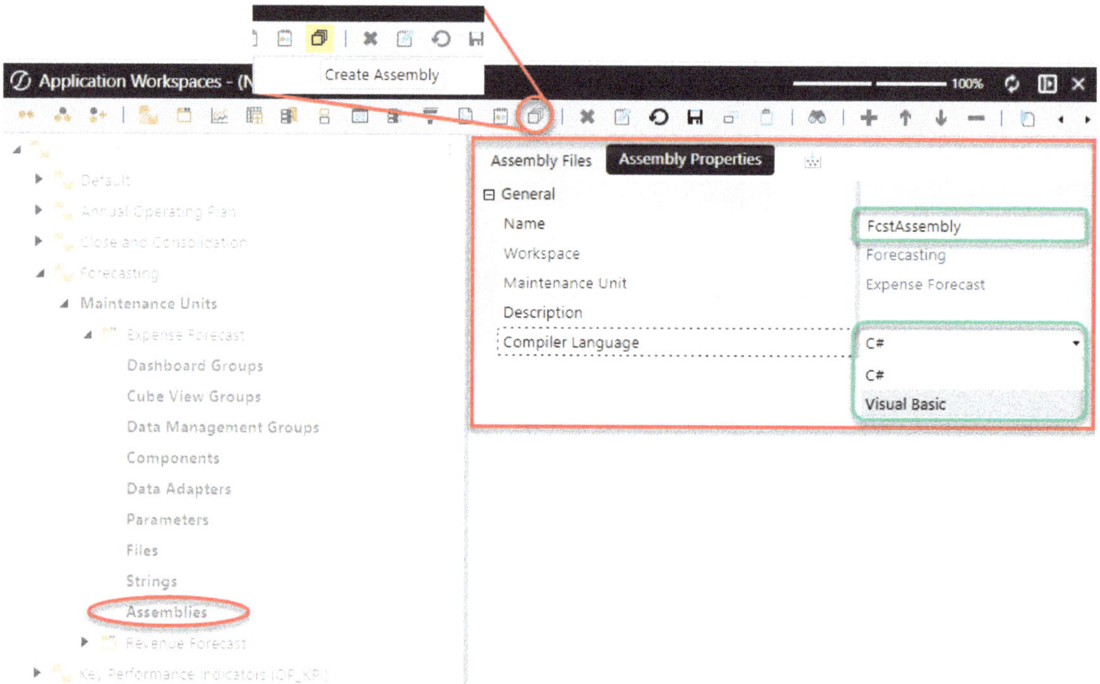

Figure 6.1

Working with Workspace Assemblies 101

Before we dive into creating Assembly business rule files, let's talk about how to navigate and work with Assemblies.

Working with Workspace Assemblies Summary

1. **Unique Assembly Names:** Assembly names must be unique within the Workspace. You cannot have the same name in two different maintenance units.
2. **Compiler Language:** All compiler language is set at the Assembly level. In other words, if your Assembly is set to C#, all files within that Assembly will use C#.
3. **Compiler Button:** When you click the Compiler button, it compiles all files within the Assembly that have not been set to Disable Compiler.
4. **Copy and Paste:** You can copy and paste Assemblies either by right-clicking on the Assembly and clicking on Copy then Paste, or by selecting the Assembly Properties tab at which point the copy button will be enabled.
5. **Delete an Assembly:** You can only delete a full Assembly by selecting the Assembly, then clicking on the Assembly Properties tab, at which point the delete button is enabled. (Note: To delete an Assembly file, right-click on the file and select Delete.)
6. **Rename an Assembly:** You can only rename an Assembly if you are on the Assembly Properties tab, at which point the rename button is enabled. (Note: All Assembly names within aW must be unique.)

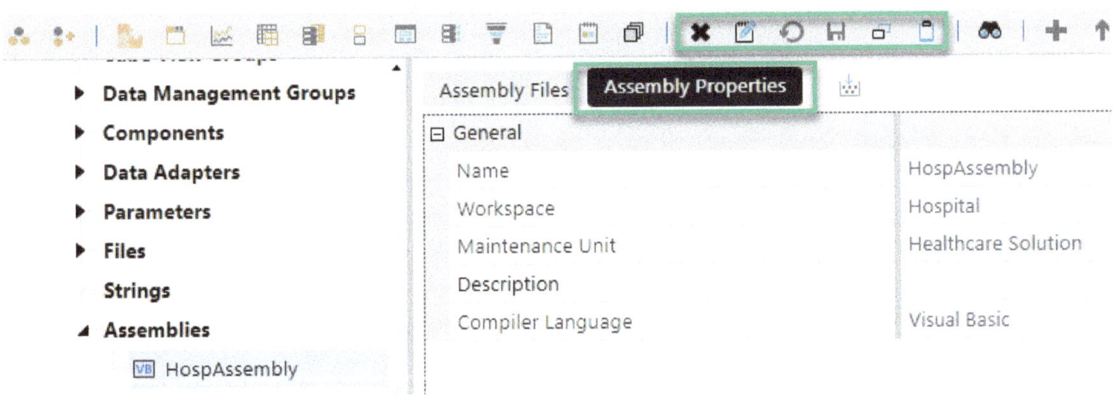

Figure 6.2

Working with Workspace Assemblies Detail

1. **Unique Assembly Names:** Assembly names must be unique within the Workspace. You cannot have the same name in two different maintenance units. If you inadvertently try to name an Assembly with a non-unique name, the system will prevent you from saving.

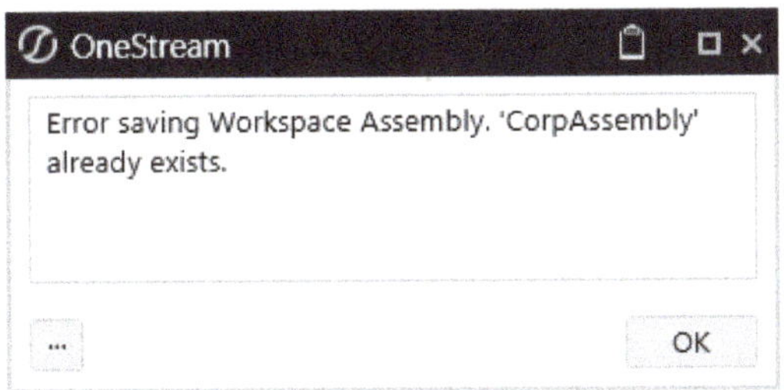

Figure 6.3

2. **Compiler Language:** The compiler language for all files is set at the Assembly level. Every file within the Assembly will have the same language.

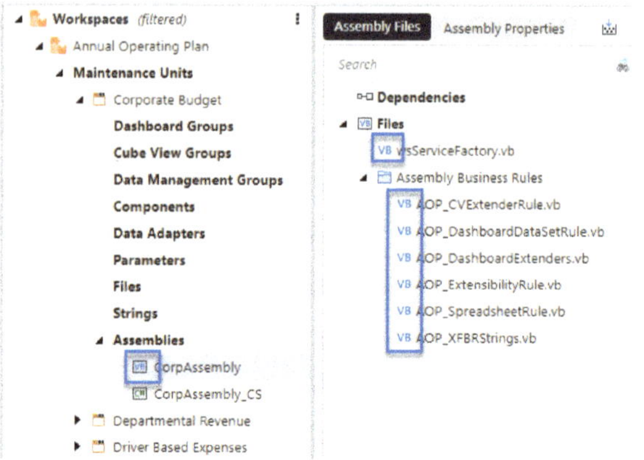

Figure 6.4

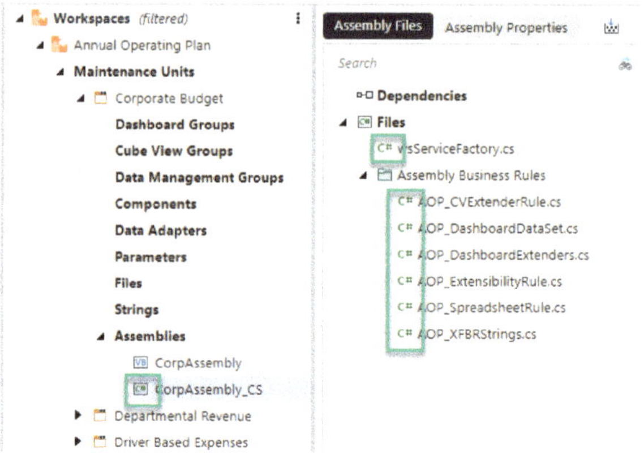

Figure 6.5

3. **Compiler Button:** The Compiler button compiles all files within the Assembly that are not marked Disabled. In this example, `TestBusinessRule_1.vb` is marked as Disabled, so the compiler will skip this file and only compile the other two `.vb` files. (Note: This is a change from how traditional business rules are compiled.)

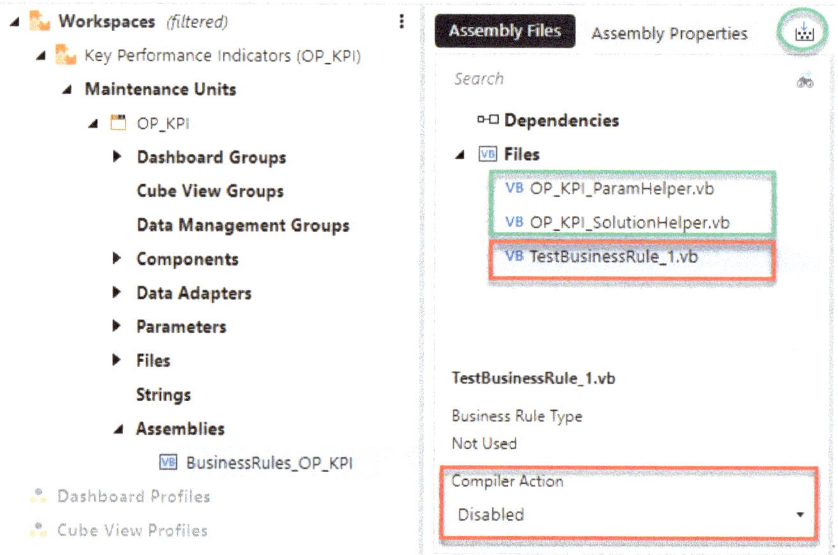

Figure 6.6

Useful tip: You can include files that are not compiled for documentation of the business rule (example: a README file).

4. Toolbar buttons are disabled when on the Assembly Files tab.

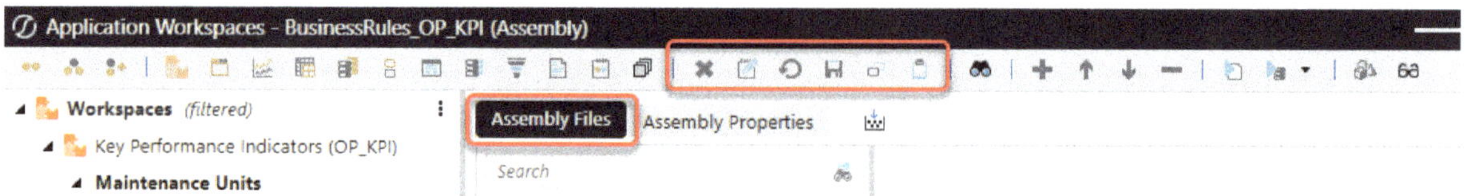

Figure 6.7

5. Toolbar buttons are active when on the Assembly Properties tab.

Figure 6.8

Encrypting Assembly Files

When you need to protect your code, you can encrypt individual Assembly files and make them password-protected. There is a setting in the Security Roles of the Application tab that needs to be enabled for this to happen.

1. **Enable Security Groups:** Enable security groups to encrypt business rules in the Security Roles section of the application.
2. **Encrypt File:** Right-click on the Assembly file to see the option to Encrypt the file to password-protect it.
3. **Encryption Icon:** The file now has an encryption icon to signal that it is encrypted; when that file is selected, no code will show.
4. **Decrypt File:** To decrypt an encrypted file, right-click on the file and select Decrypt and enter the password to remove the encryption.

Let's go through these steps in a little more detail.

Enable Security Groups

Enable security groups to encrypt business rules in the Security Roles section of the application.

The default for this security role setting is Nobody. If this is the case, you will not see an Encrypt option when right-clicking on the Assembly file.

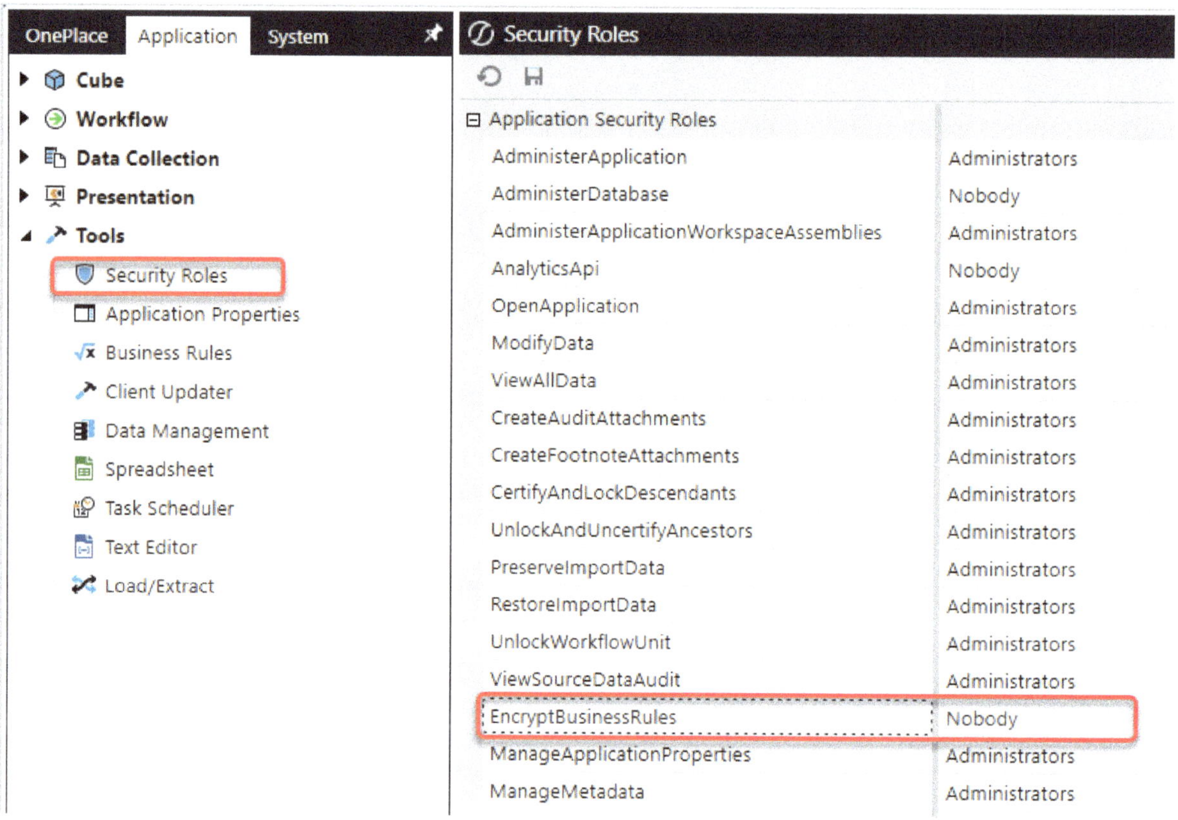

Figure 6.9

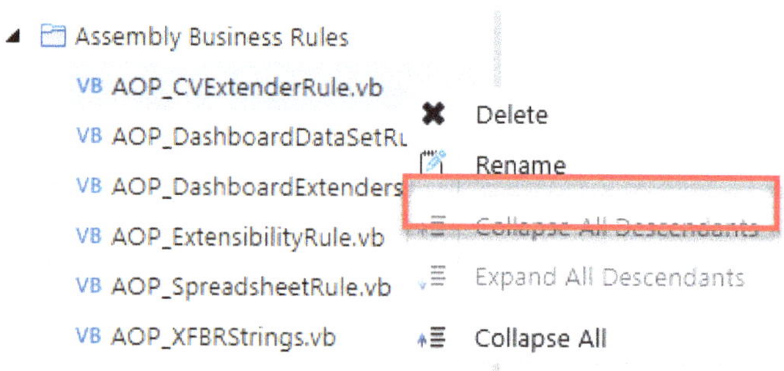

Figure 6.10

Once the appropriate security group is selected, the Encrypt selection appears in the right-click menu on the Assembly file.

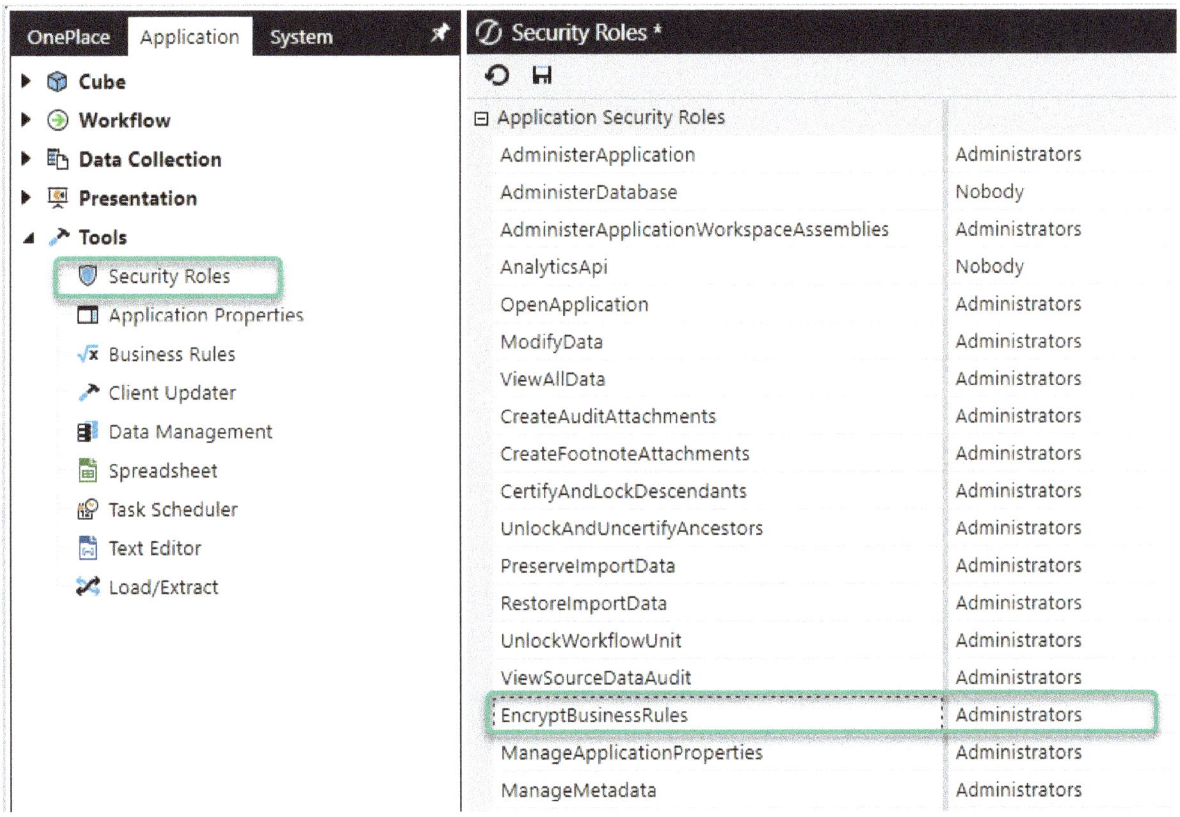

Figure 6.11

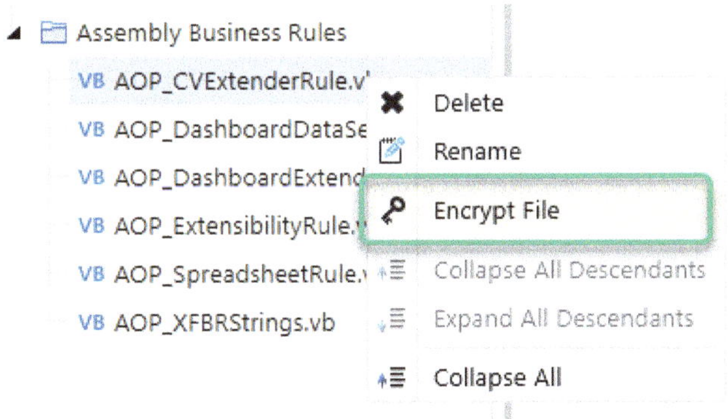

Figure 6.12

Encrypt File:
Right-click on the Assembly file to see the option to encrypt it and password-protect it.

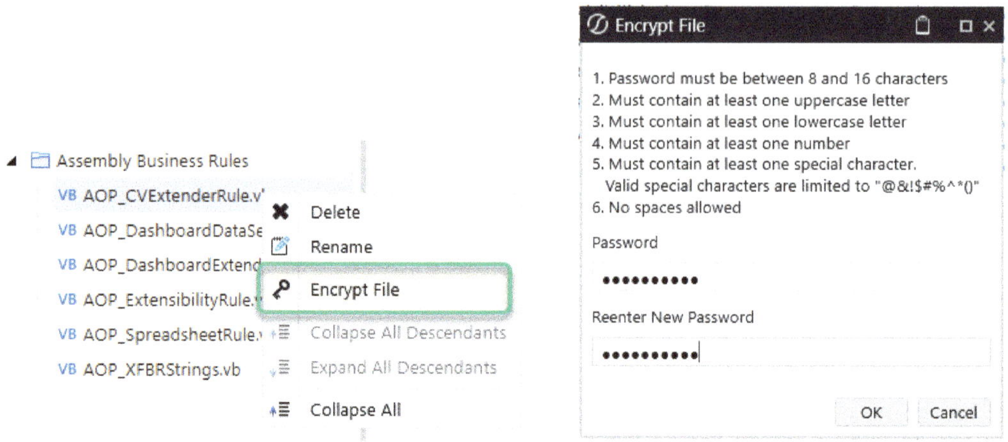

Figure 6.13

Encryption Icon:
The file now has an encryption icon to signal that it is encrypted; when that file is selected, no code will show.

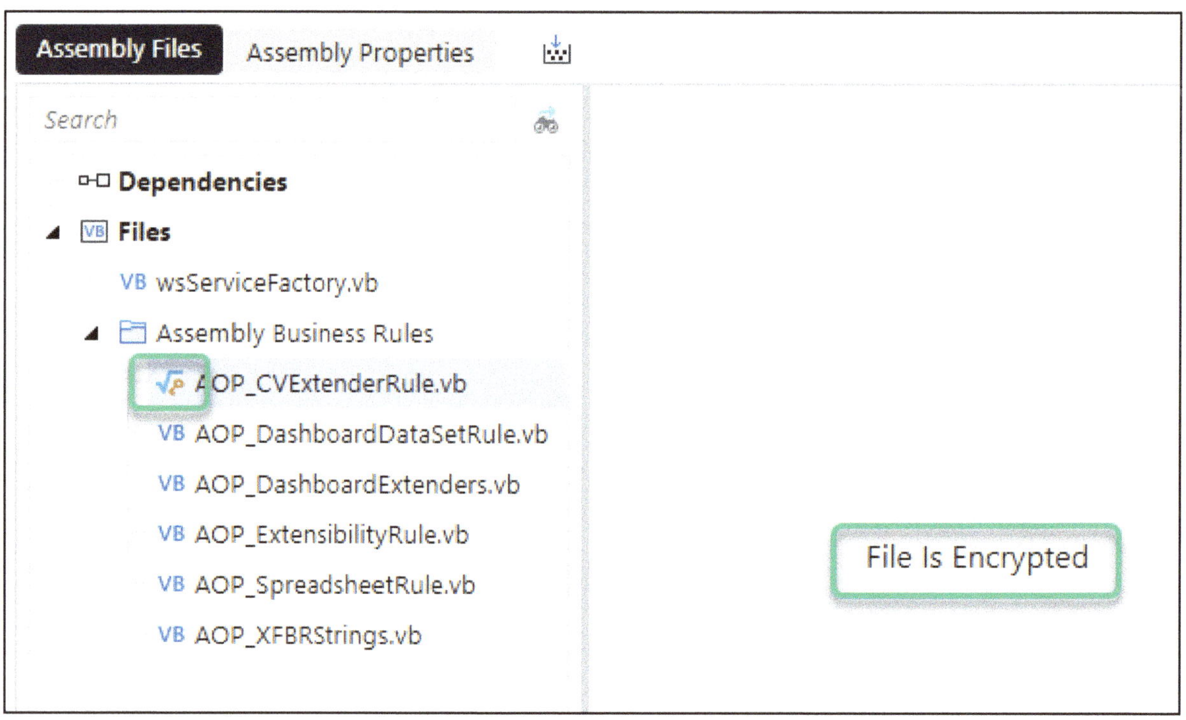

Figure 6.14

Decrypt File:
To decrypt an encrypted file, right-click on the file and select Decrypt and enter the password. Encryption is removed.

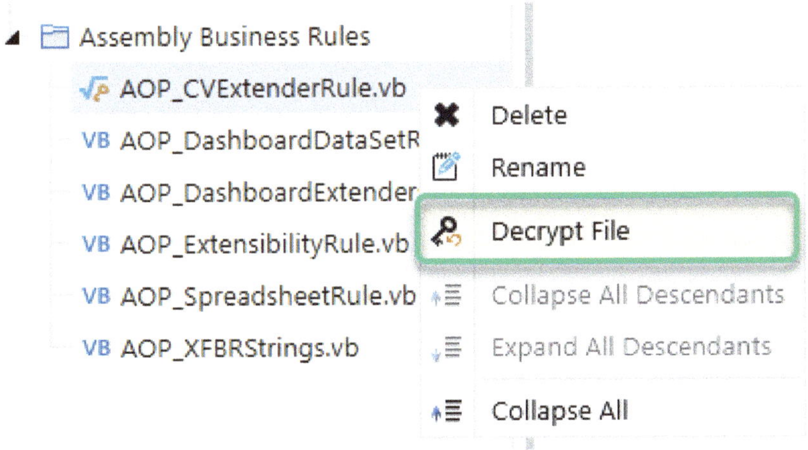

Figure 6.15

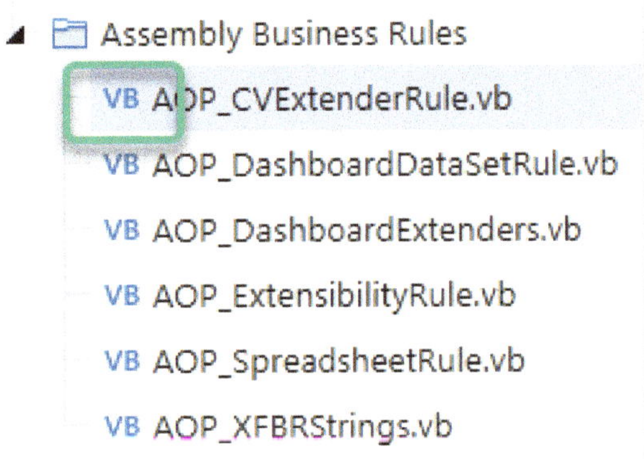

Figure 6.16

Create Assembly Business Rule

Now that we have produced an Assembly, we can create the appropriate Assembly business rule. But first, let's create a folder that will hold our business rules. This isn't technically necessary, but folders will come in handy later as we are trying to have a well-organized Assembly structure. Because it is possible to have Assembly service files in the same Assembly as the Assembly business rules, it is best to start organizing the files as we go.

Simply right-click on the `Files` icon and select Add Folder to create a folder and name it appropriately.

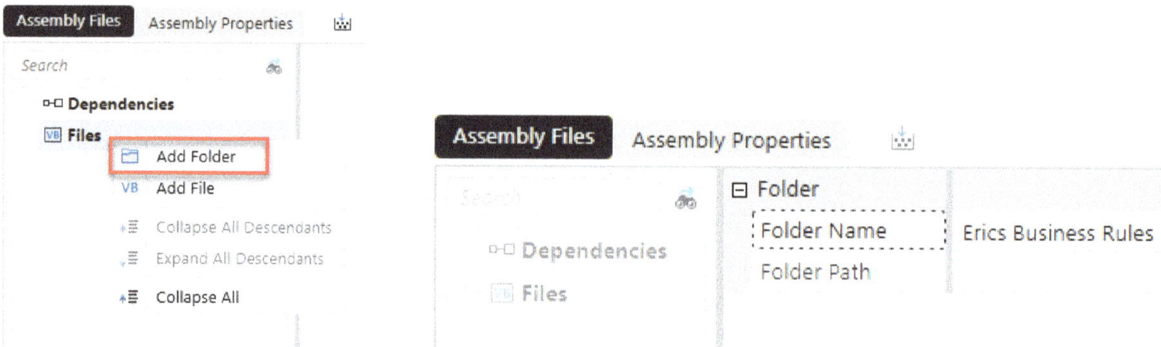

Figure 6.17

To create an Assembly business rule file under the new folder, right-click on the folder and select Add File. The Add File dialog box will prompt you to name the file, select the appropriate source code type, and choose whether to include the file in the Assembly compiler (the default is to Enable Compiling).

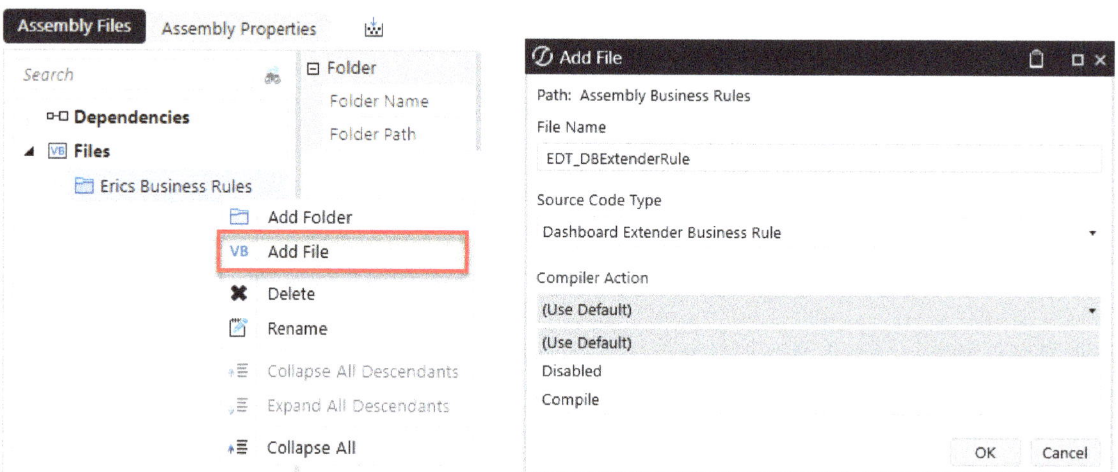

Figure 6.18

For Assembly business rules, the source code type is at the bottom of the list and has the suffix of Business Rule.

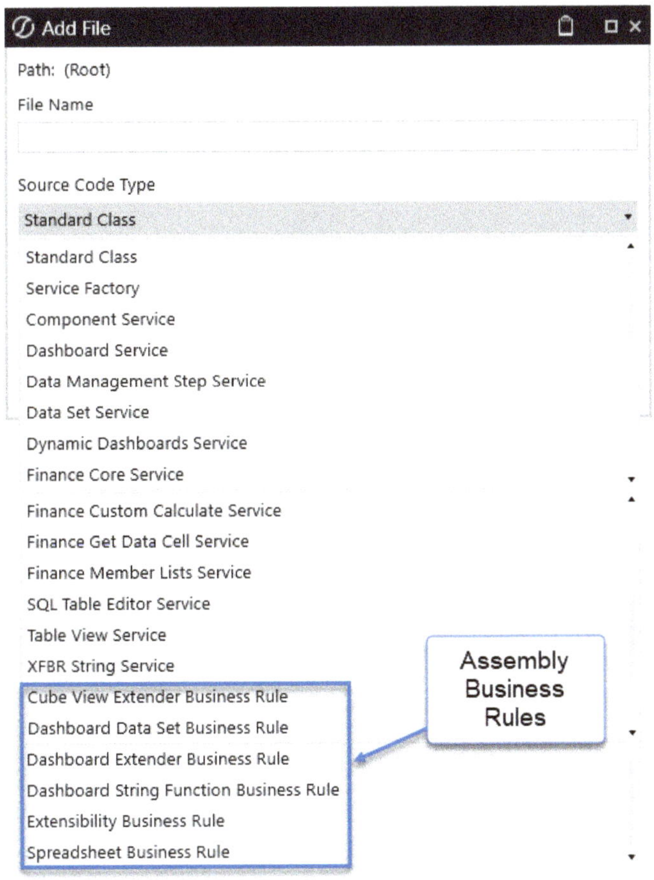

Figure 6.19

Once the file is created, OneStream prepopulates the file with the predefined classes and arguments for the source code type you selected, as well as placeholders for functions. In the screenshot example, you can see that since we selected the Dashboard Extender Business Rule source code type, the file is populated with `classes` and `args` that correlate to dashboard extender logic.

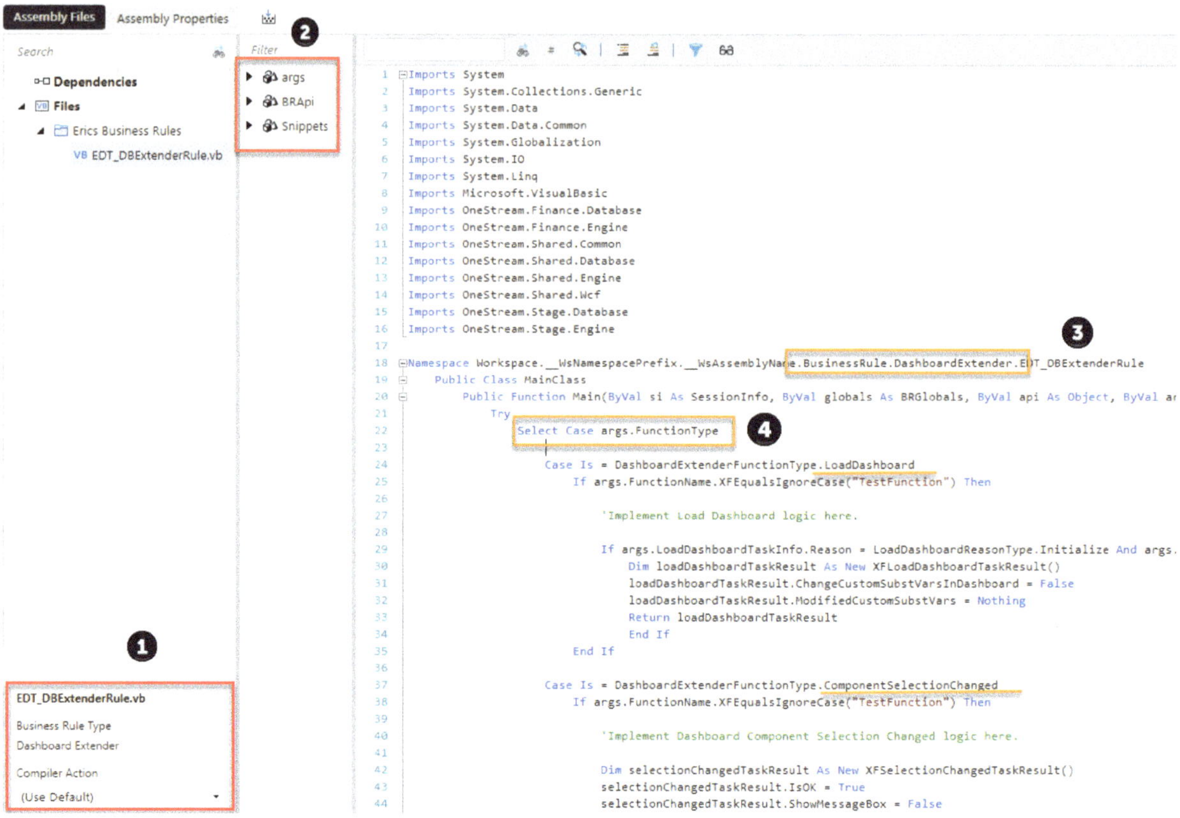

Figure 6.20

❶ When the file is created, you will see that the bottom left of the screen gives information about the file: `Business Rule Type` and `Compiler Action`. This is where you can change the compiler action.

❷ The helper section lists all the arguments available within this rule, plus the APIs available, and snippets of code to help with writing the proper syntax. Note that these helpers correlate to the code source type that was selected for the Assembly file.

❸ Within the code, you can see the code type is a `BusinessRule` and the `DashboardExtender` library of classes and functions.

❹ Some function types are listed as examples, suggesting the most common actions you can control.

The purpose of this book is to get you comfortable understanding where and how to set up Assembly files in Workspaces, but it isn't meant to be a guide on how to actually write the code to customize your application. So, at this point in your application development, you will probably begin writing your code within the Assembly business rule file and do your appropriate testing. The next section will cover where and how to execute these Assembly business rules.

Copy and Paste Nuances with Assemblies

Copying and Pasting Assemblies

When copying and pasting Assemblies, all the files and dependencies are copied and then pasted into a new Assembly that has the suffix `_Copy`. This gives the Assembly a unique name within the Workspace. All the files and dependency references within the pasted Assembly will have the same exact name since the uniqueness needs to be at the Assembly level and not the Assembly file level.

You can right-click on an Assembly to Copy and Paste, or select the Assembly Properties tab on the Assembly, and the toolbar icons allow you to copy and paste:

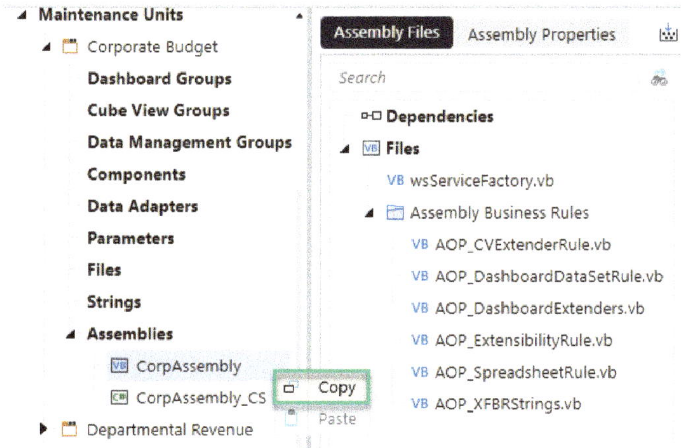

Figure 6.21

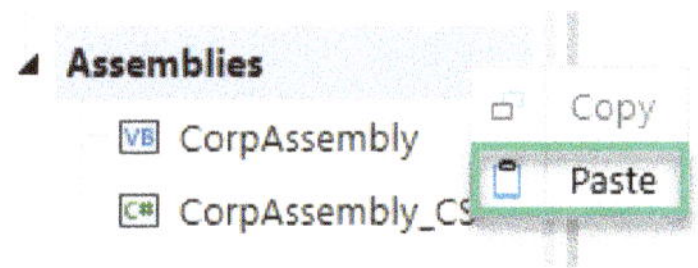

Figure 6.22

Filenames within the copied Assembly don't change.

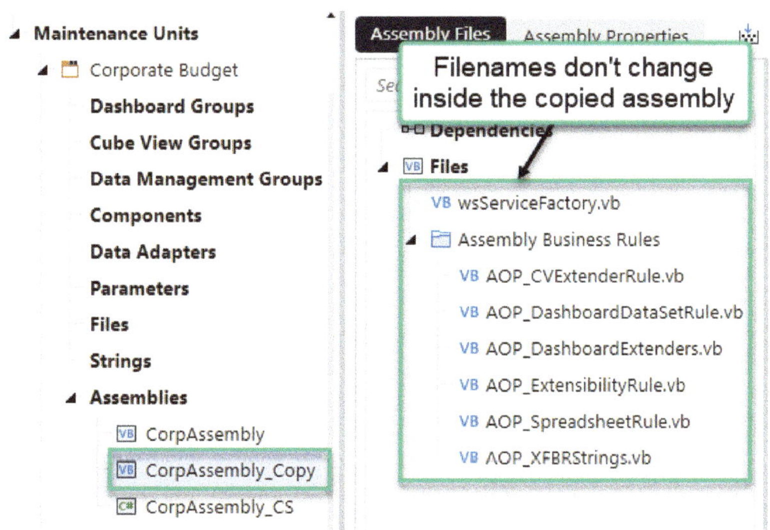

Figure 6.23

Copying and Pasting Individual Business Rule Type Files

The title of this section is deceptive because you cannot copy and paste *individual files* within an Assembly. When you right-click on an Assembly file, there are no options for copying and pasting:

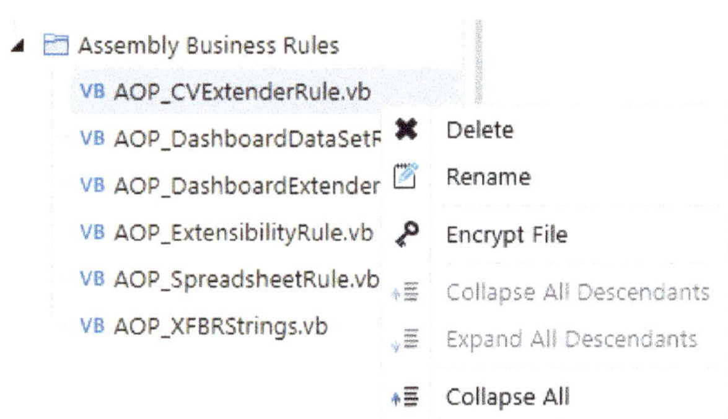

Figure 6.24

Instead, you must create a new file and copy and paste the code within the file into the new Assembly file. Highlight the code you would like to copy and right-click on the highlighted code to select Copy. When copying the code, make sure you do not include the namespace since that is unique for each Assembly file. You can grab everything between `Namespace` and `End Namespace` (note that this is true for business rule type Assembly files; for other types, you will need to consider the Public Class Name as well, where the public class must be named the same as the file).

Create a new Assembly file of the same source code type you are trying to copy.

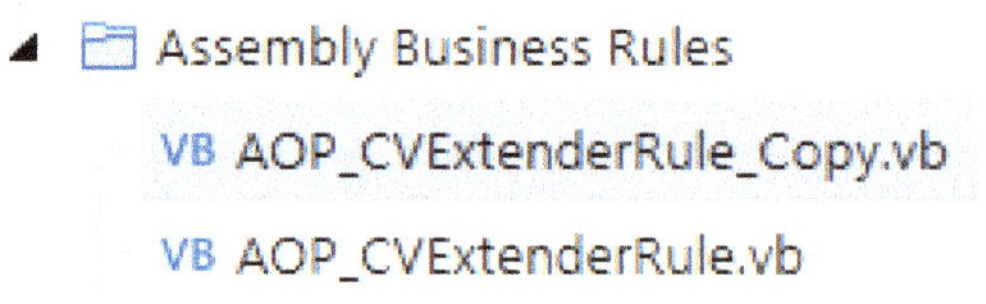

Figure 6.25

Highlight the code in the original rule between `Namespace` and `End Namespace`, right-click and Copy.

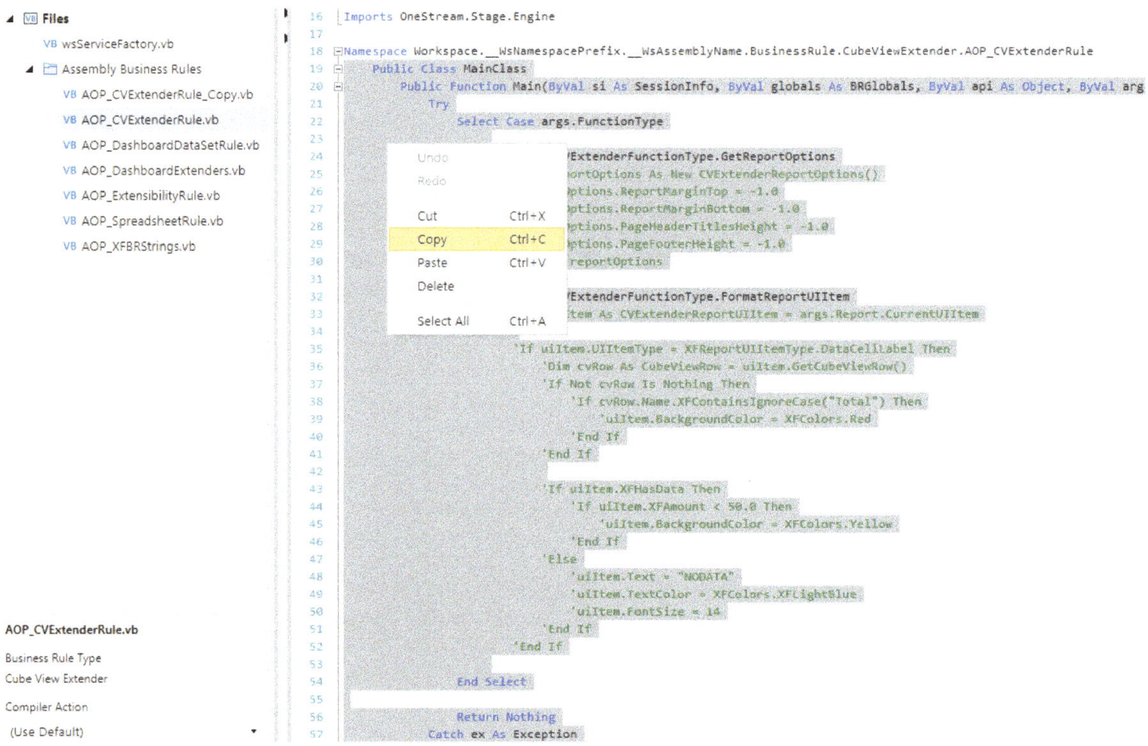

Figure 6.26

Pasting the code into the new file you created should not overwrite the namespace section since it contains the unique filename attached to this Assembly file.

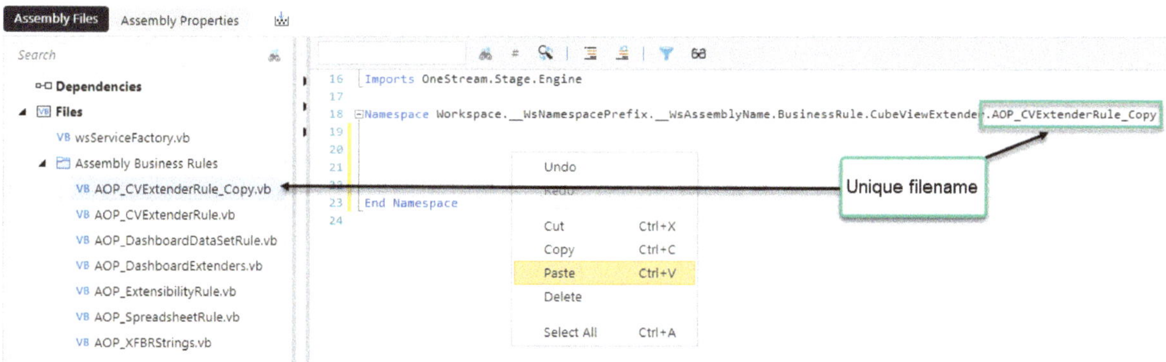

Figure 6.27

Again, this might be completely obvious to you, but if not, this hopefully clears up some confusion.

Referencing Assembly BRs

Once an Assembly business rule is created, referencing it works almost exactly the same as invoking traditional business rules, but through an updated path. Where you would once reference the business rule name, you now reference the Workspace, Assembly, and filename. Let's use an example of a dashboard extender business rule to illustrate the differences.

Syntax to call a traditional business rule:

```
{MyDashboardExtenderBRName}{MyFunction}{Param1=[MyValue1],Param2=
[MyValue2]}
```

Syntax to call an Assembly Business Rule:

```
{Workspace.WorkspaceName.AssemblyName.Filename}{MyFunction}{Param1=
[MyValue1],Param2=[MyValue2]}
```

Other options to call the same rule:

```
{Workspace.WorkspaceNamePrefix.AssemblyName.Filename}{MyFunction}{Para
m1=[MyValue1],Param2=[MyValue2]}

{Workspace.Current.AssemblyName.Filename}{MyFunction}{Param1=
[MyValue1],Param2=[MyValue2]}
```

Let's dive deeper into the references here, so we are crystal clear on how these references work with Assembly business rules.

`Workspace`: Indicates to OneStream that we are looking for an Assembly business rule in a Workspace and *not* in the central repository of traditional business rules.

`WorkspaceName`: Specifies which Workspace to look in. This will reference the Workspace that holds the business rule. There are three options you can use here:

1. You can use the actual name of the Workspace: `WorkspaceName`
2. You can use the Workspace setting Namespace Prefix as a short name to reference the same Workspace: `WorkspaceNamePrefix`
3. You can use Current if you are in the same Workspace as the Assembly business rule: `Current`

In turn,

- `AssemblyName`: This specifies which Assembly within the Workspace the business rule file is located.
- `Filename`: The name of the Assembly business rule file.
- `MyFunction`: The function within the business rule to execute.
- `NameValuePairs`: Parameters or variables that the function expects.

Here is the Assembly business rule reference example we saw in Chapter 5, which we will reiterate here:

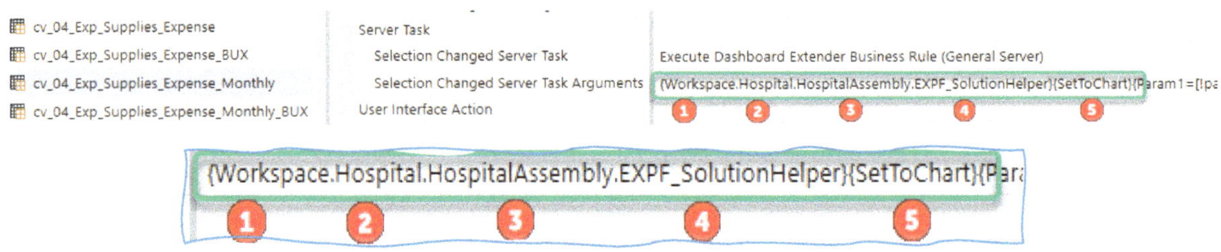

Figure 6.28

This tells OneStream to look in the Workspace ① named `Hospital` ② and look in the Assembly named `HospAssembly` ③ for an Assembly file named `EXPF_SolutionHelper` ④ and run the function `SetToChart`. ⑤ Here is where OS will go to find the code (Figure 6.29):

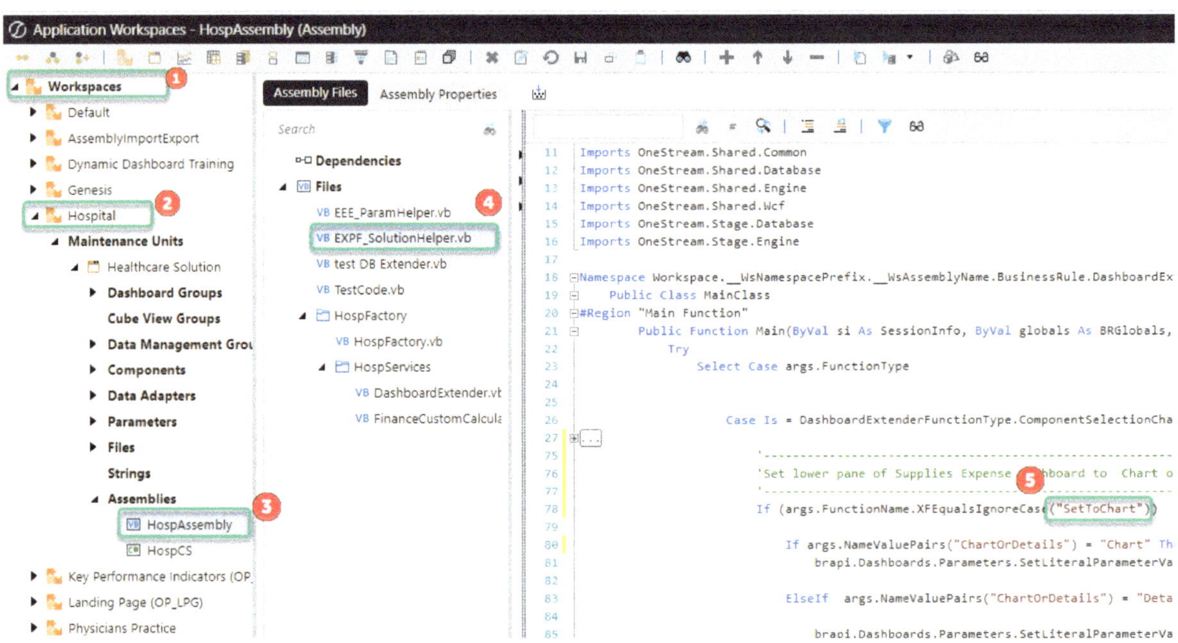

Figure 6.29

One nuance that we need to reiterate is the reference to the Workspace in position ②. This can be referenced in any of the three ways listed below.

Any of the following will work:

`{Workspace.WorkspaceName` – actual name of the Workspace.

`{Workspace.WorkspaceNamePrefix` – namespace prefix of Workspace.

`{Workspace.Current` – If you are calling the business rule from the same Workspace.

Alternative statements from the example above:

```
{Workspace.Hospital.HospAssembly.EXPF_SolutionHelper}{SetToChart}{Para
m1=|!prm_ChartOrDetail!|}

{Workspace.Hosp.HospAssembly.EXPF_SolutionHelper}{SetToChart}{Param1=|
!prm_ChartOrDetail!|}

{Workspace.Current.HospAssembly.EXPF_SolutionHelper}{SetToChart}{Param
1=|!prm_ChartOrDetail!|}
```

> **Best Practice:** It is best to reference with `Current` as it makes porting the code to other applications easier.

As a reminder, here are the Workspace settings that are being referred to in this syntax:

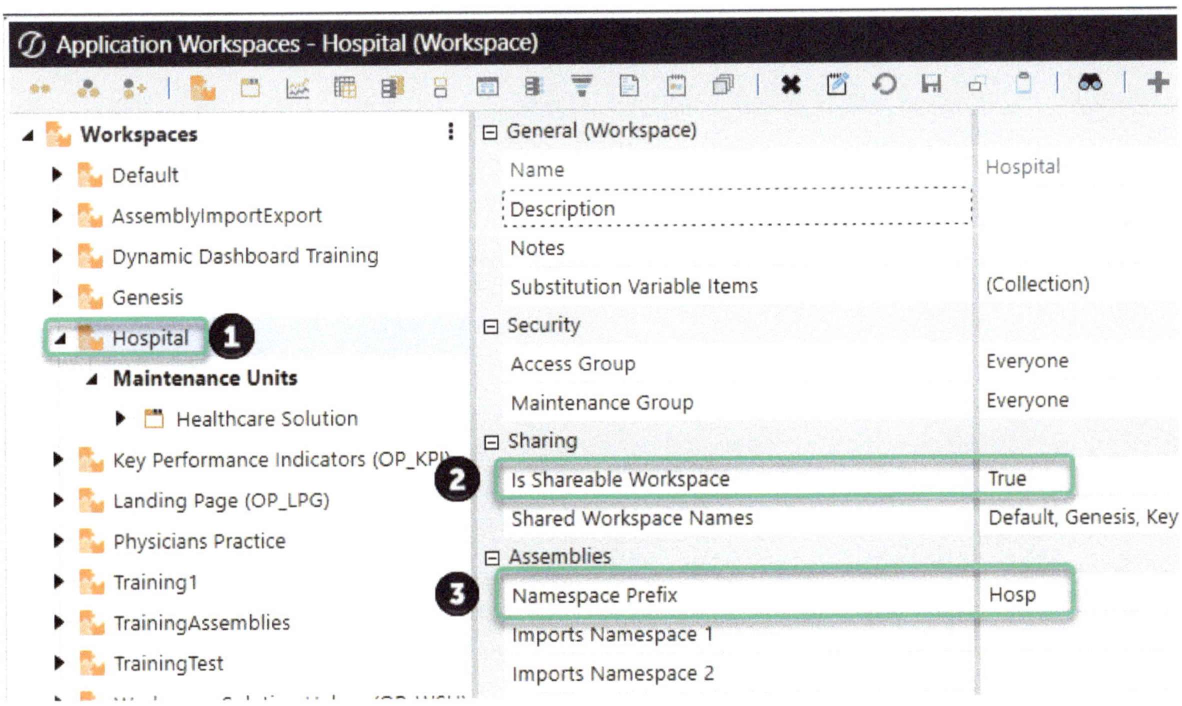

Figure 6.30

The bottom line to referencing an Assembly business rule is to ensure the system knows where the file is stored, so you need to give this information: (`Workspace.WorkspaceName.AssemblyName.Filename`) instead of just referencing the traditional business rule name (`MyDashboardExtenderBRName`).

Dependencies

If you need to use code from Assemblies in other Workspaces or from a traditional business rule outside of Workspaces, you can create a dependency to use that code in your Assembly files. Dependencies allow one Assembly file to reference any of the `Public Subs` and `Functions` in another. You can also create a dependency from an outside source as a **Prepackaged Assembly**.

These dependencies function in much the same way as referenced Assemblies do in traditional business rules. Once you have created a dependency with a shared Workspace Assembly, a business rule, or a prepackaged Assembly, you can reference it within any of your Assembly files.

> **Note:** If the source Assembly is in a different Workspace, the source Workspace must have Is Shareable Workspace set to True.

To add a dependency, just right-click on Dependencies and select Add Dependency.

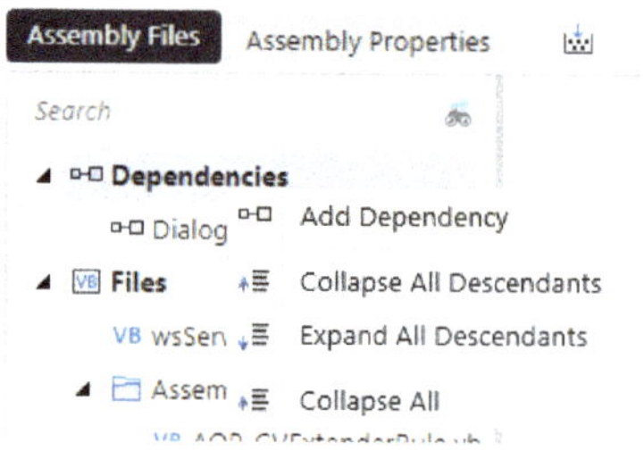

Figure 6.31

In the next sections, we will show you examples of the three different **Dependency Types**:

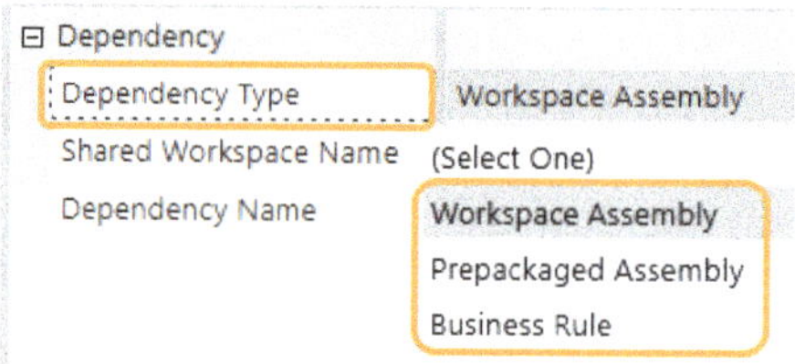

Figure 6.32

Dependency Example – Workspace Assembly

When creating a dependency to another Workspace and Assembly, the `[Shared Workspace Name]` and `[Dependency Name]` *must* match the source Workspace name and source Assembly name (as shown in Figure 6.33).

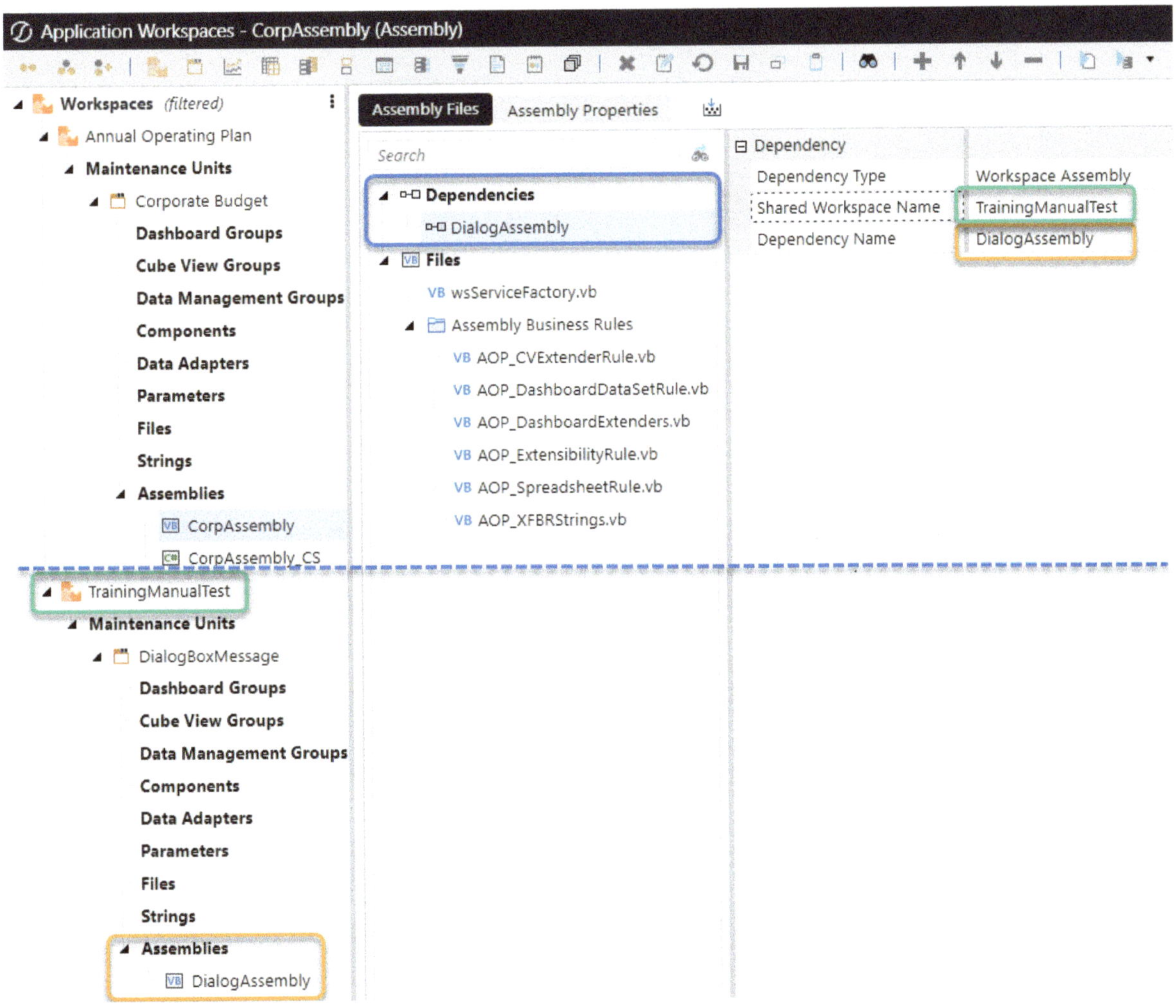

Figure 6.33

When using the Workspace Assembly dependency, after the dependency is defined, you call the public functions from the referenced Assembly into the code of the target Assembly.

1. Define a dependency to add a link to another Assembly.

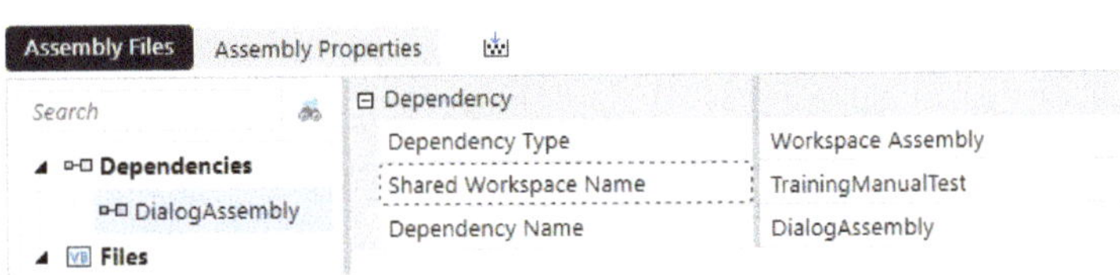

Figure 6.34

2. Reference the dependent class and call the needed functions in your target Assembly file.

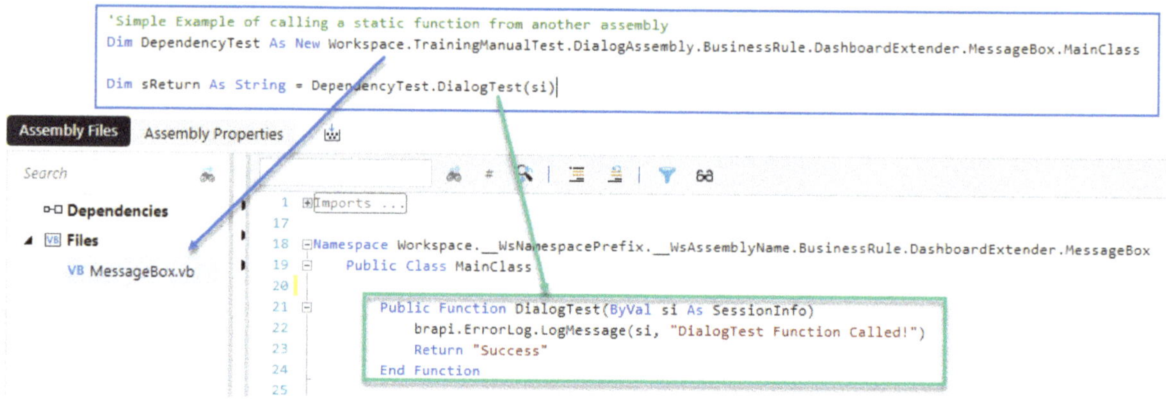

Figure 6.35

Dependency Example – Business Rule

Example of creating a dependency to a traditional business rule.

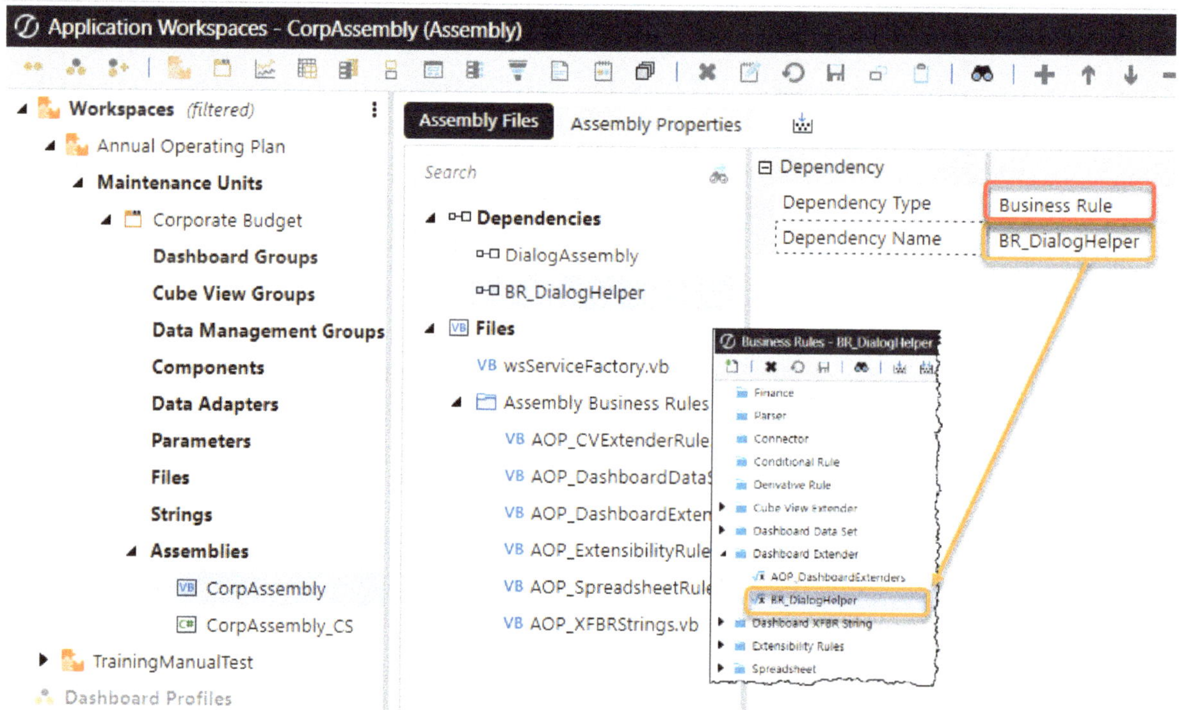

Figure 6.36

Dependency Example – Prepackaged Assembly

Here is an example of creating a dependency to a prepackaged Assembly. We are referencing the DLL package and calling the libraries in an Assembly file.

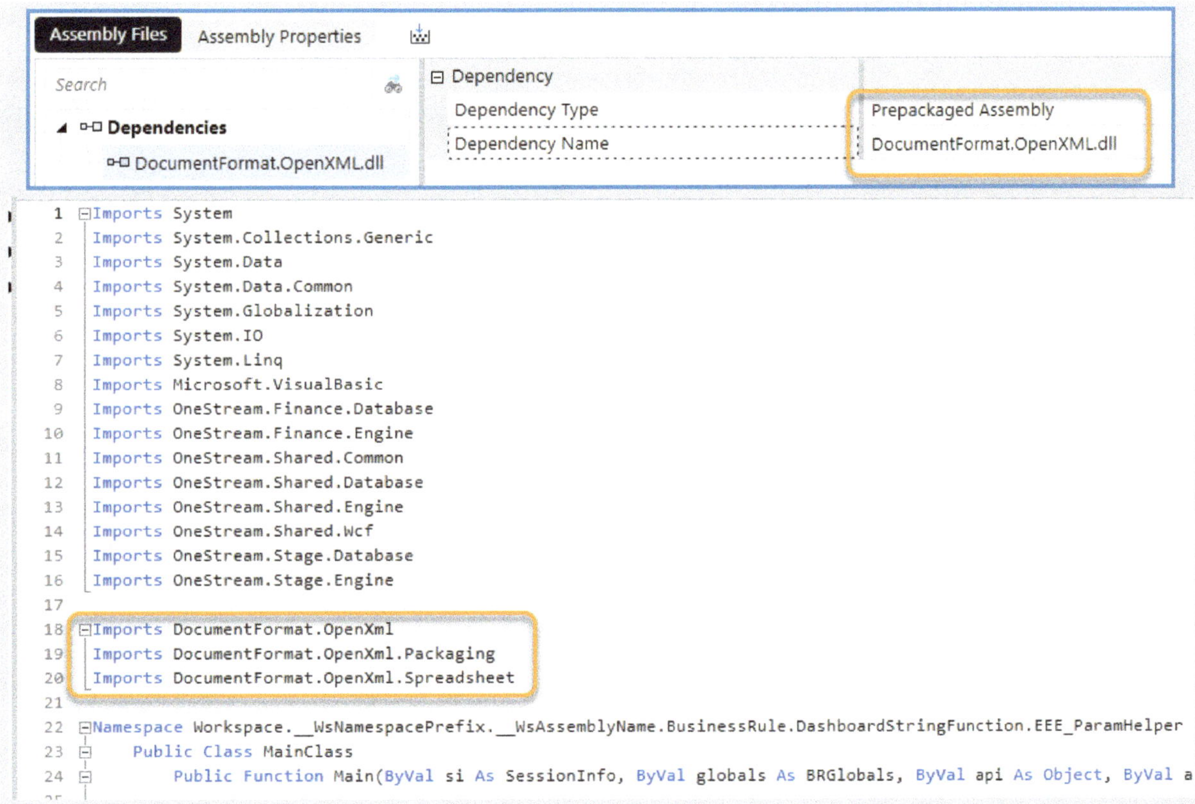

Figure 6.37

Examples of Referencing the Six Types of Assembly Business Rules

To end this chapter on Assembly business rules, I would like to show you examples of these six different business rule source code types and how to invoke them.

- Cube View Extender Business Rules
- Dashboard Data Set Business Rules
- Dashboard Extender Business Rules
- Dashboard String Function Business Rules
- Extensibility Business Rules
- Spreadsheet Business Rules

Cube View Extender Business Rules in Assembly Files

Cube View extender rules are commonly used to fine-tune the formatting of Cube Views. You can write these rules directly on a Cube View, from the Business Rules page, or through Assemblies. These rules run only on the PDF version of the Cube View.

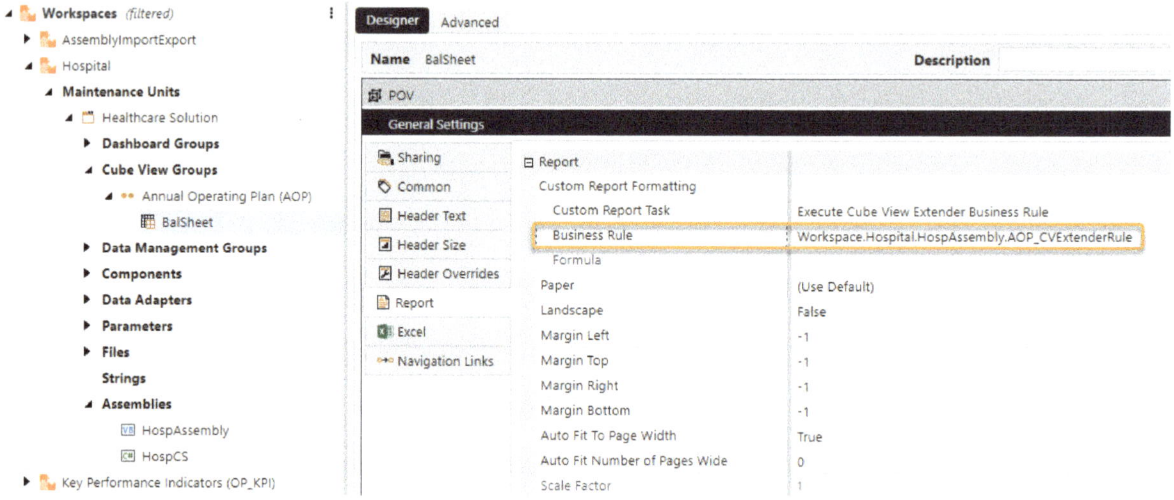

Figure 6.38

To reference a Cube View extender rule that was created as an Assembly, you should set the Cube View Custom Report Task to Execute Cube View Extender Business Rule. Refer to the rule using the following syntax:

Typical syntax for this rule type, written for the traditional Business Rules page, would be:

```
MyCubeViewExtenderRuleName
```

Because this is an Assembly business rule file, it must be modified to this syntax:

```
Workspace.WorkspaceName.AssemblyName.FileName
```

In our example, here is the syntax:

```
Workspace.Hospital.HospAssembly.AOP_CVExtenderRule
```

> **Note:** The ellipsis icon to select a business rule provides the syntax for Cube View extender business rules in Assembly files, but not the individual Assembly files. It still shows the individual traditional business rules present in the central repository Business Rules page.

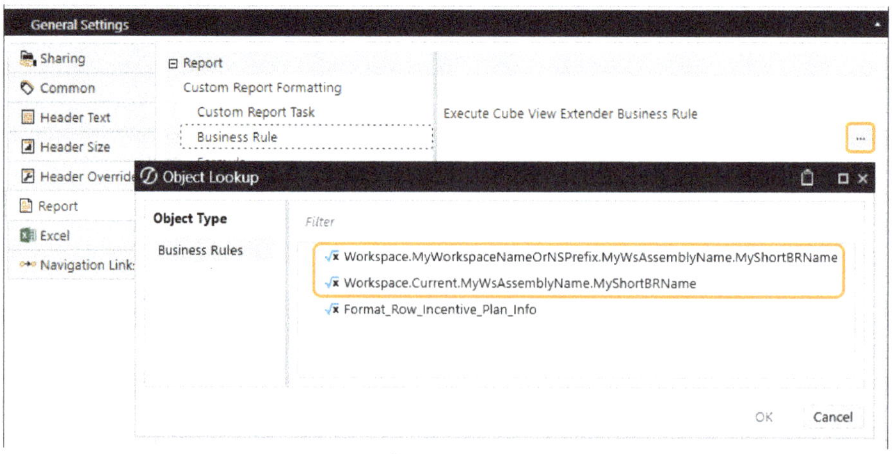

Figure 6.39

Dashboard Data Set Business Rules in Assembly Files

In this example, a method query data adapter is referencing a business rule. However, because this was created as an Assembly file, appropriate syntax must be used.

Typical syntax for this rule type, written for the traditional Business Rules page, would be:

```
{MyDataSetBRName}{DataSetName}{Param1=[MyValue1], Param2=[MyValue2]}
```

Because this is an Assembly business rule file, it must be modified to this syntax:

```
{Workspace.WorkspaceName.AssemblyName.Filename}{DataSetName}{Param1=[M
yValue1], Param2=[MyValue2]}
```

…where `WorkspaceName` can be `Current` or `Namespace Prefix`.

Dashboard Extender Business Rules

In the following example, when a button is clicked, a dashboard extender rule completes the selected Workflow Profile.

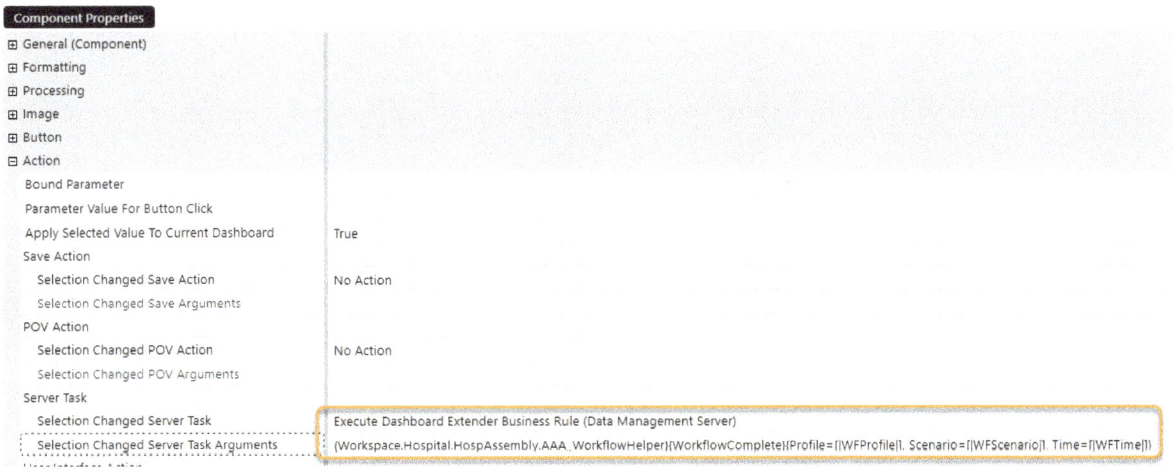

Figure 6.40

Typical syntax for this rule type, written for the traditional Business Rules page, would be:

```
{MyDashboardExtenderBRName}{MyFunction}{Param1=[MyValue1],
Param2=[MyValue2]}
```

Replace this with more specific syntax:

```
{Workspace.WorkspaceName.AssemblyName.Filename}{MyFunction}{Param1=[My
Value1], Param2=[MyValue2]}
```

…where `WorkspaceName` can be `Current` or `Namespace Prefix`.

In our example, here is the syntax:

```
{Workspace.Hospital.HospAssembly.AAA_WorkflowHelper}{WorkflowComplete}
{Profile= [|WFProfile|], Scenario=[|WFScenario|], Time=[|WFTime|]}
```

Dashboard String Function Business Rules

In the following example, we would like to execute an XFBR string function for a button component that returns True or False.

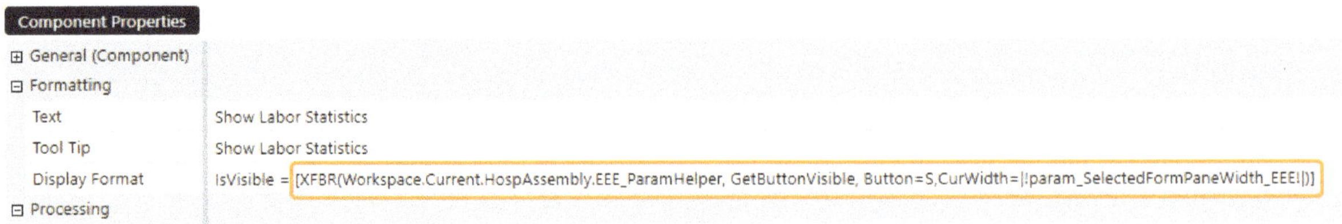

Figure 6.41

Typical syntax for this rule, written for the traditional Business Rules page, would be:

```
XFBR(RuleName,FunctionName,NameValuePairs)
```

Replace this with more specific syntax:

```
XFBR(Workspace.WorkspaceName.AssemblyName.FileName,FunctionName,NameVa
luePairs)
```

…where `WorkspaceName` can be `Current` or `Namespace Prefix`.

In our example, here is the syntax:

```
XFBR(Workspace.Current.HospAssembly.EEE_ParamHelper, GetButtonVisible,
Button=S,CurrWidth=|!param_SelectedFormPaneWidth_EEE!|)
```

Extensibility Business Rules

From the Design and Reference Guide:

Extensibility Rule

- Extensibility rules have these two types: Extender and Event Handlers. Extender rules are the most generalized type of business rule in the OneStream platform. Use these to write a simple utility function or a specific helper function called as part of a data management job. Event Handlers are exclusively called before or after a certain operation occurs within the system.

> **Important:** Full administrator rights are required to edit extensibility rules.

For an extensibility business rule example, please reference the Design and Reference Guide.

- There is an example of an Event Handler that sends an email notification after a ProcessCube event.

Spreadsheet Business Rules

Traditional business rule names are typically chosen by clicking the ellipsis icon in the Spreadsheet. But with Assembly business rules, the ellipsis gives the syntax for referencing the business rule, but not the actual names.

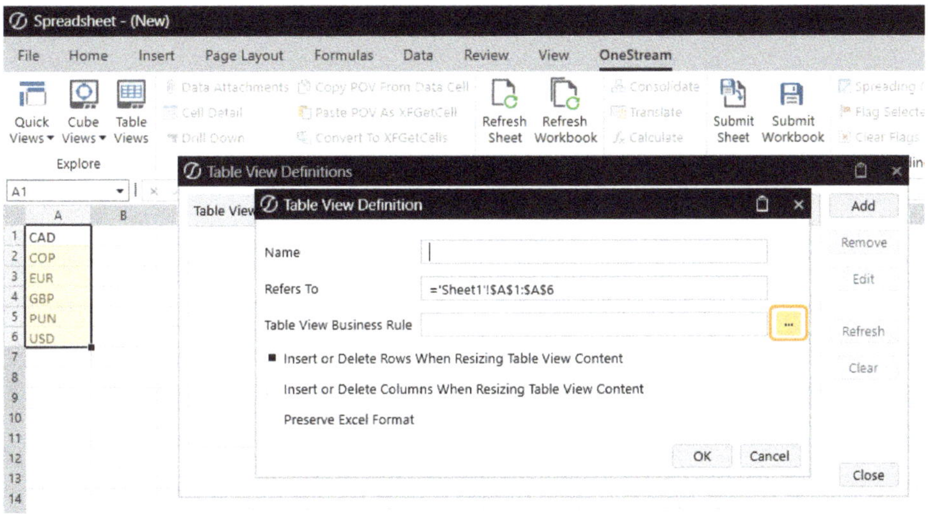

Figure 6.42

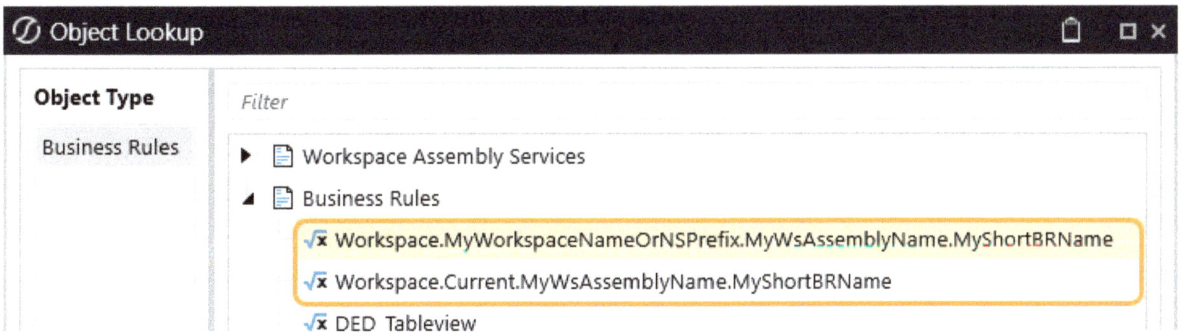

Figure 6.43

Typical syntax for this rule type, written for the traditional Business Rules page, would be:

```
MySpreadsheetRuleName
```

The Spreadsheet Assembly business rule can still be referenced using the business rules syntax:

```
Workspace.WorkspaceName.AssemblyName.FileName
```

…where `WorkspaceName` can be `Current` or `Namespace Prefix`.

In our example, here is the syntax:

```
Workspace.ESG.ESGAssembly.ESGSpreadsheetHelper
```

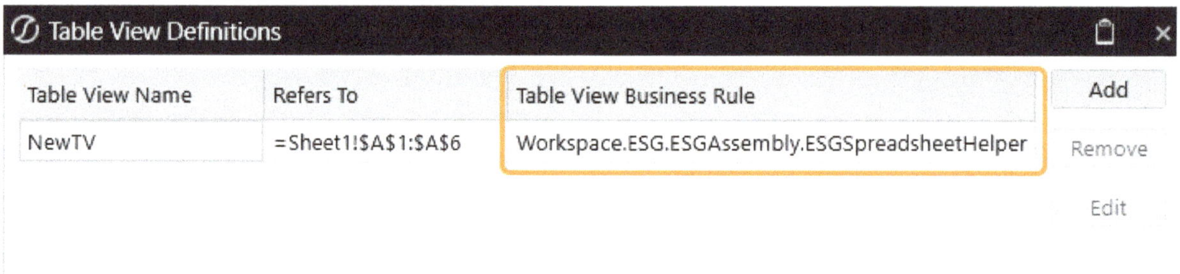

Figure 6.44

Conclusion

As we have explored, transitioning from traditional business rules to Assembly business rules in the Workspace Aware framework is not just straightforward but also beneficial for organizing and maintaining code. By segmenting different code within a Workspace, we can achieve portability, ease of use, and improved performance.

This chapter has provided a step-by-step guide on creating, maintaining, and invoking Assembly business rules, illustrating how these rules serve as a bridge between traditional business rule methods and the more structured Assembly approach. While Assembly business rules offer a seamless transition, they remain a valuable tool that you can continue to use alongside Assembly Services.

In the next chapter, we will delve deeper into Assembly Services, highlighting the key differences and demonstrating how they play a crucial role in handling finance business rules and dynamic content. Remember, the flexibility and adaptability of Assembly business rules allow you to tailor your approach to your specific needs, ensuring a smooth and efficient workflow.

By understanding and leveraging these concepts, you are well-equipped to enhance your OneStream applications and drive greater efficiency and performance in your projects!

7

Managing Assembly Services

Future of Managing Logic and Calculations in OneStream

After I had been working with Assembly business rules for a while, I got to the point of needing to write financial calculations in the Workspace. This led me to work with Assembly Services and service factories, and I am happy to say that I survived the process(!), and I'm thrilled that I made the transition.

Assembly Services not only unlock financial calculations within the Workspace but also provide access to the dynamic functionality that OneStream continues to innovate. This includes features like dynamic dashboards, dynamic dimensions, and dynamic cubes, which enable OneStream to process many operations in-memory for better performance. Beyond these advantages, they bring structure and efficiency to working within a Workspace.

In this chapter, I will attempt to bridge the gap between working in a pre-Workspace environment and working with all of the latest OneStream features, empowering you to take your application to the next level.

Understanding Assembly Services in OneStream

Transitioning to Assembly Services was challenging at first, but the benefits quickly became clear. Let's explore how these benefits come together by breaking down service factories in an easy-to-grasp way. To explain service factories in layman's terms, imagine this:

Assembly Business Rules are like multiple stand-alone stores that each sell only one type of food item. So, if you only need one type of food, this is very efficient, but to go grocery shopping for the week, you need to visit multiple stores to get all the different types of food you need (very inefficient).

A **Service Factory** is like a supermarket grocery store. When you enter and ask the worker which section has bread, she points you to the bakery section. If you ask about getting chicken, she points you to the butchery section, and so on. Now, all your grocery shopping needs are met in one place, even though there are different sections within the supermarket.

In this analogy, the supermarket represents the Service Factory, which centralizes and organizes the various services (or sections) you need, making the process more efficient and user-friendly.

From a more technical perspective, Assembly Services and service factories are designed to enhance flexibility and modularity in managing business rules and operations. A Service Factory acts as a dispatcher, routing requests to the right service for the task – whether it's managing dashboards, processing financial calculations, or executing data steps. This structure allows organizations to centralize operations, tailor services to specific contexts (such as weekday vs. weekend workflows), and streamline complex workflows with ease.

How Assembly Services Eliminate the Need for Explicit File References

In the case of Assembly Services, you no longer need to specify the file name where the code resides, as you would with traditional business rules or Assembly business rules. This concept was initially confusing for me because it wasn't clear how OneStream knew which code to execute without explicitly referencing a file.

After discussing this with a very knowledgeable colleague, Jerome Marcq, I came to understand that the system determines the correct code to run based on the context of the call. The location from which the code is invoked informs the Service Factory about the type of service requested. This eliminates the need to specify the exact Assembly file, as the Service Factory seamlessly routes the request to the correct service.

Here are three practical examples that showcase how the Service Factory routes requests based on different types of rules, ensuring each one is directed to the appropriate destination.

Example 1: Data Management Step – Custom Calculate

For a data management step defined with a Step Type of Custom Calculate, you only need to specify which Workspace to use. The system then automatically refers to the **Workspace Service Factory** to locate the Assembly service file for the **Financial Custom Calculate** service type and executes the required function. There's no need to explicitly point the data management job to a specific Assembly file – the Service Factory already knows where to route the request.

Figure 7.1 is an example of syntax within a data management step that references the Workspace, but not a specific business rule.

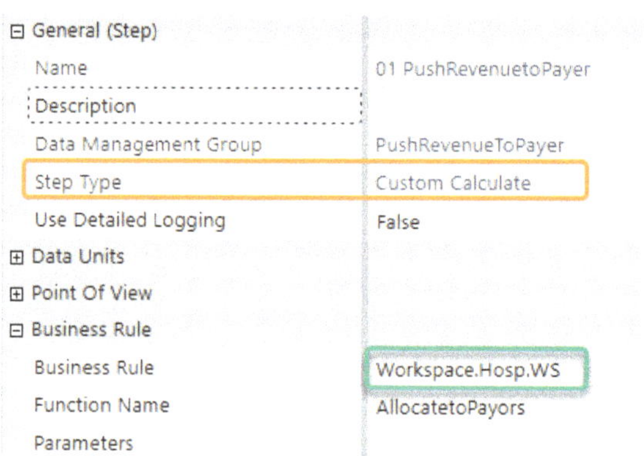

Figure 7.1

Figure 7.2 is a flow chart of how OneStream routes the request to the Service Factory and the factory routes that call to the appropriate Finance CustomCalc service file.

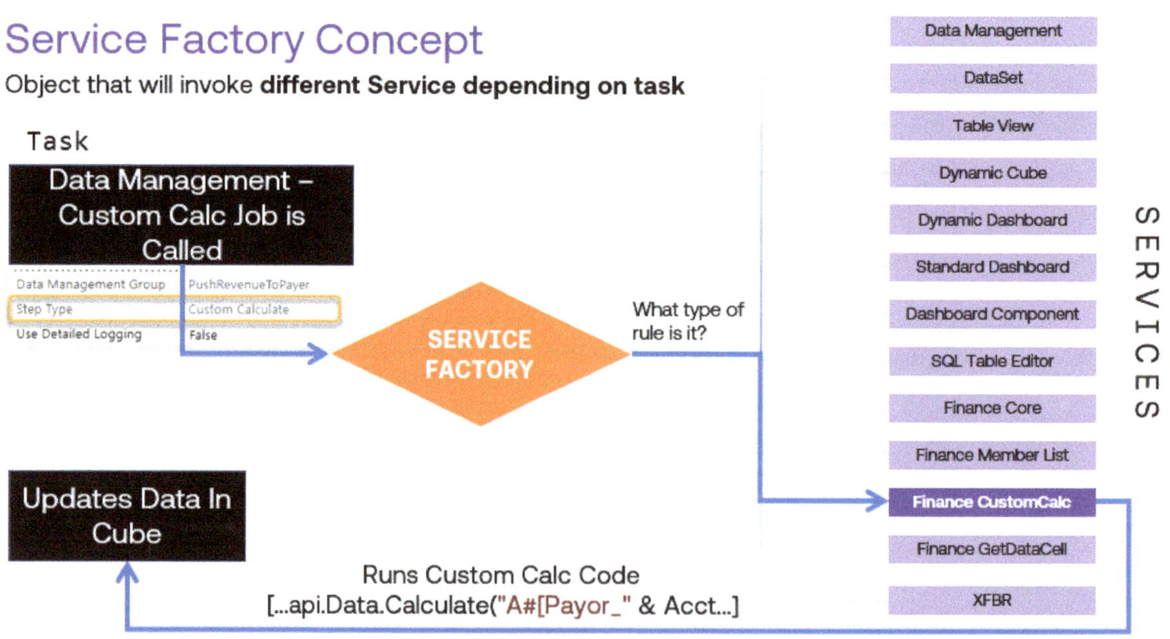

Figure 7.2

Example 2: Dashboard Extender Code Request

Let's now consider a different scenario: routing a dashboard extender code request.

When executing a server task with the Execute Dashboard Extender Business Rule option within a Cube View dashboard component, you simply indicate that the system should look in the current Workspace. From there, the system consults the Workspace Service Factory to locate the appropriate dashboard extender service file. This process occurs seamlessly, with the Service Factory routing the request to the correct service without requiring you to specify the exact name of the file.

Figure 7.3 is an example of syntax within a dashboard component that references the Workspace, but not a business rule.

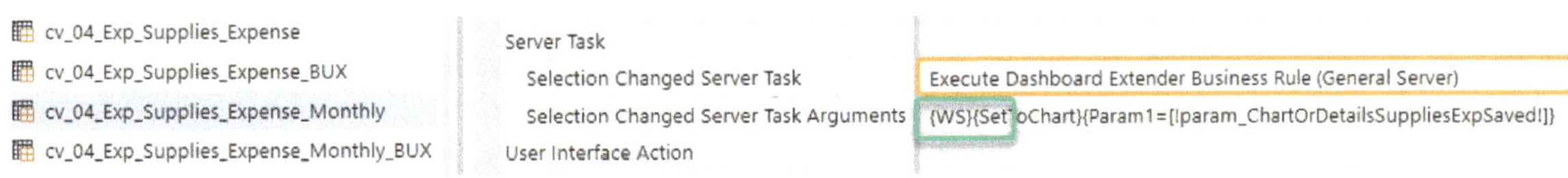

Figure 7.3

Figure 7.4 is a flow chart of how OneStream routes this request to the Service Factory and the factory routes that call to the appropriate dashboard component service file.

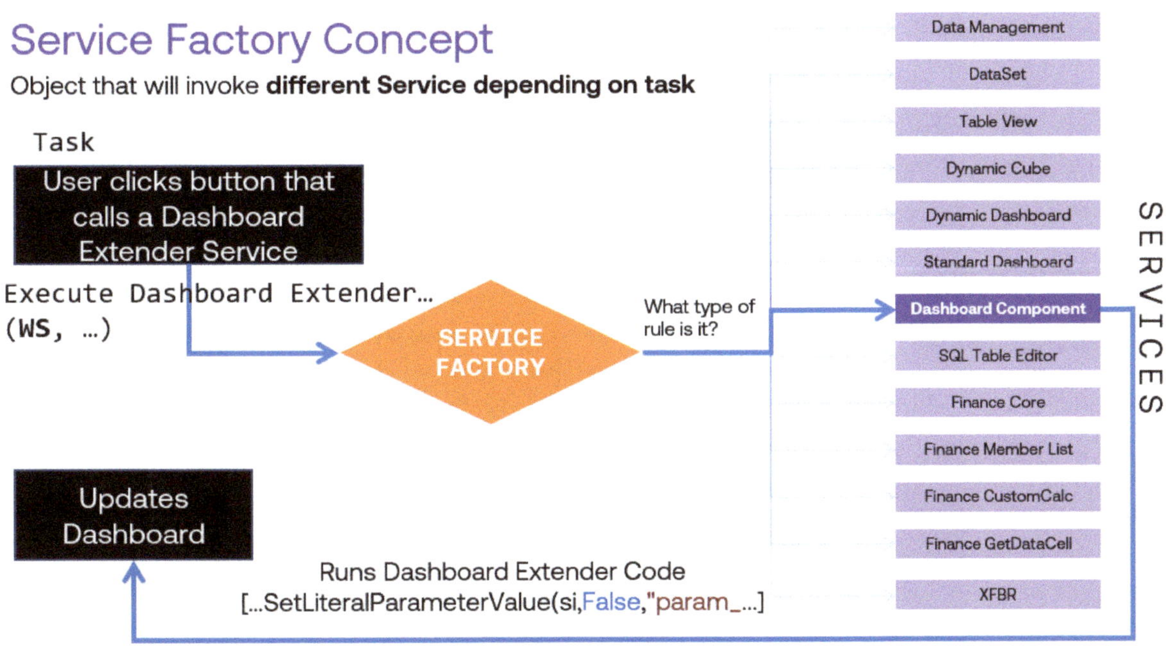

Figure 7.4

Example 3: XFBR String Function Called

Finally, let's consider a different scenario: routing an XFBR string code request.

An XFBR string function dynamically returns a text value to any OneStream setting that can accept a parameter. These rules provide enhanced flexibility compared to standard parameters or substitution variables, as they use code to generate string outputs for dashboards, Cube Views, and extensible documents. When you invoke an XFBR function and designate the current Workspace, the system automatically queries the Workspace Service Factory to locate the necessary XFBR string service file. As with the other examples, there is no need to reference the file by name – the Service Factory handles the request routing seamlessly.

Figure 7.5 is an example of syntax within an XFBR function that references the Workspace, but not a business rule.

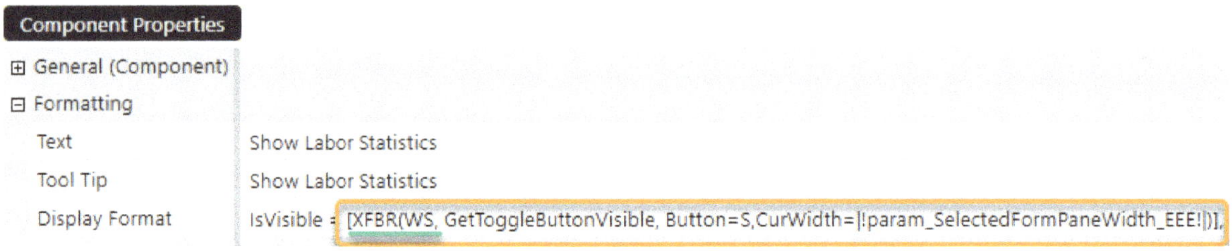

Figure 7.5

Figure 7.6 is a flow chart of how OneStream routes this request to the Service Factory and the factory routes that call to the appropriate XFBR string service file.

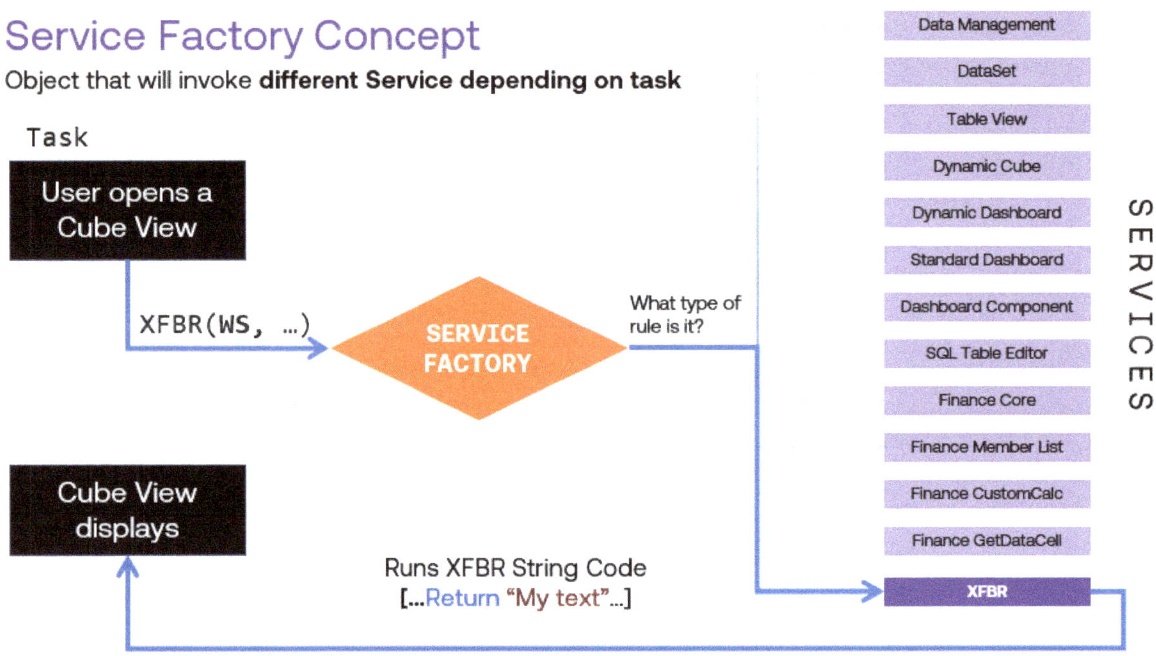

Figure 7.6

Now that we've looked at these three examples, here is a reminder of the number of services available as of version 9.0, and the transition from traditional business rules to these Assembly Services.

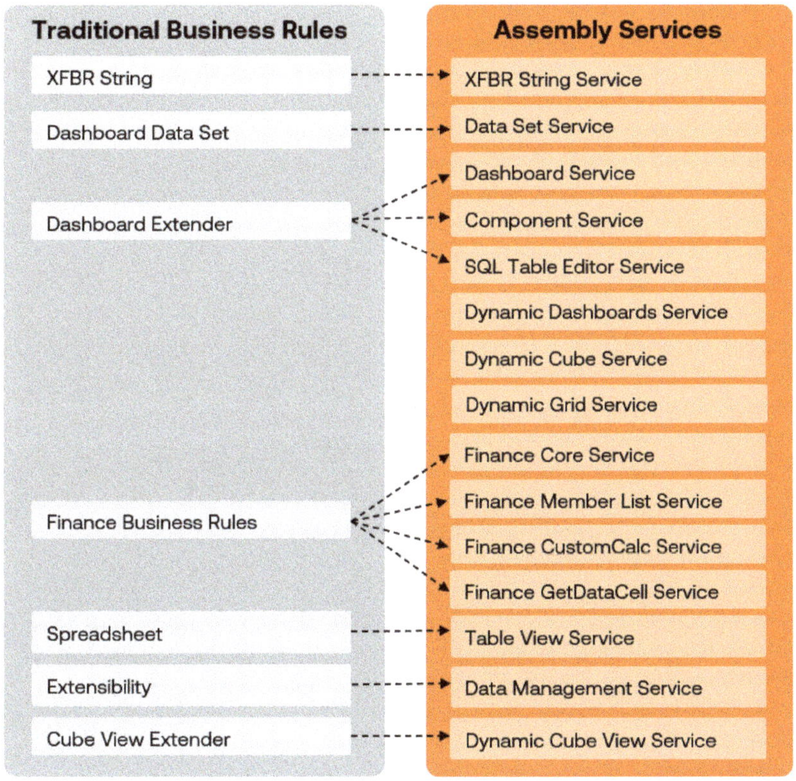

Figure 7.7

Before we move on to the details of how to set all of this up, here is an example of a comprehensive Service Factory that can route requests to multiple Assembly Services. Notice how the `Case` statement identifies the specific `WsAssemblyType` being called and determines the corresponding `Assembly Service` file. This approach ensures the appropriate service is executed based on the type of request.

> **Note:** By default, a service file contains the declaration of a class of the same name. While you can rename both independently, it's good practice to keep them aligned. What matters is the name of the class included in the file.
>
> It's important to remember that the names of the Assembly service classes must align exactly with the references in the Service Factory calls. While you can name these files and classes whatever you prefer, maintaining consistency between the class names and their references in the Service Factory is crucial for proper functionality.

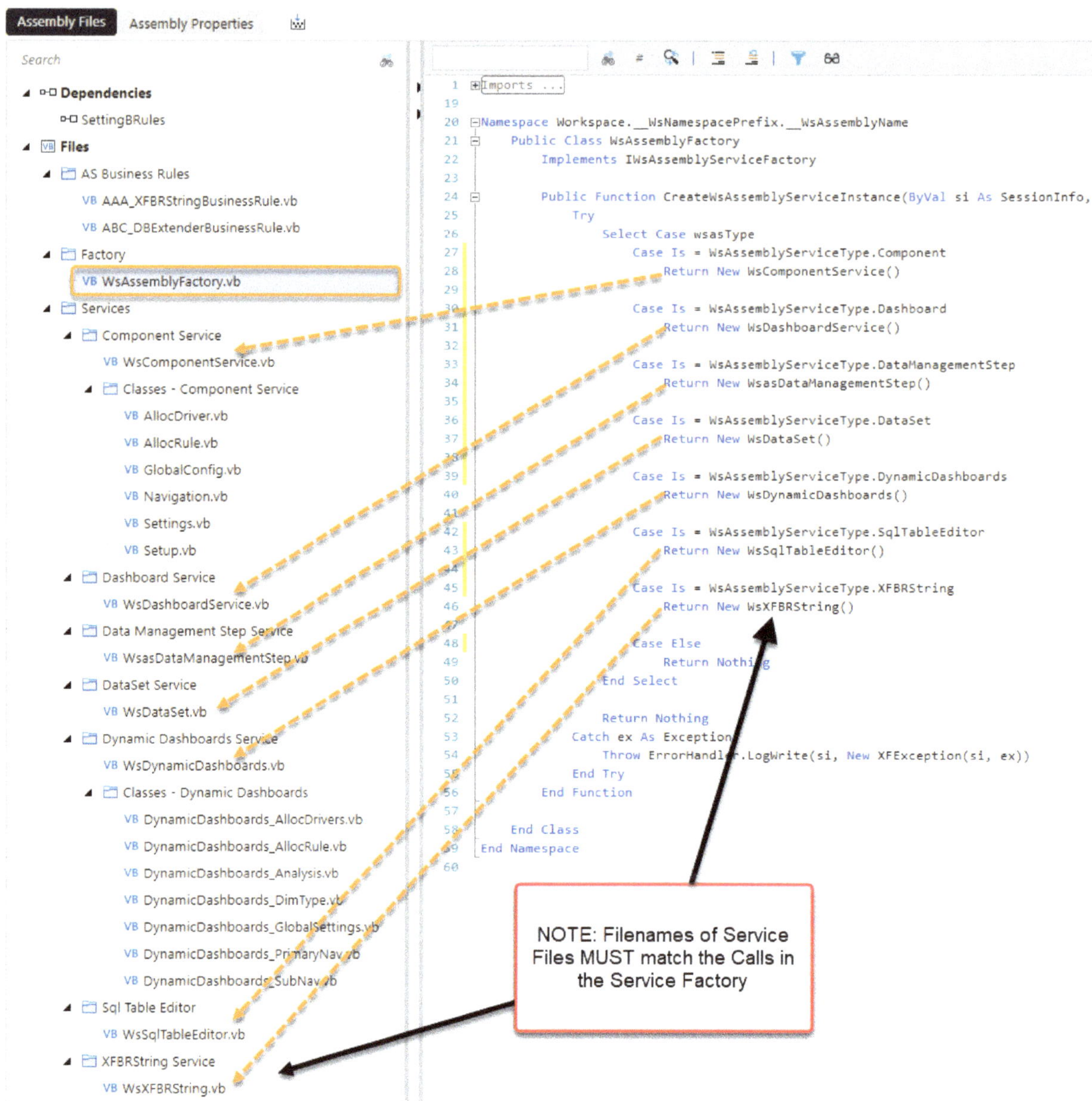

Figure 7.8

We should now have a good reference point of how Assembly Services are routed from an Assembly Service Factory, so let's dive into some specific steps of how service factories and service files are configured.

Setting up the Service Factory

Now that we understand the Service Factory is the gatekeeper for Assembly service files, we're going to walk through the process of setting one up.

It's important to note that you don't need to include all service types within a Service Factory – you can include just one if that's all you need for a particular maintenance unit's services.

The most critical requirement when creating a Service Factory is ensuring that the ServiceFile referenced in the `Return New ServiceFile()` statement matches the ServiceFile name exactly. Any mismatch will result in errors.

At its core, the Service Factory contains a function that returns a class based on the **AssemblyType** of the call's origin. While the code structure is relatively simple, there are a few key points to keep in mind:

- If you call a ServiceType in the factory, there must be a corresponding Assembly service file (and therefore class) created and enabled for compiling.
- If the file and class don't exist or are disabled for compiling, the Service Factory won't know where to retrieve the service, causing errors – even if you aren't directly calling that service type.
- If the names do not match, this is the same as the reference not existing, and this will cause errors.

> **Best Practice Suggestion:** *Organize your folder structure.* It is wise to set up a structured folder system when creating a new Assembly, as you won't be able to move files into different folders after they are created. The more organization you put into your Assembly, the easier it will be to maintain good, clean code.

A great example of a full and robust Assembly that has a nice, structured folder strategy is from the Assembly that was used above in Figure 7.8. Here, we have folders for Assembly business rules, service factories, services, individual services, and classes within the services. Here is a cleaner image of that Assembly structure (Figure 7.9):

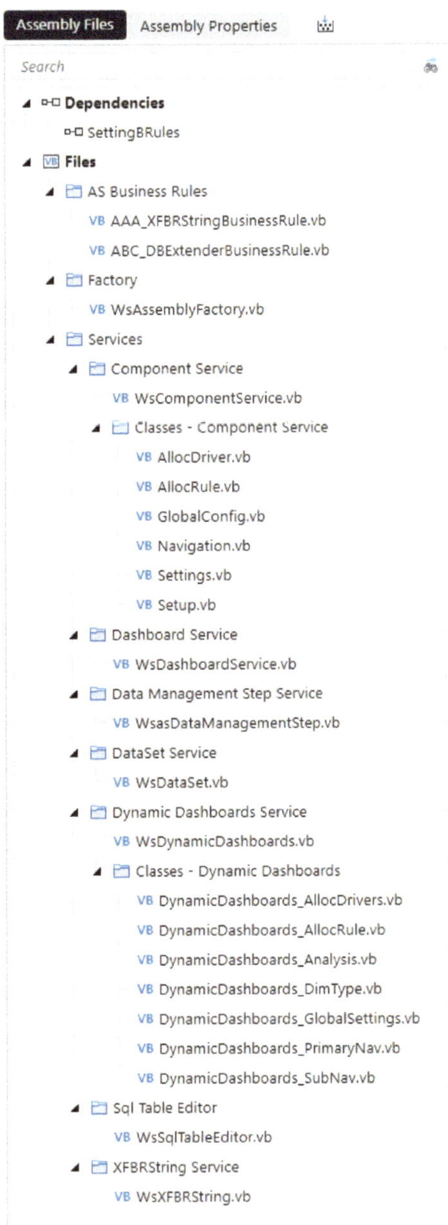

Figure 7.9

Step-by-Step Guide to Creating a Service Factory

In this next section, we will create a sample Service Factory, a component service file, and a standard class file to highlight the nuances of Assembly Services.

Summary of Steps:

1. Create the folder structure that you will need.
2. Create the Service Factory.
3. Open the Assembly service type in the Service Factory file.
4. Create the Assembly service file that corresponds to the Assembly service type (with exactly the same name).
5. Create a standard class file that the service file calls.

Steps with screenshots:

1. Create the folder structure that you will need.

It is important to have a general structure in mind when you start to keep these files well organized. Typically, I have folders for the factory, all services, individual services, and classes that the services will call.

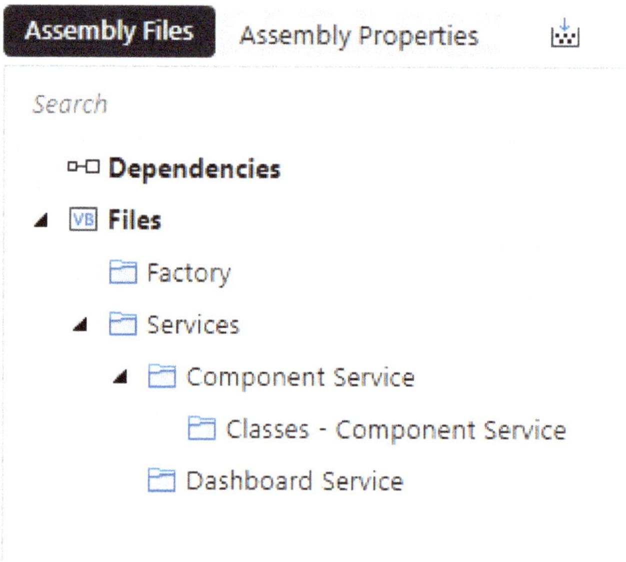

Figure 7.10

2. Create the Service Factory.

When you create the Service Factory file, right-click on the folder you want the factory file to reside in and select Service Factory as the Source Code Type:

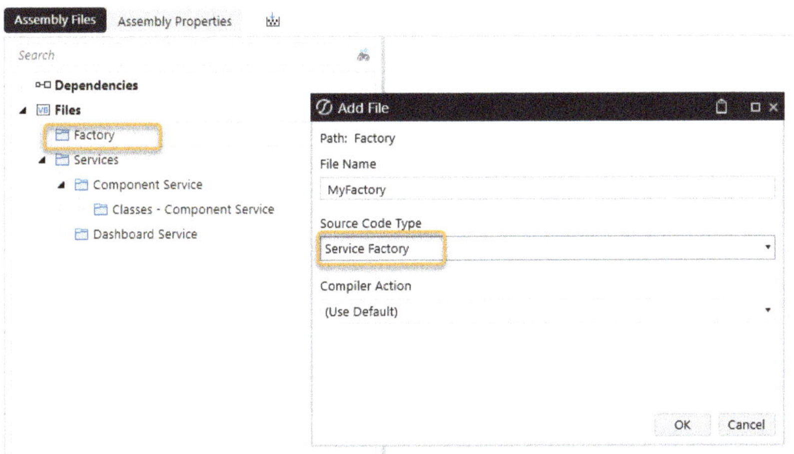

Figure 7.11

This file will be prepopulated with all of the `AssemblyServiceTypes` (these service types will continue to be expanded when new services are introduced), but the code is commented out as a starting point.

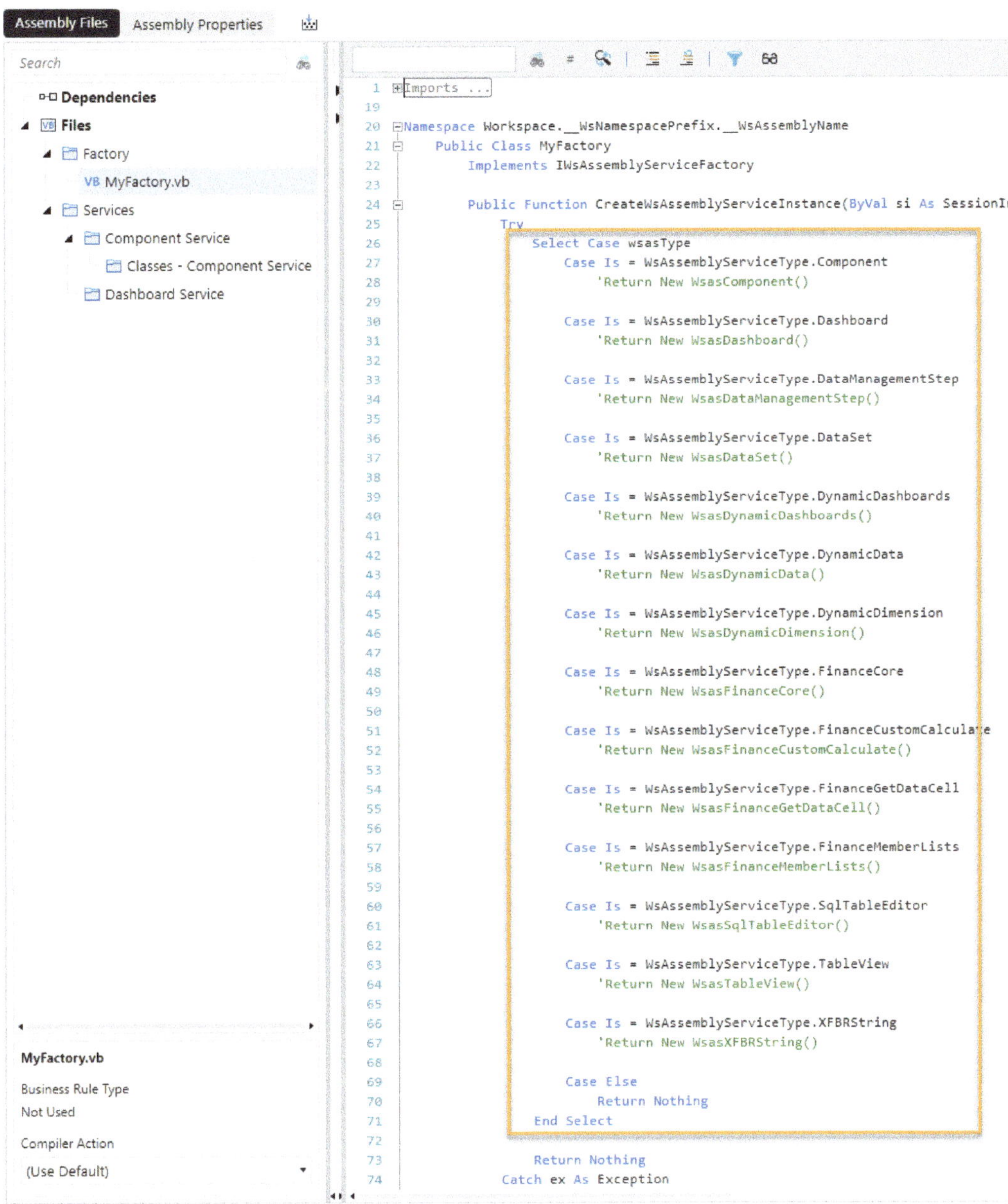

Figure 7.12

3. Open the Assembly service type in the Service Factory file.

To open up any of the service types, uncomment the appropriate line and give the `Return` value a name you would like for your corresponding service file.

From this:

```
    Select Case wsasType
        Case Is = WsAssemblyServiceType.Component
            'Return New WsasComponent()
```

Figure 7.13

To this:

```
Select Case wsasType
    Case Is = WsAssemblyServiceType.Component
        Return New EricsComponentService()
```

Figure 7.14

> **Warning:** If you open up a `ServiceType` and you don't have a matching Assembly service file, you will get errors when you try to run the Assembly factory and when you compile the Assembly, like below (Figure 7.15):

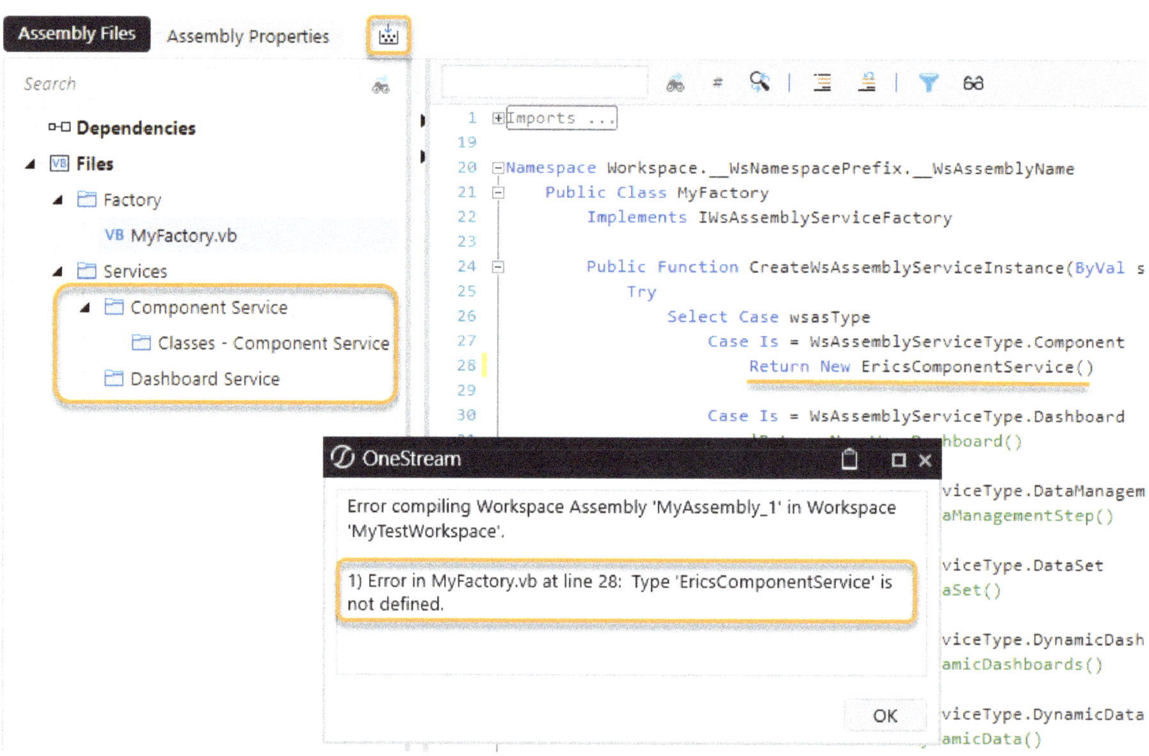

Figure 7.15

4. Create the Assembly service file that corresponds to the Assembly service type (with exactly the same name).

Right-click on the folder in which you would like the file to be placed and Add File. Add a component service file with the same name you chose in the Service Factory.

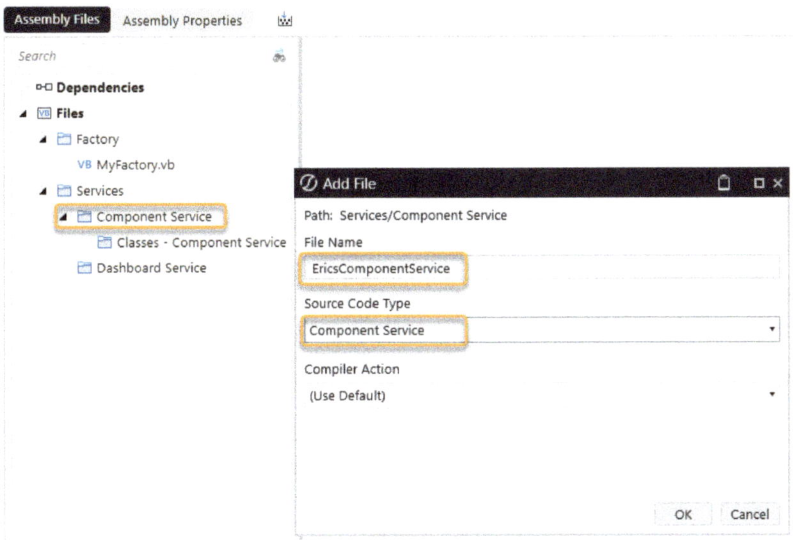

Figure 7.16

The service file will be prepopulated with pertinent libraries and classes. As we discussed in Chapter 5, a `Public Class` is created with the name of the file. This `Public Class` is how the Service Factory is able to call this file and run the code defined here.

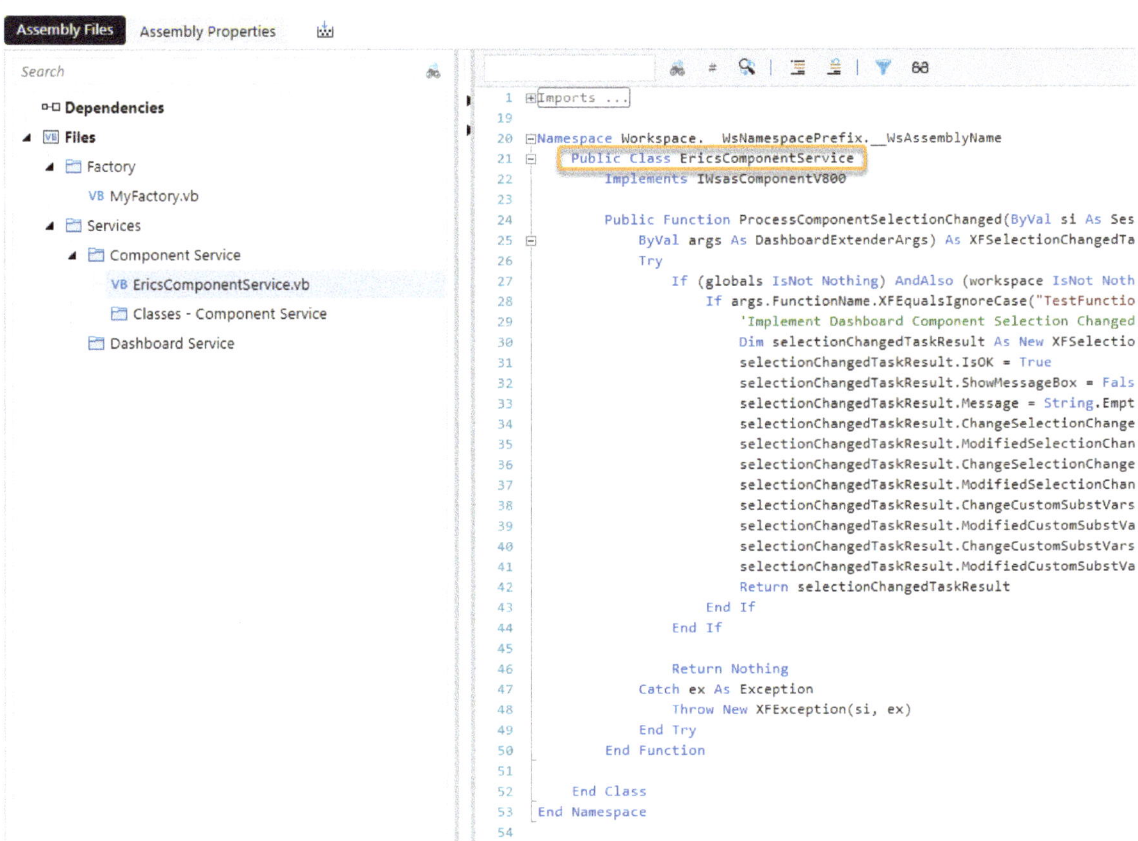

Figure 7.17

5. Create a standard class file that the service file calls.

Now, let's create a standard class file and demonstrate how to reference it from the component service file. This will showcase how modular design helps you organize and manage your code in smaller, more efficient pieces. To start, right-click on the folder where you would like the file to be placed, then select Add File and select Standard Class as the Source Code Type.

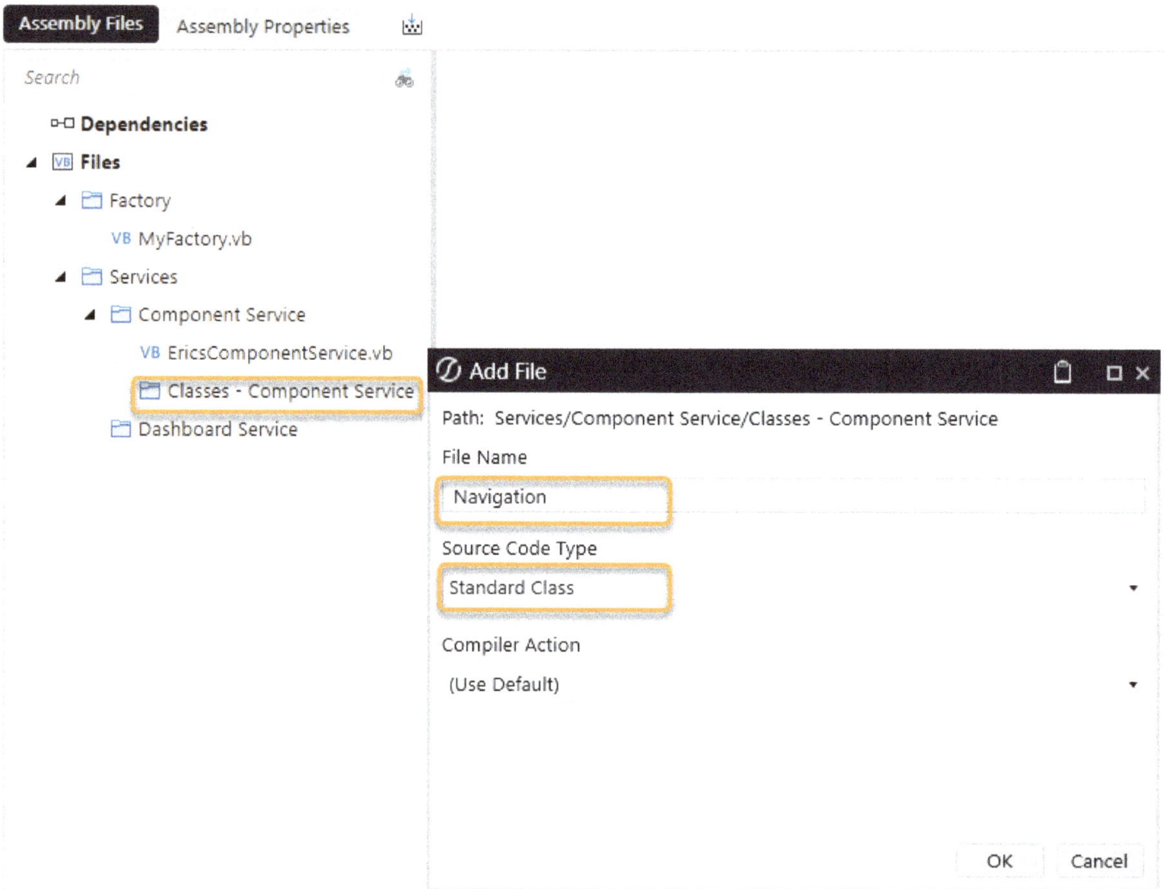

Figure 7.18

This file is defined as a public class that our other service files can use:

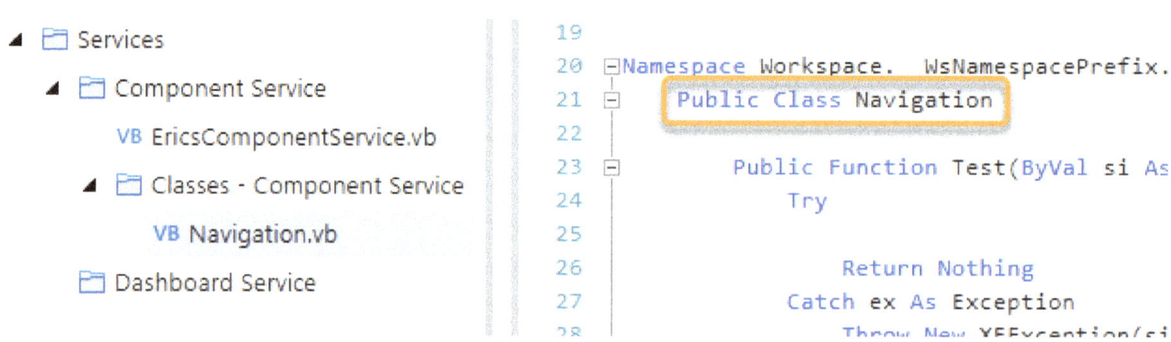

Figure 7.19

Finally, let's see how we call this new class in our service file. Because there is now a file with a `Public Class` called `Navigation`, we can create a new object from the `Navigation` class.

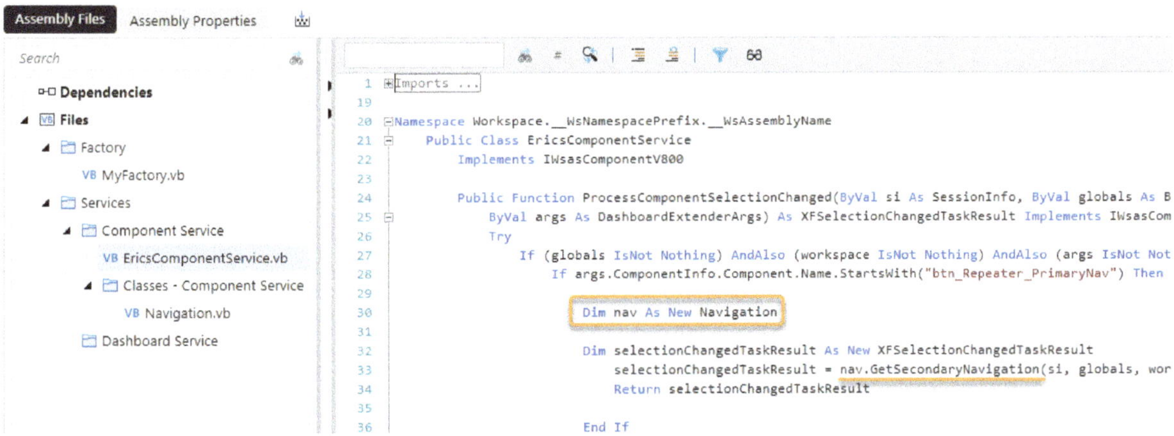

Figure 7.20

This example demonstrates how a structured approach to creating service factories, service files, and class files ensures better organization, scalability, and maintainability of your code.

Now that we've walked through the process of setting up a Service Factory, let's shift our focus to how service calls are managed and routed using OneStream's built-in mechanisms.

Invoking Assembly Services: WS vs WSMU vs Implicit

A critical part of using Assembly Services effectively is understanding the routing mechanisms provided by WS and WSMU. These tools determine how service calls are handled, ensuring that the correct Service Factory processes each request based on its scope and context.

When it comes to calling your Service Factory, WS (Workspace Service) and WSMU (Workspace Maintenance Unit) are used in different scenarios to control how and where service calls are routed. Let's break this down:

Workspace Service (WS)

- **Definition:** WS references the Service Factory specified at the Workspace level. It looks for the Service Factory specified on the Workspace that contains the object. If the Service Factory isn't defined at this level, the call will fail.
- **Use Case:** Use WS when the object you're working with has a broader scope across the Workspace, and you want the Workspace's Service Factory to handle the service call.

Workspace Maintenance Unit (WSMU)

- **Definition:** WSMU references the Service Factory specified at the maintenance unit level. It looks for the Service Factory specified on the maintenance unit that contains the object. If the Service Factory isn't defined at this level, it will search at the Workspace level. If it still can't find the Service Factory, the call will fail.
- **Use Case:** Use WSMU when the object is more granularly scoped within a specific maintenance unit, and you want that specific unit's Service Factory to handle the service call.

Inplicit

- **Definition:** Certain tools, like dynamic dashboards, do not use WS or WSMU as they implicitly look up the chain. On opening a dynamic dashboard, OneStream will look for a Service Factory with a Dynamic Dashboard Service by first looking at the maintenance unit, then at the Workspace.

- **Use Case:** Dynamic dashboards require you to provide a Service Factory either at the maintenance unit or the Workspace.

Let's explore where these settings are defined with some examples of setting the Workspace Service Factory (WS) vs the Workspace Maintenance Unit Service Factory (WSMU):

The Workspace Service Factory (WS) is defined in the Workspace Properties as Workspace Assembly Service. Figure 7.21 illustrates how the Assembly Service Factory MyAssembly_2.MyServiceFactory_2 will be called when the WS is invoked.

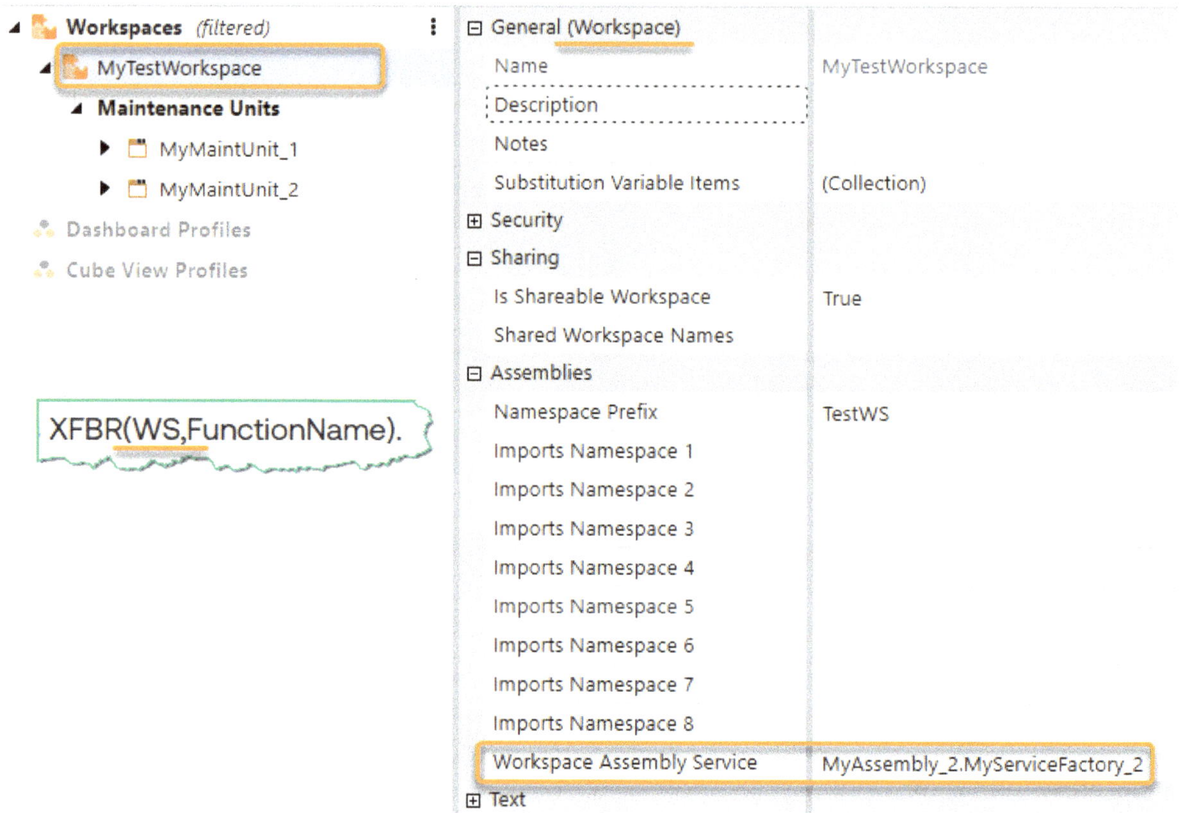

Figure 7.21

The Workspace Maintenance Unit Service Factory (WSMU) is defined in the Maintenance Unit Properties as Workspace Assembly Service. Figure 7.22 shows how the Assembly Service Factory MyAssembly_1.MyServiceFactory_1 is called when the "WSMU" is invoked.

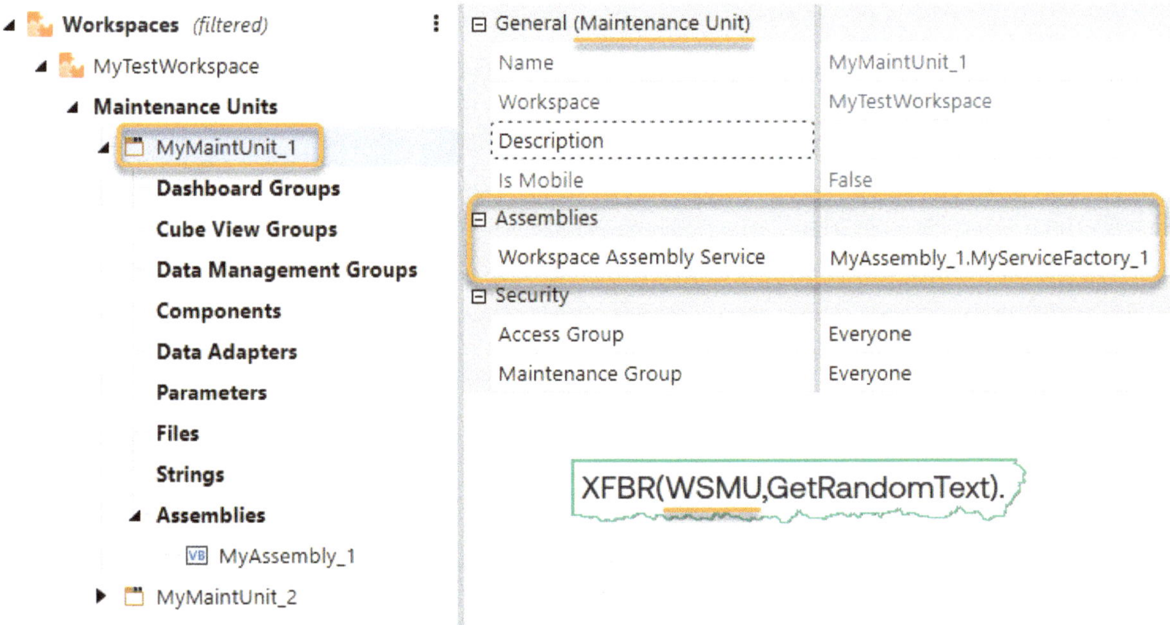

Figure 7.22

Syntax Conventions for Calling Assembly Services

Now, let's address a potentially confusing aspect: each service type in OneStream has unique syntax restrictions that govern how it can be called, which can sometimes be confusing. Below are the syntax conventions you need to understand:

- `{WS,..}` : Called when the object calling the service is in the same Workspace.
- `{WSMU,…}` : Called when the object calling the service is in the same maintenance unit.
- `{Workspace.xxxx.WS,…}` : Syntax to explicitly call a different Workspace.
- `{Workspace.xxxx.yyyy.WSMU,…}` : Syntax to explicitly call a different Workspace and/or maintenance unit.

In these examples:

- `xxxx` represents either the `workspaceName`, `workspaceNamePrefix`, or `"Current"` if the object is in the same Workspace.
- `yyyy` represents either the `maintenanceUnitName` or `"Current"` if the object is in the same maintenance unit.

It's also important to note the distinctions between the various **enclosure symbols** you may encounter in the syntax:

- **Curly brackets** `{ }` : Used to enclose certain routing instructions for Service Factory calls.
- **Parentheses** `( )` : Used to encapsulate parameters for functions, such as XFBR.
- **Square brackets** `[ ]` : Commonly used in Cube View syntax to reference member lists or functions.
- In some cases, no enclosure symbols are required, depending on the context and the service type being invoked.

Understanding and correctly applying these syntax conventions ensures the accurate routing of service requests and minimizes configuration errors.

Comparison of Syntax Restrictions for Different Service Types

Now that we've outlined the general syntax conventions, I'd like to compare and contrast how these conventions apply to different service types, using **XFBR** and **Finance GetDataCell** services as the two examples to make the point of differing syntax requirements.

XFBR Service Syntax

XFBR rules allow for multiple flexible syntax options, such as:

- `XFBR(Workspace.workspaceName.maintenanceUnitName.WSMU,MyStringFunction)`
- `XFBR(Workspace.workspaceName.WS,MyStringFunction)`
- `XFBR(Workspace.Current.maintenanceUnitName.WSMU,MyStringFunction)`
- `XFBR(Workspace.Current.Current.WSMU,MyStringFunction)`
- `XFBR(Workspace.Current.WS,MyStringFunction)`
- `XFBR(WS,MyStringFunction)`
- `XFBR(WSMU,MyStringFunction)`

Finance GetDataCell Service Syntax:

In contrast, the Finance GetDataCell service type has stricter syntax requirements. It mandates the explicit inclusion of both the `workspaceName` and `maintenanceUnitName`. You cannot simplify this by relying on just the Workspace or the "Current" keywords. For example:

```
GetDataCell("BR#
[Workspace.workspaceName.maintenanceUnitName.WSMU,MyDataCellFunction]")
```

The ultimate purpose of these different syntax methods is to ensure that OneStream can find the correct Assembly service, regardless of the context in which the spreadsheet is opened (within a dashboard of that maintenance unit or in Excel on a local computer). Because OneStream supports a variety of business rule types, each service type has tailored syntax to fit its specific use case and operational context.

Due to these nuances, I will provide a detailed list of every service type along with its syntax requirements in subsequent sections.

Detailed Syntax for all 13 Assembly Services

This section should be a good reference guide for you when making calls for an Assembly service. I hope these references and examples will help save you time as you learn the nuances of the Assembly Services approach within Workspaces.

Here are the syntax requirements for the current list of Assembly Services, in no particular order. I've also included a screenshot of where these are referenced in OneStream:

XFBR String Service

Note: This is called from anywhere within any OneStream setting that can accept a parameter.

- `XFBR(Workspace.workspaceName.maintenanceUnitName.WSMU,MyStringFunction)`
- `XFBR(Workspace.workspaceName.WS,MyStringFunction)`
- `XFBR(Workspace.Current.maintenanceUnitName.WSMU,MyStringFunction)`
- `XFBR(Workspace.Current.Current.WSMU,MyStringFunction)`
- `XFBR(Workspace.Current.WS,MyStringFunction)`
- `XFBR(WS,MyStringFunction)`

- `XFBR(WSMU,MyStringFunction)`

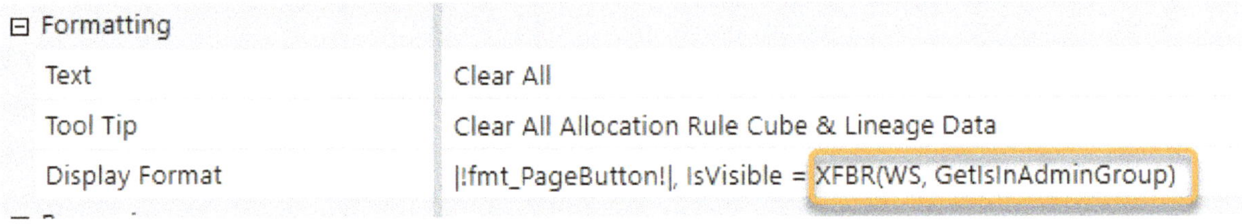

Figure 7.23

Data Set Services [Method Queries on Data Adapters]

Note: This is called from a data adapter object within a Workspace.

- `{WS}{DataSetName}{Parameter1=Value1}`
- `{WSMU}{DataSetName}{Parameter1=Value1}`

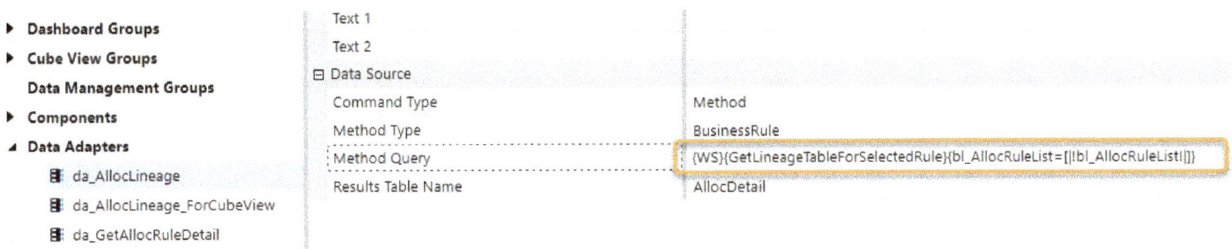

Figure 7.24

Dashboard Service [Execute Dashboard Extender Rule (General Server)]

Note: This is called from a dashboard object.

- `{Workspace.workspaceName.maintenanceUnitName.WSMU}{DBFunction}{Param="input"}`
- `{Workspace.workspaceName.WS}{DBFunction}{Param="input"}`
- `{Workspace.Current.maintenanceUnitName.WSMU}{DBFunction}{Param="input"}`
- `{Workspace.Current.Current.WSMU}{DBFunction}{Param="input"}`
- `{Workspace.Current.WS}{DBFunction}{Param="input"}`
- `{WS}{DBFunction}{Param="input"}`
- `{WSMU}{DBFunction}{Param="input"}`

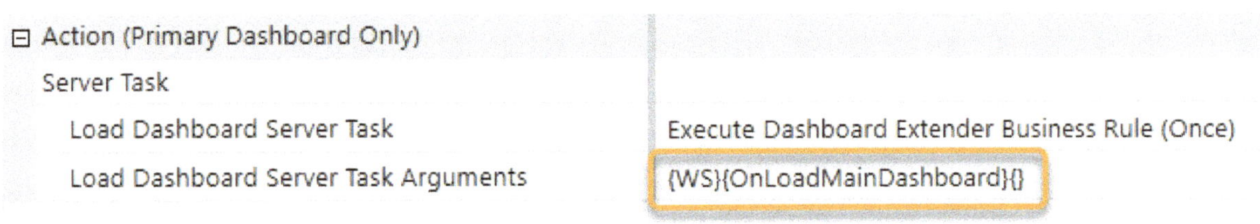

Figure 7.25

Component Service [Execute Dashboard Extender Rule (General Server)]

Note: This is called from a dashboard component, like a button, combo box, CV, etc.

- {Workspace.workspaceName.maintenanceUnitName.WSMU}{DBFunction}{Param=“input”}
- {Workspace.workspaceName.WS}{DBFunction}{Param=“input”}
- {Workspace.Current.maintenanceUnitName.WSMU}{DBFunction}{Param=“input”}
- {Workspace.Current.Current.WSMU}{DBFunction}{Param=“input”}
- {Workspace.Current.WS}{DBFunction}{Param=“input”}
- {WS}{DBFunction}{Param=“input”}
- {WSMU}{DBFunction}{Param=“input”}

Figure 7.26

SQL Table Editor Service [Execute Dashboard Extender Rule]

Note: This is called from a SQL table editor component.

- {Workspace.workspaceName.maintenanceUnitName.WSMU}{SQLFunction}{Param=“input”}
- {Workspace.workspaceName.WS}{SQLFunction}{Param=“input”}
- {Workspace.Current.maintenanceUnitName.WSMU}{SQLFunction}{Param=“input”}
- {Workspace.Current.Current.WSMU}{SQLFunction}{Param=“input”}
- {Workspace.Current.WS}{SQLFunction}{Param=“input”}
- {WS}{SQLFunction}{Param=“input”}
- {WSMU}{SQLFunction}{Param=“input”}

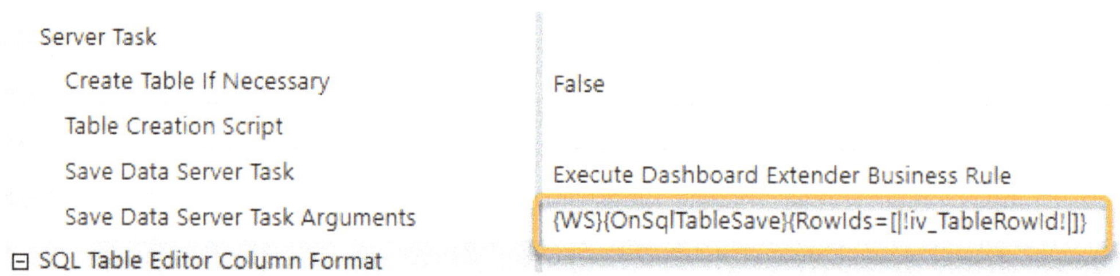

Figure 7.27

Dynamic Dashboard Service [Embedded Dynamic Dashboard Type]

Note: This is called when a dashboard of the type Embedded Dynamic is called.

- Implicit reference so no syntax for WS or WSMU – Dashboard Type = Embedded Dynamic will trigger this service when the dashboard is called.
- We will discuss this further in Chapter 8.

Figure 7.28

Dynamic Cube Service

Note: This is called when a cube with dynamic source data is called from an Assembly service.

- `Workspace.workspaceName.WS "Current" is not allowed`

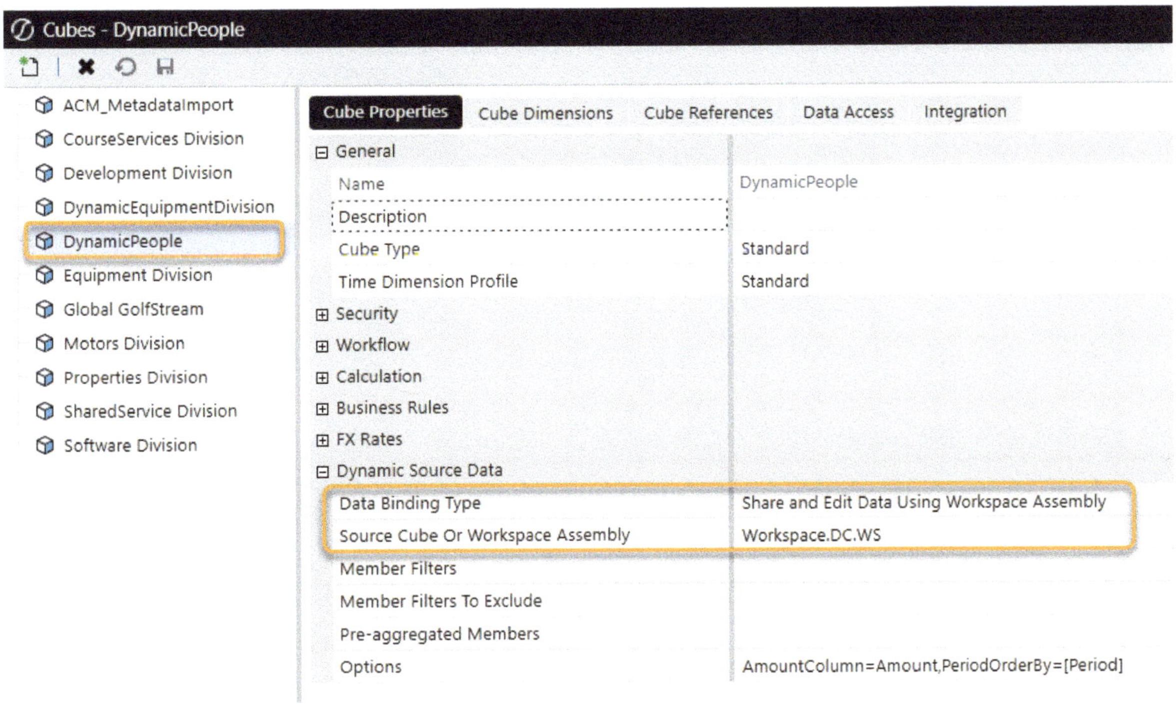

Figure 7.29

Finance Core Service [Cube Business Rules]

Note: This is called from the business rules of a cube.

- `Workspace.workspaceName.WS "Current" is not allowed`

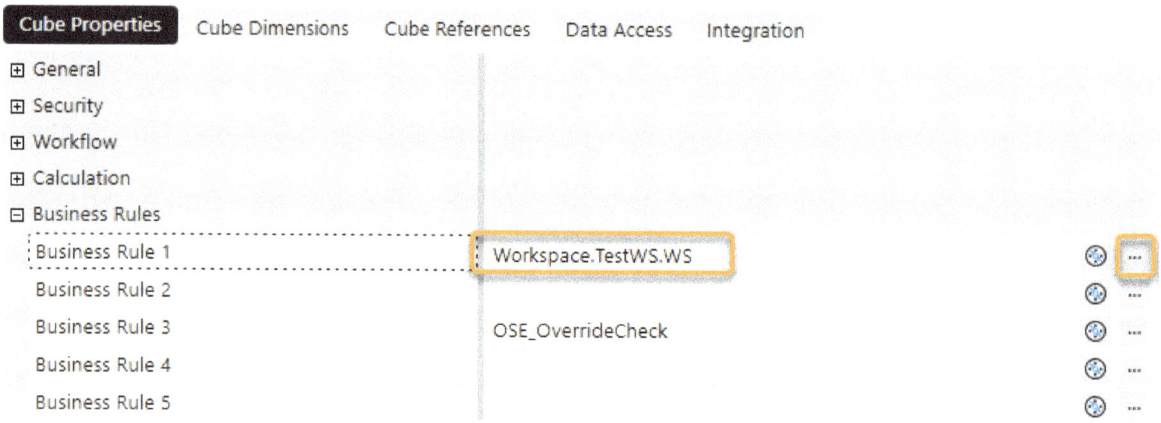

Figure 7.30

Ellipsis returns available Workspaces and syntax.

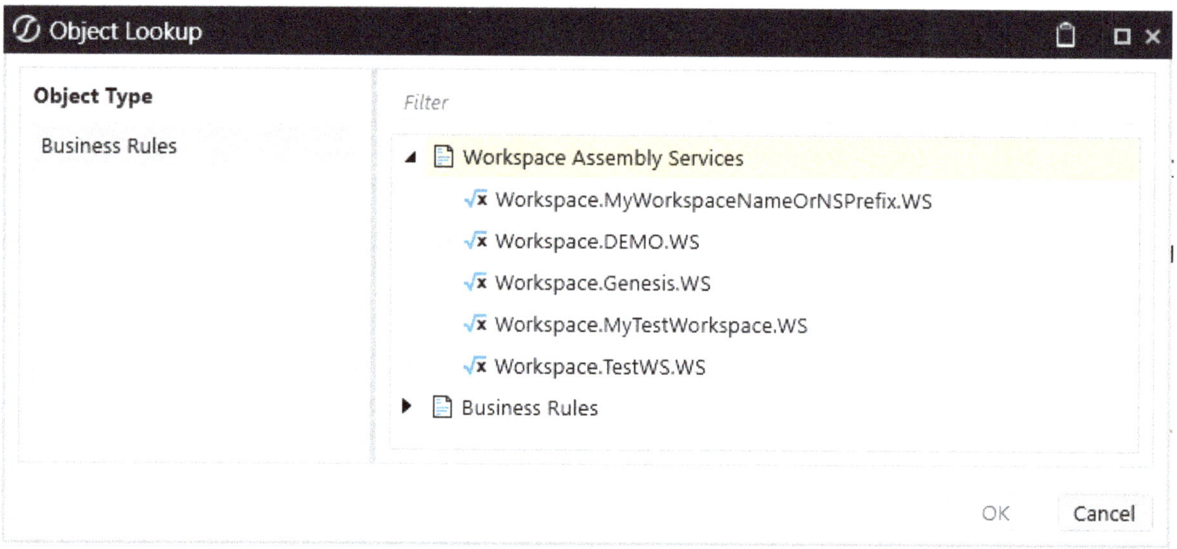

Figure 7.31

Finance Member List Service [Member Filter for Cube Views]

Note: This is called when a Cube View is retrieving a list of members.

- `[Workspace.workspaceName.maintenanceUnitName.WSMU,…] "Current" is not allowed`
- Since this reference is used within a Cube View and Cube Views may execute without a current Workspace context (and may span Workspaces), the `workspaceName` and `maintenanceUnitName` must be explicitly specified.
- The reason that `.WS` is not allowed for this service call is because Cube Views are evaluated by the Finance engine and may execute without a current Workspace context and potentially across Workspaces. A `.WS` reference relies on an implicit "Current" Workspace, which cannot be guaranteed in this execution model.

⊟ Row Members	
Member Expansion 1	
Primary Dimension Type	Entity
Member Filter	E#Root.[Workspace.Hospital.Healthcare Solution.WSMU,MyMemberList]

Figure 7.32

Finance GetDataCell Service [Member Filter for Cube Views]

Note: This is called when a Cube View is returning data for an individual cell.

- `[Workspace.workspaceName.maintenanceUnitName.WSMU,…] "Current" is not allowed`
- Since this reference is used within a Cube View and Cube Views may execute without a current Workspace context (and may span Workspaces), the `workspaceName` and `maintenanceUnitName` must be explicitly specified.
- For the same reason as the Member List service, `.WS` is not allowed; Cube Views are evaluated by the Finance engine and may execute without a current Workspace context and potentially across Workspaces. A `.WS` reference relies on an implicit "Current" Workspace, which cannot be guaranteed in this execution model.

⊟ Row Members	
Member Expansion 1	
Primary Dimension Type	Account
Member Filter	GetDataCell("BR#.[Workspace.Hospital.Healthcare Solution.WSMU,MyDataCellFunction]")Name(My Check)

Figure 7.33

Finance CustomCalc Service [Data management Step of type "Custom Calculate"]

Note: This is called when a data management job calls a Custom Calculate.

- `Workspace.workspaceName.WS`
- `Workspace.workspaceName.maintenanceUnitName.WSMU`
- Note: The Function Name is referenced on a different field.

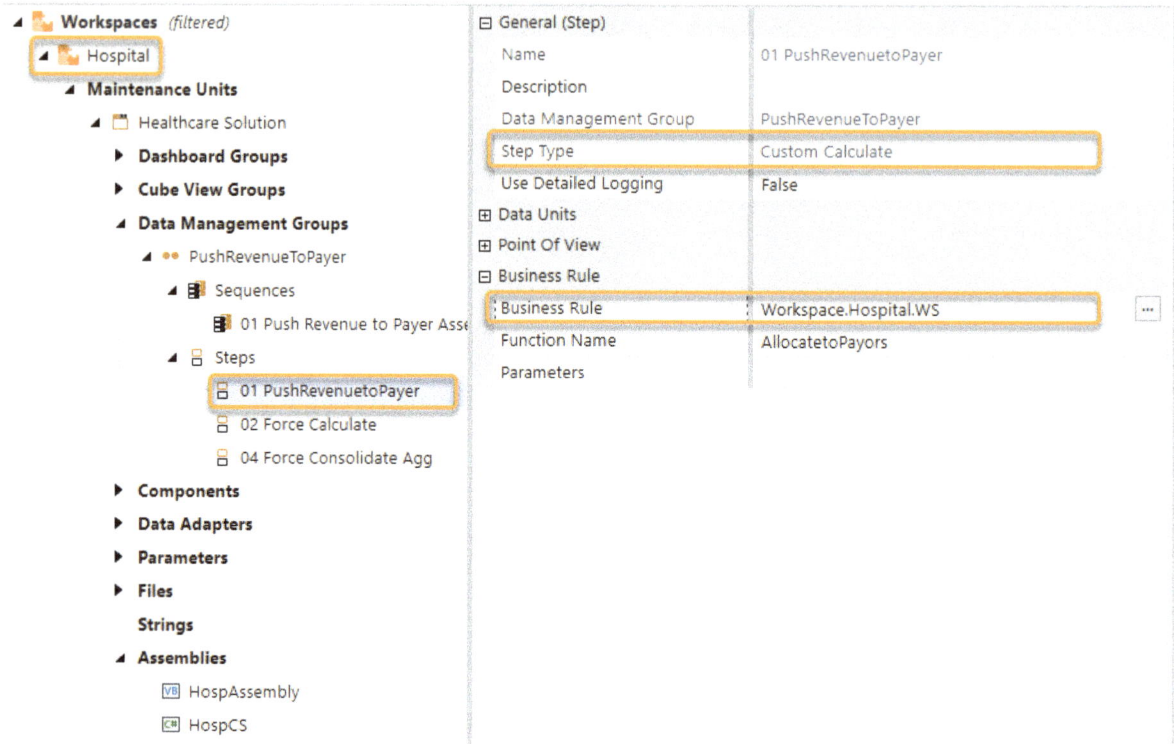

Figure 7.34

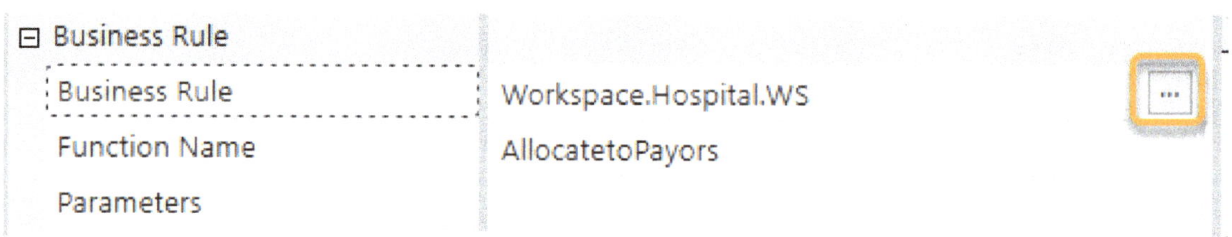

Figure 7.35

Ellipsis returns available Workspaces and syntax. Note that only the available Workspace References (WS) are listed here, but there are also Workspace Maintenance Unit references (WSMU) that are valid.

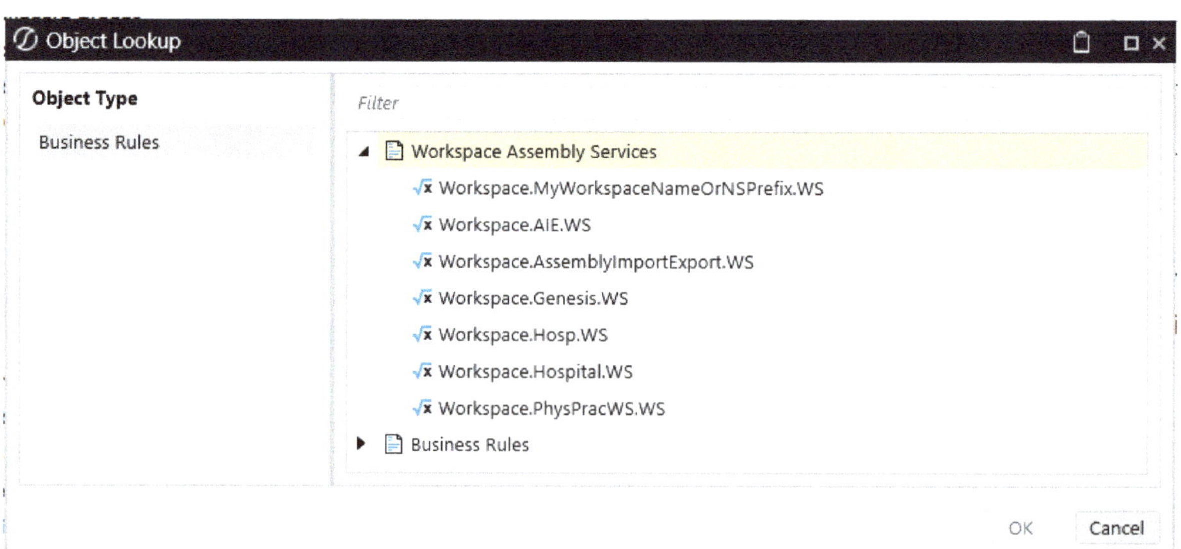

Figure 7.36

Table View Service [Spreadsheet Table View]

Note: This is called when working with table views within the Spreadsheet editor.

- `Workspace.workspaceName.maintenanceUnitName.WSMU`
- `Workspace.workspaceName.WS`
- `Workspace.Current.maintenanceUnitName.WSMU`
- `Workspace.Current.Current.WSMU`
- `Workspace.Current.WS`
- `WS`
- `WSMU`

Ellipsis gives you syntax as well as available Workspaces.

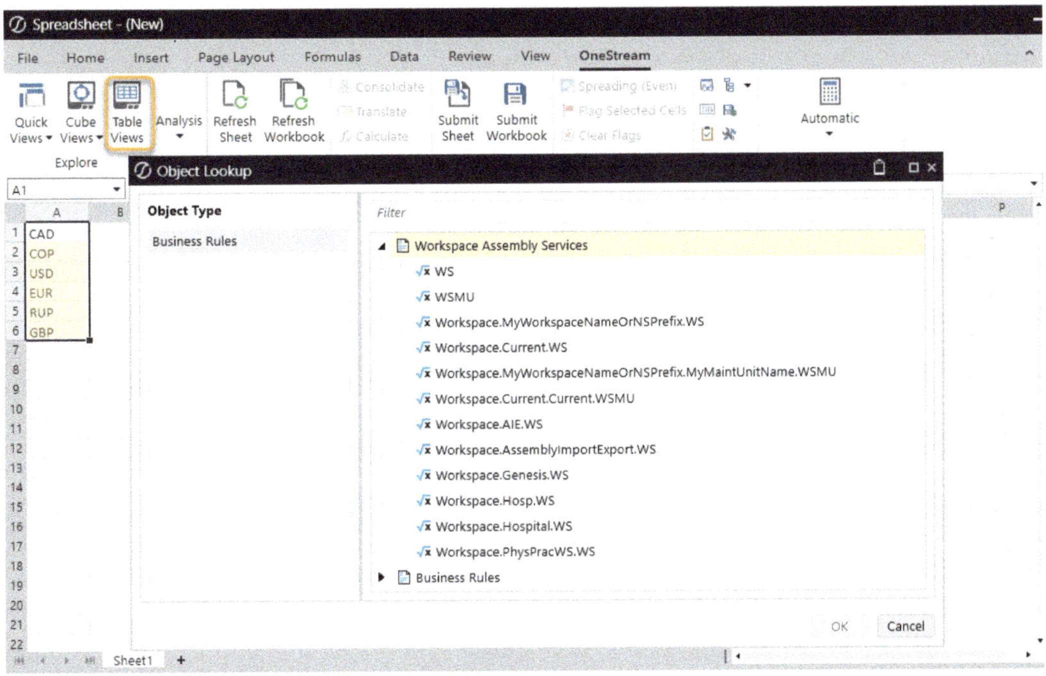

Figure 7.37

> **Note:** For table views, it is recommended to use explicit references to ensure that the spreadsheet can be opened from anywhere.

Data Management Service [Data management Step of type "Execute Business Rule"]

Note: This is called when a data management job calls an Execute business rule.

- `Workspace.workspaceName.maintenanceUnitName.WSMU`
- `Workspace.workspaceName.WS`
- `Workspace.Current.maintenanceUnitName.WSMU`
- `Workspace.Current.Current.WSMU`

Note that, as of the time of writing, the ellipsis for business rules only shows the Assembly business rule syntax and available traditional business rules. It does not show the Assembly service syntax or the available Workspaces for services.

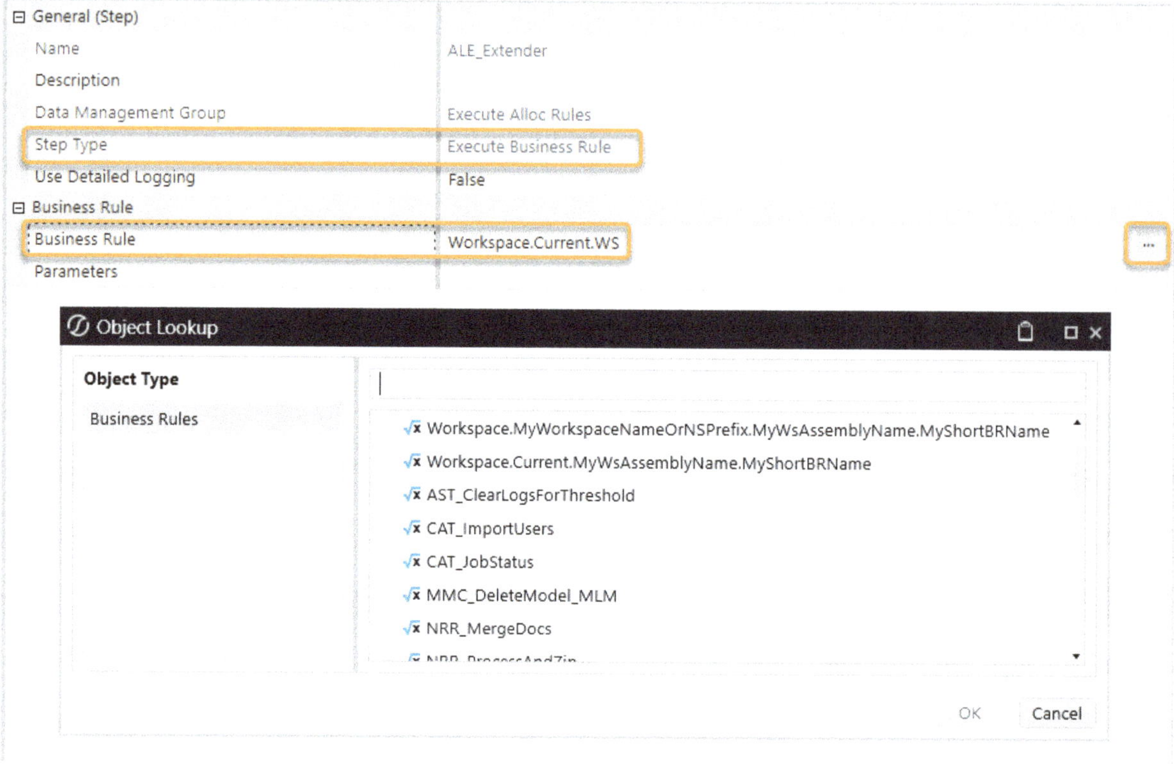

Figure 7.38

Version Control

One of the great advantages of working with Assemblies and service factories with WS and WSMU references is that they can be a great help for version control. If you have a first version of your dashboard working Assembly, say `MyAssemblyV1`, you can always choose to copy and paste your Assembly and create `MyAssemblyV2`. This will allow you to modify the code while keeping a working copy as a backup. If you want to run the dashboard using the new code, update the maintenance unit or Workspace Assembly factory once, and all components of your dashboard will use your new code. Need to revert? Simply update the reference back to the old code, and all components will start using the old working code.

WS and WSMU - Conclusion

In this section, I wanted to break down how the WS (Workspace Service) and WSMU (Workspace Maintenance Unit) work in OneStream, and why understanding them is so important. Basically, these two determine how service calls are routed to the right Service Factory. WS is your go-to for broader, Workspace-level calls, while WSMU steps in when you need more specific, granular control within a maintenance unit.

One of the great things about this system is its flexibility – you're not restricted to using service factories in the same Workspace or maintenance unit. You can call service factories from different ones as long as those Workspaces are shared, which is a handy feature when working across larger setups.

Another key point I've tried to highlight is how different service types come with their own syntax rules. For example, XFBR is more forgiving with options like "Current" keywords, whereas Finance GetDataCell requires you to explicitly name both the Workspace and maintenance unit. Knowing these nuances helps you route your service calls efficiently, no matter the type or context.

By understanding WS and WSMU, along with the unique syntax for different service types, you'll be able to configure your service factories effectively and make sure everything runs like clockwork.

Advanced Topics

Assembly Services and service factories unlock a level of flexibility in OneStream that might surprise you. In this section, we'll explore a few creative ways to configure service factories, showcasing how they can be adapted to meet unique needs. Hopefully, these examples will spark your imagination and inspire your own innovative solutions to make your application even more powerful.

Service Factory Routing

Now that we've covered the basics of setting up a standard Service Factory file, let's explore how you can take things further with creative configurations. Here is an example of a Service Factory conditioned on the 'day of the week' to select which data management step service file to return. This approach allows you to schedule long, time-intensive processes to run exclusively on weekends, ensuring smoother operations during the week.

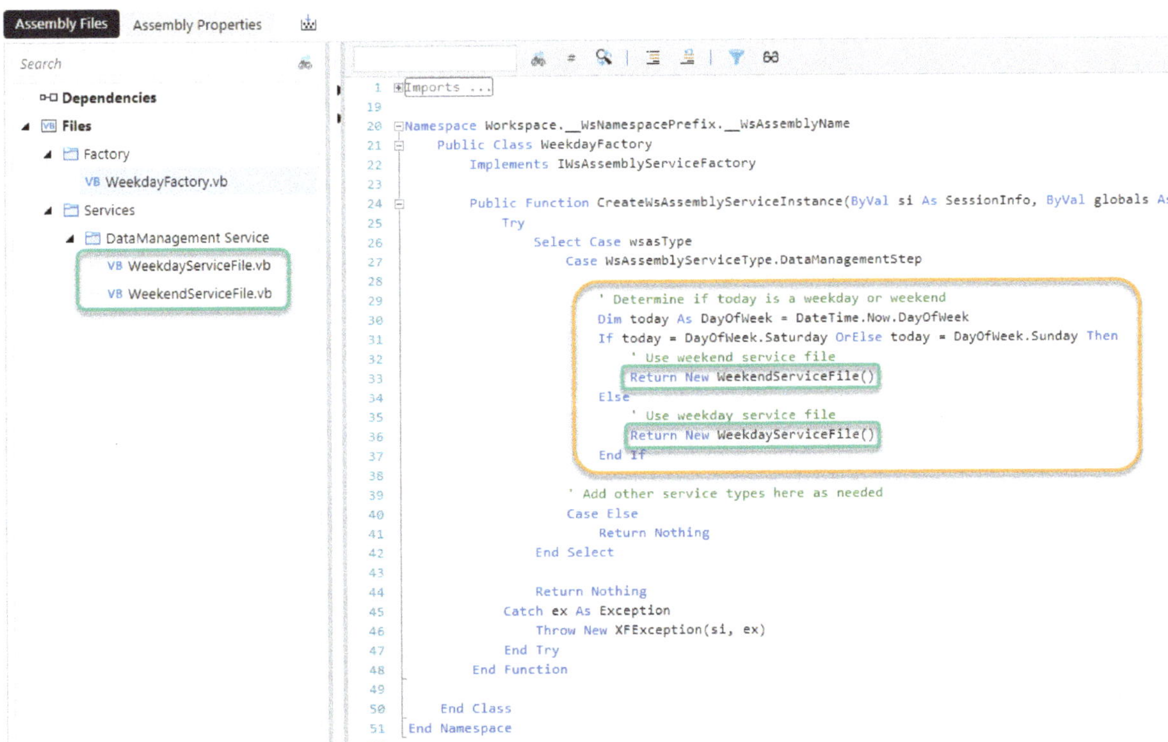

Figure 7.39

This is just one of many ways to customize service factories. Think about how you could apply similar logic to create tailored workflows and make your application even more robust and adaptable.

Advanced Orchestration

Jack Lacava, another genius here at OneStream, recently shared an inspiring blog on the OneStream Community. His article highlights a creative way to use service factories, which could be a game-changer for your Assembly service journey.

In his blog, Jack explores the idea of using nested factories, where one factory retrieves its services from another. This approach streamlines privilege-based logic and keeps your Service Factory clean and maintainable.

Jack Lacava's Blog

Factories must return service objects, of course; however, there is no rule about having to create such instances right there and then. What if I had a factory that gets its services from... another factory?

For example, let's say we want to build a particular interface in substantially different ways, depending on whether the user is an administrator or not. That setting will determine so many things that you might end up having completely different services for dashboards, components, even Custom Calculate jobs.

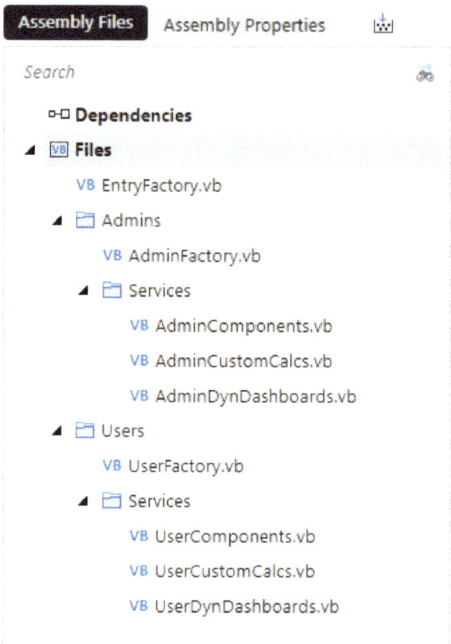

Figure 7.40

AdminFactory will dispatch to Admin services, and *UserFactory* will dispatch User services, keeping their logic very clean. And then, in *EntryFactory*, you would just delegate the choice to one factory or the other, depending on privilege checking:

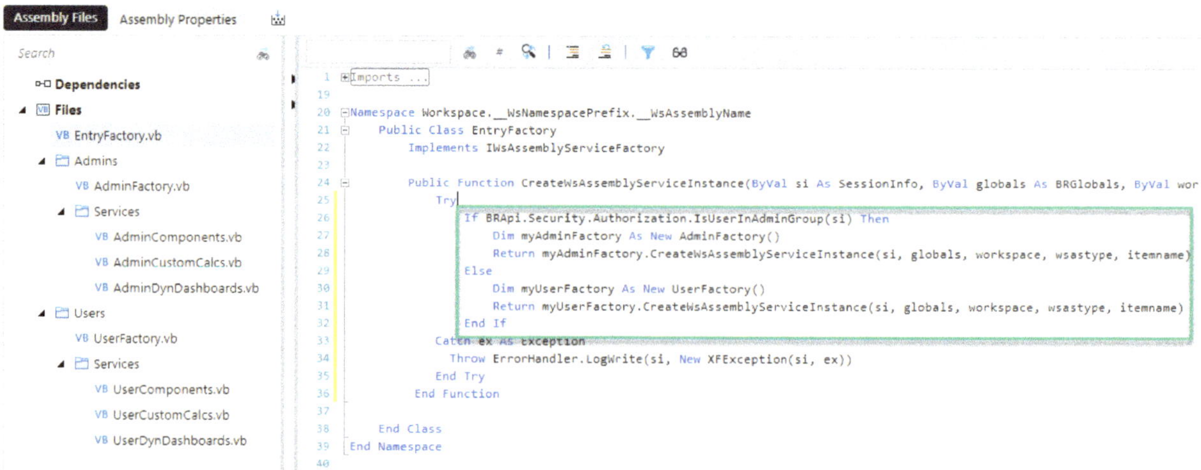

Figure 7.41

(Actual Text of Code for clarity)

```
Public Function CreateWsAssemblyServiceInstance(...) [...]
   Try
      If BRApi.Security.Authorization.IsUserInAdminGroup(si) Then
         Dim myAdminFactory As New AdminFactory()
         Return myAdminFactory.CreateWsAssemblyServiceInstance(si,
globals, workspace, wsastype, itemname)
      Else
         Dim myUserFactory As New UserFactory()
         Return myUserFactory.CreateWsAssemblyServiceInstance(si,
globals, workspace, wsastype, itemname)
      End If
   Catch ex As Exception
      Throw ErrorHandler.LogWrite(si, New XFException(si, ex))
   End Try
End Function
```

Instead of having code that checks the privilege for each individual service, polluting our class with repetitive (and error-prone) copy/pasted lines, we have one clear check at the very start of the process, and everything flows from there.

[End of Blog]

As you can see from these two examples, Assembly Services and the use of service factories can greatly improve the flexibility and control of how to run the code that controls your OneStream application. There are an infinite number of possibilities with OneStream's use of Assembly Services. Think about how you might implement similar logic to address unique challenges in your own application.

Conclusion

Wrapping it all up, Assembly Services and service factories are like the secret sauce to making your OneStream application efficient, scalable, and downright powerful. Once you grasp how WS and WSMU operate, and how they route service calls smartly, you'll feel like you've unlocked a new level of control over your application. Plus, the flexibility to call service factories across shared Workspaces or maintenance units opens up endless possibilities for larger, more complex setups.

The big takeaway here is that Assembly Services aren't just about solving today's problems – they're about future-proofing your application. With a solid understanding of these tools and some creative implementation, you'll be setting up your OneStream environment to handle anything that comes its way and build a foundation for long-term success.

8

Intro to Dynamic Dashboards

One of the game-changing innovations that OneStream introduced in association with Workspaces is the concept of dynamic dashboards. Imagine needing hundreds of dashboards that differ slightly across user groups or locations. Traditionally, this would require creating and maintaining countless components and dashboards to capture all possible variations. Dynamic dashboards eliminate this complexity by empowering you to design a single stored dashboard along with a few core components. Using its powerful in-memory capabilities, OneStream can dynamically generate all permutations on the fly when the dashboard is accessed.

For example, if your dashboards include combo boxes or buttons that vary in number across different users, you no longer need to build each variation manually. **Dynamic Dashboard Services** work behind the scenes to dynamically assemble these variations during runtime, drastically reducing manual effort and complexity.

This subject can get quite deep, given the powerful possibilities it unlocks. For this book, however, the goal is to introduce the core concepts and inspire you with the potential of dynamic dashboards – without diving too heavily into the code. More detailed guides and documentation are available for those who wish to explore further.

In this chapter, we will walk through two simple examples: first, a no-code approach using embedded dynamic repeater dashboards, followed by a more technical approach utilizing Assembly Services.

My approach to explaining dynamic dashboards will be to walk through these two examples in detail with enough information and screenshots that you will be able to replicate the logic in your own application and have this be a starting point as you try to learn these concepts.

First Concept – Embedded Dynamic Repeater Dashboards (No Code Dynamic Dashboards)

Embedded dynamic repeater dashboard types were introduced in version 8.0, and for me, it was a turning point in understanding what OneStream aimed to achieve with dynamic dashboards. The concept is simple yet transformative: you can take one stored object, use a repeater list to apply different parameters, and render an unlimited number of variations in-memory. As a developer, this means you no longer need to repeatedly replicate, modify, and store multiple objects that differ only slightly. The demonstration I will use has one stored object with multiple template parameters to render five very different buttons. Now, extrapolate that concept with multiple stored items within a dashboard and then multiple embedded dashboards, each having their own repeated items, and you then have a truly unlimited number of in-memory dashboards and components with minimal stored objects.

I'll illustrate this with a straightforward example – creating five buttons to navigate to different workflows using just one stored button.

Let me show you my first "aha" moment. Coming from pre-Workspace dashboard development, I was familiar with a dashboard only showing the components explicitly added to the Dashboard Components page. When I saw an example of a dashboard with just one button attached, I assumed that's all I'd see. So, it was impressive to run the dashboard and see five buttons appear, each configured to navigate to a different workflow.

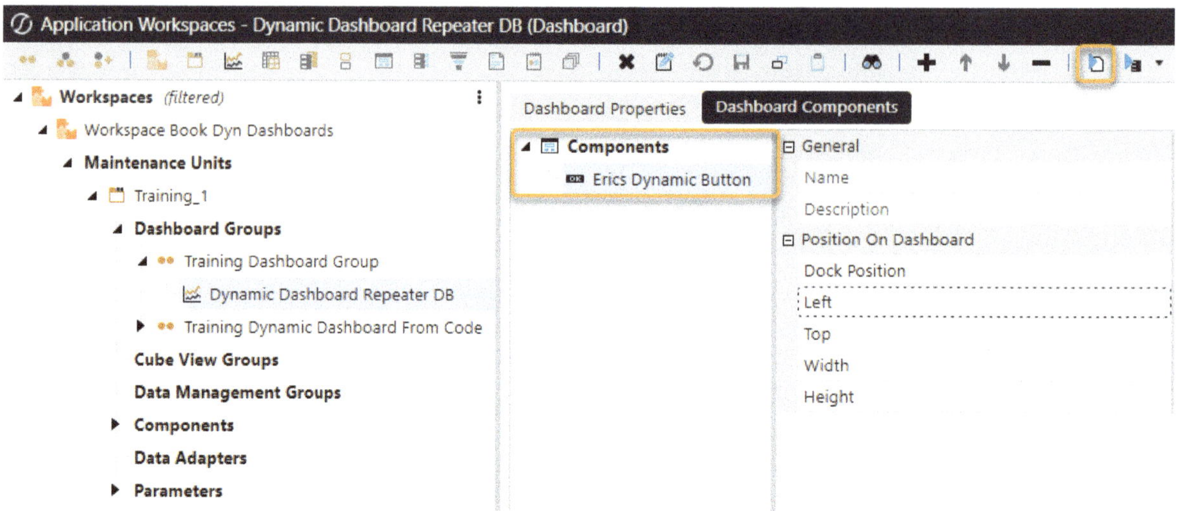

Figure 8.1

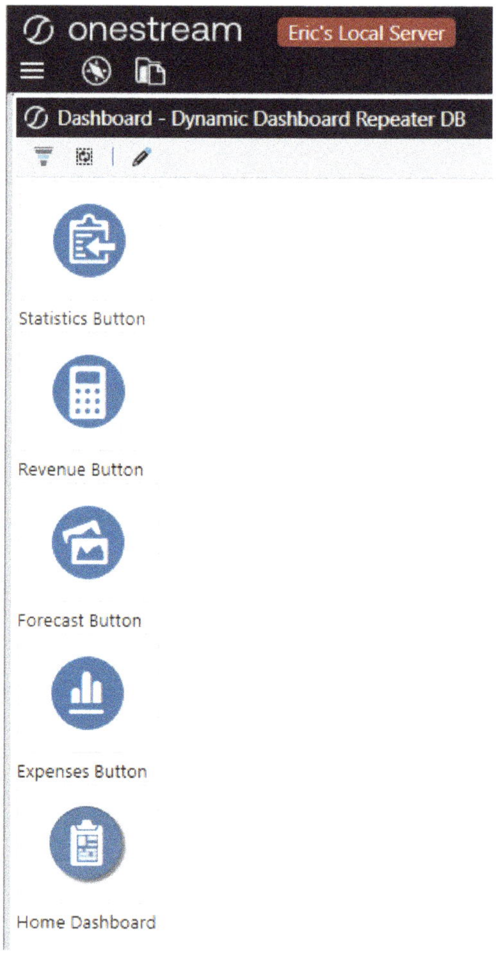

Figure 8.2

I was truly intrigued…

It turns out that OneStream introduced a new dashboard type in version 8.0 that allows for this: the **Embedded Dynamic Repeater**.

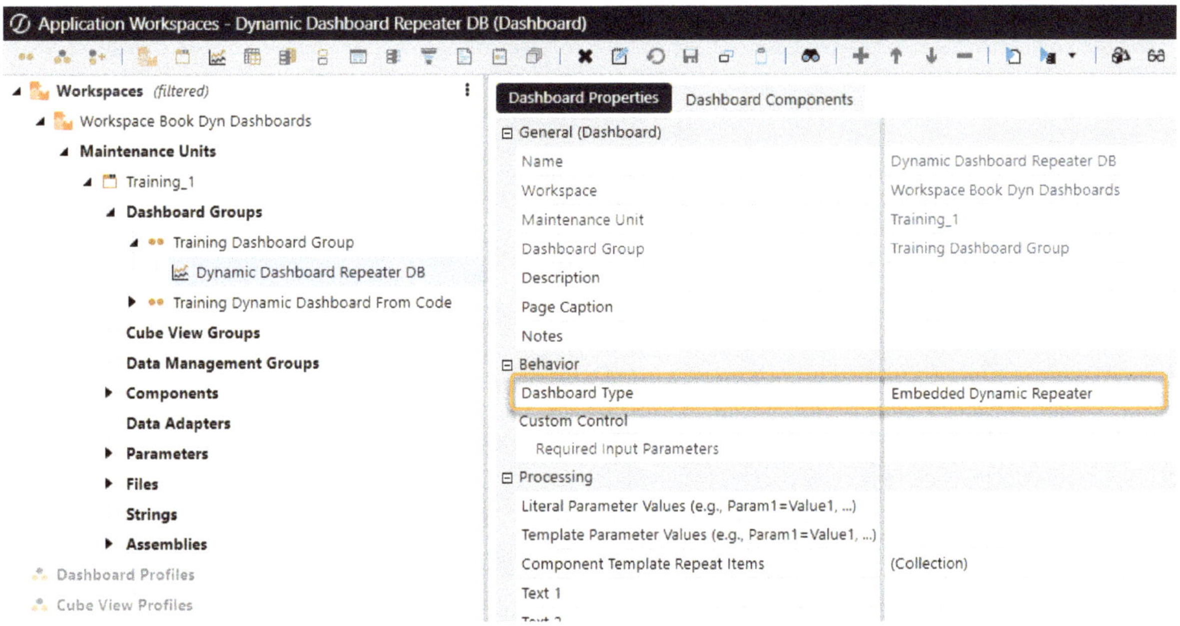

Figure 8.3

Two Key Concepts for Embedded Dynamic Repeater Dashboards

The embedded dynamic repeater dashboard type introduces two powerful concepts: **Component Template Repeat Items** and **Template Parameters**. These features enable developers to define and reuse dynamic elements, simplifying the creation of dashboards with repeated components.

Component Template Repeat Items

Component template repeat items allow developers to define lists of items that are dynamically repeated within a dashboard. This eliminates the need to manually replicate components for every variation. When creating a new dashboard, you'll find that the Component Template Repeat Items setting in the Processing group is only available for the Embedded Dynamic Repeater dashboard type. This setting is where you define the repeated items and their associated template parameters.

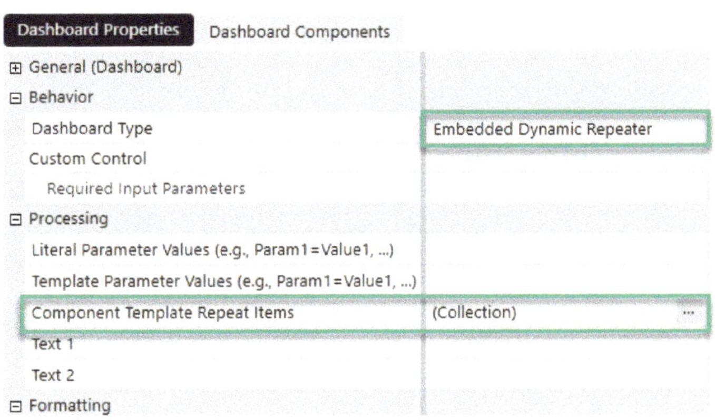

Figure 8.4

Template Parameters (i.e., Repeater List Parameters)

Template parameters, also known as repeater list parameters, are unique to embedded dynamic repeater and embedded dynamic dashboard types (discussed in the next section). These parameters allow you to dynamically substitute values within repeated components.

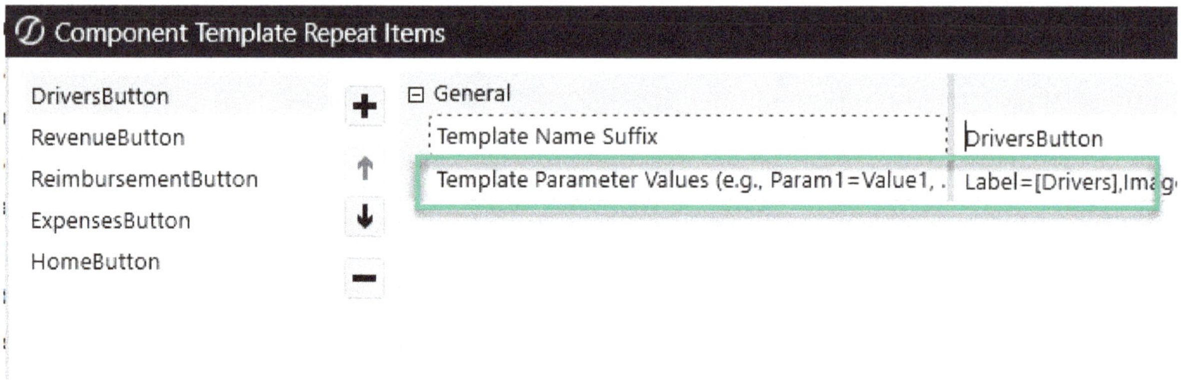

Figure 8.5

Their syntax differs from standard dashboard parameters, and it's important to use the correct format:

- Here is the new syntax to call the parameter
  `~!templateParam!~`
- Instead of the standard dashboard parameter syntax:
  `|!dashboardParam!|`

These two concepts are essential for unlocking the full potential of dynamic dashboards, allowing developers to significantly reduce complexity and enhance scalability.

Example 1 - How to Create Multiple Buttons using an Embedded Dynamic Repeater Dashboard

To showcase this concept, it is easiest to walk through a simple example that should only take about five minutes to set up. If you are coming from pre-Workspace dashboard development, this will immediately highlight the concepts behind dynamic dashboards and why they are so powerful.

In this section, I'll guide you through creating this type of dashboard – the same simple example seen in Figure 8.2, using just one stored button.

Example 1: Functional Requirement

We need to create a vertical stack dashboard with five buttons that navigate to five different Workflow Profiles and different icons using an embedded dynamic repeater dashboard type.

Example 1: Solution Steps

Pay close attention to Step 5 and how the collection needs to be set up. Step 6 showcases a new parameter type within OneStream and special syntax to call them.

1. **Create a Button**: Start by creating a button within a Workspace. You'll edit its details later.
2. **Import Image Files**: Upload the image files needed for the button icons.
3. **Prepare Workflow Steps**: Ensure the relevant workflow steps are set up in advance.
4. **Create a Dashboard**: Set the dashboard type to Embedded Dynamic Repeater.
5. **Set Up the Component Template Repeat Items**: Define a list with five items for this example.
6. **Edit the Button Parameters**: Update the button to include parameters such as (Nav, Label, image, Workflow, and POV), which are used in the Component Template Repeat Items.

7. **Add the Button to the Dashboard**: Attach the button to the dynamic repeater dashboard.
8. **Configure the Dashboard Layout**: Adjust the layout to either Vertical Stack or Grid, as needed. (Grid used in this example.)
9. **Run the Dashboard**: Test your dashboard to ensure it works as expected.
10. **Inspect in Design Mode**: Open Design Mode to review how OneStream generates the components dynamically in-memory.

Example 1: Solution Step Details

1. **Create a Button:** Start by creating a button within a Workspace. You'll edit its details later.

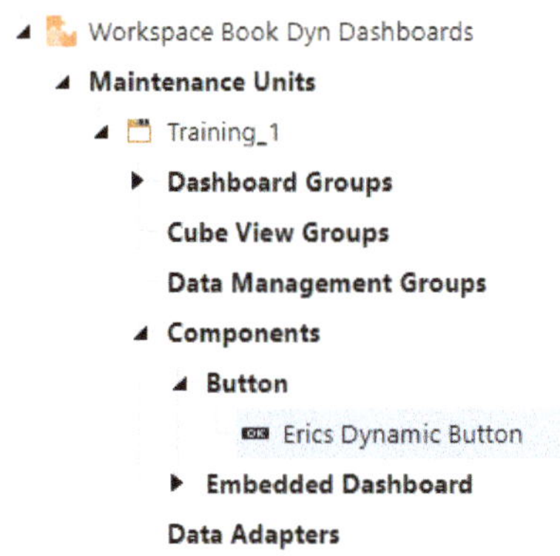

Figure 8.6

2. **Import Image Files**: Upload the image files needed for the button icons.

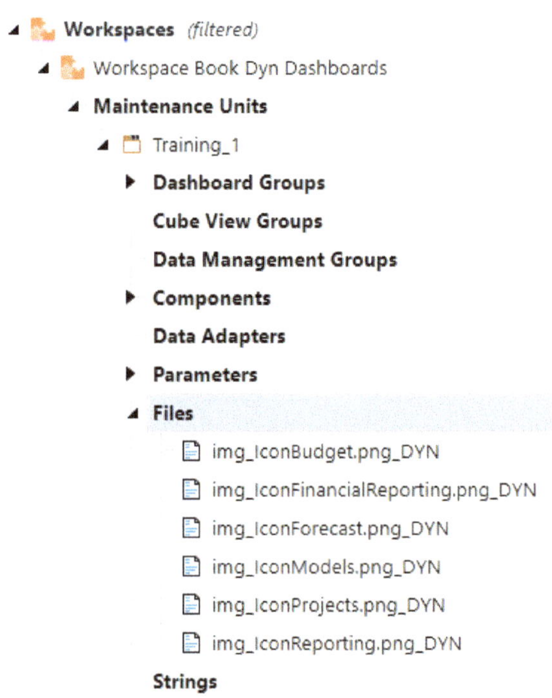

Figure 8.7

3. **Prepare Workflow Steps**: Ensure the relevant workflow steps are set up in advance. (If you are not navigating to workflow steps, skip this step and just navigate to a dashboard in step 5.) I picked a button that will be used to navigate to a specific workflow to showcase the flexibility of using these template parameters.

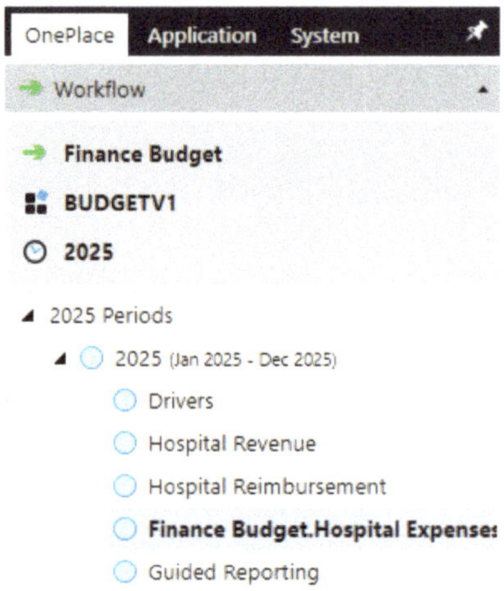

Figure 8.8

4. **Create a Dashboard**: Set the dashboard type to Embedded Dynamic Repeater.

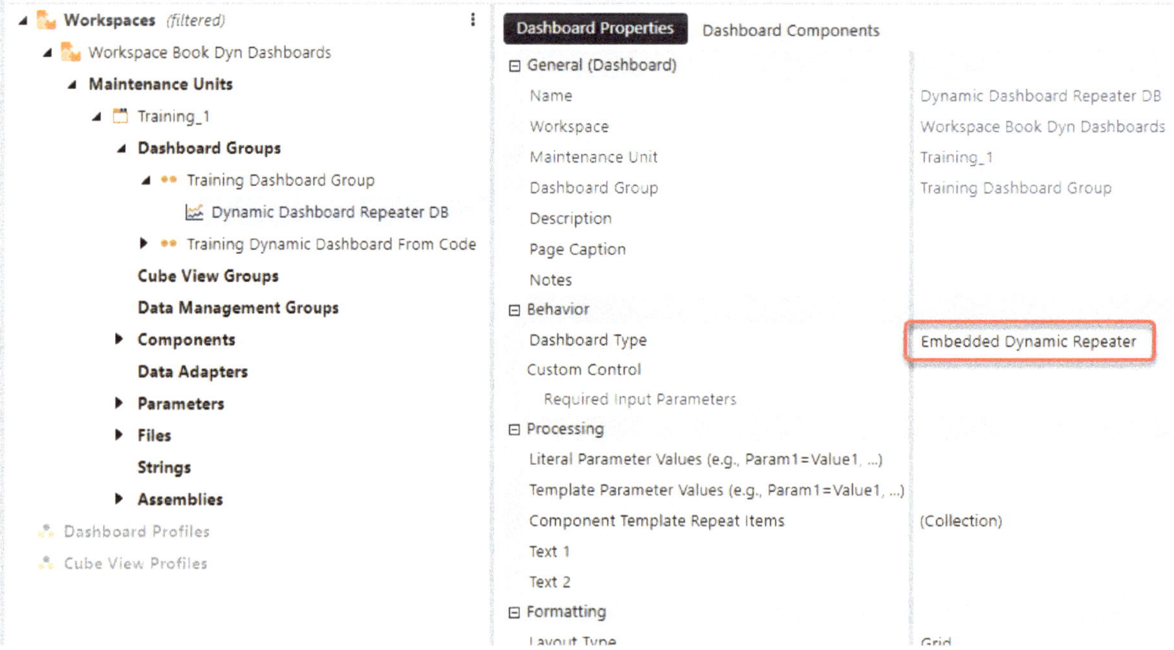

Figure 8.9

5. **Set Up the Component Template Repeat Items:** Define a list with five items for this example.

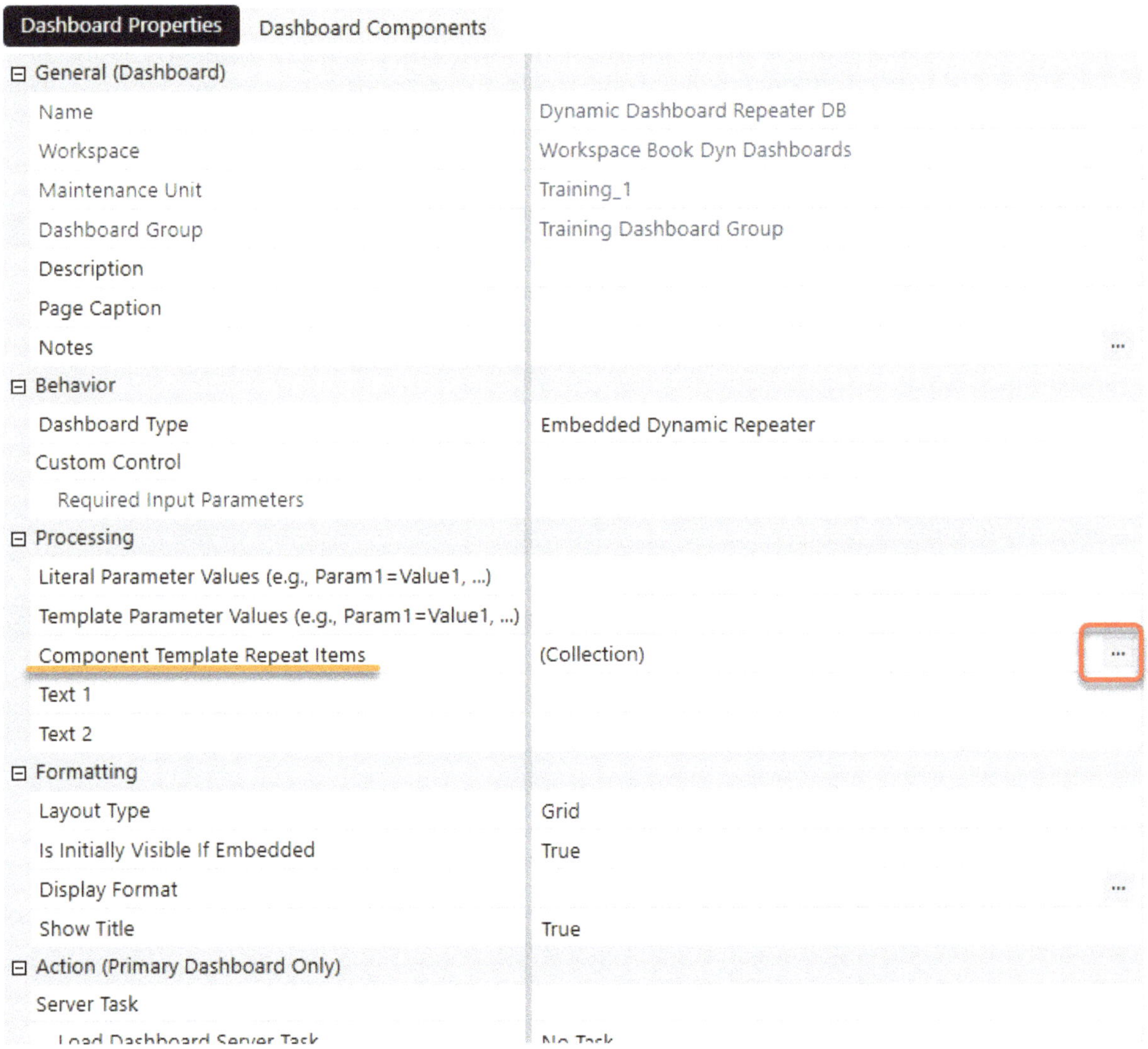

Figure 8.10

a. Create each item to be repeated. The repeater will page through each of the repeat items.

Note: The template suffix name will be the reference name and will also be used as a suffix when the buttons are rendered in-memory.

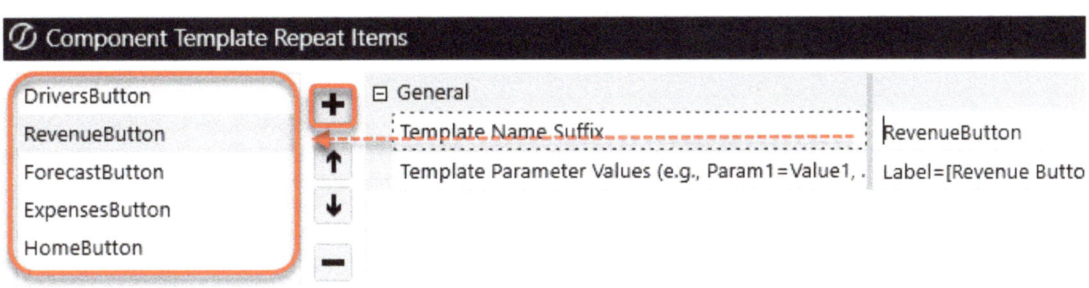

Figure 8.11

b. Create the template parameters separated by a comma (i.e., in this example, I have six parameters defined for each repeat item. These will be used in the settings of the stored button: Label, Image, Nav, WFProfile, WFScenario, and WFTime. They will all be called separately).

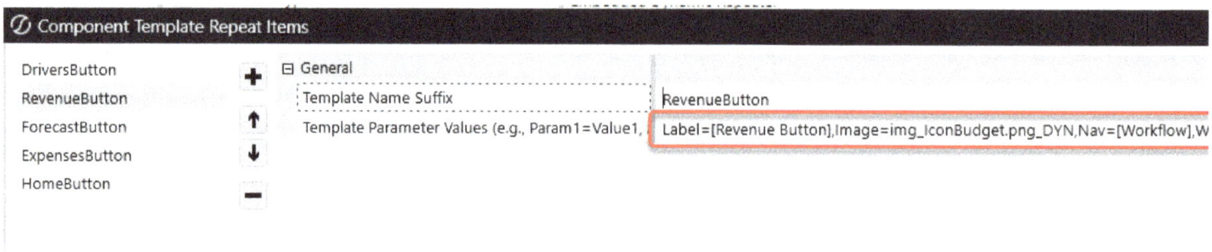

Closeup of Settings:

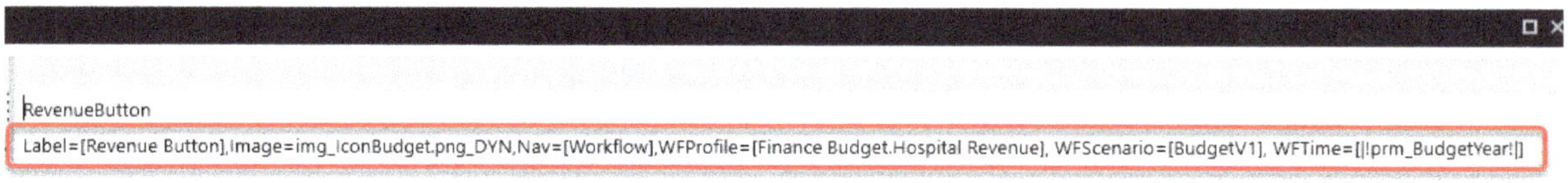

Figure 8.12

(my example)

```
Label=[Revenue Button], Image=img_IconBudget.png_DYN,
Nav=[Workflow], WFProfile=[Finance Budget.Hospital Revenue],
WFScenario=[BudgetV1], WFTime=[|!prm_BudgetYear!|]
```

> **Note 1:** The syntax when there is a space or a special character is to use square brackets `[ ]`.
>
> **Note 2:** You can use dashboard parameters inside these lists to give extra flexibility (e.g., `|!prm_BudgetYear!|`).
>
> **Note 3:** Each repeat item can have multiple template parameters separated by a comma.

c. Make sure you have the same parameter names for each repeat item (i.e., this example: Nav, Label, Image, WFProfile, WFScenario, WFTime). These will each be created as a repeater parameter that can be used in the dynamic dashboard.

6. **Edit the Button Parameters**: Update the button to include parameters such as Nav, Label, image, Workflow, and POV, which are used in the Component Template Repeat Items.

Notice that all six template parameters are used in this button; you do not have to use all of them if there is an instance that doesn't require them.

> **Important:** The syntax for calling parameters created in the Component Template Repeat Items is `~!parameter!~`

Component Properties

⊟ General (Component)	
Name	Erics Dynamic Button
Workspace	Workspace Book Dyn Dashboards
Maintenance Unit	Training_1
Description	
Component Type	Button
⊟ Formatting	
Text	~!Label!~
Tool Tip	Navigate to ~!Label!~
Display Format	Height = 110, HorizontalAlignment = Left, HorizontalContentAlignment = Center, ImageStretch = None, LabelPosition = Bc
⊟ Processing	
Template Parameter Values (e.g., Param1=Valu	
Text 1	
Text 2	
⊟ Image	
Image File Source Type	Workspace File
Image Url Or Full File Name	~!Image!~
Excel Page Number	
Excel Sheet	
Excel Named Range	
⊟ Button	
Button Type	Standard
⊟ Action	
Bound Parameter	
Parameter Value For Button Click	
Apply Selected Value To Current Dashboard	True
Save Action	
Selection Changed Save Action	No Action
Selection Changed Save Arguments	
POV Action	
Selection Changed POV Action	Change POV And Workflow
Selection Changed POV Arguments	Cube=[HospitalSystem], WFProfile=[~!WFProfile!~], WFScenario=[~!WFScenario!~], WFTime=[~!WFTime!~]
Server Task	
Selection Changed Server Task	No Task
Selection Changed Server Task Arguments	
User Interface Action	
Selection Changed User Interface Action	No Action
Dashboards To Redraw	
Dashboards To Show	
Dashboards To Hide	
Dashboard To Open In Dialog	
Dialog Initial Parameter Values	
Dialog Input Parameter Map	
Dialog Output Parameter Map	
Navigation Action	
Selection Changed Navigation Action	Open Page
Selection Changed Navigation Arguments	XFPage=~!Nav!~

Figure 8.13

7. **Add the Button to the Dashboard**: Attach the button to the dynamic repeater dashboard.

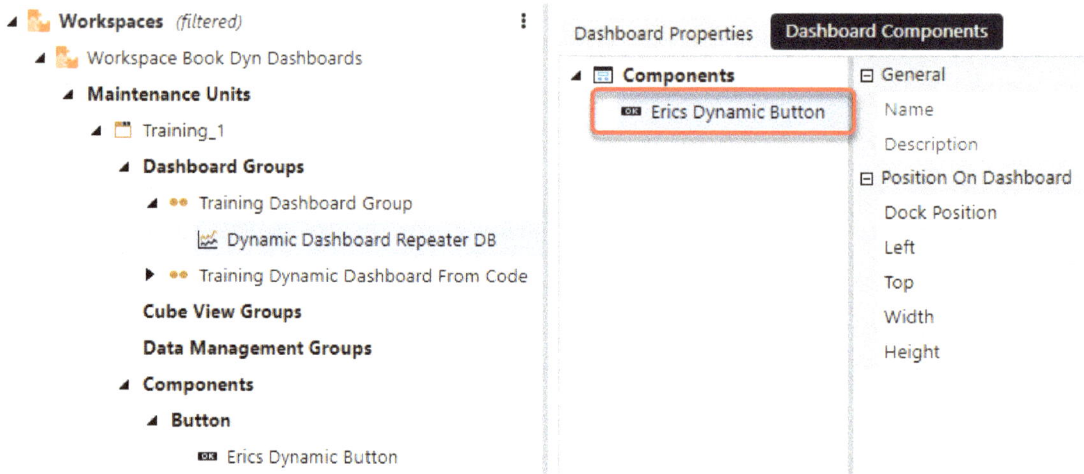

Figure 8.14

8. **Configure the Dashboard Layout**: Adjust the layout to either Vertical Stack or Grid, as needed. (Grid used in this example.)

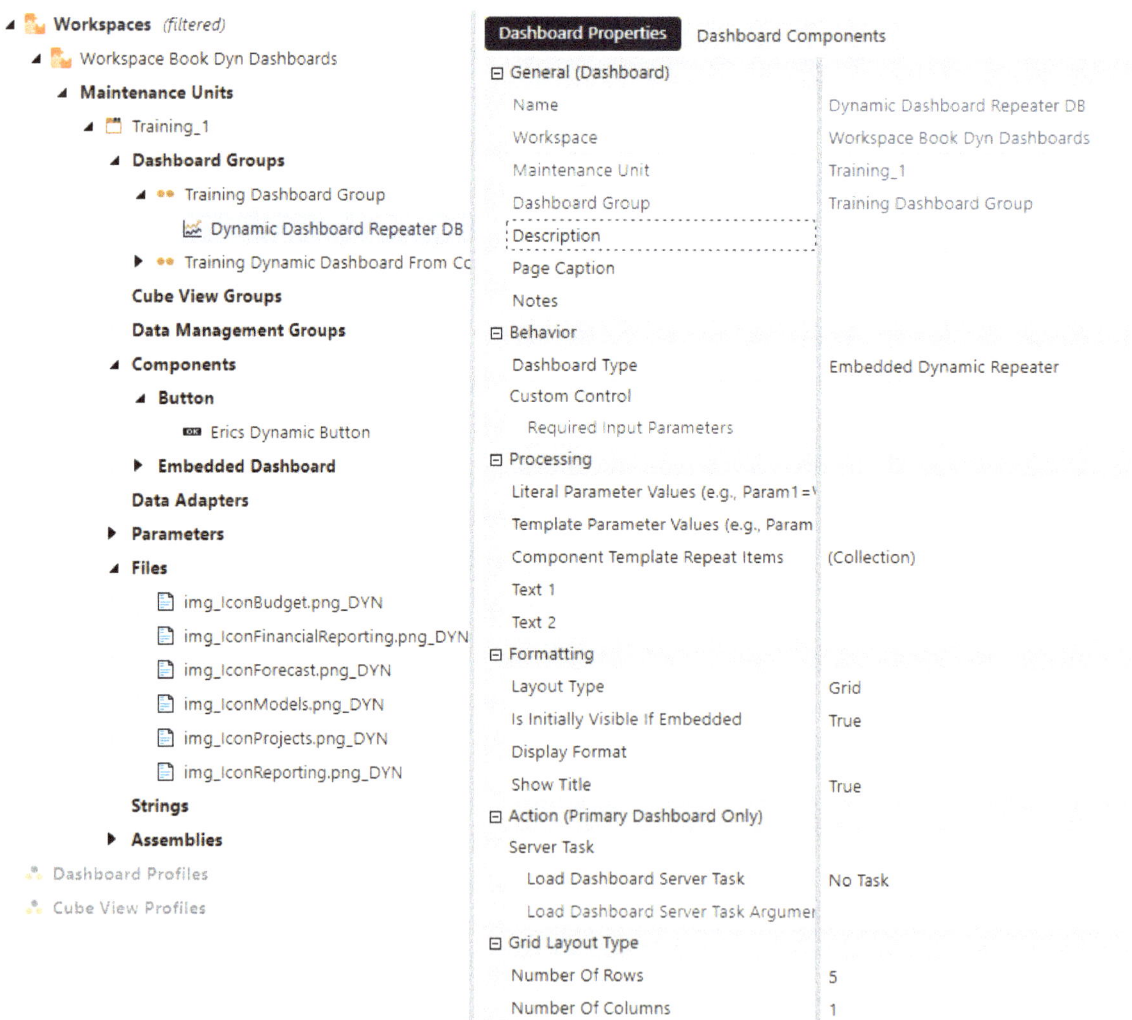

Figure 8.15

9. **Run the Dashboard**: Test your dashboard to ensure it works as expected.

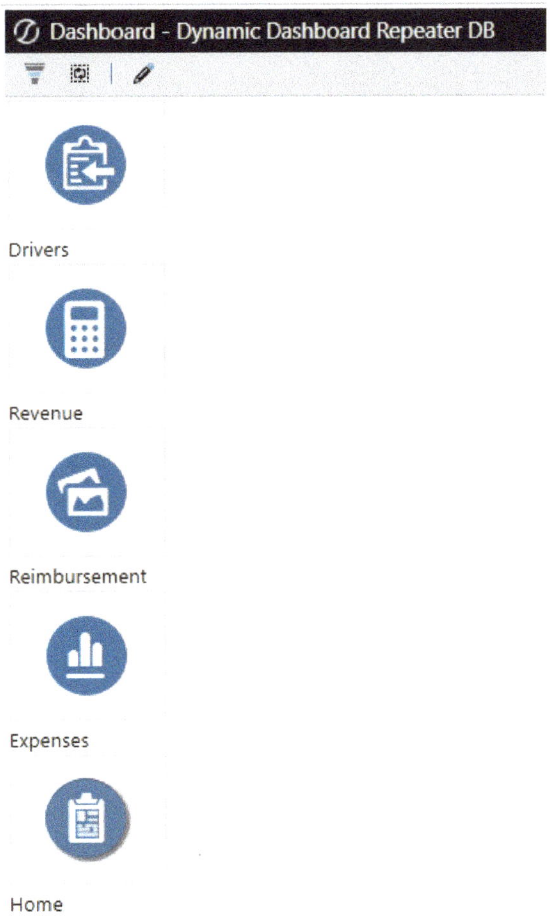

Figure 8.16

10. **Inspect in Design Mode**: Open Design Mode to review how OneStream generates the components dynamically in-memory.

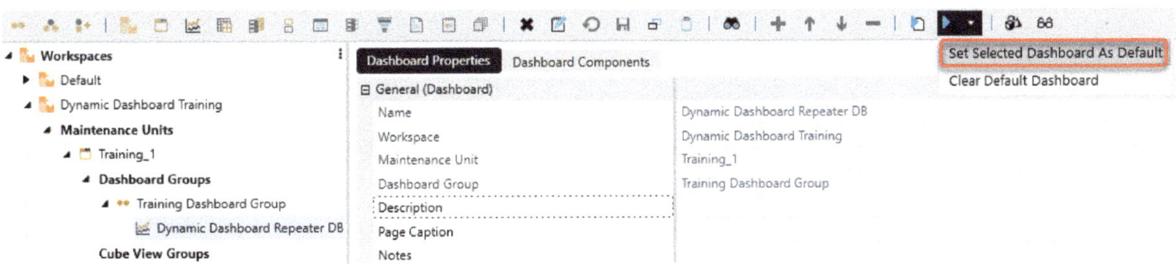

Figure 8.17

OneStream uses the collection of repeater items and cycles through them. These items that you see are in-memory, dynamic buttons that OneStream produces when the dashboard is run.

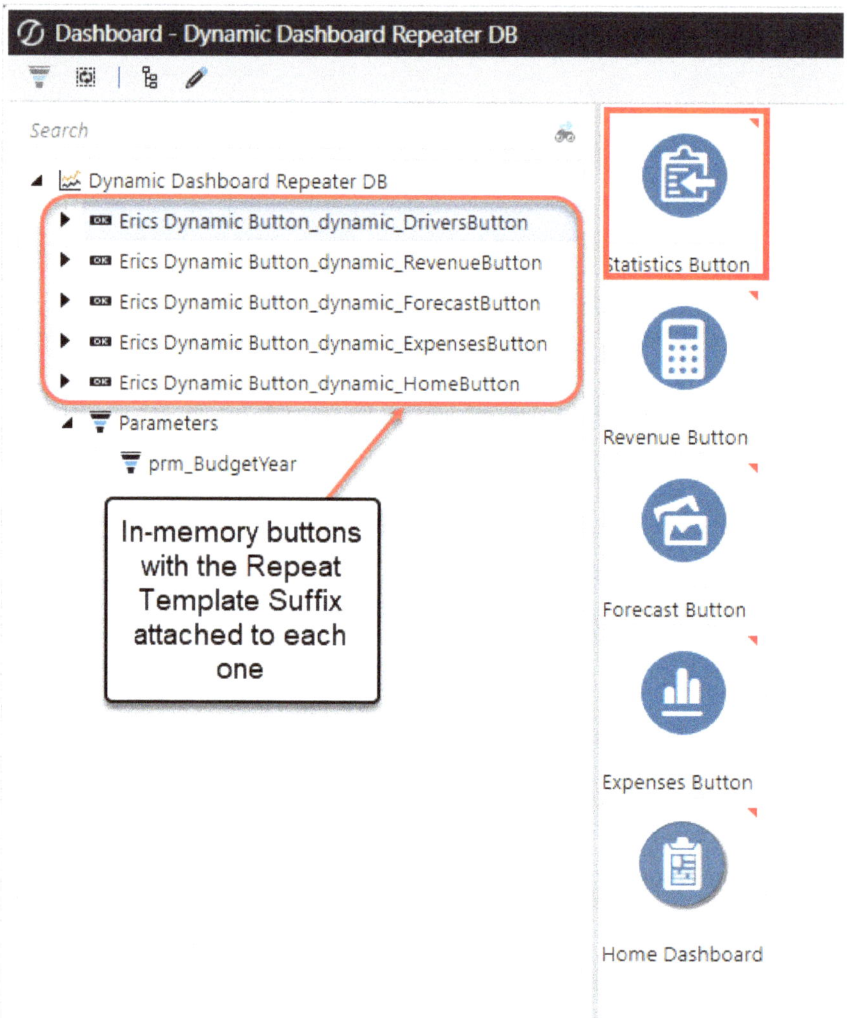

Figure 8.18

> **Note:** each of these in-memory dynamic components will have a suffix of the form: `_dynamic_"Template Name Suffix"`

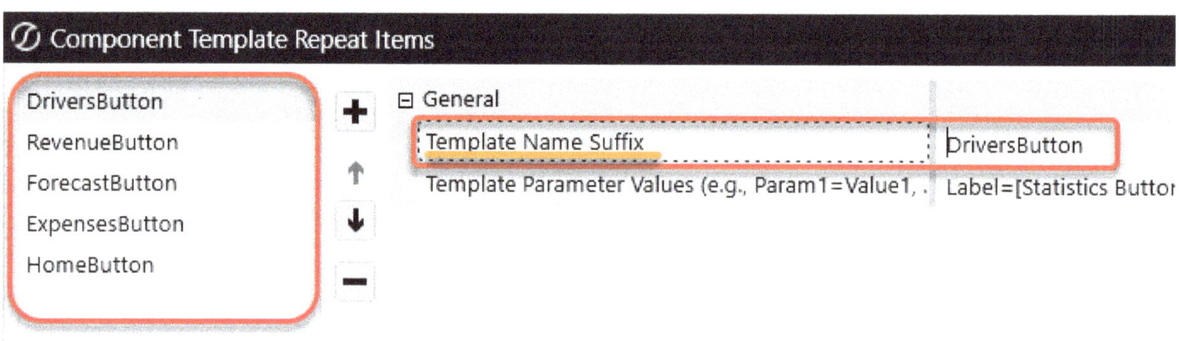

Figure 8.19

This exercise demonstrates the power of embedded dynamic repeater dashboards, showcasing how multiple dynamic dashboards can be generated effortlessly without writing a single line of code. By leveraging minimal stored objects, you've created a fully dynamic and scalable solution that adapts seamlessly to future needs. The potential of this approach is immense – enabling enterprise-level dashboards with dozens of components while significantly reducing development time and effort. This is just the beginning of what dynamic dashboards can achieve!

Second Concept – Use Service Factory and Dynamic Dashboard Services to update Repeater Arguments

Now that we've explored the underlying principle behind dynamic dashboards, let's take it a step further. In this example, we'll achieve the same outcome of creating multiple buttons from a single stored button, but this time we'll manipulate the repeater arguments programmatically, using an Assembly service file. This approach introduces greater flexibility and scalability, especially for more complex dashboard implementations.

Let me share my second "aha" moment – imagine a dashboard with *no components added*, yet which still dynamically generates an entire layout in-memory. This is the power unlocked when combining embedded dynamic dashboards and Assembly Services.

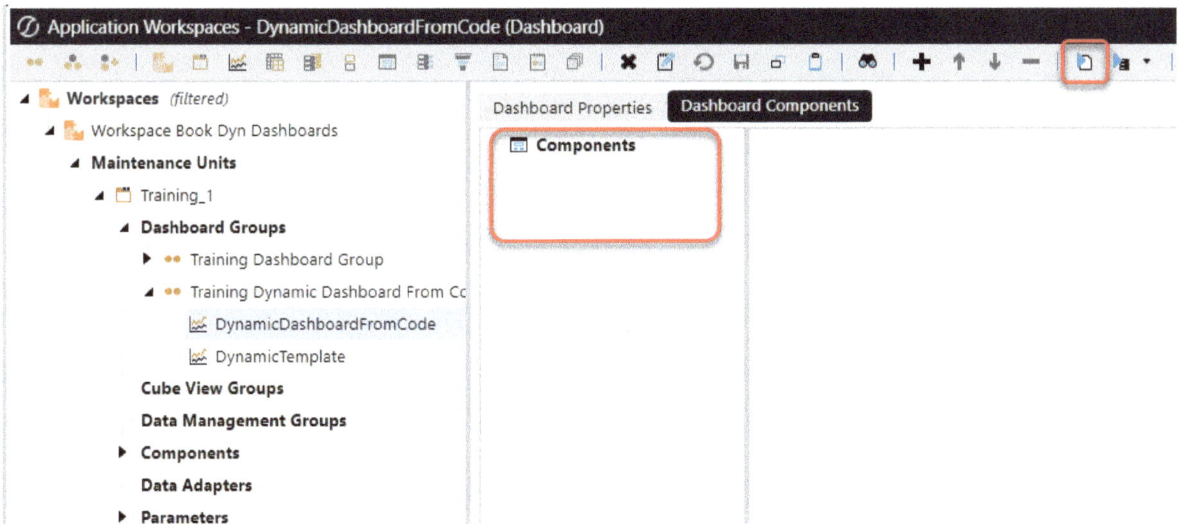

Figure 8.20

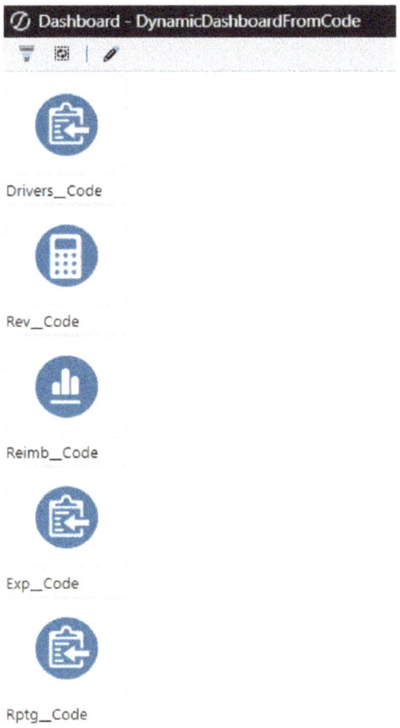

Figure 8.21

This concept goes beyond the capabilities of embedded dynamic repeaters. With Assembly Services, you gain complete control over how dashboards render in-memory, eliminating redundant development work and enabling fully customized dashboards tailored to your needs.

Example 2 – How to Create Multiple Buttons using Assembly Services with Dynamic Dashboards

Let me show you a complete walkthrough of how to create this simple dashboard using the embedded dynamic dashboard type. This example is a bit long, but it will show you every step needed to create the same dashboard. This example aims to give you a full working example of creating a dynamic dashboard through Assembly Services. To follow along, you'll need your own image files and dashboard parameters.

Functional Requirement

Create a vertical stack dashboard with five buttons that vary with the label as well as the icon image for the button. This will be achieved using Assembly Services and the embedded dynamic dashboard type.

Solution Steps

1. **Create a Button:** Start by creating a button (we'll edit its details later).
2. **Set up Template Dashboard:** Create a new dashboard, attach the button, and name the dashboard `DynamicTemplate` for this example.
3. **Create the Dynamic Dashboard:** Set up another dashboard with Dashboard Type set to Embedded Dynamic. Leave the components empty. Name it `DynamicDashboardFromCode` (for this example).
4. **Create the Assembly and Files:** Generate an Assembly, create a Service Factory file, the dynamic dashboard service file, and a standard class file named `DynamicNavBar`.
5. **Define the Service Factory:** Name the dynamic dashboard service `DynamicDashboardService` (for this example).
6. **Configure the Assembly File:** Modify the dynamic dashboard's Assembly file to look for the embedded dynamic dashboard (i.e., `DynamicDashboardFromCode`).
7. **Write the DynamicNavBar Code:** Edit the code in the `DynamicNavBar` file to programmatically manipulate the repeater arguments.
8. **Edit Button Parameters:** Update the button to include the following parameters: (`Label2`, `Image2`).
9. **Adjust Dashboard Layout:** Configure the `DynamicDashboardFromCode` dashboard layout to be either Vertical Stack or Grid, depending on your case.
10. **Update the Workspace Settings:** Ensure the Workspace settings for the Workspace Assembly Service are set correctly.
11. **Review and Test:** Review your dashboard and be amazed 😊

Solution Step Details

1. **Create a Button:** Start by creating a button (we'll edit its details later).

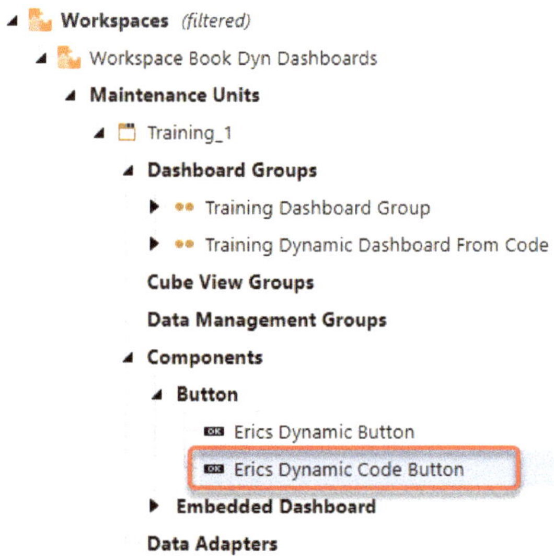

Figure 8.22

2. **Set up Template Dashboard:** Create a new dashboard, attach the button, and name the dashboard `DynamicTemplate` for this example.

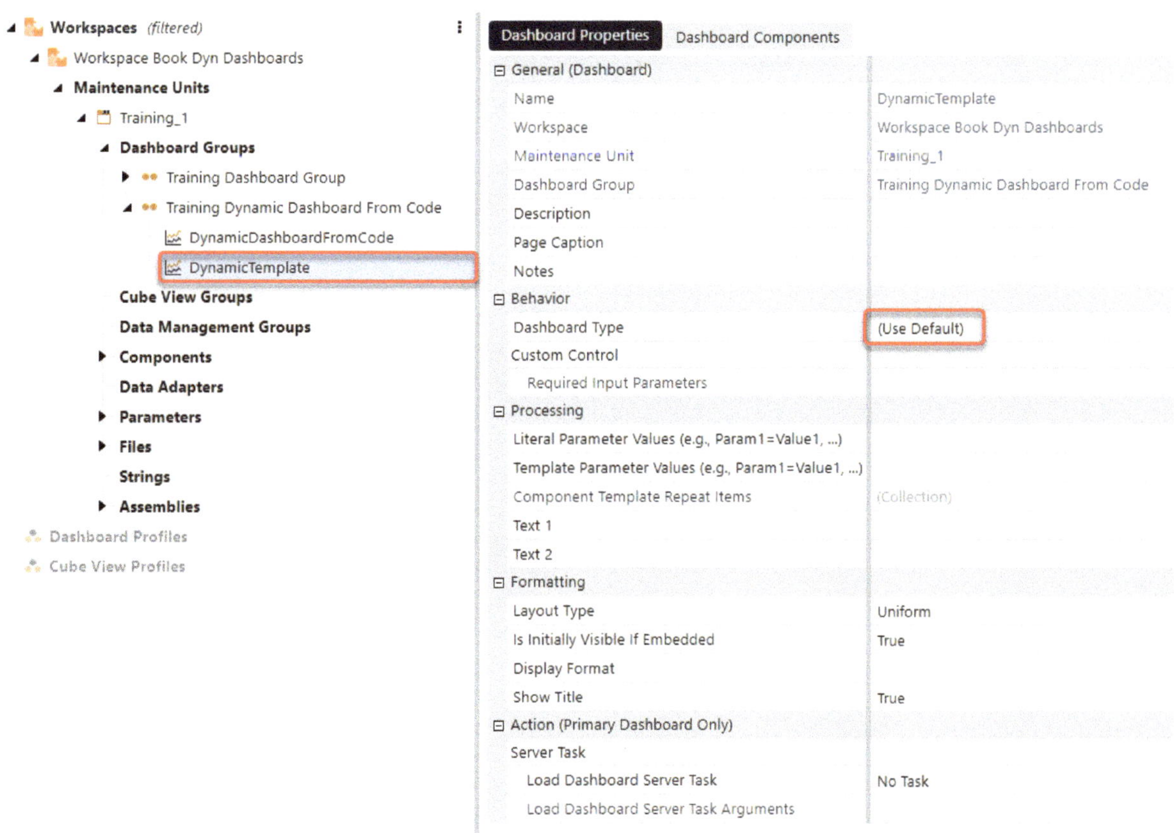

Figure 8.23

Attach the newly created button.

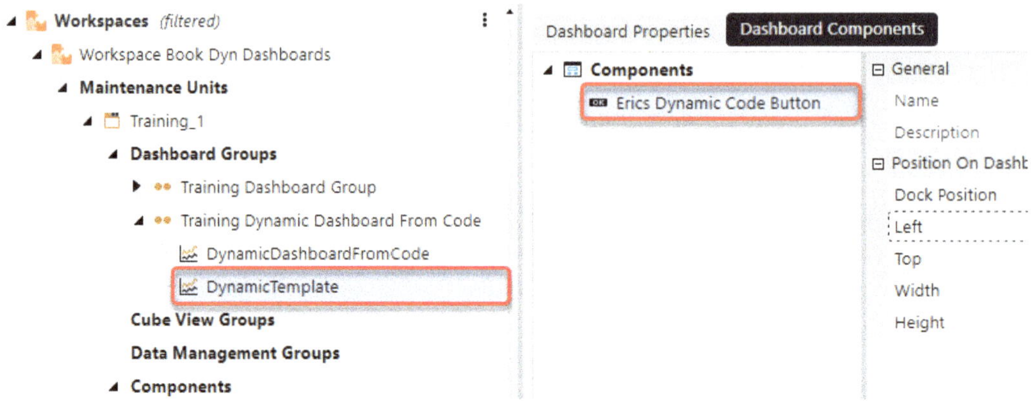

Figure 8.24

3. **Create the Dynamic Dashboard:** Set up another dashboard with Dashboard Type set to Embedded Dynamic. Leave the components empty. Name it `DynamicDashboardFromCode` (for this example).

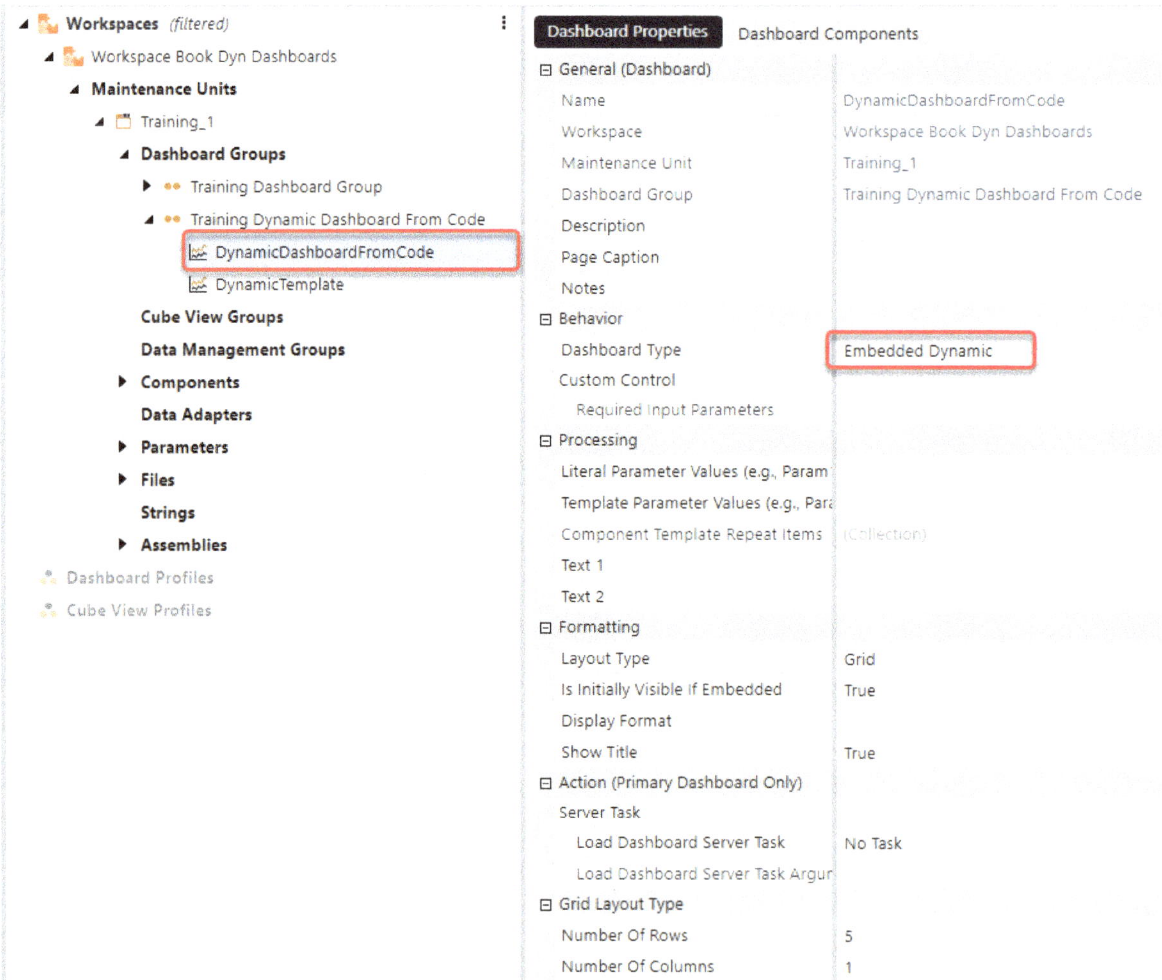

Figure 8.25

No Components

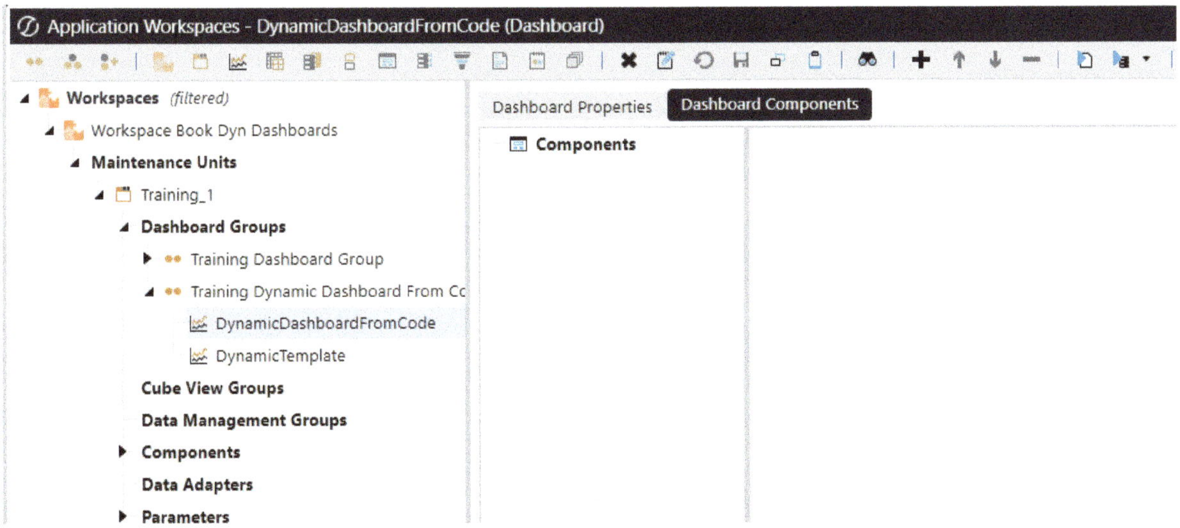

Figure 8.26

4. **Create an Assembly and Create Folders and Files**
   a. Service Factory file – named MyServiceFactory
   b. Dynamic dashboard service file – named: DynamicDashboardService
   c. Standard class file – named DynamicNavBar

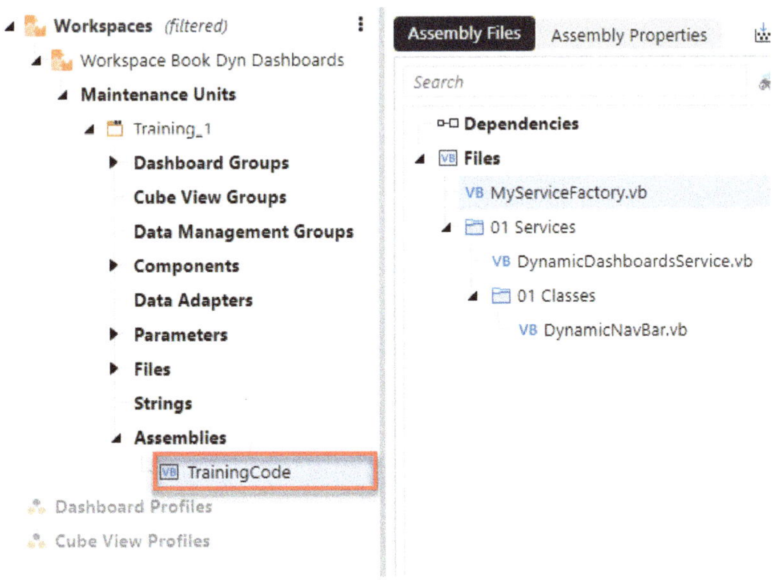

Figure 8.27

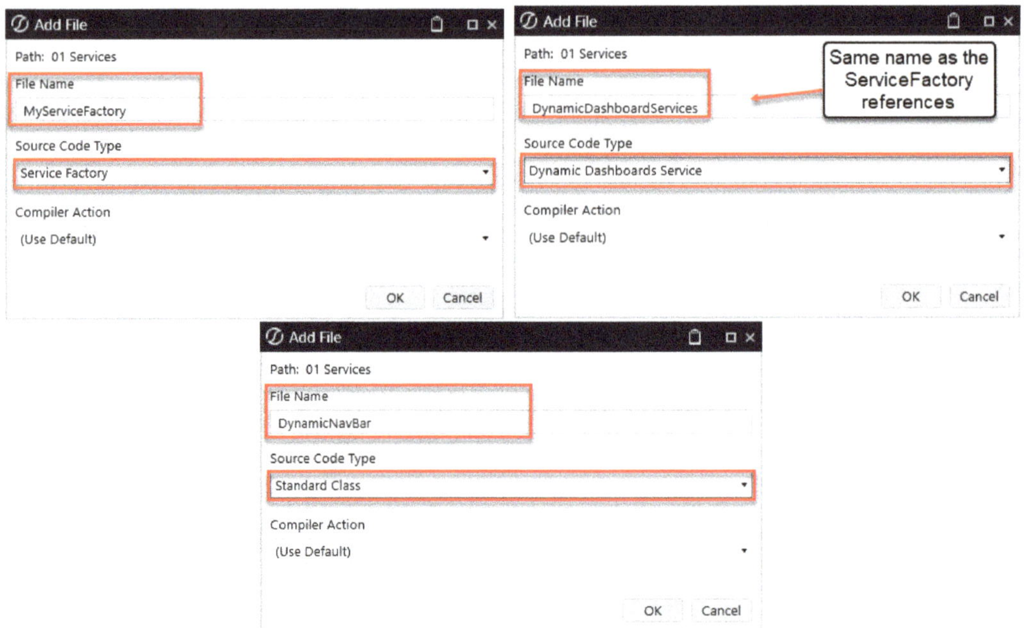

Figure 8.28

5. **Define the Service Factory:** Name the dynamic dashboard service `DynamicDashboardService` (for this example).

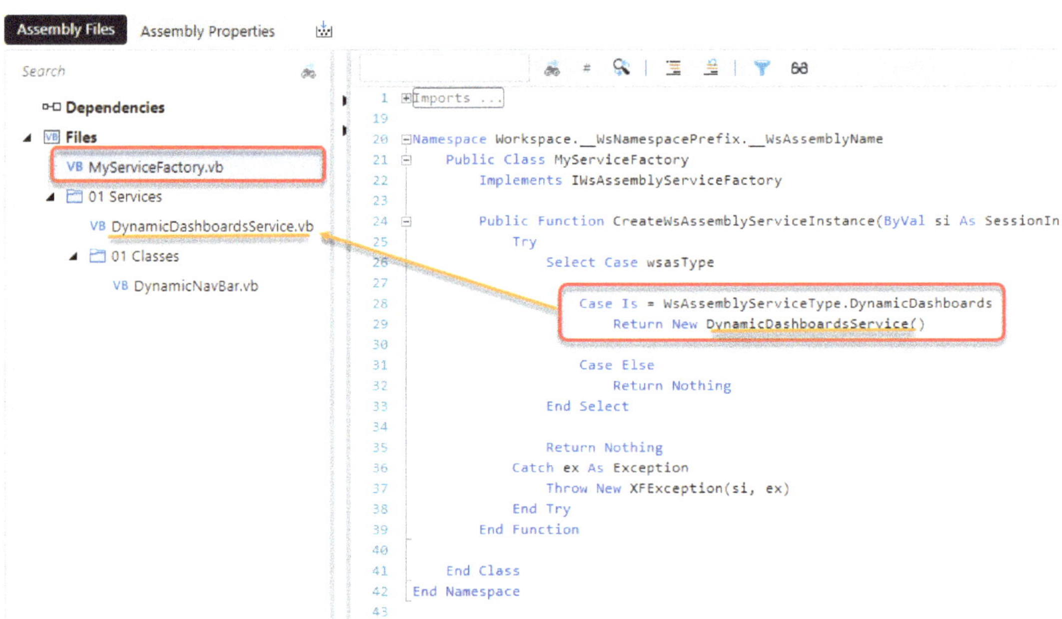

Figure 8.29

6. **Configure the Assembly File:** Modify the `DynamicDashboardsService` Assembly file to look for the embedded dynamic dashboard (i.e., `DynamicDashboardFromCode`).

Figure 8.30

Add code to the function GetDynamicComponentsForDynamicDashboard. This code references the embedded dynamic dashboard that we want – DynamicDashboardFromCode.

Then, this code calls the class DynamicNavBar.

Note: DynamicNavBar is the standard class that we created to return the dynamically repeated dashboard. You will see the full code of this class in Figure 8.32 below.

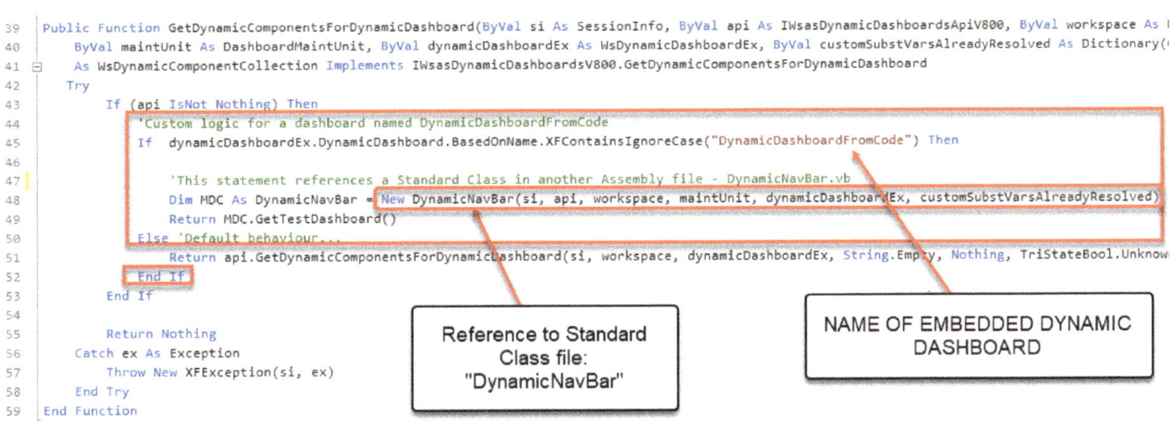

Figure 8.31

7. **Write the DynamicNavBar Code:** Edit the code in the `DynamicNavBar` file to programmatically manipulate the repeater arguments.

   Now, it's time to write the code for the `DynamicNavBar` file we just referenced. Refer to the attached screenshot of the code (Figure 8.32) for a practical example that you can replicate. To use this solution, you'll need to update it with your own image files and dashboard parameters.

   The primary goal of this code is to populate a dictionary object with all of the component repeat items and then run them dynamically against the dashboard. This ensures that the button (which is looking for these template parameters) can be configured and rendered appropriately.

   There are many ways to accomplish this in both VB.Net and C#, but this example is a straightforward approach to demonstrate the concept.

> **Note:** As a friendly reminder, I don't come from a programming background, so please be kind when you are critiquing this code 😊. Consider this a starting point for further customization, based on your specific requirements.

```
Imports ...

Namespace Workspace.__WsNamespacePrefix.__WsAssemblyName
    Public Class DynamicNavBar

        Private _si As SessionInfo
        Private _api As IWsasDynamicDashboardsApiV800
        Private _workspace As DashboardWorkspace
        Private _maintUnit As DashboardMaintUnit
        Private _dynamicDashboardEx As WsDynamicDashboardEx
        Private _customSubstVarsAlreadyResolved As Dictionary(Of String, String)

        'Consructor for the Public Function GetDynamicComponentsForDynamicDashboard
        Public Sub New(ByVal si As SessionInfo, ByVal api As IWsasDynamicDashboardsApiV800, ByVal workspace As DashboardWorkspace, _
            ByVal maintUnit As DashboardMaintUnit, ByVal dynamicDashboardEx As WsDynamicDashboardEx, _
            ByVal customSubstVarsAlreadyResolved As Dictionary(Of String, String))
            _si = si
            _api = api
            _workspace = workspace
            _maintUnit = maintUnit
            _dynamicDashboardEx = dynamicDashboardEx
            _customSubstVarsAlreadyResolved = customSubstVarsAlreadyResolved
        End Sub


' Define a class to encapsulate the component details
Public Class DashboardComponentDetails
    Public Property Label As String
    Public Property Image As String

    Public Sub New(label As String, image As String)
        Me.Label = label
        Me.Image = image
    End Sub
End Class

```

Creates a place to hold the Label and Image parameters

(Code continued below)

```
'Function to build the dynamic dashboard
Public Function GetTestDashboard() As WsDynamicComponentCollection
    Dim dynamicComponents As New List(Of WsDynamicDbrdCompMemberEx)

    ' Create a list of component details
    Dim components As New List(Of DashboardComponentDetails) From {
        New DashboardComponentDetails("Drivers_"&"|!prm_BudgetYear!|", "img_IconProjects.png_DYN"),
        New DashboardComponentDetails("Revenue_"&"|!prm_ActualYear!|", "img_IconBudget.png_DYN"),
        New DashboardComponentDetails("Reimb_"&"|!prm_ActualPriorYear!|", "img_IconForecast.png_DYN"),
        New DashboardComponentDetails("Expenses_"&"|!prm_BudgetYear!|", "img_IconReporting.png_DYN"),
        New DashboardComponentDetails("Rptg_"&"|!prm_BudgetYear!|", "img_IconModels.png_DYN")
    }

    Dim index As Integer = 0

    ' Iterate through the components and build the dynamic components
    For Each compDetails In components
        index += 1

        ' Populate Dictionary of template parameters
        Dim nextLevelSubstVarToAdd As New Dictionary(Of String, String) From {
            {"Label2", compDetails.Label},
            {"Image2", compDetails.Image}
        }

        ' Build dynamic component
        Dim dynamicComponent As WsDynamicDbrdCompMemberEx = Me.BuildDynamicComponentFromStoredComponent(
            "Embedded DynamicTemplate", "EricsButton_" & index, nextLevelSubstVarToAdd, WsDynamicItemStateType.MinimalWithTemplateParameters)

        If dynamicComponent IsNot Nothing Then
            Dim comp As DashboardComponent = dynamicComponent.DynamicComponentEx.DynamicComponent.Component
            Dim format As ComponentDisplayFormatBuilder = New ComponentDisplayFormatBuilder(comp.DisplayFormat)
            format.SetValue(ComponentDisplayFormatBuilder.constLabelItalic, "True")

            comp.DisplayFormat = format.FormatString
            dynamicComponents.Add(dynamicComponent)
        End If
    Next

    Return New WsDynamicComponentCollection(_dynamicDashboardEx, dynamicComponents)
End Function

'Helper function to build a dynamic component from a stored component
Private Function BuildDynamicComponentFromStoredComponent( storedComponentName As String, nextLevelNameSuffixToAdd As String, _
    nextLevelSubstVarToAdd As Dictionary(Of String, String),  dynamicItemStateType As WsDynamicItemStateType) As WsDynamicDbrdCompMemberEx

    Dim storedComp As DashboardDbrdCompMemberEx= _api.GetStoredComponentForDynamicDashboard(_si,_workspace,_dynamicDashboardEx.DynamicDashboard, storedComponentName)

    If (Not storedComp Is Nothing) Then
        Dim wsDynamicCompEx = _api.GetDynamicComponentForDynamicDashboard(_si, _workspace, _dynamicDashboardEx, storedComp.Component, nextLevelNameSuffixToAdd, _
            nextLevelSubstVarToAdd, TriStateBool.TrueValue, dynamicItemStateType)

        If (Not wsDynamicCompEx Is Nothing) Then
            Dim WsDynCompMember As WsDynamicDbrdCompMember = New WsDynamicDbrdCompMember()
            Return New WsDynamicDbrdCompMemberEx(WsDynCompMember, wsDynamicCompEX)
        End If
    End If
    Return Nothing
End Function

    End Class
End Namespace
```

Creates the Component Template Repeat Items

Runs the Repeat Items against the Embedded Dashboard that holds our button.

Figure 8.32

8. **Edit Button Parameters:** Update the button to include the following parameters: (`Label2`, `Image2`). As a reminder, the repeater parameter's syntax is `~!parameter!~`.

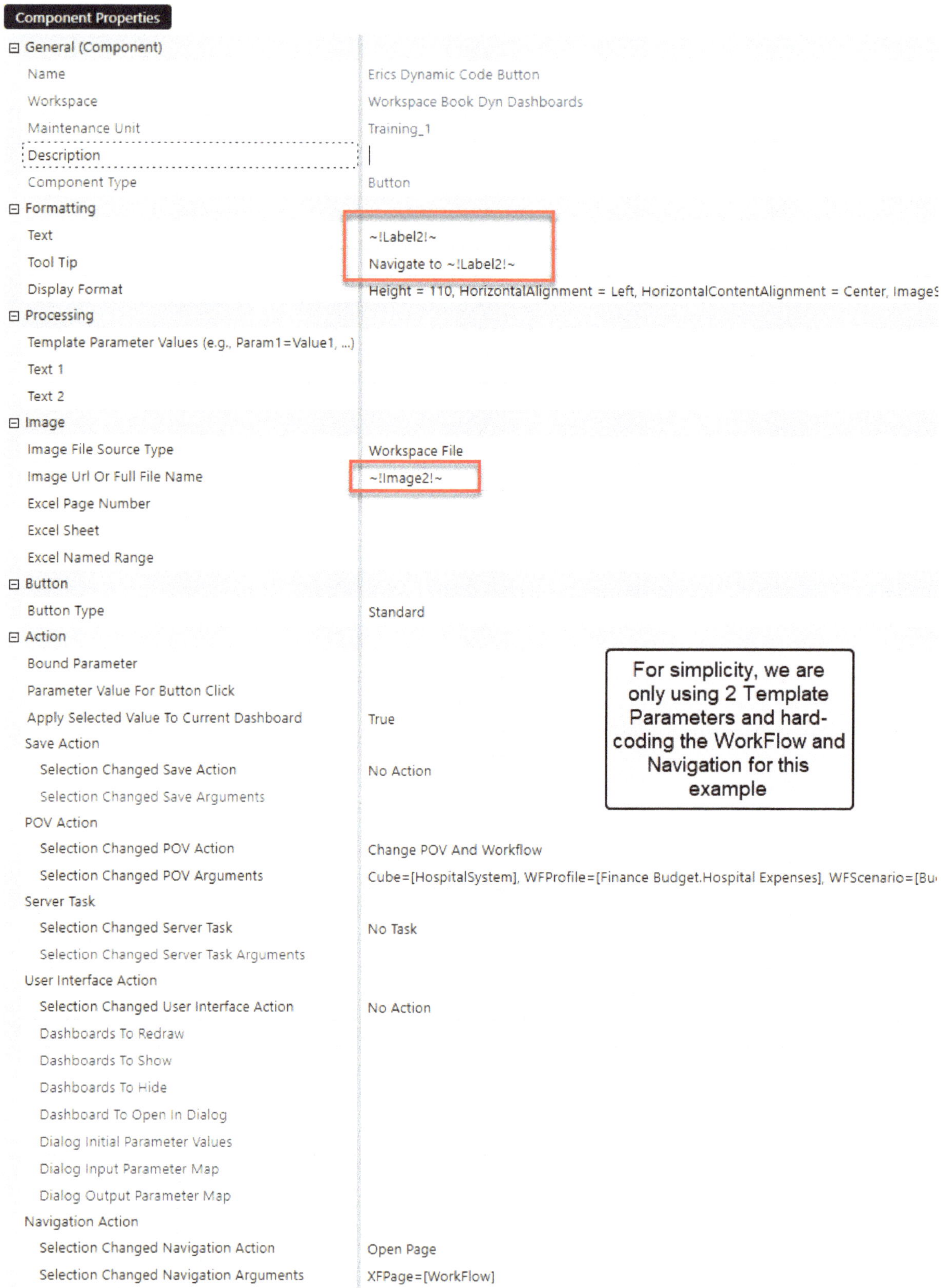

Figure 8.33

9. **Adjust Dashboard Layout:** Configure the DynamicDashboardFromCode dashboard layout to be either Vertical Stack or Grid, depending on your case. We are using Grid here.

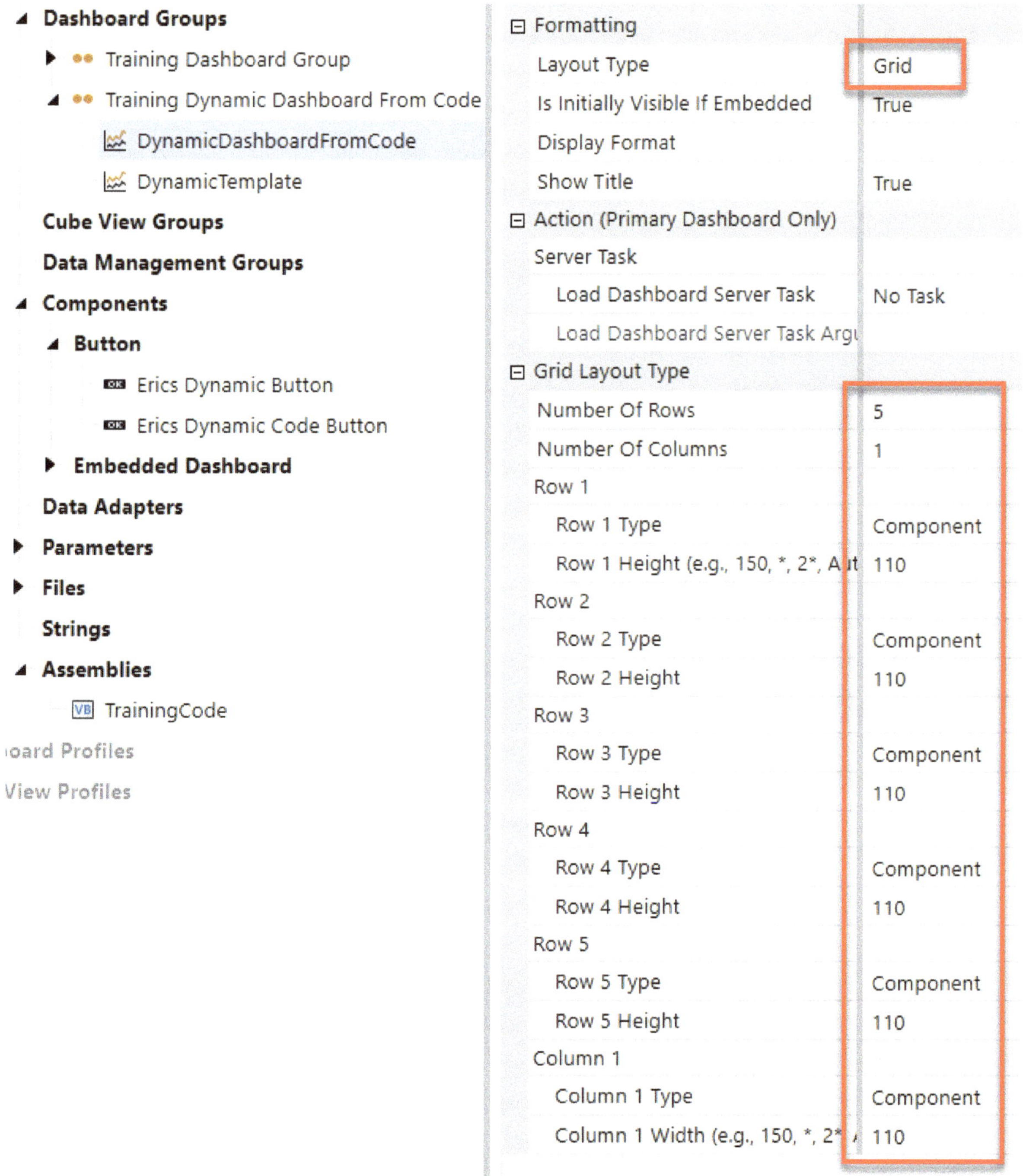

Figure 8.34

10. **Update the Workspace Settings:** Ensure you have the Workspace settings defined to your Service Factory.

> **Remember:** When you invoke an embedded dynamic dashboard type, OneStream looks in the current Workspace to see which Service Factory is defined, and then looks for the dynamic dashboard service type.

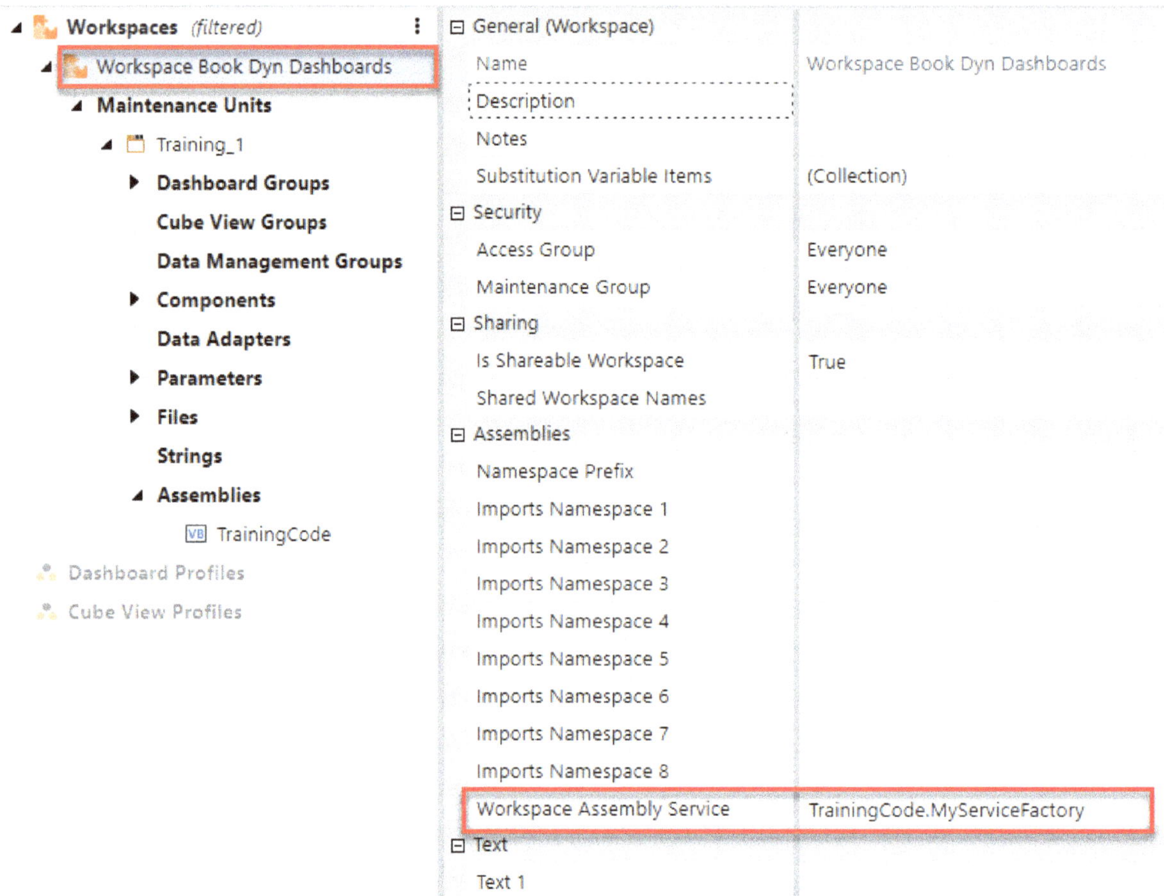

Figure 8.35

11. **Review:** Final dashboard using dynamic dashboard service *from* an Assembly factory.

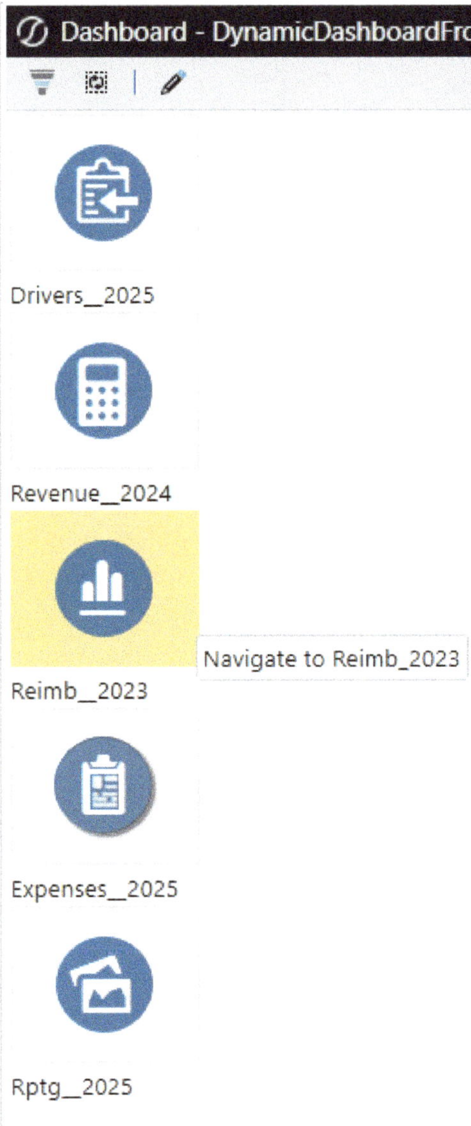

Figure 8.36

12. **Review:** View the Dashboard in Design Mode and see the dynamic buttons that came from only one stored button.

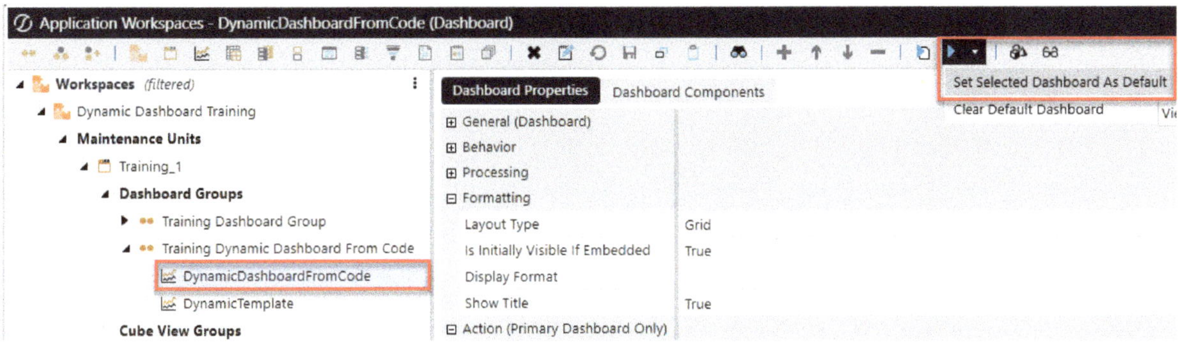

Figure 8.37

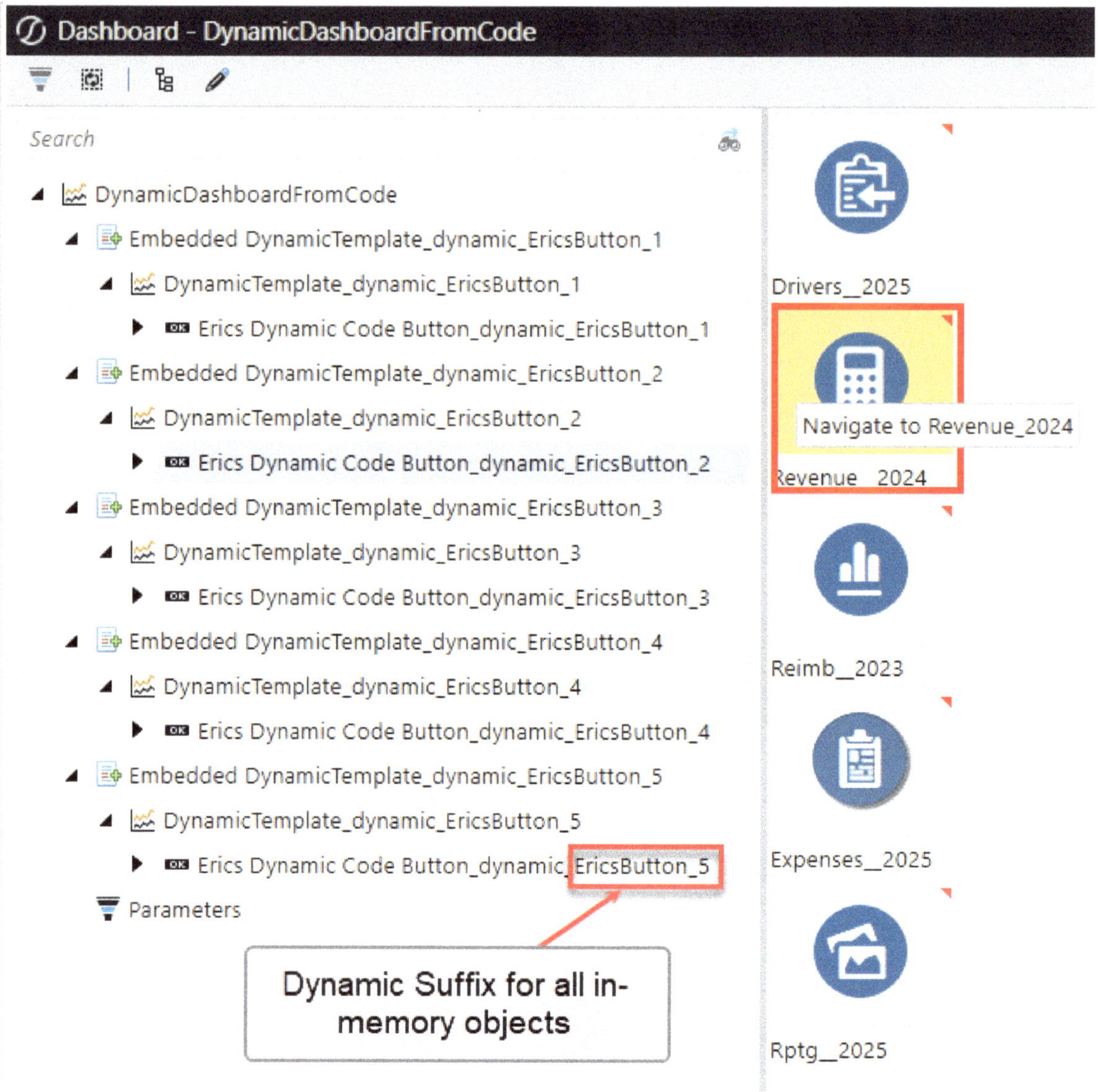

Figure 8.38

You have control over what suffix you give the dynamic objects. In this example, here is where that is defined in the DynamicNavBar.vb file:

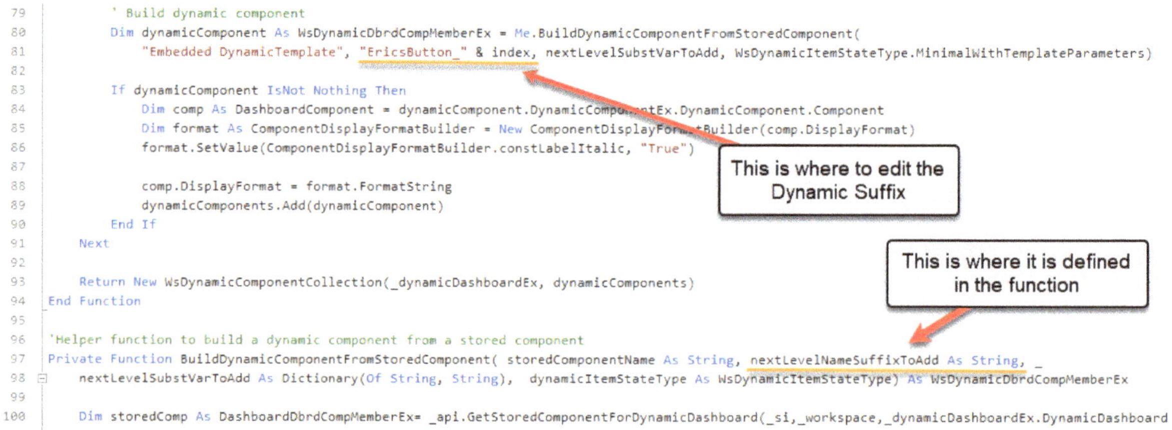

Figure 8.39

Summary of Example 2

Let's summarize the big picture of what the code is doing:

- When the embedded dynamic dashboard is invoked, OneStream searches the current Workspace for the associated solution factory.
- The Service Factory identifies the dynamic dashboard service and routes the request to the appropriate service file.
- Within the dynamic dashboard service file, it matches the dashboard's name and executes the relevant code.
- The executed code references a standard class file to define all the repeatable arguments required for the dashboard.
- Using the list of repeatable arguments, the service cycles through the embedded dynamic dashboard, dynamically binding the template parameters to the button.
- Finally, it generates and returns the in-memory repeater template parameters, enabling the dashboard to render dynamically in-memory.

Differences Between No-Code Dynamic Dashboards and Code-Based Dynamic Dashboard Services

In the previous examples, we demonstrated how dynamic dashboards can create multiple components from a single stored component, with each "in-memory" component configured using repeater parameters. Now, let's take this concept a step further.

No-Code Dynamic Dashboards, using embedded dynamic repeaters are a great starting point but are limited in scope – they can only modify settings that accept text values. This is because the template parameters defined in the component template repeat items return string variables – although great for simple use cases – lack versatility for more complex requirements.

This is where **Dynamic Dashboard Services** excel. With code-based solutions, you can modify settings that traditionally don't accept text values, such as action settings. For instance, in a button component, this could include the save action, POV action, or navigation action.

While repeater parameters allow for dynamic changes to parameterized settings, certain settings – like save settings or server task settings – could not previously be altered dynamically, leading to the need for multiple, nearly identical component copies. With Dynamic Dashboard Services, OneStream removes these limitations. Nearly all dashboard component settings can now be adjusted programmatically, in-memory, allowing you to eliminate redundancy and streamline your dashboards.

Here's an example of a button component and the wide range of settings that can now be altered dynamically in-memory (Figure 8.40):

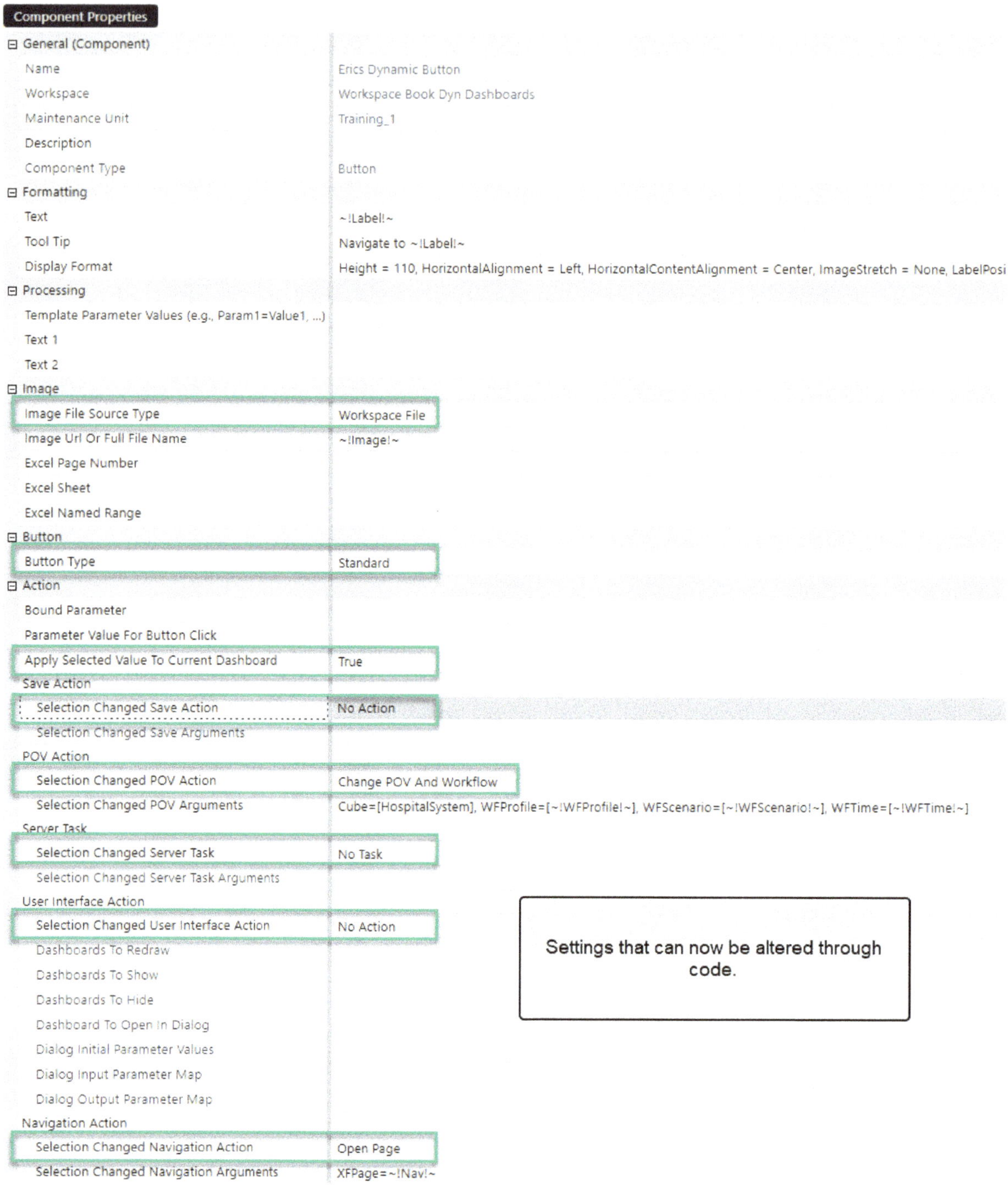

Figure 8.40

With Figure 8.40 illustrating the extensive range of settings that can now be modified dynamically, we've reached the tipping point in understanding the full capabilities of Dynamic Dashboard Services. Moving beyond foundational concepts, it's time to explore the **advanced methods and classes** that drive these dynamic interactions. While mastering these components requires some technical effort, understanding their role will unlock the ability to design even more adaptive and scalable dashboards. The next section aims to guide you through these objects and provide practical insights into how they can be leveraged to enhance your OneStream implementations.

Advanced Topics – Dynamic Methods and Classes for Dynamic Dashboard Service

Admittedly, diving into the dynamic dashboard service methods and classes can seem overwhelming at first, especially if you're unfamiliar with these concepts. However, this section is designed to gently guide you into the world of Dynamic Dashboard Services in OneStream, providing you with the resources and insights to kickstart your learning journey.

The key to mastering Dynamic Dashboard Services lies in understanding the additional methods and classes specifically built to support dynamic functionality. These tools offer tremendous flexibility and are integral to creating scalable, adaptive dashboards. Think of this section as your reference guide – highlighting the objects and methods you can leverage in your code to unlock the full potential of Dynamic Dashboard Services.

When you create a new dynamic dashboard service file, OneStream provides several default methods to help you get started. Among these, two of the most commonly used and versatile methods are:

- `GetEmbeddedDynamicDashboard`
- `GetDynamicComponentsForDynamicDashboards`

Note: Do not delete or comment out any of the default functions in the dynamic dashboard service file because they are required to be available due to the line 22 statement:
`Implements IWsasDynamicDashboardsV800`

```
20  Namespace Workspace.__WsNamespacePrefix.__WsAssemblyName
21      Public Class TestDynDashboardService
22          Implements IWsasDynamicDashboardsV800
23
24          Public Function GetEmbeddedDynamicDashboard(ByVal si As Ses
```

Figure 8.41

Let's get a detailed understanding of the two most common methods.

1. GetEmbeddedDynamicDashboard

- **Purpose**: This method is used to retrieve or generate a dynamic dashboard that is embedded within a parent dashboard or Workspace. It is typically invoked when a specific dashboard needs to be dynamically created and rendered based on the context, such as user interactions or runtime parameters.
- **Functionality**:
  - It takes in several important parameters like session information (`SessionInfo`), API context (`IWsasDynamicDashboardsApiV800`), and a reference to the parent dashboard or Workspace.
  - The method resolves the relevant template parameters, stored dashboards, or data required to construct the embedded dynamic dashboard.
  - It generates a `WsDynamicDashboardEx` object, which represents the embedded dashboard in its fully constructed form.
  - The embedded dashboard is created in-memory at runtime, allowing for a highly flexible and on-demand rendering approach.
- **Use Case**:
  - When you have a "parent" dashboard with nested components or dashboards that depend on dynamic inputs, this method helps dynamically generate the embedded dashboards as needed.

    - For example, in a financial planning application, it could be used to generate sub-dashboards for individual departments, based on user input or selected parameters.

2. GetDynamicComponentsForDynamicDashboards

- **Purpose**: This method is used to retrieve the individual components of a dynamic dashboard. It focuses on providing the building blocks (dynamic components) that make up the entire dashboard, such as charts, labels, buttons, or other UI elements.
- **Functionality**:
    - It takes inputs like session information (`SessionInfo`), API context (`IWsasDynamicDashboardsApiV800`), and the dashboard or Workspace for which the components are needed.
    - The method constructs a collection of components (e.g., `WsDynamicComponent` objects) based on predefined templates, stored components, or runtime parameters.
    - These components are dynamically created in-memory, ensuring that the dashboard layout can be customized and rendered as required.
- **Use Case**:
    - When building dashboards where each component's content, appearance, or functionality depends on dynamic data or templates, this method is used to fetch and prepare those components.
    - For example, in a reporting dashboard, it could dynamically generate components like charts for revenue, expenses, and profit, tailored to the user's selected time period or business unit.

Key Difference Between the Two:

- `GetEmbeddedDynamicDashboard`: Focuses on creating or retrieving the entire dynamic dashboard as a single entity.
- `GetDynamicComponentsForDynamicDashboards`: Focuses on creating or retrieving individual components that make up a dynamic dashboard.

Together, these methods enable a highly flexible and scalable approach to dashboard creation in OneStream, allowing developers to efficiently manage both the overall structure and granular details of dynamic dashboards.

3. Other methods similar to GetDynamicComponentsForDynamicDashboards

These are three other methods that are listed in the default dynamic dashboard service files and are run when the relevant elements, such as data adapters and parameters, are created in-memory.

- `GetDynamicAdaptersForDynamicComponent`: Creates data adapters dynamically in-memory, which are used to connect components to data sources and facilitate real-time data interaction.
- `GetDynamicCubeViewForDynamicAdapter`: Generates an in-memory data adapter by leveraging an in-memory Cube View, enabling efficient data manipulation and visualization.
- `GetDynamicParametersForDynamicComponent`: Dynamically builds parameters in-memory that can be used to filter, configure, or pass values to dashboard components at runtime.

Classes that are specific to OneStream's Dynamic Dashboard Services

There are additional classes and objects in OneStream's Dynamic Dashboard Services that are designed to provide flexibility and customization when working with dynamic dashboards. Here are a few notable ones:

WsDynamicComponent

- Represents a single dynamic component within a dashboard. It is used to define and manage individual elements, such as labels, buttons, or charts, that are dynamically created and rendered in dashboards.

WsDynamicCollection

- A collection or container that holds multiple dynamic components. It is typically used to group components together for easier management and rendering within a dynamic dashboard.

WsDynamicDbrdCompMemberEx

- An extended member of a dynamic dashboard component. This class is used to define additional properties or behaviors for components that are part of a dynamic dashboard, allowing for more customization and functionality.

WsDynamicRepeatArgs

- Represents the arguments or parameters used in a repeater dashboard. These are essential for creating multiple instances of a component dynamically, with variations in their properties or data based on the provided arguments.

WsDynamicDashboardEx

- Represents the entire dynamic dashboard, including its components and layout. It is often used as the main object for managing and rendering dashboards dynamically.

WsDynamicParameterCollection

- A collection of parameters that can be dynamically applied to components within a dashboard. This is useful for passing data or settings to multiple components at runtime.

WsDynamicComponentRepeatArgs

- Used to define arguments for repeating components dynamically. This is particularly helpful when creating dashboards with repeated elements, such as rows or columns of similar components.

WsDynamicItemStateType

- Represents the state of a dynamic item (e.g., minimal, full, or with template parameters). This is used to control how components are rendered or processed and is useful to optimize performance.

DashboardWorkspace

- While not exclusive to dynamic dashboards, this class is essential for managing the Workspace context in which dashboards and their components are created and maintained.

DashboardMaintUnit

- Represents the maintenance unit for dashboards, which is critical for organizing and managing dashboard components and Assemblies.

ComponentDisplayFormatBuilder

- A utility class for customizing the display format of dashboard components, such as labels, fonts, and styles.

XFSelection... Rules To Control Dashboard Component Behavior

XFSelection rules are the secret sauce behind making dashboards in OneStream truly interactive and responsive. This is what gives you the power to control exactly how components behave when users interact with them – whether that's saving data, triggering an action, or responding to a selection change. Think about the real-world impact: you can create dashboards that adapt seamlessly to your workflows, instantly refresh data, or take user input and transform it into actionable results. These rules are essential for building dashboards that feel intuitive and effortless to use, saving you from hours of manual tweaks and ensuring a smooth, engaging experience for the end user. By tapping into the flexibility of these rules, you can make your dashboards smarter, faster, and far more user-friendly.

XFSelectionChangedSaveType

- Defines how changes in selection are saved (e.g., automatically, manually, or not at all).

XFSelectionChangedTaskType

- Specifies the type of task triggered by a selection change (e.g., calculation, custom business rule execution, or no task).

XFSelectionChangedTaskResult

- Represents the result of a task executed due to a selection change, including success or failure details.

XFSelectionChangedUIAction

- Determines the user interface action performed when a selection changes (e.g., refreshing components or navigating dashboards).

XFSelectionChangedWorkflowAction

- Handles workflow-related actions triggered by selection changes, such as updating the Workflow POV.

XFSelectionChangedDataAction

- Manages data-related actions, such as recalculating or refreshing data sources based on selection changes.

XFSelectionChangedParameterAction

- Controls the behavior of parameters when a selection changes, including resolving template variables dynamically.

XFSelectionChangedComponentAction

- Modifies component-specific settings, such as enabling/disabling components or changing their visibility.

These rules provide granular control over dashboard behavior and interactivity.

Conclusion

Dynamic Dashboard Services in OneStream undoubtedly come with a learning curve, especially for those just beginning to explore these methods and classes. This chapter is meant to give you that initial push and provide the foundational knowledge needed to start your journey with confidence.

The *no-code approach* of embedded dynamic repeater dashboards serves as a perfect introduction. It demonstrates how powerful dynamic dashboards can be, whether you're creating something as simple as the example above, or crafting far more intricate solutions limited only by your imagination. This approach provides very good insight into what the Dynamic Dashboard Services are trying to achieve through code. By utilizing stored components and applying template parameters, you can dynamically generate multiple iterations of dashboards in-memory, precisely when they're needed.

This flexibility highlights the core purpose of Dynamic Dashboard Services: empowering users to scale and adapt their dashboards through both simplicity and advanced customization. With time and practice, you'll begin to unlock the full potential of these services, creating dynamic and efficient solutions that save time, reduce redundancy, and adapt to evolving business needs. Beyond just simplifying development, these services lay the groundwork for "future-proofing" your OneStream application, ensuring it remains agile and relevant as requirements change.

9

Sharing and Reusing Workspace Objects

What is Workspace Sharing?

In OneStream, *sharing objects between Workspaces* means you can *reference and reuse* existing components – like dashboards, data adapters, parameters, and Cube Views – across multiple Workspaces without having to duplicate them.

Communicating this powerful sharing tool to your development teams will help you realize more synergies between development efforts, and ultimately help you extend your OneStream investment.

Do I Need to Share Workspaces?

The short answer is no, you don't *need* to share Workspaces (maintaining Workspaces as private and self-contained has many advantages in terms of portability and robustness). However, there are many benefits to incorporating this practice in your application, such as making dashboard development more efficient and effective. Once you start dabbling with Workspace sharing, you'll quickly see how this feature allows you to streamline development.

Here are the benefits of sharing Workspaces within your OneStream application.

1. Leverage Existing Work

Instead of recreating dashboards or related objects from scratch in each Workspace:

- You can *link* to or *reference* objects that already exist in another Workspace.

This reduces development time, encourages reusability, and maintains consistency across projects or teams.

2. Eliminates Redundancy

Duplicating dashboard components across Workspaces leads to:

- *Multiple versions* of the same object.
- Increased storage use.
- Difficulties in updating or maintaining consistency.

Sharing allows *centralized updates* to be reflected automatically across all consuming Workspaces.

3. Ensures Consistency

When objects are shared rather than duplicated:

- Everyone is working with the *same version* of the dashboard or Cube View.
- Business logic (like calculations or parameters) is consistent across the organization.
- The risk of *data discrepancies* or misinterpretation is significantly reduced.

4. Improves Governance and Control

Sharing supports better governance by:

- Centralizing control of critical objects.
- Enabling a single source of truth.
- Making audits and updates more manageable.
- Reducing errors caused by conflicting versions.

5. Supports Scalable Development

For organizations with multiple developers or departments:

- Teams can collaborate without stepping on each other's toes with the use of a shared Workspace – a Central Library, if you will – containing objects that are meant to be shared (or extended) for consumption by other Workspaces.
- Developers can test or enhance shared components in their own Workspace before proposing changes to the central/shared version.

As you begin your OneStream journey or explore ways to make your OneStream investment work for you, there are undoubtedly areas where Workspace sharing will allow you to leverage existing work and cut down development time.

How Do I Share Workspaces?

Sharing Workspace objects can be done in several ways. As the OneStream framework continues to evolve and grow, you may find other ways of sharing Workspace objects that help facilitate more efficient development practices and streamlined application management.

Preparation

To share objects from a Workspace, the Workspace containing the shared objects (the *source* Workspace) must be configured to allow sharing by setting the Workspace property Is Shareable Workspace to True.

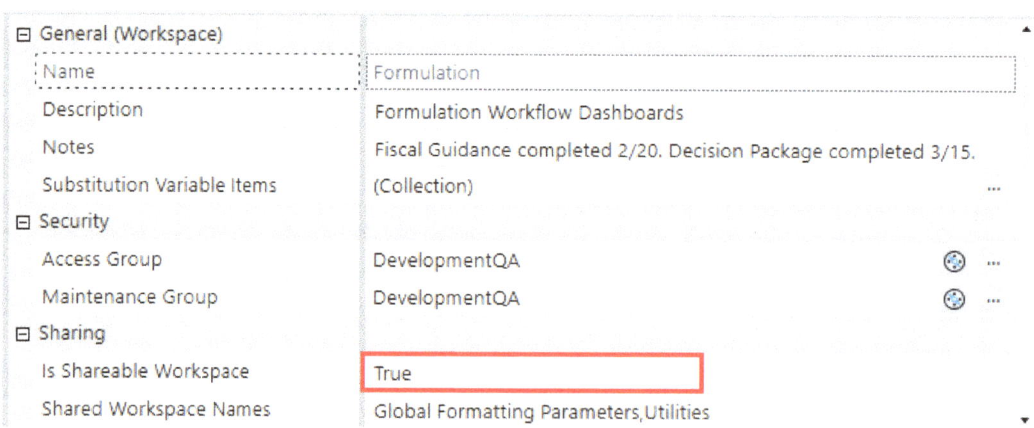

Figure 9.1

Once the source Workspace is configured, objects can be shared in two ways:

Direct Reference

When calling an object from the source Workspace into the target Workspace, reference the object using the syntax `WorkspaceName.ObjectName`.

Direct reference example – showing the object name preceded by the source Workspace name.

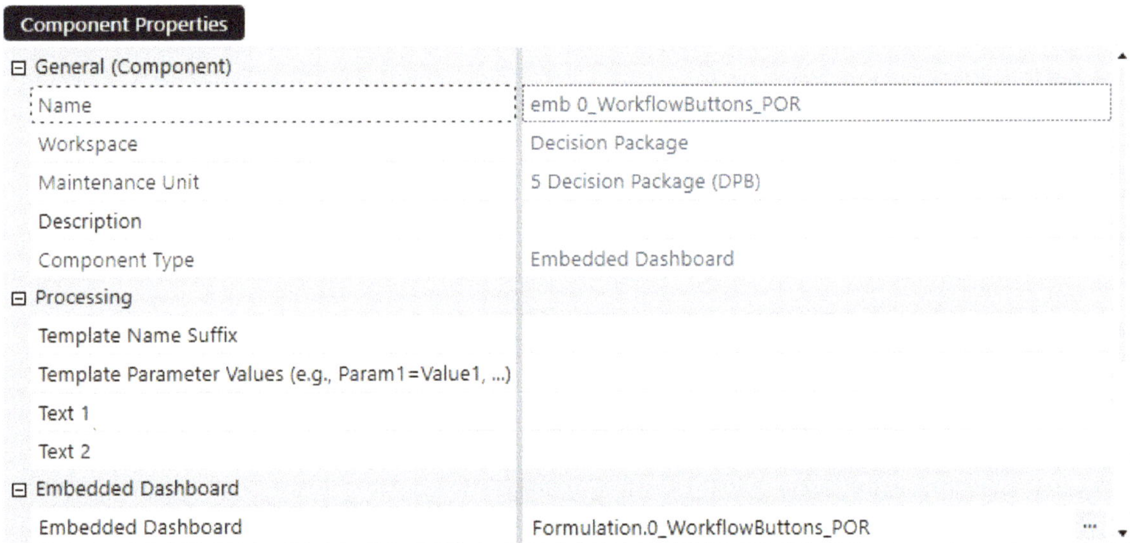

Figure 9.2

Full Workspace Share

By defining the source Workspace as a Shared Workspace in the Target Workspace property, all objects can be called using their name only.

Target Workspace definition example – showing the Formulation Workspace configured as a fully-shared Workspace.

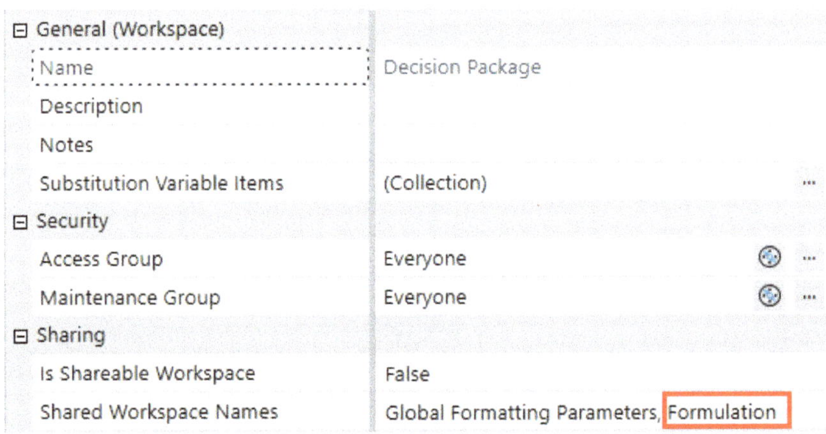

Figure 9.3

Full Workspace shared object reference – showing only the object name being called.

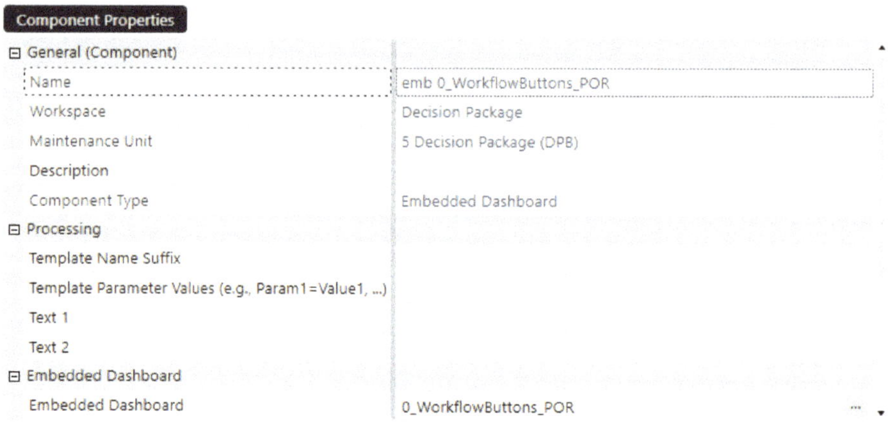

Figure 9.4

The *direct reference* approach has the advantage of making it clear where the definition of the object is stored. The *full Workspace share* makes it easier if you are planning to share multiple objects.

Let's explore two commonly used methods for sharing Workspace objects: displaying shared dashboards using embedded dashboard components, and opening dashboards in dialog boxes using button components.

Method #1 – Embedded Dashboards

To display a shared dashboard from another Workspace on your Workspace's dashboard, you'll start by creating an embedded dashboard component that can be a placeholder to nest on your dashboard.

The first step is to create an embedded dashboard component. Navigate to the Embedded Dashboard component list and click on the Create Dashboard Component button from the Workspace toolbar.

Figure 9.5

Select Embedded Dashboard from the Create Dashboard Component dialog box and click OK.

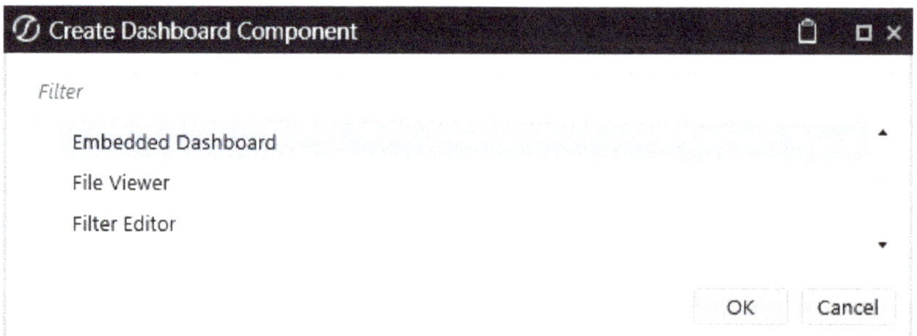

Figure 9.6

Name the embedded dashboard component and click Save. Once you have created the new component, click on the Edit button on the Embedded Dashboard property.

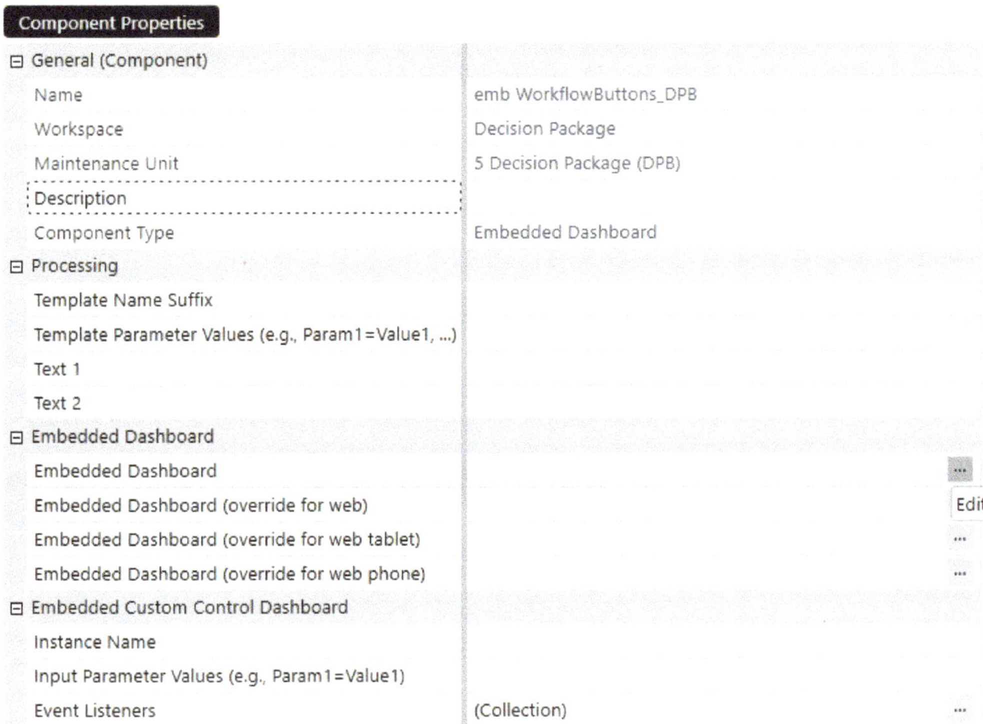

Figure 9.7

The object lookup dialog box opens, displaying which Workspaces are shared *and* to which the user has access. You may have shared Workspaces in your application that a user does not have access to, which will not be displayed until you give the user access to those specific Workspaces.

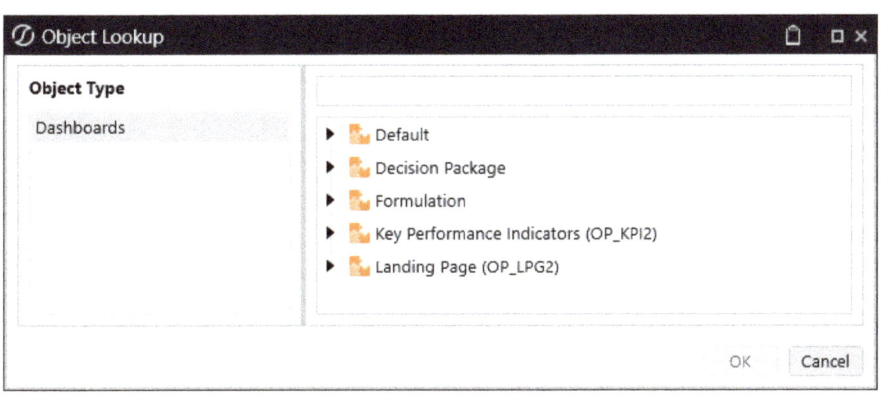

Figure 9.8

Start typing the name of the dashboard you want to reuse, and the lookup menu will filter it based on your search criteria. Once you find the desired dashboard, select it and click OK.

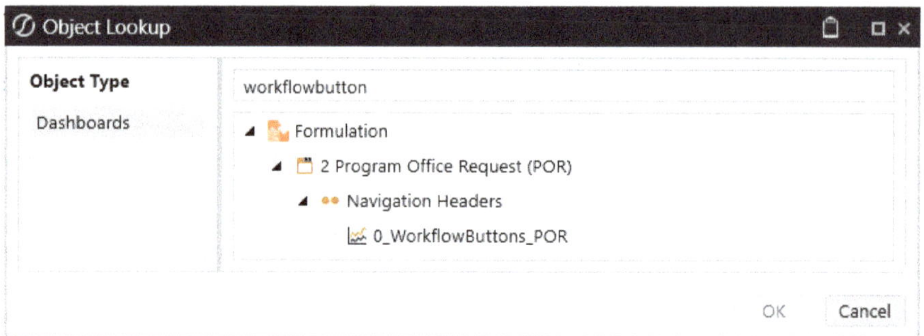

Figure 9.9

Navigate to the dashboard where you want to display the shared object and click on the Dashboard Components tab. Click the + button and select the embedded dashboard component, then click OK.

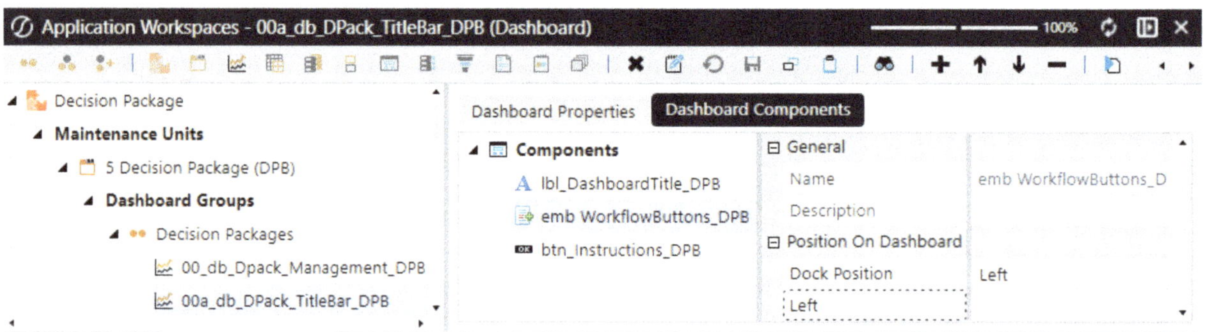

Figure 9.10

To test the dashboard and ensure it displays, click the View Dashboard button.

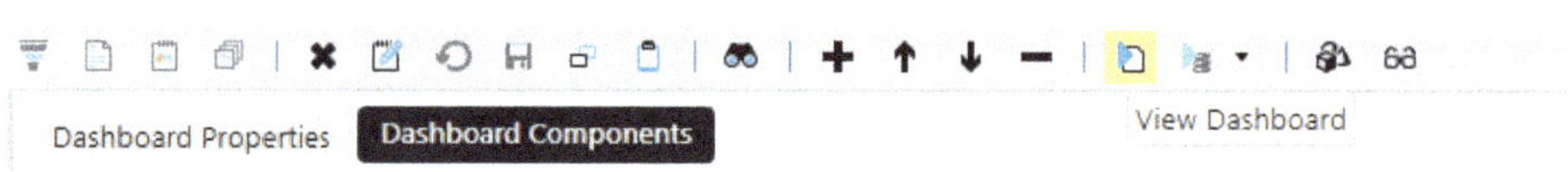

Figure 9.11

The result will display the shared dashboard.

Figure 9.12

Method #2 - Open Dialog Box with Button

Another common method of displaying shared dashboards is using a button to open a dialog box. Create a new button component and scroll down to the User Interface Action properties. From the Selection Changed User Interface Action property, select Open Dialog With No Buttons from the drop-down menu, then select the dashboard to open in Dialog from the Edit button.

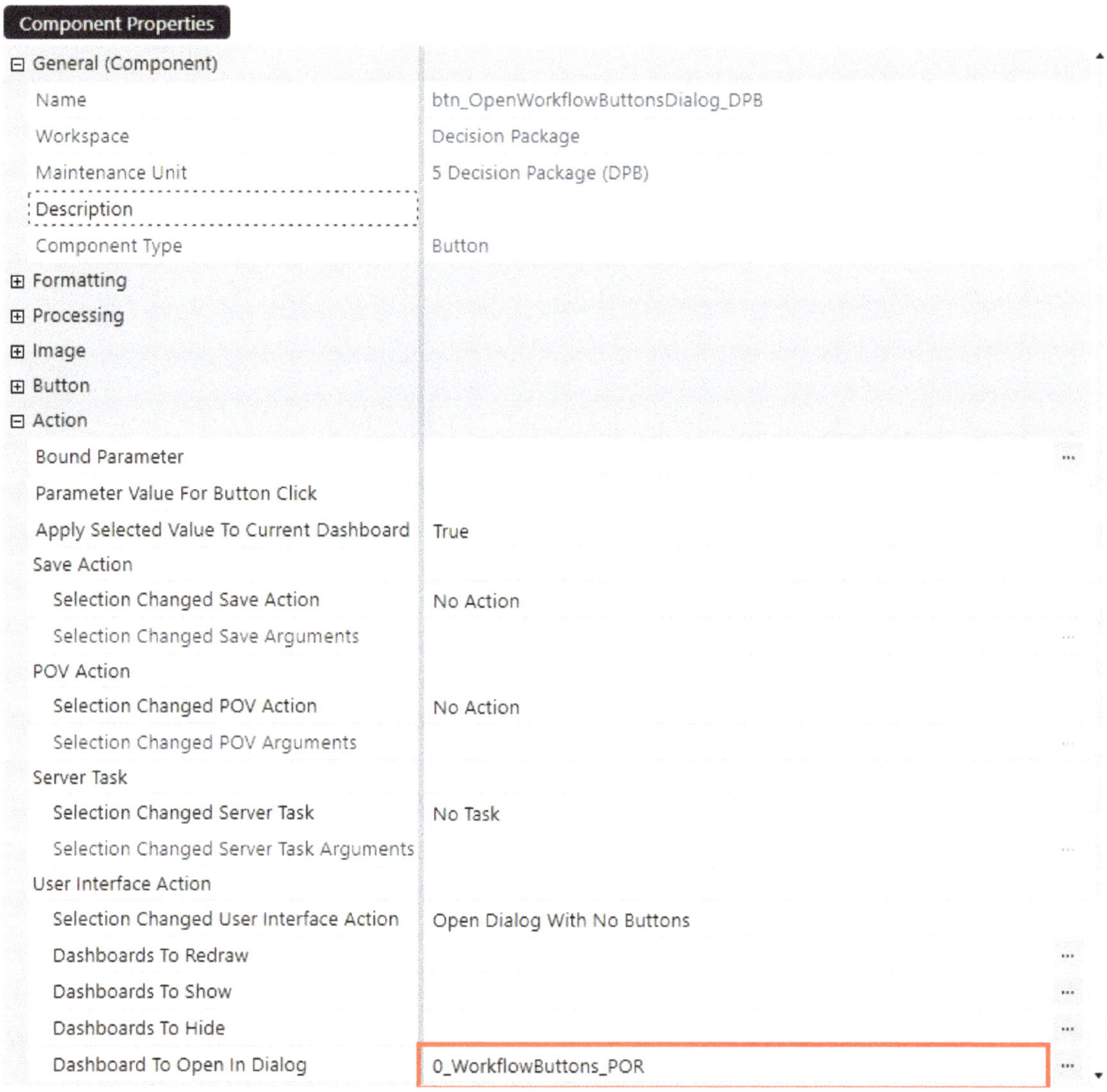

Figure 9.13

To test the button's action, attach the button to your dashboard's Dashboard Component tab using the ✚ button, and then click View Dashboard. Once you see your button on the dashboard, click it, and you should see a dialog box appear with the shared dashboard.

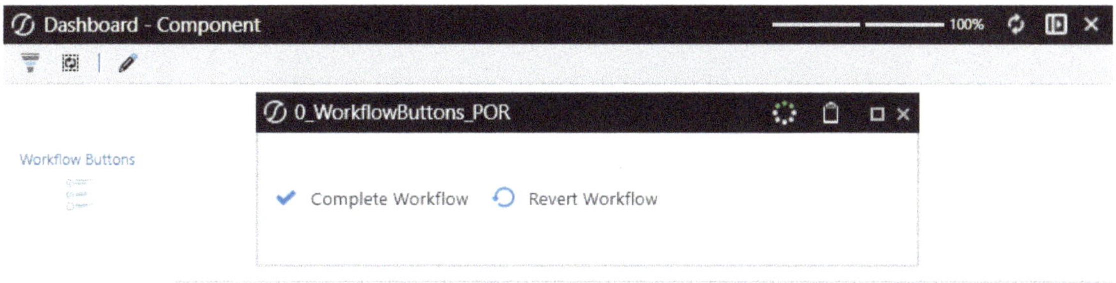

Figure 9.14

These are just some examples of how you can share objects between Workspaces, but this should give you the groundwork and inspiration to enable you to share Workspace objects to enhance your application and streamline your development.

Sharing Workspace Objects Examples

Here are a few examples of when you might want to share Workspace objects and how to properly configure your Workspaces to allow sharing. Although these are examples of use cases for sharing Workspaces and inherited objects, as you read through the examples, just imagine how much efficiency you can bring into your application by leveraging OneStream's Workspace sharing functionality. With this feature in your toolbox, aside from streamlining development, you can significantly reduce the number of redundant objects and build efforts for your organization.

Example #1 – Shared KPI Dashboard

You have two developers working on separate Workspaces. One developer is building a dynamic landing page dashboard that allows users to customize their landing page experience, and the other is building standardized KPI dashboards that will be surfaced throughout the application.

The KPI dashboard has been developed to dynamically change KPI data based on a user's Cube POV settings, and below is a sample of how the dashboard is displayed.

Figure 9.15

With this dashboard ready to share with the `Landing Page` Workspace, the Is Shareable Workspace property needs to be set to True.

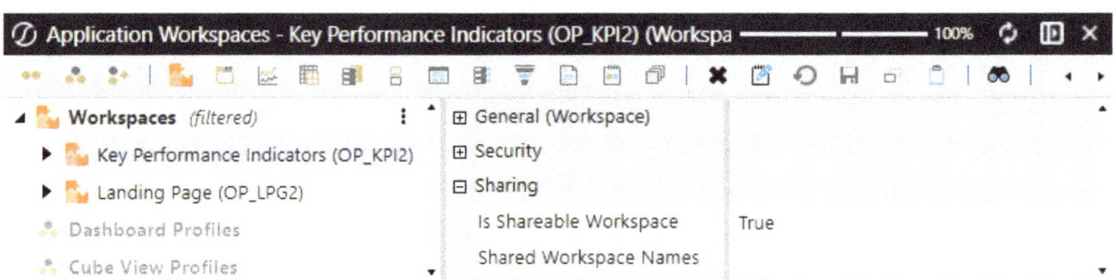

Figure 9.16

Next, we need to review the `Landing Page` Workspace and enter the `Key Performance Indicators (OP_KPI2)` Workspace name in the Shared Workspace Names property to enable the KPI dashboard to be reused on the landing page dashboards. This step is crucial to enable the systematic object lookup when referencing shared objects, as it is the driver that populates the object lookup dialog when searching for dashboards to share.

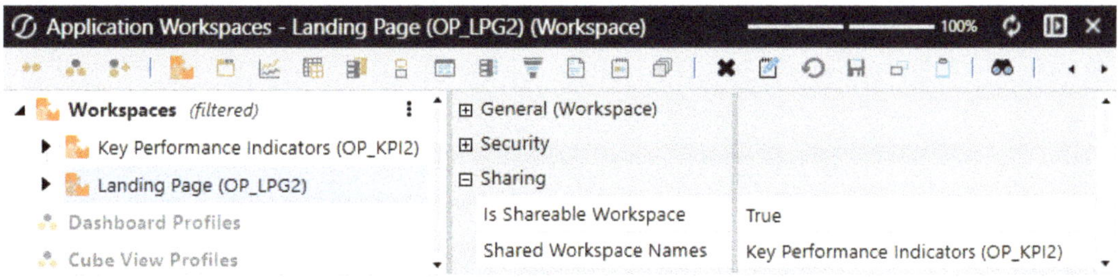

Figure 9.17

Next, we need to insert the KPI dashboard into the landing page and ensure it is visible and working as expected. To do this, we've created an embedded dashboard component and selected the KPI Dashboard named `00_Horizontal_OP_KPI2` using the dashboard object lookup function.

Below is our embedded dashboard component, where we have the selected KPI dashboard in the Embedded Dashboard property.

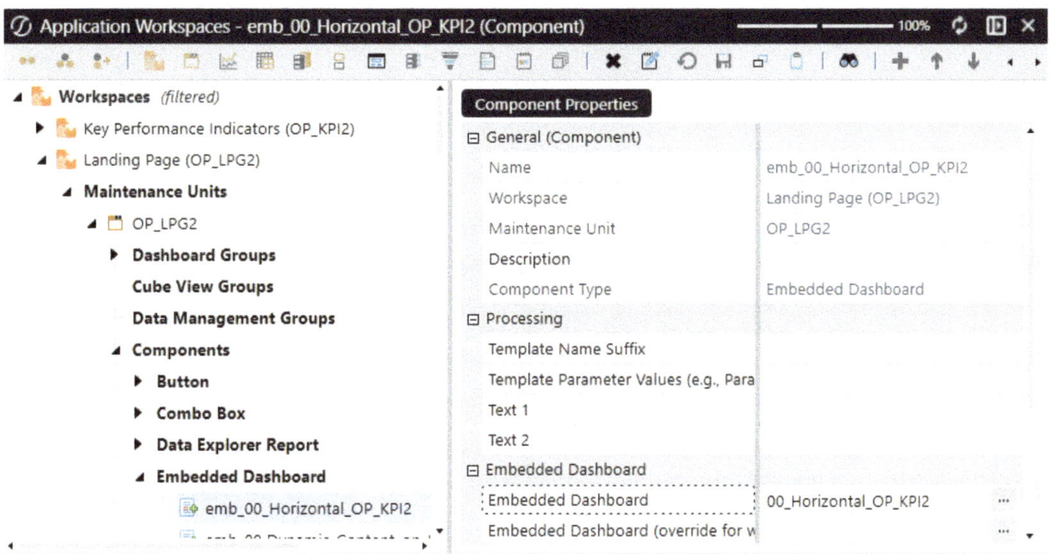

Figure 9.18

The embedded dashboard component is now available to be attached to the dashboard.

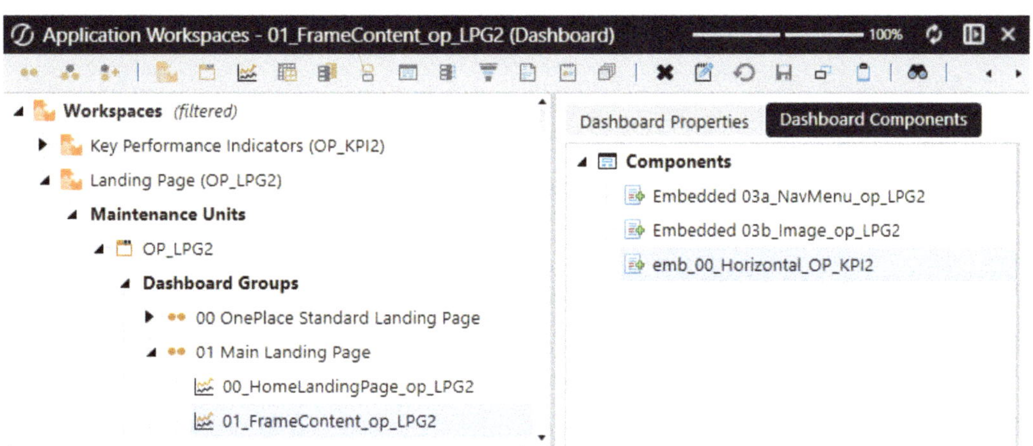

Figure 9.19

The final product displays the KPI dashboard from the independent Workspace embedded into our landing page dashboard.

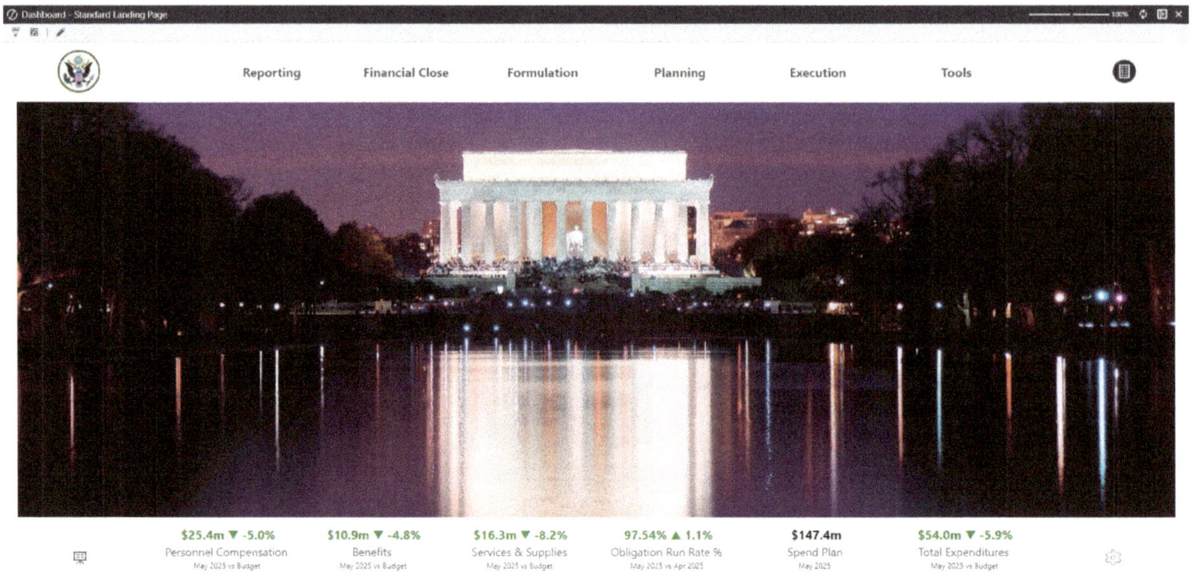

Figure 9.20

Example #2 – Shared Workflow Buttons

Your FP&A manager instructs you to add a workflow step to capture new funding requests with justification requirements during the planning process. They've provided requirements for the dashboard layout and functionality that will be developed in a new Workspace. You need to incorporate buttons that trigger workflow complete and revert actions to allow users to submit data and revert to make changes as necessary.

While the dashboard itself is completely new, you have other dashboards utilizing the same set of workflow buttons that you want to reuse instead of creating new buttons unnecessarily. The buttons you want to reuse are attached to the dashboard named `0_WorkflowButtons_POR` that is located in the Formulation Workspace; below is the dashboard you want to reuse.

Figure 9.21

In the figure below, you can see that we've created and attached the embedded dashboard component that references the workflow buttons that need to be on our new dashboard.

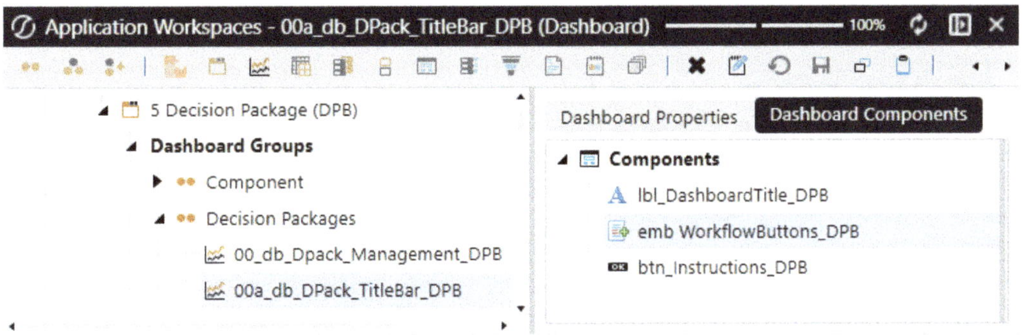

Figure 9.22

Upon running the dashboard, the shared buttons are displayed in our dashboard's header. Not only are they visible, they are functional on the dashboard, all without needing to rebuild the same buttons.

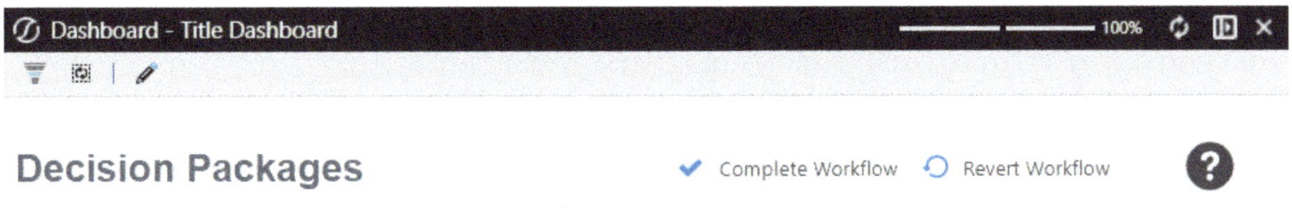

Figure 9.23

Example #3 – Shared Parameters

You've created global formatting parameters – to maintain a consistent look and feel for your users – that you want to use throughout your application. These formatting parameters are in a standalone Workspace where they are maintained by a specific user in your organization.

Below is the Workspace named `Global Formatting Parameters` with the parameters that you want to use in another Workspace. Notice that the Is Shareable Workspace property is set to True.

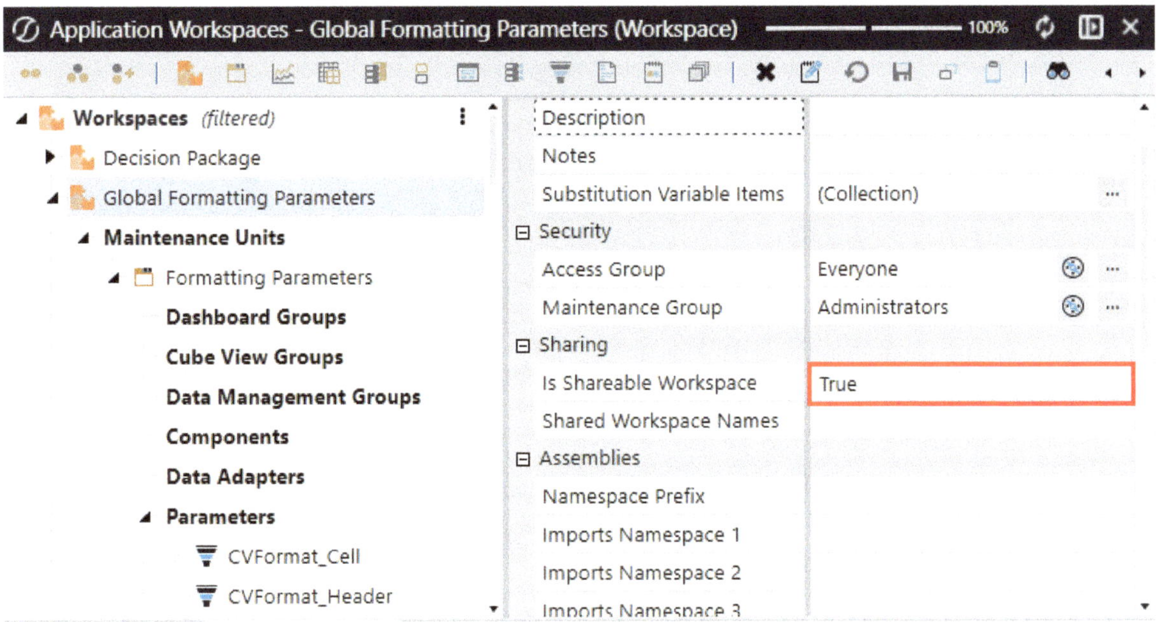

Figure 9.24

In the Workspace named `Decision Package`, you have Cube Views that you want to format to match your organization's prescribed formatting. Notice the `Global Formatting Parameters` Workspace name has been entered into the Shared Workspace Names property; this allows you to reuse the objects or parameters *from* the `Global Formatting Parameters` Workspace in the `Decision Package` Workspace.

The Is Shareable Workspace property for the `Decision Package` Workspace is intentionally set to False. Since this Workspace does not contain objects intended for use in other Workspaces, disabling sharing helps prevent accidental or unintended references from external Workspaces – acting as a safeguard for object integrity.

To simplify:

- Is Shareable Workspace controls whether the current Workspace can share its objects *with* other Workspaces.
- Shared Workspace Names defines which external Workspaces can share their objects *into* the current Workspace.

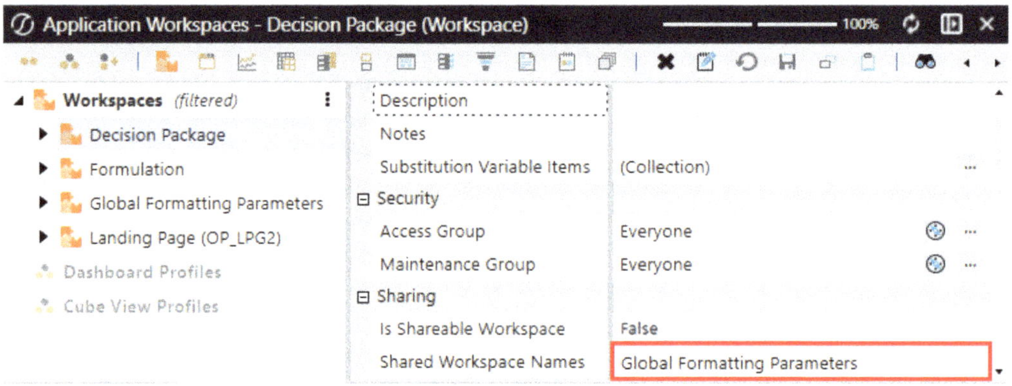

Figure 9.25

Once you've configured both the source Workspace (`Global Formatting Parameters`) and the target Workspace (`Decision Package`), you can use the parameters in your Workspace Cube Views, making formatting consistent and easily managed from the single Workspace.

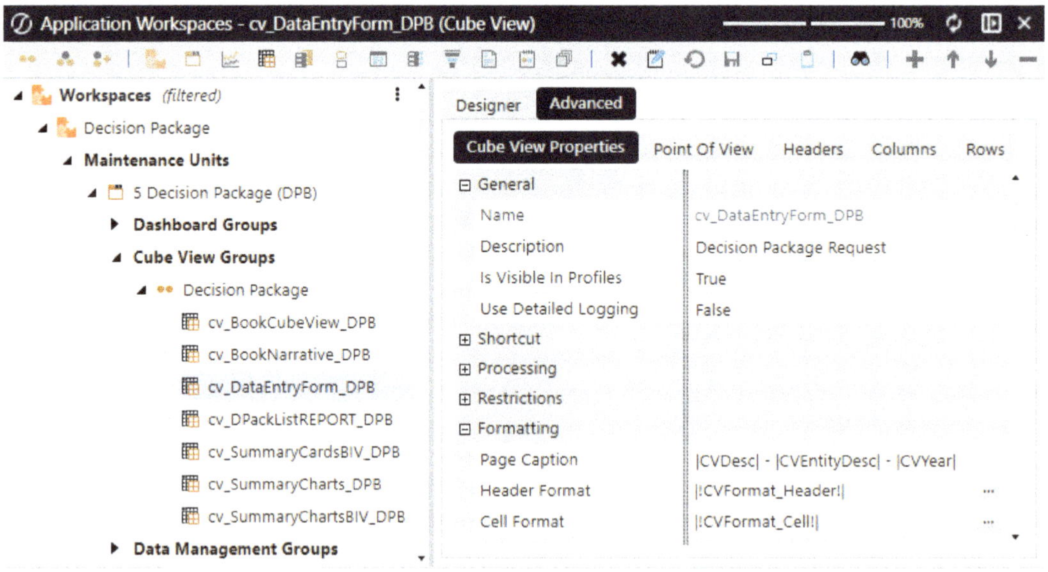

Figure 9.26

Conclusion

Sharing Workspace objects in OneStream is an incredibly useful concept that allows you to reduce the need to recreate the same objects over and over again. For advanced developers, this allows you to seamlessly integrate various intricate solutions within your application with the ability to restrict sharing as needed. For users who are new to OneStream or just starting to explore the breadth of functionality, simply understanding how sharing Workspace objects works will give you a head start in envisioning where you can take your OneStream investment.

10

End-to-End Workspace Exercise

Workspace Concept Review

In the previous chapters, we explored the core concepts of Workspaces in OneStream, including their key properties, the types of objects they contain, and how Assemblies can be used to run custom code in place of traditional business rules.

In this chapter, we'll bring all those elements together through a step-by-step exercise. You'll learn how to use Workspaces in a practical, hands-on way to maximize the value of your OneStream application.

Whether you're just getting started and want to enhance your existing application, or you're a more experienced developer seeking a flexible environment to build and deploy custom solutions, this chapter will serve as a complete guide. You'll gain a deeper understanding of how to build, manage, and expand your solutions using Workspaces in OneStream.

Workspace Overview

Before we dive into the exercise, let's review a fully configured and packaged Workspace dashboard solution to reiterate how Workspaces enhance your OneStream development experience and give you the tools to easily and quickly share solutions, collaborate, and accelerate QA times – ultimately helping make your application more efficient and realizing the benefits in an expedient way.

In this exercise, we will walk through setting up a Workspace with two maintenance units to demonstrate how development can be collaborative yet securitized by developers to limit who can modify dashboards and the content within them.

If you want to follow along with this chapter's exercise, make sure you have access to the Application tab, and the `Workspaces` page under the `Presentation` section.

Navigate to the Application tab and select `Workspaces` under the `Presentation` section.

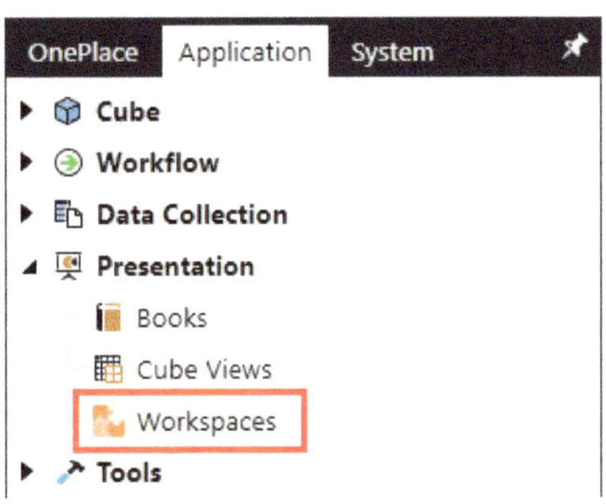

Figure 10.1

Create Workspace

In Chapter 3, we showed a step-by-step example of how to set up a new Workspace, and we will use this Workspace to build maintenance units with Assemblies, Cube Views, and data management groups, all of which can be packaged and exported for simplified solution sharing.

You may notice that we've changed the maintenance group on this Workspace from `DeveloperGroup1` to `DevelopmentQA`. This change will allow us to show multiple developers working on solutions within the same Workspace, while restricting them to only having the rights to modify their respective maintenance units. We'll show how you can apply the same security settings to maintenance units as Workspaces that we demonstrated in Chapter 2.

Also, notice that we've entered Formulation.ServiceFactory into the Workspace Assembly Service property. We've made this change to show how to appropriately call Assemblies from a specific Workspace *and* a Workspace maintenance unit. The **Workspace Assembly Service** is the name of the Assembly that contains a library of syntax files to be called from a specified action; the standard syntax for this property is `MyVBWsAssemblyName.WsAssemblyService`. Type Formulation.ServiceFactory into the field; we'll set up the Assembly later in this chapter.

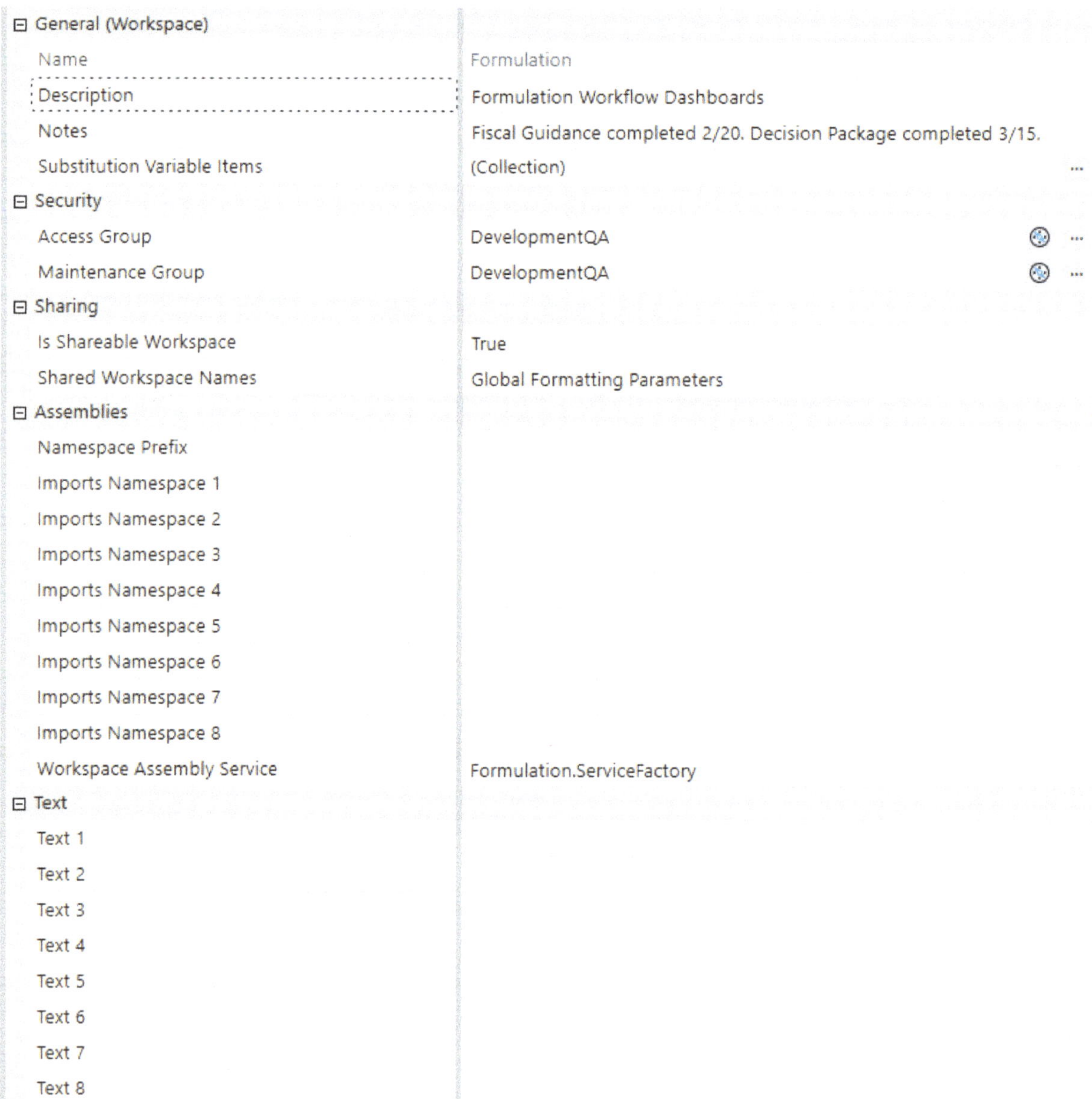

Figure 10.2

Solution #1 – Decision Packages

The first solution that we will build completely within Workspaces, including the creation of Workspace Assemblies, is called Decision Packages. This dashboard is robust, with data entry fields, rich-text narrative collection, advanced charts, and buttons that process Workspace Assembly logic, open fully formatted report books, and even send report books to email recipients.

Below is the final product that we are aiming to build. In this section, we will show how to build some of the components in this dashboard.

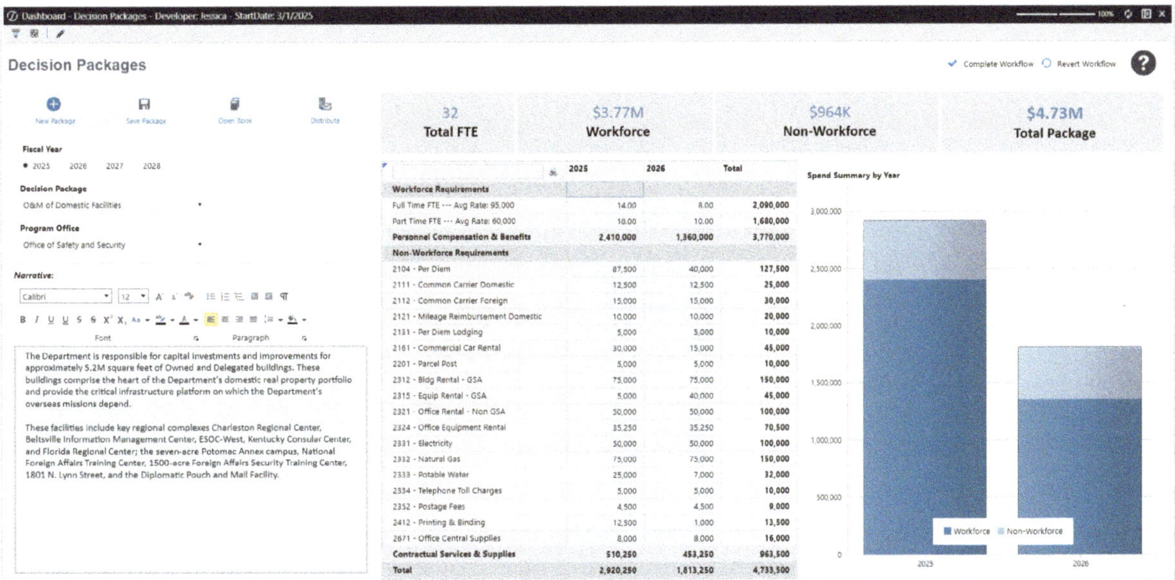

Figure 10.3

Create Maintenance Unit

Objective Review

To show how developers can collaborate within Workspaces, we'll create two maintenance units that multiple developers have access to, but each developer can only create and modify their respective maintenance unit's objects.

This dashboard will be added as a step in our Planning workflow to enter new budget requests for approval submission. We need to allow our users to create new requests, or "decision packages" that explain the amount being requested, the justification for the request, and how the funds will be allocated if approved.

Our FP&A team has provided the following requirements for the solution:

- **Data Entry Form:** Enter headcount and expense category amounts
- **Narrative Collection:** Enter justification narrative and comments

Development will require Workspace Assemblies to write calculations, execute report publishing, and email the report package.

Exercise

Click on `Maintenance Units` under the `Formulation` Workspace and click the Create Maintenance Unit button.

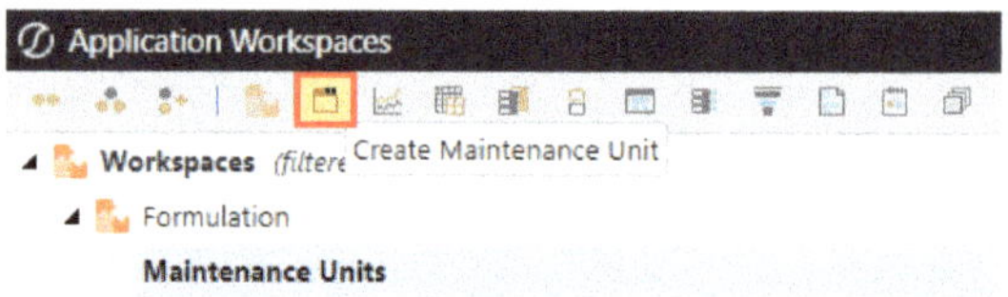

Figure 10.4

In the name field of the maintenance unit, type Decision Packages; you can also enter a description, which is optional.

Since we know that Assemblies will be used in this solution, we can proactively set up the Service Factory Assembly framework and add it to the maintenance unit to save time later. In the Workspace Assembly Service field, type DecisionPackage.ServiceFactory. After we've saved the maintenance unit, we'll create the Workspace Assembly using this naming convention.

Jessica is our developer for this solution; she belongs to both the DevelopmentQA and DeveloperGroup2 security groups, which are the groups we will assign to this maintenance unit. Click the Save button to create the new maintenance unit.

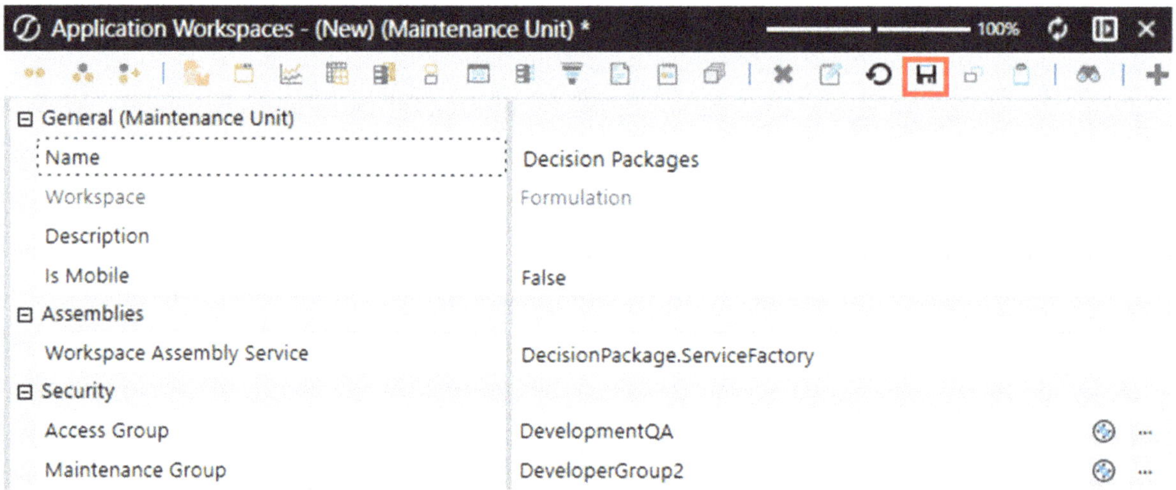

Figure 10.5

Create Cube Views

Objective Review

If you've been in the OneStream ecosystem since before the concept of Workspaces existed, you probably think Cube Views can only be created from the Cube Views page – that's no longer true.

Since version 8, OneStream introduced an enhanced framework featuring Workspace capabilities, offering a new approach to organizing Cube Views within maintenance units and, more significantly, within Workspaces. The inception of Workspace-specific Cube View groups has provided a whole new way of creating solutions without having ever to leave the Workspaces page, not to mention no longer worrying about naming conflicts that required the use of modified Cube View names.

Cube Views can be created from the `Cube Views` page or from the `Workspaces` page within `Maintenance Units`. Cube Views within the Cube View page will also display on the Workspaces page, as shown below.

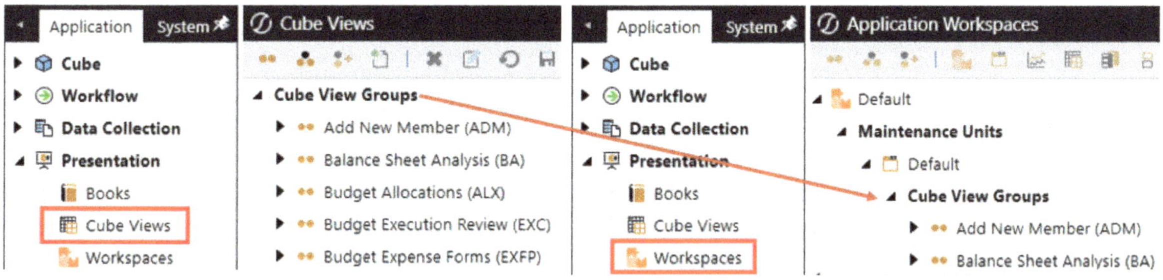

Figure 10.6

Exercise

For this exercise, the Workspace we're building is for a unique business purpose that includes Cube Views for data entry and publishing report books. Because they will not be globally used in our application, *and* we want to package the Workspace as a solution to be shared, we will create Cube Views within the maintenance unit of our new Workspace.

Click on `Cube View Groups` under the `Decision Packages` maintenance unit and click the Create Group button.

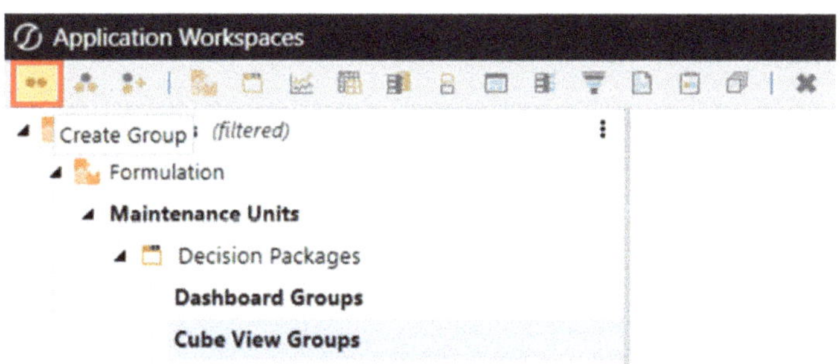

Figure 10.7

Type Decision Packages into the name field. You can enter additional text into the description field for context, but this field is optional.

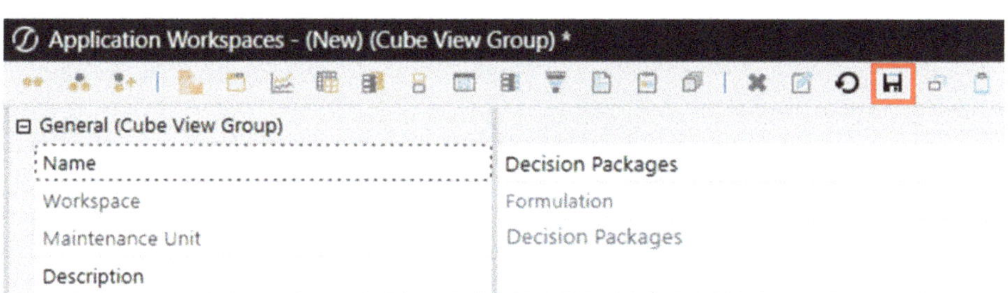

Figure 10.8

You are not limited to one Cube View group, so feel free to create as many groups as you need to help organize Cube Views within the maintenance unit. Something to keep in mind is that Cube Views are only exposed in the application when they are added to Cube View Profiles. This is meaningful for designing groups since you may have many Cube Views within a group but only want to expose certain Cube Views from a Cube View Profile.

In this scenario, I typically create two Cube View groups – one group for development/dashboard use, and another group for Cube Views that I want to make accessible from a Cube View Profile. Once you create a Cube View Profile, you can assign the Cube View group to add to the profile.

Click on the Cube View group and then click Create Cube View.

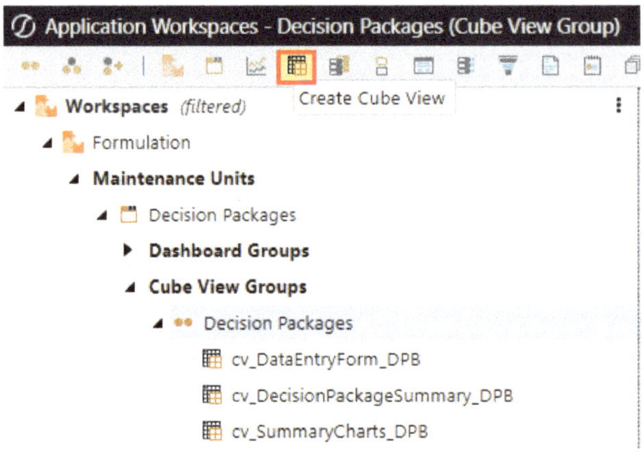

Figure 10.9

The Cube Views required for this dashboard have been created and are shown in the figure above. These will not be exposed in OnePlace or workflows, so there is no need to create a Cube View Profile to add them to for users to access.

Copying Existing Cube Views

If your application has existing Cube Views that you want to use as a starting point rather than building Cube Views from scratch, OneStream allows you to copy and paste Cube Views from one maintenance unit to another. This is something I do quite often to accelerate development by leveraging Cube Views as templates that I can quickly modify to meet design requirements.

To copy existing Cube Views to a new Workspace or maintenance unit, follow these steps:

1. Open the `Default` Workspace.
2. Expand the `Default` Maintenance Unit.
3. Expand the `Cube View Groups`.
4. Select the Cube View (or Cube Views), right-click, and select Copy.

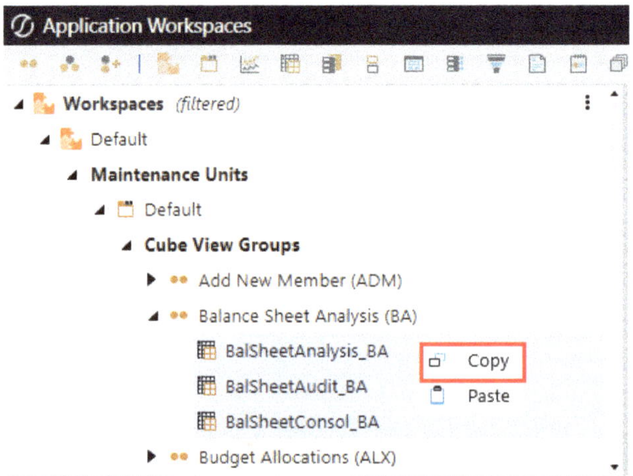

Figure 10.10

Select the Cube View group where you want to paste the Cube Views, right-click, and then select Paste. This will duplicate the Cube Views copied from the Default and append the Cube View names with `_Copy`. The duplicated Cube Views can be renamed, modified as needed, and used in the target maintenance unit's dashboard objects.

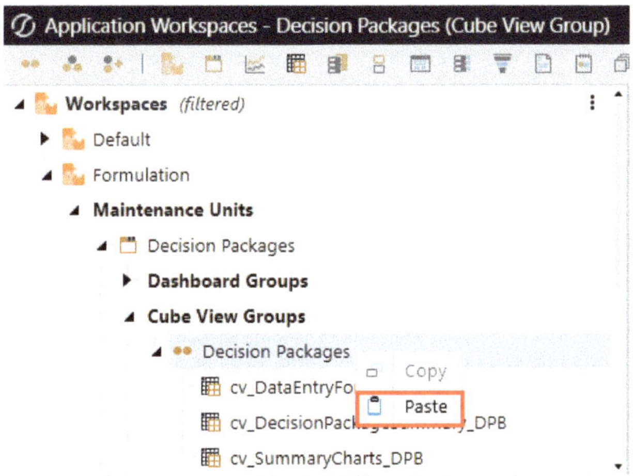

Figure 10.11

> **Note:** Cube Views in different Workspaces can use the same Cube View name; however, Cube View names *cannot* be reused within the same Workspace, even if they are in different maintenance units.

Create Data Management Groups

Objective Review

Data management groups within the Data Management page will also display on the Workspaces page, as shown below. Data management groups, like Cube Views, that are not built into specific Workspaces are displayed under the Default maintenance unit of the Default Workspace.

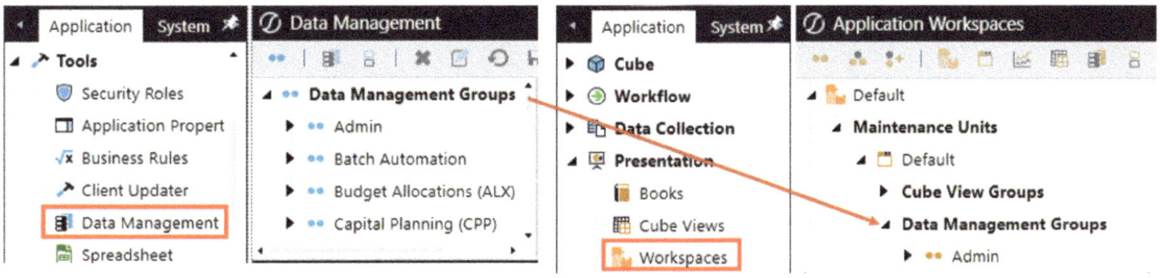

Figure 10.12

Copying Existing Data Management Objects

If your application has existing data management objects that you want to use as a starting point, rather than building the steps and sequences from scratch, OneStream allows you to copy and paste data management objects from one maintenance unit to another.

Copying data management objects is slightly different to copying Cube Views. The most notable feature is that copying a sequence will also copy the steps associated with the sequence. Another key difference is that when you copy a sequence to a different Workspace, the object names *are not* appended with _Copy when pasted. However, copying within the same Workspace to different maintenance units *will* append the name with _Copy.

To copy data management objects to a new Workspace or maintenance unit, follow these steps:

1. Open the Default Workspace.
2. Expand the Default Maintenance Unit.
3. Expand the Data Management Groups.
4. Select the sequence, right-click, and select Copy.

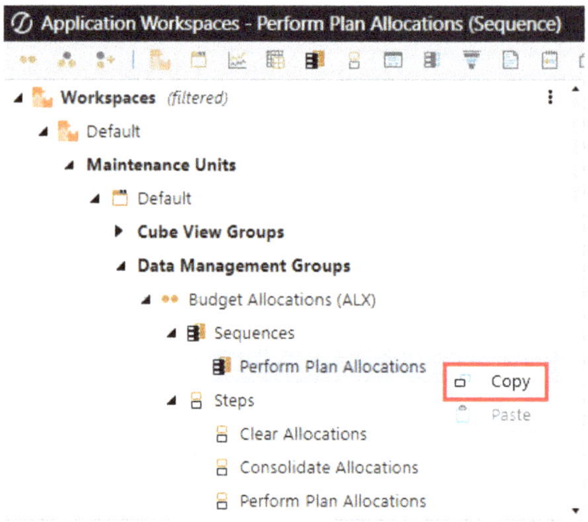

Figure 10.13

Select the data management group where you want to paste the sequence and right-click, then select Paste. This will duplicate the data management sequence *and* the steps associated with the selected sequence copied from the Default into the target maintenance unit. The duplicated Cube Views can be renamed, modified as needed, and used in the target maintenance unit's dashboard objects.

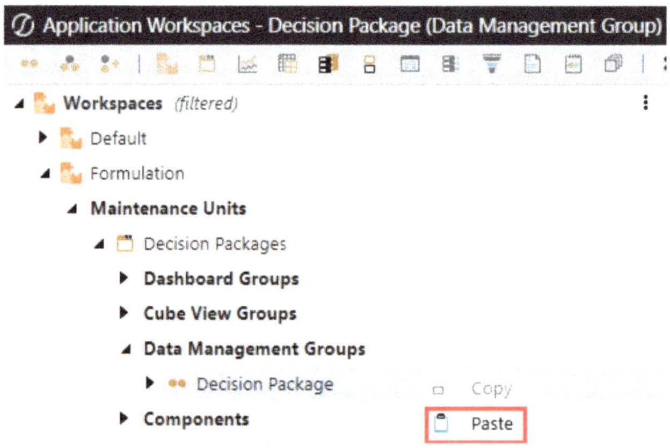

Figure 10.14

Below is a brief refresher on data management groups and their respective objectives:

- **Groups:** Where we create and organize data management objects.
- **Step:** What action needs to be executed.
- **Sequence:** How we apply the action to a component.

> **Note**: For information on what data management objects are, and how they work, go back to Chapter 4 for an overview of how these objects are structured and an explanation of how they work together.

Exercise

For this exercise, we will create a data management step to consolidate data, and a data management sequence that we will attach the step to, and reference in our Assembly to execute the applicable steps.

Click on `Data Management Groups` under the `Decision Packages` maintenance unit and click the Create Group button.

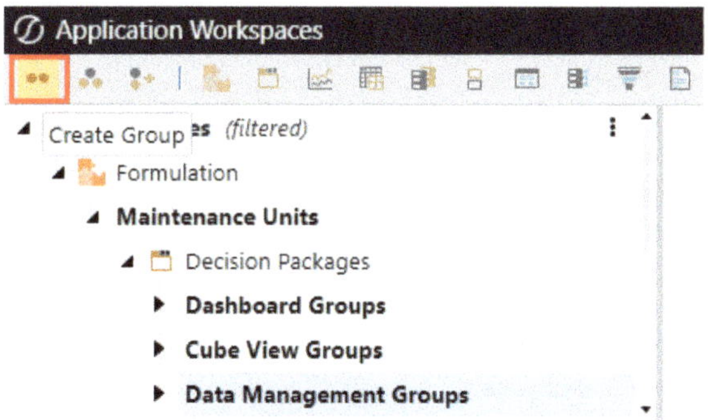

Figure 10.15

Type Decision Packages into the name field. You can enter additional text into the description field for context, but this field is optional.

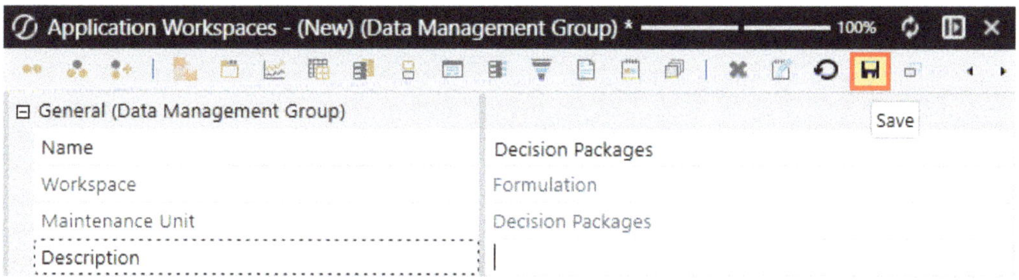

Figure 10.16

Click on `Steps` under the newly created group and then click the Create Step button.

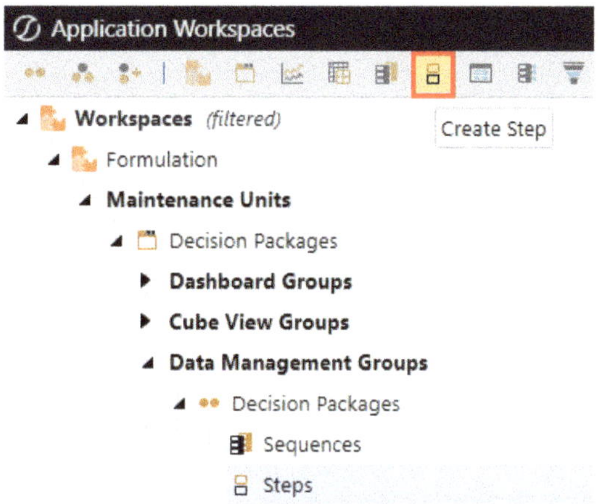

Figure 10.17

Select Calculate from the Create Step dialog box, then click OK.

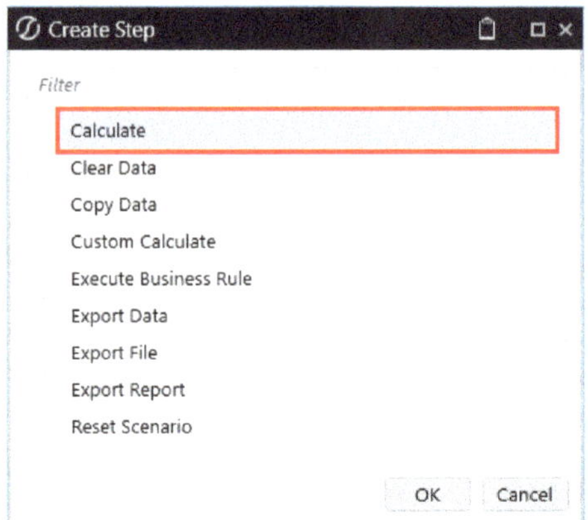

Figure 10.18

This step will be configured to consolidate data for the defined Scenario and Time at the parent entity.

Name: Consolidate Packages

Description (optional): Leave this blank or add your own description

Calculation Type: Select Consolidate from the Calculation Type drop-down menu

Data Units: Define the target intersection to run the consolidation

The result should look like the figure below; click Save to create the step.

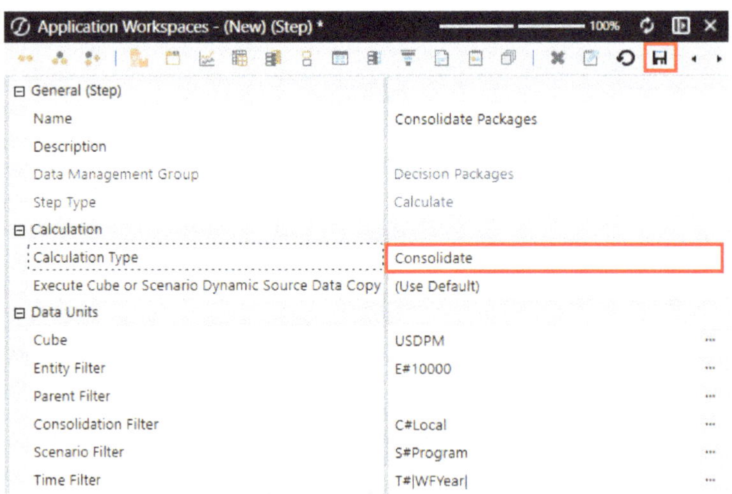

Figure 10.19

Next, we need to create a sequence to which we will add the step; this sequence will be referenced in our Assembly to execute when a button is clicked.

Click on `Sequences` and then click the Create Sequence button.

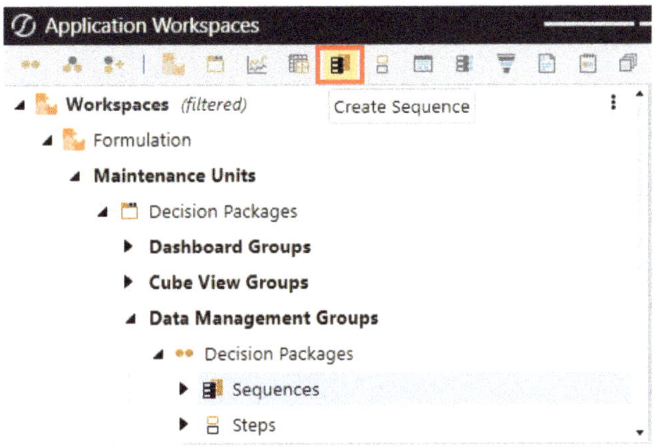

Figure 10.20

Type in a name for the sequence; you can also enter a description, which is optional. We named our Sequence `Consolidate Decision Packages`; this name will be referenced in our Assembly.

A recent enhancement to the OneStream framework is the ability to enable email notifications configured from the UI, as shown below.

> **Important:** An email connection must be configured in your server configuration to enable notifications. Contact your administrator if the **Notification Connection** drop-down menu is blank.

Notifications can be sent to specific users *or* security groups; click Edit on the Notification Users and Groups property to select the desired user or group. Notifications are event-based; select the Notification Event Type drop-down menu to choose one of the available options: 1. On Success, 2. On Failure, 3. On Success or Failure.

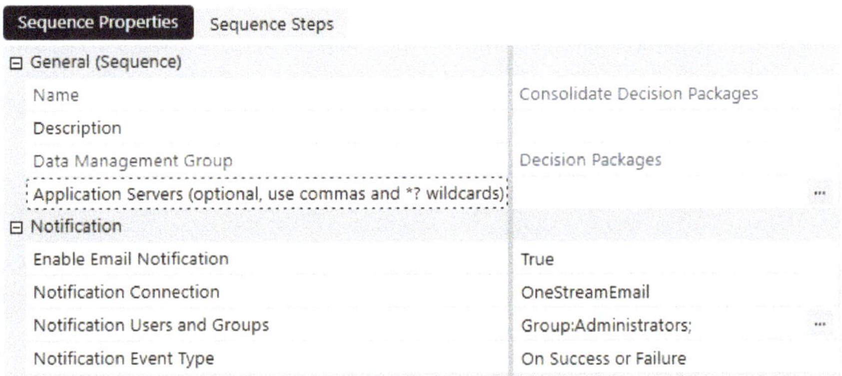

Figure 10.21

Select the Sequence Steps tab and click the **+** button to add the Consolidate Packages step to the sequence. Click Save to create the sequence.

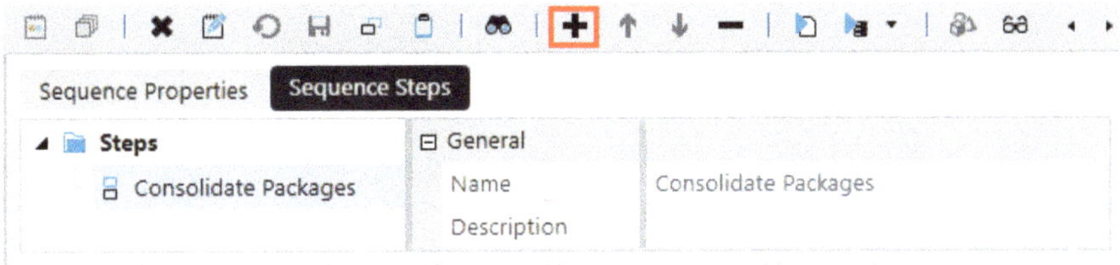

Figure 10.22

Create Assemblies

Objective Review

Assemblies are another method for executing actions and processing code. OneStream's Workspaces provide an alternative entry point for developing code without leaving the Workspaces page. You now have the ability to use Assemblies where business rules were called – making it much easier and quicker to share/export complete dashboard solutions with syntax from the Assemblies packaged.

Exercise

Click `Assemblies` under the `Decision Packages` maintenance unit and click Create Assembly.

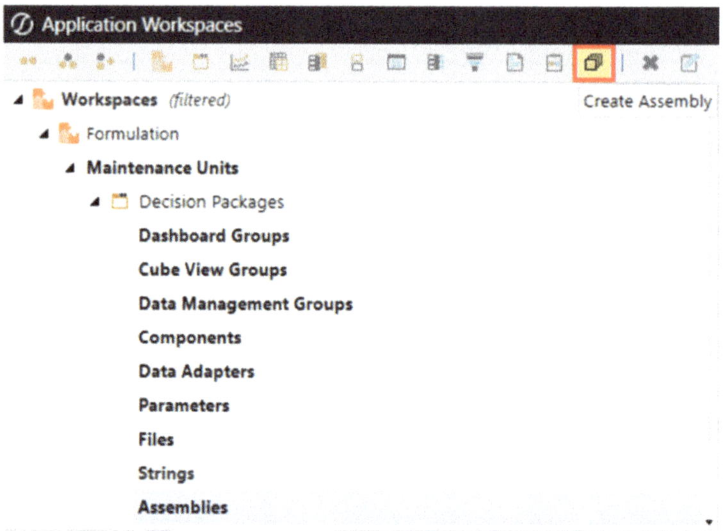

Figure 10.23

Type DecisionPackage into the Assembly Name. Remember that the name in the maintenance unit's Workspace Assembly Service property *must* match the Assembly name. Type Decision Package Rules & Calculations into the description; this field is optional.

Select the Compiler Language drop-down menu to view the languages available and select your preferred language. OneStream's development framework is currently compatible with two languages: Visual Basic (VB) and C#. The files created within the Assembly will be configured in the defined selection, depending on the compiler language selected.

Developers are free to choose their preferred language throughout the application – this is especially useful when you have different developers with different preferences. It is recommended to coordinate among your team, however, as a consistent language will help collaboration.

We selected Visual Basic since that's my preferred language. Click Save to create the Assembly.

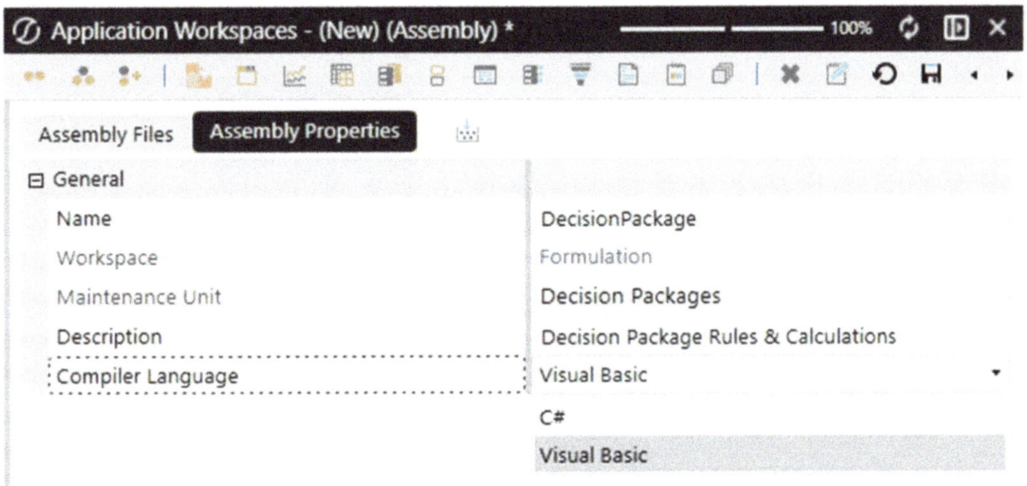

Figure 10.24

Changing Compiler Languages

Once the Assembly is saved, you will not be able to change the language. However, you *can* create a new Assembly and select the language you prefer.

For example, if you create the DecisionPackage Assembly using the Visual Basic language but then decide you want to develop in C#, you can create a new Assembly and name it `DecisionPackageCS`. In this scenario, you would simply modify the maintenance unit's Workspace Assembly Service property to reflect the new Assembly name: `DecisionPackageCS.ServiceFactory`.

Adding Files to the Assembly

The last part of the DecisionPackage.ServiceFactory syntax is what we will name the Assembly file. To create the file, click on the Assembly Files tab and right-click on Files, then select Add File.

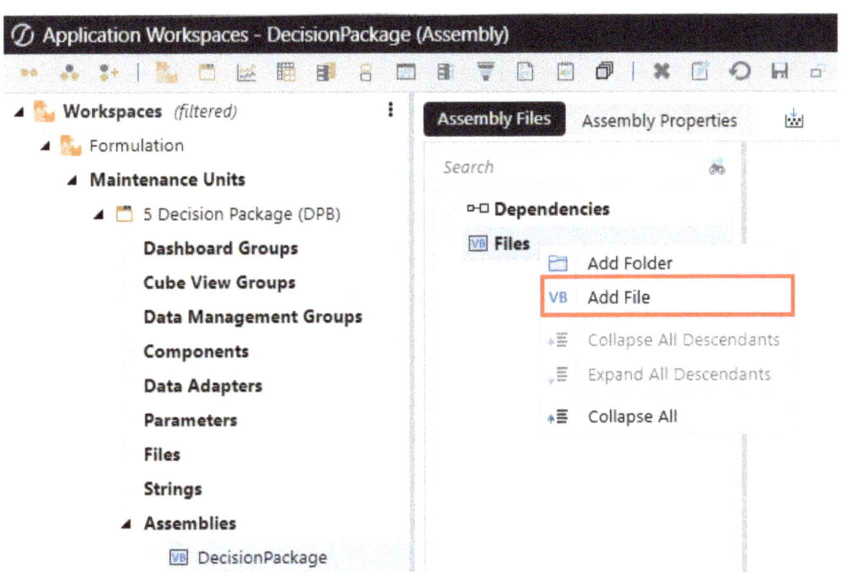

Figure 10.25

Type ServiceFactory into the File Name; remember that this *must* match the maintenance unit's Workspace Assembly Service property, as it is the entry point for processing code from the Service Factory. Click the Source Code Type drop-down menu and select Service Factory, then click OK.

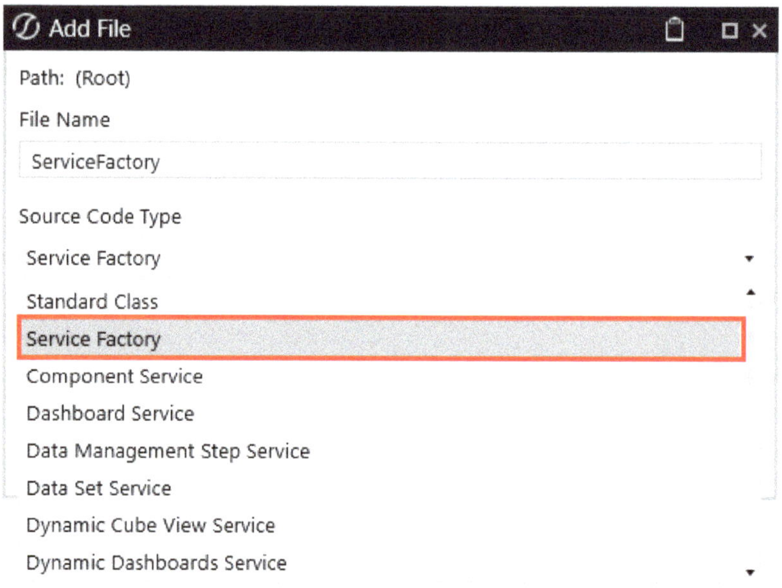

Figure 10.26

The Service Factory will produce a list of service types you can use as a directory for creating and linking new services. For this exercise, we've kept only the services that we'll use for this solution in order to reduce the clutter and focus on the services we are actually using.

```
Imports ...

Namespace Workspace.__WsNamespacePrefix.__WsAssemblyName
    Public Class ServiceFactory
        Implements IWsAssemblyServiceFactory

        Public Function CreateWsAssemblyServiceInstance(ByVal si As SessionInfo, ByVal globals As BRGlob
            Try
                Select Case wsasType
                    Case Is = WsAssemblyServiceType.Component
                        Return New ComponentService()

                    Case Is = WsAssemblyServiceType.FinanceCustomCalculate
                        Return New FinanceCustomCalculateService()

                    Case Else
                        Return Nothing
                End Select
```

Figure 10.27

Staying with the theme of keeping our example neat and organized, we've created a folder to store the service files we *will* use. Click on Files, right-click, and select Add Folder.

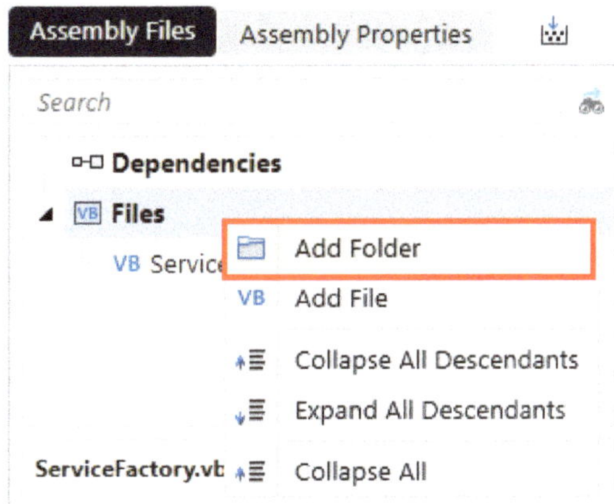

Figure 10.28

Type Services into the Folder Name, then click Save.

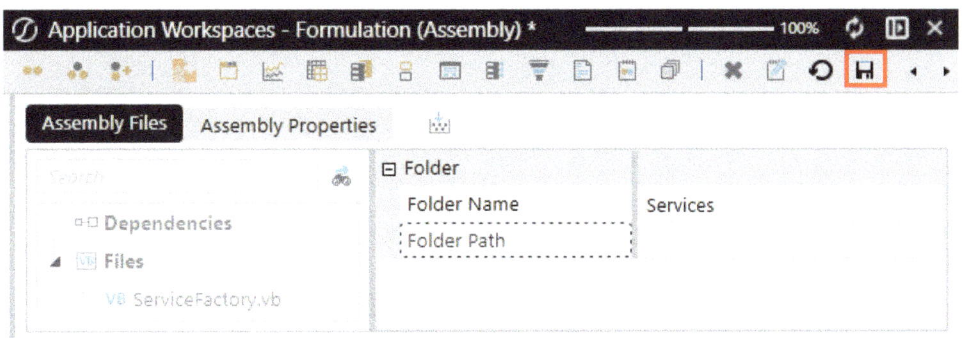

Figure 10.29

Note: Folders are a great tool to organize code, especially if you are building an advanced solution that will require many different files. It is recommended to agree standards on how to organize files in your team to improve maintainability over time. As an example, the root can be split between factory files (Service Factory and all service files), page-specific files (code that is used to build or to be executed in the context of a specific dashboard), and shared files (code that can be reused and in which any change might impact any part of the solution).

Now, we'll create the service files used in our solution:

- **FinanceCustomCalculateService:** Where we will write our custom calculations.
- **ComponentService:** Where we will write our code to publish and email the report book.

Select the newly added Services folder, right-click and select Add File. Type FinanceCustomCalculateService into the File Name. Click the Source Code Type drop-down menu and select Finance Custom Calculate Service. Click OK.

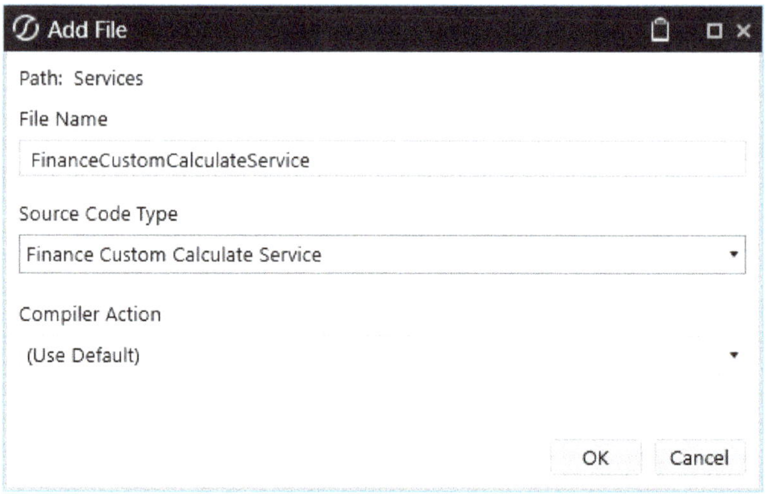

Figure 10.30

The finance custom calculate code used in this Assembly was already written in a finance business rule from the Business Rules page, so all we did here was copy the functions from the business rule and paste them into the Assembly's Public Sub.

Our custom calculate file has two functions: `SaveDecisionPackage` and `GetValues`. The `SaveDecisionPackage` function will be called from a button, and the `GetValues` function will be called from a combo box.

```
If args.CustomCalculateArgs.FunctionName.XFEqualsIgnoreCase("SaveDecisionPackage") Then

    Dim OrgValue    As String = args.CustomCalculateArgs.NameValuePairs.XFGetValue("Ent")
    Dim ModsValue   As String = args.CustomCalculateArgs.NameValuePairs.XFGetValue("UD5")
    Dim TimeValue   As String = args.CustomCalculateArgs.NameValuePairs.XFGetValue("Time")

    api.Data.ClearCalculatedData("A#1101:S#Program:E#[" & OrgValue & "]:U1#10001:U2#[Measure 1.1.1]:U5#[" & Moc
    api.Data.ClearCalculatedData("A#1131:S#Program:E#[" & OrgValue & "]:U1#10001:U2#[Measure 1.1.1]:U5#[" & Moc

    api.Data.Calculate("S#Program:A#1101:O#Import:E#[" & OrgValue & "]:U1#10001:U2#[Measure 1.1.1]:U5#[" & Mod:
    api.Data.Calculate("S#Program:A#1131:O#Import:E#[" & OrgValue & "]:U1#10001:U2#[Measure 1.1.1]:U5#[" & Mod:

    Dim NarrativeTime       As String = BRApi.Dashboards.Parameters.GetLiteralParameterValue(si,False, Currentl
    Dim DPDescriptionPOV    As String = "V#AuditComment:S#Program:A#DecisionPackage:F#EndBal:O#Forms:E#[" & Or
    Dim DPNarrativePOV      As String = "V#Footnote:S#Program:A#DecisionPackage:F#EndBal:O#Forms:E#[" & OrgVal
    Dim DPNarrative         As String = args.CustomCalculateArgs.NameValuePairs.XFGetValue("Narr")

    If Not DPNarrative  = "|!Narrative!|" Then api.Data.SetDataAttachmentText(DPNarrativePOV,DPNarrative,False
    brapi.Dashboards.Parameters.SetLiteralParameterValue(si,False, CurrentWorkspace, "Narrative",DPNarrative)

    Dim customSubstVars = New Dictionary(Of String, String)(StringComparer.InvariantCultureIgnoreCase)
    Dim workspaceName As Guid = BRApi.Dashboards.Workspaces.GetWorkspaceIDFromName(si, False, "Formulation")
    Dim objTaskActivityItem As TaskActivityItem = BRApi.Utilities.ExecuteDataMgmtSequence(si, workspaceName, "(

End If


If args.CustomCalculateArgs.FunctionName.XFEqualsIgnoreCase("GetValues") Then

    Dim OrgValue    As String = args.CustomCalculateArgs.NameValuePairs.XFGetValue("Ent")
    Dim ModsValue   As String = args.CustomCalculateArgs.NameValuePairs.XFGetValue("UD5")
    Dim TimeValue   As String = args.CustomCalculateArgs.NameValuePairs.XFGetValue("Time")
    Dim NarrativeTime As String = BRApi.Dashboards.Parameters.GetLiteralParameterValue(si,False, CurrentWorksp
    BRApi.Dashboards.Parameters.SetLiteralParameterValue(si, False, CurrentWorkspace, "NarrativeTime", TimeVal

    Dim DPNarrativePOV  As String = "V#Footnote:S#Program:A#DecisionPackage:F#EndBal:O#Forms:E#[" & OrgValue &
    Dim CVNarrative     As String = api.Data.GetDataCellEx(DPNarrativePOV).DataCellAnnotation
    brapi.Dashboards.Parameters.SetLiteralParameterValue(si,False, CurrentWorkspace, "Narrative",CVNarrative)

End If
```

Figure 10.31

Repeat the step to add a new file under the Services folder and type ComponentService into the File Name. Click the Source Code Type drop-down menu and select Component Service. Click OK.

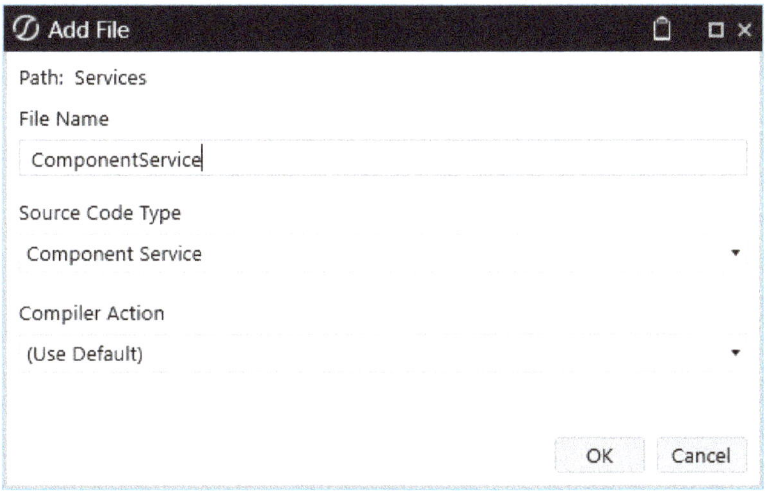

Figure 10.32

The next file we'll use in our solution was formerly a dashboard extender business rule, which we converted into a **Component Service** that is called from the Service Factory.

We'll configure a dashboard button to run this component service, allowing users to quickly and easily send a report book via email to recipients using security groups. This is just an example of a component service being called from the Service Factory, with the purpose of demonstrating how Assemblies can do just as much, if not more, than currently with traditional business rules.

```
Namespace Workspace.__WsNamespacePrefix.__WsAssemblyName
    Public Class ComponentService
        Implements IWsasComponentV800

        Public Function ProcessComponentSelectionChanged(ByVal si As SessionInfo, ByVal globals As BRGlobals, ByVal works|
            ByVal args As DashboardExtenderArgs) As XFSelectionChangedTaskResult Implements IWsasComponentV800.ProcessCom|
            Try
                If args.FunctionName.Equals("MailBook", StringComparison.InvariantCultureIgnoreCase) Then
                    Dim dashboardNames As List(Of String) = Me.GetDashboardNameList(si, globals, args)
                    Dim pdfFilePath As String = Me.CreateCombinedPdf(si, globals, args, dashboardNames, True)
                    Dim emailDistCount As Integer = 0
                    If pdfFilePath <> String.Empty Then
                        Dim bookName As String = "Department Resource Request"
                        emailDistCount = Me.ProcessEmailDistribtion(si, bookName, pdfFilePath)
                    End If
                    Dim selectionChangedTaskResult As New XFSelectionChangedTaskResult()
                    selectionChangedTaskResult.IsOK = True
                    selectionChangedTaskResult.ShowMessageBox = True
                    If pdfFilePath = String.Empty Then
                        selectionChangedTaskResult.Message = "Report file could not be created, book was NOT published."
                    Else
                        selectionChangedTaskResult.Message = "Report book was published and distributed to (" & emailDist(
                    End If
                End If
                Return Nothing
            Catch ex As Exception
                Throw ErrorHandler.LogWrite(si, New XFException(si, ex))
            End Try
        End Function

"Book Publishing Helper Functions"

"Book Distribution Helper Function"

"Common Helper Functions"

    End Class
End Namespace
```

Figure 10.33

Once you've created your service files, the result will look something like this.

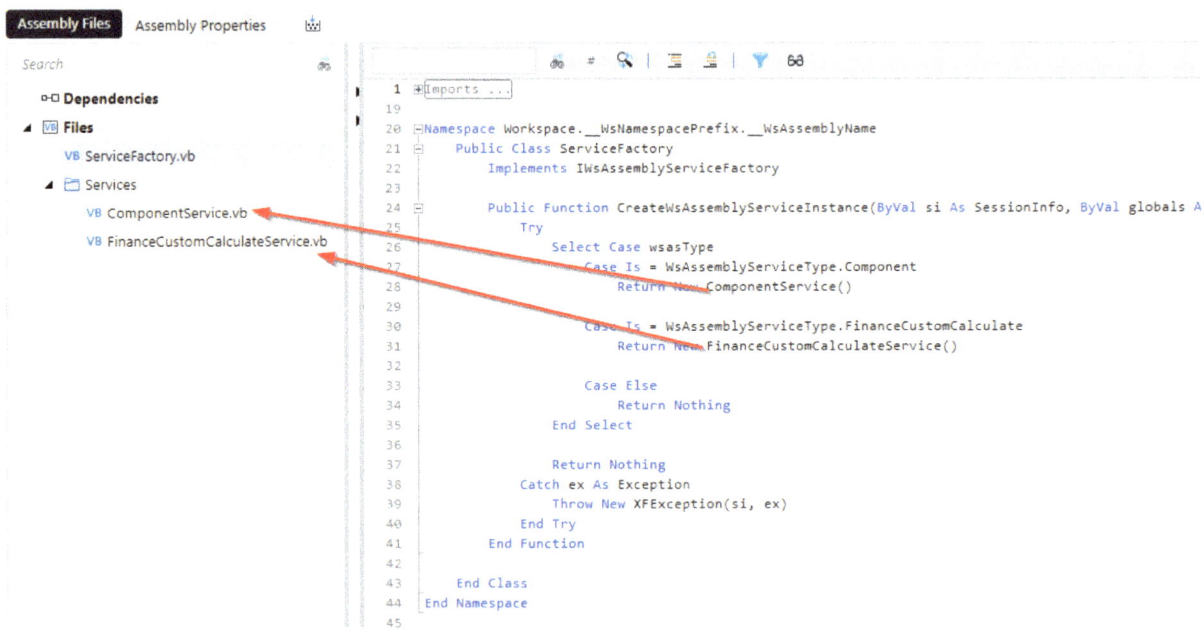

Figure 10.34

Create Components

Objective Review

In Chapter 4, we showed examples of existing OneStream dashboard components, ideas, and tips for when you would use each of them, and how they generally display when processed on a dashboard. The intention of showing the displayed components was to familiarize you with what's available to use in your solutions and to get you thinking about how you would use them in your dashboard solutions.

The figure below shows the components that are used to build the Decision Packages dashboard. In the following section, we'll go under the covers to explain how to create these components to update your dashboard, process code from the Assembly file, and hopefully give you inspiration to enhance your own dashboards.

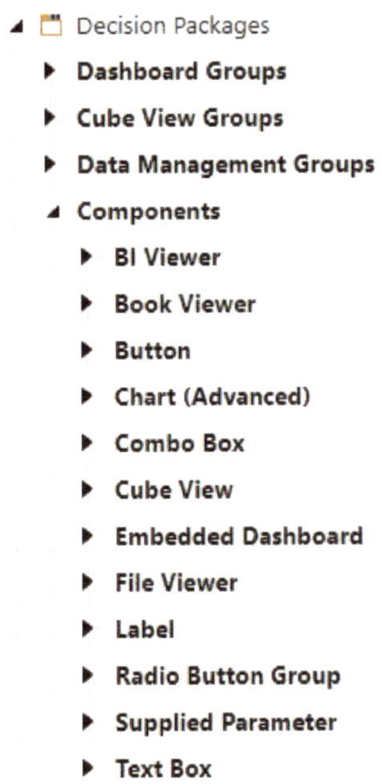

Figure 10.35

Exercise

For this exercise, we'll show how to build components that interact with the user to process code, update dashboards using parameters for filtering, and which components call the Assembly logic, with examples of how to maintain them.

We'll focus on the components that users will interact with, including the following:

- **Cube View** – Enter data into a Cube View form.
- **Button** – Save work, calculate data, and send report books via email.
- **Combo Box** – Change the dashboard data with a combo box which also retrieves **Text Box Annotation** for the selected member.
- **Radio Button Group** – Toggle time selection to plan out years.

Cube View

This form, displayed on the dashboard, is a Cube View component used to collect information, specifically financial data that will contribute to the new funding being requested. In this solution, users enter FTEs and dollar amounts for the specific spending accounts being requested. The Personnel expense is calculated in the Assembly using the FTE input number multiplied by the Avg Rate stored by a manager and displayed on the employee type Cube View row.

Cells with a light blue background indicate writeable cells; all other cells are calculated or aggregated. Cube Views used as forms can be designed with different colors indicating writable vs non-writable cells within the Cube View's cell format configuration.

	2025	2026	Total
Workforce Requirements			
Full Time FTE --- Avg Rate: 95,000	14.00	8.00	**2,090,000**
Part Time FTE --- Avg Rate: 60,000	18.00	10.00	**1,680,000**
Personnel Compensation & Benefits	**2,410,000**	**1,360,000**	**3,770,000**
Non-Workforce Requirements			
2104 - Per Diem	87,500	40,000	**127,500**
2111 - Common Carrier Domestic	12,500	12,500	**25,000**
2112 - Common Carrier Foreign	15,000	15,000	**30,000**
2121 - Mileage Reimbursement Domestic	10,000	10,000	**20,000**
2131 - Per Diem Lodging	5,000	5,000	**10,000**
2161 - Commercial Car Rental	30,000	15,000	**45,000**
2201 - Parcel Post	5,000	5,000	**10,000**
2312 - Bldg Rental - GSA	75,000	75,000	**150,000**
2315 - Equip Rental - GSA	5,000	40,000	**45,000**
2321 - Office Rental - Non GSA	50,000	50,000	**100,000**
2324 - Office Equipment Rental	35,250	35,250	**70,500**
2331 - Electricity	50,000	50,000	**100,000**
2332 - Natural Gas	75,000	75,000	**150,000**
2333 - Potable Water	25,000	7,000	**32,000**
2334 - Telephone Toll Charges	5,000	5,000	**10,000**
2352 - Postage Fees	4,500	4,500	**9,000**
2412 - Printing & Binding	12,500	1,000	**13,500**
2671 - Office Central Supplies	8,000	8,000	**16,000**
Contractual Services & Supplies	**510,250**	**453,250**	**963,500**
Total	**2,920,250**	**1,813,250**	**4,733,500**

Figure 10.36

From the Cube View configuration POV, the parameters are highlighted below; this is how parameters are passed into the form using a radio button group and combo box components to update the form on the dashboard, using the same form for a number of intersections.

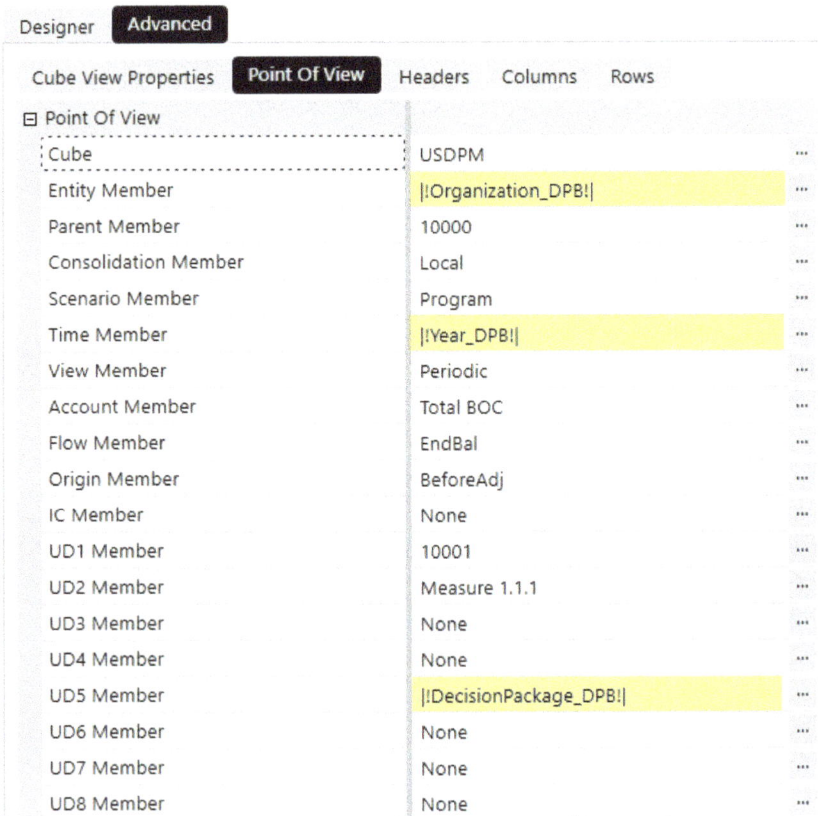

Figure 10.37

To create this component, select `Components` under the `Decision Packages` maintenance unit and click Create Dashboard Component.

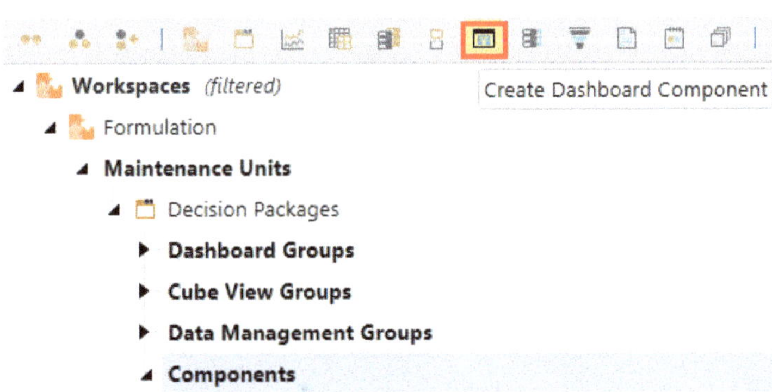

Figure 10.38

Select Cube View from the Create Dashboard Component dialog box, then click OK.

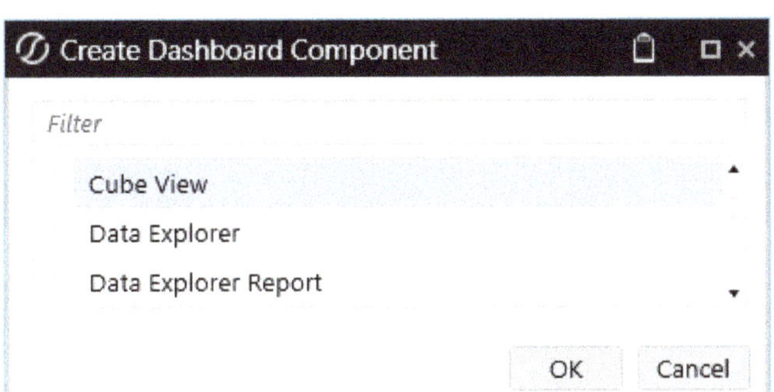

Figure 10.39

Button

After a user enters data into the Cube View form, they'll click the Save Package button on the dashboard. For the user, this is just a Save button, but behind the scenes, the button is checking the maintenance unit's Workspace Assembly Service property for the appropriate Assembly name.

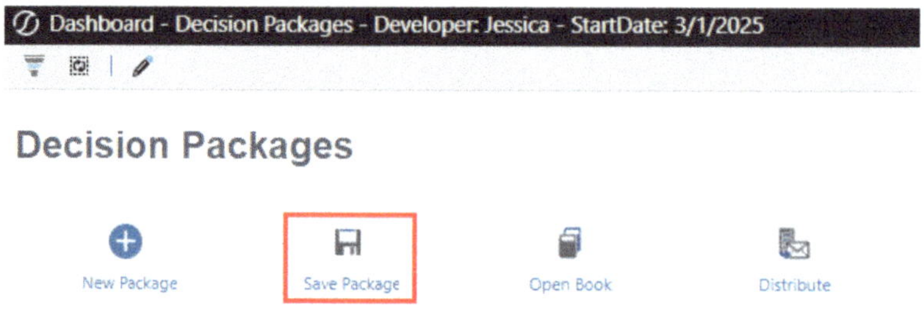

Figure 10.40

To create this component, select `Components` under the `Decision Packages` maintenance unit and click Create Dashboard Component.

Select Button from the Create Dashboard Component dialog box, then click OK.

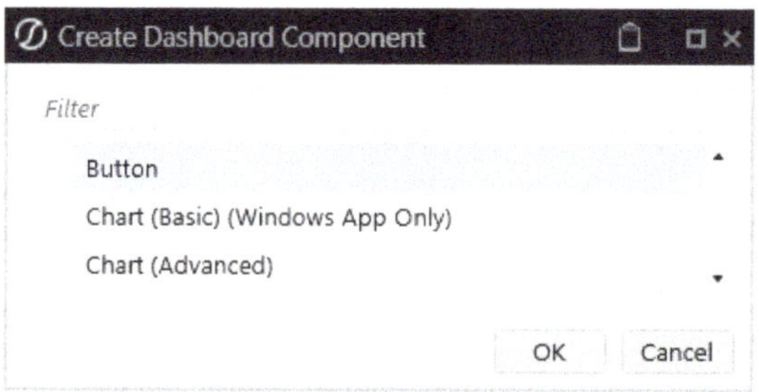

Figure 10.41

The button properties are configured to *Save Data for All Components* and process the server task shown in the figure below. Assemblies can be called from the Workspace *or* the maintenance unit, which is indicated in the server task argument.

- When Assembly is called from a Workspace: `Workspace.Current.Decision Packages.WS`
- When Assembly is called from a maintenance unit: `Workspace.Current.Decision Packages.WSMU`

Since we've wired the Assembly to the maintenance unit, we would use the WSMU suffix.

- **Server Changed Server Task:** Execute custom calculate business rule
- **Server Changed Server Task Argument**: `{Workspace.Current.Decision Packages.WSMU}{SaveDecisionPackage}{Narr=[|!Narrative!|],Time=|!Year_DPB!|,Ent=|!Organization_DPB!|,UD5=|!DecisionPackage_DPB!|}`

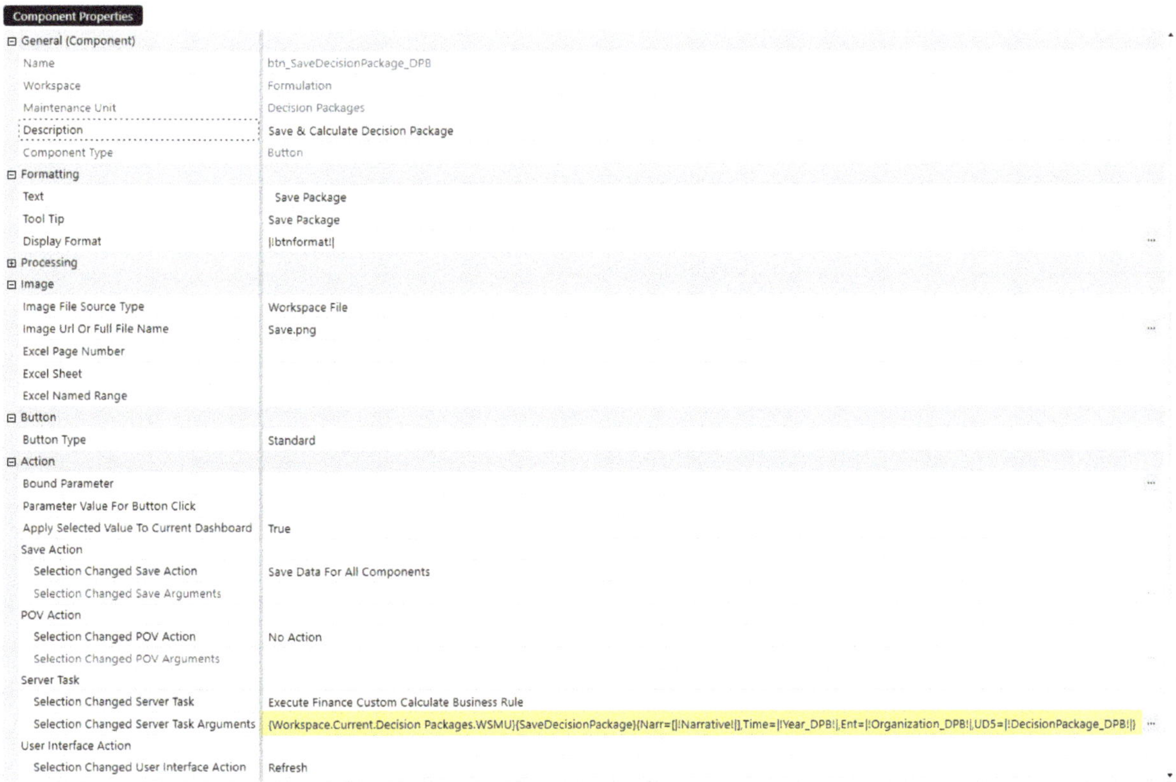

Figure 10.42

Below is the lineage of the Assembly logic being called from the button when clicked. With the Service Factory configured with the associate service files, developers don't need to hunt and peck for the right business rule and function; they can rely on the **Workspace Assembly Service Factory** to route the code as intended, simply by aligning their Assembly files.

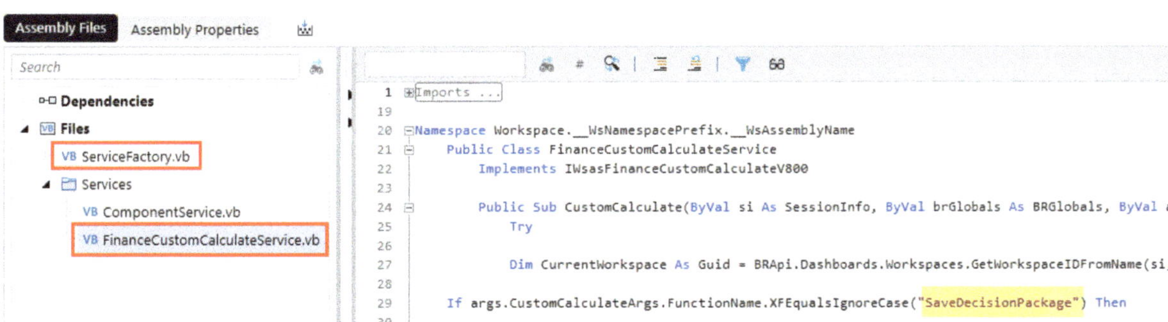

Figure 10.43

Combo box

Users can change member selections using a combo box, which refreshes the dashboard with the selected member; they just see the data update on the dashboard while – behind the scenes – this action is processing code routed from the Assembly.

Figure 10.44

To create this component, select `Components` under the `Decision Packages` maintenance unit and click Create Dashboard Component. Select Combo Box from the Create Dashboard Component dialog box, then click OK.

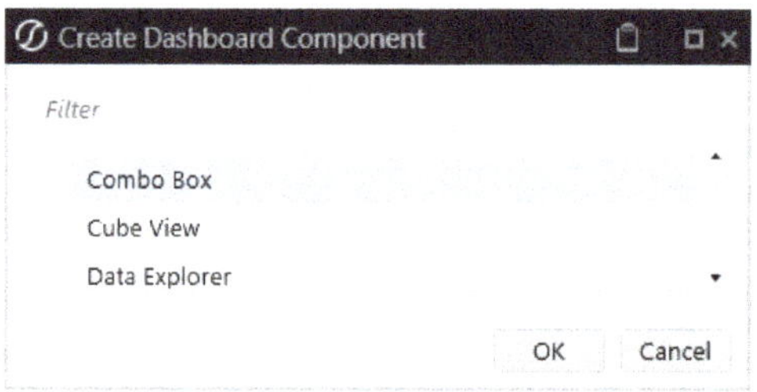

Figure 10.45

The combo box component triggers the `GetValues` function from our Assembly, using the following server task component configuration.

- **Server Changed Server Task:** Execute custom calculate business rule
- **Server Changed Server Task Argument**: `{Workspace.Current.Decision Packages.WSMU}{GetValues}{Narr=[|!Narrative!|],Time=|!Year_DPB!|,Ent=|!Organization_DPB!|,UD5=|!DecisionPackage_DPB!|}`

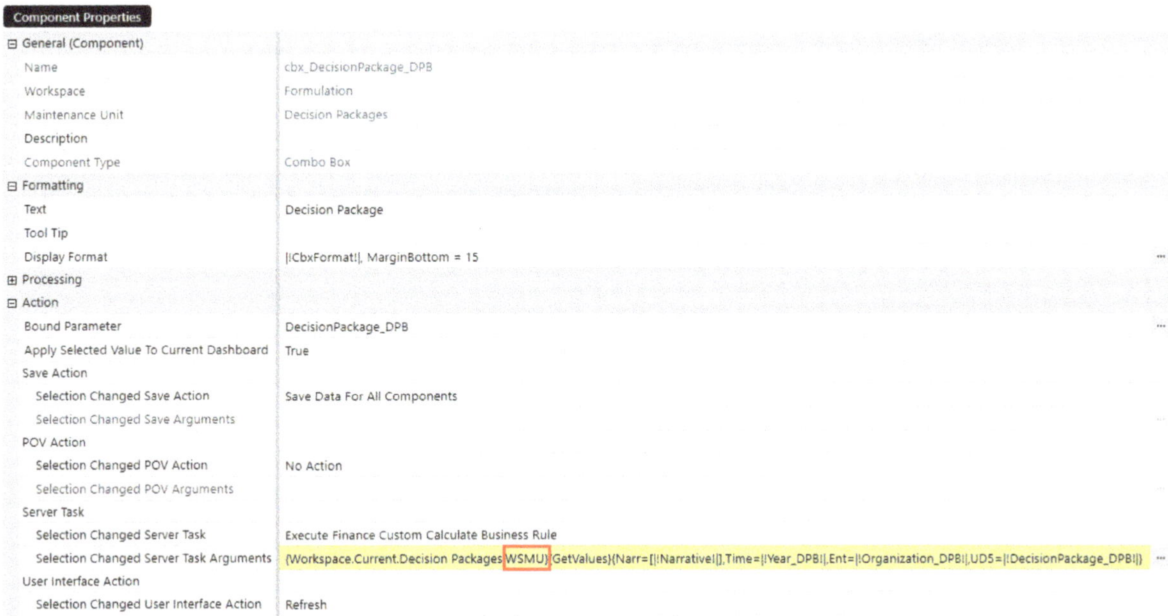

Figure 10.46

Radio Button Group

To give the user some variety, we've created a radio button group component to toggle the year in which we are entering data. The component defaults the year to 2025, which is the `|WFYear|` as set on the default property of the `Year_DPB` parameter.

Figure 10.47

To create this component, select `Components` under the `Decision Packages` maintenance unit and click Create Dashboard Component.

Select Radio Button Group from the Create Dashboard Component dialog box, then click OK.

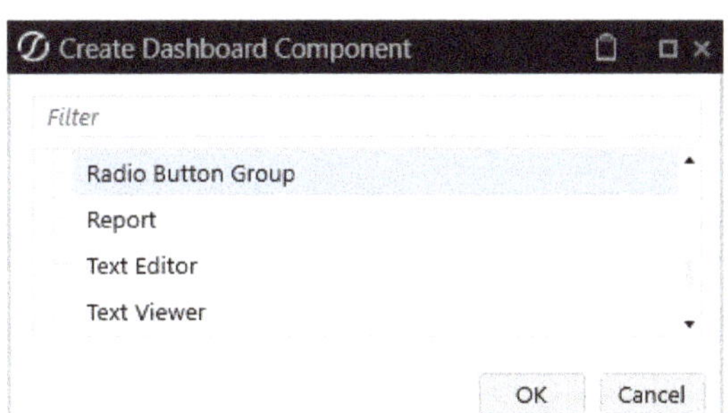

Figure 10.48

The figure below shows the Year_DPB parameter that's been passed into our component. The Default Value is optional, though we've set it as |WFYear| to display the user's workflow year when the dashboard is initialized.

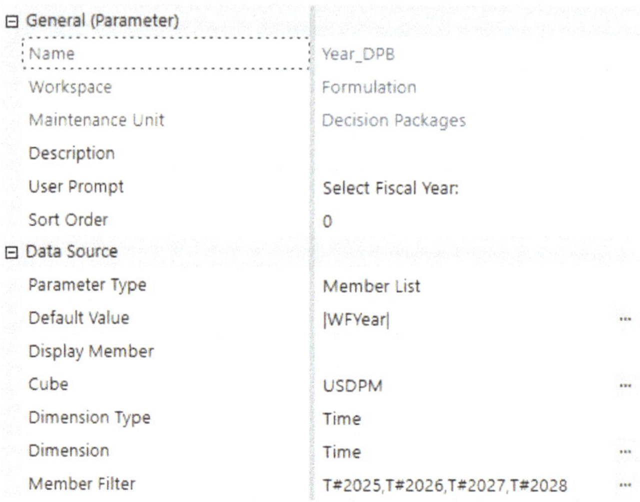

Figure 10.49

The component configuration is displayed below. The Year_DPB parameter has been inserted into the **Bound Parameter** property, effectively controlling the members (year) displayed from the component when the dashboard is processed.

We've configured this component to process the `GetValues` function from our Workspace Assembly.

- **Server Changed Server Task:** Execute custom calculate business rule
- **Server Changed Server Task Argument**:`{Workspace.Current.Decision Packages.WSMU}{GetValues}{Narr=[|!Narrative!|],Time=|!Year_DPB!|,Ent=|!Organization_DPB!|,UD5=|!DecisionPackage_DPB!|}`

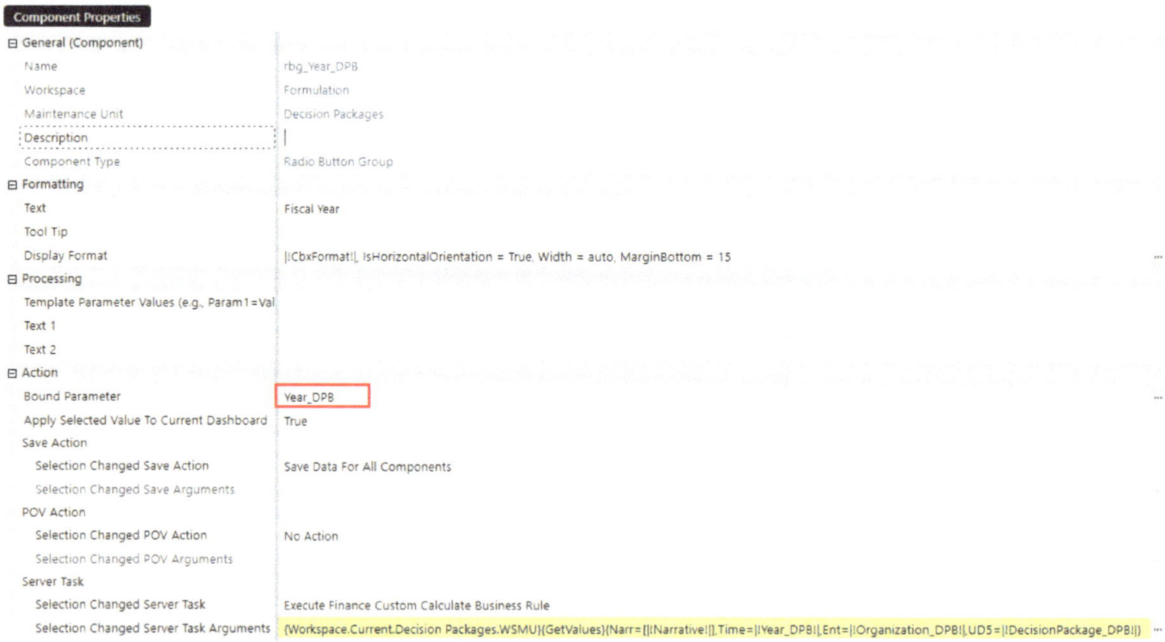

Figure 10.50

The radio button group and combo box components essentially have the same functionality; they both trigger the `SaveDecisionPackage` function from the Assembly – just using different components to show options (consider this when designing and building your dashboard solutions).

Solution #2 – Fiscal Guidance

The second solution that we will build completely within our Formulation Workspace is called Fiscal Guidance. This dashboard is much simpler, with fewer components than our first solution, but the components we are using on this dashboard are just as powerful. This is like seeding a long-range plan with prior year balances rolled forward, and then multiplying them by percentages the user enters.

Below is the final product we are aiming for. In this exercise, we'll see how to build some of the components of this dashboard.

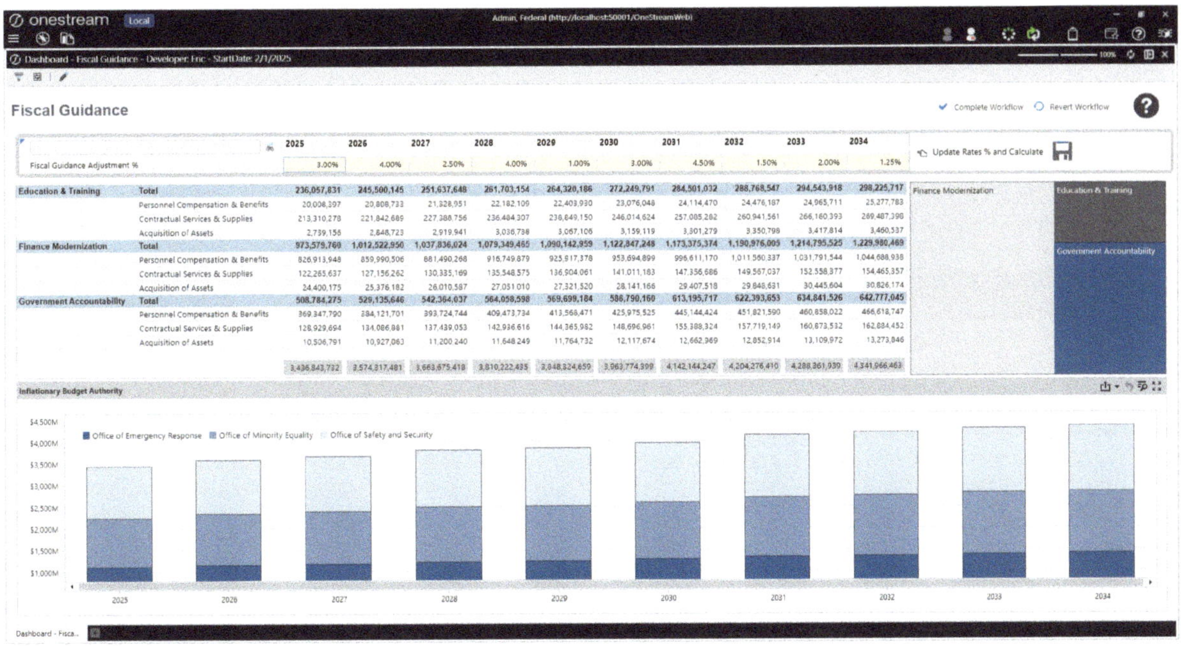

Figure 10.51

Create Maintenance Unit

Objective Review

The first maintenance unit we'll create is used to calculate Fiscal Guidance. Our developer, Eric, will be building the solution. This dashboard's purpose is to calculate the impact of inflation % year-over-year for a 10-year forecast.

Exercise

Click on `Maintenance Units` under the `Formulation` Workspace and click the Create Maintenance Unit button.

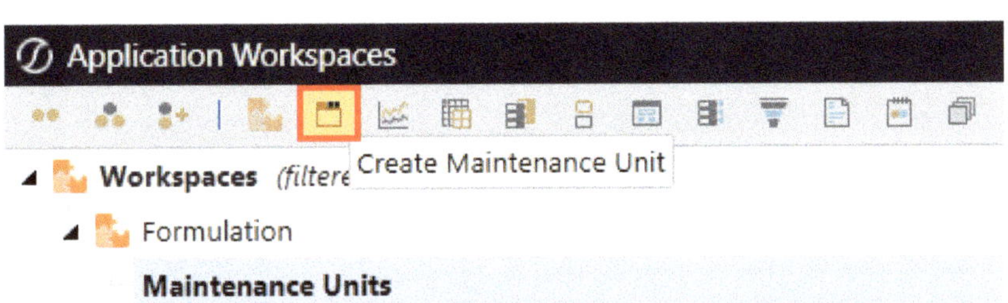

Figure 10.52

In the name field of the Maintenance Unit, type in Fiscal Guidance. The description field is optional for adding more context as desired; for now, we will leave this blank.

We will leverage Assemblies to trigger custom calculate actions for this dashboard. However, to show the difference between calling syntax from a Workspace vs. a Workspace Maintenance Unit, we will call the Assembly rule file from the Formulation Workspace, where we assigned the Workspace Assembly Service named Formulation.ServiceFactory.

Select the Access Group and Maintenance Group security groups to which you want to give these rights. For this exercise, we will select the DevelopmentQA security group as the Access Group on both maintenance units, allowing both developers to access/view both solutions. In contrast, the maintenance unit's Maintenance Group will differ – essentially restricting each developer from accidentally modifying one another's dashboards. Eric belongs to both the DevelopmentQA and DeveloperGroup1 security groups, so these are the security groups we'll assign to the maintenance unit.

You can modify these properties later if you don't have security groups configured yet.

Click the Save button to create the new maintenance unit.

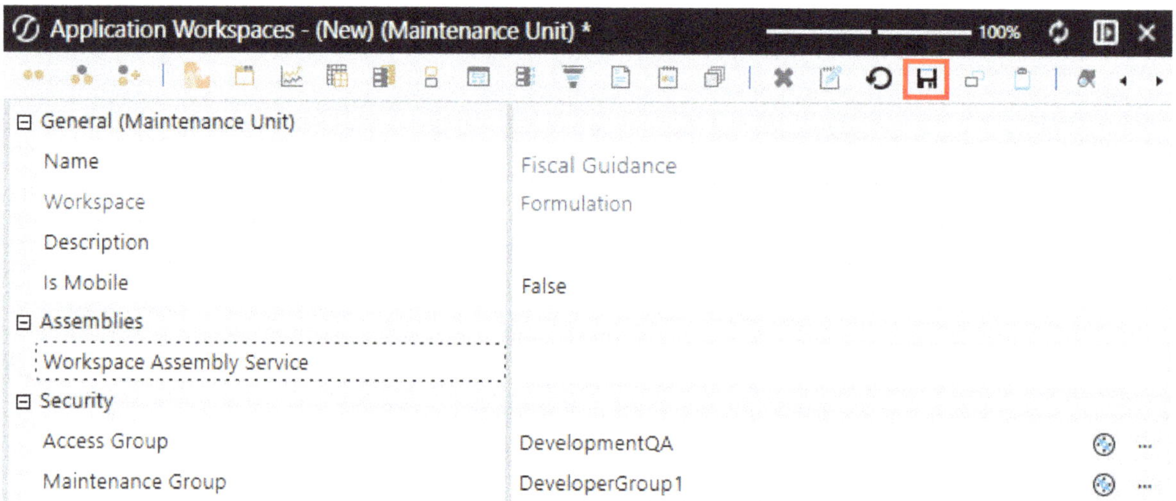

Figure 10.53

Create Cube Views

Objective Review

The fiscal guidance dashboard will contain two Cube Views. The first will be used for data entry, where users will enter and/or adjust inflation % to adjust the future year's budget authority. The second Cube View will show users the inflation % impact on accounts and programs. We will also use this Cube View for a BI Viewer component to visualize the data, allowing users to quickly see the impact of inflation % changes.

Exercise

Click on `Cube View Groups` under the `Fiscal Guidance` maintenance unit and click the Create Group button.

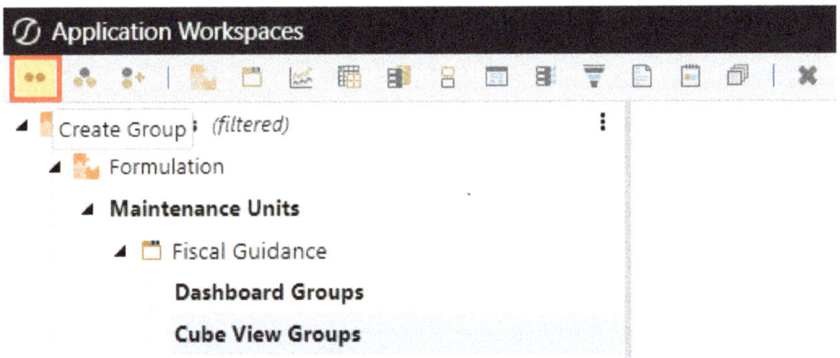

Figure 10.54

Type Fiscal Guidance into the Name field; the Description is optional.

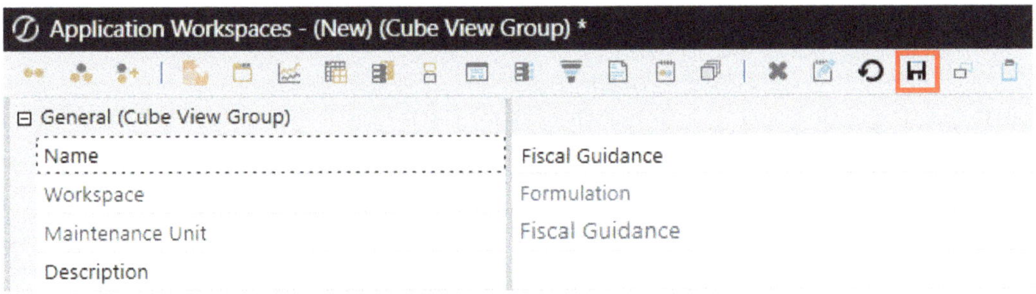

Figure 10.55

Click on the `Fiscal Guidance` Cube View group and click the Create Cube View button.

We've created the two Cube Views required for this dashboard (shown in the figure below). The Cube View named `cv_FiscalGuidanceRates_FGR` will be used to display the data entry form for users to enter the inflation %, while the Cube View named `cv_FiscalGuidance_FGR` will display the results of the calculated impact.

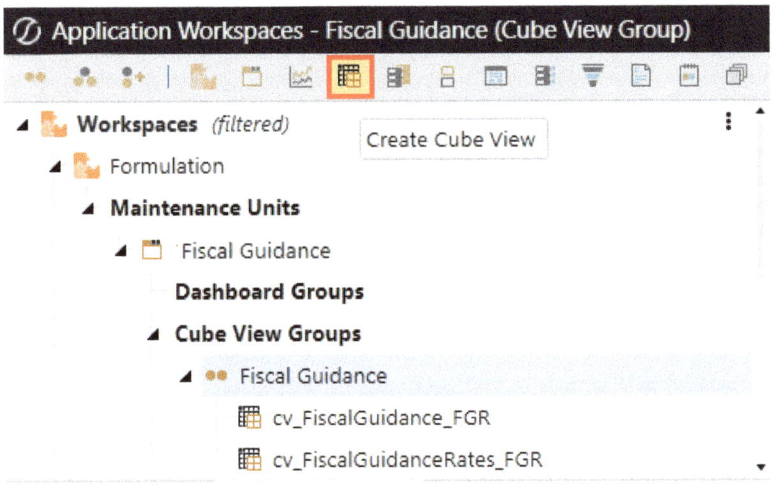

Figure 10.56

Create Data Management Groups

Objective Review

Our dashboard will include a button that will process code that triggers a custom calculate function from the **Workspace Assembly's Service Factory** upon user click. To configure our button to call the Assembly, we need a data management sequence that calculates the forecasted years.

Data management groups consist of **Sequences** and **Steps**. Data management steps are the vehicle for processing various functions, including calculations, consolidations, executing business rules, and processing custom calculation logic. Conversely, data management sequences are the vehicles that dashboard components use to trigger actions. In a nutshell, steps are the actions that are added to sequences – sequences can consist of as many steps as needed.

Our next task is creating the data management objects to facilitate the Assembly rule from a button, which will require us to create the following data management objects:

- **Groups:** Where we create and organize data management objects.
- **Step:** Where we call the custom calculation script from our Assembly.
- **Sequence:** How we apply the action to a button.

Exercise

Click on Data Management Groups and then click the Create Group button.

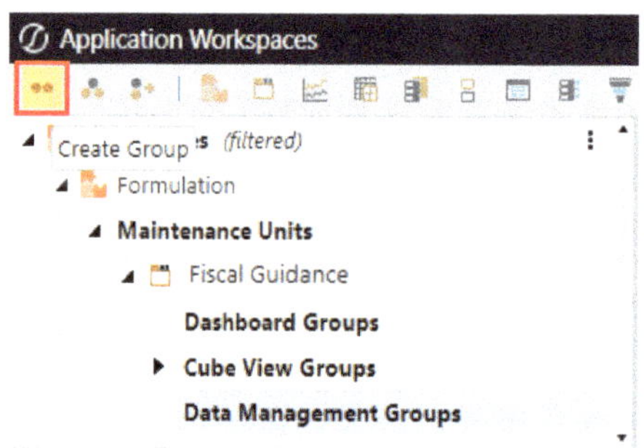

Figure 10.57

Type Button Actions into the Name, then click Save. The Description field is optional for adding more context to the group's purpose; for this exercise, we will leave this blank.

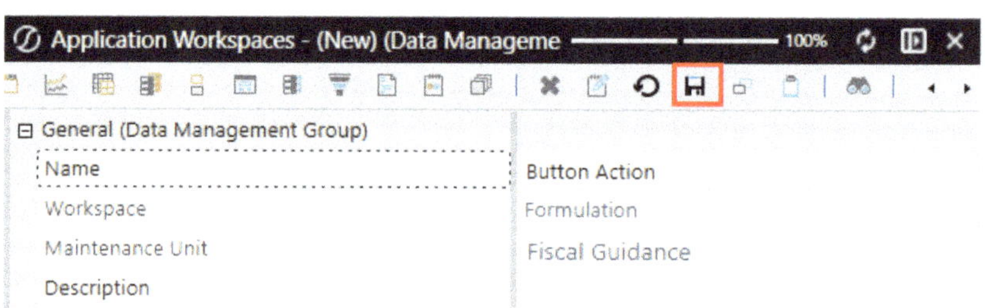

Figure 10.58

Click on Steps and then click the Create Step button.

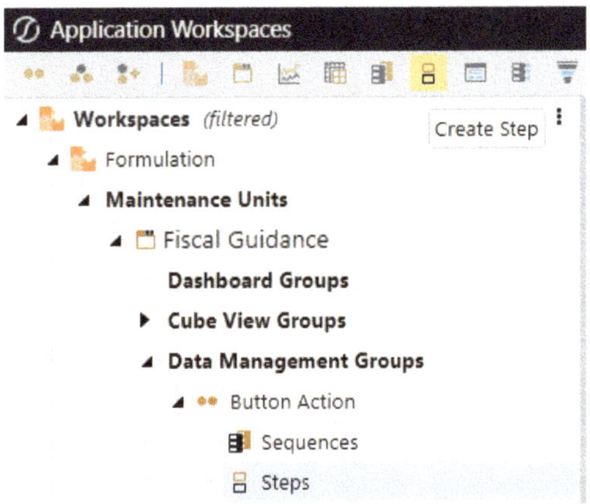

Figure 10.59

Select Custom Calculate from the Create Step dialog box, then click OK.

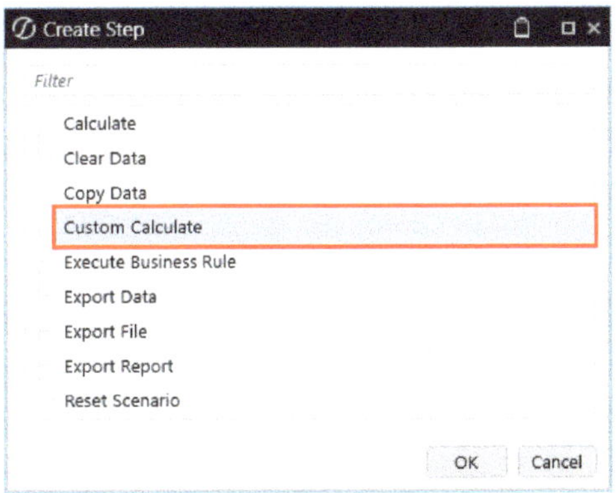

Figure 10.60

Custom Calculate Data Management Step Properties Explained

Here's a breakdown of the syntax used in the four-part Assembly logic:

Method: Workspace

Workspace Name: Workspace Name where the Assembly is located. Alternatively, you can enter Current if the Assembly is in the same Workspace as the data management step being processed.

Maintenance Unit: Name of the maintenance unit where the Assembly is located.

Service Factory Location: WS if the Service Factory is configured on the Workspace; WSMU if the Service Factory is configured on the Workspace's maintenance unit.

Name: Enter the name of the step that is being processed

Description: Optional field for adding more context or explanation of the step

Data Units: Target intersections where you are writing data and calculations

Business Rule: Enter the business rule or Workspace Assembly name, and type in the function name that contains the code your step will process

Since we are using Workspace Assemblies to build our processing code, the business rule field must contain a valid Workspace format: `Workspace.Current.Fiscal Guidance.WS`

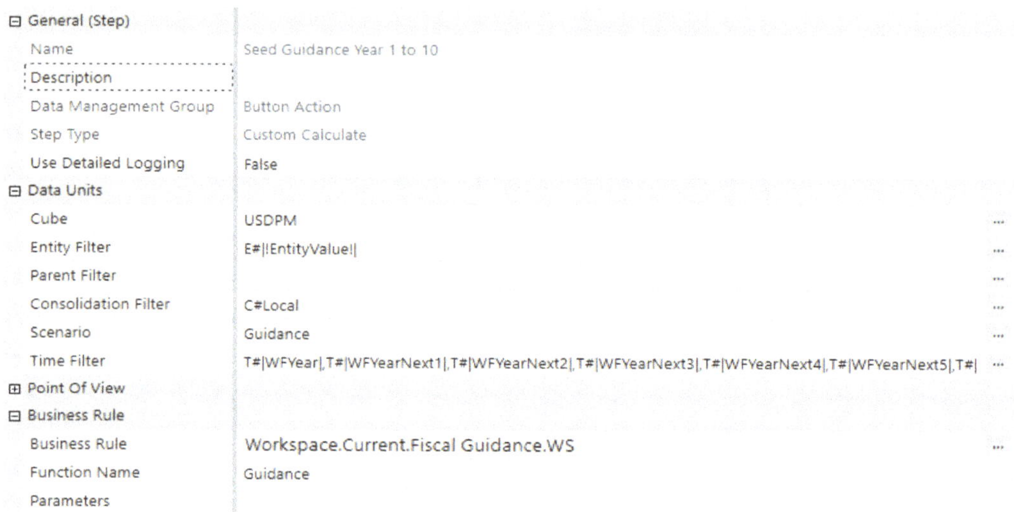

Figure 10.61

Next, we need to create the sequence that we will add the step to and eventually use to configure our dashboard button. Click on Sequences and then click the Create Sequence button.

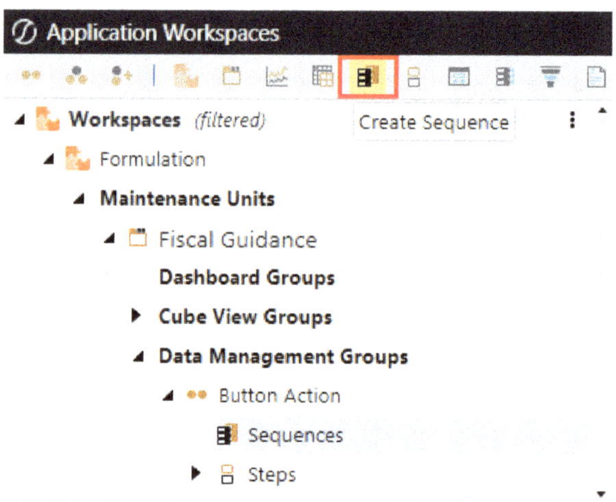

Figure 10.62

Type in a name for the sequence; you can also enter a description, which is optional. We named our sequence Seed Fiscal Guidance; this name will be used to configure our button action.

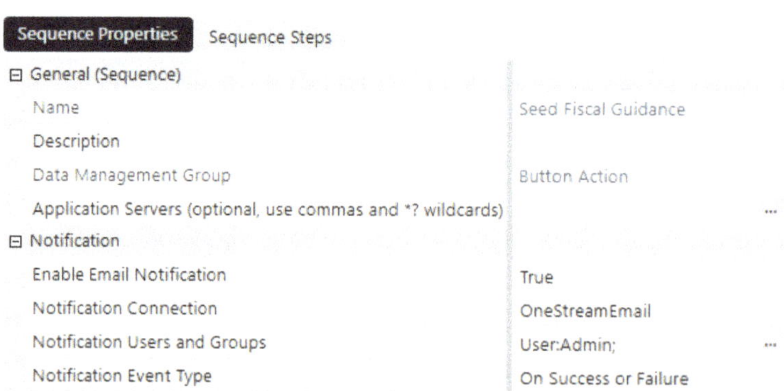

Figure 10.63

Select the Sequence Steps tab and click the + button to add the Seed Guidance Year 1 to 10 step to the sequence. Click Save to create the sequence.

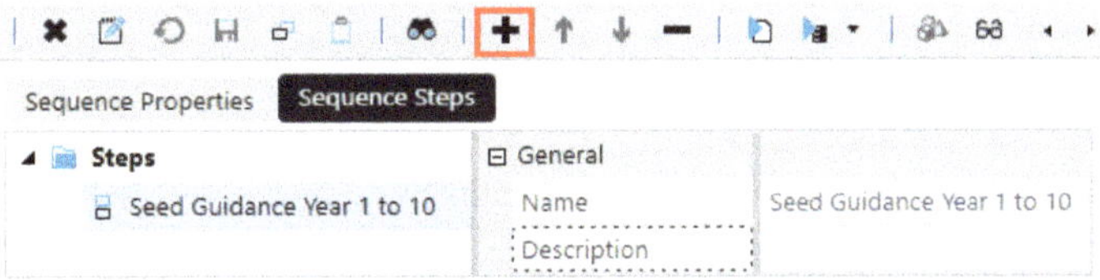

Figure 10.64

Create Assembly

Objective Review

Assemblies, in their simplest form, are another method for triggering actions. Previously, syntax was called from the business rules page. With OneStream's Workspaces, though, you now have the ability to use Assemblies where business rules were called – making it much easier and quicker to share/export full dashboard solutions with syntax from the Assemblies packaged.

Exercise

Click on `Assemblies` and click the Create Assembly button.

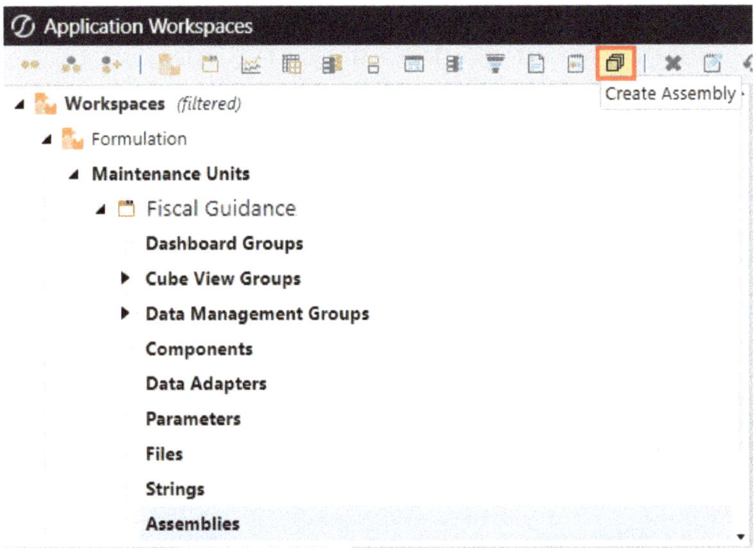

Figure 10.65

Type Formulation into the Name field, and type Formulation Rules in the Description (optional). When creating new Assemblies, the default compiler language is C#. Change the drop-down selection to Visual Basic, and then click Save.

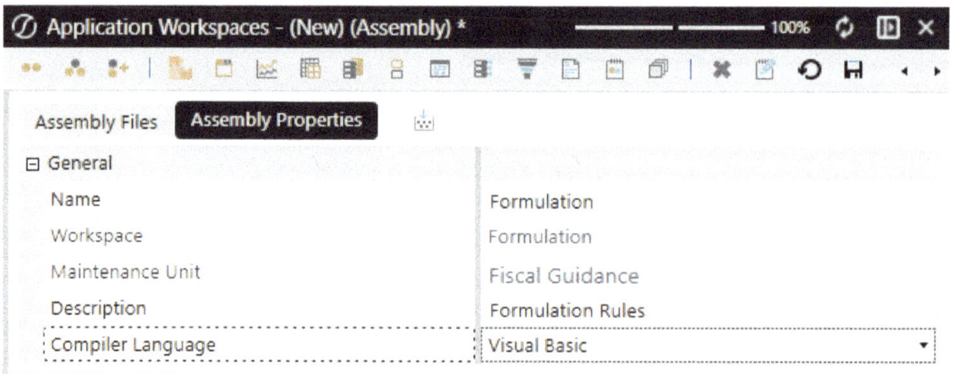

Figure 10.66

Navigate to the Assembly Files tab and right-click on Files, then click Add File.

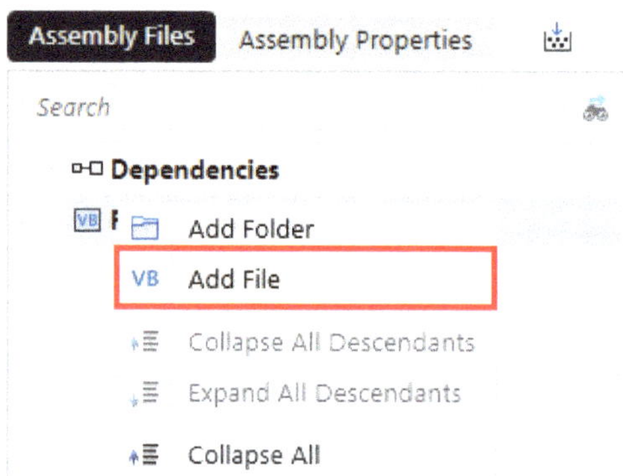

Figure 10.67

Type ServiceFactory into the Name, then select Service Factory from the Source Code Type drop-down menu, then click OK.

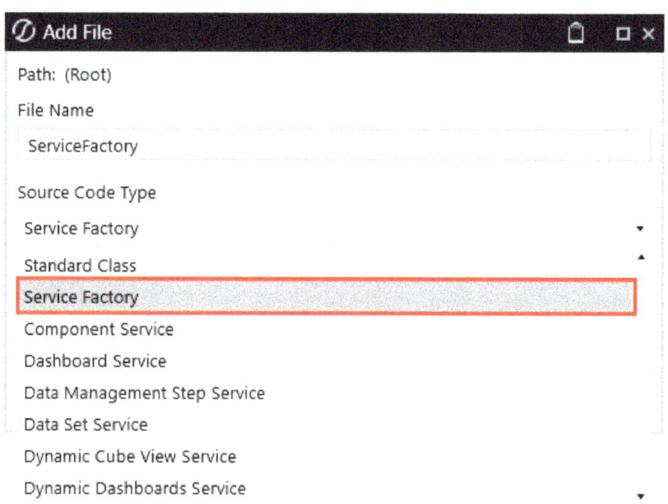

Figure 10.68

The **Source Code Type** selection will determine the sample syntax provided when creating new files. When you add a new Assembly file with the **Service Factory Source Code Type** selected,

OneStream automatically populates the file with placeholders for each standard Service Factory Workspace Assembly type.

Although each Assembly type is listed in the initial Service Factory file, the Assembly will not process any syntax until you make the syntax active. In other words, there is no harm in leaving the Assembly types 'as-is' in the Service Factory, since they will not be processed or triggered unless you enable them.

For advanced developers reading this, you are likely to understand the concept of uncommenting and commenting out syntax to make lines in your file active or not.

For those new to development and writing code, or if you are just getting acquainted with developing in different languages, OneStream's flexible framework provides the ability to write code in Visual Basic, C#, or a combination of the two coding languages. The beauty of this is that you are not forced to write your code in a single language, especially if you're comfortable with one language and not the other. Personally, I find Visual Basic easier for writing code, and more importantly, easier to read. However, most true developers I've worked with prefer C#.

The concept of turning lines of code on/off within your Assembly is straightforward; the character used to enable code lines is determined by the language you're writing your code in.

The following section's screenshots highlight the difference between turning lines of code on/off in Visual Basic vs C#.

Visual Basic

Comment-out code: Use an apostrophe (') before the row to make inactive.

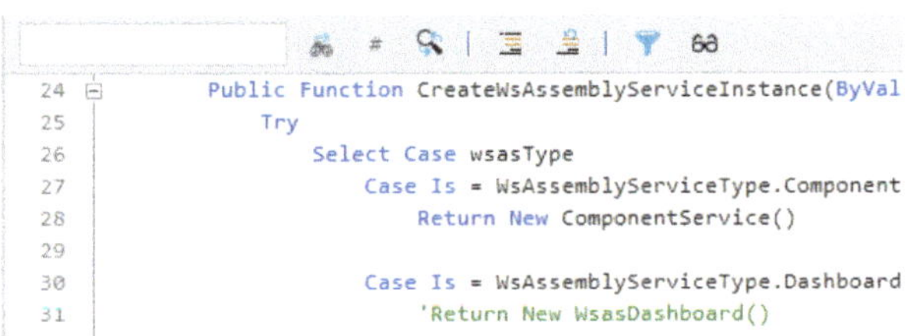

C#

Comment-out code: Use double backslash (//) before the row to make inactive.

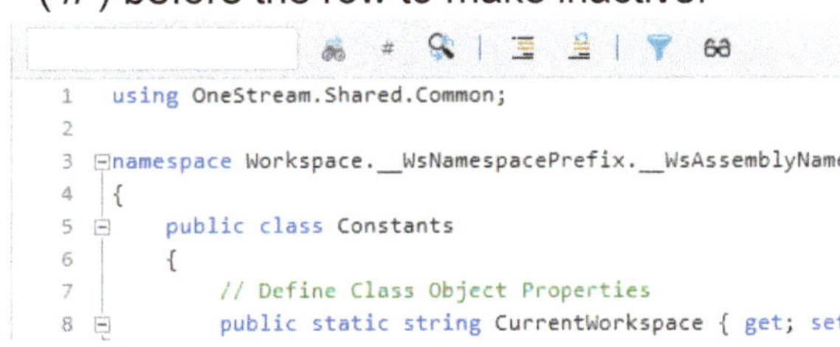

Figure 10.69

In both languages, code that has been commented-out (made inactive) will display as green text.

With the basic knowledge of what code in your Assemblies will and will not be processed, we can easily identify lines of code within the Service Factory Assembly file that we want to make active.

For this solution exercise, we need to create a custom calculate rule to process calculations upon saving data entry in our dashboard's forms. The Service Factory's library is shown below for reference, but for simplicity, we will focus on the **Custom Calculate** type to explain how the Service Factory can dynamically call the appropriate code based on the Workspace's configuration.

Scroll down to where the Finance Custom Calculate case syntax is located:

```
Case Is = WsAssemblyServiceType.FinanceCustomCalculate
```

Immediately below this line of code, uncomment (remove the ' before) the line of code:

```
Return New WsasFinanceCustomCalculate()
```

This is what the code should look like once you've modified the row to enable the script to be processed.

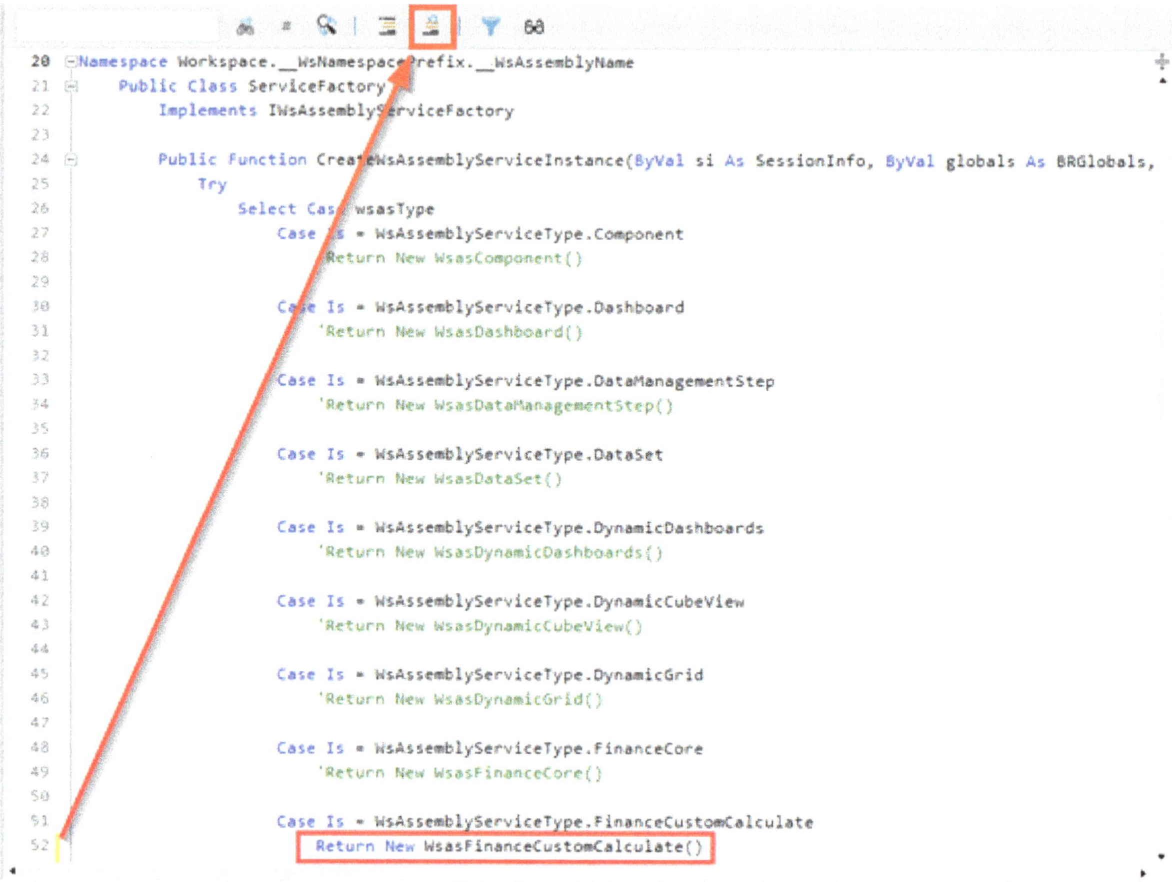

Figure 10.70

Now that we've made the line of code active, we need to create the file that the Service Factory points to in order to process the appropriate function; otherwise, nothing will happen when the Service Factory is called.

In an effort to keep our Assemblies organized and easy to navigate to specific sections of the code, we can create folders within the Assembly that group or structure the Assembly in a way that users will find more intuitive (in order to find specific code to modify or build upon).

Folders are purely for organization; feel free to name them whatever makes most sense to you in your development. I like to name folders in a way that groups types of rules to make troubleshooting and modifying code more intuitive.

For example, below is a sample Assembly organized by `11_Services` and `2_Process`. The `11_Services` folder contains code that is processed from the Service Factory, and the `2_Process` folder contains code that is processed from specific service files. When creating folders, you only need to enter the Folder Name. The Folder Path field is not editable, rather it populates the lineage once you save the new folder, as shown in the next figure.

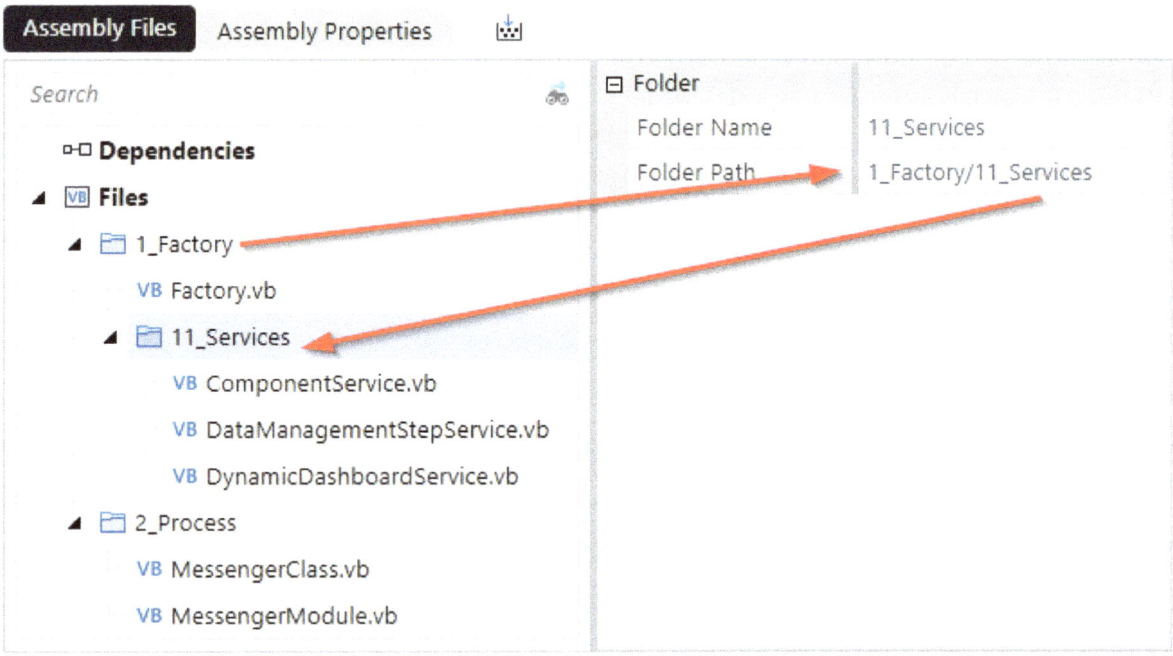

Figure 10.71

Organizing and naming Assembly files is ultimately up to you. The most important thing to remember when naming files is that the service file names *must* match the Service Factory `Return` statements.

Click on Files, right-click, and select Add Folder.

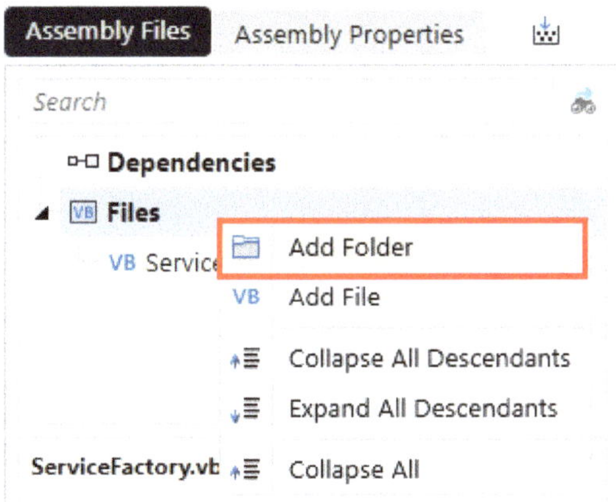

Figure 10.72

Type Services into the Folder Name, then click Save.

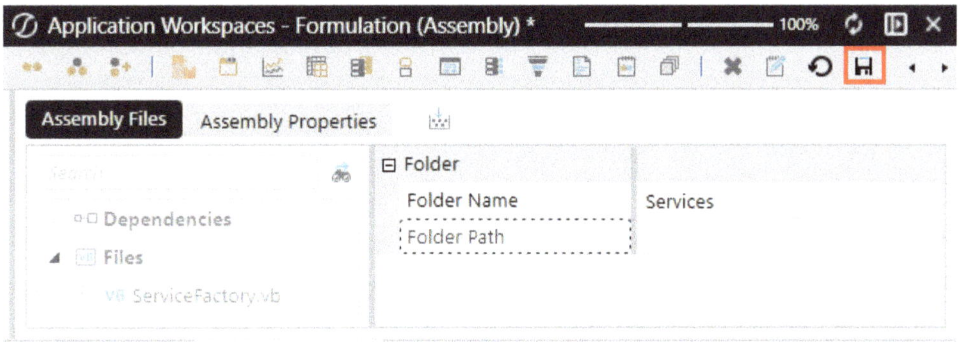

Figure 10.73

Right-click on the Services folder and select Add File.

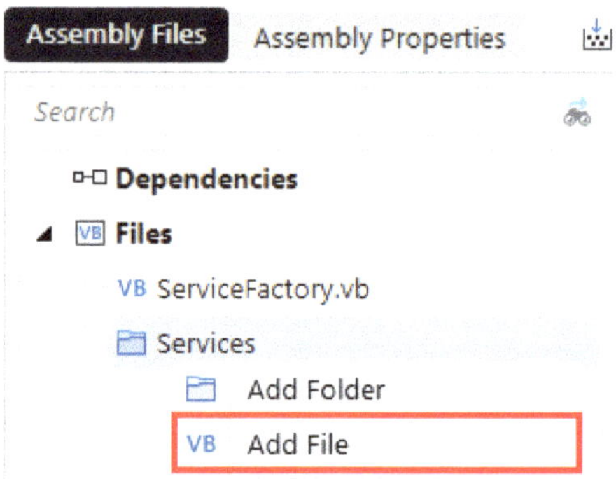

Figure 10.74

In order to call the `Case` statement from the Service Factory, the name of the service must match the name of the `Case` statement referenced in the `ServiceFactory` Assembly.

Type WsAssemblyServiceType into the File Name (as reflected in row 52 of the ServiceFactory rule), then select Finance Custom Calculate Service from the Source Code Type drop-down menu. Click OK.

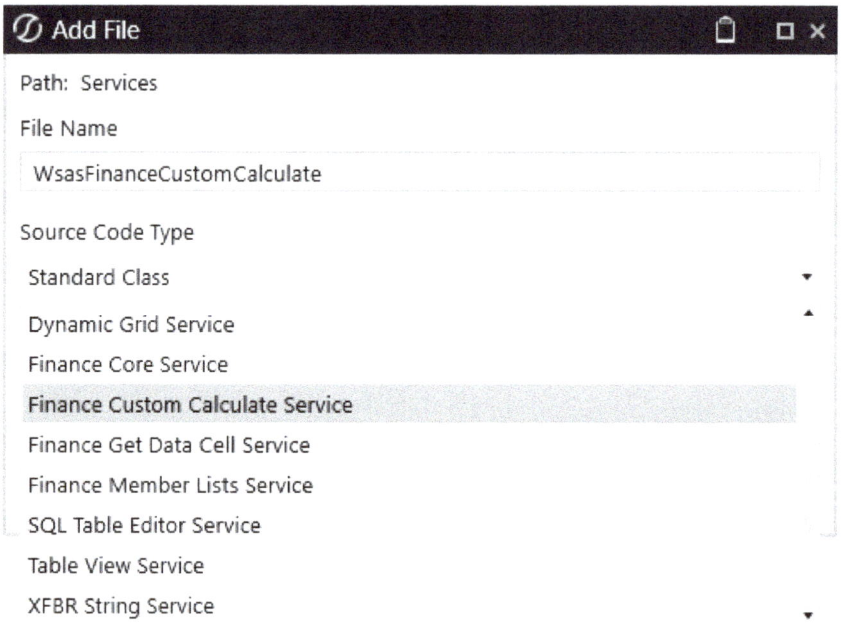

Figure 10.75

The source code type selected in the previous step provides the shell of the pre-defined rule type. Depending on the source code type selected for the file, you will see different syntax templates.

Row 21 of the syntax in the figure below shows the name of the file created and referenced in the ServiceFactory file named `WsasFinanceCustomCalculate`.

Directly below the `Try` syntax on row 25 is where you will start writing your own syntax. For this exercise, we've written custom calculation logic into the Assembly to calculate the impact of inflation.

To systematically call this syntax from a dashboard's button component, we will also need to create a data management sequence in the following steps that processes the function called `Guidance`, as shown in row 26 of the figure below.

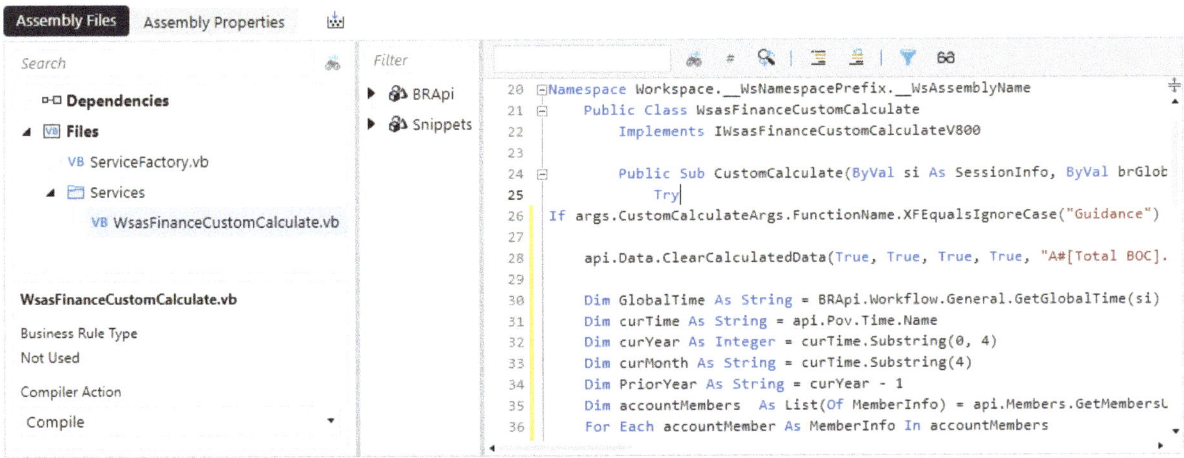

Figure 10.76

Create Components

Objective Review

The figure below shows the components that are used to build the Fiscal Guidance dashboard. In the following exercise section, we'll go under the covers to explain how to create these components to update your dashboard and process code from the Assembly file.

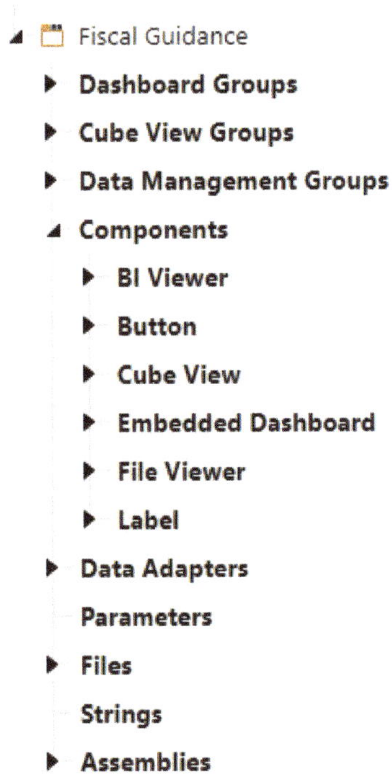

Figure 10.77

Exercise

For this exercise, we'll focus on the primary components that require user interaction.

- **Cube View:** Enter data into a Cube View form
- **Button:** Save work, process custom calculation logic

Cube View

This form, displayed on the dashboard, is a Cube View component used to collect Fiscal Guidance Adjustment %, implying inflation predictions' impact on future years' fund values.

Cells with a yellow cornsilk background indicate that they are writeable; users can enter or update these.

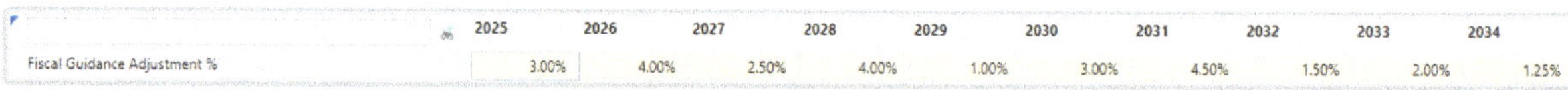

Figure 10.78

To create this component, select Components under the Decision Packages maintenance unit and click Create Dashboard Component.

Select Cube View from the Create Dashboard Component dialog box, then click OK.

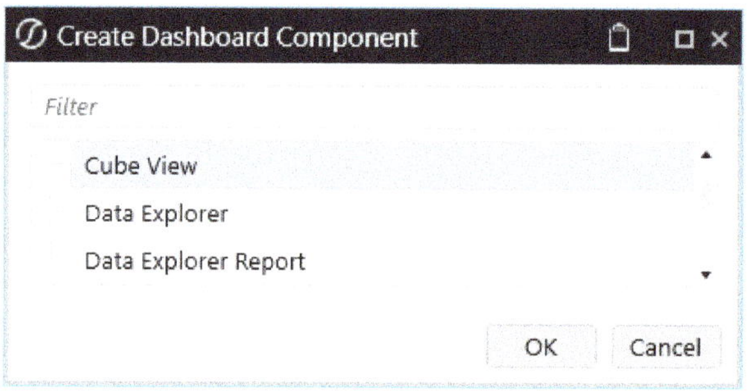

Figure 10.79

Button

After a user enters or modifies the percentage input form, they'll click the Update Rates % and Calculate button on the dashboard.

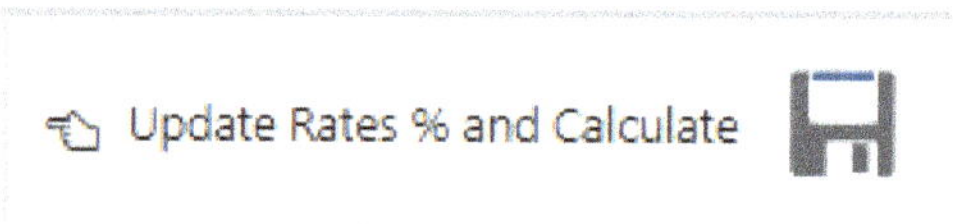

Figure 10.80

To create this component, select Components under the Fiscal Guidance maintenance unit and click Create Dashboard Component.

Select Button from the Create Dashboard Component dialog box, then click OK.

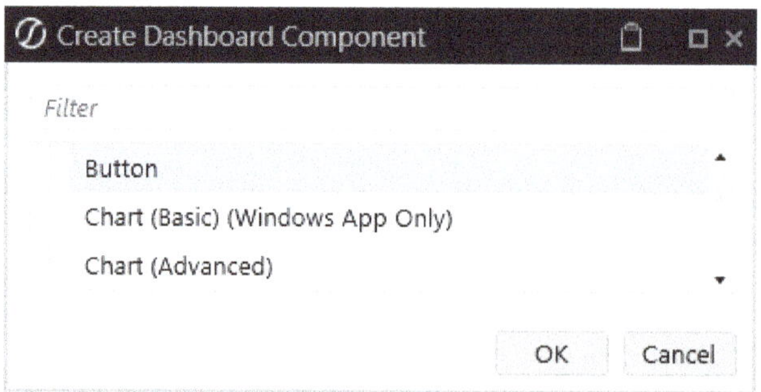

Figure 10.81

The button properties are configured to **Save Data for All Components** and process the server task shown in the figure below. In the Decision Packages solution, we showed how to build a button to execute a custom calculate business rule from the server task options. For this solution, we'll show how to call a data management sequence to process Assembly logic with a custom calculate step.

Server Changed Server Task: Execute Data Management Sequence

Server Changed Server Task Argument: `{Seed Fiscal Guidance}{}`

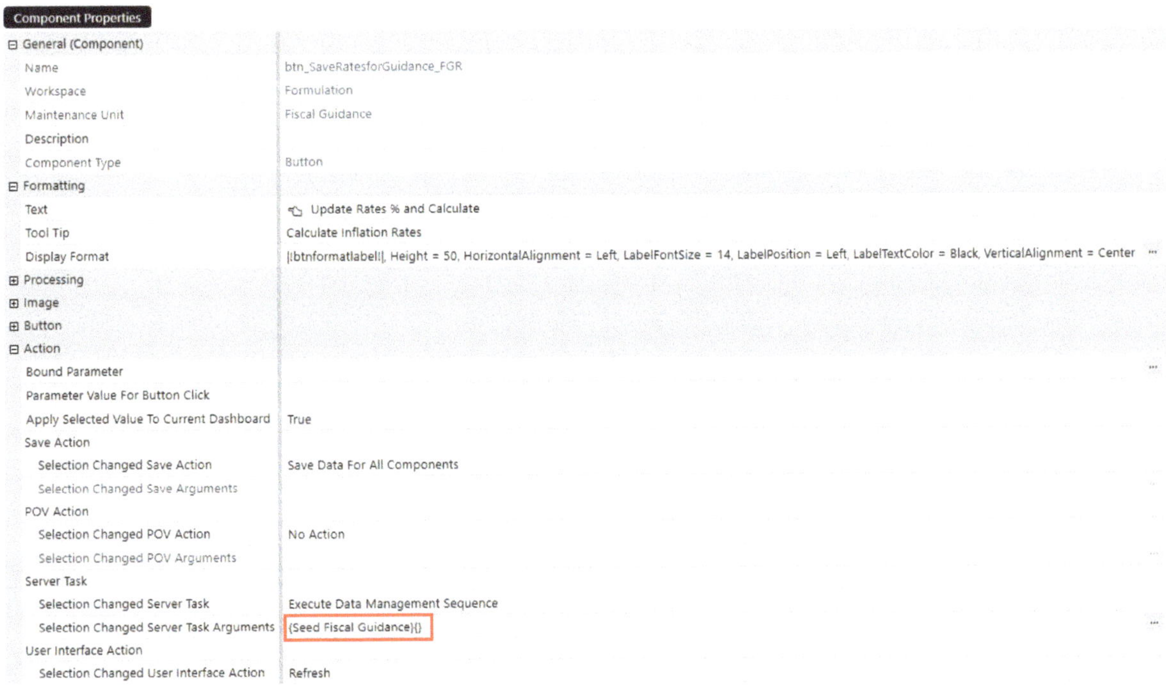

Figure 10.82

In the Create Data Management Groups section above, we created a step that called an Assembly function using the Service Factory. That sequence, named Seed Fiscal Guidance, contains a step named Seed Guidance Year 1 to 10.

Notice the business rule in the data management step is configured with `Workspace.Current.Fiscal Guidance.WS.` The syntax here is `WS` instead of `WSMU`, since the Assembly is wired to the Workspace itself.

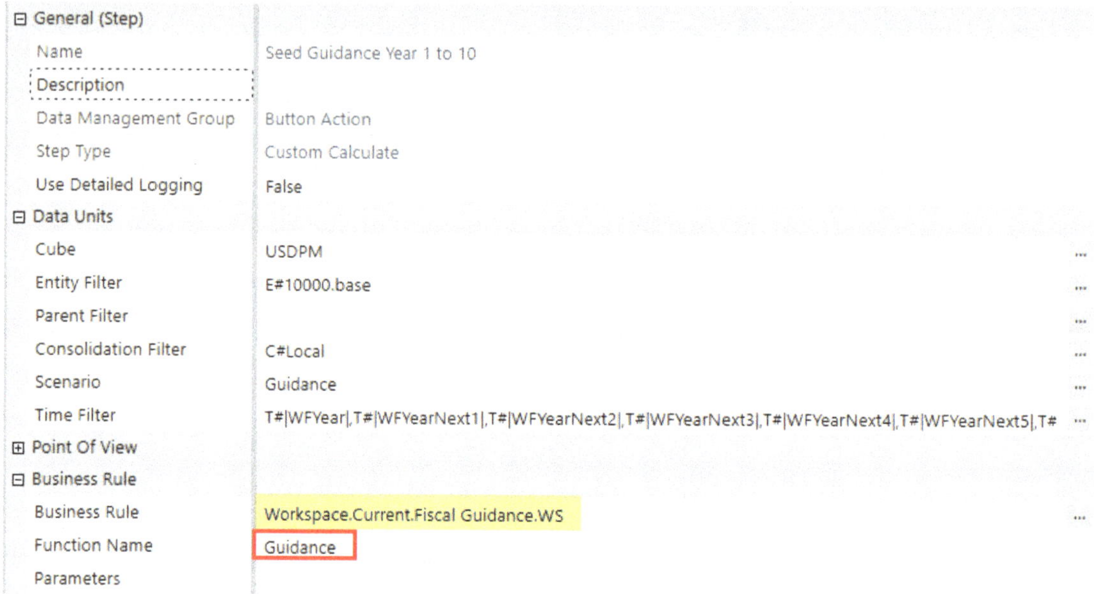

Figure 10.83

Navigate back to the Formulation Workspace and notice where we originally configured the Assembly name and location.

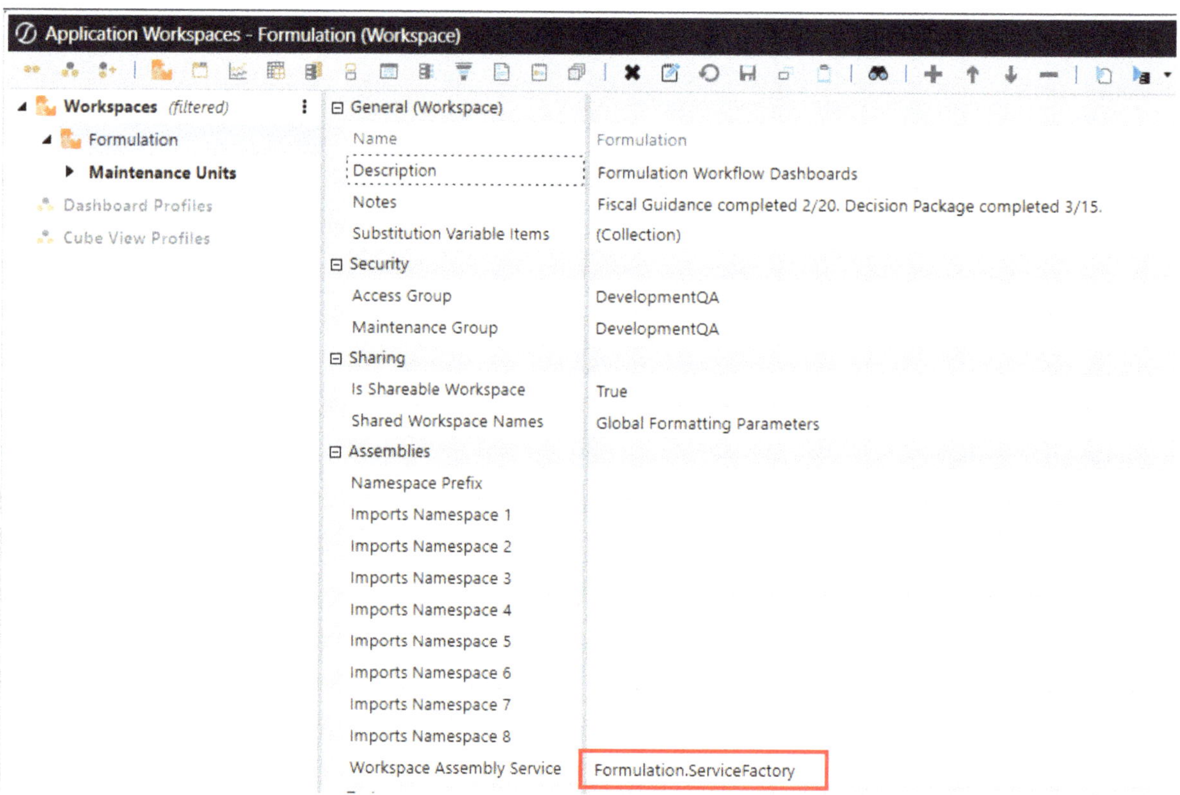

Figure 10.84

Porting Solutions

Thanks to Workspaces and Workspace Assemblies, exporting solutions has never been easier in OneStream. Let's look at the steps required to export our solution *before* Workspaces provided a central location to build and extend our solutions.

Before Workspaces

Exporting files from OneStream has always been an easy task, but for developers building robust solutions that need to be exported for sharing or testing, the task of capturing all necessary files can be daunting – and prone to error if you forget to export even one file that the solution requires.

To export files, navigate to the Application tab and select Load/Extract under the Tools section.

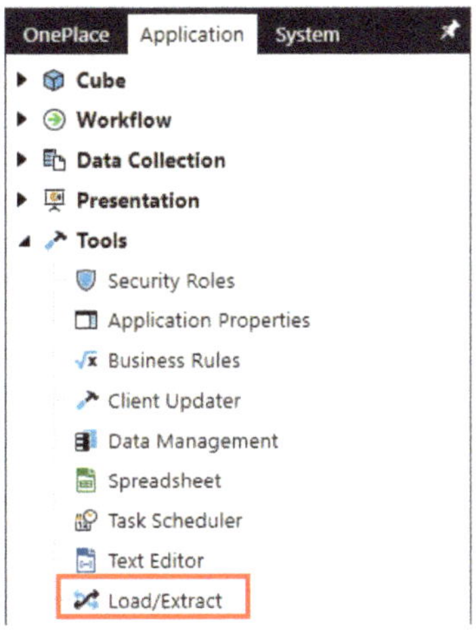

10.85

Before Workspaces existed, you had to export multiple file types and hope you didn't miss any files for the solution to function (when importing to another application or sharing the solution with others).

It was a multi-step process to get each file. The Decision Package solution, for example, required repeating the export step to get the following files out of the application.

1. Export Cube Views
2. Export Data Management
3. Export Business Rules
4. Export Dashboards

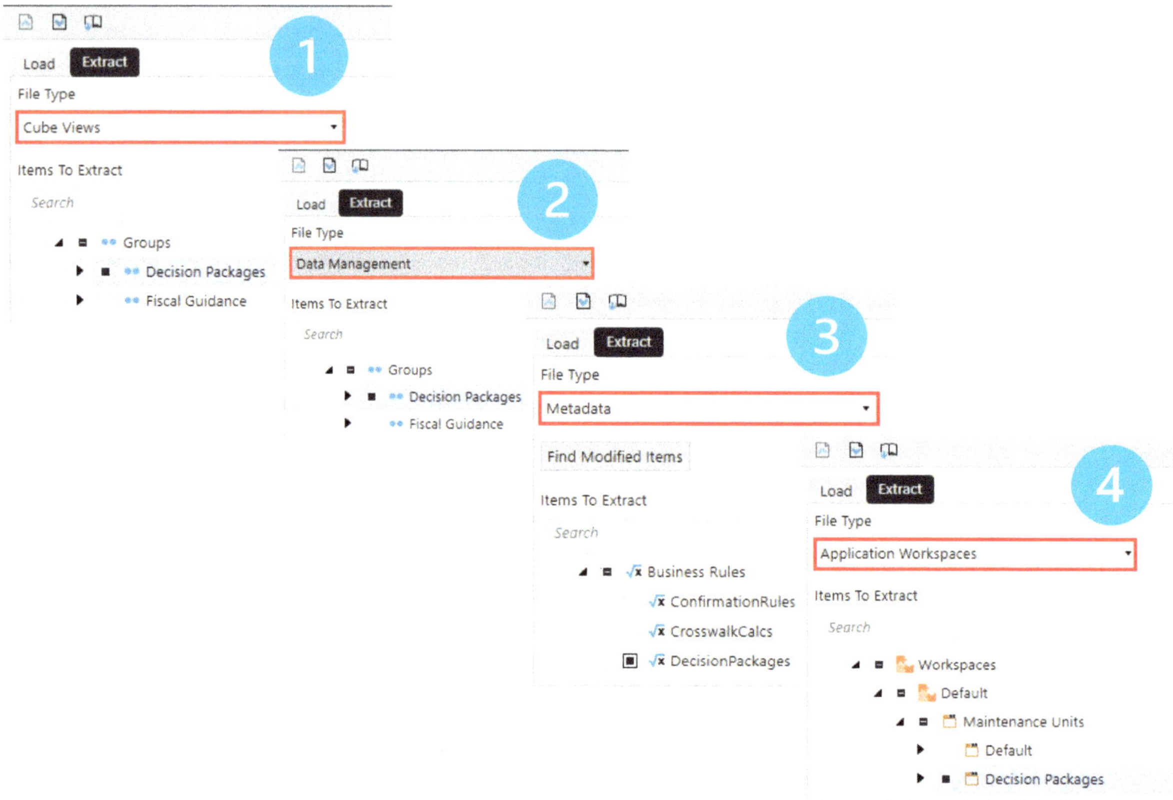

Figure 10.86

After Workspaces

When solutions are developed completely within the Workspace, this task requires only one step.

1. Export Workspaces

To export a Workspace, select the Application Workspaces file type from the drop-down menu. Unselect the top item and click the specific Workspace you want to export. Much easier!

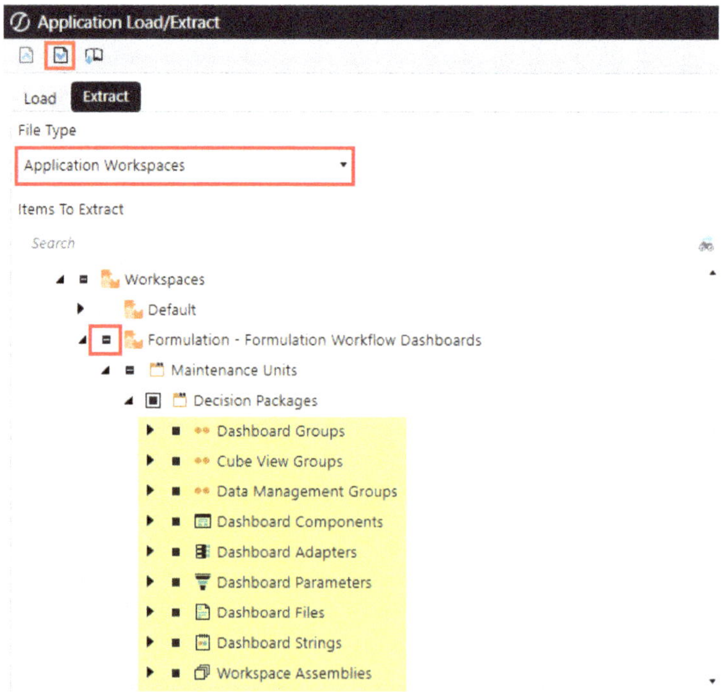

Figure 10.87

Conclusion

This end-to-end exercise clearly demonstrates how OneStream Workspaces empower users across all roles… developers, administrators, and business users alike. By consolidating development, configuration, and deployment into a single, intuitive interface, Workspaces streamline the entire solution lifecycle. Developers benefit from modular design through maintenance units and Assemblies, enabling secure, collaborative development without code conflicts. Administrators gain efficiency through simplified packaging and deployment, reducing the risk of missing components during exports. Business users experience more responsive, interactive dashboards that are easier to navigate and tailored to their needs.

Ultimately, Workspaces foster a more agile, secure, and scalable environment for building and managing enterprise solutions. Whether you're creating complex financial models or simple data entry forms, Workspaces provide the structure and flexibility to deliver high-quality solutions faster and with greater confidence!

11 Troubleshooting Workspaces and Assemblies

Developing OneStream applications with a Workspace approach unlocks endless possibilities and empowers you to create dynamic, adaptable solutions. As with any advanced toolset, there may be times when everything seems properly set up, yet something doesn't work as expected. These moments, however, are opportunities to learn, grow, and sharpen your skills. Whether that's something straightforward, like configuring a combo box from another Workspace, or tackling a more intricate challenge, such as refining a dynamic dashboard service.

This chapter is here to support you through those challenges. Together, we'll explore some of the common errors you might encounter and uncover practical strategies to address them. While not exhaustive, this guide aims to equip you with a solid foundation, ensuring you feel prepared to resolve issues and move forward with confidence. Let's dive in!

Troubleshooting Approach

Most of the Workspace and Assembly development that we do relies on a simple philosophy: we try to start small, stay focused, and test regularly. With this in mind, we'll first cover the essential areas where confusion often arises. Many times, the issue is a slight syntax error that can be frustrating, but very relieving when you find it and realize that your logic was correct all along. Other times, it could be a particular setting that wasn't turned on when it needed to be.

You'll also encounter scenarios involving reference errors when you are trying to reference objects in another Workspace, and in some cases, the same Workspace. We will try to give examples of the most common errors and even touch on some more technical issues like dependencies within the Assemblies. From experience, we can confidently say that the more you engage with Workspaces and Assemblies, the easier it becomes to anticipate and overcome these challenges. With every hurdle cleared, you'll grow more adept at preventing them altogether.

Common Workspace Issues

OneStream's out-of-the-box security framework is a robust slice security model that allows nearly every object in the application to be securitized, allowing administrators to grant and/or restrict user access and maintenance rights with a fine-tooth comb.

This security model is incredibly powerful in controlling user access to data and metadata; this also extends to Workspace development, allowing you to leverage your existing model by layering in security groups specific to your development teams. Reviewing your security model when modifying configuration – to allow your developers access to only areas you deem appropriate within the application – is essential. Here are some examples of security restrictions that may limit users from accessing and modifying Workspaces, and the security configuration settings to troubleshoot.

User Cannot Access Workspaces

The first step in setting up your developers for success is granting them access to the Workspace Admin page. If users do not see the Application tab with the Workspaces option when they log in to OneStream, they most likely do not have the appropriate security group assignment.

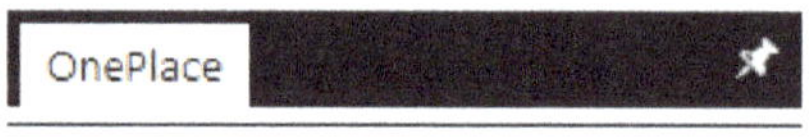

Figure 11.1

To access the Workspaces administration page in OneStream, users must belong to the security group assigned to the WorkspaceAdminPage property, located under the Application User Interface Role settings from the Security Roles page.

Once the user is added to the security group assigned to the WorkspaceAdminPage property, they will see the Workspaces option under the Application tab.

Figure 11.2

User Cannot Create Workspaces

As you start utilizing Workspaces in your development, you'll want to consider *who* should have the ability to create new Workspaces. Do you want to allow your developers to create new Workspaces? Or, do you want to only allow administrators to create Workspaces when they are needed?

Depending on your development teams and number of users, you may want to limit Workspace creation to certain users in order to control which Workspaces are in your library to avoid clutter.

To create new Workspaces in OneStream, users must belong to the security group assigned to the ManageApplicationWorkspaces property, located under the Application Security Role settings from the Security Roles page.

Users who *are* assigned to this security group have the ability to click the Create Workspace button.

Figure 11.3

Users who *are not* assigned to this security group will see the Create Workspace button, but will not have the ability to click the button.

Figure 11.4

User Cannot Modify Workspace Assemblies

Developers building solutions in OneStream will most likely need to create and modify Workspace Assemblies. However, depending on the scope of their work and their expertise, you may want to limit who can modify Assemblies. For example, if you have multiple developers working in the same Workspace but only want to allow Developer #1 to modify Assemblies, then you would need to assign Developer #1 to a separate security group role to restrict the other developers from making changes to Assemblies that are not approved.

To create or modify Workspace Assemblies, users must belong to the security group assigned to the AdministerApplicationWorkspaceAssemblies property from the Application Security Roles.

Users with Workspace access will see any existing Workspace Assemblies; however, they will only be able to create or modify Assemblies if they are in the appropriate security group. If they are not in the security group with rights to modify Assemblies, they will see a dialog box like the one below, telling them that they are not authorized to make changes.

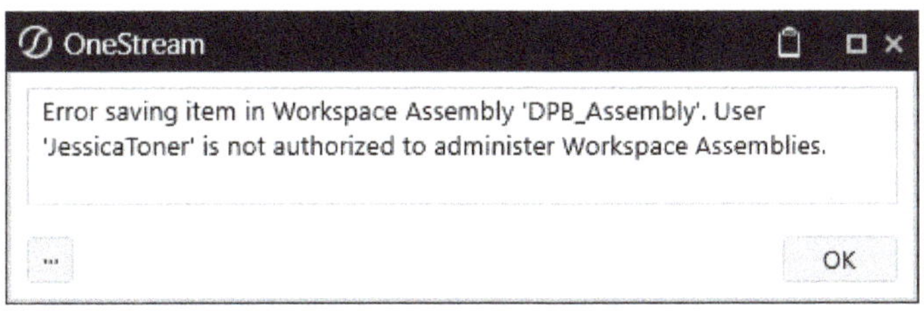

Figure 11.5

Error When Using Shared Object

To reuse any object from another Workspace, the share settings must be properly set. As an example, let's look at creating an embedded dashboard component and select the dashboard you want to reuse from the embedded dashboard selector. In the figure below, you want to reuse a help document that is located within the Landing Page (`OP_LPG2`) Workspace.

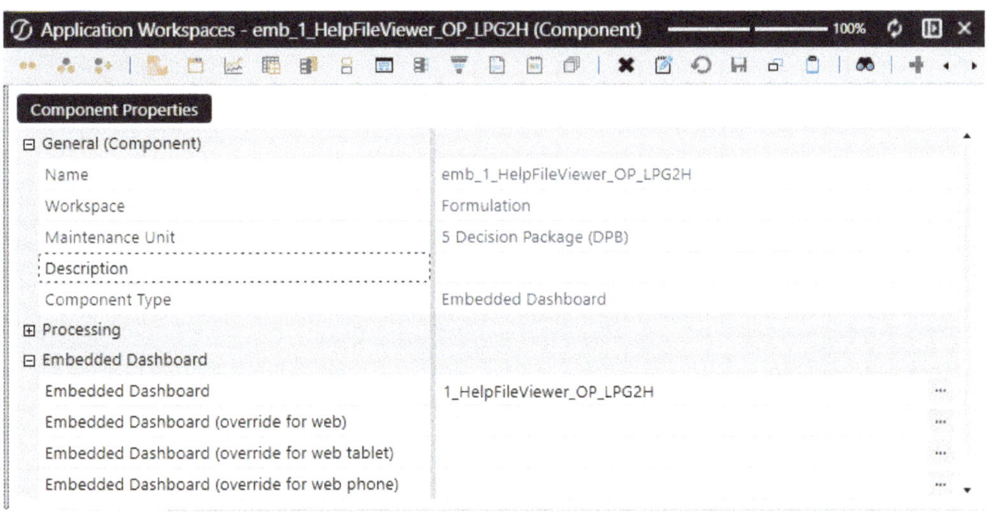

Figure 11.6

After attaching the embedded dashboard component to our dashboard, we get the following error message upon viewing the dashboard.

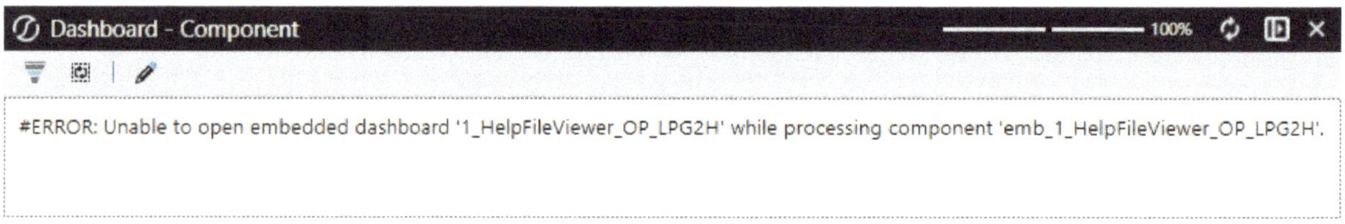

Figure 11.7

What is causing this error? There are two places to check your configuration to fix this error.

Is Shareable Workspace

In order to reuse objects from another Workspace, the Workspace that you are sharing *from* must have the Is Shareable Workspace property set to True. In the example below, we see that the Workspace we are sharing from is set to False. You would fix this error by changing this to True.

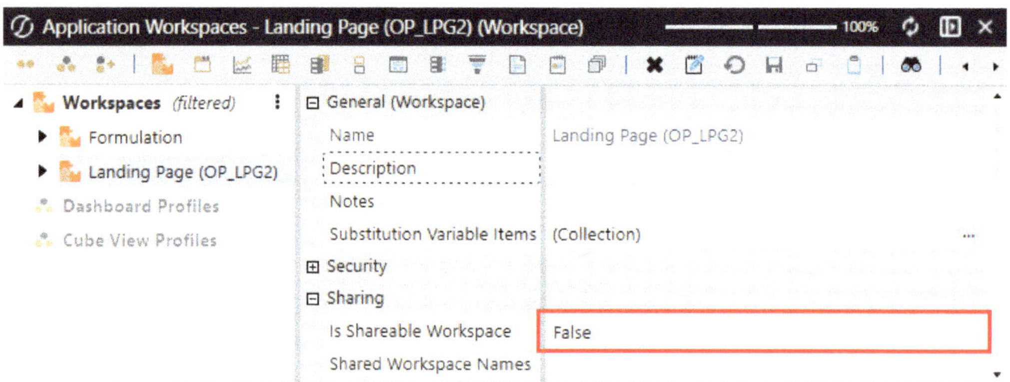

Figure 11.8

Shared Workspace Names

In order to reuse objects from another Workspace, the Workspace that you are sharing *from* must be listed in your *current Workspace's* Shared Workspace Names property. In the example below, you would fix this error by entering the Workspace name from which you are reusing the object.

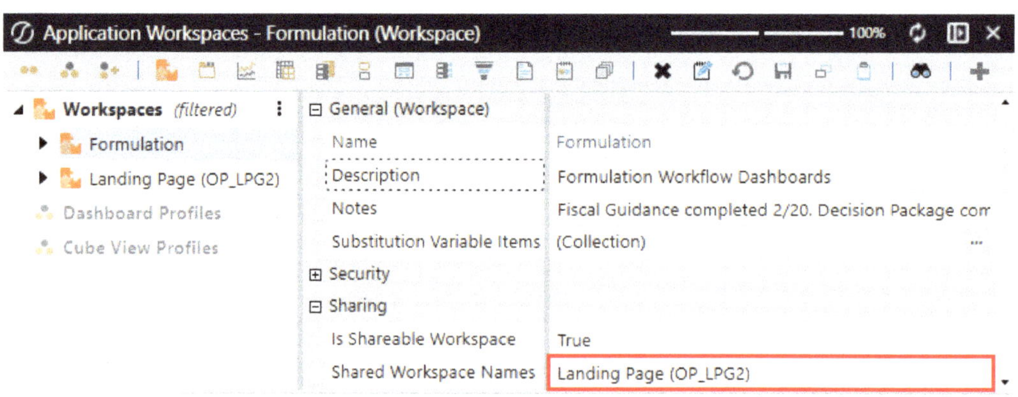

Figure 11.9

Once you've fixed the Workspace sharing properties, the dashboard will display the desired result.

Figure 11.10

Common Assembly Issues

Calling Assembly Business Rules and Assembly Services

The most common issue when working with Assemblies and Service Factories is getting the correct syntax for all the different types of calls. There are a lot of syntax variations between all the calls from Assembly business rules and Assembly Services.

Please go back to Chapter 6 and look through the detailed list of the six types of Assembly business rules and the required syntax:

- Cube View Extender Business Rules
- Dashboard Data Set Business Rules
- Dashboard Extender Business Rules
- Dashboard String Function Business Rules
- Extensibility Business Rules
- Spreadsheet Business Rules

In chapter 7, we have a detailed list of syntax variations for the current 13 types of Assembly Services.

- Component Service
- Dashboard Service
- Data Management Service
- Data Set Service
- Dynamic Dashboards Service
- Dynamic Cube Service
- Finance Core Service
- Finance Custom Calculate Service
- Finance Get Data Cell Service
- Finance Member Lists Service
- SQL Table Editor Service
- Table View Service
- XFBR String Service

Common Dependency Errors

Dependencies are a powerful strategy for building efficient code within Assemblies, but they can sometimes lead to errors if not managed correctly. Below, we outline common issues and their resolutions.

Common Dependency Errors

Undefined Classes: Compilation errors like "class is not defined" often occur due to:

- Incorrect definitions of the referenced Workspace or Assembly.
- Syntax errors when referencing classes and functions.

Here's an example of a typical error message:

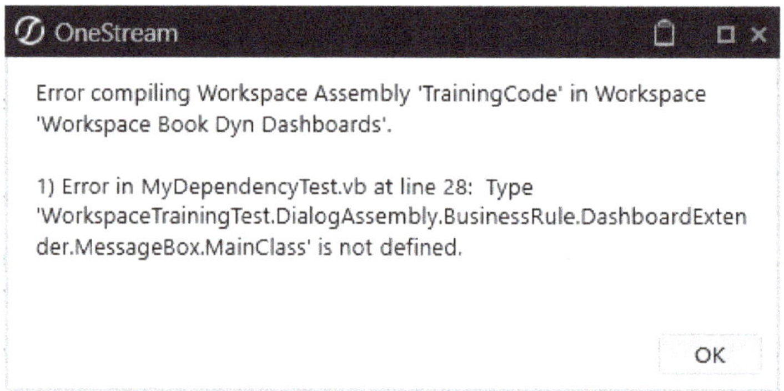

Figure 11.11

Since the error doesn't specify whether the issue lies in the dependency definition or the syntax, start by verifying the dependency definition. Let's look at dependencies defined as Workspace Assemblies first, and then go over dependencies defined as traditional business rules.

Dependency Calling another Workspace Assembly

Defining Dependency

When defining a dependency from another Assembly, you define the dependency as a Workspace Assembly and give the Workspace Name and Assembly Name of the location of the Assembly business rule. It's very important to give the referenced Assembly the correct name.

To reference an Assembly from another Workspace, follow these steps:

1. **Specify as a Workspace Assembly**:
    - Set the Shared Workspace Name to match the actual Workspace name.
    - Define the Dependency Name as the referenced Assembly's name.

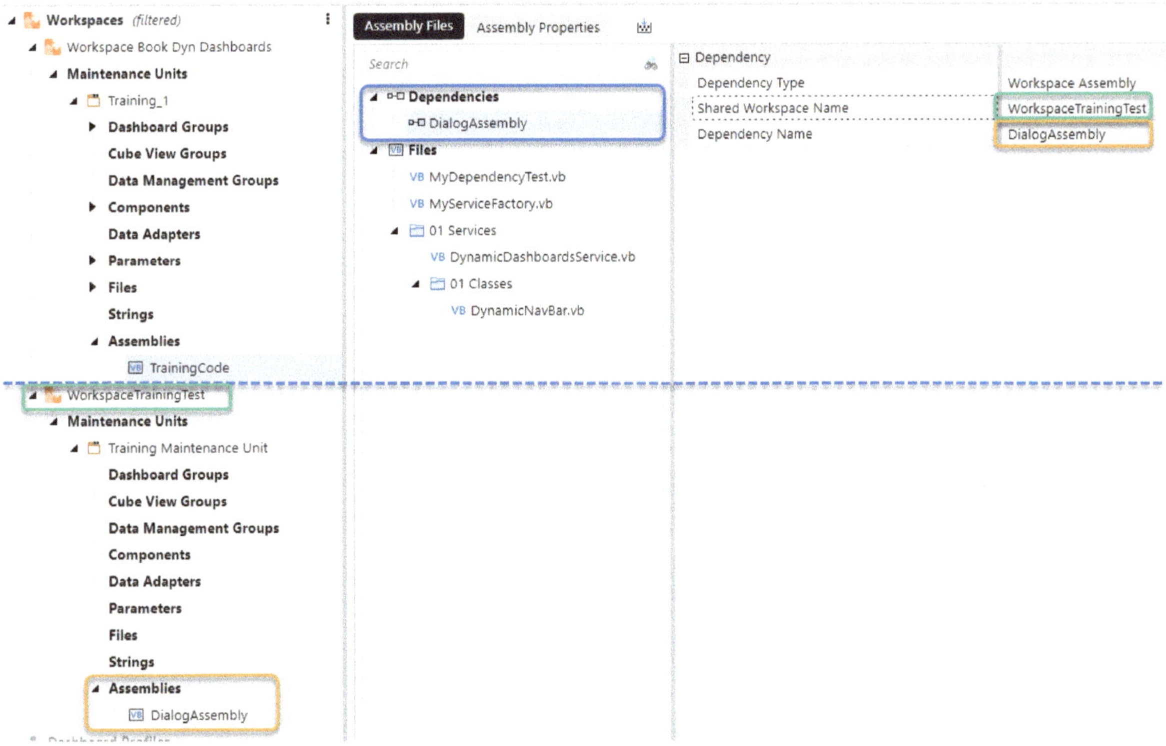

Figure 11.12

Key Details:

- **Shared Workspace Name:** Must match the exact Workspace name (not the namespace prefix).
- **Dependency Name:** Must match the Assembly name being referenced.

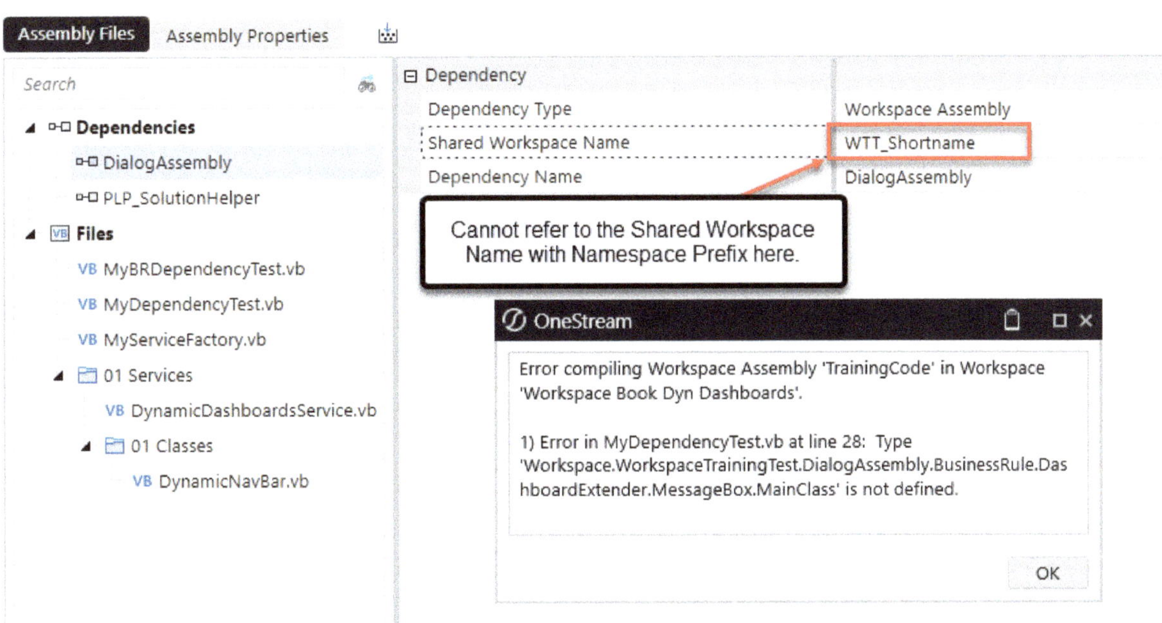

Figure 11.13

In the dependency definition, Shared Workspace Name MUST be the actual Workspace name and not the namespace prefix.

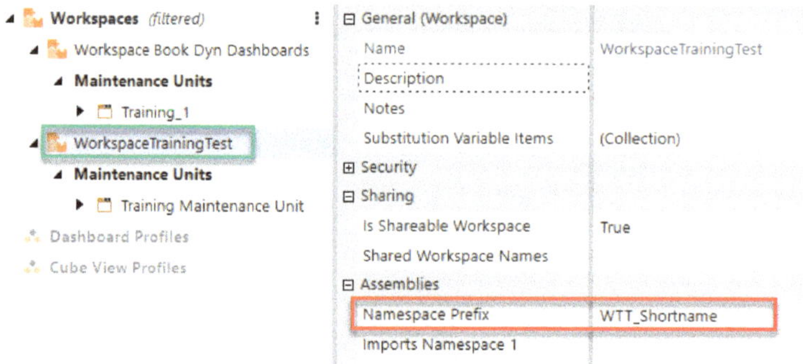

Figure 11.14

Dependency name must be the Assembly name being referenced.

Referencing Classes and Methods in a Dependency

Once you've successfully defined the dependency, you'll need to use the correct syntax to reference classes and methods from the dependent Assembly. Follow this structure:

1. **Create an Object**: Use the `Dim` keyword to create an object from the dependency, referencing the Workspace, Assembly, and class hierarchy.

Syntax:

```
Dim yourObjectName As New
Workspace.WorkspaceName(orNamespacePrefix).AssemblyName.BusinessRule.
DashboardExtender.YourFileName.YourClassName
```

Example:

```
Dim DependencyTest As New
Workspace.WorkspaceTrainingTest.DialogAssembly.BusinessRule.
DashboardExtender.MessageBox.MainClass
```

2. **Access Public Methods and Functions:** Once your object is created, you can call public functions or subs within the class by referencing the object.

Example:

```
Dim sReturn As String = DependencyTest.DialogTest(si)
```

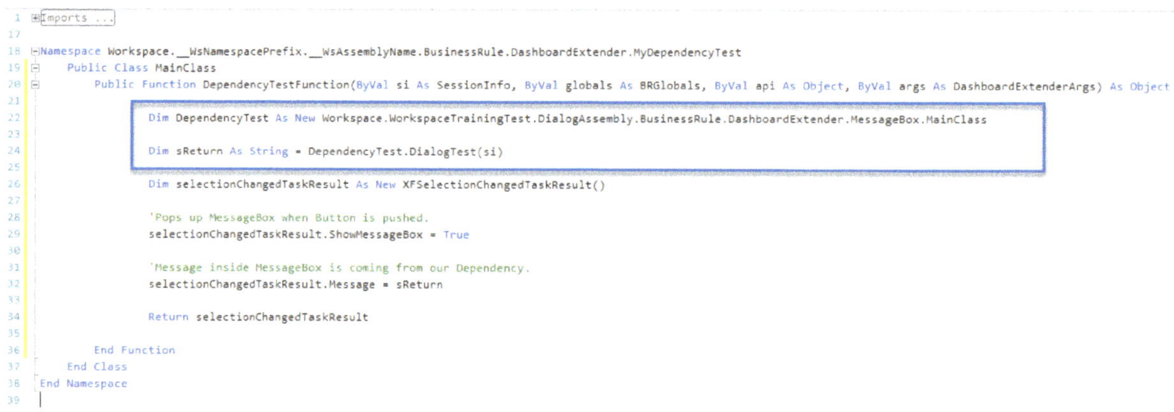

Figure 11.15

Key Notes:

- **Workspace Name vs. Namespace Prefix**: If your dependent Workspace has a namespace prefix defined, you must use the namespace prefix instead of the actual Workspace name in your code. Using the Workspace name will cause an error in this case.
- **Consistent Naming**: Ensure that the Workspace, Assembly, and class names match exactly with their definitions to avoid compilation errors.

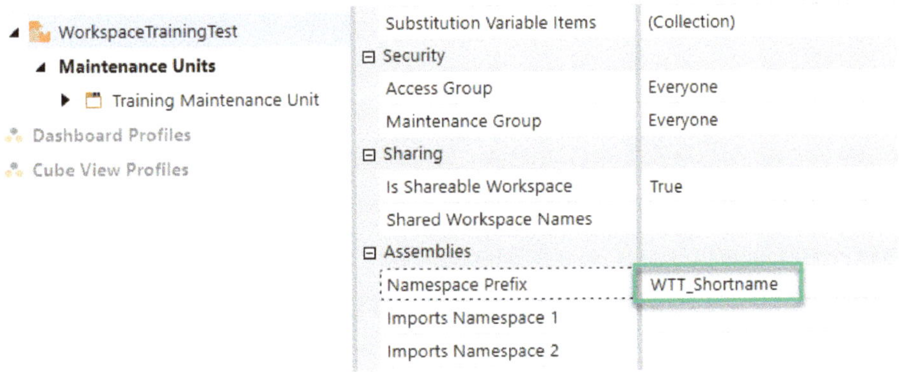

Figure 11.16

Use a namespace prefix in code.

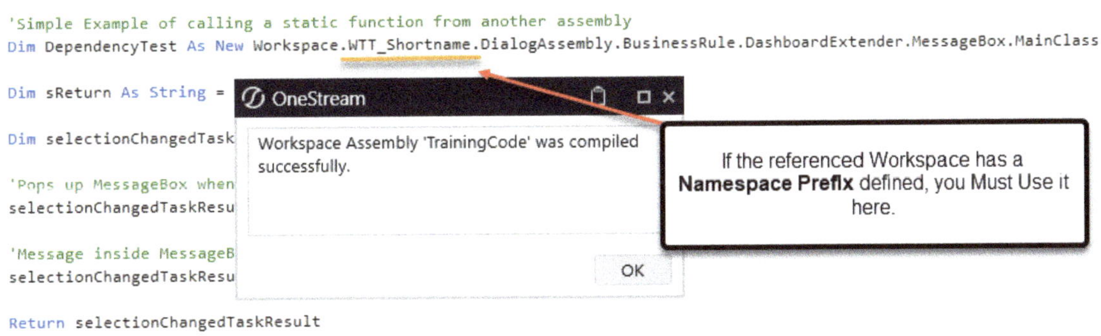

Figure 11.17

If the Workspace has a namespace prefix defined, putting in the actual Workspace name will throw an error. If the Workspace does not have a namespace prefix, the actual Workspace name works as expected.

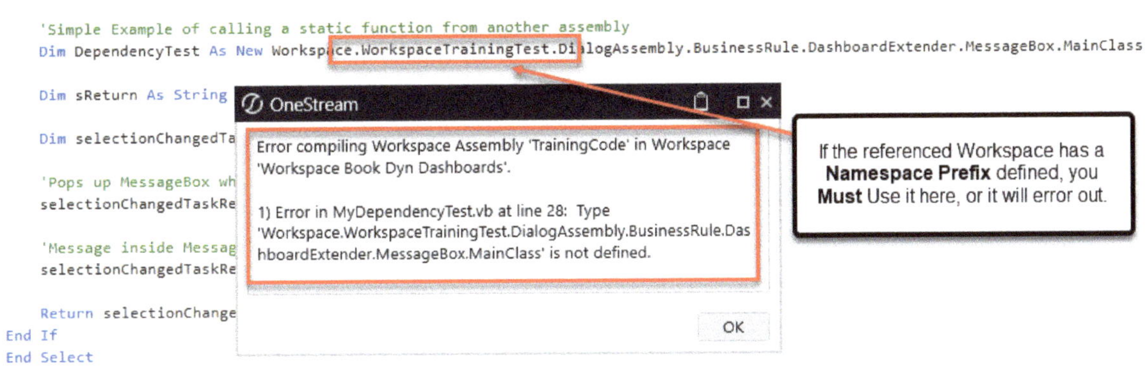

Figure 11.18

Advanced Description of Namespace Prefix Dependency Error

When working with dependencies, errors related to namespace prefixes can arise, preventing your rule from compiling. Here's a detailed technical explanation of the issue and how to address it.

Understanding the Issue

If the referenced Workspace has a namespace prefix defined, VB.NET substitutes the *namespace prefix* in the fully qualified namespace when resolving the dependency. This replacement often breaks the reference, as the target code expects the original Workspace name.

Example Behavior:

- Referenced Workspace: WorkspaceTrainingTest
- Namespace Prefix: WTT_Shortname

Dependency Code Example:

In this case, when the target code is trying to run the dependency with this line of code in Figure 11.19:

```
'Simple Example of calling a static function from another assembly
Dim DependencyTest As New Workspace.WorkspaceTrainingTest.DialogAssembly.BusinessRule.DashboardExtender.MessageBox.MainClass
```

Figure 11.19

What is actually run:

```
Workspace.WTT_Shortname.DialogAssembly.BusinessRule.DashboardExtender.
MessageBox.MainClass
```

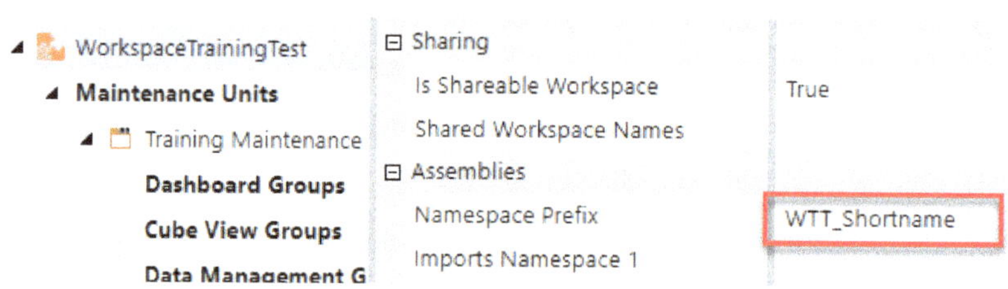

Figure 11.20

In this scenario, the target code searches for WorkspaceTrainingTest, but the dependency code sends WTT_Shortname instead, causing a mismatch and breaking the reference.

The dependency code sends the namespace prefix because of the default variable in `Namespace` of `__WsNamespacePrefix`, as shown in Figure 11.21. This variable gets replaced by the namespace prefix if it exists, or the actual Workspace name if there is no namespace prefix.

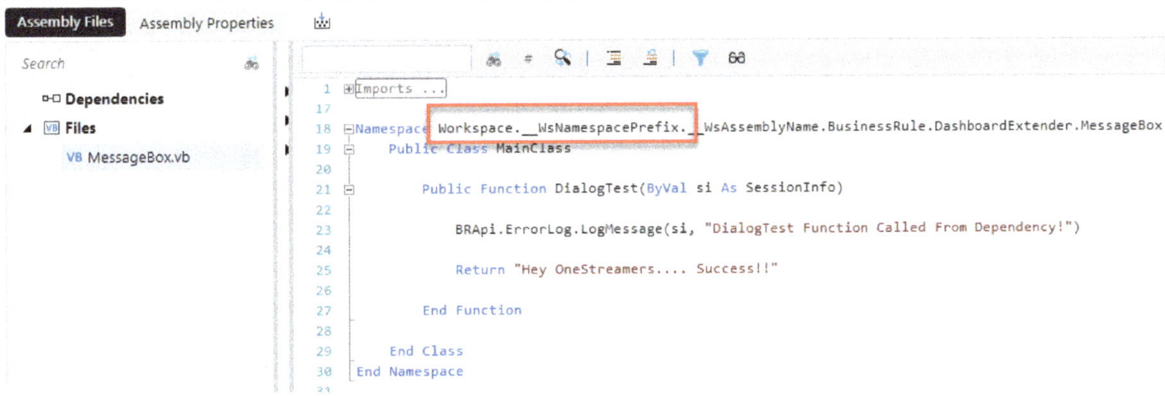

Figure 11.21

Fixing the Error

To resolve namespace prefix errors, you can **Update the Target Code** and replace the Workspace name in your target code with the **Namespace Prefix** defined for the referenced Workspace. For example:

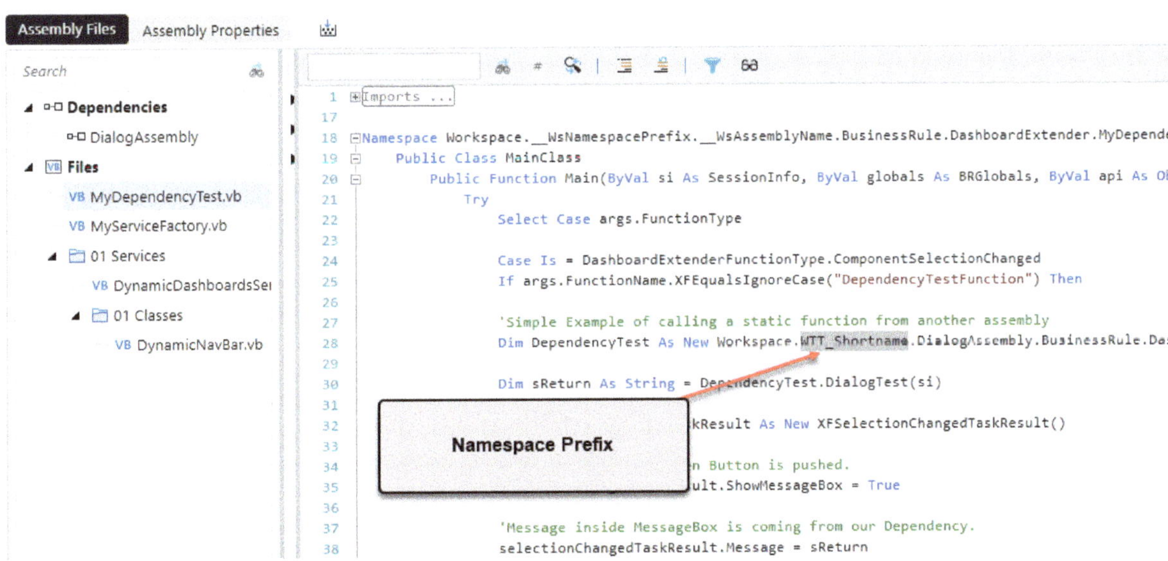

Figure 11.22

Dependency Calling a Traditional Business Rule

When defining a dependency with a dependency type of Business Rule, this refers specifically to a traditional business rule. In this case, the dependency name should be set to the name of the business rule itself.

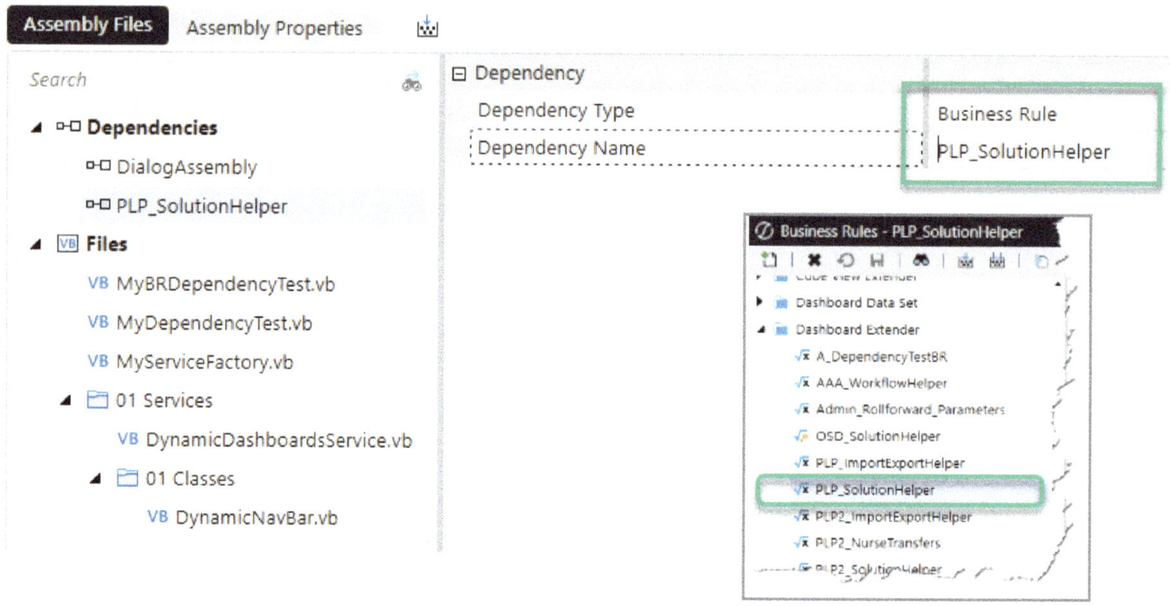

Figure 11.23

Syntax for Calling the Dependency

To reference the traditional business rule as a dependency, use the following syntax:

```
OneStream.BusinessRule.DashboardExtender.SharedRulename.
SharedClassName
```

Example:

```
OneStream.BusinessRule.DashboardExtender.PLP_SolutionHelper.MainClass
```

This demonstrates the proper approach to calling a traditional business rule as a dependency within your code.

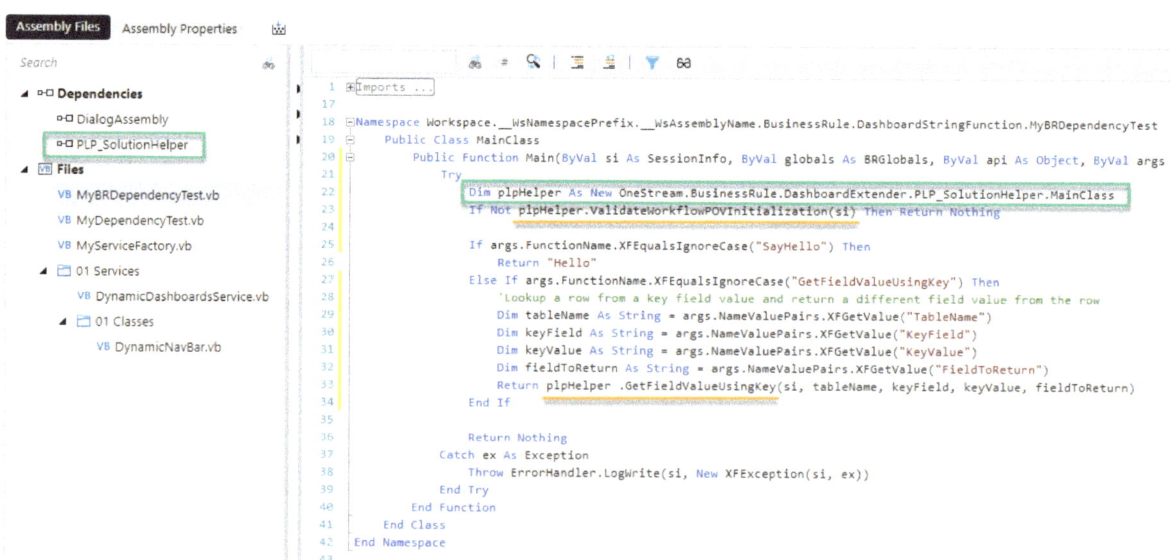

Figure 11.24

Additional Note:

- Ensure the business rule name and class name match exactly as defined in your configuration.

Traditional Business Rule Referencing Assemblies

When using a traditional business rule, the syntax for **referenced Assemblies** in the business rule properties differs from the syntax used for other business rules or external DLL files. An incorrectly referenced Assembly entry will result in the following error when attempting to call a class in a Workspace Assembly:

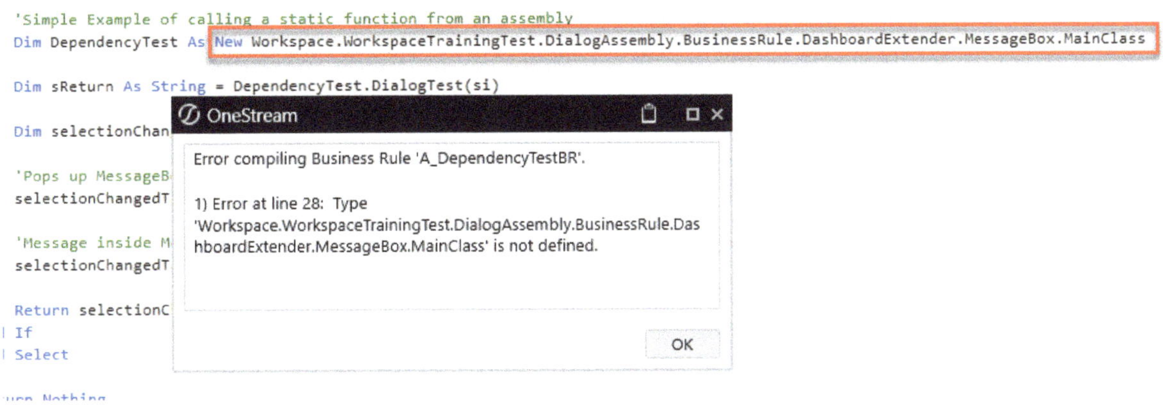

Figure 11.25

Correct Syntax for Referencing an Assembly BR

To reference an Assembly Business Rule (BR) correctly, follow these steps:

1. **Define the Referenced Assembly:** In the Referenced Assemblies field, use the following syntax:

```
WS\Workspace.YourWorkspaceName.YourAssemblyName
```

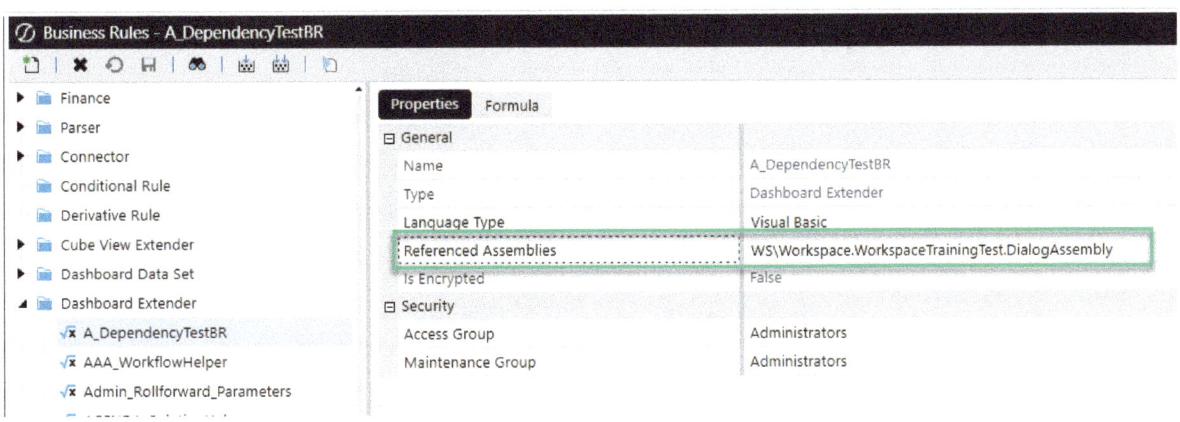

Figure 11.26

2. **Call Classes and Methods:** Use the same convention to define and reference classes within the Workspace Assembly:

Syntax:

```
Dim yourClassName As
Workspace.YourWorkspaceName.YourAssemblyName.BusinessRule.
DashboardExtender.YourFileName.MainClass
```

Example (Figure 11.27):

```
Dim DependencyTest As
Workspace.WorkspaceTrainingTest.DialogAssembly.BusinessRule.
DashboardExtender.MessageBox.MainClass
```

> **Note:** Typically, the referenced business rules are dashboard extender types, and you need to include this type in the reference when you are calling the ClassName (e.g., `.BusinessRule.DashboardExtender.`).

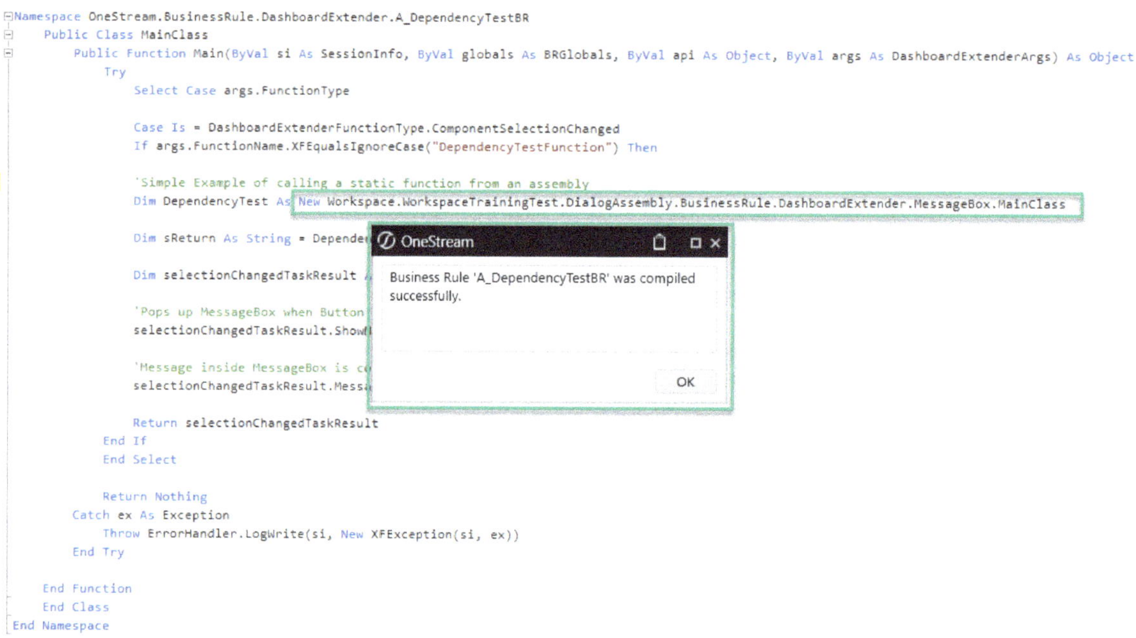

Figure 11.27

> **Note:** If calling the same rule in multiple places within your business rule, you can save some typing by adding `Imports Workspace.WorkspaceTrainingTest.DialogAssembly.BusinessRule.DashboardExtender` to the list of imported libraries at the top. Then you just need to reference `Yourfilename.MainClass`. (e.g., Figure 11.28.)

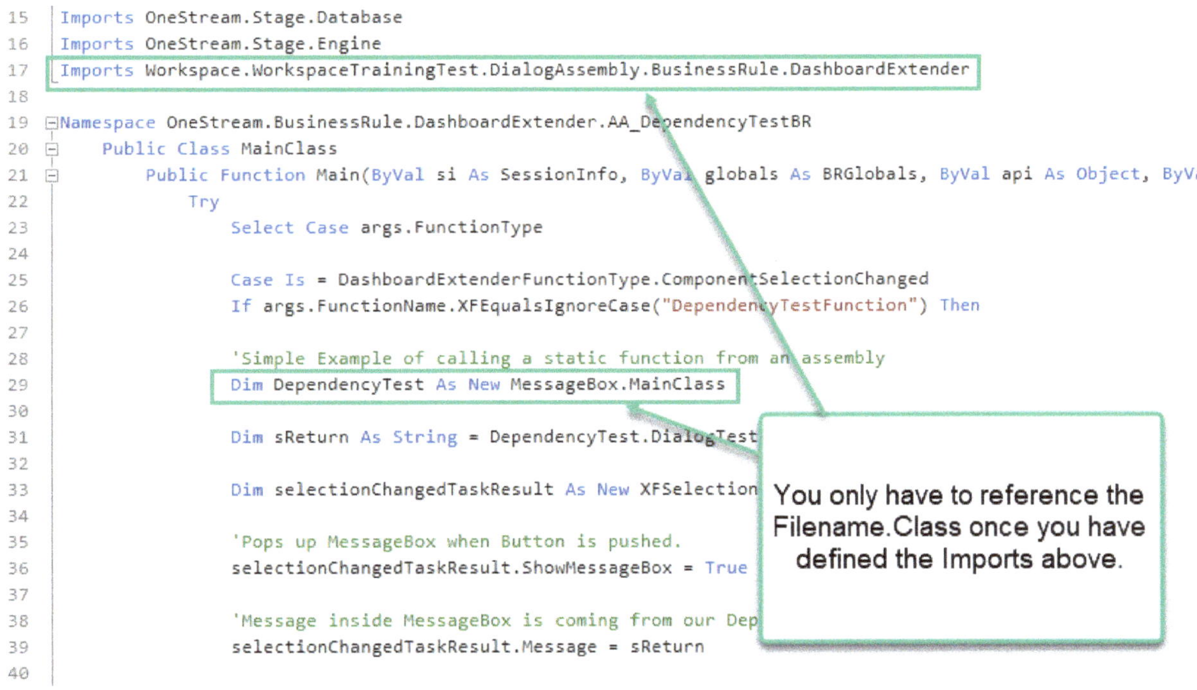

Figure 11.28

Working Example of a Workspace Assembly Dependency

In this section, I will walk through a full working example of using an Assembly dashboard extender business rule as a dependency, so you can see all the screens and references working.

Example to Solve

Create a button that shows a dialog box with a message, where the message is generated from a dependency.

Example: Solution Steps

1. Create an Assembly dashboard extender business rule that calls a MessageBox with a static message.
2. In a different Workspace, create a dependency that references the Workspace and Assembly of the code we just created.
3. Create an Assembly dashboard extender business rule that will reference the function in step 1.
4. Create a button that executes the Assembly dashboard extender business rule of step 3.
5. Create a dashboard that has that one button on it.
6. Execute the dashboard and test the button.

Example: Solution Step Details:

1. Create an Assembly dashboard extender business rule that calls a MessageBox with a static message.

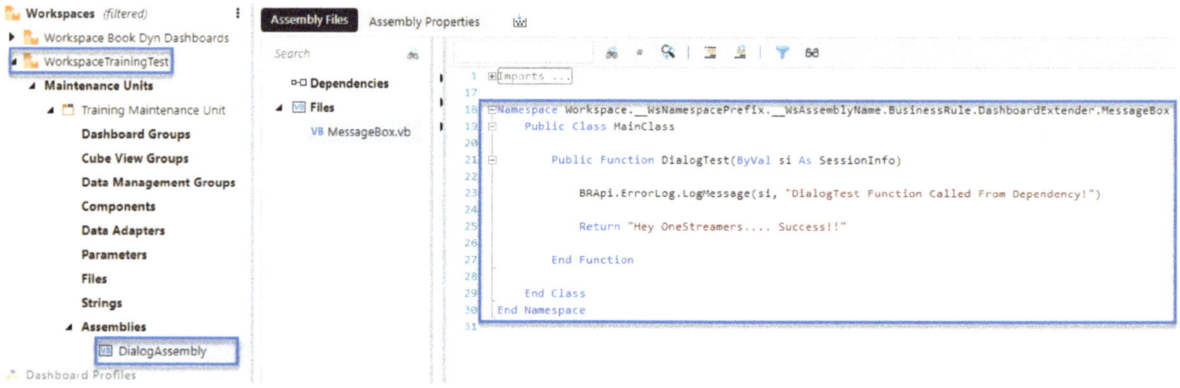

Figure 11.29

2. In a different Workspace, create a dependency that references the Workspace and Assembly of the code we just created.

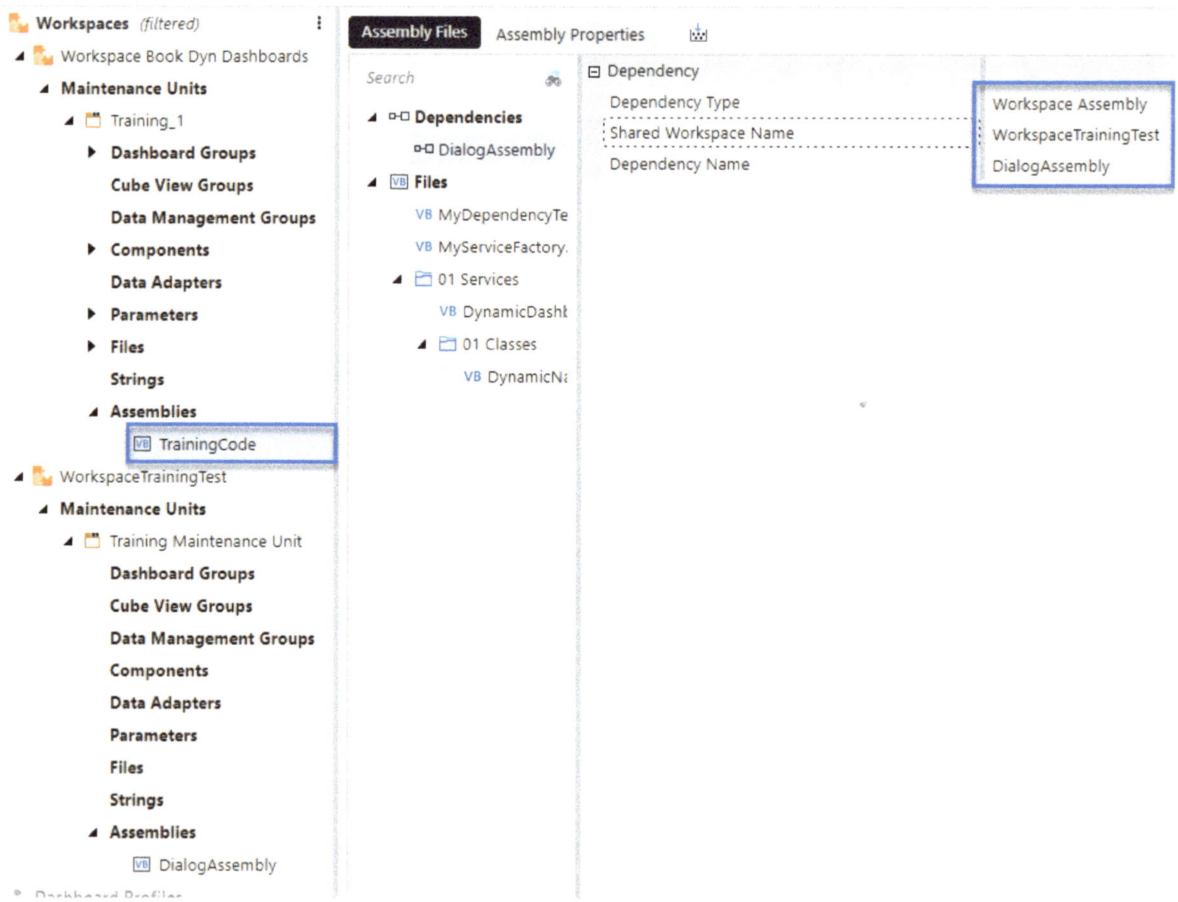

Figure 11.30

3. Create an Assembly dashboard extender business rule that will reference the function in step 1.

```
Imports ...

Namespace Workspace.__WsNamespacePrefix.__WsAssemblyName.BusinessRule.DashboardExtender.MyDependencyTest
    Public Class MainClass
        Public Function Main(ByVal si As SessionInfo, ByVal globals As BRGlobals, ByVal api As Object, ByVal args As DashboardExtenderArgs) As Object
            Try
                Select Case args.FunctionType

                Case Is = DashboardExtenderFunctionType.ComponentSelectionChanged
                If args.FunctionName.XFEqualsIgnoreCase("DependencyTestFunction") Then

                'Simple Example of calling a static function from another assembly
                Dim DependencyTest As New Workspace.WorkspaceTrainingTest.DialogAssembly.BusinessRule.DashboardExtender.MessageBox.MainClass

                Dim sReturn As String = DependencyTest.DialogTest(si)

                Dim selectionChangedTaskResult As New XFSelectionChangedTaskResult()

                'Pops up MessageBox when Button is pushed.
                selectionChangedTaskResult.ShowMessageBox = True

                'Message inside MessageBox is coming from our Dependency.
                selectionChangedTaskResult.Message = sReturn

                Return selectionChangedTaskResult
            End If
            End Select

            Return Nothing
        Catch ex As Exception
            Throw ErrorHandler.LogWrite(si, New XFException(si, ex))
        End Try

    End Function
    End Class
End Namespace
```

Figure 11.31

4. Create a button that executes the Assembly dashboard extender business rule of step 3.

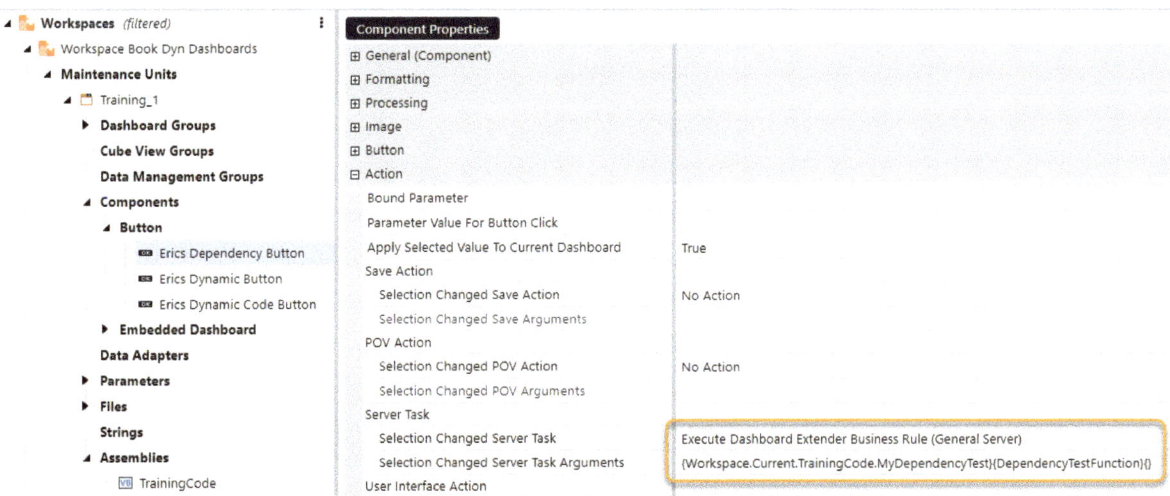

Figure 11.32

5. Create a dashboard with that one button.

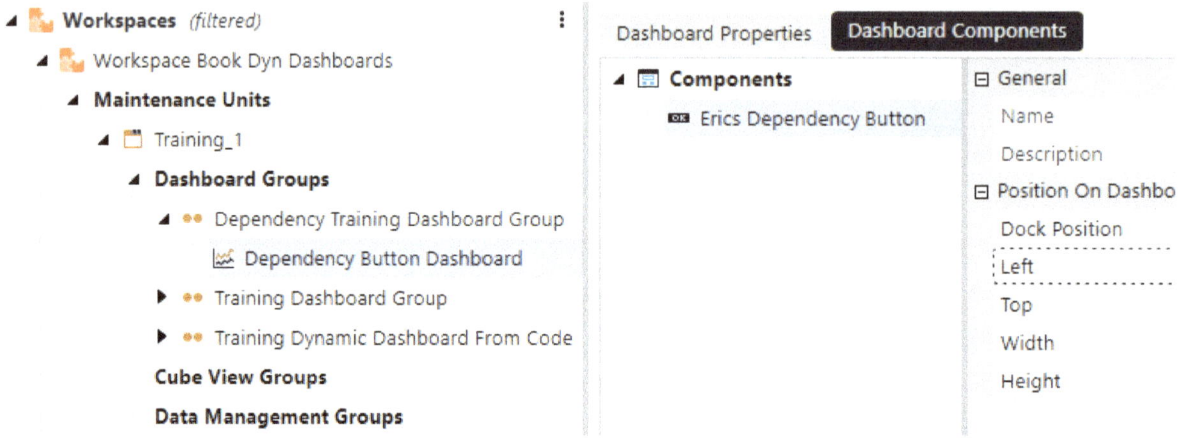

Figure 11.33

6. Execute the dashboard and test the button.

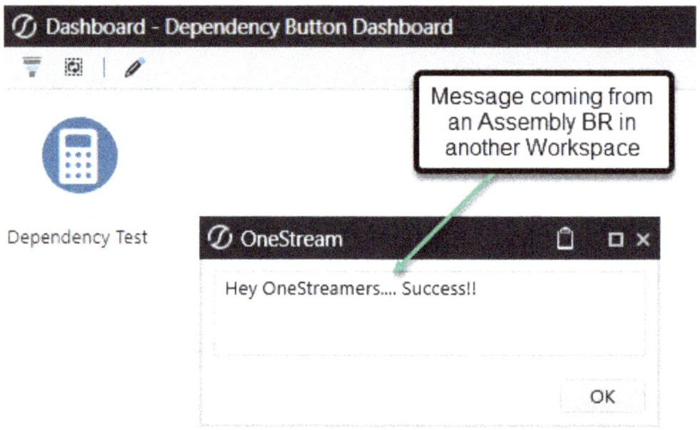

Figure 11.34

Renaming Assemblies and Assembly Files

If you need to rename anything around Assemblies, there are some things to keep in mind to keep your application running smoothly. One crucial point to note: *references are not updated automatically when renaming.* You must manually update all references to the renamed items.

In general, when you need to rename an Assembly or an Assembly file, try to follow these guidelines.

Guidelines for Renaming Assemblies and Files

Follow these best practices to ensure smooth transitions:

- **Search and Update References:**
  - After renaming, perform a thorough search across your Workspace and Assemblies for references to the old file name and update them to the new name.
- **Workspace Editor Updates:**
  - Update the Workspace Editor to reflect the renamed file. Ensure the Assembly is listed under its new name.
- **Test in Isolation:**
  - Test the renamed Assembly independently to confirm proper execution before integrating it with other components.

- **Document Changes:**
    - Maintain a naming convention document or change log to track renamed files and their corresponding updates.

With these principles in mind, let's dive into specific scenarios for renaming Assemblies and files.

Renaming an Assembly

When renaming an Assembly, ensure that you update the following references:

1. **Workspace Settings:**
    - Update the Workspace Assembly Service settings to reflect the new Assembly name.

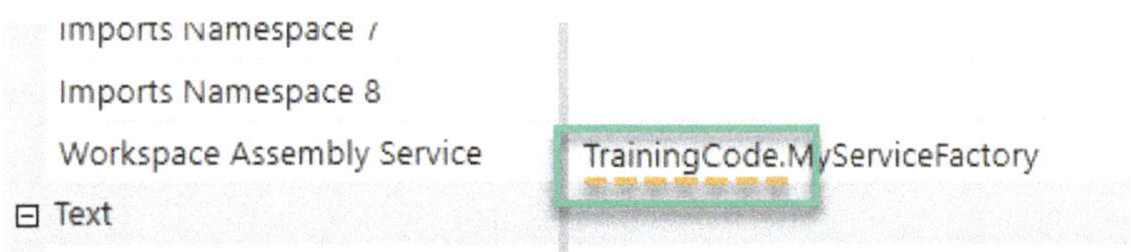

Figure 11.35

2. **Maintenance Unit Settings:**
    - Update references in the maintenance unit settings to ensure alignment with the renamed Assembly.

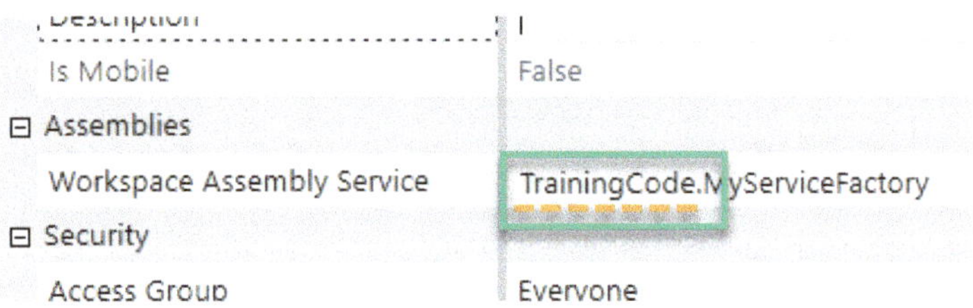

Figure 11.36

3. **Component References:**
    - Update any Workspace component that is referencing code within this Assembly and has a reference such as:

```
{Workspace.WorkspaceName.AssemblyName.Filename}{MyFunction}{Param1=
[MyValue1],Param2=[MyValue2]}
```

4. **Dependencies:**
    - Check for dependencies in other Assemblies that reference the renamed Assembly and update their definitions.

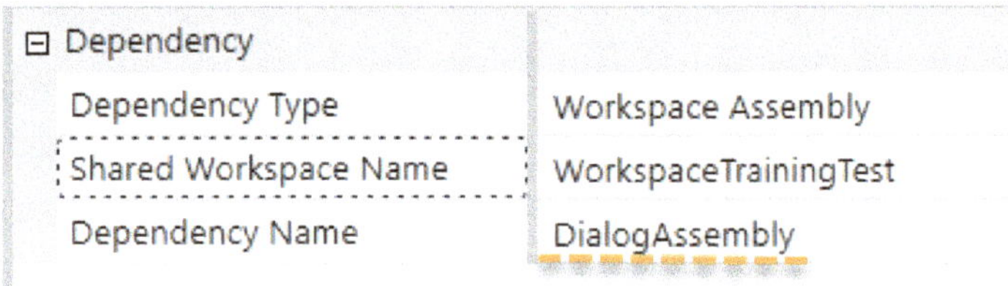

Figure 11.37

5. **References Within Code:**
   - Update any references in your code that use the renamed Assembly files. For example:

```
'Simple Example of calling a static function from another assembly
Dim DependencyTest As New Workspace.WorkspaceTrainingTest.DialogAssembly.BusinessRule.DashboardExtender.MessageBox.MainClass
```

Figure 11.38

Renaming an Assembly Service Factory File

Renaming an Assembly Service Factory file requires careful attention due to the way OneStream defines classes within the file. Key considerations include ensuring the file and its Public Class are aligned to avoid errors.

Key Steps for Renaming:

1. **Update the Public Class within the File:**
   - Renaming a file DOES NOT automatically rename the Public Class inside that file. After renaming the Service Factory file, ensure the Public Class inside the file is updated to match the new filename.

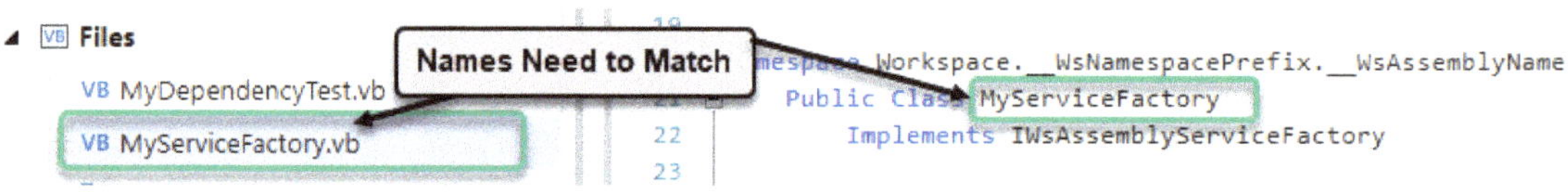

Figure 11.39

2. **Workspace Settings:**
   - Update Workspace Assembly Service settings to reflect the new filename.

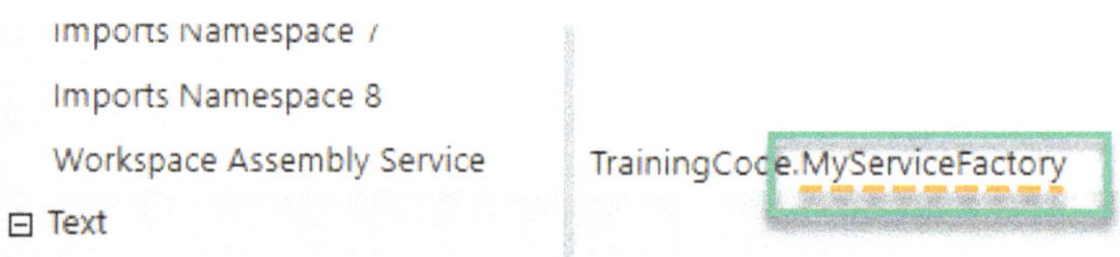

Figure 11.40

3. **Maintenance Unit Settings:**
   - Check and update all Workspace Assembly Service settings within maintenance units.

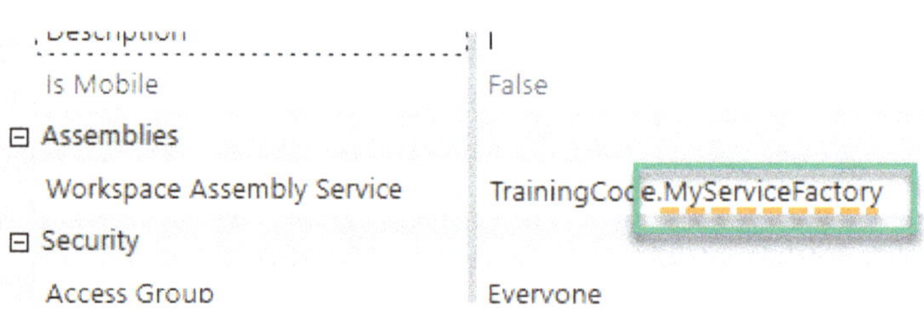

Figure 11.41

4. **Components References:**
   - Update any Workspace components that reference the factory. Ensure all dependencies and references are consistent with the new name.

Renaming an Assembly Service File

Renaming an Assembly service file requires careful attention – similar to Service Factory files – due to the way OneStream defines classes within the files. Additionally, you must update the Service Factory reference to reflect the new name.

1. **Update the Public Class within the File:**
   - Renaming a file does not automatically rename the Public Class inside it. Update the Public Class within the file to match the new filename.

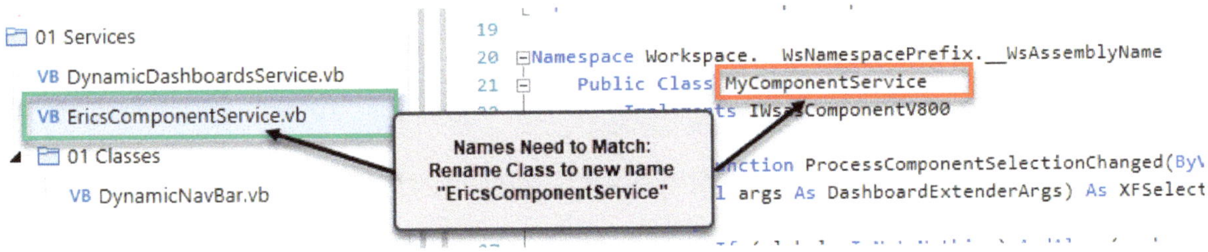

Figure 11.42

2. **Rename the Service Factory Reference:**
   - Renaming the file does not update its reference in the Service Factory. Ensure you update the reference to this service in the Service Factory.

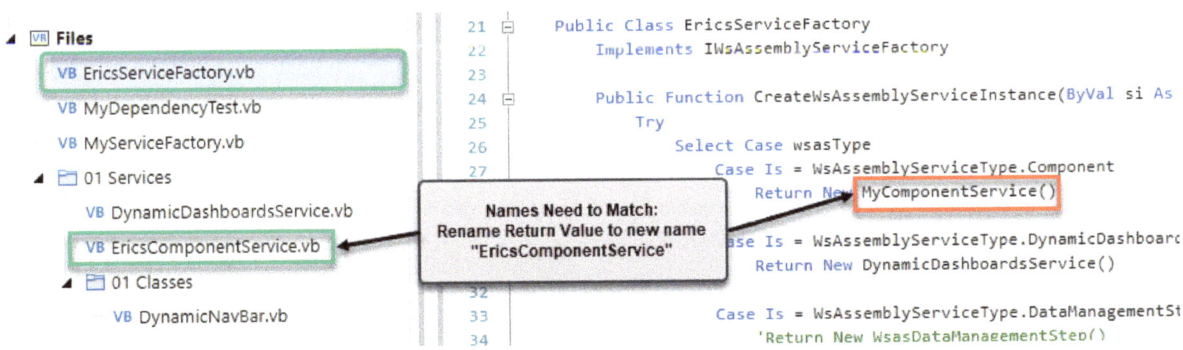

Figure 11.43

Rename an Assembly Business Rule File

When renaming an Assembly business rule file, you'll need to update multiple references to ensure functionality. These updates include arguments within the file, other code files, and dashboard component references.

1. **Update the Namespace Within the File:**
   - The name of an Assembly business rule file must equal the *namespace* inside the file:

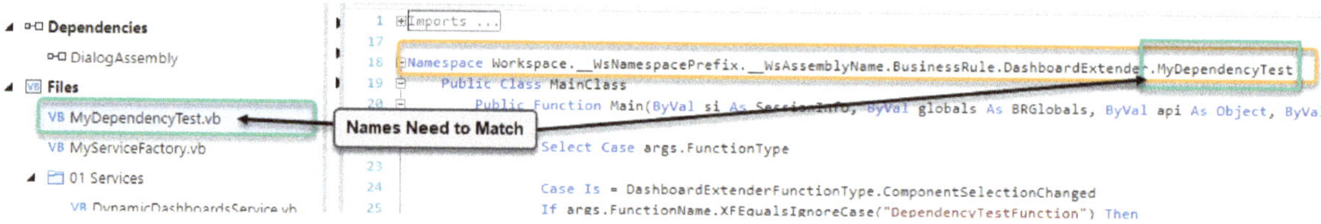

Figure 11.44

2. **Update References in Other Code Files:**
   - Locate and update all references to the renamed Assembly business rule file in other code files.

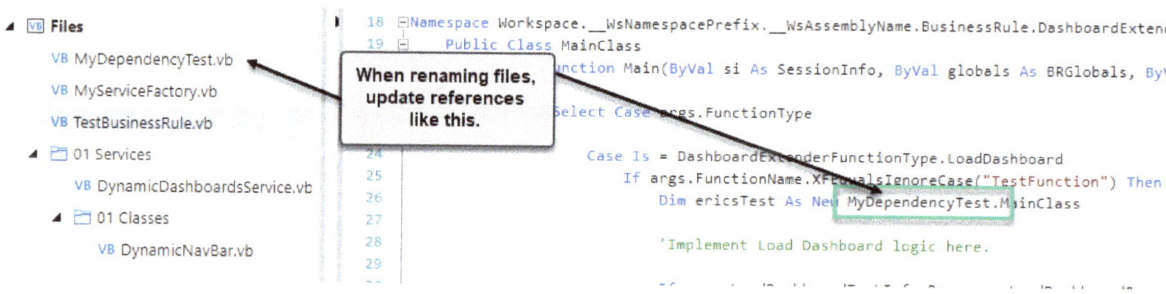

Figure 11.45

3. **Update Component References:**
   - Update any Workspace component that references the Assembly business rule file. Here's an example of the syntax:

```
{Workspace.WorkspaceName.AssemblyName.Filename}{MyFunction}{Param1=
[MyValue1],Param2=[MyValue2]}
```

Key Notes for Renaming Assemblies and Files

When renaming Assemblies, files, or related components in OneStream, keep these overarching principles in mind to ensure a smooth process:

- **Manually Update All References**: References to renamed items – such as files, classes, namespaces, and dependencies – are not updated automatically. Perform a thorough search and update them manually across your Workspace, including settings, components, and code.
- **Maintain Consistency**: Ensure that file names, class names, and namespaces are consistent to prevent compilation errors or broken dependencies.
- **Test Thoroughly**: Test renamed Assemblies, files, and their dependencies in isolation to confirm proper functionality before reintegrating them with other components.
- **Keep Records**: Maintain a naming convention document or change log to track renamed files and their corresponding updates. This can streamline troubleshooting and future updates.

Conclusion

Troubleshooting Workspaces and Assemblies can sometimes feel like navigating a maze, but every challenge is an opportunity to learn and grow. Those "why won't this work?" moments might be frustrating at first, but the sense of accomplishment when you finally uncover the solution is second to none. Whether it's perfecting syntax, resolving dependencies, or deciphering those tricky reference errors, each success brings you one step closer to mastering the Workspace approach.

Jessica and I have been through this journey ourselves. We've tackled unexpected errors and, through persistence and problem-solving, gained invaluable insights. Over time, we've learned to anticipate potential hiccups, streamline our process, and even enjoy the problem-solving process. Because of these experiences, we've become more confident and capable OneStream developers, and we know the same will happen for you. With every hurdle you clear, you'll gain the tools and instincts to handle whatever comes next – and before you know it, you'll naturally start to recognize and resolve these challenges before they even occur. Keep troubleshooting, keep learning, and keep building – you've got this!

12

The Future of Workspaces in OneStream

In the ever-changing world of OneStream, Workspaces and Assemblies have become the go-to tools for developers. Why? Because they streamline complex development processes, making implementations clearer, more intuitive, and more flexible. These aren't just technical components – they're stepping stones to building smarter, scalable solutions that anticipate what's around the corner. As businesses continue to push the limits of what can be done, these tools are ready to step up and redefine how we approach development.

OneStream has always been about innovation – it's part of our DNA. From starting out as a unified corporate performance management platform to growing into a dynamic ecosystem for developers, OneStream has consistently raised the bar. Just think about milestones like Assembly Services or Dynamic Dashboards – they're perfect examples of how OneStream combines innovation with practicality, always staying ahead of what's needed.

So, where do we go from here? This chapter is all about exploring what's next for Workspaces. Imagine AI-assisted development creating dashboards, and Cube Views from input into a chatbot, or Assembly files directly accessible from powerful IDEs. These advancements aren't just concepts – they're opportunities waiting to happen. And, together, they promise to take efficiency, creativity, and collaboration to new heights. In short, the future of OneStream is shaping up to be more exciting than ever!

With this innovative foundation in place, it's clear that Workspaces and Assemblies are just the beginning of what OneStream has to offer. To truly understand the potential ahead, we must dive deeper into one of the most exciting areas of development – **Dynamic Services** with in-memory data and dashboards. These groundbreaking tools are set to transform how developers and users interact with data, making dashboards more intelligent, intuitive, and impactful than ever before.

Concept 1: Dynamic Services Capabilities – Transforming User Interactions

Today's businesses face rapidly changing environments, requiring tools and systems that actively evolve and innovate to meet new challenges. While companies used to concentrate on adaptability, this only focuses on being reactive to change as it happens. Evolving dynamically goes a step further, proactively anticipating shifts and making adjustments ahead of time.

This ability to grow and improve alongside complex organizational needs ensures businesses remain competitive and effective in an ever-shifting landscape. OneStream's dynamic services embody this proactive evolution. As discussed in Chapter 8 with dynamic dashboards, these services encompass dynamic grids, Cube Views, cubes, and dimensions, forming the backbone of an agile and forward-thinking development framework.

By enabling applications that predict needs, adapt to evolving requirements, and drive smarter decision-making, dynamic services offer real-time updates, multidimensional analysis, and hierarchical flexibility, paving the way for innovative enterprise solutions that keep businesses ahead of the curve.

By the time this book gets published, OneStream will have already released multiple new dynamic services that will transform the way organizations can leverage OneStream. Moving from here and beyond, OneStream will continue to invest R&D into creating additional dynamic services.

Here is a list of known dynamic services that will be coming out.

Dynamic Grids

This component maintains the core functionality of the SQL Table Editor component while enhancing the flexibility of data presentation and end-user interaction. The dynamic grid component displays data in a tabular format from a Workspace Assembly-driven data source. Each column represents a field, and each row represents a record. This grid enables you to read data from any source, transform that data, and write it back to any specified target. This offers a flexible and high-performance feature for managing datasets of any shape or size. It supports paging, dynamic columns, and custom formatting.

Key Features:

- **Flexible data transformation:** Read, write, and transform data from any source using Workspace Assemblies.
- **Volume performance:** Manage large datasets efficiently with paging.
- **Dynamic columns:** Add, remove, and modify columns.
- **Custom formatting:** Apply custom formatting to data for better visualization.

Use Cases:

- **Real-Time Data Manipulation:** Users can modify datasets directly within the grid, enabling quick adjustments during financial planning or scenario modeling.
- **Customizable Views:** Developers can offer tailored grid interfaces, providing only the columns or rows relevant to specific users or tasks.
- **On-The-Fly Table Creation:** Businesses can dynamically generate tables to explore different data perspectives without needing full database rebuilds. Tables could even be virtual, reading and saving data from simple dashboard parameters or files!

The result is a powerful tool that blends the robustness of SQL with the flexibility of modern user interfaces, fostering a seamless bridge between raw data and actionable insights.

Dynamic Cube Views Services

Dynamic Cube Views in OneStream revolutionize data presentation by dynamically tailoring what data is displayed, based on factors like user attributes and security settings. This ensures that each user sees only the relevant information they are authorized to access, without requiring the manual creation of multiple static Cube Views.

By replacing the need for numerous similar but slightly varied Cube Views, dynamic Cube Views significantly streamline administration and reduce redundancy. With this capability, a single stored Cube View can dynamically produce hundreds of permutations, offering immense flexibility while maintaining simplicity and efficiency in dashboard development. This innovation enhances both the developer's and the end user's experience by providing tailored, secure, and scalable data visualization solutions.

Dynamic Data, Dimensions, and Cubes

The **Dynamic Data Assembly Service** type in OneStream is a powerful capability designed to enhance how data is retrieved, assembled, and rendered dynamically within applications. This service allows for highly configurable and responsive data handling to and from any source system. By leveraging this service, developers can construct solutions that eliminate the need for static, predefined datasets, enabling real-time adaptability to changes in user requirements or organizational structures.

The dynamic data Assembly service significantly reduces redundancy and simplifies data management by assembling data on the fly, and allows real-time data refreshing without additional data imports. This not only improves efficiency but also supports the creation of scalable and flexible applications that can handle complex, multidimensional business scenarios.

Dynamic dimensions in OneStream enable the creation of in-memory dimensional structures that serve as the foundation for dynamic cubes. These dimensions are defined and stored temporarily in memory rather than being fixed within the application's underlying configuration. This flexibility allows developers to construct dimensions based on contextual factors, without the need for alternate hierarchies that can clutter your application.

Dynamic cubes leverage these in-memory dimensions to generate multidimensional datasets that act as **virtual cubes**. While these cubes are not physically stored, they emulate the functionality of traditional cubes, allowing developers and users to report on, analyze, and interact with data as if it were part of an actual cube structure. This capability facilitates real-time analytics, enabling businesses to adapt to evolving requirements without the overhead of static configuration or prebuilt data structures.

As an example, for those of you familiar with OneStream's People Planning solution, you understand that you can have employee-level data in a relational flat table called a 'Register'. Imagine being able to create an Employee dimension on the fly, in-memory, and reporting on the register data as if it were sitting in a multidimensional cube. All without affecting the performance of any stored data cube. The possibilities are endless.

The combination of dynamic dimensions and dynamic cubes streamlines development workflows, eliminates redundancy, and enhances performance by creating adaptable, scalable solutions for complex data environments. It allows organizations to quickly assemble tailored datasets that align with their needs, while maintaining the power and flexibility of multidimensional reporting.

Dynamic Services Impact

The introduction of dynamic dashboard service capabilities has fundamentally altered the landscape of application development and user interaction within OneStream. Similarly, OneStream will continue to empower businesses with dynamic services like dynamic grids, Cube Views, cubes, and dimensions. Developers can build solutions that are not only responsive to user needs but also highly performant and capable of evolving alongside the organization.

Concept 2: Expansion of the Component Library

OneStream has demonstrated a consistent commitment to enhancing its dashboard development toolkit by continuously expanding the **Component Library**. This ongoing innovation is exemplified by recent additions like the **Menu Component**, which streamlines navigation through customizable frameworks tailored to user roles and business requirements.

These advancements not only address specific challenges faced by developers but also embody a broader vision of efficiency and scalability. The steady growth of the component library reflects OneStream's dedication to empowering developers with diverse and cutting-edge tools, laying the groundwork for more advanced and collaborative dashboard features in the future. Such progress underscores OneStream's resolve to innovate and provide high-quality solutions that meet the evolving demands of businesses and users alike.

Future Directions

OneStream is always looking to develop new dashboard components and actively recruits suggestions from customers and partners through our OneStream **IdeaStream** website, which allows customers and partners to contribute their ideas, share feedback, and propose enhancements for OneStream products and solutions. By encouraging user-driven suggestions, IdeaStream ensures that OneStream's development roadmap is guided by the real-world needs and experiences of its users. This platform exemplifies OneStream's commitment to continuously refining and evolving its offerings to better support businesses in achieving their goals.

Here is a list of the current dashboard components, illustrating the sheer volume of existing dashboard development tools that OneStream has already completed, and giving you an idea of OneStream's commitment to continuing to enhance and innovate our capabilities:

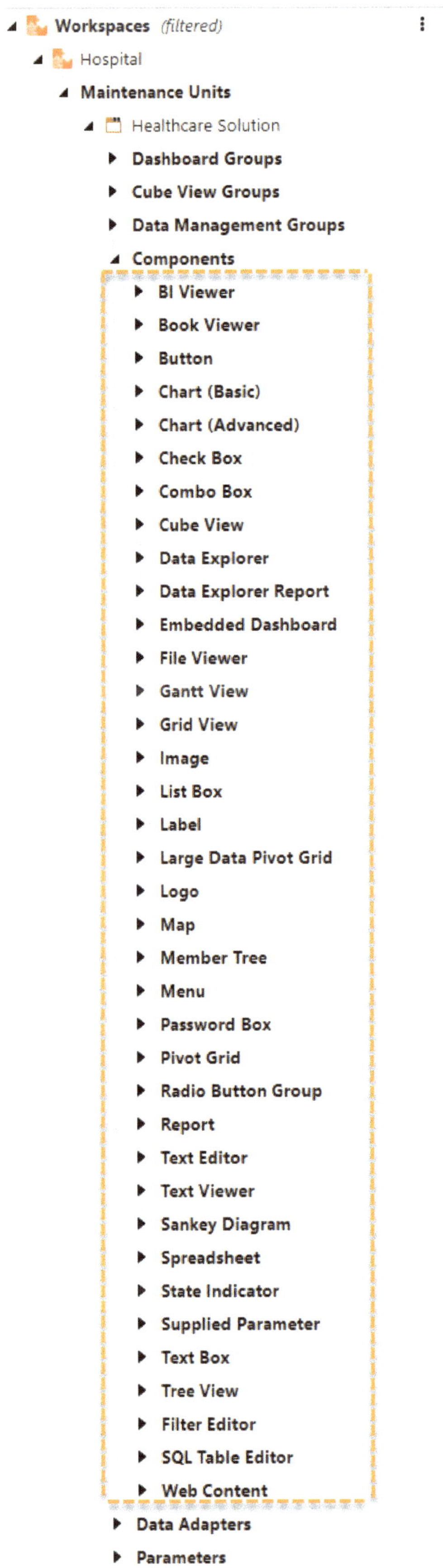

Figure 12.1

The continued expansion of the component library represents a critical opportunity for OneStream to continue aligning development capabilities with the complexities of modern business processes. As the library grows, it will strengthen OneStream's ability to support scalable, innovative solutions that serve both developers and users effectively.

Concept 3: AI-Assisted Dashboard Creation – The Next Frontier

One very exciting stream of development that OneStream is actively developing is AI capabilities within the OneStream Platform. There are many AI workstreams currently being developed at OneStream, but the one I would like to discuss is the introduction of AI capabilities to help users build dashboards.

From Manual to AI-Assisted

Dashboard development has come a long way from painstaking manual assembly to more streamlined, component-based approaches. However, even with these advancements, building a dashboard still requires significant time, effort, and expertise.

Now, imagine a paradigm shift: a future where AI takes on much of the heavy lifting, transforming the developer's role from manual creator to strategic collaborator. With AI-assisted dashboard creation, developers can move beyond tedious setup tasks and focus instead on refining insights, enhancing user experiences, and unlocking new capabilities. New users to OneStream will also benefit from accelerating dashboard creation in a more wizard-based approach. This evolution represents not just an incremental improvement but a revolutionary step forward in application development within OneStream.

AI and Assembly Services

The recent introduction of Assembly Services and Dynamic Dashboards has laid the groundwork for integrating AI into OneStream's development ecosystem. These innovations have provided developers with a modular, extensible framework that supports dynamic behavior and real-time adaptability – perfect conditions for harnessing AI's potential.

How Assembly Services Might Enable AI Integration

- Assembly Services offer modularity and scalability, ensuring that AI-powered components can be easily integrated into existing applications.
- Dynamic dashboards provide a flexible canvas where AI can analyze data structures and generate tailored suggestions, enabling fluid and intuitive development workflows.

The synergy between these foundational elements sets the stage for AI to become an essential partner in building smarter, faster, and more impactful dashboards!

Concept 4: IDE Integration

Integration with IDEs (e.g., Visual Studio)

OneStream is exploring a number of approaches to make it easier for developers to access our code with external IDEs, to improve the development experience and lifecycle management. A virtual file share would serve as the foundation for integrating OneStream with widely used Integrated Development Environments (IDEs) like Visual Studio. This integration would dramatically elevate developer workflows, empowering OneStream developers to leverage features typically reserved for traditional programming.

How IDE Integration Enhances Development

IntelliSense

Developers can access powerful IntelliSense functionality for autocompleting code, identifying methods and classes, and reducing errors while writing Assembly code. This greatly improves speed and accuracy during development.

Advanced Debugging Tools

Real-time debugging capabilities will enable developers to pinpoint issues in their Assemblies with precision. Breakpoints, call stack inspection, and variable tracking will simplify troubleshooting.

Code Linting

IDE-based linting tools can analyze code for issues or inefficiencies, ensuring that Assemblies are optimized for performance and maintainability.

Assembly Testing

Developers will be able to compile their Assemblies directly within the IDE, using robust testing frameworks to validate functionality before deployment.

With IDE integration, OneStream will incorporate industry-best development practices, providing developers with tools to innovate faster while maintaining high standards of quality.

Concept 5: Genesis: Empowering Creativity and Accelerating Value

Genesis is OneStream's groundbreaking no-code solution, designed to unlock the full potential of your OneStream investment. It transforms the way dashboards are developed by enabling users to design and build dashboards without needing to write a single line of code. By offering reusable, templated layouts called **Content Blocks**, Genesis empowers users to bring their creative visions to life while eliminating complexity.

With Genesis, the speed of innovation reaches new heights. Power users can adapt existing content or create new dashboards – streamlining development and accelerating time to value. Built on OneStream's unified platform and data model, Genesis not only fosters rapid deployment but also ensures strict governance and security to build trust across the organization.

This solution represents a leap forward in usability, accessibility, and innovation, empowering development teams and power users to design highly curated experiences that evolve alongside business needs. By bridging functionality with user creativity, Genesis sets the stage for an era of rapid, impactful development that aligns with the pace of modern enterprise demands.

Conclusion: Embracing the Future

The potential for OneStream to revolutionize Workspaces and Assemblies is immense, with a continuously expanding roadmap of goals that promise to redefine the platform. While these capabilities may not yet be fully realized, the vision is bold, and the possibilities are inspiring.

The concept of dynamic services sets the stage for a new level of adaptability and interactivity. Envisioning tools like dynamic grids, Cube Views, and dimensions offers a glimpse of what's possible: dashboards and data that respond to change in real time, allowing users to analyze and interact with data with unprecedented agility. These innovations aim to empower organizations to be more responsive, efficient, and effective.

The component library offers tremendous potential to accelerate development and improve application capabilities. By expanding this library with advanced charting tools and cross-application collaboration features, OneStream aspires to provide developers with a rich toolkit for creating cutting-edge solutions. Each new addition enhances how developers approach their work, streamlining efforts and enabling greater customization.

Integrating AI-assisted dashboard creation into OneStream's ecosystem is an exciting frontier. The goal is to harness AI to simplify and enhance dashboard development, from suggesting layouts and placing components to surfacing AI-driven insights. This vision anticipates a future where AI becomes a collaborative partner, helping developers produce dashboards that are not only faster to build but also smarter and more user-centric.

The dream of a virtual file share and IDE integration represents a transformative leap forward for developers. By creating seamless compatibility with tools like Visual Studio, OneStream will open new doors for collaboration, efficiency, and innovation. Features like IntelliSense, advanced debugging, and integrated testing are on the horizon, aimed at elevating OneStream development to match the flexibility and power of industry-standard tools.

Genesis introduces a powerful no-code solution that unlocks the full potential of your OneStream investment. By accelerating time to value, Genesis provides users with a flexible structure to quickly develop and deploy solutions tailored to their needs. Genesis empowers users to bring their creative vision to life with intuitive tools, eliminating the need to learn complex coding. Whether refining Cube Views or crafting dashboards, Genesis enables innovation at the speed of business, fostering efficiency and customization that drive impactful results.

These goals reflect OneStream's aspiration to bridge gaps and push boundaries, aligning the platform with the evolving needs of developers and organizations alike. While all of these innovations may not be here today, they illuminate the path forward, offering a vision of where OneStream is headed.

As these ideas take shape, it will be up to developers and users to embrace change, adapt to new tools, and lead the charge in this era of transformation. The journey to realize these goals may be challenging, but the rewards will be extraordinary – a platform that empowers creativity, amplifies efficiency, and delivers unparallcled solutions. The future of Workspaces and Assemblies is not yet written, but the opportunities ahead are boundless!

Index

OneStream Planning: The Why, How and When

OneStream is a world-class Intelligent Finance Platform that handles the complex planning, consolidation, reporting and other requirements of mid-sized to large enterprises. Whether in retail, financial services, manufacturing or other industries, the OneStream platform provides the means to integrate multiple data sources and utilize a wide range of tools and methodologies to improve business processes and performance. Through OneStream, organizations benefit from unified, real-time, enterprise-wide planning and forecasting.

Aimed at OneStream Planning practitioners, administrators, implementors, and power users alike, as well as Financial close and consolidations practitioners, *OneStream Planning: The Why, How and When* is the first standalone book in the performance management space to cover the power and potential of Planning in OneStream. Drawing from real-world deployments, the book is rooted in easily understood business use cases, and explains approaches (with code) through a comprehensive exploration of the solution. All this is offered within a framework of top functional and technical practice as informed by the authors' decades-long consulting and application development experiences.

- Which should I do – Import or Direct Load, Consolidate or Aggregate?
- How do Data Buffers really work; what is Eval and why should I care? Which approach is fastest and does it really matter?
- Why Multiyear Scenarios should never be Yearly
- Can Thing Planning run in the Spreadsheet? (It can.)
- Combining REST API and Analytic Blend
- Slice Security down to the very tiniest slice
- Pivot Grid or Large Pivot Grid, that is the question
- A book filled with clear use cases
- Exhaustively tested and verified solutions, and extensive source code
- Undocumented features and functionality covered, along with functional and technical good practices

OneStream Finance Rules and Calculations Handbook

Hundreds of companies have turned to OneStream to solve complex planning, consolidation and operational reporting needs. OneStream's unique ability to provide a multitude of solutions across dozens of industries is largely due to its dynamic Finance Engine which provides the capability to add industry- and company-specific business intelligence to data. Employing the full power of the Finance Engine allows companies to extend the platform and fully exploit the power of their investment.

Aimed at everyone from novices to seasoned veterans, this handbook—by OneStream Distinguished Architect Jon Golembiewski—will break down the Finance Engine and outline how to write Finance Business Rules and Calculations. Its insights will help propel OneStream applications to the next level.

- Fundamentals of the Finance Engine
- Detailed breakdown of the Cube and Data
- A look under the hood of the Api.Data.Calculate function
- Techniques for tackling complex calculation requirements
- How to use the Custom Calculate function to make calculations dynamic
- How to write calculations for optimal performance
- How to troubleshoot calculations
- How to solve and avoid common errors and pitfalls
- Real-world calculation examples with detailed explanations
- A full application with all referenced code examples is available to download

OneStream Financial Close Handbook

OneStream provides a market-leading Intelligent Finance Platform that reduces the complexity of financial operations. It unifies corporate performance management (CPM) processes such as planning, financial close & consolidation, reporting and analytics through a single, extensible solution.

The OneStream Financial Close Handbook – written by expert authors – is a practical book for implementors, administrators, and end-users, that dives into the Financial Close with a specific focus on the Account Reconciliations and Transaction Matching solutions.

The Account Reconciliations solution is a complete package that plugs into the Financial Close Workflow to leverage data that already resides within the consolidation application, whilst Transaction Matching helps accounting teams automate the collection and matching of large numbers of transactions across multiple sources.

With these solutions, OneStream Financial Close delivers the four key pillars of a good reconciliation process: Visibility, Standardization, Efficiency and Control.

In this book:

- Get a better understanding of the Financial Close process, and how OneStream delivers a streamlined, automated solution.
- Learn how to implement Account Reconciliations through detailed project phases, and accompanying case studies.
- Get to grips with the administration of Account Reconciliations, including settings, security, and auditing.
- Deep dive into the Account Reconciliation Solution from the End User's perspective, including how to prepare a Reconciliation, the sign-off and approval process, and overall reporting and monitoring capabilities.
- Learn what Transaction Matching is, plus how to build, test, and implement OneStream's highly automated system.
- Understand how to administer Transaction Matching through global options, access control, match sets, data sets, rules, and more!

OneStream Advanced Reporting and Dashboards

OneStream is a world-class Intelligent Finance Platform that empowers organizations to have confidence in their data and make decisions that maximize business impact. It is used by enterprises all over the world to streamline financial close, consolidation, planning, reporting and analysis, and drive effective business decisions – all based on near real-time data.

The user experience is the point of contact with the platform, and while OneStream comes with a powerful standard UI, one of its greatest strengths is its ability to create bespoke reports and custom dashboards. Like our customers, each OneStream application is unique – whether you're a novice or have experience with CPM solutions, OneStream provides the flexibility to tailor a solution to meet your needs. Concepts discussed in this book are intended to help you understand the unlimited possibilities of designing your ultimate user experience.

Written for administrators, dashboard and report designers, plus end users, and filled with background knowledge and step-by-step guides, this book deep dives into Cube Views, dashboards, reporting, and highlights the tools and tricks that will take user experiences to a new level. We examine how leveraging the full power of the OneStream Platform will help you move beyond the standard interface, align your end-user experiences with your business and process requirements, promote user adoption through efficiency and ease of use, and truly maximize the value of your OneStream implementation.

By the end of this book, you will have a deep understanding of the components that drive the user experience and how and when to use them. You'll walk away with a plethora of tools and ideas to incorporate into your application to deliver your very own user experience.

In this book, we will:

- Design and build Cube Views, based on data entry and reporting needs.
- Discuss the use of Cube View extender business rules to expose advanced formatting capabilities.
- Explore how navigation links and drill to dashboard functionality provide intuitive analysis.
- Identify the benefits of configuring personalized home pages to ensure user adoption.
- Create working role-based dashboards inspired by real-world customer requirements.

OneStream Administrator Handbook

Administrators are integral to the day-by-day operations and overall wellbeing of a **company's financial ecosystem.** Although each OneStream application is unique, the challenges that administrators face when managing the OneStream platform remain similar when it comes to processes and troubleshooting.

Whether you are a novice or seasoned administrator, this book examines key concepts to help you understand and manage the financial and data processes of your OneStream application. Written for administrators, this book is filled with technical and functional contexts – whether syntax-related to business rules or general accounting concepts – and dives into practical examples and use cases that provide guidance and insights into commonly encountered themes.

By the end of this book, you will have a deep understanding and appreciation of the capabilities that the OneStream platform offers, and have the tools needed to tackle the wide variety of administrative actions that may surface. In this book, we will cover:

- Components within OneStream, such as application properties, metadata, and workflow
- Data troubleshooting for missing or off data, whether that is related to integration setup, workflow setup, calculation adjustments in business rules, or more.
- Translations involving cube and metadata settings, plus the loading and viewing of FX rates.
- The security framework, and all the nooks and crannies that can be secured within OneStream.
- Constraining and locking data through systems-level and process-level controls.
- Considerations – as companies mature – for the updating of new or existing business processes.

OneStream Foundation Handbook [Second Edition]

In this practical second edition of the OneStream Foundation Handbook – comprising more than 15% new and revised content – The Architect Factory team at OneStream Software explains each part of an implementation, and the design of solutions. Readers will learn the core guiding principles for implementing OneStream from the company's top team of experts.

Beyond offering a training guide, the focus of this book is on the 'why' of design and building an application. While the foundational principles of building a solid, scalable OneStream application have remained largely unchanged, updates contained in this second edition reflect implemented software enhancements, along with the ongoing development of the OneStream landscape.

- Manage your Implementation with the OneStream methodology
- Understand Design and Build concepts
- Build solutions for the Consolidation of financial data, and develop Planning models
- Create Data Integration solutions that will feed your models
- Develop Workflows to guide and manage your End-Users
- Advance your solutions with Rules and Security
- Take advantage of detailed Data Reporting using tools such as Analytic Blend and Advanced Excel functionality
- Tune Performance, and optimize your application
- New content on Workspaces, Smart Integration, Dashboard design, and more
- Over 180 updated images

The information contained within this book is relevant to software version 8.4.0.

OneStream Security Essentials

Protecting your OneStream investment and data – while making your end-user experience optimal – is fundamental to getting the most out of OneStream.

This OneStream mini-book offers practical guidance, analogies, and in-depth information to help you design, test, and maintain a robust security model. Whether your company is small, large, public, or private, this book delivers the background and tools to meet your company's unique security and data requirements. Whether you are a consultant guiding implementations, a developer building solutions, or an administrator managing day-to-day operations, you'll gain a deep understanding of:

- What's possible with OneStream security
- How to define a Security Model tailored to your company's needs
- Extending security with Custom Use Cases (aka Slice Security and more)
- Reporting off your Security Framework and Application Tables
- Effective Testing and Maintenance strategies for optimal results

From practical advice on security group nesting and naming conventions to detailed information on database tables, API calls, and sample code, this mini-book is your one-stop shop for mastering OneStream security quickly and effectively!

OneStream Fundamentals

OneStream is an intelligent finance platform used by many mid-sized to large enterprises worldwide for consolidation, planning, and reporting. It spans numerous industries, including financial services, energy, retail, and manufacturing. Understanding how the OneStream platform enhances business processes and performance begins here.

This focused and concise starter guide is aimed at individuals who are new to corporate performance management and OneStream, serving as an introduction to the OneStream journey. It starts by identifying the components that make up the platform, then provides a learning roadmap covering metadata, data import, consolidation and planning calculations, workflow, reporting, project methodologies, and troubleshooting.

In this book, you will learn:

- All about Members, Dimensions, and Cube Views
- How to import different Types of Data and build Transformation Rules
- What Calculations offer, and how to create them
- The Power of Workflows
- An introduction to Genesis
- Reporting, including Spreadsheets, Report Books, and Dashboards
- How to troubleshoot problems, such as configuration errors and reporting issues
- Plus much more!

Get up and running with OneStream with this OneStream Fundamentals mini-book!

www.ingramcontent.com/pod-product-compliance
Ingram Content Group UK Ltd.
Pitfield, Milton Keynes, MK11 3LW, UK
UKHW061845041026
15591UKWH00015B/914

9 781068 333842